THE CITY OF GOD

BOOKS I-XII

SAINT AUGUSTINE OF HIPPO

ALICIA EDITIONS

TRANSLATOR'S PREFACE

"Rome having been stormed and sacked by the Goths under Alaric their king,[1] the worshipers of false gods, or pagans, as we commonly call them, made an attempt to attribute this calamity to the Christian religion, and began to blaspheme the true God with even more than their wonted bitterness and acerbity. It was this which kindled my zeal for the house of God, and prompted me to undertake the defense of the city of God against the charges and misrepresentations of its assailants. This work was in my hands for several years, owing to the interruptions occasioned by many other affairs which had a prior claim on my attention, and which I could not defer. However, this great undertaking was at last completed in twenty-two books. Of these, the first five refute those who fancy that the polytheistic worship is necessary in order to secure worldly prosperity, and that all these overwhelming calamities have befallen us in consequence of its prohibition. In the following five books I address myself to those who admit that such calamities have at all times attended, and will at all times attend, the human race, and that they constantly recur in forms more or less disastrous, varying only in the scenes, occasions, and persons on whom they light, but, while admitting this, maintain that the worship of the gods is advantageous for the life to come. In these ten books, then, I refute these two opinions, which are as groundless as they are antagonistic to the Christian religion.

"But that no one might have occasion to say, that though I had refuted the tenets of other men, I had omitted to establish my own, I devote to this object the second part of this work, which comprises twelve books, although I have not scrupled, as occasion offered, either to advance my own opinions in the first ten books, or to demolish the arguments of my opponents in the last twelve. Of these twelve books, the first four contain an account of the origin of these two cities—the city of God and the city of the world. The second four treat of their history or progress; the third and last four, of their deserved destinies. And so, though all these twenty-two books refer to both cities, yet I have named them after the better city, and called them *The City of God*."

Such is the account given by Augustine himself[2] of the occasion and plan of this his greatest work. But in addition to this explicit information, we learn from the correspondence[3] of Augustine, that it was due to the importunity of his friend Marcellinus that this defense of Christianity extended beyond the limits of a few letters. Shortly before the fall of Rome, Marcellinus had been sent to Africa by the Emperor Honorius to arrange a settlement of the differences between the Donatists and the Catholics. This brought him into contact not only with Augustine, but with Volusian, the proconsul of Africa, and a man of rare intelligence and candor. Finding that Volusian, though as yet a pagan, took an interest in the Christian religion, Marcellinus set his heart on converting him to the true faith. The details of the subsequent significant intercourse between the learned and courtly bishop and the two imperial statesmen, are unfortunately almost entirely lost to us; but the impression conveyed by the extant correspondence is, that Marcellinus was the means of bringing his two friends into communication with one another. The first overture was on Augustine's part, in the shape of a simple and manly request that Volusian would carefully peruse the Scriptures, accompanied by a frank offer to do his best to solve any difficulties that might arise from such a course of inquiry. Volusian accordingly enters into correspondence with Augustine; and in order to illustrate the kind of difficulties experienced by men in his position, he gives some graphic notes of a conversation in which he had recently taken part at a gathering of some of his friends. The difficulty to which most weight is attached in this letter is the apparent impossibility of believing in the Incarnation. But a letter which Marcellinus immediately dispatched to Augustine, urging him to reply to Volusian at large, brought the intelligence that the difficulties and objections to Christianity were thus limited merely out of a courteous regard to the preciousness of the bishop's time, and the vast number of his engagements. This letter, in short, brought out the important fact, that a removal of speculative doubts would not suffice for the conversion of such men as Volusian, whose life was one with the life of the empire. Their difficulties were rather political, historical, and social. They could not see how the reception of the Christian rule of life was compatible with the interests of Rome as the mistress of the world.[4] And thus Augustine was led to take a more distinct and wider view of the whole relation which Christianity bore to the old state of things—moral, political, philosophical, and religious—and was gradually drawn on to undertake the elaborate work now presented to the English reader, and which may more appropriately than any other of his writings be called his masterpiece[5] or life-work. It was begun the very year of Marcellinus's death, A.D. 413, and was issued in detached portions from time to time, until its completion in the year 426. It thus occupied the maturest years of Augustine's life —from his fifty-ninth to his seventy-second year.[6]

From this brief sketch, it will be seen that though the accompanying work is essentially an Apology, the Apologetic of Augustine can be no mere rehabilitation of the somewhat threadbare, if not effete, arguments of Justin and Tertullian.[7] In fact, as Augustine considered what was required of him— to expound the Christian faith, and justify it to enlightened men: to distinguish it from, and show its superiority to, all those forms of truth, philosophical or popular, which were then striving for the mastery, or at least for standing room; to set before the world's eye a vision of glory that might win the regard even of men who were dazzled by the fascinating splendor of a worldwide empire—he recognized that a task was laid before him to which even his powers might prove unequal—a task certainly which would afford ample scope for his learning, dialectic, philosophical grasp and acumen, eloquence, and faculty of exposition.

But it is the occasion of this great Apology which invests it at once with grandeur and vitality. After more than eleven hundred years of steady and triumphant progress, Rome had been taken and sacked. It is difficult for us to appreciate, impossible to overestimate, the shock which was thus communicated from center to circumference of the whole known world. It was generally believed, not only by the heathen, but also by many of the most liberal minded of the Christians, that the destruction of Rome would be the prelude to the destruction of the world.[8] Even Jerome, who might have been supposed to be embittered against the proud mistress of the world by her inhospitality to himself, cannot conceal his profound emotion on hearing of her fall. "A terrible rumor," he says, "reaches me from the west telling of Rome besieged, bought for gold, besieged again, life and property perishing together. My voice falters, sobs stifle the words I dictate; for she is a captive, that city which enthralled the world."[9] Augustine is never so theatrical as Jerome in the expression of his feeling, but he is equally explicit in lamenting the fall of Rome as a great calamity: and while he does not scruple to ascribe her recent disgrace to the profligate manners, the effeminacy, and the pride of her citizens, he is not without hope that, by a return to the simple, hardy, and honorable mode of life which characterized the early Romans, she may still be restored to much of her former prosperity.[10] But as Augustine contemplates the ruins of Rome's greatness, and feels in common with all the world at this crisis, the instability of the strongest governments, the insufficiency of the most authoritative statesmanship, there hovers over these ruins the splendid vision of the city of God "coming down out of heaven, adorned as a bride for her husband." The old social system is crumbling away on all sides, but in its place he seems to see a pure Christendom arising. He sees that human history and human destiny are not wholly identified with the history of any earthly power—not though it be as cosmopolitan as the empire of Rome.[11] He directs the attention of men to the fact that there is another kingdom on earth—a city which has foundations, whose builder and maker is God. He teaches men to take profounder views of history, and shows them how from the first the city of God, or community of God's people, has lived alongside of the kingdoms of this world and their glory, and has been silently increasing, "crescit occulto velut arbor ævo." He demonstrates that the superior morality, the true doctrine, the heavenly origin of this city, ensure it success; and over against this, he depicts the silly or contradictory theorizings of the pagan philosophers, and the unhinged morals of the people, and puts it to all candid men to say, whether in the presence of so manifestly sufficient a cause for Rome's downfall, there is room for imputing it to the spread of Christianity. He traces the antagonism of these two grand communities of rational creatures back to their first divergence in the fall of the angels, and down to the consummation of all things in the last judgment and eternal destination of the good and evil. In other words, The City of God is "the first real effort to produce a philosophy of history,"[12] to exhibit historical events in connection with their true causes, and in their real sequence. This plan of the work is not only a great conception, but it is accompanied with many practical advantages; the chief of which is, that it admits, and even requires, a full treatment of those doctrines of our faith that are more directly historical—the doctrines of creation, the fall, the incarnation, the connection between the Old and New Testaments, and the doctrine of "the last things."[13]

The effect produced by this great work it is impossible to determine with accuracy. Beugnot, with an absoluteness which we should condemn as presumption in any less competent authority, declares that its effect can only have been very slight.[14] Probably its effect would be silent and slow; telling first upon cultivated minds, and only indirectly upon the people. Certainly its effect must have been weakened by the interrupted manner of its publication. It is an easier task to estimate its intrinsic value. But on this also patristic and literary authorities widely differ. Dupin admits that it is very pleasant reading, owing to the surprising variety of matters which are introduced to illustrate and forward the argument, but censures the author for discussing very useless questions, and for adducing reasons which could satisfy no one who was not already convinced.[15] Huet also speaks of the book as "un amas confus d'excellents materiaux; c'est de l'or en barre et en lingots."[16] L'Abbé Flottes censures these opinions as unjust, and cites with approbation the unqualified eulogy of Pressensé.[17] But probably the popularity of the book is its best justification. This popularity may be measured by the circumstance that, between the year 1467 and the end of the fifteenth century, no fewer than twenty editions were called for, that is to say, a fresh edition every eighteen months.[18] And in the interesting series of letters that passed between Ludovicus Vives and Erasmus, who had engaged him to write a commentary on *The City of God* for his edition of Augustine's works, we find Vives pleading for a separate edition of this work, on the plea that, of all the writings of Augustine, it was almost the only one read by patristic students, and might therefore naturally be expected to have a much wider circulation.[19]

If it were asked to what this popularity is due, we should be disposed to attribute it mainly to the great variety of ideas, opinions, and facts that are here brought before the reader's mind. Its importance as a contribution to the history of opinion cannot be overrated. We find in it not only indications or explicit enouncement of the author's own views upon almost every important topic which occupied his thoughts, but also a compendious exhibition of the ideas which most powerfully influenced the life at that age. It thus becomes, as Poujoulat says, "comme l'encyclopédie du cinquième siècle." All that is valuable, together with much indeed that is not so, in the religion and philosophy of the classical nations of antiquity, is reviewed. And on some branches of these subjects it has, in the judgment of one well qualified to judge, "preserved more than the whole surviving Latin literature." It is true we are sometimes wearied by the too elaborate refutation of opinions which to a modern mind seem self-evident absurdities; but if these opinions were actually prevalent in the fifth century, the historical inquirer will not quarrel with the form in which his information is conveyed, nor will commit the absurdity of attributing to Augustine the foolishness of these opinions, but rather the credit of exploding them. That Augustine is a well-informed and impartial critic, is evinced by the courteousness and candor which he uniformly displays to his opponents, by the respect he won from the heathen themselves, and by his own early life. The most rigorous criticism has found him at fault regarding matters of fact only in some very rare instances, which can be easily accounted for. His learning would not indeed stand comparison with what is accounted such in our day: his life was too busy, and too devoted to the poor and to the spiritually necessitous, to admit of any extraordinary acquisition. He had access to no literature but the Latin; or at least he had only sufficient Greek to enable him to refer to Greek authors on points of importance, and not enough to enable him to read their writings with ease and pleasure.[20] But he had a profound knowledge of his own time, and a familiar acquaintance not only with the Latin poets, but with many other authors, some of whose writings are now lost to us, save the fragments preserved through his quotations.

But the interest attaching to *The City of God* is not merely historical. It is the earnestness and ability with which he develops his own philosophical and theological views which gradually fascinate the reader, and make him see why the world has set this among the few greatest books of all time. The fundamental lines of the Augustinian theology are here laid down in a comprehensive and interesting form. Never was thought so abstract expressed in language so popular. He handles metaphysical problems with the unembarrassed ease of Plato, with all Cicero's accuracy and acuteness, and more than Cicero's profundity. He is never more at home than when exposing the incompetency of Neoplatonism, or demonstrating the harmony of Christian doctrine and true philosophy. And though there are in *The City of God*, as in all ancient books, things that seem to us childish and barren, there are also the most surprising anticipations of modern speculation. There is an earnest grappling with those problems which are continually reopened because they underlie man's relation to God and the spiritual world—the problems which are not peculiar to any one century. As we read these animated discussions,

> *The fourteen centuries fall away*
> *Between us and the Afric saint,*
> *And at his side we urge, today,*
> *The immemorial quest and old complaint.*

*No outward sign to us is given,
From sea or earth comes no reply;
Hushed as the warm Numidian heaven,
He vainly questioned bends our
   frozen sky.*

It is true, the style of the book is not all that could be desired: there are passages which can possess an interest only to the antiquarian; there are others with nothing to redeem them but the glow of their eloquence; there are many repetitions; there is an occasional use of arguments "plus ingenieux que solides," as M. Saisset says. Augustine's great admirer, Erasmus, does not scruple to call him a writer "obscuræ, subtilitatis et parum amœnæ prolixitatis";[21] but "the toil of penetrating the apparent obscurities will be rewarded by finding a real wealth of insight and enlightenment."

Some who have read the opening chapters of *The City of God* may have considered it would be a waste of time to proceed; but no one, we are persuaded, ever regretted reading it all. The book has its faults; but it effectually introduces us to the most influential of theologians and the greatest popular teacher; to a genius that cannot nod for many lines together; to a reasoner whose dialectic is more formidable, more keen and sifting, than that of Socrates or Aquinas; to a saint whose ardent and genuine devotional feeling bursts up through the severest argumentation; to a man whose kindliness and wit, universal sympathies and breadth of intelligence, lend piquancy and vitality to the most abstract dissertation.

The propriety of publishing a translation of so choice a specimen of ancient literature needs no defense. As Poujoulat very sensibly remarks, there are not a great many men nowadays who will read a work in Latin of twenty-two books. Perhaps there are fewer still who ought to do so. With our busy neighbors in France, this work has been a prime favorite for four hundred years. There may be said to be eight independent translations of it into the French tongue, though some of these are in part merely revisions. One of these translations has gone through as many as four editions. The most recent is that which forms part of the Nisard series; but the best, so far as we have seen, is that of the accomplished professor of philosophy in the College of France, Emile Saisset. This translation is indeed all that can be desired: here and there an omission occurs, and about one or two renderings a difference of opinion may exist; but the exceeding felicity and spirit of the whole show it to have been a labor of love, the fond homage of a disciple proud of his master. The preface of M. Saisset is one of the most valuable contributions ever made to the understanding of Augustine's philosophy.[22]

Of English translations there has been an unaccountable poverty. Only one exists,[23] and this so exceptionally bad, so unlike the racy translations of the seventeenth century in general, so inaccurate, and so frequently unintelligible, that it is not impossible it may have done something toward giving the English public a distaste for the book itself. That the present translation also might be improved, we know; that many men were fitter for the task, on the score of scholarship, we are very sensible; but that anyone would have executed it with intenser affection and veneration for the author, we are not prepared to admit. A few notes have been added where it appeared to be necessary. Some are original, some from the Benedictine Augustine, and the rest from the elaborate commentary of Vives.[24]

**Marcus Dods.
Glasgow, 1871.**

---

1. A.D. 410.
2. *Retract.* 2.43.
3. *Ep.* 132–38.
4. See some admirable remarks on this subject in the useful work of Beugnot, *Histoire de la Destruction du Paganism*, 2.83 et seqq.
5. As Waterland (4.760) does call it, adding that it is "his most learned, most correct, and most elaborate work."
6. For proof, see the Benedictine Preface.
7. "Hitherto the Apologies had been framed to meet particular exigencies: they were either brief and pregnant statements of the Christian doctrines; refutations of prevalent calumnies; invectives against the follies and crimes of paganism; or confutations of anti-Christian works like those of Celsus, Porphyry, or Julian, closely following their course of argument, and rarely expanding into general and comprehensive views of the great conflict."—Milman *History of Christianity*, vol. 3, ch. 10. We are not acquainted with any more complete preface to *The City of God* than is contained in the two or three pages which Milman has devoted to this subject.
8. See the interesting remarks of Lactantius *Inst. Div.* 7.25.
9. "Hæret vox et singultus intercipiunt verba dictantis. Capitur urbs quæ totum cepit orbem."—Jerome 4.783.
10. See below, 4.7.
11. This is well brought out by Merivale, *Conversion of the Roman Empire*, p. 145, etc.
12. Ozanam, *History of Civilization in the Fifth Century* (English trans.), 2.160.

13. Abstracts of the work at greater or lesser length are given by Dupin, Bindemann, Böhringer, Poujoulat, Ozanam, and others.
14. His words are "Plus on examine la Cité de Dieu, plus on reste convaincu que cet ouvrage dût exercea tres-peu d'influence sur l'esprit des paiens" (2.122); and this though he thinks one cannot but be struck with the grandeur of the ideas it contains.
15. Dupin, History of Ecclesiastical Writers, 1.406.
16. Huetiana, p. 24.
17. Flottes, Etudes sur S. Augustin (Paris, 1861), pp. 154–56, one of the most accurate and interesting even of French monographs on theological writers.
18. These editions will be found detailed in the second volume of Schoenemann's Bibliotheca Pat.
19. His words (Ep. 6) are quite worth quoting: "Cura rogo te, ut excudantur aliquot centena exemplarium istius operis a reliquo Augustini corpore separata; nam multi erunt studiosi qui Augustinum totum emere vel nollent, vel non poterunt, quia non egebunt, seu quia tantum pecuniænon habebunt. Scio enim fere a deditis studiis istis elegantioribus præter hoc Augustini opus nullum fere aliud legi ejusdem autoris."
20. The fullest and fairest discussion of the very simple yet never settled question of Augustine's learning will be found in Nourrisson's Philosophie de S. Augustin 2.92–100.
21. Erasmi Epistolœ 20.2.
22. A large part of it has been translated in Saisset's Pantheism (Clark, Edinburgh).
23. By J. H., published in 1610, and again in 1620, with Vives's commentary.
24. As the letters of Vives are not in every library, we give his comico-pathetic account of the result of his Augustinian labors on his health: "Ex quo Augustinum perfeci, nunquam valui ex sententia; proximâ vero hebdomade et hac, fracto corpore cuncto, et nervis lassitudine quadam et debilitate dejectis, in caput decem turres incumbere mihi videntur incidendo pondere, ac mole intolerabili; isti sunt fructus studiorum, et merces pulcherrimi laboris; quid labor et benefacta juvant?"

BOOK ONE

ARGUMENT

Augustine censures the pagans, who attributed the calamities of the world, and especially the recent sack of Rome by the Goths, to the Christian religion, and its prohibition of the worship of the gods. He speaks of the blessings and ills of life, which then, as always, happened to good and bad men alike. Finally, he rebukes the shamelessness of those who cast up to the Christians that their women had been violated by the soldiers.

PREFACE, EXPLAINING HIS DESIGN IN UNDERTAKING THIS WORK

The glorious city of God is my theme in this work, which you, my dearest son Marcellinus, suggested, and which is due to you by my promise. I have undertaken its defense against those who prefer their own gods to the Founder of this city—a city surpassingly glorious, whether we view it as it still lives by faith in this fleeting course of time, and sojourns as a stranger in the midst of the ungodly, or as it shall dwell in the fixed stability of its eternal seat, which it now with patience waits for, expecting until "righteousness shall return unto judgment,"[1] and it obtain, by virtue of its excellence, final victory and perfect peace. A great work this, and an arduous; but God is my helper. For I am aware what ability is requisite to persuade the proud how great is the virtue of humility, which raises us, not by a quite human arrogance, but by a divine grace, above all earthly dignities that totter on this shifting scene. For the King and Founder of this city of which we speak, has in Scripture uttered to His people a dictum of the divine law in these words: "God resisteth the proud, but giveth grace unto the humble."[2] But this, which is God's prerogative, the inflated ambition of a proud spirit also affects, and dearly loves that this be numbered among its attributes, to

> *Show pity to the humbled soul,*
> *And crush the sons of pride.*[3]

And therefore, as the plan of this work we have undertaken requires, and as occasion offers, we must speak also of the earthly city, which, though it be mistress of the nations, is itself ruled by its lust of rule.

---

1. Ps. 94:15, rendered otherwise in English versions.
2. Jas. 4:6 and 1 Pet. 5:5.
3. Virgil *Æneid* 6.854.

1. OF THE ADVERSARIES OF THE NAME OF CHRIST, WHOM THE BARBARIANS FOR CHRIST'S SAKE SPARED WHEN THEY STORMED THE CITY

For to this earthly city belong the enemies against whom I have to defend the city of God. Many of them, indeed, being reclaimed from their ungodly error, have become sufficiently creditable citizens of this city; but many are so inflamed with hatred against it, and are so ungrateful to its Redeemer for His signal benefits, as to forget that they would now be unable to utter a single word to its prejudice, had they not found in its sacred places, as they fled from the enemy's steel, that life in which they now boast themselves. Are not those very Romans, who were spared by the barbarians through their respect for Christ, become enemies to the name of Christ? The reliquaries of the martyrs and the churches of the apostles bear witness to this; for in the sack of the city they were open sanctuary for all who fled to them, whether Christian or pagan. To their very threshold the bloodthirsty enemy raged; there his murderous fury owned a limit. Thither did such of the enemy as had any pity convey those to whom they had given quarter, lest any less mercifully disposed might fall upon them. And, indeed, when even those murderers who everywhere else showed themselves pitiless came to those spots where that was forbidden which the license of war permitted in every other place, their furious rage for slaughter was bridled, and their eagerness to take prisoners was quenched. Thus escaped multitudes who now reproach the Christian religion, and impute to Christ the ills that have befallen their city; but the preservation of their own life—a boon which they owe to the respect entertained for Christ by the barbarians—they attribute not to our Christ, but to their own good luck. They ought rather, had they any right perceptions, to attribute the severities and hardships inflicted by their enemies, to that divine Providence which is wont to reform the depraved manners of men by chastisement, and which exercises with similar afflictions the righteous and praiseworthy—either translating them, when they have passed through the trial, to a better world, or detaining them still on earth for ulterior purposes. And they ought to attribute it to the spirit of these Christian times, that, contrary to the custom of war, these bloodthirsty barbarians spared them, and spared them for Christ's sake, whether this mercy was actually shown in promiscuous places, or in those places specially dedicated to Christ's name, and of which the very largest were selected as sanctuaries, that full scope might thus be given to the expansive compassion which desired that a large multitude might find shelter there. Therefore ought they to give God thanks, and with sincere confession flee for refuge to His name, that so they may escape the punishment of eternal fire—they who with lying lips took upon them this name, that they might escape the punishment of present destruction. For of those whom you see insolently and shamelessly insulting the servants of Christ, there are numbers who would not have escaped that destruction and slaughter had they not pretended that they themselves were Christ's servants. Yet now, in ungrateful pride and most impious madness, and at the risk of being punished in everlasting darkness, they perversely oppose that name under which they fraudulently protected themselves for the sake of enjoying the light of this brief life.

2. THAT IT IS QUITE CONTRARY TO THE USAGE OF WAR, THAT THE VICTORS SHOULD SPARE THE VANQUISHED FOR THE SAKE OF THEIR GODS

There are histories of numberless wars, both before the building of Rome and since its rise and the extension of its dominion; let these be read, and let one instance be cited in which, when a city had been taken by foreigners, the victors spared those who were found to have fled for sanctuary to the temples of their gods;[1] or one instance in which a barbarian general gave orders that none should be put to the sword who had been found in this or that temple. Did not Æneas see

> *Dying Priam at the shrine,*
> *Staining the hearth he made divine?*[2]
> *Did not Diomedes and Ulysses*
> *Drag with red hands, the sentry slain,*
> *Her fateful image from your fane,*
> *Her chaste locks touch, and stain*
>   *with gore*
> *The virgin coronal she wore?*[3]

Neither is that true which follows, that
Thenceforth the tide of fortune changed,
And Greece grew weak.[4]

For after this they conquered and destroyed Troy with fire and sword; after this they beheaded Priam as he fled to the altars. Neither did Troy perish because it lost Minerva. For what had Minerva herself first lost, that she should perish? Her guards perhaps? No doubt; just her guards. For as soon as they were slain, she could be stolen. It was not, in fact, the men who were preserved by the image, but the image by the men. How, then, was she invoked to defend the city and the citizens, she who could not defend her own defenders?

---

1. The Benedictines remind us that Alexander and Xenophon, at least on some occasions, did so.
2. Virgil *Æneid* 2.501–502. The renderings of Virgil are from Conington.
3. Ibid., 2.166.
4. Ibid.

3. THAT THE ROMANS DID NOT SHOW THEIR USUAL SAGACITY WHEN THEY TRUSTED THAT THEY WOULD BE BENEFITED BY THE GODS WHO HAD BEEN UNABLE TO DEFEND TROY

And these be the gods to whose protecting care the Romans were delighted to entrust their city! O too, too piteous mistake! And they are enraged at us when we speak thus about their gods, though, so far from being enraged at their own writers, they part with money to learn what they say; and, indeed, the very teachers of these authors are reckoned worthy of a salary from the public purse, and of other honors. There is Virgil, who is read by boys, in order that this great poet, this most famous and approved of all poets, may impregnate their virgin minds, and may not readily be forgotten by them, according to that saying of Horace,

The fresh cask long keeps its first tang.[1]

Well, in this Virgil, I say, Juno is introduced as

hostile to the Trojans, and stirring up Æolus, the king of the winds, against them in the words,

> *A race I hate now plows the sea,*
> *Transporting Troy to Italy,*
> *And home-gods conquered*[2] ...

And ought prudent men to have entrusted the defense of Rome to these conquered gods? But it will be said, this was only the saying of Juno, who, like an angry woman, did not know what she was saying. What, then, says Æneas himself—Æneas who is so often designated "pious"? Does he not say,

> *"Lo! Panthus, 'scaped from death by*
> *flight,*
> *Priest of Apollo on the height,*
> *His conquered gods with trembling hands*
> *He bears, and shelter swift demands"?*[3]

Is it not clear that the gods (whom he does not scruple to call "conquered") were rather entrusted to Æneas than he to them, when it is said to him,

> *"The gods of her domestic shrines*
> *Your country to your care consigns"?*[4]

If, then, Virgil says that the gods were such as these, and were conquered, and that when conquered they could not escape except under the protection of a man, what a madness is it to suppose that Rome had been wisely entrusted to these guardians, and could not have been taken unless it had lost them! Indeed, to worship conquered gods as protectors and champions, what is this but to worship, not good divinities, but evil omens?[5] Would it not be wiser to believe, not that Rome would never have fallen into so great a calamity had not they first perished, but rather that they would have perished long since had not Rome preserved them as long as she could? For who does not see, when he thinks of it, what a foolish assumption it is that they could not be vanquished under vanquished defenders, and that they only perished because they had lost their guardian gods, when, indeed, the only cause of their perishing was that they chose for their protectors gods condemned to perish? The poets, therefore, when they composed and sang these things about the conquered gods, had no intention to invent falsehoods, but uttered, as honest men, what the truth extorted from them. This, however, will be carefully and copiously discussed in another and more fitting place. Meanwhile I will briefly, and to the best of my ability, explain what I meant to say about these ungrateful men who blasphemously impute to Christ the calamities which they deservedly suffer in consequence of their own wicked ways, while that which is for Christ's sake spared them in spite of their wickedness they do not even take the trouble to notice; and in their mad and blasphemous insolence, they use against His name those very lips wherewith they falsely claimed that same name that their lives might be spared. In the places consecrated to Christ, where for His sake no enemy would injure them, they restrained their tongues that they might be safe and protected; but no sooner do they emerge from these sanctuaries, than they unbridle these tongues to hurl against Him curses full of hate.

---

1. Horace *Ep.* 1.2.69.
2. Æneid 1.71.
3. Ibid., 2.319.
4. Ibid., 2.293.
5. "Non numina bona, sed omina mala."

4. OF THE ASYLUM OF JUNO IN TROY, WHICH SAVED NO ONE FROM THE GREEKS; AND OF THE CHURCHES OF THE APOSTLES, WHICH PROTECTED FROM THE BARBARIANS ALL WHO FLED TO THEM

Troy itself, the mother of the Roman people, was not able, as I have said, to protect its own citizens in the sacred places of their gods from the fire and sword of the Greeks, though the Greeks worshiped the same gods. Not only so, but

> *Phœnix and Ulysses fell*
> *In the void courts by Juno's cell*
> *Were set the spoil to keep;*
> *Snatched from the burning shrines away,*
> *There Ilium's mighty treasure lay,*
> *Rich altars, bowls of massy gold,*
> *And captive raiment, rudely rolled*
> *In one promiscuous heap;*
> *While boys and matrons, wild with fear,*
> *In long array were standing near.*[1]

In other words, the place consecrated to so great

a goddess was chosen, not that from it none might be led out a captive, but that in it all the captives might be immured. Compare now this "asylum"—the asylum not of an ordinary god, not of one of the rank and file of gods, but of Jove's own sister and wife, the queen of all the gods—with the churches built in memory of the apostles. Into it were collected the spoils rescued from the blazing temples and snatched from the gods, not that they might be restored to the vanquished, but divided among the victors; while into these was carried back, with the most religious observance and respect, everything which belonged to them, even though found elsewhere. There liberty was lost; here preserved. There bondage was strict; here strictly excluded. Into that temple men were driven to become the chattels of their enemies, now lording it over them; into these churches men were led by their relenting foes, that they might be at liberty. In fine, the gentle[2] Greeks appropriated that temple of Juno to the purposes of their own avarice and pride; while these churches of Christ were chosen even by the savage barbarians as the fit scenes for humility and mercy. But perhaps, after all, the Greeks did in that victory of theirs spare the temples of those gods whom they worshiped in common with the Trojans, and did not dare to put to the sword or make captive the wretched and vanquished Trojans who fled thither; and perhaps Virgil, in the manner of poets, has depicted what never really happened? But there is no question that he depicted the usual custom of an enemy when sacking a city.

1. Virgil *Æneid*. 2.761.
2. Though *levis* was the word usually employed to signify the inconstancy of the Greeks, it is evidently here used, in opposition to *immanis* of the following clause, to indicate that the Greeks were more civilized than the barbarians, and not relentless, but, as we say, easily moved.

5. CÆSAR'S STATEMENT REGARDING THE UNIVERSAL CUSTOM OF AN ENEMY WHEN SACKING A CITY

Even Cæsar himself gives us positive testimony regarding this custom; for, in his deliverance in the senate about the conspirators, he says (as Sallust, a historian of distinguished veracity, writes[1]) "that virgins and boys are violated, children torn from the embrace of their parents, matrons subjected to whatever should be the pleasure of the conquerors, temples and houses plundered, slaughter and burning rife; in fine, all things filled with arms, corpses, blood, and wailing." If he had not mentioned temples here, we might suppose that enemies were in the habit of sparing the dwellings of the gods. And the Roman temples were in danger of these disasters, not from foreign foes, but from Catiline and his associates, the most noble senators and citizens of Rome. But these, it may be said, were abandoned men, and the parricides of their fatherland.

1. *Sallust De Conj. Cat. 51.*

6. THAT NOT EVEN THE ROMANS, WHEN THEY TOOK CITIES, SPARED THE CONQUERED IN THEIR TEMPLES

Why, then, need our argument take note of the many nations who have waged wars with one another, and have nowhere spared the conquered in the temples of their gods? Let us look at the practice of the Romans themselves; let us, I say, recall and review the Romans, whose chief praise it has been "to spare the vanquished and subdue the proud," and that they preferred "rather to forgive than to revenge an injury";[1] and among so many and great cities which they have stormed, taken, and overthrown for the extension of their dominion, let us be told what temples they were accustomed to exempt, so that whoever took refuge in them was free. Or have they really done this, and has the fact been suppressed by the historians of these events? Is it to be believed, that men who sought out with the greatest eagerness points they could praise, would omit those which, in their own estimation, are the most signal proofs of piety? Marcus Marcellus, a distinguished Roman, who took Syracuse, a most splendidly adorned city, is reported to have bewailed its coming ruin, and to have shed his own tears over it before he spilled its blood. He took steps also to preserve the chastity even of his enemy. For before he gave orders for the storming of the city, he issued an edict forbidding the violation of any free person. Yet the city was sacked according to the custom of war; nor do we anywhere read, that even by so chaste and gentle a commander orders were given that no one should be injured who had fled to this or that temple. And this certainly would by no means have been omitted, when neither his weeping nor his edict preservative of chastity could be passed in silence. Fabius, the conqueror of the city of Tarentum, is praised for abstaining from making booty of the images. For when his secretary proposed the question to him, what he wished done with the statues of the gods, which had been taken in large numbers, he veiled his moderation under a joke. For he asked of what sort they were; and when they reported to him that there were not only many large images, but some of them armed, "Oh," says he, "let us leave with the Tarentines their angry gods." Seeing, then, that the writers of Roman history could not pass in silence, neither the weeping of the one general nor the laughing of the other, neither the chaste pity of the one nor the facetious moderation of the other, on what occasion would it be omitted, if, for the honor of any of their enemy's gods, they had shown this particular form of leniency, that in any temple slaughter or captivity was prohibited?

---

1. Ibid., 9.

7. THAT THE CRUELTIES WHICH OCCURRED IN THE SACK OF ROME WERE IN ACCORDANCE WITH THE CUSTOM OF WAR, WHEREAS THE ACTS OF CLEMENCY RESULTED FROM THE INFLUENCE OF CHRIST'S NAME

All the spoiling, then, which Rome was exposed to in the recent calamity—all the slaughter, plundering, burning, and misery—was the result of the custom of war. But what was novel, was that savage barbarians showed themselves in so gentle a guise, that the largest churches were chosen and set apart for the purpose of being filled with the people to whom quarter was given, and that in them none were slain, from them none forcibly dragged; that into them many were led by their relenting enemies to be set at liberty, and that from them none were led into slavery by merciless foes. Whoever does not see that this is to be attributed to the name of Christ, and to the Christian temper, is blind; whoever sees this, and gives no praise, is ungrateful; whoever hinders anyone from praising it, is mad. Far be it from any prudent man to impute this clemency to the barbarians. Their fierce and bloody minds were awed, and bridled, and marvelously tempered by Him who so long before said by His prophet, "I will visit their transgression with the rod, and their iniquities with stripes; nevertheless My lovingkindness will I not utterly take from them."[1]

---

1. Ps. 89:32.

8. OF THE ADVANTAGES AND DISADVANTAGES WHICH OFTEN INDISCRIMINATELY ACCRUE TO GOOD AND WICKED MEN

Will someone say, Why, then, was this divine compassion extended even to the ungodly and ungrateful? Why, but because it was the mercy of Him who daily "maketh His sun to rise on the evil and on the good, and sendeth rain on the just and on the unjust."[1] For though some of these men, taking thought of this, repent of their wickedness and reform, some, as the apostle says, "despising the riches of His goodness and long-suffering, after their hardness and impenitent heart, treasure up unto themselves wrath against the day of wrath and revelation of the righteous judgment of God, who will render to every man according to his deeds";[2] nevertheless does the patience of God still invite the wicked to repentance, even as the scourge of God educates the good to patience. And so, too, does the mercy of God embrace the good that it may cherish them, as the severity of God arrests the wicked to punish them.

To the divine Providence it has seemed good to prepare in the world to come for the righteous good things, which the unrighteous shall not enjoy; and for the wicked evil things, by which the good shall not be tormented. But as for the good things of this life, and its ills, God has willed that these should be common to both; that we might not too eagerly covet the things which wicked men are seen equally to enjoy, nor shrink with an unseemly fear from the ills which even good men often suffer.

There is, too, a very great difference in the purpose served both by those events which we call adverse and those called prosperous. For the good man is neither uplifted with the good things of time, nor broken by its ills; but the wicked man, because he is corrupted by this world's happiness, feels himself punished by its unhappiness.[3] Yet often, even in the present distribution of temporal things, does God plainly evince His own interference. For if every sin were now visited with manifest punishment, nothing would seem to be reserved for the final judgment; on the other hand, if no sin received now a plainly divine punishment, it would be concluded that there is no divine Providence at all. And so of the good things of this life: if God did not by a very visible liberality confer these on some of those persons who ask for them, we should say that these good things were not at His disposal; and if He gave them to all who sought them, we should suppose that such were the only rewards of His service; and such a service would make us not godly, but greedy rather, and covetous. Wherefore, though good and bad men suffer alike, we must not suppose that there is no difference between the men themselves, because there is no difference in what they both suffer. For even in the likeness of the sufferings, there remains an unlikeness in the sufferers; and though exposed to the same anguish, virtue and vice are not the same thing. For as the same fire causes gold to glow brightly, and chaff to smoke; and under the same flail the straw is beaten small, while the grain is cleansed; and as the lees are not mixed with the oil, though squeezed out of the vat by the same pressure, so the same violence of affliction proves, purges, clarifies the good, but damns, ruins, exterminates the wicked. And thus it is that in the same affliction the wicked detest God and blaspheme, while the good pray and praise. So material a difference does it make, not what ills are suffered, but what kind of man suffers them. For, stirred up with the same movement, mud exhales a horrible stench, and ointment emits a fragrant odor.

---

1. Matt. 5:45.
2. Rom. 2:4.
3. *So Cyprian (Contra Demetrianum) says, "Pœnam de adversis mundi ille sentit, cui et lætitia et gloria omnis in mundo est."*

9. OF THE REASONS FOR ADMINISTERING CORRECTION TO BAD AND GOOD TOGETHER

What, then, have the Christians suffered in that calamitous period, which would not profit everyone who duly and faithfully considered the following circumstances? First of all, they must humbly consider those very sins which have provoked God to fill the world with such terrible disasters; for although they be far from the excesses of wicked, immoral, and ungodly men, yet they do not judge themselves so clean removed from all faults as to be too good to suffer for these even temporal ills. For every man, however laudably he lives, yet yields in some points to the lust of the flesh. Though he does not fall into gross enormity of wickedness, and abandoned viciousness, and abominable profanity, yet he slips into some sins, either rarely or so much the more frequently as the sins seem of less account. But not to mention this, where can we readily find a man who holds in fit and just estimation those persons on account of whose revolting pride, luxury, and avarice, and cursed iniquities and impiety, God now smites the earth as His predictions threatened? Where is the man who lives with them in the style in which it becomes us to live with them? For often we wickedly blind ourselves to the occasions of teaching and admonishing them, sometimes even of reprimanding and chiding them, either because we shrink from the labor or are ashamed to offend them, or because we fear to lose good friendships, lest this should stand in the way of our advancement, or injure us in some worldly matter, which either our covetous disposition desires to obtain, or our weakness shrinks from losing. So that, although the conduct of wicked men is distasteful to the good, and therefore they do not fall with them into that damnation which in the next life awaits such persons, yet, because they spare their damnable sins through fear, therefore, even though their own sins be slight and venial, they are justly scourged with the wicked in this world, though in eternity they quite escape punishment. Justly, when God afflicts them in common with the wicked, do they find this life bitter, through love of whose sweetness they declined to be bitter to these sinners.

If anyone forbears to reprove and find fault with those who are doing wrong, because he seeks a more seasonable opportunity, or because he fears they may be made worse by his rebuke, or that other weak persons may be disheartened from endeavoring to lead a good and pious life, and may be driven from the faith—this man's omission seems to be occasioned not by covetousness, but by a charitable consideration. But what is blameworthy is, that they who themselves revolt from the conduct of the wicked, and live in quite another fashion, yet spare those faults in other men which they ought to reprehend and wean them from; and spare them because they fear to give offense, lest they should injure their interests in those things which good men may innocently and legitimately use—though they use them more greedily than becomes persons who are strangers in this world, and profess the hope of a heavenly country. For not only the weaker brethren who enjoy married life, and have children (or desire to have them), and own houses and establishments, whom the apostle addresses in the churches, warning and instructing them how they should live, both the wives with their husbands, and the husbands with their wives, the children with their parents, and parents with their children, and servants with their masters, and masters with their servants—not only do these weaker brethren gladly obtain and grudgingly lose many earthly and temporal things on account of which they dare not offend men whose polluted and wicked life greatly displeases them; but those also who live at a higher level, who are not entangled in the meshes of married life, but use meager food and raiment, do often take thought of their own safety and good name, and abstain from finding fault with the wicked, because they fear their wiles and violence. And although they do not fear them to such an extent as to be drawn to the commission of like iniquities, no, not by any threats or violence soever; yet those very deeds which they refuse to share in the commission of they often decline to find fault with, when possibly they might by finding fault prevent their commission. They abstain from interference, because they fear that, if it fail of good effect, their own safety or reputation may be damaged or destroyed; not because they see that their preservation and good name are needful, that they may be able to influence those who need their instruction, but rather because they weakly relish the flattery and respect of men, and fear the judgments of the people, and the pain or death of the body; that is to say, their nonintervention is the result of selfishness, and not of love.

Accordingly this seems to me to be one principal reason why the good are chastised along with the wicked, when God is pleased to visit with temporal punishments the profligate manners of a community. They are punished together, not because they have spent an equally corrupt life, but because the good as well as the wicked, though not equally with them, love this present life; while they ought to hold it cheap, that the wicked, being admonished and reformed by their example, might lay hold of life eternal. And if they will not be the companions of the good in seeking life everlasting, they should be loved as enemies, and be dealt with patiently. For so long as they live, it remains uncertain whether they may not come to a better mind. These selfish persons have more cause to fear than those to whom it was said through the prophet, "He is taken away in his iniquity, but his blood will I require at the watchman's hand."[1] For watchmen or overseers of the people are appointed in churches, that they may unsparingly rebuke sin. Nor is that man guiltless of the sin we speak of, who, though he be not a watchman, yet sees in the conduct of those with whom the relationships of this life bring him into contact, many things that should be blamed, and yet overlooks them, fearing to give offense, and lose such worldly blessings as may legitimately be desired, but which he too eagerly grasps. Then, lastly, there is another reason why the good are afflicted with temporal calamities—the reason which Job's case exemplifies: that the human spirit may be proved, and that it may be manifested with what fortitude of pious trust, and with how unmercenary a love, it cleaves to God.[2]

---

1. Ezek. 33:6.
2. Cf. with this chapter the first homily of Chrysostom to the people of Antioch.

10. THAT THE SAINTS LOSE NOTHING IN LOSING TEMPORAL GOODS

These are the considerations which one must keep in view, that he may answer the question whether any evil happens to the faithful and godly which cannot be turned to profit. Or shall we say that the question is needless, and that the apostle is vaporing when he says, "We know that all things work together for good to them that love God"?[1]

They lost all they had. Their faith? Their godliness? The possessions of the hidden man of the heart, which in the sight of God are of great price?[2] Did they lose these? For these are the wealth of Christians, to whom the wealthy apostle said, "Godliness with contentment is great gain. For we brought nothing into this world, and it is certain we can carry nothing out. And having food and raiment, let us be therewith content. But they that will be rich fall into temptation and a snare, and into many foolish and hurtful lusts, which drown men in destruction and perdition. For the love of money is the root of all evil; which, while some coveted after, they have erred from the faith, and pierced themselves through with many sorrows."[3]

They, then, who lost their worldly all in the sack of Rome, if they owned their possessions as they had been taught by the apostle, who himself was poor without, but rich within—that is to say, if they used the world as not using it—could say in the words of Job, heavily tried, but not overcome: "Naked came I out of my mother's womb, and naked shall I return thither: the LORD gave, and the LORD hath taken away; as it pleased the LORD, so has it come to pass: blessed be the name of the LORD."[4] Like a good servant, Job counted the will of his Lord his great possession, by obedience to which his soul was enriched; nor did it grieve him to lose, while yet living, those goods which he must shortly leave at his death. But as to those feebler spirits who, though they cannot be said to prefer earthly possessions to Christ, do yet cleave to them with a somewhat immoderate attachment, they have discovered by the pain of losing these things how much they were sinning in loving them. For their grief is of their own making; in the words of the apostle quoted above, "They have pierced themselves through with many sorrows." For it was well that they who had so long despised these verbal admonitions should receive the teaching of experience. For when the apostle says, "They that will be rich fall into temptation," and so on, what he blames in riches is not the possession of them, but the desire of them. For elsewhere he says, "Charge them that are rich in this world, that they be not high-minded, nor trust in uncertain riches, but in the living God, who giveth us richly all things to enjoy; that they do good, that they be rich in good works, ready to distribute, willing to communicate; laying up in store for themselves a good foundation against the time to come, that they may lay hold on eternal life."[5] They who were making such a use of their property have been consoled for light losses by great gains, and have had more pleasure in those possessions which they have securely laid past, by freely giving them away, than grief in those which they entirely lost by an anxious and selfish hoarding of them. For nothing could perish on earth save what they would be ashamed to carry away from earth. Our Lord's injunction runs, "Lay not up for yourselves treasures upon earth, where moth and rust doth corrupt, and where thieves break through and steal; but lay up for yourselves treasures in heaven, where neither moth nor rust doth corrupt, and where thieves do not break through nor steal: for where your treasure is, there will your heart be also."[6] And they who have listened to this injunction have proved in the time of tribulation how well they were advised in not despising this most trustworthy teacher, and most faithful and mighty guardian of their treasure. For if many were glad that their treasure was stored in places which the enemy chanced not to light upon, how much better founded was the joy of those who, by the counsel of their God, had fled with their treasure to a citadel which no enemy can possibly reach! Thus our Paulinus, bishop of Nola,[7] who voluntarily abandoned vast wealth and became quite poor, though abundantly rich in holiness, when the barbarians sacked Nola, and took him prisoner, used silently to pray, as he afterward told me, "O Lord, let me not be troubled for gold and silver, for where all my treasure is Thou knowest." For all his treasure was where he had been taught to hide and store it by Him who had also foretold that these calamities would happen in the world. Consequently those persons who obeyed their Lord, when He warned them where and how to lay up treasure, did not lose even their earthly possessions in the invasion of the barbarians; while those who are now repenting that they did not obey Him have learned the right use of earthly goods, if not by the wisdom which would have prevented their loss, at least by the experience which follows it.

But some good and Christian men have been put to the torture, that they might be forced to deliver up their goods to the enemy. They could indeed neither deliver nor lose that good which made themselves good. If, however, they preferred torture to the surrender of the mammon of iniquity, then I say they were not good men. Rather they should have been reminded that, if they suffered so severely for the sake of money, they should endure all torment, if need be, for Christ's sake; that they might be taught to love Him rather who enriches with eternal felicity all who suffer for Him, and not silver and gold, for which it was pitiable to suffer, whether they preserved it by telling a lie or lost it by telling the truth. For under these tortures no one lost Christ by confessing Him, no one preserved wealth save by denying its existence. So that possibly the torture which taught them that they should set their affections on a possession they could not lose, was more useful than those possessions which, without any useful fruit at all, disquieted and tormented their anxious owners. But then we are reminded that some were tortured who had no wealth to surrender, but who were not believed when they said so. These too, however, had perhaps some craving for wealth, and were not willingly poor with a holy resignation; and to such it had to be made plain, that not the actual possession alone, but also the desire of wealth, deserved such excruciating pains. And even if they were destitute of any hidden stores of gold and silver, because they were living in hopes of a better life—I know not indeed if any such person was tortured on the supposition that he had wealth; but if so, then certainly in confessing, when put to the question, a holy poverty, he confessed Christ. And though it was scarcely to be expected that the barbarians should believe him, yet no confessor of a holy poverty could be tortured without receiving a heavenly reward.

Again, they say that the long famine laid many a Christian low. But this, too, the faithful turned to good uses by a pious endurance of it. For those whom famine killed outright it rescued from the ills of this life, as a kindly disease would have done; and those who were only hunger-bitten were taught to live more sparingly, and inured to longer fasts.

---

1. Rom. 8:28.

2. 1 Pet. 3:4.
3. 1 Tim. 6:6–10.
4. Job 1:21.
5. 1 Tim. 6:17–19.
6. Matt. 6:19–21.
7. Paulinus was a native of Bordeaux, and both by inheritance and marriage acquired great wealth, which, after his conversion in his thirty-sixth year, he distributed to the poor. He became bishop of Nola in A.D. 409, being then in his fifty-sixth year. Nola was taken by Alaric shortly after the sack of Rome.

11. OF THE END OF THIS LIFE, WHETHER IT IS MATERIAL THAT IT BE LONG DELAYED

But, it is added, many Christians were slaughtered, and were put to death in a hideous variety of cruel ways. Well, if this be hard to bear, it is assuredly the common lot of all who are born into this life. Of this at least I am certain, that no one has ever died who was not destined to die sometime. Now the end of life puts the longest life on a par with the shortest. For of two things which have alike ceased to be, the one is not better, the other worse—the one greater, the other less.[1] And of what consequence is it what kind of death puts an end to life, since he who has died once is not forced to go through the same ordeal a second time? And as in the daily casualties of life every man is, as it were, threatened with numberless deaths, so long as it remains uncertain which of them is his fate, I would ask whether it is not better to suffer one and die, than to live in fear of all? I am not unaware of the poor-spirited fear which prompts us to choose rather to live long in fear of so many deaths, than to die once and so escape them all; but the weak and cowardly shrinking of the flesh is one thing, and the well-considered and reasonable persuasion of the soul quite another. That death is not to be judged an evil which is the end of a good life; for death becomes evil only by the retribution which follows it. They, then, who are destined to die, need not be careful to inquire what death they are to die, but into what place death will usher them. And since Christians are well aware that the death of the godly pauper whose sores the dogs licked was far better than of the wicked rich man who lay in purple and fine linen, what harm could these terrific deaths do to the dead who had lived well?

---

1. Much of a kindred nature might be gathered from the Stoics. Antoninus says (2.14): "Though thou shouldest be going to live three thousand years, and as many times ten thousand years, still remember that no man loses any other life than this which he now lives, nor lives any other than this which he now loses. The longest and the shortest are thus brought to the same."

12. OF THE BURIAL OF THE DEAD: THAT THE DENIAL OF IT TO CHRISTIANS DOES THEM NO INJURY

Further still[1], we are reminded that in such a carnage as then occurred, the bodies could not even be buried. But godly confidence is not appalled by so ill-omened a circumstance; for the faithful bear in mind that assurance has been given that not a hair of their head shall perish, and that, therefore, though they even be devoured by beasts, their blessed resurrection will not hereby be hindered. The Truth would nowise have said, "Fear not them which kill the body, but are not able to kill the soul,"[2] if anything whatever that an enemy could do to the body of the slain could be detrimental to the future life. Or will someone perhaps take so absurd a position as to contend that those who kill the body are not to be feared before death, and lest they kill the body, but after death, lest they deprive it of burial? If this be so, then that is false which Christ says, "Be not afraid of them that kill the body, and after that have no more that they can do";[3] for it seems they can do great injury to the dead body. Far be it from us to suppose that the Truth can be thus false. They who kill the body are said "to do something," because the deathblow is felt, the body still having sensation; but after that, they have no more that they can do, for in the slain body there is no sensation. And so there are indeed many bodies of Christians lying unburied; but no one has separated them from heaven, nor from that earth which is all filled with the presence of Him who knows whence He will raise again what He created. It is said, indeed, in the psalm: "The dead bodies of Thy servants have they given to be meat unto the fowls of the heaven, the flesh of Thy saints unto the beasts of the earth. Their blood have they shed like water round about Jerusalem; and there was none to bury them."[4] But this was said rather to exhibit the cruelty of those who did these things, than the misery of those who suffered them. To the eyes of men this appears a harsh and doleful lot, yet "precious in the sight of the LORD is the death of His saints."[5] Wherefore all these last offices and ceremonies that concern the dead, the careful funeral arrangements, and the equipment of the tomb, and the pomp of obsequies, are rather the solace of the living than the comfort of the dead. If a costly burial does any good to a wicked man, a squalid burial, or none at all, may harm the godly. His crowd of domestics furnished the purple-clad Dives with a funeral gorgeous in the eye of man; but in the sight of God that was a more sumptuous funeral which the ulcerous pauper received at the hands of the angels, who did not carry him out to a marble tomb, but bore him aloft to Abraham's bosom.

The men against whom I have undertaken to defend the city of God laugh at all this. But even their own philosophers[6] have despised a careful burial; and often whole armies have fought and fallen for their earthly country without caring to inquire whether they would be left exposed on the field of battle, or become the food of wild beasts. Of this noble disregard of sepulture poetry has well said: "He who has no tomb has the sky for his vault."[7] How much less ought they to insult over the unburied bodies of Christians, to whom it has been promised that the flesh itself shall be restored, and the body formed anew, all the members of it being gathered not only from the earth, but from the most secret recesses of any other of the elements in which the dead bodies of men have lain hid!

---

1. Augustine expresses himself more fully on this subject in his tract *De cura pro mortuis gerenda.*
2. Matt. 10:28.
3. Luke 12:4.
4. Ps. 79:2–3.
5. Ps. 116:15.
6. Diogenes especially, and his followers. See also Seneca *De Tranq.* 14 and *Ep.* 92; and in Cicero's *Tusc. Disp.* 1.43, the answer of Theodorus, the Cyrenian philosopher, to Lysimachus, who threatened him with the cross: "Threaten that to your courtiers; it is of no consequence to Theodorus whether he rot in the earth or in the air."
7. Lucan *Pharsalia* 7.819, of those whom Cæsar forbade to be buried after the battle of Pharsalia.

13. REASONS FOR BURYING THE BODIES OF THE SAINTS

Nevertheless the bodies of the dead are not on this account to be despised and left unburied; least of all the bodies of the righteous and faithful, which have been used by the Holy Spirit as His organs and instruments for all good works. For if the dress of a father, or his ring, or anything he wore, be precious to his children, in proportion to the love they bore him, with how much more reason ought we to care for the bodies of those we love, which they wore far more closely and intimately than any clothing! For the body is not an extraneous ornament or aid, but a part of man's very nature. And therefore to the righteous of ancient times the last offices were piously rendered, and sepulchres provided for them, and obsequies celebrated;[1] and they themselves, while yet alive, gave commandment to their sons about the burial, and, on occasion, even about the removal of their bodies to some favorite place.[2] And Tobit, according to the angel's testimony, is commended, and is said to have pleased God by burying the dead.[3] Our Lord Himself, too, though He was to rise again the third day, applauds, and commends to our applause, the good work of the religious woman who poured precious ointment over His limbs, and did it against His burial.[4] And the gospel speaks with commendation of those who were careful to take down His body from the cross, and wrap it lovingly in costly cerements, and see to its burial.[5] These instances certainly do not prove that corpses have any feeling; but they show that God's providence extends even to the bodies of the dead, and that such pious offices are pleasing to Him, as cherishing faith in the resurrection. And we may also draw from them this wholesome lesson, that if God does not forget even any kind office which loving care pays to the unconscious dead, much more does He reward the charity we exercise toward the living. Other things, indeed, which the holy patriarchs said of the burial and removal of their bodies, they meant to be taken in a prophetic sense; but of these we need not here speak at large, what we have already said being sufficient. But if the want of those things which are necessary for the support of the living, as food and clothing, though painful and trying, does not break down the fortitude and virtuous endurance of good men, nor eradicate piety from their souls, but rather renders it more fruitful, how much less can the absence of the funeral, and of the other customary attentions paid to the dead, render those wretched who are already reposing in the hidden abodes of the blessed! Consequently, though in the sack of Rome and of other towns the dead bodies of the Christians were deprived of these last offices, this is neither the fault of the living, for they could not render them; nor an infliction to the dead, for they cannot feel the loss.

---

1. Gen. 25:9; 35:29, etc.
2. Gen. 47:29; 50:24.
3. Tob. 12:12.
4. Matt. 26:10–13.
5. John 19:38.

14. OF THE CAPTIVITY OF THE SAINTS, AND THAT DIVINE CONSOLATION NEVER FAILED THEM THEREIN

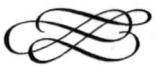

But, say they, many Christians were even led away captive. This indeed were a most pitiable fate, if they could be led away to any place where they could not find their God. But for this calamity also sacred Scripture affords great consolation. The three youths[1] were captives; Daniel was a captive; so were other prophets: and God, the Comforter, did not fail them. And in like manner He has not failed His own people in the power of a nation which, though barbarous, is yet human; He who did not abandon the prophet[2] in the belly of a monster. These things, indeed, are turned to ridicule rather than credited by those with whom we are debating; though they believe what they read in their own books, that Arion of Methymna, the famous lyrist,[3] when he was thrown overboard, was received on a dolphin's back and carried to land. But that story of ours about the prophet Jonah is far more incredible—more incredible because more marvelous, and more marvelous because a greater exhibition of power.

---

1. Dan. 3.
2. Jonah.
3. "Second to none," as he is called by Herodotus, who first of all tells his well-known story (*Clio.* 23–24).

15. OF REGULUS, IN WHOM WE HAVE AN EXAMPLE OF THE VOLUNTARY ENDURANCE OF CAPTIVITY FOR THE SAKE OF RELIGION; WHICH YET DID NOT PROFIT HIM, THOUGH HE WAS A WORSHIPER OF THE GODS

But among their own famous men they have a very noble example of the voluntary endurance of captivity in obedience to a religious scruple. Marcus Attilius Regulus, a Roman general, was a prisoner in the hands of the Carthaginians. But they, being more anxious to exchange their prisoners with the Romans than to keep them, sent Regulus as a special envoy with their own ambassadors to negotiate this exchange, but bound him first with an oath, that if he failed to accomplish their wish, he would return to Carthage. He went and persuaded the senate to the opposite course, because he believed it was not for the advantage of the Roman republic to make an exchange of prisoners. After he had thus exerted his influence, the Romans did not compel him to return to the enemy; but what he had sworn he voluntarily performed. But the Carthaginians put him to death with refined, elaborate, and horrible tortures. They shut him up in a narrow box, in which he was compelled to stand, and in which finely sharpened nails were fixed all round about him, so that he could not lean upon any part of it without intense pain; and so they killed him by depriving him of sleep.[1] With justice, indeed, do they applaud the virtue which rose superior to so frightful a fate. However, the gods he swore by were those who are now supposed to avenge the prohibition of their worship, by inflicting these present calamities on the human race. But if these gods, who were worshiped specially in this behalf, that they might confer happiness in this life, either willed or permitted these punishments to be inflicted on one who kept his oath to them, what more cruel punishment could they in their anger have inflicted on a perjured person? But why may I not draw from my reasoning a double inference? Regulus certainly had such reverence for the gods, that for his oath's sake he would neither remain in his own land nor go elsewhere, but without hesitation returned to his bitterest enemies. If he thought that this course would be advantageous with respect to this present life, he was certainly much deceived, for it brought his life to a frightful termination. By his own example, in fact, he taught that the gods do not secure the temporal happiness of their worshipers; since he himself, who was devoted to their worship, as both conquered in battle and taken prisoner, and then, because he refused to act in violation of the oath he had sworn by them, was tortured and put to death by a new, and hitherto unheard of, and all too horrible kind of punishment. And on the supposition that the worshipers of the gods are rewarded by felicity in the life to come, why, then, do they calumniate the influence of Christianity? Why do they assert that this disaster has overtaken the city because it has ceased to worship its gods, since, worship them as assiduously as it may, it may yet be as unfortunate as Regulus was? Or will someone carry so wonderful a blindness to the extent of wildly attempting, in the face of the evident truth, to contend that though one man might be unfortunate, though a worshiper of the gods, yet a whole city could not be so? That is to say, the power of their gods is better adapted to preserve multitudes than individuals—as if a multitude were not composed of individuals.

But if they say that M. Regulus, even while a prisoner and enduring these bodily torments, might yet enjoy the blessedness of a virtuous soul,[2] then let them recognize that true virtue by which a city also may be blessed. For the blessedness of a community and of an individual flow from the same source; for a community is nothing else than a harmonious collection of individuals. So that I am not concerned meantime to discuss what kind of virtue Regulus possessed; enough, that by his very noble example they are forced to own that the gods are to be worshiped not for the sake of bodily comforts or external advantages; for he preferred to lose all such things rather than offend the gods by whom he had sworn. But what can we make of men who glory in having such a citizen, but dread having a city like him? If they do not dread this, then let them acknowledge that some such calamity as befell Regulus may also befall a community, though they be worshiping their gods as diligently as he; and let them no longer throw the blame of their misfortunes on Christianity. But as our present concern is with those Christians who were taken prisoners, let those who take occasion from this calamity to revile our most wholesome religion in a fashion not less imprudent than impudent, consider this and hold their peace; for if it was no reproach to their gods that a most punctilious worshiper of theirs should, for the sake of keeping his oath to them, be deprived of his native land without hope of finding another, and fall into the hands of his enemies, and be put to death by a long-drawn and exquisite torture, much less ought the Christian name to be charged with the captivity of those who believe in its power, since they, in confident expectation of a heavenly country, know that they are pilgrims even in their own homes.

---

1. Augustine here uses the words of Cicero (*"vigilando peremerunt"*), who refers to Regulus (*In Pisonem* 19). Aulus Gellius, quoting Tubero and Tuditanus (6.4), adds some further particulars regarding these tortures.
2. As the Stoics generally would affirm.

16. OF THE VIOLATION OF THE CONSECRATED AND OTHER CHRISTIAN VIRGINS, TO WHICH THEY WERE SUBJECTED IN CAPTIVITY AND TO WHICH THEIR OWN WILL GAVE NO CONSENT; AND WHETHER THIS CONTAMINATED THEIR SOULS

But they fancy they bring a conclusive charge against Christianity, when they aggravate the horror of captivity by adding that not only wives and unmarried maidens, but even consecrated virgins, were violated. But truly, with respect to this, it is not Christian faith, nor piety, nor even the virtue of chastity, which is hemmed into any difficulty; the only difficulty is so to treat the subject as to satisfy at once modesty and reason. And in discussing it we shall not be so careful to reply to our accusers as to comfort our friends. Let this, therefore, in the first place, be laid down as an unassailable position, that the virtue which makes the life good has its throne in the soul, and thence rules the members of the body, which becomes holy in virtue of the holiness of the will; and that while the will remains firm and unshaken, nothing that another person does with the body, or upon the body, is any fault of the person who suffers it, so long as he cannot escape it without sin. But as not only pain may be inflicted, but lust gratified on the body of another, whenever anything of this latter kind takes place, shame invades even a thoroughly pure spirit from which modesty has not departed—shame, lest that act which could not be suffered without some sensual pleasure, should be believed to have been committed also with some assent of the will.

17. OF SUICIDE COMMITTED THROUGH FEAR OF PUNISHMENT OR DISHONOR

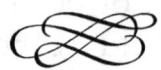

And consequently, even if some of these virgins killed themselves to avoid such disgrace, who that has any human feeling would refuse to forgive them? And as for those who would not put an end to their lives, lest they might seem to escape the crime of another by a sin of their own, he who lays this to their charge as a great wickedness is himself not guiltless of the fault of folly. For if it is not lawful to take the law into our own hands, and slay even a guilty person, whose death no public sentence has warranted, then certainly he who kills himself is a homicide, and so much the guiltier of his own death, as he was more innocent of that offense for which he doomed himself to die. Do we justly execrate the deed of Judas, and does truth itself pronounce that by hanging himself he rather aggravated than expiated the guilt of that most iniquitous betrayal, since, by despairing of God's mercy in his sorrow that worked death, he left to himself no place for a healing penitence? How much more ought he to abstain from laying violent hands on himself who has done nothing worthy of such a punishment! For Judas, when he killed himself, killed a wicked man; but he passed from this life chargeable not only with the death of Christ, but with his own: for though he killed himself on account of his crime, his killing himself was another crime. Why, then, should a man who has done no ill do ill to himself, and by killing himself kill the innocent to escape another's guilty act, and perpetrate upon himself a sin of his own, that the sin of another may not be perpetrated on him?

18. OF THE VIOLENCE WHICH MAY BE DONE TO THE BODY BY ANOTHER'S LUST, WHILE THE MIND REMAINS INVIOLATE

But is there a fear that even another's lust may pollute the violated? It will not pollute, if it be another's: if it pollute, it is not another's, but is shared also by the polluted. But since purity is a virtue of the soul, and has for its companion virtue the fortitude which will rather endure all ills than consent to evil; and since no one, however magnanimous and pure, has always the disposal of his own body, but can control only the consent and refusal of his will, what sane man can suppose that, if his body be seized and forcibly made use of to satisfy the lust of another, he thereby loses his purity? For if purity can be thus destroyed, then assuredly purity is no virtue of the soul; nor can it be numbered among those good things by which the life is made good, but among the good things of the body, in the same category as strength, beauty, sound and unbroken health, and, in short, all such good things as may be diminished without at all diminishing the goodness and rectitude of our life. But if purity be nothing better than these, why should the body be periled that it may be preserved? If, on the other hand, it belongs to the soul, then not even when the body is violated is it lost. No more, the virtue of holy continence, when it resists the uncleanness of carnal lust, sanctifies even the body, and therefore when this continence remains unsubdued, even the sanctity of the body is preserved, because the will to use it holily remains, and, so far as lies in the body itself, the power also.

For the sanctity of the body does not consist in the integrity of its members, nor in their exemption from all touch; for they are exposed to various accidents which do violence to and wound them, and the surgeons who administer relief often perform operations that sicken the spectator. A midwife, suppose, has (whether maliciously or accidentally, or through unskillfulness) destroyed the virginity of some girl, while endeavoring to ascertain it: I suppose no one is so foolish as to believe that, by this destruction of the integrity of one organ, the virgin has lost anything even of her bodily sanctity. And thus, so long as the soul keeps this firmness of purpose which sanctifies even the body, the violence done by another's lust makes no impression on this bodily sanctity, which is preserved intact by one's own persistent continence. Suppose a virgin violates the oath she has sworn to God, and goes to meet her seducer with the intention of yielding to him, shall we say that as she goes she is possessed even of bodily sanctity, when already she has lost and destroyed that sanctity of soul which sanctifies the body? Far be it from us to so misapply words. Let us rather draw this conclusion, that while the sanctity of the soul remains even when the body is violated, the sanctity of the body is not lost; and that, in like manner, the sanctity of the body is lost when the sanctity of the soul is violated, though the body itself remains intact. And therefore a woman who has been violated by the sin of another, and without any consent of her own, has no cause to put herself to death; much less has she cause to commit suicide in order to avoid such violation, for in that case she commits certain homicide to prevent a crime which is uncertain as yet, and not her own.

19. OF LUCRETIA, WHO PUT AN END TO HER LIFE BECAUSE OF THE OUTRAGE DONE HER

This, then, is our position, and it seems sufficiently lucid. We maintain that when a woman is violated while her soul admits no consent to the iniquity, but remains inviolably chaste, the sin is not hers, but his who violates her. But do they against whom we have to defend not only the souls, but the sacred bodies too of these outraged Christian captives—do they, perhaps, dare to dispute our position? But all know how loudly they extol the purity of Lucretia, that noble matron of ancient Rome. When King Tarquin's son had violated her body, she made known the wickedness of this young profligate to her husband Collatinus, and to Brutus her kinsman, men of high rank and full of courage, and bound them by an oath to avenge it. Then, heartsick, and unable to bear the shame, she put an end to her life. What shall we call her? An adulteress, or chaste? There is no question which she was. Not more happily than truly did a declaimer say of this sad occurrence: "Here was a marvel: there were two, and only one committed adultery." Most forcibly and truly spoken. For this declaimer, seeing in the union of the two bodies the foul lust of the one, and the chaste will of the other, and giving heed not to the contact of the bodily members, but to the wide diversity of their souls, says: "There were two, but the adultery was committed only by one."

But how is it, that she who was no partner to the crime bears the heavier punishment of the two? For the adulterer was only banished along with his father; she suffered the extreme penalty. If that was not impurity by which she was unwillingly ravished, then this is not justice by which she, being chaste, is punished. To you I appeal, you laws and judges of Rome. Even after the perpetration of great enormities, you do not suffer the criminal to be slain untried. If, then, one were to bring to your bar this case, and were to prove to you that a woman not only untried, but chaste and innocent, had been killed, would you not visit the murderer with punishment proportionably severe? This crime was committed by Lucretia; that Lucretia so celebrated and lauded slew the innocent, chaste, outraged Lucretia. Pronounce sentence. But if you cannot, because there does not appear anyone whom you can punish, why do you extol with such unmeasured laudation her who slew an innocent and chaste woman? Assuredly you will find it impossible to defend her before the judges of the realms below, if they be such as your poets are fond of representing them; for she is among those

> *Who guiltless sent themselves to doom,*
> *And all for loathing of the day,*
> *In madness threw their lives away.*
> *And if she with the others wishes to return,*
> *Fate bars the way: around their keep*
> *The slow unlovely waters creep,*
> *And bind with ninefold chain.*[1]

Or perhaps she is not there, because she slew herself conscious of guilt, not of innocence? She herself alone knows her reason; but what if she was betrayed by the pleasure of the act, and gave some consent to Sextus, though so violently abusing her, and then was so affected with remorse, that she thought death alone could expiate her sin? Even though this were the case, she ought still to have held her hand from suicide, if she could with her false gods have accomplished a fruitful repentance. However, if such were the state of the case, and if it were false that there were two, but one only committed adultery; if the truth were that both were involved in it, one by open assault, the other by secret consent, then she did not kill an innocent woman; and therefore her erudite defenders may maintain that she is not among that class of the dwellers below "who guiltless sent themselves to doom." But this case of Lucretia is in such a dilemma, that if you extenuate the homicide, you confirm the adultery: if you acquit her of adultery, you make the charge of homicide heavier; and there is no way out of the dilemma, when one asks, if she was adulterous, why praise her? If chaste, why slay her?

Nevertheless, for our purpose of refuting those who are unable to comprehend what true sanctity is, and who therefore insult over our outraged Christian women, it is enough that in the instance of this noble Roman matron it was said in her praise, "There were two, but the adultery was the crime of only one." For Lucretia was confidently believed to be superior to the contamination of any consenting thought to the adultery. And accordingly, since she killed herself for being subjected to an outrage in which she had no guilty part, it is obvious that this act of hers was prompted not by the love of purity, but by the overwhelming burden of her shame. She was ashamed that so foul a crime had been perpetrated upon her, though without her abetting; and this matron, with the Roman love of glory in her veins, was seized with a proud dread that, if she continued to live, it would be supposed she willingly did not resent the wrong that had been done her. She could not exhibit to men her conscience, but she judged that her self-inflicted punishment would testify her state of mind; and she burned with shame at the thought that her patient endurance of the foul affront that another had done her should be construed into complicity with him. Not such was the decision of the Christian women who suffered as she did, and yet survive. They declined to avenge upon themselves the guilt of others, and so add crimes of their own to those crimes in which they had no share. For this they would have done had their shame driven them to homicide, as the lust of their enemies had driven them to adultery. Within their own souls, in the witness of their own conscience, they enjoy the glory of chastity. In the sight of God, too, they are esteemed pure, and this contents them; they ask no more: it suffices them to have opportunity of doing good, and they decline to evade the distress of human suspicion, lest they thereby deviate from the divine law.

---

1. Virgil *Æneid* 6.434.

20. THAT CHRISTIANS HAVE NO AUTHORITY FOR COMMITTING SUICIDE IN ANY CIRCUMSTANCES WHATEVER

It is not without significance, that in no passage of the holy canonical books there can be found either divine precept or permission to take away our own life, whether for the sake of entering on the enjoyment of immortality, or of shunning, or ridding ourselves of anything whatever. No, the law, rightly interpreted, even prohibits suicide, where it says, "Thou shalt not kill." This is proved especially by the omission of the words "thy neighbor," which are inserted when false witness is forbidden: "Thou shalt not bear false witness against thy neighbor." Nor yet should anyone on this account suppose he has not broken this commandment if he has borne false witness only against himself. For the love of our neighbor is regulated by the love of ourselves, as it is written, "Thou shalt love thy neighbor as thyself." If, then, he who makes false statements about himself is not less guilty of bearing false witness than if he had made them to the injury of his neighbor; although in the commandment prohibiting false witness only his neighbor is mentioned, and persons taking no pains to understand it might suppose that a man was allowed to be a false witness to his own hurt; how much greater reason have we to understand that a man may not kill himself, since in the commandment, "Thou shalt not kill," there is no limitation added nor any exception made in favor of anyone, and least of all in favor of him on whom the command is laid! And so some attempt to extend this command even to beasts and cattle, as if it forbade us to take life from any creature. But if so, why not extend it also to the plants, and all that is rooted in and nourished by the earth? For though this class of creatures have no sensation, yet they also are said to live, and consequently they can die; and therefore, if violence be done them, can be killed. So, too, the apostle, when speaking of the seeds of such things as these, says, "That which thou sowest is not quickened except it die"; and in the psalm it is said, "He killed their vines with hail." Must we therefore reckon it a breaking of this commandment, "Thou shalt not kill," to pull a flower? Are we thus insanely to countenance the foolish error of the Manichæans? Putting aside, then, these ravings, if, when we say, "Thou shalt not kill," we do not understand this of the plants, since they have no sensation, nor of the irrational animals that fly, swim, walk, or creep, since they are dissociated from us by their want of reason, and are therefore by the just appointment of the Creator subjected to us to kill or keep alive for our own uses; if so, then it remains that we understand that commandment simply of man. The commandment is, "Thou shalt not kill man"; therefore neither another nor yourself, for he who kills himself still kills nothing else than man.

21. OF THE CASES IN WHICH WE MAY PUT MEN TO DEATH WITHOUT INCURRING THE GUILT OF MURDER

However, there are some exceptions made by the divine authority to its own law, that men may not be put to death. These exceptions are of two kinds, being justified either by a general law, or by a special commission granted for a time to some individual. And in this latter case, he to whom authority is delegated, and who is but the sword in the hand of him who uses it, is not himself responsible for the death he deals. And, accordingly, they who have waged war in obedience to the divine command, or in conformity with His laws, have represented in their persons the public justice or the wisdom of government, and in this capacity have put to death wicked men; such persons have by no means violated the commandment, "Thou shalt not kill." Abraham indeed was not merely deemed guiltless of cruelty, but was even applauded for his piety, because he was ready to slay his son in obedience to God, not to his own passion.

And it is reasonably enough made a question, whether we are to esteem it to have been in compliance with a command of God that Jephthah killed his daughter, because she met him when he had vowed that he would sacrifice to God whatever first met him as he returned victorious from battle. Samson, too, who drew down the house on himself and his foes together, is justified only on this ground, that the Spirit who worked wonders by him had given him secret instructions to do this. With the exception, then, of these two classes of cases, which are justified either by a just law that applies generally, or by a special intimation from God Himself, the fountain of all justice, whoever kills a man, either himself or another, is implicated in the guilt of murder.

22. THAT SUICIDE CAN NEVER BE PROMPTED BY MAGNANIMITY

But they who have laid violent hands on themselves are perhaps to be admired for their greatness of soul, though they cannot be applauded for the soundness of their judgment. However, if you look at the matter more closely, you will scarcely call it greatness of soul, which prompts a man to kill himself rather than bear up against some hardships of fortune, or sins in which he is not implicated. Is it not rather proof of a feeble mind, to be unable to bear either the pains of bodily servitude or the foolish opinion of the vulgar? And is not that to be pronounced the greater mind, which rather faces than flees the ills of life, and which, in comparison of the light and purity of conscience, holds in small esteem the judgment of men, and specially of the vulgar, which is frequently involved in a mist of error? And, therefore, if suicide is to be esteemed a magnanimous act, none can take higher rank for magnanimity than that Cleombrotus, who (as the story goes), when he had read Plato's book in which he treats of the immortality of the soul, threw himself from a wall, and so passed from this life to that which he believed to be better. For he was not hard pressed by calamity, nor by any accusation, false or true, which he could not very well have lived down; there was, in short, no motive but only magnanimity urging him to seek death, and break away from the sweet detention of this life. And yet that this was a magnanimous rather than a justifiable action, Plato himself, whom he had read, would have told him; for he would certainly have been forward to commit, or at least to recommend suicide, had not the same bright intellect which saw that the soul was immortal, discerned also that to seek immortality by suicide was to be prohibited rather than encouraged.

Again, it is said many have killed themselves to prevent an enemy doing so. But we are not inquiring whether it has been done, but whether it ought to have been done. Sound judgment is to be preferred even to examples, and indeed examples harmonize with the voice of reason; but not all examples, but those only which are distinguished by their piety, and are proportionately worthy of imitation. For suicide we cannot cite the example of patriarchs, prophets, or apostles; though our Lord Jesus Christ, when He admonished them to flee from city to city if they were persecuted, might very well have taken that occasion to advise them to lay violent hands on themselves, and so escape their persecutors. But seeing He did not do this, nor proposed this mode of departing this life, though He were addressing His own friends for whom He had promised to prepare everlasting mansions, it is obvious that such examples as are produced from the "nations that forget God," give no warrant of imitation to the worshipers of the one true God.

23. WHAT WE ARE TO THINK OF THE EXAMPLE OF CATO, WHO SLEW HIMSELF BECAUSE UNABLE TO ENDURE CÆSAR'S VICTORY

Besides Lucretia, of whom enough has already been said, our advocates of suicide have some difficulty in finding any other prescriptive example, unless it be that of Cato, who killed himself at Utica. His example is appealed to, not because he was the only man who did so, but because he was so esteemed as a learned and excellent man, that it could plausibly be maintained that what he did was and is a good thing to do. But of this action of his, what can I say but that his own friends, enlightened men as he, prudently dissuaded him, and therefore judged his act to be that of a feeble rather than a strong spirit, and dictated not by honorable feeling forestalling shame, but by weakness shrinking from hardships? Indeed, Cato condemns himself by the advice he gave to his dearly loved son. For if it was a disgrace to live under Cæsar's rule, why did the father urge the son to this disgrace, by encouraging him to trust absolutely to Cæsar's generosity? Why did he not persuade him to die along with himself? If Torquatus was applauded for putting his son to death, when contrary to orders he had engaged, and engaged successfully, with the enemy, why did conquered Cato spare his conquered son, though he did not spare himself? Was it more disgraceful to be a victor contrary to orders, than to submit to a victor contrary to the received ideas of honor? Cato, then, cannot have deemed it to be shameful to live under Cæsar's rule; for had he done so, the father's sword would have delivered his son from this disgrace. The truth is, that his son, whom he both hoped and desired would be spared by Cæsar, was not more loved by him than Cæsar was envied the glory of pardoning him (as indeed Cæsar himself is reported to have said[1]); or if envy is too strong a word, let us say he was *ashamed* that this glory should be his.

---

1. Plutarch *Life of Cato* 72.

24. THAT IN THAT VIRTUE IN WHICH REGULUS EXCELS CATO, CHRISTIANS ARE PREEMINENTLY DISTINGUISHED

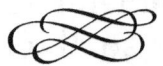

Our opponents are offended at our preferring to Cato the saintly Job, who endured dreadful evils in his body rather than deliver himself from all torment by self-inflicted death; or other saints, of whom it is recorded in our authoritative and trustworthy books that they bore captivity and the oppression of their enemies rather than commit suicide. But their own books authorize us to prefer to Marcus Cato, Marcus Regulus. For Cato had never conquered Cæsar; and when conquered by him, disdained to submit himself to him, and that he might escape this submission put himself to death. Regulus, on the contrary, had formerly conquered the Carthaginians, and in command of the army of Rome had won for the Roman republic a victory which no citizen could bewail, and which the enemy himself was constrained to admire; yet afterward, when he in his turn was defeated by them, he preferred to be their captive rather than to put himself beyond their reach by suicide. Patient under the domination of the Carthaginians, and constant in his love of the Romans, he neither deprived the one of his conquered body, nor the other of his unconquered spirit. Neither was it love of life that prevented him from killing himself. This was plainly enough indicated by his unhesitatingly returning, on account of his promise and oath, to the same enemies whom he had more grievously provoked by his words in the senate than even by his arms in battle. Having such a contempt of life, and preferring to end it by whatever torments excited enemies might contrive, rather than terminate it by his own hand, he could not more distinctly have declared how great a crime he judged suicide to be. Among all their famous and remarkable citizens, the Romans have no better man to boast of than this, who was neither corrupted by prosperity, for he remained a very poor man after winning such victories; nor broken by adversity, for he returned intrepidly to the most miserable end. But if the bravest and most renowned heroes, who had but an earthly country to defend, and who, though they had but false gods, yet rendered them a true worship, and carefully kept their oath to them; if these men, who by the custom and right of war put conquered enemies to the sword, yet shrank from putting an end to their own lives even when conquered by their enemies; if, though they had no fear at all of death, they would yet rather suffer slavery than commit suicide, how much rather must Christians, the worshipers of the true God, the aspirants to a heavenly citizenship, shrink from this act, if in God's providence they have been for a season delivered into the hands of their enemies to prove or to correct them! And certainly, Christians subjected to this humiliating condition will not be deserted by the Most High, who for their sakes humbled Himself. Neither should they forget that they are bound by no laws of war, nor military orders, to put even a conquered enemy to the sword; and if a man may not put to death the enemy who has sinned, or may yet sin against him, who is so infatuated as to maintain that he may kill himself because an enemy has sinned, or is going to sin, against him?

25. THAT WE SHOULD NOT ENDEAVOR BY SIN TO OBVIATE SIN

But, we are told, there is ground to fear that, when the body is subjected to the enemy's lust, the insidious pleasure of sense may entice the soul to consent to the sin, and steps must be taken to prevent so disastrous a result. And is not suicide the proper mode of preventing not only the enemy's sin, but the sin of the Christian so allured? Now, in the first place, the soul which is led by God and His wisdom, rather than by bodily concupiscence, will certainly never consent to the desire aroused in its own flesh by another's lust. And, at all events, if it be true, as the truth plainly declares, that suicide is a detestable and damnable wickedness, who is such a fool as to say, "Let us sin now, that we may obviate a possible future sin; let us now commit murder, lest we perhaps afterward should commit adultery"? If we are so controlled by iniquity that innocence is out of the question, and we can at best but make a choice of sins, is not a future and uncertain adultery preferable to a present and certain murder? Is it not better to commit a wickedness which penitence may heal, than a crime which leaves no place for healing contrition? I say this for the sake of those men or women who fear they may be enticed into consenting to their violator's lust, and think they should lay violent hands on themselves, and so prevent, not another's sin, but their own. But far be it from the mind of a Christian confiding in God, and resting in the hope of His aid; far be it, I say, from such a mind to yield a shameful consent to pleasures of the flesh, howsoever presented. And if that lustful disobedience, which still dwells in our mortal members, follows its own law irrespective of our will, surely its motions in the body of one who rebels against them are as blameless as its motions in the body of one who sleeps.

26. THAT IN CERTAIN PECULIAR CASES THE EXAMPLES OF THE SAINTS ARE NOT TO BE FOLLOWED

But, they say, in the time of persecution some holy women escaped those who menaced them with outrage, by casting themselves into rivers which they knew would drown them; and having died in this manner, they are venerated in the church catholic as martyrs. Of such persons I do not presume to speak rashly. I cannot tell whether there may not have been vouchsafed to the church some divine authority, proved by trustworthy evidences, for so honoring their memory: it may be that it is so. It may be they were not deceived by human judgment, but prompted by divine wisdom, to their act of self-destruction. We know that this was the case with Samson. And when God enjoins any act, and intimates by plain evidence that He has enjoined it, who will call obedience criminal? Who will accuse so religious a submission? But then every man is not justified in sacrificing his son to God, because Abraham was commendable in so doing. The soldier who has slain a man in obedience to the authority under which he is lawfully commissioned is not accused of murder by any law of his state; no, if he has not slain him, it is then he is accused of treason to the state, and of despising the law. But if he has been acting on his own authority, and at his own impulse, he has in this case incurred the crime of shedding human blood. And thus he is punished for doing without orders the very thing he is punished for neglecting to do when he has been ordered. If the commands of a general make so great a difference, shall the commands of God make none? He, then, who knows it is unlawful to kill himself, may nevertheless do so if he is ordered by Him whose commands we may not neglect. Only let him be very sure that the divine command has been signified. As for us, we can become privy to the secrets of conscience only insofar as these are disclosed to us, and so far only do we judge: "No one knoweth the things of a man, save the spirit of man which is in him." But this we affirm, this we maintain, this we every way pronounce to be right, that no man ought to inflict on himself voluntary death, for this is to escape the ills of time by plunging into those of eternity; that no man ought to do so on account of another man's sins, for this were to escape a guilt which could not pollute him, by incurring great guilt of his own; that no man ought to do so on account of his own past sins, for he has all the more need of this life that these sins may be healed by repentance; that no man should put an end to this life to obtain that better life we look for after death, for those who die by their own hand have no better life after death.

27. WHETHER VOLUNTARY DEATH SHOULD BE SOUGHT IN ORDER TO AVOID SIN

There remains one reason for suicide which I mentioned before, and which is thought a sound one—namely, to prevent one's falling into sin either through the blandishments of pleasure or the violence of pain. If this reason were a good one, then we should be impelled to exhort men at once to destroy themselves, as soon as they have been washed in the laver of regeneration, and have received the forgiveness of all sin. Then is the time to escape all future sin, when all past sin is blotted out. And if this escape be lawfully secured by suicide, why not then specially? Why does any baptized person hold his hand from taking his own life? Why does any person who is freed from the hazards of this life again expose himself to them, when he has power so easily to rid himself of them all, and when it is written, "He who loveth danger shall fall into it"?¹ Why does he love, or at least face, so many serious dangers, by remaining in this life from which he may legitimately depart? But is anyone so blinded and twisted in his moral nature, and so far astray from the truth, as to think that, though a man ought to make away with himself for fear of being led into sin by the oppression of one man, his master, he ought yet to live, and so expose himself to the hourly temptations of this world, both to all those evils which the oppression of one master involves, and to numberless other miseries in which this life inevitably implicates us? What reason, then, is there for our consuming time in those exhortations by which we seek to animate the baptized, either to virginal chastity, or vidual continence, or matrimonial fidelity, when we have so much more simple and compendious a method of deliverance from sin, by persuading those who are fresh from baptism to put an end to their lives, and so pass to their Lord pure and well conditioned? If anyone thinks that such persuasion should be attempted, I say not he is foolish, but mad. With what face, then, can he say to any man, "Kill yourself, lest to your small sins you add a heinous sin, while you live under an unchaste master, whose conduct is that of a barbarian"? How can he say this, if he cannot without wickedness say, "Kill yourself, now that you are washed from all your sins, lest you fall again into similar or even aggravated sins, while you live in a world which has such power to allure by its unclean pleasures, to torment by its horrible cruelties, to overcome by its errors and terrors"? It is wicked to say this; it is therefore wicked to kill oneself. For if there could be any just cause of suicide, this were so. And since not even this is so, there is none.

---

1. Ecclus. 3:27.

28. BY WHAT JUDGMENT OF GOD THE ENEMY WAS PERMITTED TO INDULGE HIS LUST ON THE BODIES OF CONTINENT CHRISTIANS

Let not your life, then, be a burden to you, ye faithful servants of Christ, though your chastity was made the sport of your enemies. You have a grand and true consolation, if you maintain a good conscience, and know that you did not consent to the sins of those who were permitted to commit sinful outrage upon you. And if you should ask why this permission was granted, indeed it is a deep providence of the Creator and Governor of the world; and "unsearchable are His judgments, and His ways past finding out."[1] Nevertheless, faithfully interrogate your own souls, whether you have not been unduly puffed up by your integrity, and continence, and chastity; and whether you have not been so desirous of the human praise that is accorded to these virtues, that you have envied some who possessed them. I, for my part, do not know your hearts, and therefore I make no accusation; I do not even hear what your hearts answer when you question them. And yet, if they answer that it is as I have supposed it might be, do not marvel that you have lost that by which you can win men's praise, and retain that which cannot be exhibited to men. If you did not consent to sin, it was because God added His aid to His grace that it might not be lost, and because shame before men succeeded to human glory that it might not be loved. But in both respects even the fainthearted among you have a consolation, approved by the one experience, chastened by the other; justified by the one, corrected by the other. As to those whose hearts, when interrogated, reply that they have never been proud of the virtue of virginity, widowhood, or matrimonial chastity, but, condescending to those of low estate, rejoiced with trembling in these gifts of God, and that they have never envied anyone the like excellences of sanctity and purity, but rose superior to human applause, which is wont to be abundant in proportion to the rarity of the virtue applauded, and rather desired that their own number be increased, than that by the smallness of their numbers each of them should be conspicuous; even such faithful women, I say, must not complain that permission was given to the barbarians so grossly to outrage them; nor must they allow themselves to believe that God overlooked their character when He permitted acts which no one with impunity commits. For some most flagrant and wicked desires are allowed free play at present by the secret judgment of God, and are reserved to the public and final judgment. Moreover, it is possible that those Christian women, who are unconscious of any undue pride on account of their virtuous chastity, whereby they sinlessly suffered the violence of their captors, had yet some lurking infirmity which might have betrayed them into a proud and contemptuous bearing, had they not been subjected to the humiliation that befell them in the taking of the city. As, therefore, some men were removed by death, that no wickedness might change their disposition, so these women were outraged lest prosperity should corrupt their modesty. Neither those women then, who were already puffed up by the circumstance that they were still virgins, nor those who might have been so puffed up had they not been exposed to the violence of the enemy, lost their chastity, but rather gained humility; the former were saved from pride already cherished, the latter from pride that would shortly have grown upon them.

We must further notice that some of those sufferers may have conceived that continence is a bodily good, and abides so long as the body is inviolate, and did not understand that the purity both of the body and the soul rests on the steadfastness of the will strengthened by God's grace, and cannot be forcibly taken from an unwilling person. From this error they are probably now delivered. For when they reflect how conscientiously they served God, and when they settle again to the firm persuasion that He can in nowise desert those who so serve Him, and so invoke His aid; and when they consider, what they cannot doubt, how pleasing to

Him is chastity, they are shut up to the conclusion that He could never have permitted these disasters to befall His saints, if by them that saintliness could be destroyed which He Himself had bestowed upon them, and delights to see in them.

---

1. Rom. 11:33.

29. WHAT THE SERVANTS OF CHRIST SHOULD SAY IN REPLY TO THE UNBELIEVERS WHO CAST IN THEIR TEETH THAT CHRIST DID NOT RESCUE THEM FROM THE FURY OF THEIR ENEMIES

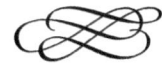

The whole family of God, most high and most true, has therefore a consolation of its own—a consolation which cannot deceive, and which has in it a surer hope than the tottering and falling affairs of earth can afford. They will not refuse the discipline of this temporal life, in which they are schooled for life eternal; nor will they lament their experience of it, for the good things of earth they use as pilgrims who are not detained by them, and its ills either prove or improve them. As for those who insult over them in their trials, and when ills befall them say, "Where is thy God?"[1] we may ask them where their gods are when they suffer the very calamities for the sake of avoiding which they worship their gods, or maintain they ought to be worshiped; for the family of Christ is furnished with its reply: our God is everywhere present, wholly everywhere; not confined to any place. He can be present unperceived, and be absent without moving; when He exposes us to adversities, it is either to prove our perfections or correct our imperfections; and in return for our patient endurance of the sufferings of time, He reserves for us an everlasting reward. But who are you, that we should deign to speak with you even about your own gods, much less about our God, who is "to be feared above all gods? For all the gods of the nations are idols; but the LORD made the heavens."[2]

---

1. Ps. 42:10.
2. Ps. 96:4–5.

30. THAT THOSE WHO COMPLAIN OF CHRISTIANITY REALLY DESIRE TO LIVE WITHOUT RESTRAINT IN SHAMEFUL LUXURY

If the famous Scipio Nasica were now alive, who was once your pontiff, and was unanimously chosen by the senate, when, in the panic created by the Punic war, they sought for the best citizen to entertain the Phrygian goddess, he would curb this shamelessness of yours, though you would perhaps scarcely dare to look upon the countenance of such a man. For why in your calamities do you complain of Christianity, unless because you desire to enjoy your luxurious license unrestrained, and to lead an abandoned and profligate life without the interruption of any uneasiness or disaster? For certainly your desire for peace, and prosperity, and plenty is not prompted by any purpose of using these blessings honestly, that is to say, with moderation, sobriety, temperance, and piety; for your purpose rather is to run riot in an endless variety of sottish pleasures, and thus to generate from your prosperity a moral pestilence which will prove a thousandfold more disastrous than the fiercest enemies. It was such a calamity as this that Scipio, your chief pontiff, your best man in the judgment of the whole senate, feared when he refused to agree to the destruction of Carthage, Rome's rival; and opposed Cato, who advised its destruction. He feared security, that enemy of weak minds, and he perceived that a wholesome fear would be a fit guardian for the citizens. And he was not mistaken; the event proved how wisely he had spoken. For when Carthage was destroyed, and the Roman republic delivered from its great cause of anxiety, a crowd of disastrous evils forthwith resulted from the prosperous condition of things. First concord was weakened, and destroyed by fierce and bloody seditions; then followed, by a concatenation of baleful causes, civil wars, which brought in their train such massacres, such bloodshed, such lawless and cruel proscription and plunder, that those Romans who, in the days of their virtue, had expected injury only at the hands of their enemies, now that their virtue was lost, suffered greater cruelties at the hands of their fellow citizens. The lust of rule, which with other vices existed among the Romans in more unmitigated intensity than among any other people, after it had taken possession of the more powerful few, subdued under its yoke the rest, worn and wearied.

31. BY WHAT STEPS THE PASSION FOR GOVERNING INCREASED AMONG THE ROMANS

For at what stage would that passion rest when once it has lodged in a proud spirit, until by a succession of advances it has reached even the throne. And to obtain such advances nothing avails but unscrupulous ambition. But unscrupulous ambition has nothing to work upon, save in a nation corrupted by avarice and luxury. Moreover, a people becomes avaricious and luxurious by prosperity; and it was this which that very prudent man Nasica was endeavoring to avoid when he opposed the destruction of the greatest, strongest, wealthiest city of Rome's enemy. He thought that thus fear would act as a curb on lust, and that lust being curbed would not run riot in luxury, and that luxury being prevented avarice would be at an end; and that these vices being banished, virtue would flourish and increase the great profit of the state; and liberty, the fit companion of virtue, would abide unfettered. For similar reasons, and animated by the same considerate patriotism, that same chief pontiff of yours—I still refer to him who was adjudged Rome's best man without one dissentient voice—threw cold water on the proposal of the senate to build a circle of seats round the theatre, and in a very weighty speech warned them against allowing the luxurious manners of Greece to sap the Roman manliness, and persuaded them not to yield to the enervating and emasculating influence of foreign licentiousness. So authoritative and forcible were his words, that the senate was moved to prohibit the use even of those benches which hitherto had been customarily brought to the theatre for the temporary use of the citizens.[1] How eagerly would such a man as this have banished from Rome the scenic exhibitions themselves, had he dared to oppose the authority of those whom he supposed to be gods! For he did not know that they were malicious devils; or if he did, he supposed they should rather be propitiated than despised. For there had not yet been revealed to the Gentiles the heavenly doctrine which should purify their hearts by faith, and transform their natural disposition by humble godliness, and turn them from the service of proud devils to seek the things that are in heaven, or even above the heavens.

---

1. Originally the spectators had to stand, and now (according to Livy *Ep.* 48) the old custom was restored.

32. OF THE ESTABLISHMENT OF SCENIC ENTERTAINMENTS

Know then, ye who are ignorant of this, and ye who feign ignorance be reminded, while you murmur against Him who has freed you from such rulers, that the scenic games, exhibitions of shameless folly and license, were established at Rome, not by men's vicious cravings, but by the appointment of your gods. Much more pardonably might you have rendered divine honors to Scipio than to such gods as these. The gods were not so moral as their pontiff. But give me now your attention, if your mind, inebriated by its deep potations of error, can take in any sober truth. The gods enjoined that games be exhibited in their honor to stay a physical pestilence; their pontiff prohibited the theatre from being constructed, to prevent a moral pestilence. If, then, there remains in you sufficient mental enlightenment to prefer the soul to the body, choose whom you will worship. Besides, though the pestilence was stayed, this was not because the voluptuous madness of stage plays had taken possession of a warlike people hitherto accustomed only to the games of the circus; but these astute and wicked spirits, foreseeing that in due course the pestilence would shortly cease, took occasion to infect, not the bodies, but the morals of their worshipers, with a far more serious disease. And in this pestilence these gods find great enjoyment, because it benighted the minds of men with so gross a darkness and dishonored them with so foul a deformity, that even quite recently (will posterity be able to credit it?) some of those who fled from the sack of Rome and found refuge in Carthage were so infected with this disease, that day after day they seemed to contend with one another who should most madly run after the actors in the theatres.

33. THAT THE OVERTHROW OF ROME HAS NOT CORRECTED THE VICES OF THE ROMANS

O, infatuated men, what is this blindness, or rather madness, which possesses you? How is it that while, as we hear, even the eastern nations are bewailing your ruin, and while powerful states in the most remote parts of the earth are mourning your fall as a public calamity, you yourselves should be crowding to the theatres, should be pouring into them and filling them; and, in short, be playing a madder part now than ever before? This was the foul plague-spot, this the wreck of virtue and honor that Scipio sought to preserve you from when he prohibited the construction of theatres; this was his reason for desiring that you might still have an enemy to fear, seeing as he did how easily prosperity would corrupt and destroy you. He did not consider that republic flourishing whose walls stand, but whose morals are in ruins. But the seductions of evil-minded devils had more influence with you than the precautions of prudent men. Hence the injuries you do, you will not permit to be imputed to you: but the injuries you suffer, you impute to Christianity. Depraved by good fortune, and not chastened by adversity, what you desire in the restoration of a peaceful and secure state, is not the tranquility of the commonwealth, but the impunity of your own vicious luxury. Scipio wished you to be hard pressed by an enemy, that you might not abandon yourselves to luxurious manners; but so abandoned are you, that not even when crushed by the enemy is your luxury repressed. You have missed the profit of your calamity; you have been made most wretched, and have remained most profligate.

34. OF GOD'S CLEMENCY IN MODERATING THE RUIN OF THE CITY

And that you are yet alive is due to God, who spares you that you may be admonished to repent and reform your lives. It is He who has permitted you, ungrateful as you are, to escape the sword of the enemy, by calling yourselves His servants, or by finding asylum in the sacred places of the martyrs.

It is said that Romulus and Remus, in order to increase the population of the city they founded, opened a sanctuary in which every man might find asylum and absolution of all crime—a remarkable foreshadowing of what has recently occurred in honor of Christ. The destroyers of Rome followed the example of its founders. But it was not greatly to their credit that the latter, for the sake of increasing the number of their citizens, did that which the former have done, lest the number of their enemies should be diminished.

35. OF THE SONS OF THE CHURCH WHO ARE HIDDEN AMONG THE WICKED, AND OF FALSE CHRISTIANS WITHIN THE CHURCH

Let these and similar answers (if any fuller and fitter answers can be found) be given to their enemies by the redeemed family of the Lord Christ, and by the pilgrim city of King Christ. But let this city bear in mind, that among her enemies lie hid those who are destined to be fellow citizens, that she may not think it a fruitless labor to bear what they inflict as enemies until they become confessors of the faith. So, too, as long as she is a stranger in the world, the city of God has in her communion, and bound to her by the sacraments, some who shall not eternally dwell in the lot of the saints. Of these, some are not now recognized; others declare themselves, and do not hesitate to make common cause with our enemies in murmuring against God, whose sacramental badge they wear. These men you may today see thronging the churches with us, tomorrow crowding the theatres with the godless. But we have the less reason to despair of the reclamation even of such persons, if among our most declared enemies there are now some, unknown to themselves, who are destined to become our friends. In truth, these two cities are entangled together in this world, and intermixed until the last judgment effects their separation. I now proceed to speak, as God shall help me, of the rise, progress, and end of these two cities; and what I write, I write for the glory of the city of God, that, being placed in comparison with the other, it may shine with a brighter luster.

36. WHAT SUBJECTS ARE TO BE HANDLED IN THE FOLLOWING DISCOURSE

But I have still some things to say in confutation of those who refer the disasters of the Roman republic to our religion, because it prohibits the offering of sacrifices to the gods. For this end I must recount all, or as many as may seem sufficient, of the disasters which befell that city and its subject provinces, before these sacrifices were prohibited; for all these disasters they would doubtless have attributed to us, if at that time our religion had shed its light upon them, and had prohibited their sacrifices. I must then go on to show what social well-being the true God, in whose hand are all kingdoms, vouchsafed to grant to them that their empire might increase. I must show why He did so, and how their false gods, instead of at all aiding them, greatly injured them by guile and deceit. And, lastly, I must meet those who, when on this point convinced and confuted by irrefragable proofs, endeavor to maintain that they worship the gods, not hoping for the present advantages of this life, but for those which are to be enjoyed after death. And this, if I am not mistaken, will be the most difficult part of my task, and will be worthy of the loftiest argument; for we must then enter the lists with the philosophers, not the mere common herd of philosophers, but the most renowned, who in many points agree with ourselves, as regarding the immortality of the soul, and that the true God created the world, and by His providence rules all He has created. But as they differ from us on other points, we must not shrink from the task of exposing their errors, that, having refuted the gainsaying of the wicked with such ability as God may vouchsafe, we may assert the city of God, and true piety, and the worship of God, to which alone the promise of true and everlasting felicity is attached. Here, then, let us conclude, that we may enter on these subjects in a fresh book.

BOOK TWO

ARGUMENT

In this book Augustine reviews those calamities which the Romans suffered before the time of Christ, and while the worship of the false gods was universally practiced; and demonstrates that, far from being preserved from misfortune by the gods, the Romans have been by them overwhelmed with the only, or at least the greatest, of all calamities—the corruption of manners, and the vices of the soul.

1. OF THE LIMITS WHICH MUST BE PUT TO THE NECESSITY OF REPLYING TO AN ADVERSARY

If the feeble mind of man did not presume to resist the clear evidence of truth, but yielded its infirmity to wholesome doctrines, as to a health-giving medicine, until it obtained from God, by its faith and piety, the grace needed to heal it, they who have just ideas, and express them in suitable language, would need to use no long discourse to refute the errors of empty conjecture. But this mental infirmity is now more prevalent and hurtful than ever, to such an extent that even after the truth has been as fully demonstrated as man can prove it to man, they hold for the very truth their own unreasonable fancies, either on account of their great blindness, which prevents them from seeing what is plainly set before them, or on account of their opinionative obstinacy, which prevents them from acknowledging the force of what they do see. There therefore frequently arises a necessity of speaking more fully on those points which are already clear, that we may, as it were, present them not to the eye, but even to the touch, so that they may be felt even by those who close their eyes against them. And yet to what end shall we ever bring our discussions, or what bounds can be set to our discourse, if we proceed on the principle that we must always reply to those who reply to us? For those who are either unable to understand our arguments, or are so hardened by the habit of contradiction, that though they understand they cannot yield to them, reply to us, and, as it is written, "speak hard things,"[1] and are incorrigibly vain. Now, if we were to propose to confute their objections as often as they with brazen face chose to disregard our arguments, and so often as they could by any means contradict our statements, you see how endless, and fruitless, and painful a task we should be undertaking. And therefore I do not wish my writings to be judged even by you, my son Marcellinus, nor by any of those others at whose service this work of mine is freely and in all Christian charity put, if at least you intend always to require a reply to every exception which you hear taken to what you read in it; for so you would become like those silly women of whom the apostle says that they are "always learning, and never able to come to the knowledge of the truth."[2]

---

1. Ps. 94:4.
2. 2 Tim. 3:7.

2. RECAPITULATION OF THE CONTENTS OF THE FIRST BOOK

In the foregoing book, having begun to speak of the city of God, to which I have resolved, heaven helping me, to consecrate the whole of this work, it was my first endeavor to reply to those who attribute the wars by which the world is being devastated, and especially the recent sack of Rome by the barbarians, to the religion of Christ, which prohibits the offering of abominable sacrifices to devils. I have shown that they ought rather to attribute it to Christ, that for His name's sake the barbarians, in contravention of all custom and law of war, threw open as sanctuaries the largest churches, and in many instances showed such reverence to Christ, that not only His genuine servants, but even those who in their terror feigned themselves to be so, were exempted from all those hardships which by the custom of war may lawfully be inflicted. Then out of this there arose the question, why wicked and ungrateful men were permitted to share in these benefits; and why, too, the hardships and calamities of war were inflicted on the godly as well as on the ungodly. And in giving a suitably full answer to this large question, I occupied some considerable space, partly that I might relieve the anxieties which disturb many when they observe that the blessings of God, and the common and daily human casualties, fall to the lot of bad men and good without distinction; but mainly that I might minister some consolation to those holy and chaste women who were outraged by the enemy, in such a way as to shock their modesty, though not to sully their purity, and that I might preserve them from being ashamed of life, though they have no guilt to be ashamed of. And then I briefly spoke against those who with a most shameless wantonness insult over those poor Christians who were subjected to those calamities, and especially over those broken-hearted and humiliated, though chaste and holy women; these fellows themselves being most depraved and unmanly profligates, quite degenerate from the genuine Romans, whose famous deeds are abundantly recorded in history, and everywhere celebrated, but who have found in their descendants the greatest enemies of their glory. In truth, Rome, which was founded and increased by the labors of these ancient heroes, was more shamefully ruined by their descendants, while its walls were still standing, than it is now by the razing of them. For in this ruin there fell stones and timbers; but in the ruin those profligates effected, there fell, not the mural, but the moral bulwarks and ornaments of the city, and their hearts burned with passions more destructive than the flames which consumed their houses. Thus I brought my first book to a close. And now I go on to speak of those calamities which that city itself, or its subject provinces, have suffered since its foundation; all of which they would equally have attributed to the Christian religion, if at that early period the doctrine of the gospel against their false and deceiving gods had been as largely and freely proclaimed as now.

3. THAT WE NEED ONLY TO READ HISTORY IN ORDER TO SEE WHAT CALAMITIES THE ROMANS SUFFERED BEFORE THE RELIGION OF CHRIST BEGAN TO COMPETE WITH THE WORSHIP OF THE GODS

But remember that, in recounting these things, I have still to address myself to ignorant men; so ignorant, indeed, as to give birth to the common saying, "Drought and Christianity go hand in hand."[1] There are indeed some among them who are thoroughly well educated men, and have a taste for history, in which the things I speak of are open to their observation; but in order to irritate the uneducated masses against us, they feign ignorance of these events, and do what they can to make the vulgar believe that those disasters, which in certain places and at certain times uniformly befall mankind, are the result of Christianity, which is being everywhere diffused, and is possessed of a renown and brilliancy which quite eclipse their own gods.[2] Let them then, along with us, call to mind with what various and repeated disasters the prosperity of Rome was blighted, before ever Christ had come in the flesh, and before His name had been blazoned among the nations with that glory which they vainly grudge. Let them, if they can, defend their gods in this article, since they maintain that they worship them in order to be preserved from these disasters, which they now impute to us if they suffer in the least degree. For why did these gods permit the disasters I am to speak of to fall on their worshipers before the preaching of Christ's name offended them, and put an end to their sacrifices?

---

1. "*Pluvia defit, causa Christiani.*" Similar accusations and similar replies may be seen in the celebrated passage of Tertullian's *Apol.* 40, and in the eloquent exordium of Arnobius *C. Gentes.*
2. Augustine is supposed to refer to Symmachus, who similarly accused the Christians in his address to the emperor Valentinianus in the year 384. At Augustine's request, Paulus Orosius wrote his history in confutation of Symmachus's charges.

4. THAT THE WORSHIPERS OF THE GODS NEVER RECEIVED FROM THEM ANY HEALTHY MORAL PRECEPTS, AND THAT IN CELEBRATING THEIR WORSHIP ALL SORTS OF IMPURITIES WERE PRACTICED

First of all, we would ask why their gods took no steps to improve the morals of their worshipers. That the true God should neglect those who did not seek His help, that was but justice; but why did those gods, from whose worship ungrateful men are now complaining that they are prohibited, issue no laws which might have guided their devotees to a virtuous life? Surely it was but just, that such care as men showed to the worship of the gods, the gods on their part should have to the conduct of men. But, it is replied, it is by his own will a man goes astray. Who denies it? But nonetheless was it incumbent on these gods, who were men's guardians, to publish in plain terms the laws of a good life, and not to conceal them from their worshipers. It was their part to send prophets to reach and convict such as broke these laws, and publicly to proclaim the punishments which await evildoers, and the rewards which may be looked for by those that do well. Did ever the walls of any of their temples echo to any such warning voice? I myself, when I was a young man, used sometimes to go to the sacrilegious entertainments and spectacles; I saw the priests raving in religious excitement, and heard the choristers; I took pleasure in the shameful games which were celebrated in honor of gods and goddesses, of the virgin Cœlestis,[1] and Berecynthia,[2] the mother of all the gods. And on the holy day consecrated to her purification, there were sung before her couch productions so obscene and filthy for the ear—I do not say of the mother of the gods, but of the mother of any senator or honest man—no, so impure, that not even the mother of the foul-mouthed players themselves could have formed one of the audience. For natural reverence for parents is a bond which the most abandoned cannot ignore. And, accordingly, the lewd actions and filthy words with which these players honored the mother of the gods, in presence of a vast assemblage and audience of both sexes, they could not for very shame have rehearsed at home in presence of their own mothers. And the crowds that were gathered from all quarters by curiosity, offended modesty must, I should suppose, have scattered in the confusion of shame. If these are sacred rites, what is sacrilege? If this is purification, what is pollution? This festivity was called the Tables,[3] as if a banquet were being given at which unclean devils might find suitable refreshment. For it is not difficult to see what kind of spirits they must be who are delighted with such obscenities, unless, indeed, a man be blinded by these evil spirits passing themselves off under the name of gods, and either disbelieves in their existence, or leads such a life as prompts him rather to propitiate and fear them than the true God.

---

1. Tertullian (*Apol.* 24) mentions Cœlestis as specially worshiped in Africa. Augustine mentions her again in the twenty-sixth chapter of this book, and in other parts of his works.
2. Berecynthia is one of the many names of Rhea or Cybele. Livy (29.11) relates that the image of Cybele was brought to Rome the day before the ides of April, which was accordingly dedicated as her feast day. The image, it seems, had to be washed in the stream Almon, a tributary of the Tiber, before being placed in the temple of Victory; and each year, as the festival returned, the washing was repeated with much pomp at the same spot. Hence Lucan's line (1.600), "*Et lotam parvo revocant Almone Cybelen,*" and the elegant verses of Ovid (*Fast.* 4.337 et seq.).
3. *Fercula,* dishes or courses.

5. OF THE OBSCENITIES PRACTICED IN HONOR OF THE MOTHER OF THE GODS

In this matter I would prefer to have as my assessors in judgment, not those men who rather take pleasure in these infamous customs than take pains to put an end to them, but that same Scipio Nasica who was chosen by the senate as the citizen most worthy to receive in his hands the image of that demon Cybele, and convey it into the city. He would tell us whether he would be proud to see his own mother so highly esteemed by the state as to have divine honors adjudged to her; as the Greeks and Romans and other nations have decreed divine honors to men who had been of material service to them, and have believed that their mortal benefactors were thus made immortal, and enrolled among the gods.[1] Surely he would desire that his mother should enjoy such felicity were it possible. But if we proceeded to ask him whether, among the honors paid to her, he would wish such shameful rites as these to be celebrated, would he not at once exclaim that he would rather his mother lay stone-dead, than survive as a goddess to lend her ear to these obscenities? Is it possible that he who was of so severe a morality, that he used his influence as a Roman senator to prevent the building of a theatre in that city dedicated to the manly virtues, would wish his mother to be propitiated as a goddess with words which would have brought the blush to her cheek when a Roman matron? Could he possibly believe that the modesty of an estimable woman would be so transformed by her promotion to divinity, that she would suffer herself to be invoked and celebrated in terms so gross and immodest, that if she had heard the like while alive upon earth, and had listened without stopping her ears and hurrying from the spot, her relatives, her husband, and her children would have blushed for her? Therefore, the mother of the gods being such a character as the most profligate man would be ashamed to have for his mother, and meaning to enthrall the minds of the Romans, demanded for her service their best citizen, not to ripen him still more in virtue by her helpful counsel, but to entangle him by her deceit, like her of whom it is written, "The adulteress will hunt for the precious soul."[2] Her intent was to puff up this high-souled man by an apparently divine testimony to his excellence, in order that he might rely upon his own eminence in virtue, and make no further efforts after true piety and religion, without which natural genius, however brilliant, vapors into pride and comes to nothing. For what but a guileful purpose could that goddess demand the best man seeing that in her own sacred festivals she requires such obscenities as the best men would be covered with shame to hear at their own tables?

---

1. See Cicero *De Nat. Deor.* 2.24.
2. Prov. 6:26.

6. THAT THE GODS OF THE PAGANS NEVER INCULCATED HOLINESS OF LIFE

This is the reason why those divinities quite neglected the lives and morals of the cities and nations who worshiped them, and threw no dreadful prohibition in their way to hinder them from becoming utterly corrupt, and to preserve them from those terrible and detestable evils which visit not harvests and vintages, not house and possessions, not the body which is subject to the soul, but the soul itself, the spirit that rules the whole man. If there was any such prohibition, let it be produced, let it be proved. They will tell us that purity and probity were inculcated upon those who were initiated in the mysteries of religion, and that secret incitements to virtue were whispered in the ear of the elite; but this is an idle boast. Let them show or name to us the places which were at any time consecrated to assemblages in which, instead of the obscene songs and licentious acting of players, instead of the celebration of those most filthy and shameless Fugalia[1] (well called Fugalia, since they banish modesty and right feeling), the people were commanded in the name of the gods to restrain avarice, bridle impurity, and conquer ambition; where, in short, they might learn in that school which Persius vehemently lashes them to, when he says: "Be taught, ye abandoned creatures, and ascertain the causes of things; what we are, and for what end we are born; what is the law of our success in life; and by what art we may turn the goal without making shipwreck; what limit we should put to our wealth, what we may lawfully desire, and what uses filthy lucre serves; how much we should bestow upon our country and our family; learn, in short, what God meant you to be, and what place He has ordered you to fill."[2] Let them name to us the places where such instructions were wont to be communicated from the gods, and where the people who worshiped them were accustomed to resort to hear them, as we can point to our churches built for this purpose in every land where the Christian religion is received.

---

1. Fugalia. Vives is uncertain to what feast Augustine refers. Censorinus understands him to refer to a feast celebrating the expulsion of the kings from Rome. This feast, however (celebrated on February 24), was commonly called *Regifugium*.
2. Persius *Sat.* 3.66–72.

7. THAT THE SUGGESTIONS OF PHILOSOPHERS ARE PRECLUDED FROM HAVING ANY MORAL EFFECT, BECAUSE THEY HAVE NOT THE AUTHORITY WHICH BELONGS TO DIVINE INSTRUCTION, AND BECAUSE MAN'S NATURAL BIAS TO EVIL INDUCES HIM RATHER TO FOLLOW THE EXAMPLES OF THE GODS THAN TO OBEY THE PRECEPTS OF MEN

But will they perhaps remind us of the schools of the philosophers, and their disputations? In the first place, these belong not to Rome, but to Greece; and even if we yield to them that they are now Roman, because Greece itself has become a Roman province, still the teachings of the philosophers are not the commandments of the gods, but the discoveries of men, who, at the prompting of their own speculative ability, made efforts to discover the hidden laws of nature, and the right and wrong in ethics, and in dialectic what was consequent according to the rules of logic, and what was inconsequent and erroneous. And some of them, by God's help, made great discoveries; but when left to themselves they were betrayed by human infirmity, and fell into mistakes. And this was ordered by divine Providence, that their pride might be restrained, and that by their example it might be pointed out that it is humility which has access to the highest regions. But of this we shall have more to say, if the Lord God of truth permit, in its own place.[1] However, if the philosophers have made any discoveries which are sufficient to guide men to virtue and blessedness, would it not have been greater justice to vote divine honors to them? Were it not more accordant with every virtuous sentiment to read Plato's writings in a "Temple of Plato," than to be present in the temples of devils to witness the priests of Cybele[2] mutilating themselves, the effeminate being consecrated, the raving fanatics cutting themselves, and whatever other cruel or shameful, or shamefully cruel or cruelly shameful, ceremony is enjoined by the ritual of such gods as these? Were it not a more suitable education, and more likely to prompt the youth to virtue, if they heard public recitals of the laws of the gods, instead of the vain laudation of the customs and laws of their ancestors? Certainly all the worshipers of the Roman gods, when once they are possessed by what Persius calls "the burning poison of lust,"[3] prefer to witness the deeds of Jupiter rather than to hear what Plato taught or Cato censured. Hence the young profligate in Terence, when he sees on the wall a fresco representing the fabled descent of Jupiter into the lap of Danaë in the form of a golden shower, accepts this as authoritative precedent for his own licentiousness, and boasts that he is an imitator of God. "And what God?" he says. "He who with his thunder shakes the loftiest temples. And was I, a poor creature compared to him, to make bones of it? No; I did it, and with all my heart."[4]

---

1. See below, books 8–12.
2. *Galli*, the castrated priests of Cybele, who were named after the river Gallus, in Phrygia, the water of which was supposed to intoxicate or madden those who drank it. According to Vitruvius (8.3), there was a similar fountain in Paphlagonia. Apuleius (*Golden Ass* 8) gives a graphic and humorous description of the dress, dancing, and imposture of these priests; mentioning, among other things, that they lashed themselves with whips and cut themselves with knives till the ground was wet with blood.
3. Persius *Sat*. 3.37.
4. Terence *Eun*. 3.5.36; and cf. the similar allusion in Aristophanes *Clouds* 1033–1034. It may be added that the argument of this chapter was largely used by the wiser of the heathen themselves. Dionysius of Halicarnassus (2.20) and Seneca (*De Brev. Vit.* 16) make the very same complaint; and it will be remembered that his adoption of this reasoning was one of the grounds on which Euripides was suspected of atheism.

8. THAT THE THEATRICAL EXHIBITIONS PUBLISHING THE SHAMEFUL ACTIONS OF THE GODS, PROPITIATED RATHER THAN OFFENDED THEM

But, someone will interpose, these are the fables of poets, not the deliverances of the gods themselves. Well, I have no mind to arbitrate between the lewdness of theatrical entertainments and of mystic rites; only this I say, and history bears me out in making the assertion, that those same entertainments, in which the fictions of poets are the main attraction, were not introduced in the festivals of the gods by the ignorant devotion of the Romans, but that the gods themselves gave the most urgent commands to this effect, and indeed extorted from the Romans these solemnities and celebrations in their honor. I touched on this in the preceding book, and mentioned that dramatic entertainments were first inaugurated at Rome on occasion of a pestilence, and by authority of the pontiff. And what man is there who is not more likely to adopt, for the regulation of his own life, the examples that are represented in plays which have a divine sanction, rather than the precepts written and promulgated with no more than human authority? If the poets gave a false representation of Jove in describing him as adulterous, then it were to be expected that the chaste gods should in anger avenge so wicked a fiction, in place of encouraging the games which circulated it. Of these plays, the most inoffensive are comedies and tragedies, that is to say, the dramas which poets write for the stage, and which, though they often handle impure subjects, yet do so without the filthiness of language which characterizes many other performances; and it is these dramas which boys are obliged by their seniors to read and learn as a part of what is called a liberal and gentlemanly education.[1]

---

1. This sentence recalls Augustine's own experience as a boy, which he bewails in his *Confessions*.

9. THAT THE POETICAL LICENSE WHICH THE GREEKS, IN OBEDIENCE TO THEIR GODS, ALLOWED, WAS RESTRAINED BY THE ANCIENT ROMANS

The opinion of the ancient Romans on this matter is attested by Cicero in his work *De Republica,* in which Scipio, one of the interlocutors, says, "The lewdness of comedy could never have been suffered by audiences, unless the customs of society had previously sanctioned the same lewdness." And in the earlier days the Greeks preserved a certain reasonableness in their license, and made it a law, that whatever comedy wished to say of anyone, it must say it of him by name. And so in the same work of Cicero's, Scipio says, "Whom has it not aspersed? Nay, whom has it not worried? Whom has it spared? Allow that it may assail demagogues and factions, men injurious to the commonwealth—a Cleon, a Cleophon, a Hyperbolus. That is tolerable, though it had been more seemly for the public censor to brand such men, than for a poet to lampoon them; but to blacken the fame of Pericles with scurrilous verse, after he had with the utmost dignity presided over their state alike in war and in peace, was as unworthy of a poet, as if our own Plautus or Nævius were to bring Publius and Cneius Scipio on the comic stage, or as if Cæcilius were to caricature Cato." And then a little after he goes on: "Though our Twelve Tables attached the penalty of death only to a very few offenses, yet among these few this was one: if any man should have sung a pasquinade, or have composed a satire calculated to bring infamy or disgrace on another person. Wisely decreed. For it is by the decisions of magistrates, and by a well-informed justice, that our lives ought to be judged, and not by the flighty fancies of poets; neither ought we to be exposed to hear calumnies, save where we have the liberty of replying, and defending ourselves before an adequate tribunal." This much I have judged it advisable to quote from the fourth book of Cicero's *De Republica;* and I have made the quotation word for word, with the exception of some words omitted, and some slightly transposed, for the sake of giving the sense more readily. And certainly the extract is pertinent to the matter I am endeavoring to explain. Cicero makes some further remarks, and concludes the passage by showing that the ancient Romans did not permit any living man to be either praised or blamed on the stage. But the Greeks, as I said, though not so moral, were more logical in allowing this license which the Romans forbade; for they saw that their gods approved and enjoyed the scurrilous language of low comedy when directed not only against men, but even against themselves; and this, whether the infamous actions imputed to them were the fictions of poets, or were their actual iniquities commemorated and acted in the theatres. And would that the spectators had judged them worthy only of laughter, and not of imitation! Manifestly it had been a stretch of pride to spare the good name of the leading men and the common citizens, when the very deities did not grudge that their own reputation should be blemished.

10. THAT THE DEVILS, IN SUFFERING EITHER FALSE OR TRUE CRIMES TO BE LAID TO THEIR CHARGE, MEANT TO DO MEN A MISCHIEF

It is alleged, in excuse of this practice, that the stories told of the gods are not true, but false, and mere inventions, but this only makes matters worse, if we form our estimate by the morality our religion teaches; and if we consider the malice of the devils, what more wily and astute artifice could they practice upon men? When a slander is uttered against a leading statesman of upright and useful life, is it not reprehensible in proportion to its untruth and groundlessness? What punishment, then, shall be sufficient when the gods are the objects of so wicked and outrageous an injustice? But the devils, whom these men repute gods, are content that even iniquities they are guiltless of should be ascribed to them, so long as they may entangle men's minds in the meshes of these opinions, and draw them on along with themselves to their predestinated punishment: whether such things were actually committed by the men whom these devils, delighting in human infatuation, cause to be worshiped as gods, and in whose stead they, by a thousand malign and deceitful artifices, substitute themselves, and so receive worship; or whether, though they were really the crimes of men, these wicked spirits gladly allowed them to be attributed to higher beings, that there might seem to be conveyed from heaven itself a sufficient sanction for the perpetration of shameful wickedness. The Greeks, therefore, seeing the character of the gods they served, thought that the poets should certainly not refrain from showing up human vices on the stage, either because they desired to be like their gods in this, or because they were afraid that, if they required for themselves a more unblemished reputation than they asserted for the gods, they might provoke them to anger.

11. THAT THE GREEKS ADMITTED PLAYERS TO OFFICES OF STATE, ON THE GROUND THAT MEN WHO PLEASED THE GODS SHOULD NOT BE CONTEMPTUOUSLY TREATED BY THEIR FELLOWS

It was a part of this same reasonableness of the Greeks which induced them to bestow upon the actors of these same plays no inconsiderable civic honors. In the above-mentioned book of the *De Republica*, it is mentioned that Æschines, a very eloquent Athenian, who had been a tragic actor in his youth, became a statesman, and that the Athenians again and again sent another tragedian, Aristodemus, as their plenipotentiary to Philip. For they judged it unbecoming to condemn and treat as infamous persons those who were the chief actors in the scenic entertainments which they saw to be so pleasing to the gods. No doubt this was immoral of the Greeks, but there can be as little doubt they acted in conformity with the character of their gods; for how could they have presumed to protect the conduct of the citizens from being cut to pieces by the tongues of poets and players, who were allowed, and even enjoined by the gods, to tear their divine reputation to tatters? And how could they hold in contempt the men who acted in the theatres those dramas which, as they had ascertained, gave pleasure to the gods whom they worshiped? No, how could they but grant to them the highest civic honors? On what plea could they honor the priests who offered for them acceptable sacrifices to the gods, if they branded with infamy the actors who in behalf of the people gave to the gods that pleasure or honor which they demanded, and which, according to the account of the priests, they were angry at not receiving. Labeo,[1] whose learning makes him an authority on such points, is of opinion that the distinction between good and evil deities should find expression in a difference of worship; that the evil should be propitiated by bloody sacrifices and doleful rites, but the good with a joyful and pleasant observance, as, for example (as he says himself), with plays, festivals, and banquets.[2] All this we shall, with God's help, hereafter discuss. At present, and speaking to the subject on hand, whether all kinds of offerings are made indiscriminately to all the gods, as if all were good (and it is an unseemly thing to conceive that there are evil gods; but these gods of the pagans are all evil, because they are not gods, but evil spirits), or whether, as Labeo thinks, a distinction is made between the offerings presented to the different gods, the Greeks are equally justified in honoring alike the priests by whom the sacrifices are offered, and the players by whom the dramas are acted, that they may not be open to the charge of doing an injury to all their gods, if the plays are pleasing to all of them, or (which were still worse) to their good gods, if the plays are relished only by them.

---

1. Labeo, a jurist of the time of Augustus, learned in law and antiquities, and the author of several works much prized by his own and some succeeding ages. The two articles in Smith's *Dictionary* on Antistius and Cornelius Labeo should be read.
2. Lectisternia, feasts in which the images of the gods were laid on pillows in the streets, and all kinds of food set before them.

12. THAT THE ROMANS, BY REFUSING TO THE POETS THE SAME LICENSE IN RESPECT OF MEN WHICH THEY ALLOWED THEM IN THE CASE OF THE GODS, SHOWED A MORE DELICATE SENSITIVENESS REGARDING THEMSELVES THAN REGARDING THE GODS

The Romans, however, as Scipio boasts in that same discussion, declined having their conduct and good name subjected to the assaults and slanders of the poets, and went so far as to make it a capital crime if anyone should dare to compose such verses. This was a very honorable course to pursue, so far as they themselves were concerned, but in respect of the gods it was proud and irreligious: for they knew that the gods not only tolerated, but relished, being lashed by the injurious expressions of the poets, and yet they themselves would not suffer this same handling; and what their ritual prescribed as acceptable to the gods, their law prohibited as injurious to themselves. How then, Scipio, do you praise the Romans for refusing this license to the poets, so that no citizen could be calumniated, while you know that the gods were not included under this protection? Do you count your senate house worthy of so much higher a regard than the Capitol? Is the one city of Rome more valuable in your eyes than the whole heaven of gods, that you prohibit your poets from uttering any injurious words against a citizen, though they may with impunity cast what imputations they please upon the gods, without the interference of senator, censor, prince, or pontiff? It was, forsooth, intolerable that Plautus or Nævius should attack Publius and Cneius Scipio, insufferable that Cæcilius should lampoon Cato; but quite proper that your Terence should encourage youthful lust by the wicked example of supreme Jove.

13. THAT THE ROMANS SHOULD HAVE UNDERSTOOD THAT GODS WHO DESIRED TO BE WORSHIPED IN LICENTIOUS ENTERTAINMENTS WERE UNWORTHY OF DIVINE HONOR

But Scipio, were he alive, would possibly reply: "How could we attach a penalty to that which the gods themselves have consecrated? For the theatrical entertainments in which such things are said, and acted, and performed, were introduced into Roman society by the gods, who ordered that they should be dedicated and exhibited in their honor." But was not this, then, the plainest proof that they were no true gods, nor in any respect worthy of receiving divine honors from the republic? Suppose they had required that in their honor the citizens of Rome should be held up to ridicule, every Roman would have resented the hateful proposal. How then, I would ask, can they be esteemed worthy of worship, when they propose that their own crimes be used as material for celebrating their praises? Does not this artifice expose them, and prove that they are detestable devils?

Thus the Romans, though they were superstitious enough to serve as gods those who made no secret of their desire to be worshiped in licentious plays, yet had sufficient regard to their hereditary dignity and virtue, to prompt them to refuse to players any such rewards as the Greeks accorded them. On this point we have this testimony of Scipio, recorded in Cicero: "They [the Romans] considered comedy and all theatrical performances as disgraceful, and therefore not only debarred players from offices and honors open to ordinary citizens, but also decreed that their names should be branded by the censor, and erased from the roll of their tribe." An excellent decree, and another testimony to the sagacity of Rome; but I could wish their prudence had been more thoroughgoing and consistent. For when I hear that if any Roman citizen chose the stage as his profession, he not only closed to himself every laudable career, but even became an outcast from his own tribe, I cannot but exclaim: This is the true Roman spirit, this is worthy of a state jealous of its reputation. But then someone interrupts my rapture, by inquiring with what consistency players are debarred from all honors, while plays are counted among the honors due to the gods? For a long while the virtue of Rome was uncontaminated by theatrical exhibitions;[1] and if they had been adopted for the sake of gratifying the taste of the citizens, they would have been introduced hand in hand with the relaxation of manners. But the fact is, that it was the gods who demanded that they should be exhibited to gratify them. With what justice, then, is the player excommunicated by whom God is worshiped? On what pretext can you at once adore him who exacts, and brand him who acts these plays? This, then, is the controversy in which the Greeks and Romans are engaged. The Greeks think they justly honor players, because they worship the gods who demand plays; the Romans, on the other hand, do not suffer an actor to disgrace by his name his own plebeian tribe, far less the senatorial order. And the whole of this discussion may be summed up in the following syllogism. The Greeks give us the major premise: If such gods are to be worshiped, then certainly such men may be honored. The Romans add the minor: But such men must by no means be honored. The Christians draw the conclusion: Therefore such gods must by no means be worshiped.

---

1. According to Livy (7.2), theatrical exhibitions were introduced in the year 392 A.U.C. Before that time, he says, there had only been the games of the circus. The Romans sent to Etruria for players, who were called *histriones, hister* being the Tuscan word for a player. Other particulars are added by Livy.

14. THAT PLATO, WHO EXCLUDED POETS FROM A WELL-ORDERED CITY, WAS BETTER THAN THESE GODS WHO DESIRE TO BE HONORED BY THEATRICAL PLAYS

We have still to inquire why the poets who write the plays, and who by the law of the Twelve Tables are prohibited from injuring the good name of the citizens, are reckoned more estimable than the actors, though they so shamefully asperse the character of the gods? Is it right that the actors of these poetical and God-dishonoring effusions be branded, while their authors are honored? Must we not here award the palm to a Greek, Plato, who, in framing his ideal republic,[1] conceived that poets should be banished from the city as enemies of the state? He could not brook that the gods be brought into disrepute, nor that the minds of the citizens be depraved and besotted, by the fictions of the poets. Compare now human nature as you see it in Plato, expelling poets from the city that the citizens be uninjured, with the divine nature as you see it in these gods exacting plays in their own honor. Plato strove, though unsuccessfully, to persuade the light-minded and lascivious Greeks to abstain from so much as writing such plays; the gods used their authority to extort the acting of the same from the dignified and sober-minded Romans. And not content with having them acted, they had them dedicated to themselves, consecrated to themselves, solemnly celebrated in their own honor. To which, then, would it be more becoming in a state to decree divine honors—to Plato, who prohibited these wicked and licentious plays, or to the demons who delighted in blinding men to the truth of what Plato unsuccessfully sought to inculcate?

This philosopher, Plato, has been elevated by Labeo to the rank of a demigod, and set thus upon a level with such as Hercules and Romulus. Labeo ranks demigods higher than heroes, but both he counts among the deities. But I have no doubt that he thinks this man whom he reckons a demigod worthy of greater respect not only than the heroes, but also than the gods themselves. The laws of the Romans and the speculations of Plato have this resemblance, that the latter pronounce a wholesale condemnation of poetical fictions, while the former restrain the license of satire, at least so far as men are the objects of it. Plato will not suffer poets even to dwell in his city: the laws of Rome prohibit actors from being enrolled as citizens; and if they had not feared to offend the gods who had asked the services of the players, they would in all likelihood have banished them altogether. It is obvious, therefore, that the Romans could not receive, nor reasonably expect to receive, laws for the regulation of their conduct from their gods, since the laws they themselves enacted far surpassed and put to shame the morality of the gods. The gods demand stage plays in their own honor; the Romans exclude the players from all civic honors;[2] the former commanded that they should be celebrated by the scenic representation of their own disgrace; the latter commanded that no poet should dare to blemish the reputation of any citizen. But that demigod Plato resisted the lust of such gods as these, and showed the Romans what their genius had left incomplete; for he absolutely excluded poets from his ideal state, whether they composed fictions with no regard to truth, or set the worst possible examples before wretched men under the guise of divine actions. We for our part, indeed, reckon Plato neither a god nor a demigod; we would not even compare him to any of God's holy angels; nor to the truth-speaking prophets, nor to any of the apostles or martyrs of Christ, no, not to any faithful Christian man. The reason of this opinion of ours we will, God prospering us, render in its own place. Nevertheless, since they wish him to be considered a demigod, we think he certainly is more entitled to that rank, and is every way superior, if not to Hercules and Romulus (though no historian could ever narrate nor any poet sing of him that he had killed his brother, or committed any crime), yet certainly to Priapus, or a Cynocephalus,[3] or the Fever[4]—divinities whom the Romans have partly received from foreigners, and partly consecrated by homegrown rites. How, then, could gods such as these be expected to promulgate good and wholesome laws, either for the prevention of moral and social evils, or for their eradication where they had already sprung up?—gods who used their influence even to sow and cherish profligacy, by appointing that deeds truly or falsely ascribed to them should be published to the people by means of theatrical exhibitions, and by thus gratuitously fanning the flame of human lust with the breath of a seemingly divine approbation. In vain does Cicero, speaking of poets, exclaim against this state of things in these words: "When the plaudits and acclamation of the people, who sit as infallible judges, are won by the poets, what darkness benights the mind, what fears invade, what passions inflame it!"[5]

---

1. See the *Republic* 3.
2. Cf. Tertullian *De Spect.* 22.
3. The Egyptian gods represented with dogs' heads, called by Lucan (8.832) *semicanes deos*.
4. The Fever had, according to Vives, three altars in Rome. See Cicero *De Nat. Deor.* 3.25 and Ælian *Var. Hist.* 12.11.
5. Cicero *De Rep.* 5. Cf. the third *Tusc. Disp.* 2.

15. THAT IT WAS VANITY, NOT REASON, WHICH CREATED SOME OF THE ROMAN GODS

But is it not manifest that vanity rather than reason regulated the choice of some of their false gods? This Plato, whom they reckon a demigod, and who used all his eloquence to preserve men from the most dangerous spiritual calamities, has yet not been counted worthy even of a little shrine; but Romulus, because they can call him their own, they have esteemed more highly than many gods, though their secret doctrine can allow him the rank only of a demigod. To him they allotted a flamen, that is to say, a priest of a class so highly esteemed in their religion (distinguished, too, by their conical mitres), that for only three of their gods were flamens appointed—the Flamen Dialis for Jupiter, Martialis for Mars, and Quirinalis for Romulus (for when the ardor of his fellow citizens had given Romulus a seat among the gods, they gave him this new name Quirinus). And thus by this honor Romulus has been preferred to Neptune and Pluto, Jupiter's brothers, and to Saturn himself, their father. They have assigned the same priesthood to serve him as to serve Jove; and in giving Mars (the reputed father of Romulus) the same honor, is this not rather for Romulus's sake than to honor Mars?

16. THAT IF THE GODS HAD REALLY POSSESSED ANY REGARD FOR RIGHTEOUSNESS, THE ROMANS SHOULD HAVE RECEIVED GOOD LAWS FROM THEM, INSTEAD OF HAVING TO BORROW THEM FROM OTHER NATIONS

Moreover, if the Romans had been able to receive a rule of life from their gods, they would not have borrowed Solon's laws from the Athenians, as they did some years after Rome was founded; and yet they did not keep them as they received them, but endeavored to improve and amend them.[1] Although Lycurgus pretended that he was authorized by Apollo to give laws to the Lacedemonians, the sensible Romans did not choose to believe this, and were not induced to borrow laws from Sparta. Numa Pompilius, who succeeded Romulus in the kingdom, is said to have framed some laws, which, however, were not sufficient for the regulation of civic affairs. Among these regulations were many pertaining to religious observances, and yet he is not reported to have received even these from the gods. With respect, then, to moral evils, evils of life and conduct—evils which are so mighty, that, according to the wisest pagans,[2] by them states are ruined while their cities stand uninjured—their gods made not the smallest provision for preserving their worshipers from these evils, but, on the contrary, took special pains to increase them, as we have previously endeavored to prove.

---

1. In the year 299 A.U.C., three ambassadors were sent from Rome to Athens to copy Solon's laws, and acquire information about the institutions of Greece. On their return the Decemviri were appointed to draw up a code; and finally, after some tragic interruptions, the celebrated Twelve Tables were accepted as the fundamental statutes of Roman law (*fons universi publici privatique juris*). These were graven on brass, and hung up for public information. Livy 3.31–34.
2. Possibly he refers to Plautus's *Persa* 4.4.11–14.

17. OF THE RAPE OF THE SABINE WOMEN, AND OTHER INIQUITIES PERPETRATED IN ROME'S PALMIEST DAYS

But possibly we are to find the reason for this neglect of the Romans by their gods, in the saying of Sallust, that "equity and virtue prevailed among the Romans not more by force of laws than of nature."[1] I presume it is to this inborn equity and goodness of disposition we are to ascribe the rape of the Sabine women. What, indeed, could be more equitable and virtuous, than to carry off by force, as each man was fit, and without their parents' consent, girls who were strangers and guests, and who had been decoyed and entrapped by the pretense of a spectacle! If the Sabines were wrong to deny their daughters when the Romans asked for them, was it not a greater wrong in the Romans to carry them off after that denial? The Romans might more justly have waged war against the neighboring nation for having refused their daughters in marriage when they first sought them, than for having demanded them back when they had stolen them. War should have been proclaimed at first; it was then that Mars should have helped his warlike son, that he might by force of arms avenge the injury done him by the refusal of marriage, and might also thus win the women he desired. There might have been some appearance of "right of war" in a victor carrying off, in virtue of this right, the virgins who had been without any show of right denied him; whereas there was no "right of peace" entitling him to carry off those who were not given to him, and to wage an unjust war with their justly enraged parents. One happy circumstance was indeed connected with this act of violence, namely, that though it was commemorated by the games of the circus, yet even this did not constitute it a precedent in the city or realm of Rome. If one would find fault with the results of this act, it must rather be on the ground that the Romans made Romulus a god in spite of his perpetrating this iniquity; for one cannot reproach them with making this deed any kind of precedent for the rape of women.

Again, I presume it was due to this natural equity and virtue, that after the expulsion of King Tarquin, whose son had violated Lucretia, Junius Brutus the consul forced Lucius Tarquinius Collatinus, Lucretia's husband and his own colleague, a good and innocent man, to resign his office and go into banishment, on the one sole charge that he was of the name and blood of the Tarquins. This injustice was perpetrated with the approval, or at least connivance, of the people, who had themselves raised to the consular office both Collatinus and Brutus. Another instance of this equity and virtue is found in their treatment of Marcus Camillus. This eminent man, after he had rapidly conquered the Veians, at that time the most formidable of Rome's enemies, and who had maintained a ten years' war, in which the Roman army had suffered the usual calamities attendant on bad generalship, after he had restored security to Rome, which had begun to tremble for its safety, and after he had taken the wealthiest city of the enemy, had charges brought against him by the malice of those that envied his success, and by the insolence of the tribunes of the people; and seeing that the city bore him no gratitude for preserving it, and that he would certainly be condemned, he went into exile, and even in his absence was fined ten thousand *asses*. Shortly after, however, his ungrateful country had again to seek his protection from the Gauls. But I cannot now mention all the shameful and iniquitous acts with which Rome was agitated, when the aristocracy attempted to subject the people, and the people resented their encroachments, and the advocates of either party were actuated rather by the love of victory than by any equitable or virtuous consideration.

---

1. Sallust *De Conj. Cat.* 9. Cf. the similar saying of Tacitus regarding the chastity of the Germans: "*Plusque ibi boni mores valent, quam alibi bonæ leges*" (*Germ.* 19).

18. WHAT THE HISTORY OF SALLUST REVEALS REGARDING THE LIFE OF THE ROMANS, EITHER WHEN STRAITENED BY ANXIETY OR RELAXED IN SECURITY

I will therefore pause, and adduce the testimony of Sallust himself, whose words in praise of the Romans (that "equity and virtue prevailed among them not more by force of laws than of nature") have given occasion to this discussion. He was referring to that period immediately after the expulsion of the kings, in which the city became great in an incredibly short space of time. And yet this same writer acknowledges in the first book of his history, in the very exordium of his work, that even at that time, when a very brief interval had elapsed after the government had passed from kings to consuls, the more powerful men began to act unjustly, and occasioned the defection of the people from the patricians, and other disorders in the city. For after Sallust had stated that the Romans enjoyed greater harmony and a purer state of society between the second and third Punic wars than at any other time, and that the cause of this was not their love of good order, but their fear lest the peace they had with Carthage might be broken (this also, as we mentioned, Nasica contemplated when he opposed the destruction of Carthage, for he supposed that fear would tend to repress wickedness, and to preserve wholesome ways of living), he then goes on to say: "Yet, after the destruction of Carthage, discord, avarice, ambition, and the other vices which are commonly generated by prosperity, more than ever increased." If they "increased," and that "more than ever," then already they had appeared, and had been increasing. And so Sallust adds this reason for what he said. "For," he says, "the oppressive measures of the powerful, and the consequent secessions of the plebs from the patricians, and other civil dissensions, had existed from the first, and affairs were administered with equity and well-tempered justice for no longer a period than the short time after the expulsion of the kings, while the city was occupied with the serious Tuscan war and Tarquin's vengeance." You see how, even in that brief period after the expulsion of the kings, fear, he acknowledges, was the cause of the interval of equity and good order. They were afraid, in fact, of the war which Tarquin waged against them, after he had been driven from the throne and the city, and had allied himself with the Tuscans. But observe what he adds: "After that, the patricians treated the people as their slaves, ordering them to be scourged or beheaded just as the kings had done, driving them from their holdings, and harshly tyrannizing over those who had no property to lose. The people, overwhelmed by these oppressive measures, and most of all by exorbitant usury, and obliged to contribute both money and personal service to the constant wars, at length took arms and seceded to Mount Aventine and Mount Sacer, and thus obtained for themselves tribunes and protective laws. But it was only the second Punic war that put an end on both sides to discord and strife." You see what kind of men the Romans were, even so early as a few years after the expulsion of the kings; and it is of these men he says, that "equity and virtue prevailed among them not more by force of law than of nature."

Now, if these were the days in which the Roman republic shows fairest and best, what are we to say or think of the succeeding age, when, to use the words of the same historian, "changing little by little from the fair and virtuous city it was, it became utterly wicked and dissolute"? This was, as he mentions, after the destruction of Carthage. Sallust's brief sum and sketch of this period may be read in his own history, in which he shows how the profligate manners which were propagated by prosperity resulted at last even in civil wars. He says: "And from this time the primitive manners, instead of undergoing an insensible alteration as hitherto they had done, were swept away as by a torrent: the young men were so depraved by luxury and avarice, that it may justly be said that no father had a son who could either preserve his own patrimony, or keep his hands off other men's." Sallust adds a number of particulars about the vices of Sylla, and the debased condition of the republic in general; and other writers make similar observations, though in much less striking language.

However, I suppose you now see, or at least anyone who gives his attention has the means of seeing, in what a sink of iniquity that city was plunged before the advent of our heavenly King. For these things happened not only before Christ had begun to teach, but before He was even born of the virgin. If, then, they dare not impute to their gods the grievous evils of those former times, more tolerable before the destruction of Carthage, but intolerable and dreadful after it, although it was the gods who by their malign craft instilled into the minds of men the conceptions from which such dreadful vices branched out on all sides, why do they impute these present calamities to Christ, who teaches life-giving truth, and forbids us to worship false and deceitful gods, and who, abominating and condemning with His divine authority those wicked and hurtful lusts of men, gradually withdraws His own people from a world that is corrupted by these vices, and is falling into ruins, to make of them an eternal city, whose glory rests not on the acclamations of vanity, but on the judgment of truth?

19. OF THE CORRUPTION WHICH HAD GROWN UPON THE ROMAN REPUBLIC BEFORE CHRIST ABOLISHED THE WORSHIP OF THE GODS

Here, then, is this Roman republic, "which has changed little by little from the fair and virtuous city it was, and has become utterly wicked and dissolute." It is not I who am the first to say this, but their own authors, from whom we learned it for a fee, and who wrote it long before the coming of Christ. You see how, before the coming of Christ, and after the destruction of Carthage, "the primitive manners, instead of undergoing insensible alteration, as hitherto they had done, were swept away as by a torrent; and how depraved by luxury and avarice the youth were." Let them now, on their part, read to us any laws given by their gods to the Roman people, and directed against luxury and avarice. And would that they had only been silent on the subjects of chastity and modesty, and had not demanded from the people indecent and shameful practices, to which they lent a pernicious patronage by their so-called divinity.

Let them read our commandments in the Prophets, Gospels, Acts of the Apostles, or Epistles; let them peruse the large number of precepts against avarice and luxury which are everywhere read to the congregations that meet for this purpose, and which strike the ear, not with the uncertain sound of a philosophical discussion, but with the thunder of God's own oracle pealing from the clouds. And yet they do not impute to their gods the luxury and avarice, the cruel and dissolute manners, that had rendered the republic utterly wicked and corrupt, even before the coming of Christ; but whatever affliction their pride and effeminacy have exposed them to in these latter days, they furiously impute to our religion. If the kings of the earth and all their subjects, if all princes and judges of the earth, if young men and maidens, old and young, every age, and both sexes; if they whom the Baptist addressed, the publicans and the soldiers, were all together to hearken to and observe the precepts of the Christian religion regarding a just and virtuous life, then should the republic adorn the whole earth with its own felicity, and attain in life everlasting to the pinnacle of kingly glory. But because this man listens and that man scoffs, and most are enamored of the blandishments of vice rather than the wholesome severity of virtue, the people of Christ, whatever be their condition—whether they be kings, princes, judges, soldiers, or provincials, rich or poor, bond or free, male or female—are enjoined to endure this earthly republic, wicked and dissolute as it is, that so they may by this endurance win for themselves an eminent place in that most holy and august assembly of angels and republic of heaven, in which the will of God is the law.

20. OF THE KIND OF HAPPINESS AND LIFE TRULY DELIGHTED IN BY THOSE WHO INVEIGH AGAINST THE CHRISTIAN RELIGION

But the worshipers and admirers of these gods delight in imitating their scandalous iniquities, and are nowise concerned that the republic be less depraved and licentious. Only let it remain undefeated, they say, only let it flourish and abound in resources; let it be glorious by its victories, or still better, secure in peace; and what matters it to us? This is our concern, that every man be able to increase his wealth so as to supply his daily prodigalities, and so that the powerful may subject the weak for their own purposes. Let the poor court the rich for a living, and that under their protection they may enjoy a sluggish tranquility; and let the rich abuse the poor as their dependants, to minister to their pride. Let the people applaud not those who protect their interests, but those who provide them with pleasure. Let no severe duty be commanded, no impurity forbidden. Let kings estimate their prosperity, not by the righteousness, but by the servility of their subjects. Let the provinces stand loyal to the kings, not as moral guides, but as lords of their possessions and purveyors of their pleasures; not with a hearty reverence, but a crooked and servile fear. Let the laws take cognizance rather of the injury done to another man's property, than of that done to one's own person. If a man be a nuisance to his neighbor, or injure his property, family, or person, let him be actionable; but in his own affairs let everyone with impunity do what he will in company with his own family, and with those who willingly join him. Let there be a plentiful supply of public prostitutes for everyone who wishes to use them, but specially for those who are too poor to keep one for their private use. Let there be erected houses of the largest and most ornate description: in these let there be provided the most sumptuous banquets, where everyone who pleases may, by day or night, play, drink, vomit,[1] dissipate. Let there be everywhere heard the rustling of dancers, the loud, immodest laughter of the theatre; let a succession of the most cruel and the most voluptuous pleasures maintain a perpetual excitement. If such happiness is distasteful to any, let him be branded as a public enemy; and if any attempt to modify or put an end to it let him be silenced, banished, put an end to. Let these be reckoned the true gods, who procure for the people this condition of things, and preserve it when once possessed. Let them be worshiped as they wish; let them demand whatever games they please, from or with their own worshipers; only let them secure that such felicity be not imperiled by foe, plague, or disaster of any kind. What sane man would compare a republic such as this, I will not say to the Roman Empire, but to the palace of Sardanapalus, the ancient king who was so abandoned to pleasures, that he caused it to be inscribed on his tomb, that now that he was dead, he possessed only those things which he had swallowed and consumed by his appetites while alive? If these men had such a king as this, who, while self-indulgent, should lay no severe restraint on them, they would more enthusiastically consecrate to him a temple and a flamen than the ancient Romans did to Romulus.

---

1. The same collocation of words is used by Cicero with reference to the well-known mode of renewing the appetite in use among the Romans.

21. CICERO'S OPINION OF THE ROMAN REPUBLIC

But if our adversaries do not care how foully and disgracefully the Roman republic be stained by corrupt practices, so long only as it holds together and continues in being, and if they therefore pooh-pooh the testimony of Sallust to its "utterly wicked and profligate" condition, what will they make of Cicero's statement, that even in his time it had become entirely extinct, and that there remained extant no Roman republic at all? He introduces Scipio (the Scipio who had destroyed Carthage) discussing the republic, at a time when already there were presentiments of its speedy ruin by that corruption which Sallust describes. In fact, at the time when the discussion took place, one of the Gracchi, who, according to Sallust, was the first great instigator of seditions, had already been put to death. His death, indeed, is mentioned in the same book. Now Scipio, at the end of the second book, says: "As among the different sounds which proceed from lyres, flutes, and the human voice, there must be maintained a certain harmony which a cultivated ear cannot endure to hear disturbed or jarring, but which may be elicited in full and absolute concord by the modulation even of voices very unlike one another; so, where reason is allowed to modulate the diverse elements of the state, there is obtained a perfect concord from the upper, lower, and middle classes as from various sounds; and what musicians call harmony in singing, is concord in matters of state, which is the strictest bond and best security of any republic, and which by no ingenuity can be retained where justice has become extinct." Then, when he had expatiated somewhat more fully, and had more copiously illustrated the benefits of its presence and the ruinous effects of its absence upon a state, Pilus, one of the company present at the discussion, struck in and demanded that the question should be more thoroughly sifted, and that the subject of justice should be freely discussed for the sake of ascertaining what truth there was in the maxim which was then becoming daily more current, that "the republic cannot be governed without injustice." Scipio expressed his willingness to have this maxim discussed and sifted, and gave it as his opinion that it was baseless, and that no progress could be made in discussing the republic unless it was established, not only that this maxim, that "the republic cannot be governed without injustice," was false, but also that the truth is, that it cannot be governed without the most absolute justice. And the discussion of this question, being deferred till the next day, is carried on in the third book with great animation. For Pilus himself undertook to defend the position that the republic cannot be governed without injustice, at the same time being at special pains to clear himself of any real participation in that opinion. He advocated with great keenness the cause of injustice against justice, and endeavored by plausible reasons and examples to demonstrate that the former is beneficial, the latter useless, to the republic. Then, at the request of the company, Lælius attempted to defend justice, and strained every nerve to prove that nothing is so hurtful to a state as injustice; and that without justice a republic can neither be governed, nor even continue to exist.

When this question has been handled to the satisfaction of the company, Scipio reverts to the original thread of discourse, and repeats with commendation his own brief definition of a republic, that it is the weal of the people. "The people" he defines as being not every assemblage or mob, but an assemblage associated by a common acknowledgment of law, and by a community of interests. Then he shows the use of definition in debate; and from these definitions of his own he gathers that a republic, or "weal of the people," then exists only when it is well and justly governed, whether by a monarch, or an aristocracy, or by the whole people. But when the monarch is unjust, or, as the Greeks say, a tyrant; or the aristocrats are unjust, and form a faction; or the people themselves are unjust, and become, as Scipio for want of a better name calls them, themselves the tyrant, then the republic is not only blemished (as had been proved the day before), but by legitimate deduction from those definitions, it altogether ceases to be. For it could not be the people's weal when a tyrant factiously lorded it over the state; neither would the people be any longer a people if it were unjust, since it would no longer answer the definition of a people—"an assemblage associated by a common acknowledgment of law, and by a community of interests."

When, therefore, the Roman republic was such as Sallust described it, it was not "utterly wicked and profligate," as he says, but had altogether ceased to exist, if we are to admit the reasoning of that debate maintained on the subject of the republic by its best representatives. Tully himself, too, speaking not in the person of Scipio or anyone else, but uttering his own sentiments, uses the following language in the beginning of the fifth book, after quoting a line from the poet Ennius, in which he said, "Rome's severe morality and her citizens are her safeguard." "This verse," says Cicero, "seems to me to have all the sententious truthfulness of an oracle. For neither would the citizens have availed without the morality of the community, nor would the morality of the commons without outstanding men have availed either to establish or so long to maintain in vigor so grand a republic with so wide and just an empire. Accordingly, before our day, the hereditary usages formed our foremost men, and they on their part retained the usages and institutions of their fathers. But our age, receiving the republic as a *chef-d'œuvre* of another age which has already begun to grow old, has not merely neglected to restore the colors of the original, but has not even been at the pains to preserve so much as the general outline and most outstanding features. For what survives of that primitive morality which the poet called Rome's safeguard? It is so obsolete and forgotten, that, far from practicing it, one does not even know it. And of the citizens what shall I say? Morality has perished through poverty of great men; a poverty for which we must not only assign a reason, but for the guilt of which we must answer as criminals charged with a capital crime. For it is through our vices, and not by any mishap, that we retain only the name of a republic, and have long since lost the reality."

This is the confession of Cicero, long indeed after the death of Africanus, whom he introduced as an interlocutor in his work *De Republica*, but still before the coming of Christ. Yet, if the disasters he bewails had been lamented after the Christian religion had been diffused, and had begun to prevail, is there a man of our adversaries who would not have thought that they were to be imputed to the Christians? Why, then, did their gods not take steps then to prevent the decay and extinction of that republic, over the loss of which Cicero, long before Christ had come in the flesh, sings so lugubrious a dirge? Its admirers have need to inquire whether, even in the days of primitive men and morals, true justice flourished in it; or was it not perhaps even then, to use the casual expression of Cicero, rather a colored painting than the living reality? But, if God will, we shall consider this elsewhere. For I mean in its own place to show that—according to the definitions in which Cicero himself, using Scipio as his mouthpiece, briefly propounded what a republic is, and what a people is, and according to many testimonies, both of his own lips and of those who took part in that same debate—Rome never was a republic, because true justice had never a place in it. But accepting the more feasible definitions of a republic, I grant there was a republic of a certain kind, and certainly much better administered by the more ancient Romans than by their modern representatives. But the fact is, true justice has no existence save in that republic whose founder and ruler is Christ, if at least any choose to call this a republic; and indeed we cannot deny that it is the people's weal. But if perchance this name, which has become familiar in other connections, be considered alien to our common parlance, we may at all events say that in this city is true justice; the city of which Holy Scripture says, "Glorious things are said of thee, O city of God."

22. THAT THE ROMAN GODS NEVER TOOK ANY STEPS TO PREVENT THE REPUBLIC FROM BEING RUINED BY IMMORALITY

But what is relevant to the present question is this, that however admirable our adversaries say the republic was or is, it is certain that by the testimony of their own most learned writers it had become, long before the coming of Christ, utterly wicked and dissolute, and indeed had no existence, but had been destroyed by profligacy. To prevent this, surely these guardian gods ought to have given precepts of morals and a rule of life to the people by whom they were worshiped in so many temples, with so great a variety of priests and sacrifices, with such numberless and diverse rites, so many festal solemnities, so many celebrations of magnificent games. But in all this the demons only looked after their own interest, and cared not at all how their worshipers lived, or rather were at pains to induce them to lead an abandoned life, so long as they paid these tributes to their honor, and regarded them with fear. If anyone denies this, let him produce, let him point to, let him read the laws which the gods had given against sedition, and which the Gracchi transgressed when they threw everything into confusion; or those Marius, and Cinna, and Carbo broke when they involved their country in civil wars, most iniquitous and unjustifiable in their causes, cruelly conducted, and yet more cruelly terminated; or those which Sylla scorned, whose life, character, and deeds, as described by Sallust and other historians, are the abhorrence of all mankind. Who will deny that at that time the republic had become extinct?

Possibly they will be bold enough to suggest in defense of the gods, that they abandoned the city on account of the profligacy of the citizens, according to the lines of Virgil:

> *Gone from each fane, each sacred shrine,*
> *Are those who made this realm divine.*[1]

But, firstly, if it be so, then they cannot complain against the Christian religion, as if it were that which gave offense to the gods and caused them to abandon Rome, since the Roman immorality had long ago driven from the altars of the city a cloud of little gods, like as many flies. And yet where was this host of divinities, when, long before the corruption of the primitive morality, Rome was taken and burned by the Gauls? Perhaps they were present, but asleep? For at that time the whole city fell into the hands of the enemy, with the single exception of the Capitoline hill; and this too would have been taken, had not—the watchful geese aroused the sleeping gods! And this gave occasion to the festival of the goose, in which Rome sank nearly to the superstition of the Egyptians, who worship beasts and birds. But of these adventitious evils which are inflicted by hostile armies or by some disaster, and which attach rather to the body than the soul, I am not meanwhile disputing. At present I speak of the decay of morality, which at first almost imperceptibly lost its brilliant hue, but afterward was wholly obliterated, was swept away as by a torrent, and involved the republic in such disastrous ruin, that though the houses and walls remained standing the leading writers do not scruple to say that the republic was destroyed. Now, the departure of the gods "from each fane, each sacred shrine," and their abandonment of the city to destruction, was an act of justice, if their laws inculcating justice and a moral life had been held in contempt by that city. But what kind of gods were these, pray, who declined to live with a people who worshiped them, and whose corrupt life they had done nothing to reform?

---

1. Virgil *Æneid* 2.351–352.

23. THAT THE VICISSITUDES OF THIS LIFE ARE DEPENDENT NOT ON THE FAVOR OR HOSTILITY OF DEMONS, BUT ON THE WILL OF THE TRUE GOD

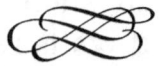

But, further, is it not obvious that the gods have abetted the fulfillment of men's desires, instead of authoritatively bridling them? For Marius, a low-born and self-made man, who ruthlessly provoked and conducted civil wars, was so effectually aided by them, that he was seven times consul, and died full of years in his seventh consulship, escaping the hands of Sylla, who immediately afterward came into power. Why, then, did they not also aid him, so as to restrain him from so many enormities? For if it is said that the gods had no hand in his success, this is no trivial admission that a man can attain the dearly coveted felicity of this life even though his own gods be not propitious; that men can be loaded with the gifts of fortune as Marius was, can enjoy health, power, wealth, honors, dignity, length of days, though the gods be hostile to him; and that, on the other hand, men can be tormented as Regulus was, with captivity, bondage, destitution, watchings, pain, and cruel death, though the gods be his friends. To concede this is to make a compendious confession that the gods are useless, and their worship superfluous. If the gods have taught the people rather what goes clean counter to the virtues of the soul, and that integrity of life which meets a reward after death; if even in respect of temporal and transitory blessings they neither hurt those whom they hate nor profit whom they love, why are they worshiped, why are they invoked with such eager homage? Why do men murmur in difficult and sad emergencies, as if the gods had retired in anger? And why, on their account, is the Christian religion injured by the most unworthy calumnies? If in temporal matters they have power either for good or for evil, why did they stand by Marius, the worst of Rome's citizens, and abandon Regulus, the best? Does this not prove themselves to be most unjust and wicked? And even if it be supposed that for this very reason they are the rather to be feared and worshiped, this is a mistake; for we do not read that Regulus worshiped them less assiduously than Marius. Neither is it apparent that a wicked life is to be chosen, on the ground that the gods are supposed to have favored Marius more than Regulus. For Metellus, the most highly esteemed of all the Romans, who had five sons in the consulship, was prosperous even in this life; and Catiline, the worst of men, reduced to poverty and defeated in the war his own guilt had aroused, lived and perished miserably. Real and secure felicity is the peculiar possession of those who worship that God by whom alone it can be conferred.

It is thus apparent, that when the republic was being destroyed by profligate manners, its gods did nothing to hinder its destruction by the direction or correction of its manners, but rather accelerated its destruction by increasing the demoralization and corruption that already existed. They need not pretend that their goodness was shocked by the iniquity of the city, and that they withdrew in anger. For they were there, sure enough; they are detected, convicted: they were equally unable to break silence so as to guide others, and to keep silence so as to conceal themselves. I do not dwell on the fact that the inhabitants of Minturnæ took pity on Marius, and commended him to the goddess Marica in her grove, that she might give him success in all things, and that from the abyss of despair in which he then lay he forthwith returned unhurt to Rome, and entered the city the ruthless leader of a ruthless army; and they who wish to know how bloody was his victory, how unlike a citizen, and how much more relentlessly than any foreign foe he acted, let them read the histories. But this, as I said, I do not dwell upon; nor do I attribute the bloody bliss of Marius to, I know not what Minturnian goddess [Marica], but rather to the secret providence of God, that the mouths of our adversaries might be shut, and that they who are not led by passion, but by prudent consideration of events, might be delivered from error. And even if the demons have any power in these matters, they have only that power which the secret decree of the Almighty allots to them, in order that we may not set too great store by earthly prosperity, seeing it is oftentimes vouchsafed even to wicked men like Marius; and that we may not, on the other hand, regard it as an evil, since we see that many good and pious worshipers of the one true God are, in spite of the demons preeminently successful; and, finally, that we may not suppose that these unclean spirits are either to be propitiated or feared for the sake of earthly blessings or calamities: for as wicked men on earth cannot do all they would, so neither can these demons, but only insofar as they are permitted by the decree of Him whose judgments are fully comprehensible, justly reprehensible by none.

24. OF THE DEEDS OF SYLLA, IN WHICH THE DEMONS BOASTED THAT HE HAD THEIR HELP

It is certain that Sylla—whose rule was so cruel that, in comparison with it, the preceding state of things which he came to avenge was regretted—when first he advanced toward Rome to give battle to Marius, found the auspices so favorable when he sacrificed, that, according to Livy's account, the augur Postumius expressed his willingness to lose his head if Sylla did not, with the help of the gods, accomplish what he designed. The gods, you see, had not departed from "every fane and sacred shrine," since they were still predicting the issue of these affairs, and yet were taking no steps to correct Sylla himself. Their presages promised him great prosperity but no threatenings of theirs subdued his evil passions. And then, when he was in Asia conducting the war against Mithridates, a message from Jupiter was delivered to him by Lucius Titius, to the effect that he would conquer Mithridates; and so it came to pass. And afterward, when he was meditating a return to Rome for the purpose of avenging in the blood of the citizens injuries done to himself and his friends, a second message from Jupiter was delivered to him by a soldier of the sixth legion, to the effect that it was he who had predicted the victory over Mithridates, and that now he promised to give him power to recover the republic from his enemies, though with great bloodshed. Sylla at once inquired of the soldier what form had appeared to him; and, on his reply, recognized that it was the same as Jupiter had formerly employed to convey to him the assurance regarding the victory over Mithridates. How, then, can the gods be justified in this matter for the care they took to predict these shadowy successes, and for their negligence in correcting Sylla, and restraining him from stirring up a civil war so lamentable and atrocious, that it not merely disfigured, but extinguished, the republic? The truth is, as I have often said, and as Scripture informs us, and as the facts themselves sufficiently indicate, the demons are found to look after their own ends only, that they may be regarded and worshiped as gods, and that men may be induced to offer to them a worship which associates them with their crimes, and involves them in one common wickedness and judgment of God.

Afterward, when Sylla had come to Tarentum, and had sacrificed there, he saw on the head of the victim's liver the likeness of a golden crown. Thereupon the same soothsayer Postumius interpreted this to signify a signal victory, and ordered that he only should eat of the entrails. A little afterward, the slave of a certain Lucius Pontius cried out, "I am Bellona's messenger; the victory is yours, Sylla!" Then he added that the Capitol should be burned. As soon as he had uttered this prediction he left the camp, but returned the following day more excited than ever, and shouted, "The Capitol is fired!" And fired indeed it was. This it was easy for a demon both to foresee and quickly to announce. But observe, as relevant to our subject, what kind of gods they are under whom these men desire to live, who blaspheme the Saviour that delivers the wills of the faithful from the dominion of devils. The man cried out in prophetic rapture, "The victory is yours, Sylla!" And to certify that he spoke by a divine spirit, he predicted also an event which was shortly to happen, and which indeed did fall out, in a place from which he in whom this spirit was speaking was far distant. But he never cried, "Forbear thy villainies, Sylla!"—the villainies which were committed at Rome by that victor to whom a golden crown on the calf's liver had been shown as the divine evidence of his victory. If such signs as this were customarily sent by just gods, and not by wicked demons, then certainly the entrails he consulted should rather have given Sylla intimation of the cruel disasters that were to befall the city and himself. For that victory was not so conducive to his exaltation to power, as it was fatal to his ambition; for by it he became so insatiable in his desires, and was rendered so arrogant and reckless by prosperity, that he may be said rather to have inflicted a moral destruction on himself than corporal destruction on his enemies. But these truly woeful and deplorable calamities the gods gave him no previous hint of, neither by entrails, augury, dream, nor prediction. For they feared his amendment more than his defeat. Yes, they took good care that this glorious conqueror of his own fellow citizens should be conquered and led captive by his own infamous vices, and should thus be the more submissive slave of the demons themselves.

25. HOW POWERFULLY THE EVIL SPIRITS INCITE MEN TO WICKED ACTIONS, BY GIVING THEM THE QUASIDIVINE AUTHORITY OF THEIR EXAMPLE

Now, who does not hereby comprehend—unless he has preferred to imitate such gods rather than by divine grace to withdraw himself from their fellowship—who does not see how eagerly these evil spirits strive by their example to lend, as it were, divine authority to crime? Is not this proved by the fact that they were seen in a wide plain in Campania rehearsing among themselves the battle which shortly after took place there with great bloodshed between the armies of Rome? For at first there were heard loud crashing noises, and afterward many reported that they had seen for some days together two armies engaged. And when this battle ceased, they found the ground all indented with just such footprints of men and horses as a great conflict would leave. If, then, the deities were veritably fighting with one another, the civil wars of men are sufficiently justified; yet, by the way, let it be observed that such pugnacious gods must be very wicked or very wretched. If, however, it was but a sham fight, what did they intend by this, but that the civil wars of the Romans should seem no wickedness, but an imitation of the gods? For already the civil wars had begun; and before this, some lamentable battles and execrable massacres had occurred. Already many had been moved by the story of the soldier, who, on stripping the spoils of his slain foe, recognized in the stripped corpse his own brother, and, with deep curses on civil wars, slew himself there and then on his brother's body. To disguise the bitterness of such tragedies, and kindle increasing ardor in this monstrous warfare, these malign demons, who were reputed and worshiped as gods, fell upon this plan of revealing themselves in a state of civil war, that no compunction for fellow citizens might cause the Romans to shrink from such battles, but that the human criminality might be justified by the divine example. By a like craft, too, did these evil spirits command that scenic entertainments, of which I have already spoken, should be instituted and dedicated to them. And in these entertainments the poetical compositions and actions of the drama ascribed such iniquities to the gods, that everyone might safely imitate them, whether he believed the gods had actually done such things, or, not believing this, yet perceived that they most eagerly desired to be represented as having done them. And that no one might suppose, that in representing the gods as fighting with one another, the poets had slandered them, and imputed to them unworthy actions, the gods themselves, to complete the deception, confirmed the compositions of the poets by exhibiting their own battles to the eyes of men, not only through actions in the theatres, but in their own persons on the actual field.

We have been forced to bring forward these facts, because their authors have not scrupled to say and to write that the Roman republic had already been ruined by the depraved moral habits of the citizens, and had ceased to exist before the advent of our Lord Jesus Christ. Now this ruin they do not impute to their own gods, though they impute to our Christ the evils of this life, which cannot ruin good men, be they alive or dead. And this they do, though our Christ has issued so many precepts inculcating virtue and restraining vice; while their own gods have done nothing whatever to preserve that republic that served them, and to restrain it from ruin by such precepts, but have rather hastened its destruction, by corrupting its morality through their pestilent example. No one, I fancy, will now be bold enough to say that the republic was then ruined because of the departure of the gods "from each fane, each sacred shrine," as if they were the friends of virtue, and were offended by the vices of men. No, there are too many presages from entrails, auguries, soothsayings, whereby they boastingly proclaimed themselves prescient of future events and controllers of the fortune of war—all which prove them to have been present. And had they been indeed absent the Romans would never in these civil wars have been so far transported by their own passions as they were by the instigations of these gods.

26. THAT THE DEMONS GAVE IN SECRET CERTAIN OBSCURE INSTRUCTIONS IN MORALS, WHILE IN PUBLIC THEIR OWN SOLEMNITIES INCULCATED ALL WICKEDNESS

Seeing that this is so—seeing that the filthy and cruel deeds, the disgraceful and criminal actions of the gods, whether real or feigned, were at their own request published, and were consecrated, and dedicated in their honor as sacred and stated solemnities; seeing they vowed vengeance on those who refused to exhibit them to the eyes of all, that they might be proposed as deeds worthy of imitation, why is it that these same demons, who by taking pleasure in such obscenities, acknowledge themselves to be unclean spirits, and by delighting in their own villainies and iniquities, real or imaginary, and by requesting from the immodest, and extorting from the modest, the celebration of these licentious acts, proclaim themselves instigators to a criminal and lewd life—why, I ask, are they represented as giving some good moral precepts to a few of their own elect, initiated in the secrecy of their shrines? If it be so, this very thing only serves further to demonstrate the malicious craft of these pestilent spirits. For so great is the influence of probity and chastity, that all men, or almost all men, are moved by the praise of these virtues; nor is any man so depraved by vice, but he has some feeling of honor left in him. So that, unless the devil sometimes transformed himself, as Scripture says, into an angel of light,[1] he could not compass his deceitful purpose. Accordingly, in public, a bold impurity fills the ear of the people with noisy clamor; in private, a feigned chastity speaks in scarce audible whispers to a few: an open stage is provided for shameful things, but on the praiseworthy the curtain falls: grace hides, disgrace flaunts: a wicked deed draws an overflowing house, a virtuous speech finds scarce a hearer, as though purity were to be blushed at, impurity boasted of. Where else can such confusion reign, but in devils' temples? Where, but in the haunts of deceit? For the secret precepts are given as a sop to the virtuous, who are few in number; the wicked examples are exhibited to encourage the vicious, who are countless.

Where and when those initiated in the mysteries of Cœlestis received any good instructions, we know not. What we do know is, that before her shrine, in which her image is set, and amid a vast crowd gathering from all quarters, and standing closely packed together, we were intensely interested spectators of the games which were going on, and saw, as we pleased to turn the eye, on this side a grand display of harlots, on the other the virgin goddess; we saw this virgin worshiped with prayer and with obscene rites. There we saw no shamefaced mimes, no actress overburdened with modesty; all that the obscene rites demanded was fully complied with. We were plainly shown what was pleasing to the virgin deity, and the matron who witnessed the spectacle returned home from the temple a wiser woman. Some, indeed, of the more prudent women turned their faces from the immodest movements of the players, and learned the art of wickedness by a furtive regard. For they were restrained, by the modest demeanor due to men, from looking boldly at the immodest gestures; but much more were they restrained from condemning with chaste heart the sacred rites of her whom they adored. And yet this licentiousness—which, if practiced in one's home, could only be done there in secret—was practiced as a public lesson in the temple; and if any modesty remained in men, it was occupied in marveling that wickedness which men could not unrestrainedly commit should be part of the religious teaching of the gods, and that to omit its exhibition should incur the anger of the gods. What spirit can that be, which by a hidden inspiration stirs men's corruption, and goads them to adultery, and feeds on the full-fledged iniquity, unless it be the same that finds pleasure in such religious ceremonies, sets in the temples images of devils, and loves to see in play the images of vices; that whispers in secret some righteous sayings to deceive the few who are good, and scatters in public invitations to profligacy, to gain possession of the millions who are wicked?

1. 2 Cor. 11:14.

27. THAT THE OBSCENITIES OF THOSE PLAYS WHICH THE ROMANS CONSECRATED IN ORDER TO PROPITIATE THEIR GODS, CONTRIBUTED LARGELY TO THE OVERTHROW OF PUBLIC ORDER

Cicero, a weighty man, and a philosopher in his way, when about to be made edile, wished the citizens to understand[1] that, among the other duties of his magistracy, he must propitiate Flora by the celebration of games. And these games are reckoned devout in proportion to their lewdness. In another place,[2] and when he was now consul, and the state in great peril, he says that games had been celebrated for ten days together, and that nothing had been omitted which could pacify the gods: as if it had not been more satisfactory to irritate the gods by temperance, than to pacify them by debauchery; and to provoke their hate by honest living, than soothe it by such unseemly grossness. For no matter how cruel was the ferocity of those men who were threatening the state, and on whose account the gods were being propitiated, it could not have been more hurtful than the alliance of gods who were won with the foulest vices. To avert the danger which threatened men's bodies, the gods were conciliated in a fashion that drove virtue from their spirits; and the gods did not enroll themselves as defenders of the battlements against the besiegers, until they had first stormed and sacked the morality of the citizens. This propitiation of such divinities—a propitiation so wanton, so impure, so immodest, so wicked, so filthy, whose actors the innate and praiseworthy virtue of the Romans disabled from civic honors, erased from their tribe, recognized as polluted and made infamous—this propitiation, I say, so foul, so detestable, and alien from every religious feeling, these fabulous and ensnaring accounts of the criminal actions of the gods, these scandalous actions which they either shamefully and wickedly committed, or more shamefully and wickedly feigned, all this the whole city learned in public both by the words and gestures of the actors. They saw that the gods delighted in the commission of these things, and therefore believed that they wished them not only to be exhibited to them, but to be imitated by themselves. But as for that good and honest instruction which they speak of, it was given in such secrecy, and to so few (if indeed given at all), that they seemed rather to fear it might be divulged, than that it might not be practiced.

---

1. Cicero *In Verrem* 6.8.
2. Cicero *In Cat.* 3.8.

28. THAT THE CHRISTIAN RELIGION IS HEALTH GIVING

They, then, are but abandoned and ungrateful wretches, in deep and fast bondage to that malign spirit, who complain and murmur that men are rescued by the name of Christ from the hellish thralldom of these unclean spirits, and from a participation in their punishment, and are brought out of the night of pestilential ungodliness into the light of most healthful piety. Only such men could murmur that the masses flock to the churches and their chaste acts of worship, where a seemly separation of the sexes is observed; where they learn how they may so spend this earthly life, as to merit a blessed eternity hereafter; where Holy Scripture and instruction in righteousness are proclaimed from a raised platform in presence of all, that both they who do the word may hear to their salvation, and they who do it not may hear to judgment. And though some enter who scoff at such precepts, all their petulance is either quenched by a sudden change, or is restrained through fear or shame. For no filthy and wicked action is there set forth to be gazed at or to be imitated; but either the precepts of the true God are recommended, His miracles narrated, His gifts praised, or His benefits implored.

29. AN EXHORTATION TO THE ROMANS TO RENOUNCE PAGANISM

This, rather, is the religion worthy of your desires, O admirable Roman race—the progeny of your Scævolas and Scipios, of Regulus, and of Fabricius. This rather covet, this distinguish from that foul vanity and crafty malice of the devils. If there is in your nature any eminent virtue, only by true piety is it purged and perfected, while by impiety it is wrecked and punished. Choose now what you will pursue, that your praise may be not in yourself, but in the true God, in whom is no error. For of popular glory you have had your share; but by the secret providence of God, the true religion was not offered to your choice. Awake, it is now day; as you have already awaked in the persons of some in whose perfect virtue and sufferings for the true faith we glory: for they, contending on all sides with hostile powers, and conquering them all by bravely dying, have purchased for us this country of ours with their blood; to which country we invite you, and exhort you to add yourselves to the number of the citizens of this city, which also has a sanctuary[1] of its own in the true remission of sins. Do not listen to those degenerate sons of yours who slander Christ and Christians, and impute to them these disastrous times, though they desire times in which they may enjoy rather impunity for their wickedness than a peaceful life. Such has never been Rome's ambition even in regard to her earthly country. Lay hold now on the celestial country, which is easily won, and in which you will reign truly and forever. For there shall you find no vestal fire, no Capitoline stone, but the one true God.

> *No date, no goal will here ordain:*
> *But grant an endless, boundless reign.*[2]

No longer, then, follow after false and deceitful gods; abjure them rather, and despise them, bursting forth into true liberty. Gods they are not, but malignant spirits, to whom your eternal happiness will be a sore punishment. Juno, from whom you deduce your origin according to the flesh, did not so bitterly grudge Rome's citadels to the Trojans, as these devils whom yet you repute gods, grudge an everlasting seat to the race of mankind. And you yourself have in no wavering voice passed judgment on them, when you did pacify them with games, and yet did account as infamous the men by whom the plays were acted. Suffer us, then, to assert your freedom against the unclean spirits who had imposed on your neck the yoke of celebrating their own shame and filthiness. The actors of these divine crimes you have removed from offices of honor; supplicate the true God, that He may remove from you those gods who delight in their crimes—a most disgraceful thing if the crimes are really theirs, and a most malicious invention if the crimes are feigned. Well done, in that you have spontaneously banished from the number of your citizens all actors and players. Awake more fully: the majesty of God cannot be propitiated by that which defiles the dignity of man. How, then, can you believe that gods who take pleasure in such lewd plays, belong to the number of the holy powers of heaven, when the men by whom these plays are acted are by yourselves refused admission into the number of Roman citizens even of the lowest grade? Incomparably more glorious than Rome is that heavenly city in which for victory you have truth; for dignity, holiness; for peace, felicity; for life, eternity. Much less does it admit into its society such gods, if you do blush to admit into yours such men. Wherefore, if you would attain to the blessed city, shun the society of devils. They who are propitiated by deeds of shame are unworthy of the worship of right-hearted men. Let these, then, be obliterated from your worship by the cleansing of the Christian religion, as those men were blotted from your citizenship by the censor's mark.

But, so far as regards carnal benefits, which are the only blessings the wicked desire to enjoy, and carnal miseries, which alone they shrink from enduring, we will show in the following book that the demons have not the power they are supposed to have; and although they had it, we ought rather on that account to despise these blessings, than for the sake of them to worship those gods, and by worshiping them to miss the attainment of these blessings they grudge us. But that they have not even this power which is ascribed to them by those who worship them for the sake of temporal advantages, this, I say, I will prove in the following book; so let us here close the present argument.

---

1. Alluding to the sanctuary given to all who fled to Rome in its early days.
2. Virgil *Æneid* 1.278.

BOOK THREE

ARGUMENT

As in the foregoing book Augustine has proved regarding moral and spiritual calamities, so in this book he proves regarding external and bodily disasters, that since the foundation of the city the Romans have been continually subject to them; and that even when the false gods were worshiped without a rival, before the advent of Christ, they afforded no relief from such calamities.

1. OF THE ILLS WHICH ALONE THE WICKED FEAR, AND WHICH THE WORLD CONTINUALLY SUFFERED, EVEN WHEN THE GODS WERE WORSHIPED

Of moral and spiritual evils, which are above all others to be deprecated, I think enough has already been said to show that the false gods took no steps to prevent the people who worshiped them from being overwhelmed by such calamities, but rather aggravated the ruin. I see I must now speak of those evils which alone are dreaded by the heathen—famine, pestilence, war, pillage, captivity, massacre, and the like calamities, already enumerated in the first book. For evil men account those things alone evil which do not make men evil; neither do they blush to praise good things, and yet to remain evil among the good things they praise. It grieves them more to own a bad house than a bad life, as if it were man's greatest good to have everything good but himself. But not even such evils as were alone dreaded by the heathen were warded off by their gods, even when they were most unrestrictedly worshiped. For in various times and places before the advent of our Redeemer, the human race was crushed with numberless and sometimes incredible calamities; and at that time what gods but those did the world worship, if you except the one nation of the Hebrews, and, beyond them, such individuals as the most secret and most just judgment of God counted worthy of divine grace?[1] But that I may not be prolix, I will be silent regarding the heavy calamities that have been suffered by any other nations, and will speak only of what happened to Rome and the Roman Empire, by which I mean Rome properly so called, and those lands which already, before the coming of Christ, had by alliance or conquest become, as it were, members of the body of the state.

---

1. Cf. Augustine *Ep. ad Deogratias* 102, 13; and *De Præd. Sanct.* 19.

2. WHETHER THE GODS, WHOM THE GREEKS AND ROMANS WORSHIPED IN COMMON, WERE JUSTIFIED IN PERMITTING THE DESTRUCTION OF ILIUM

First, then, why was Troy or Ilium, the cradle of the Roman people (for I must not overlook nor disguise what I touched upon in the first book[1]), conquered, taken, and destroyed by the Greeks, though it esteemed and worshiped the same gods as they? Priam, some answer, paid the penalty of the perjury of his father Laomedon.[2] Then it is true that Laomedon hired Apollo and Neptune as his workmen. For the story goes that he promised them wages, and then broke his bargain. I wonder that famous diviner Apollo toiled at so huge a work, and never suspected Laomedon was going to cheat him of his pay. And Neptune too, his uncle, brother of Jupiter, king of the sea, it really was not seemly that he should be ignorant of what was to happen. For he is introduced by Homer[3] (who lived and wrote before the building of Rome) as predicting something great of the posterity of Æneas, who in fact founded Rome. And as Homer says, Neptune also rescued Æneas in a cloud from the wrath of Achilles, though (according to Virgil[4])

> *All his will was to destroy*
> *His own creation, perjured Troy.*

Gods, then, so great as Apollo and Neptune, in ignorance of the cheat that was to defraud them of their wages, built the walls of Troy for nothing but thanks and thankless people.[5] There may be some doubt whether it is not a worse crime to believe such persons to be gods, than to cheat such gods. Even Homer himself did not give full credence to the story; for while he represents Neptune, indeed, as hostile to the Trojans, he introduces Apollo as their champion, though the story implies that both were offended by that fraud. If, therefore, they believe their fables, let them blush to worship such gods; if they discredit the fables, let no more be said of the "Trojan perjury"; or let them explain how the gods hated Trojan, but loved Roman perjury. For how did the conspiracy of Catiline, even in so large and corrupt a city, find so abundant a supply of men whose hands and tongues found them a living by perjury and civic broils? What else but perjury corrupted the judgments pronounced by so many of the senators? What else corrupted the people's votes and decisions of all causes tried before them? For it seems that the ancient practice of taking oaths has been preserved even in the midst of the greatest corruption, not for the sake of restraining wickedness by religious fear, but to complete the tale of crimes by adding that of perjury.

1. See above, 1.4.
2. *Virgil Georg. 1.502, "Laomedonteæ luimus perjuria Trojæ."*
3. Homer *Iliad* 20.293 et seqq.
4. Virgil *Æneid* 5.810–811.
5. *"Gratis et ingratis."*

3. THAT THE GODS COULD NOT BE OFFENDED BY THE ADULTERY OF PARIS, THIS CRIME BEING SO COMMON AMONG THEMSELVES

There is no ground, then, for representing the gods (by whom, as they say, that empire stood, though they are proved to have been conquered by the Greeks) as being enraged at the Trojan perjury. Neither, as others again plead in their defense, was it indignation at the adultery of Paris that caused them to withdraw their protection from Troy. For their habit is to be instigators and instructors in vice, not its avengers. "The city of Rome," says Sallust, "was first built and inhabited, as I have heard, by the Trojans, who, flying their country, under the conduct of Æneas, wandered about without making any settlement."[1] If, then, the gods were of opinion that the adultery of Paris should be punished, it was chiefly the Romans, or at least the Romans also, who should have suffered; for the adultery was brought about by Æneas's mother. But how could they hate in Paris a crime which they made no objection to in their own sister Venus, who (not to mention any other instance) committed adultery with Anchises, and so became the mother of Æneas? Is it because in the one case Menelaus[2] was aggrieved, while in the other Vulcan[3] connived at the crime? For the gods, I fancy, are so little jealous of their wives, that they make no scruple of sharing them with men. But perhaps I may be suspected of turning the myths into ridicule, and not handling so weighty a subject with sufficient gravity. Well, then, let us say that Æneas is not the son of Venus. I am willing to admit it; but is Romulus any more the son of Mars? For why not the one as well as the other? Or is it lawful for gods to have intercourse with women, unlawful for men to have intercourse with goddesses? A hard, or rather an incredible condition, that what was allowed to Mars by the law of Venus, should not be allowed to Venus herself by her own law. However, both cases have the authority of Rome; for Cæsar in modern times believed no less that he was descended from Venus,[4] than the ancient Romulus believed himself the son of Mars.

---

1. *Sallust De Conj. Cat. 6.*
2. Helen's husband.
3. Venus's husband.
4. Suetonius, in his *Life of Julius Cæsar* (6), relates that, in pronouncing a funeral oration in praise of his aunt Julia, Cæsar claimed for the Julian gens to which his family belonged a descent from Venus, through Iulus, son of Æneas.

4. OF VARRO'S OPINION, THAT IT IS USEFUL FOR MEN TO FEIGN THEMSELVES THE OFFSPRING OF THE GODS

Someone will say, "But do you believe all this?" Not I indeed. For even Varro, a very learned heathen, all but admits that these stories are false, though he does not boldly and confidently say so. But he maintains it is useful for states that brave men believe, though falsely, that they are descended from the gods; for that thus the human spirit, cherishing the belief of its divine descent, will both more boldly venture into great enterprises, and will carry them out more energetically, and will therefore by its very confidence secure more abundant success. You see how wide a field is opened to falsehood by this opinion of Varro's, which I have expressed as well as I could in my own words; and how comprehensible it is, that many of the religions and sacred legends should be feigned in a community in which it was judged profitable for the citizens that lies should be told even about the gods themselves.

5. THAT IT IS NOT CREDIBLE THAT THE GODS SHOULD HAVE PUNISHED THE ADULTERY OF PARIS, SEEING THEY SHOWED NO INDIGNATION AT THE ADULTERY OF THE MOTHER OF ROMULUS

But whether Venus could bear Æneas to a human father Anchises, or Mars beget Romulus of the daughter of Numitor, we leave as unsettled questions. For our own Scriptures suggest the very similar question, whether the fallen angels had sexual intercourse with the daughters of men, by which the earth was at that time filled with giants, that is, with enormously large and strong men. At present, then, I will limit my discussion to this dilemma: If that which their books relate about the mother of Æneas and the father of Romulus be true, how can the gods be displeased with men for adulteries which, when committed by themselves, excite no displeasure? If it is false, not even in this case can the gods be angry that men should really commit adulteries, which, even when falsely attributed to the gods, they delight in. Moreover, if the adultery of Mars be discredited, that Venus also may be freed from the imputation, then the mother of Romulus is left unshielded by the pretext of a divine seduction. For Sylvia was a vestal priestess, and the gods ought to avenge this sacrilege on the Romans with greater severity than Paris's adultery on the Trojans. For even the Romans themselves in primitive times used to go so far as to bury alive any vestal who was detected in adultery, while women unconsecrated, though they were punished, were never punished with death for that crime; and thus they more earnestly vindicated the purity of shrines they esteemed divine, than of the human bed.

6. THAT THE GODS EXACTED NO PENALTY FOR THE FRATRICIDAL ACT OF ROMULUS

I add another instance: If the sins of men so greatly incensed those divinities, that they abandoned Troy to fire and sword to punish the crime of Paris, the murder of Romulus's brother ought to have incensed them more against the Romans than the cajoling of a Greek husband moved them against the Trojans: fratricide in a newly born city should have provoked them more than adultery in a city already flourishing. It makes no difference to the question we now discuss, whether Romulus ordered his brother to be slain, or slew him with his own hand; it is a crime which many shamelessly deny, many through shame doubt, many in grief disguise. And we shall not pause to examine and weigh the testimonies of historical writers on the subject. All agree that the brother of Romulus was slain, not by enemies, not by strangers. If it was Romulus who either commanded or perpetrated this crime, Romulus was more truly the head of the Romans than Paris of the Trojans; why then did he who carried off another man's wife bring down the anger of the gods on the Trojans, while he who took his brother's life obtained the guardianship of those same gods? If, on the other hand, that crime was not worked either by the hand or will of Romulus, then the whole city is chargeable with it, because it did not see to its punishment, and thus committed, not fratricide, but parricide, which is worse. For both brothers were the founders of that city, of which the one was by villainy prevented from being a ruler. So far as I see, then, no evil can be ascribed to Troy which warranted the gods in abandoning it to destruction, nor any good to Rome which accounts for the gods visiting it with prosperity; unless the truth be, that they fled from Troy because they were vanquished, and took themselves to Rome to practice their characteristic deceptions there. Nevertheless they kept a footing for themselves in Troy, that they might deceive future inhabitants who repeopled these lands; while at Rome, by a wider exercise of their malignant arts, they exulted in more abundant honors.

7. OF THE DESTRUCTION OF ILIUM BY FIMBRIA, A LIEUTENANT OF MARIUS

And surely we may ask what wrong poor Ilium had done, that, in the first heat of the civil wars of Rome, it should suffer at the hand of Fimbria, the veriest villain among Marius's partisans, a more fierce and cruel destruction than the Grecian sack.[1] For when the Greeks took it many escaped, and many who did not escape were suffered to live, though in captivity. But Fimbria from the first gave orders that not a life should be spared, and burned up together the city and all its inhabitants. Thus was Ilium requited, not by the Greeks, whom she had provoked by wrongdoing; but by the Romans, who had been built out of her ruins; while the gods, adored alike of both sides, did simply nothing, or, to speak more correctly, could do nothing. Is it then true, that at this time also, after Troy had repaired the damage done by the Grecian fire, all the gods by whose help the kingdom stood, "forsook each fane, each sacred shrine"?

But if so, I ask the reason; for in my judgment, the conduct of the gods was as much to be reprobated as that of the townsmen to be applauded. For these closed their gates against Fimbria, that they might preserve the city for Sylla, and were therefore burned and consumed by the enraged general. Now, up to this time, Sylla's cause was the more worthy of the two; for till now he used arms to restore the republic, and as yet his good intentions had met with no reverses. What better thing, then, could the Trojans have done? What more honorable, what more faithful to Rome, or more worthy of her relationship, than to preserve their city for the better part of the Romans, and to shut their gates against a parricide of his country? It is for the defenders of the gods to consider the ruin which this conduct brought on Troy. The gods deserted an adulterous people, and abandoned Troy to the fires of the Greeks, that out of her ashes a chaster Rome might arise. But why did they a second time abandon this same town, allied now to Rome, and not making war upon her noble daughter, but preserving a most steadfast and pious fidelity to Rome's most justifiable faction? Why did they give her up to be destroyed, not by the Greek heroes, but by the basest of the Romans? Or, if the gods did not favor Sylla's cause, for which the unhappy Trojans maintained their city, why did they themselves predict and promise Sylla such successes? Must we call them flatterers of the fortunate, rather than helpers of the wretched? Troy was not destroyed, then, because the gods deserted it. For the demons, always watchful to deceive, did what they could. For, when all the statues were overthrown and burned together with the town, Livy tells us that only the image of Minerva is said to have been found standing uninjured amid the ruins of her temple; not that it might be said in their praise, "The gods who made this realm divine," but that it might not be said in their defense, They are "gone from each fane, each sacred shrine": for that marvel was permitted to them, not that they might be proved to be powerful, but that they might be convicted of being present.

---

1. Livy 83, one of the lost books; and Appian, in *Mithridat*.

8. WHETHER ROME OUGHT TO HAVE BEEN ENTRUSTED TO THE TROJAN GODS

Where, then, was the wisdom of entrusting Rome to the Trojan gods, who had demonstrated their weakness in the loss of Troy? Will someone say that, when Fimbria stormed Troy, the gods were already resident in Rome? How, then, did the image of Minerva remain standing? Besides, if they were at Rome when Fimbria destroyed Troy, perhaps they were at Troy when Rome itself was taken and set on fire by the Gauls. But as they are very acute in hearing, and very swift in their movements, they came quickly at the cackling of the goose to defend at least the Capitol, though to defend the rest of the city they were too long in being warned.

9. WHETHER IT IS CREDIBLE THAT THE PEACE DURING THE REIGN OF NUMA WAS BROUGHT ABOUT BY THE GODS

It is also believed that it was by the help of the gods that the successor of Romulus, Numa Pompilius, enjoyed peace during his entire reign, and shut the gates of Janus, which are customarily kept open[1] during war. And it is supposed he was thus requited for appointing many religious observances among the Romans. Certainly that king would have commanded our congratulations for so rare a leisure, had he been wise enough to spend it on wholesome pursuits, and, subduing a pernicious curiosity, had sought out the true God with true piety. But as it was, the gods were not the authors of his leisure; but possibly they would have deceived him less had they found him busier. For the more disengaged they found him, the more they themselves occupied his attention. Varro informs us of all his efforts, and of the arts he employed to associate these gods with himself and the city; and in its own place, if God will, I shall discuss these matters. Meanwhile, as we are speaking of the benefits conferred by the gods, I readily admit that peace is a great benefit; but it is a benefit of the true God, which, like the sun, the rain, and other supports of life, is frequently conferred on the ungrateful and wicked. But if this great boon was conferred on Rome and Pompilius by their gods, why did they never afterward grant it to the Roman Empire during even more meritorious periods? Were the sacred rites more efficient at their first institution than during their subsequent celebration? But they had no existence in Numa's time, until he added them to the ritual; whereas afterward they had already been celebrated and preserved, that benefit might arise from them. How, then, is it that those forty-three, or as others prefer it, thirty-nine years of Numa's reign, were passed in unbroken peace, and yet that afterward, when the worship was established, and the gods themselves, who were invoked by it, were the recognized guardians and patrons of the city, we can with difficulty find during the whole period, from the building of the city to the reign of Augustus, one year—that, namely, which followed the close of the first Punic war—in which, for a marvel, the Romans were able to shut the gates of war?[2]

---

1. The gates of Janus were not the gates of a temple, but the gates of a passage called Janus, which was used only for military purposes; shut therefore in peace, open in war.
2. The year of the Consuls T. Manlius and C. Atilius, 519 A.U.C.

10. WHETHER IT WAS DESIRABLE THAT THE ROMAN EMPIRE SHOULD BE INCREASED BY SUCH A FURIOUS SUCCESSION OF WARS, WHEN IT MIGHT HAVE BEEN QUIET AND SAFE BY FOLLOWING IN THE PEACEFUL WAYS OF NUMA

Do they reply that the Roman Empire could never have been so widely extended, nor so glorious, save by constant and unintermitting wars? A fit argument, truly! Why must a kingdom be distracted in order to be great? In this little world of man's body, is it not better to have a moderate stature, and health with it, than to attain the huge dimensions of a giant by unnatural torments, and when you attain it to find no rest, but to be pained the more in proportion to the size of your members? What evil would have resulted, or rather what good would not have resulted, had those times continued which Sallust sketched, when he says, "At first the kings (for that was the first title of empire in the world) were divided in their sentiments: part cultivated the mind, others the body: at that time the life of men was led without covetousness; everyone was sufficiently satisfied with his own!"[1] Was it requisite, then, for Rome's prosperity, that the state of things which Virgil reprobates should succeed:

> *"At length stole on a baser age,*
> *And war's indomitable rage,*
> *And greedy lust of gain"*?[2]

But obviously the Romans have a plausible defense for undertaking and carrying on such disastrous wars—to wit, that the pressure of their enemies forced them to resist, so that they were compelled to fight, not by any greed of human applause, but by the necessity of protecting life and liberty. Well, let that pass. Here is Sallust's account of the matter: "For when their state, enriched with laws, institutions, territory, seemed abundantly prosperous and sufficiently powerful, according to the ordinary law of human nature, opulence gave birth to envy. Accordingly, the neighboring kings and states took arms and assaulted them. A few allies lent assistance; the rest, struck with fear, kept aloof from dangers. But the Romans, watchful at home and in war, were active, made preparations, encouraged one another, marched to meet their enemies—protected by arms their liberty, country, parents. Afterward, when they had repelled the dangers by their bravery, they carried help to their allies and friends, and procured alliances more by conferring than by receiving favors."[3] This was to build up Rome's greatness by honorable means.

But, in Numa's reign, I would know whether the long peace was maintained in spite of the incursions of wicked neighbors, or if these incursions were discontinued that the peace might be maintained? For if even then Rome was harassed by wars, and yet did not meet force with force, the same means she then used to quiet her enemies without conquering them in war, or terrifying them with the onset of battle, she might have used always, and have reigned in peace with the gates of Janus shut. And if this was not in her power, then Rome enjoyed peace not at the will of her gods, but at the will of her neighbors round about, and only so long as they cared to provoke her with no war, unless perhaps these pitiful gods will dare to sell to one man as their favor what lies not in their power to bestow, but in the will of another man. These demons, indeed, insofar as they are permitted, can terrify or incite the minds of wicked men by their own peculiar wickedness. But if they always had this power, and if no action were taken against their efforts by a more secret and higher power, they would be supreme to give peace or the victories of war, which almost always fall out through some human emotion, and frequently in opposition to the will of the gods, as is proved not only by lying legends, which scarcely hint or signify any grain of truth, but even by Roman history itself.

---

1. *Sallust De Conj. Cat. 2.*
2. Virgil *Æneid* 8.326–327.
3. *Sallust De Conj. Cat. 6.*

11. OF THE STATUE OF APOLLO AT CUMÆ, WHOSE TEARS ARE SUPPOSED TO HAVE PORTENDED DISASTER TO THE GREEKS, WHOM THE GOD WAS UNABLE TO SUCCOR

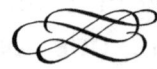

And it is still this weakness of the gods which is confessed in the story of the Cuman Apollo, who is said to have wept for four days during the war with the Achæans and King Aristonicus. And when the augurs were alarmed at the portent, and had determined to cast the statue into the sea, the old men of Cumæ interposed, and related that a similar prodigy had occurred to the same image during the wars against Antiochus and against Perseus, and that by a decree of the senate, gifts had been presented to Apollo, because the event had proved favorable to the Romans. Then soothsayers were summoned who were supposed to have greater professional skill, and they pronounced that the weeping of Apollo's image was propitious to the Romans, because Cumæ was a Greek colony, and that Apollo was bewailing (and thereby presaging) the grief and calamity that was about to light upon his own land of Greece, from which he had been brought. Shortly afterward it was reported that King Aristonicus was defeated and made prisoner—a defeat certainly opposed to the will of Apollo; and this he indicated by even shedding tears from his marble image. And this shows us that, though the verses of the poets are mythical, they are not altogether devoid of truth, but describe the manners of the demons in a sufficiently fit style. For in Virgil, Diana mourned for Camilla,[1] and Hercules wept for Pallas doomed to die.[2] This is perhaps the reason why Numa Pompilius, too, when, enjoying prolonged peace, but without knowing or inquiring from whom he received it, he began in his leisure to consider to what gods he should entrust the safekeeping and conduct of Rome, and not dreaming that the true, almighty, and most high God cares for earthly affairs, but recollecting only that the Trojan gods which Æneas had brought to Italy had been able to preserve neither the Trojan nor Lavinian kingdom founded by Æneas himself, concluded that he must provide other gods as guardians of fugitives and helpers of the weak, and add them to those earlier divinities who had either come over to Rome with Romulus, or when Alba was destroyed.

---

1. Virgil *Æneid* 11.532.
2. Ibid., 10.464.

12. THAT THE ROMANS ADDED A VAST NUMBER OF GODS TO THOSE INTRODUCED BY NUMA, AND THAT THEIR NUMBERS HELPED THEM NOT AT ALL

But though Pompilius introduced so ample a ritual, yet did not Rome see fit to be content with it. For as yet Jupiter himself had not his chief temple—it being King Tarquin who built the Capitol. And Æsculapius left Epidaurus for Rome, that in this foremost city he might have a finer field for the exercise of his great medical skill.[1] The mother of the gods, too, came I know not whence from Pessinus; it being unseemly that, while her son presided on the Capitoline hill, she herself should lie hid in obscurity. But if she is the mother of all the gods, she not only followed some of her children to Rome, but left others to follow her. I wonder, indeed, if she were the mother of Cynocephalus, who a long while afterward came from Egypt. Whether also the goddess Fever was her offspring, is a matter for her grandson Æsculapius[2] to decide. But of whatever breed she be, the foreign gods will not presume, I trust, to call a goddess baseborn who is a Roman citizen. Who can number the deities to whom the guardianship of Rome was entrusted? Indigenous and imported, both of heaven, earth, hell, seas, fountains, rivers; and, as Varro says, gods certain and uncertain, male and female: for, as among animals, so among all kinds of gods are there these distinctions. Rome, then, enjoying the protection of such a cloud of deities, might surely have been preserved from some of those great and horrible calamities, of which I can mention but a few. For by the great smoke of her altars she summoned to her protection, as by a beacon fire, a host of gods, for whom she appointed and maintained temples, altars, sacrifices, priests, and thus offended the true and most high God, to whom alone all this ceremonial is lawfully due. And, indeed, she was more prosperous when she had fewer gods; but the greater she became, the more gods she thought she should have, as the larger ship needs to be manned by a larger crew. I suppose she despaired of the smaller number, under whose protection she had spent comparatively happy days, being able to defend her greatness. For even under the kings (with the exception of Numa Pompilius, of whom I have already spoken), how wicked a contentiousness must have existed to occasion the death of Romulus's brother!

---

1. Livy 10.47.
2. Being son of Apollo.

13. BY WHAT RIGHT OR AGREEMENT THE ROMANS OBTAINED THEIR FIRST WIVES

How is it that neither Juno, who with her husband Jupiter even then cherished

Rome's sons, the nation of the gown,[1]

nor Venus herself, could assist the children of the loved Æneas to find wives by some right and equitable means? For the lack of this entailed upon the Romans the lamentable necessity of stealing their wives, and then waging war with their fathers-in-law; so that the wretched women, before they had recovered from the wrong done them by their husbands, were dowried with the blood of their fathers. "But the Romans conquered their neighbors." Yes; but with what wounds on both sides, and with what sad slaughter of relatives and neighbors! The war of Cæsar and Pompey was the contest of only one father-in-law with one son-in-law; and before it began, the daughter of Cæsar, Pompey's wife, was already dead. But with how keen and just an accent of grief does Lucan[2] exclaim: "I sing that worse than civil war waged in the plains of Emathia, and in which the crime was justified by the victory!"

The Romans, then, conquered that they might, with hands stained in the blood of their fathers-in-law, wrench the miserable girls from their embrace—girls who dared not weep for their slain parents, for fear of offending their victorious husbands; and while yet the battle was raging, stood with their prayers on their lips, and knew not for whom to utter them. Such nuptials were certainly prepared for the Roman people not by Venus, but Bellona; or possibly that infernal fury Alecto had more liberty to injure them now that Juno was aiding them, than when the prayers of that goddess had excited her against Æneas. Andromache in captivity was happier than these Roman brides. For though she was a slave, yet, after she had become the wife of Pyrrhus, no more Trojans fell by his hand; but the Romans slew in battle the very fathers of the brides they fondled. Andromache, the victor's captive, could only mourn, not fear, the death of her people. The Sabine women, related to men still combatants, feared the death of their fathers when their husbands went out to battle, and mourned their death as they returned, while neither their grief nor their fear could be freely expressed. For the victories of their husbands, involving the destruction of fellow townsmen, relatives, brothers, fathers, caused either pious agony or cruel exultation. Moreover, as the fortune of war is capricious, some of them lost their husbands by the sword of their parents, while others lost husband

and father together in mutual destruction. For the Romans by no means escaped with impunity, but they were driven back within their walls, and defended themselves behind closed gates; and when the gates were opened by guile, and the enemy admitted into the town, the Forum itself was the field of a hateful and fierce engagement of fathers-in-law and sons-in-law. The ravishers were indeed quite defeated, and, flying on all sides to their houses, sullied with new shame their original shameful and lamentable triumph. It was at this juncture that Romulus, hoping no more from the valor of his citizens, prayed Jupiter that they might stand their ground; and from this occasion the god gained the name of Stator. But not even thus would the mischief have been finished, had not the ravished women themselves flashed out with disheveled hair, and cast themselves before their parents, and thus disarmed their just rage, not with the arms of victory, but with the supplications of filial affection. Then Romulus, who could not brook his own brother as a colleague, was compelled to accept Titus Tatius, king of the Sabines, as his partner on the throne. But how long would he who misliked the fellowship of his own twin brother endure a stranger? So, Tatius being slain, Romulus remained sole king, that he might be the greater god. See what rights of marriage these were that fomented unnatural wars. These were the Roman leagues of kindred, relationship, alliance, religion. This was the life of the city so abundantly protected by the gods. You see how many severe things might be said on this theme; but our purpose carries us past them, and requires our discourse for other matters.

---

1. Virgil Æneid 1.286.
2. Lucan *Pharsalia* 5.1.

14. OF THE WICKEDNESS OF THE WAR WAGED BY THE ROMANS AGAINST THE ALBANS, AND OF THE VICTORIES WON BY THE LUST OF POWER

But what happened after Numa's reign, and under the other kings, when the Albans were provoked into war, with sad results not to themselves alone, but also to the Romans? The long peace of Numa had become tedious; and with what endless slaughter and detriment of both states did the Roman and Alban armies bring it to an end! For Alba, which had been founded by Ascanius, son of Æneas, and which was more properly the mother of Rome than Troy herself, was provoked to battle by Tullus Hostilius, king of Rome, and in the conflict both inflicted and received such damage, that at length both parties wearied of the struggle. It was then devised that the war should be decided by the combat of three twin brothers from each army: from the Romans the three Horatii stood forward, from the Albans the three Curiatii. Two of the Horatii were overcome and disposed of by the Curiatii; but by the remaining Horatius the three Curiatii were slain. Thus Rome remained victorious, but with such a sacrifice that only one survivor returned to his home. Whose was the loss on both sides? Whose the grief, but of the offspring of Æneas, the descendants of Ascanius, the progeny of Venus, the grandsons of Jupiter? For this, too, was a "worse than civil" war, in which the belligerent states were mother and daughter. And to this combat of the three twin brothers there was added another atrocious and horrible catastrophe. For as the two nations had formerly been friendly (being related and neighbors), the sister of the Horatii had been betrothed to one of the Curiatii; and she, when she saw her brother wearing the spoils of her betrothed, burst into tears, and was slain by her own brother in his anger. To me, this one girl seems to have been more humane than the whole Roman people. I cannot think her to blame for lamenting the man to whom already she had plighted her troth, or, as perhaps she was doing, for grieving that her brother should have slain him to whom he had promised his sister. For why do we praise the grief of Æneas (in Virgil[1]) over the enemy cut down even by his own hand? Why did Marcellus shed tears over the city of Syracuse, when he recollected, just before he destroyed, its magnificence and meridian glory, and thought upon the common lot of all things? I demand, in the name of humanity, that if men are praised for tears shed over enemies conquered by themselves, a weak girl should not be counted criminal for bewailing her lover slaughtered by the hand of her brother. While, then, that maiden was weeping for the death of her betrothed inflicted by her brother's hand, Rome was rejoicing that such devastation had been worked on her mother state, and that she had purchased a victory with such an expenditure of the common blood of herself and the Albans.

Why allege to me the mere names and words of "glory" and "victory"? Tear off the disguise of wild delusion, and look at the naked deeds: weigh them naked, judge them naked. Let the charge be brought against Alba, as Troy was charged with adultery. There is no such charge, none like it found: the war was kindled only in order that there

> *Might sound in languid ears the cry*
> *Of Tullus and of victory.*[2]

This vice of restless ambition was the sole motive to that social and parricidal war—a vice which Sallust brands in passing; for when he has spoken with brief but hearty commendation of those primitive times in which life was spent without covetousness, and everyone was sufficiently satisfied with what he had, he goes on: "But after Cyrus in Asia, and the Lacedemonians and Athenians in Greece, began to subdue cities and nations, and to account the lust of sovereignty a sufficient ground for war, and to reckon that the greatest glory consisted in the greatest empire";[3] and so on, as I need not now quote. This lust of sovereignty disturbs and consumes the human race with frightful ills. By this lust Rome was overcome when she triumphed over Alba, and praising her own crime, called it glory. For, as our Scriptures say, "the wicked boasteth of his heart's desire, and blesseth the covetous, whom the LORD abhorreth."[4] Away, then, with these deceitful masks, these deluding whitewashes, that things may be truthfully seen and scrutinized. Let no man tell me that this and the other was a "great" man, because he fought and conquered so and so. Gladiators fight and conquer, and this barbarism has its meed of praise; but I think it were better to take the consequences of any sloth, than to seek the glory won by such arms. And if two gladiators entered the arena to fight, one being father, the other his son, who would endure such a spectacle? Who would not be revolted by it? How, then, could that be a glorious war which a daughter state waged against its mother? Or did it constitute a difference, that the battlefield was not an arena, and that the wide plains were filled with the carcasses not of two gladiators, but of many of the flower of two nations; and that those contests were viewed not by the amphitheatre, but by the whole world, and furnished a profane spectacle both to those alive at the time, and to their posterity, so long as the fame of it is handed down?

Yet those gods, guardians of the Roman Empire, and, as it were, theatric spectators of such contests as these, were not satisfied until the sister of the Horatii was added by her brother's sword as a third victim from the Roman side, so that Rome herself, though she won the day, should have as many deaths to mourn. Afterward, as a fruit of the victory, Alba was destroyed, though it was there the Trojan gods had formed a third asylum after Ilium had been sacked by the Greeks, and after they had left

Lavinium, where Æneas had founded a kingdom in a land of banishment. But probably Alba was destroyed because from it too the gods had migrated, in their usual fashion, as Virgil says:

> *Gone from each fane, each sacred shrine,*
> *Are those who made this realm divine.*[5]

Gone, indeed, and from now their third asylum, that Rome might seem all the wiser in committing herself to them after they had deserted three other cities. Alba, whose king Amulius had banished his brother, displeased them; Rome, whose king Romulus had slain his brother, pleased them. But before Alba was destroyed, its population, they say, was amalgamated with the inhabitants of Rome so that the two cities were one. Well, admitting it was so, yet the fact remains that the city of Ascanius, the third retreat of the Trojan gods, was destroyed by the daughter city. Besides, to effect this pitiful conglomerate of the war's leavings, much blood was spilled on both sides. And how shall I speak in detail of the same wars, so often renewed in subsequent reigns, though they seemed to have been finished by great victories; and of wars that time after time were brought to an end by great slaughters, and which yet time after time were renewed by the posterity of those who had made peace and struck treaties? Of this calamitous history we have no small proof, in the fact that no subsequent king closed the gates of war; and therefore with all their tutelar gods, no one of them reigned in peace.

1. Virgil *Æneid* 10.821, of Lausus:
    "But when Anchises' son surveyed
    The fair, fair face so ghastly made,
    He groaned, by tenderness unmanned,
    And stretched the sympathizing hand," etc.
2. Ibid., 6.813.
3. *Sallust De Conj. Cat. 2.*
4. Ps. 10:3.
5. Virgil *Æneid* 2.351–352.

15. WHAT MANNER OF LIFE AND DEATH THE ROMAN KINGS HAD

And what was the end of the kings themselves? Of Romulus, a flattering legend tells us that he was assumed into heaven. But certain Roman historians relate that he was torn in pieces by the senate for his ferocity, and that a man, Julius Proculus, was suborned to give out that Romulus had appeared to him, and through him commanded the Roman people to worship him as a god; and that in this way the people, who were beginning to resent the action of the senate, were quieted and pacified. For an eclipse of the sun had also happened; and this was attributed to the divine power of Romulus by the ignorant multitude, who did not know that it was brought about by the fixed laws of the sun's course: though this grief of the sun might rather have been considered proof that Romulus had been slain, and that the crime was indicated by this deprivation of the sun's light; as, in truth, was the case when the Lord was crucified through the cruelty and impiety of the Jews. For it is sufficiently demonstrated that this latter obscuration of the sun did not occur by the natural laws of the heavenly bodies, because it was then the Jewish Passover, which is held only at full moon, whereas natural eclipses of the sun happen only at the last quarter of the moon. Cicero, too, shows plainly enough that the apotheosis of Romulus was imaginary rather than real, when, even while he is praising him in one of Scipio's remarks in the *De Republica,* he says: "Such a reputation had he acquired, that when he suddenly disappeared during an eclipse of the sun, he was supposed to have been assumed into the number of the gods, which could be supposed of no mortal who had not the highest reputation for virtue."[1] By these words, "he suddenly disappeared," we are to understand that he was mysteriously made away with by the violence either of the tempest or of a murderous assault. For their other writers speak not only of an eclipse, but of a sudden storm also, which certainly either afforded opportunity for the crime, or itself made an end of Romulus. And of Tullus Hostilius, who was the third king of Rome, and who was himself destroyed by lightning, Cicero in the same book says, that "he was not supposed to have been deified by this death, possibly because the Romans were unwilling to vulgarize the promotion they were assured or persuaded of in the case of Romulus, lest they should bring it into contempt by gratuitously assigning it to all and sundry." In one of his invectives,[2] too, he says, in round terms, "The founder of this city, Romulus, we have raised to immortality and divinity by kindly celebrating his services"; implying that his deification was not real, but reputed, and called so by courtesy on account of his virtues. In the dialogue *Hortensius,* too, while speaking of the regular eclipses of the sun, he says that they "produce the same darkness as covered the death of Romulus, which happened during an eclipse of the sun." Here you see he does not at all shrink from speaking of his "death," for Cicero was more of a reasoner than a eulogist.

The other kings of Rome, too, with the exception of Numa Pompilius and Ancus Marcius, who died natural deaths, what horrible ends they had! Tullus Hostilius, the conqueror and destroyer of Alba, was, as I said, himself and all his house consumed by lightning. Priscus Tarquinius was slain by his predecessor's sons. Servius Tullius was foully murdered by his son-in-law Tarquinius Superbus, who succeeded him on the throne. Nor did so flagrant a parricide committed against Rome's best king drive from their altars and shrines those gods who were said to have been moved by Paris's adultery to treat poor Troy in this style, and abandon it to the fire and sword of the Greeks. No, the very Tarquin who had murdered was allowed to succeed his father-in-law. And this infamous parricide, during the reign he had secured by murder, was allowed to triumph in many victorious wars, and to build the Capitol from their spoils; the gods meanwhile not departing, but abiding, and abetting, and suffering their king Jupiter to preside and reign over them in that very splendid Capitol, the work of a parricide. For he did not build the Capitol in the days of his innocence, and then suffer banishment for subsequent crimes; but to that reign during which he built the Capitol, he won his way by unnatural crime. And when he was afterward banished by the Romans, and forbidden the city, it was not for his own but his son's wickedness in the affair of Lucretia—a crime perpetrated not only without his cognizance, but in his absence. For at that time he was besieging Ardea and fighting Rome's battles; and we cannot say what he would have done had he been aware of his son's crime. Notwithstanding, though his opinion was neither inquired into nor ascertained, the people stripped him of royalty; and when he returned to Rome with his army, it was admitted, but he was excluded, abandoned by his troops, and the gates shut in his face. And yet, after he had appealed to the neighboring states, and tormented the Romans with calamitous but unsuccessful wars, and when he was deserted by the ally on whom he most depended, despairing of regaining the kingdom, he lived a retired and quiet life for fourteen years, as it is reported, in Tusculum, a Roman town, where he grew old in his wife's company, and at last terminated his days in a much more desirable fashion than his father-in-law, who had perished by the hand of his son-in-law; his own daughter abetting, if report be true. And this Tarquin the Romans called, not the Cruel, nor the Infamous, but the Proud; their own pride perhaps resenting his tyrannical airs. So little did they make of his murdering their best king, his own father-in-law, that they elected him their own king. I wonder if it was not even more criminal in them to reward so bountifully so great a criminal. And yet there was no word of the gods abandoning the altars; unless, perhaps, someone will say in defense of the gods, that they remained at Rome for the purpose of punishing the Romans, rather than of aiding and profiting them, seducing them by empty victories, and wearing them out by severe wars. Such was the life of the Romans under the kings during the much praised epoch of the state which extends to the expulsion of Tarquinius Superbus in the 243rd year, during which all those victories, which were bought with so much blood and such disasters, hardly pushed Rome's dominion twenty miles from the city; a territory which would by no means bear comparison with that of any petty Gætulian state.

---

1. Cicero *De Rep.* 2.10.
2. Cicero *In Cat.* 3.2.

16. OF THE FIRST ROMAN CONSULS, THE ONE OF WHOM DROVE THE OTHER FROM THE COUNTRY, AND SHORTLY AFTER PERISHED AT ROME BY THE HAND OF A WOUNDED ENEMY, AND SO ENDED A CAREER OF UNNATURAL MURDERS

To this epoch let us add also that of which Sallust says, that it was ordered with justice and moderation, while the fear of Tarquin and of a war with Etruria was impending. For so long as the Etrurians aided the efforts of Tarquin to regain the throne, Rome was convulsed with distressing war. And therefore he says that the state was ordered with justice and moderation, through the pressure of fear, not through the influence of equity. And in this very brief period, how calamitous a year was that in which consuls were first created, when the kingly power was abolished! They did not fulfill their term of office. For Junius Brutus deprived his colleague Lucius Tarquinius Collatinus, and banished him from the city; and shortly after he himself fell in battle, at once slaying and slain, having formerly put to death his own sons and his brothers-in-law, because he had discovered that they were conspiring to restore Tarquin. It is this deed that Virgil shudders to record, even while he seems to praise it; for when he says:

> *And call his own rebellious seed*
> *For menaced liberty to bleed,*
> *he immediately exclaims,*
> *Unhappy father! howsoe'er*
> *The deed be judged by after days;*

that is to say, let posterity judge the deed as they please, let them praise and extol the father who slew his sons, he is unhappy. And then he adds, as if to console so unhappy a man:

> *His country's love shall all o'erbear,*
> *And unextinguished thirst of praise."*[1]

In the tragic end of Brutus, who slew his own sons, and though he slew his enemy, Tarquin's son, yet could not survive him, but was survived by Tarquin the elder, does not the innocence of his colleague Collatinus seem to be vindicated, who, though a good citizen, suffered the same punishment as Tarquin himself, when that tyrant was banished? For Brutus himself is said to have been a relative[2] of Tarquin. But Collatinus had the misfortune to bear not only the blood, but the name of Tarquin. To change his name, then, not his country, would have been his fit penalty: to abridge his name by this word, and be called simply L. Collatinus. But he was not compelled to lose what he could lose without detriment, but was stripped of the honor of the first consulship, and was banished from the land he loved. Is this, then, the glory of Brutus—this injustice, alike detestable and profitless to the republic? Was it to this he was driven by "his country's love, and unextinguished thirst of praise"?

When Tarquin the tyrant was expelled, L. Tarquinius Collatinus, the husband of Lucretia, was created consul along with Brutus. How justly the people acted, in looking more to the character than the name of a citizen! How unjustly Brutus acted, in depriving of honor and country his colleague in that new office, whom he might have deprived of his name, if it were so offensive to him! Such were the ills, such the disasters, which fell out when the government was "ordered with justice and moderation." Lucretius, too, who succeeded Brutus, was carried off by disease before the end of that same year. So P. Valerius, who succeeded Collatinus, and M. Horatius, who filled the vacancy occasioned by the death of Lucretius, completed that disastrous and funereal year, which had five consuls. Such was the year in which the Roman republic inaugurated the new honor and office of the consulship.

---

1. Virgil *Æneid* 6.820, etc.
2. His nephew.

17. OF THE DISASTERS WHICH VEXED THE ROMAN REPUBLIC AFTER THE INAUGURATION OF THE CONSULSHIP, AND OF THE NONINTERVENTION OF THE GODS OF ROME

After this, when their fears were gradually diminished—not because the wars ceased, but because they were not so furious—that period in which things were "ordered with justice and moderation" drew to an end, and there followed that state of matters which Sallust thus briefly sketches: "Then began the patricians to oppress the people as slaves, to condemn them to death or scourging, as the kings had done, to drive them from their holdings, and to tyrannize over those who had no property to lose. The people, overwhelmed by these oppressive measures, and most of all by usury, and obliged to contribute both money and personal service to the constant wars, at length took arms and seceded to Mount Aventine and Mount Sacer, and thus secured for themselves tribunes and protective laws. But it was only the second Punic war that put an end on both sides to discord and strife."[1] But why should I spend time in writing such things, or make others spend it in reading them? Let the terse summary of Sallust suffice to intimate the misery of the republic through all that long period till the second Punic war—how it was distracted from without by unceasing wars, and torn with civil broils and dissensions. So that those victories they boast were not the substantial joys of the happy, but the empty comforts of wretched men, and seductive incitements to turbulent men to concoct disasters upon disasters. And let not the good and prudent Romans be angry at our saying this; and indeed we need neither deprecate nor denounce their anger, for we know they will harbor none. For we speak no more severely than their own authors, and much less elaborately and strikingly; yet they diligently read these authors, and compel their children to learn them. But they who are angry, what would they do to me were I to say what Sallust says? "Frequent mobs, seditions, and at last civil wars, became common, while a few leading men on whom the masses were dependent, affected supreme power under the seemly pretense of seeking the good of senate and people; citizens were judged good or bad without reference to their loyalty to the republic (for all were equally corrupt); but the wealthy and dangerously powerful were esteemed good citizens, because they maintained the existing state of things." Now, if those historians judged that an honorable freedom of speech required that they should not be silent regarding the blemishes of their own state, which they have in many places loudly applauded in their ignorance of that other and true city in which citizenship is an everlasting dignity; what does it become us to do, whose liberty ought to be so much greater, as our hope in God is better and more assured, when they impute to our Christ the calamities of this age, in order that men of the less instructed and weaker sort may be alienated from that city in which alone eternal and blessed life can be enjoyed? Nor do we utter against their gods anything more horrible than their own authors do, whom they read and circulate. For, indeed, all that we have said we have derived from them, and there is much more to say of a worse kind which we are unable to say.

Where, then, were those gods who are supposed to be justly worshiped for the slender and delusive prosperity of this world, when the Romans, who were seduced to their service by lying wiles, were harassed by such calamities? Where were they when Valerius the consul was killed while defending the Capitol, that had been fired by exiles and slaves? He was himself better able to defend the temple of Jupiter, than that crowd of divinities with their most high and mighty king, whose temple he came to the rescue of were able to defend him. Where were they when the city, worn out with unceasing seditions, was waiting in some kind of calm for the return of the ambassadors who had been sent to Athens to borrow laws, and was desolated by dreadful famine and pestilence? Where were they when the people, again distressed with famine, created for the first time a prefect of the market; and when Spurius Melius, who, as the famine increased, distributed corn to the famishing masses, was accused of aspiring to royalty, and at the instance of this same prefect, and on the authority of the superannuated dictator L. Quintius, was put to death by Quintus Servilius, master of the horse—an event which occasioned a serious and dangerous riot? Where were they when that very severe pestilence visited Rome, on account of which the people, after long and wearisome and useless supplications of the helpless gods, conceived the idea of celebrating Lectisternia, which had never been done before; that is to say, they set couches in honor of the gods, which accounts for the name of this sacred rite, or rather sacrilege?[2] Where were they when, during ten successive years of reverses, the Roman army suffered frequent and great losses among the Veians and would have been destroyed but for the succor of Furius Camillus, who was afterward banished by an ungrateful country? Where were they when the Gauls took, sacked, burned, and desolated Rome? Where were they when that memorable pestilence worked such destruction, in which Furius Camillus too perished, who first defended the ungrateful republic from the Veians, and afterward saved it from the Gauls? No, during this plague, they introduced a new pestilence of scenic entertainments, which spread its more fatal contagion, not to the bodies, but the morals of the Romans? Where were they when another frightful pestilence visited the city—I mean the poisonings imputed to an incredible number of noble Roman matrons, whose characters were infected with a disease more fatal than any plague? Or when both consuls at the head of the army were beset by the

Samnites in the Caudine Forks, and forced to strike a shameful treaty, six hundred Roman knights being kept as hostages; while the troops, having laid down their arms, and being stripped of everything, were made to pass under the yoke with one garment each? Or when, in the midst of a serious pestilence, lightning struck the Roman camp and killed many? Or when Rome was driven, by the violence of another intolerable plague, to send to Epidaurus for Æsculapius as a god of medicine; since the frequent adulteries of Jupiter in his youth had not perhaps left this king of all who so long reigned in the Capitol, any leisure for the study of medicine? Or when, at one time, the Lucanians, Brutians, Samnites, Tuscans, and Senonian Gauls conspired against Rome, and first slew her ambassadors, then overthrew an army under the prætor, putting to the sword thirteen thousand men, besides the commander and seven tribunes? Or when the people, after the serious and long-continued disturbances at Rome, at last plundered the city and withdrew to Janiculus; a danger so grave, that Hortensius was created dictator—an office which they had recourse to only in extreme emergencies; and he, having brought back the people, died while yet he retained his office—an event without precedent in the case of any dictator, and which was a shame to those gods who had now Æsculapius among them?

At that time, indeed, so many wars were everywhere engaged in, that through scarcity of soldiers they enrolled for military service the *proletarii*, who received this name, because, being too poor to equip for military service, they had leisure to beget offspring.[3] Pyrrhus, king of Greece, and at that time of widespread renown, was invited by the Tarentines to enlist himself against Rome. It was to him that Apollo, when consulted regarding the issue of his enterprise, uttered with some pleasantry so ambiguous an oracle, that whichever alternative happened, the god himself should be counted divine. For he so worded the oracle[4] that whether Pyrrhus was conquered by the Romans, or the Romans by Pyrrhus, the soothsaying god would securely await the issue. And then what frightful massacres of both armies ensued! Yet Pyrrhus remained conqueror, and would have been able now to proclaim Apollo a true diviner, as he understood the oracle, had not the Romans been the conquerors in the next engagement. And while such disastrous wars were being waged, a terrible disease broke out among the women. For the pregnant women died before delivery. And Æsculapius, I fancy, excused himself in this matter on the ground that he professed to be archphysician, not midwife. Cattle, too, similarly perished; so that it was believed that the whole race of animals was destined to become extinct. Then what shall I say of that memorable winter in which the weather was so incredibly severe, that in the Forum frightfully deep snow lay for forty days together, and the Tiber was frozen? Had such things happened in our time, what accusations we should have heard from our enemies! And that other great pestilence, which raged so long and carried off so many; what shall I say of it? Spite of all the drugs of Æsculapius, it only grew worse in its second year, till at last recourse was had to the Sibylline books—

a kind of oracle which, as Cicero says in his *De Divinatione,* owes significance to its interpreters, who make doubtful conjectures as they can or as they wish. In this instance, the cause of the plague was said to be that so many temples had been used as private residences. And thus Æsculapius for the present escaped the charge of either ignominious negligence or want of skill. But why were so many allowed to occupy sacred tenements without interference, unless because supplication had long been addressed in vain to such a crowd of gods, and so by degrees the sacred places were deserted of worshipers, and being thus vacant, could without offense be put at least to some human uses? And the temples, which were at that time laboriously recognized and restored that the plague might be stayed, fell afterward into disuse, and were again devoted to the same human uses. Had they not thus lapsed into obscurity, it could not have been pointed to as proof of Varro's great erudition, that in his work on sacred places he cites so many that were unknown. Meanwhile, the restoration of the temples procured no cure of the plague, but only a fine excuse for the gods.

---

1. Sallust *Hist.* 1.
2. Lectisternia, from *lectus,* a couch, and *sterno,* I spread.
3. Proletarius, from *proles,* offspring.
4. *The oracle ran: Dico te, Pyrrhe, vincere posse Romanos.*

18. THE DISASTERS SUFFERED BY THE ROMANS IN THE PUNIC WARS, WHICH WERE NOT MITIGATED BY THE PROTECTION OF THE GODS

In the Punic wars, again, when victory hung so long in the balance between the two kingdoms, when two powerful nations were straining every nerve and using all their resources against one another, how many smaller kingdoms were crushed, how many large and flourishing cities were demolished, how many states were overwhelmed and ruined, how many districts and lands far and near were desolated! How often were the victors on either side vanquished! What multitudes of men, both of those actually in arms and of others, were destroyed! What huge navies, too, were crippled in engagements, or were sunk by every kind of marine disaster! Were we to attempt to recount or mention these calamities, we should become writers of history. At that period Rome was mightily perturbed, and resorted to vain and ludicrous expedients. On the authority of the Sibylline books, the secular games were reappointed, which had been inaugurated a century before, but had faded into oblivion in happier times. The games consecrated to the infernal gods were also renewed by the pontiffs; for they, too, had sunk into disuse in the better times. And no wonder; for when they were renewed, the great abundance of dying men made all hell rejoice at its riches, and give itself up to sport: for certainly the ferocious wars, and disastrous quarrels, and bloody victories—now on one side, and now on the other—though most calamitous to men, afforded great sport and a rich banquet to the devils. But in the first Punic war there was no more disastrous event than the Roman defeat in which Regulus was taken. We made mention of him in the two former books as an incontestably great man, who had before conquered and subdued the Carthaginians, and who would have put an end to the first Punic war, had not an inordinate appetite for praise and glory prompted him to impose on the worn-out Carthaginians harder conditions than they could bear. If the unlooked-for captivity and unseemly bondage of this man, his fidelity to his oath, and his surpassingly cruel death, do not bring a blush to the face of the gods, it is true that they are brazen and bloodless.

Nor were there wanting at that time very heavy disasters within the city itself. For the Tiber was extraordinarily flooded, and destroyed almost all the lower parts of the city; some buildings being carried away by the violence of the torrent, while others were soaked to rottenness by the water that stood round them even after the flood was gone. This visitation was followed by a fire which was still more destructive, for it consumed some of the loftier buildings round the Forum, and spared not even its own proper temple, that of Vesta, in which virgins chosen for this honor, or rather for this punishment, had been employed in conferring, as it were, everlasting life on fire, by ceaselessly feeding it with fresh fuel. But at the time we speak of, the fire in the temple was not content with being kept alive: it raged. And when the virgins, scared by its vehemence, were unable to save those fatal images which had already brought destruction on three cities[1] in which they had been received, Metellus the priest, forgetful of his own safety, rushed in and rescued the sacred things, though he was half roasted in doing so. For either the fire did not recognize even him, or else the goddess of fire was there —a goddess who would not have fled from the fire supposing she had been there. But here you see how a man could be of greater service to Vesta than she could be to him. Now if these gods could not avert the fire from themselves, what help against flames or flood could they bring to the state of which they were the reputed guardians? Facts have shown that they were useless. These objections of ours would be idle if our adversaries maintained that their idols are consecrated rather as symbols of things eternal, than to secure the blessings of time; and that thus, though the symbols, like all material and visible things, might perish, no damage thereby resulted to the things for the sake of which they had been consecrated, while, as for the images themselves, they could be renewed again for the same purposes they had formerly served. But with lamentable blindness, they suppose that, through the intervention of perishable gods, the earthly well-being and temporal prosperity of the state can be preserved from perishing. And so, when they are reminded that even when the gods remained among them this well-being and prosperity were blighted, they blush to change the opinion they are unable to defend.

---

1. Troy, Lavinia, Alba.

19. OF THE CALAMITY OF THE SECOND PUNIC WAR, WHICH CONSUMED THE STRENGTH OF BOTH PARTIES

As to the second Punic war, it were tedious to recount the disasters it brought on both the nations engaged in so protracted and shifting a war, that (by the acknowledgment even of those writers who have made it their object not so much to narrate the wars as to eulogize the dominion of Rome) the people who remained victorious were less like conquerors than conquered. For, when Hannibal poured out of Spain over the Pyrenees, and overran Gaul, and burst through the Alps, and during his whole course gathered strength by plundering and subduing as he went, and inundated Italy like a torrent, how bloody were the wars, and how continuous the engagements, that were fought! How often were the Romans vanquished! How many towns went over to the enemy, and how many were taken and subdued! What fearful battles there were, and how often did the defeat of the Romans shed luster on the arms of Hannibal! And what shall I say of the wonderfully crushing defeat at Cannæ, where even Hannibal, cruel as he was, was yet sated with the blood of his bitterest enemies, and gave orders that they be spared? From this field of battle he sent to Carthage three bushels of gold rings, signifying that so much of the rank of Rome had that day fallen, that it was easier to give an idea of it by measure than by numbers and that the frightful slaughter of the common rank and file whose bodies lay undistinguished by the ring, and who were numerous in proportion to their meanness, was rather to be conjectured than accurately reported. In fact, such was the scarcity of soldiers after this, that the Romans impressed their criminals on the promise of impunity, and their slaves by the bribe of liberty, and out of these infamous classes did not so much recruit as create an army. But these slaves, or, to give them all their titles, these freedmen who were enlisted to do battle for the republic of Rome, lacked arms. And so they took arms from the temples, as if the Romans were saying to their gods: lay down those arms you have held so long in vain, if by chance our slaves may be able to use to purpose what you, our gods, have been impotent to use. At that time, too, the public treasury was too low to pay the soldiers, and private resources were used for public purposes; and so generously did individuals contribute of their property, that, saving the gold ring and bulla which each wore, the pitiful mark of his rank, no senator, and much less any of the other orders and tribes, reserved any gold for his own use. But if in our day they were reduced to this poverty, who would be able to endure their reproaches, barely endurable as they are now, when more money is spent on actors for the sake of a superfluous gratification, than was then disbursed to the legions?

20. OF THE DESTRUCTION OF THE SAGUNTINES, WHO RECEIVED NO HELP FROM THE ROMAN GODS, THOUGH PERISHING ON ACCOUNT OF THEIR FIDELITY TO ROME

But among all the disasters of the second Punic war, there occurred none more lamentable, or calculated to excite deeper complaint, than the fate of the Saguntines. This city of Spain, eminently friendly to Rome, was destroyed by its fidelity to the Roman people. For when Hannibal had broken treaty with the Romans, he sought occasion for provoking them to war, and accordingly made a fierce assault upon Saguntum. When this was reported at Rome, ambassadors were sent to Hannibal, urging him to raise the siege; and when this remonstrance was neglected, they proceeded to Carthage, lodged complaint against the breaking of the treaty, and returned to Rome without accomplishing their object. Meanwhile the siege went on; and in the eighth or ninth month, this opulent but ill-fated city, dear as it was to its own state and to Rome, was taken, and subjected to treatment which one cannot read, much less narrate, without horror. And yet, because it bears directly on the matter in hand, I will briefly touch upon it. First, then, famine wasted the Saguntines, so that even human corpses were eaten by some: so at least it is recorded. Subsequently, when thoroughly worn out, that they might at least escape the ignominy of falling into the hands of Hannibal, they publicly erected a huge funeral pile, and cast themselves into its flames, while at the same time they slew their children and themselves with the sword. Could these gods, these debauchees and gourmands, whose mouths water for fat sacrifices, and whose lips utter lying divinations—could they not do anything in a case like this? Could they not interfere for the preservation of a city closely allied to the Roman people, or prevent it perishing for its fidelity to that alliance of which they themselves had been the mediators? Saguntum, faithfully keeping the treaty it had entered into before these gods, and to which it had firmly bound itself by an oath, was besieged, taken, and destroyed by a perjured person. If afterward, when Hannibal was close to the walls of Rome, it was the gods who terrified him with lightning and tempest, and drove him to a distance, why, I ask, did they not thus interfere before? For I make bold to say, that this demonstration with the tempest would have been more honorably made in defense of the allies of Rome—who were in danger on account of their reluctance to break faith with the Romans, and had no resources of their own—than in defense of the Romans themselves, who were fighting in their own cause, and had abundant resources to oppose Hannibal. If, then, they had been the guardians of Roman prosperity and glory, they would have preserved that glory from the stain of this Saguntine disaster; and how silly it is to believe that Rome was preserved from destruction at the hands of Hannibal by the guardian care of those gods who were unable to rescue the city of Saguntum from perishing through its fidelity to the alliance of Rome. If the population of Saguntum had been Christian, and had suffered as it did for the Christian faith (though, of course, Christians would not have used fire and sword against their own persons), they would have suffered with that hope which springs from faith in Christ—the hope not of a brief temporal reward, but of unending and eternal bliss. What, then, will the advocates and apologists of these gods say in their defense, when charged with the blood of these Saguntines; for they are professedly worshiped and invoked for this very purpose of securing prosperity in this fleeting and transitory life? Can anything be said but what was alleged in the case of Regulus's death? For though there is a difference between the two cases, the one being an individual, the other a whole community, yet the cause of destruction was in both cases the keeping of their plighted troth. For it was this which made Regulus willing to return to his enemies, and this which made the Saguntines unwilling to revolt to their enemies. Does, then, the keeping of faith provoke the gods to anger? Or is it possible that not only individuals, but even entire communities, perish while the gods are propitious to them? Let our adversaries choose which alternative they will. If, on the one hand, those gods are enraged at the keeping of faith, let them enlist perjured persons as their worshipers. If, on the other hand, men and states can suffer great and terrible calamities, and at last perish while favored by the gods, then does their worship not produce happiness as its fruit. Let those, therefore, who suppose that they have fallen into distress because their religious worship has been abolished, lay aside their anger; for it were quite possible that did the gods not only remain with them, but regard them with favor, they might yet be left to mourn an unhappy lot, or might, even like Regulus and the Saguntines, be horribly tormented, and at last perish miserably.

21. OF THE INGRATITUDE OF ROME TO SCIPIO, ITS DELIVERER, AND OF ITS MANNERS DURING THE PERIOD WHICH SALLUST DESCRIBES AS THE BEST

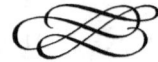

Omitting many things, that I may not exceed the limits of the work I have proposed to myself, I come to the epoch between the second and last Punic wars, during which, according to Sallust, the Romans lived with the greatest virtue and concord. Now, in this period of virtue and harmony, the great Scipio, the liberator of Rome and Italy, who had with surprising ability brought to a close the second Punic war—that horrible, destructive, dangerous contest—who had defeated Hannibal and subdued Carthage, and whose whole life is said to have been dedicated to the gods, and cherished in their temples—this Scipio, after such a triumph, was obliged to yield to the accusations of his enemies, and to leave his country, which his valor had saved and liberated, to spend the remainder of his days in the town of Liternum, so indifferent to a recall from exile, that he is said to have given orders that not even his remains should lie in his ungrateful country. It was at that time also that the proconsul Cn. Manlius, after subduing the Galatians, introduced into Rome the luxury of Asia, more destructive than all hostile armies. It was then that iron bedsteads and expensive carpets were first used; then, too, that female singers were admitted at banquets, and other licentious abominations were introduced. But at present I meant to speak, not of the evils men voluntarily practice, but of those they suffer in spite of themselves. So that the case of Scipio, who succumbed to his enemies, and died in exile from the country he had rescued, was mentioned by me as being pertinent to the present discussion; for this was the reward he received from those Roman gods whose temples he saved from Hannibal, and who are worshiped only for the sake of securing temporal happiness. But since Sallust, as we have seen, declares that the manners of Rome were never better than at that time, I therefore judged it right to mention the Asiatic luxury then introduced, that it might be seen that what he says is true, only when that period is compared with the others during which the morals were certainly worse, and the factions more violent. For at that time—I mean between the second and third Punic war—that notorious Lex Voconia was passed, which prohibited a man from making a woman, even an only daughter, his heir; than which law I am at a loss to conceive what could be more unjust. It is true that in the interval between these two Punic wars the misery of Rome was somewhat less. Abroad, indeed, their forces were consumed by wars, yet also consoled by victories; while at home there were not such disturbances as at other times. But when the last Punic war had terminated in the utter destruction of Rome's rival, which quickly succumbed to the other Scipio, who thus earned for himself the surname of Africanus, then the Roman republic was overwhelmed with such a host of ills, which sprang from the corrupt manners induced by prosperity and security, that the sudden overthrow of Carthage is seen to have injured Rome more seriously than her long-continued hostility. During the whole subsequent period down to the time of Cæsar Augustus, who seems to have entirely deprived the Romans of liberty—a liberty, indeed, which in their own judgment was no longer glorious, but full of broils and dangers, and which now was quite enervated and languishing—and who submitted all things again to the will of a monarch, and infused as it were a new life into the sickly old age of the republic, and inaugurated a fresh regime; during this whole period, I say, many military disasters were sustained on a variety of occasions, all of which I here pass by. There was specially the treaty of Numantia, blotted as it was with extreme disgrace; for the sacred chickens, they say, flew out of the coop, and thus augured disaster to Mancinus the consul; just as if, during all these years in which that little city of Numantia had withstood the besieging army of Rome, and had become a terror to the republic, the other generals had all marched against it under unfavorable auspices.

22. OF THE EDICT OF MITHRIDATES, COMMANDING THAT ALL ROMAN CITIZENS FOUND IN ASIA SHOULD BE SLAIN

These things, I say, I pass in silence; but I can by no means be silent regarding the order given by Mithridates, king of Asia, that on one day all Roman citizens residing anywhere in Asia (where great numbers of them were following their private business) should be put to death: and this order was executed. How miserable a spectacle was then presented, when each man was suddenly and treacherously murdered wherever he happened to be, in the field or on the road, in the town, in his own home, or in the street, in market or temple, in bed or at table! Think of the groans of the dying, the tears of the spectators, and even of the executioners themselves. For how cruel a necessity was it that compelled the hosts of these victims, not only to see these abominable butcheries in their own houses, but even to perpetrate them: to change their countenance suddenly from the bland kindliness of friendship, and in the midst of peace set about the business of war; and, shall I say, give and receive wounds, the slain being pierced in body, the slayer in spirit! Had all these murdered persons, then, despised auguries? Had they neither public nor household gods to consult when they left their homes and set out on that fatal journey? If they had not, our adversaries have no reason to complain of these Christian times in this particular, since long ago the Romans despised auguries as idle. If, on the other hand, they did consult omens, let them tell us what good they got thereby, even when such things were not prohibited, but authorized, by human, if not by divine law.

23. OF THE INTERNAL DISASTERS WHICH VEXED THE ROMAN REPUBLIC, AND FOLLOWED A PORTENTOUS MADNESS WHICH SEIZED ALL THE DOMESTIC ANIMALS

But let us now mention, as succinctly as possible, those disasters which were still more vexing, because nearer home; I mean those discords which are erroneously called civil, since they destroy civil interests. The seditions had now become urban wars, in which blood was freely shed, and in which parties raged against one another, not with wrangling and verbal contention, but with physical force and arms. What a sea of Roman blood was shed, what desolations and devastations were occasioned in Italy by wars social, wars servile, wars civil! Before the Latins began the social war against Rome, all the animals used in the service of man—dogs, horses, asses, oxen, and all the rest that are subject to man—suddenly grew wild, and forgot their domesticated tameness, forsook their stalls and wandered at large, and could not be closely approached either by strangers or their own masters without danger. If this was a portent, how serious a calamity must have been portended by a plague which, whether portent or no, was in itself a serious calamity! Had it happened in our day, the heathen would have been more rabid against us than their animals were against them.

24. OF THE CIVIL DISSENSION OCCASIONED BY THE SEDITION OF THE GRACCHI

The civil wars originated in the seditions which the Gracchi excited regarding the agrarian laws; for they were minded to divide among the people the lands which were wrongfully possessed by the nobility. But to reform an abuse of so long standing was an enterprise full of peril, or rather, as the event proved, of destruction. For what disasters accompanied the death of the elder Gracchus! What slaughter ensued when, shortly after, the younger brother met the same fate! For noble and ignoble were indiscriminately massacred; and this not by legal authority and procedure, but by mobs and armed rioters. After the death of the younger Gracchus, the consul Lucius Opimius, who had given battle to him within the city, and had defeated and put to the sword both himself and his confederates, and had massacred many of the citizens, instituted a judicial examination of others, and is reported to have put to death as many as three thousand men. From this it may be gathered how many fell in the riotous encounters, when the result even of a judicial investigation was so bloody. The assassin of Gracchus himself sold his head to the consul for its weight in gold, such being the previous agreement. In this massacre, too, Marcus Fulvius, a man of consular rank, with all his children, was put to death.

25. OF THE TEMPLE OF CONCORD, WHICH WAS ERECTED BY A DECREE OF THE SENATE ON THE SCENE OF THESE SEDITIONS AND MASSACRES

A pretty decree of the senate it was, truly, by which the temple of Concord was built on the spot where that disastrous rising had taken place, and where so many citizens of every rank had fallen. I suppose it was that the monument of the Gracchi's punishment might strike the eye and affect the memory of the pleaders. But what was this but to deride the gods, by building a temple to that goddess who, had she been in the city, would not have suffered herself to be torn by such dissensions? Or was it that Concord was chargeable with that bloodshed because she had deserted the minds of the citizens, and was therefore incarcerated in that temple? For if they had any regard to consistency, why did they not rather erect on that site a temple of Discord? Or is there a reason for Concord being a goddess while Discord is none? Does the distinction of Labeo hold here, who would have made the one a good, the other an evil deity?

—a distinction which seems to have been suggested to him by the mere fact of his observing at Rome a temple to Fever as well as one to Health. But, on the same ground, Discord as well as Concord ought to be deified. A hazardous venture the Romans made in provoking so wicked a goddess, and in forgetting that the destruction of Troy had been occasioned by her taking offense. For, being indignant that she was not invited with the other gods [to the nuptials of Peleus and Thetis], she created dissension among the three goddesses by sending in the golden apple, which occasioned strife in heaven, victory to Venus, the rape of Helen, and the destruction of Troy. Wherefore, if she was perhaps offended that the Romans had not thought her worthy of a temple among the other gods in their city, and therefore disturbed the state with such tumults, to how much fiercer passion would she be roused when she saw the temple of her adversary erected on the scene of that massacre, or, in other words, on the scene of her own handiwork! Those wise and learned men are enraged at our laughing at these follies; and yet, being worshipers of good and bad divinities alike, they cannot escape this dilemma about Concord and Discord: either they have neglected the worship of these goddesses, and preferred Fever and War, to whom there are shrines erected of great antiquity, or they have worshiped them, and after all Concord has abandoned them, and Discord has tempestuously hurled them into civil wars.

26. OF THE VARIOUS KINDS OF WARS WHICH FOLLOWED THE BUILDING OF THE TEMPLE OF CONCORD

But they supposed that, in erecting the temple of Concord within the view of the orators, as a memorial of the punishment and death of the Gracchi, they were raising an effectual obstacle to sedition. How much effect it had, is indicated by the still more deplorable wars that followed. For after this the orators endeavored not to avoid the example of the Gracchi, but to surpass their projects; as did Lucius Saturninus, a tribune of the people, and Caius Servilius the prætor, and some time after Marcus Drusus, all of whom stirred seditions which first of all occasioned bloodshed, and then the social wars by which Italy was grievously injured, and reduced to a piteously desolate and wasted condition. Then followed the servile war and the civil wars; and in them what battles were fought, and what blood was shed, so that almost all the peoples of Italy, which formed the main strength of the Roman Empire, were conquered as if they were barbarians! Then even historians themselves find it difficult to explain how the servile war was begun by a very few, certainly less than seventy gladiators, what numbers of fierce and cruel men attached themselves to these, how many of the Roman generals this band defeated, and how it laid waste many districts and cities. And that was not the only servile war: the province of Macedonia, and subsequently Sicily and the seacoast, were also depopulated by bands of slaves. And who can adequately describe either the horrible atrocities which the pirates first committed, or the wars they afterward maintained against Rome?

27. OF THE CIVIL WAR BETWEEN MARIUS AND SYLLA

But when Marius, stained with the blood of his fellow citizens, whom the rage of party had sacrificed, was in his turn vanquished and driven from the city, it had scarcely time to breathe freely, when, to use the words of Cicero, "Cinna and Marius together returned and took possession of it. Then, indeed, the foremost men in the state were put to death, its lights quenched. Sylla afterward avenged this cruel victory; but we need not say with what loss of life, and with what ruin to the republic."[1] For of this vengeance, which was more destructive than if the crimes which it punished had been committed with impunity, Lucan says: "The cure was excessive, and too closely resembled the disease. The guilty perished, but when none but the guilty survived: and then private hatred and anger, unbridled by law, were allowed free indulgence."[2] In that war between Marius and

Sylla, besides those who fell in the field of battle, the city, too, was filled with corpses in its streets, squares, markets, theatres, and temples; so that it is not easy to reckon whether the victors slew more before or after victory, that they might be, or because they were, victors. As soon as Marius triumphed, and returned from exile, besides the butcheries everywhere perpetrated, the head of the consul Octavius was exposed on the rostrum; Cæsar and Fimbria were assassinated in their own houses; the two Crassi, father and son, were murdered in one another's sight; Bebius and Numitorius were disemboweled by being dragged with hooks; Catulus escaped the hands of his enemies by drinking poison; Merula, the flamen of Jupiter, cut his veins and made a libation of his own blood to his god. Moreover, everyone whose salutation Marius did not answer by giving his hand, was at once cut down before his face.

---

1. Cicero *In Cat.* 3 sub. fin.
2. Lucan *Pharsalia* 2.142–146.

28. OF THE VICTORY OF SYLLA, THE AVENGER OF THE CRUELTIES OF MARIUS

Then followed the victory of Sylla, the so-called avenger of the cruelties of Marius. But not only was his victory purchased with great bloodshed; but when hostilities were finished, hostility survived, and the subsequent peace was bloody as the war. To the former and still recent massacres of the elder Marius, the younger Marius and Carbo, who belonged to the same party, added greater atrocities. For when Sylla approached, and they despaired not only of victory, but of life itself, they made a promiscuous massacre of friends and foes. And, not satisfied with staining every corner of Rome with blood, they besieged the senate, and led forth the senators to death from the curia as from a prison. Mucius Scævola the pontiff was slain at the altar of Vesta, which he had clung to because no spot in Rome was more sacred than her temple; and his blood well-nigh extinguished the fire which was kept alive by the constant care of the virgins.

Then Sylla entered the city victorious, after having slaughtered in the Villa Publica, not by combat, but by an order, seven thousand men who had surrendered, and were therefore unarmed; so fierce was the rage of peace itself, even after the rage of war was extinct. Moreover, throughout the whole city every partisan of Sylla slew whom he pleased, so that the number of deaths went beyond computation, till it was suggested to Sylla that he should allow some to survive, that the victors might not be destitute of subjects. Then this furious and promiscuous licence to murder was checked, and much relief was expressed at the publication of the proscription list, containing though it did the death warrant of two thousand men of the highest ranks, the senatorial and equestrian. The large number was indeed saddening, but it was consolatory that a limit was fixed; nor was the grief at the numbers slain so great as the joy that the rest were secure. But this very security, hard-hearted as it was, could not but bemoan the exquisite torture applied to some of those who had been doomed to die. For one was torn to pieces by the unarmed hands of the executioners; men treating a living man more savagely than wild beasts are used to tear an abandoned corpse. Another had his eyes dug out, and his limbs cut away bit by bit, and was forced to live a long while, or rather to die a long while, in such torture. Some celebrated cities were put up to auction, like farms; and one was collectively condemned to slaughter, just as an individual criminal would be condemned to death. These things were done in peace when the war was over, not that victory might be more speedily obtained, but that, after being obtained, it might not be thought lightly of. Peace vied with war in cruelty, and surpassed it: for while war overthrew armed hosts, peace slew the defenseless. War gave liberty to him who was attacked, to strike if he could; peace granted to the survivors not life, but an unresisting death.

29. A COMPARISON OF THE DISASTERS WHICH ROME EXPERIENCED DURING THE GOTHIC AND GALLIC INVASIONS, WITH THOSE OCCASIONED BY THE AUTHORS OF THE CIVIL WARS

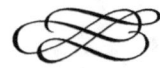

What fury of foreign nations, what barbarian ferocity, can compare with this victory of citizens over citizens? Which was more disastrous, more hideous, more bitter to Rome: the recent Gothic and the old Gallic invasion, or the cruelty displayed by Marius and Sylla and their partisans against men who were members of the same body as themselves? The Gauls, indeed, massacred all the senators they found in any part of the city except the Capitol, which alone was defended; but they at least sold life to those who were in the Capitol, though they might have starved them out if they could not have stormed it. The Goths, again, spared so many senators, that it is the more surprising that they killed any. But Sylla, while Marius was still living, established himself as conqueror in the Capitol, which the Gauls had not violated, and thence issued his death warrants; and when Marius had escaped by flight, though destined to return more fierce and bloodthirsty than ever, Sylla issued from the Capitol even decrees of the senate for the slaughter and confiscation of the property of many citizens. Then, when Sylla left, what did the Marian faction hold sacred or spare, when they gave no quarter even to Mucius, a citizen, a senator, a pontiff, and though clasping in piteous embrace the very altar in which, they say, reside the destinies of Rome? And that final proscription list of Sylla's, not to mention countless other massacres, dispatched more senators than the Goths could even plunder.

30. OF THE CONNECTION OF THE WARS WHICH WITH GREAT SEVERITY AND FREQUENCY FOLLOWED ONE ANOTHER BEFORE THE ADVENT OF CHRIST

With what effrontery, then, with what assurance, with what impudence, with what folly, or rather insanity, do they refuse to impute these disasters to their own gods, and impute the present to our Christ! These bloody civil wars, more distressing, by the avowal of their own historians, than any foreign wars, and which were pronounced to be not merely calamitous, but absolutely ruinous to the republic, began long before the coming of Christ, and gave birth to one another; so that a concatenation of unjustifiable causes led from the wars of Marius and Sylla to those of Sertorius and Catiline, of whom the one was proscribed, the other brought up by Sylla; from this to the war of Lepidus and Catulus, of whom the one wished to rescind, the other to defend the acts of Sylla; from this to the war of Pompey and Cæsar, of whom Pompey had been a partisan of Sylla, whose power he equaled or even surpassed, while Cæsar condemned Pompey's power because it was not his own, and yet exceeded it when Pompey was defeated and slain. From him the chain of civil wars extended to the second Cæsar, afterward called Augustus, and in whose reign Christ was born. For even Augustus himself waged many civil wars; and in these wars many of the foremost men perished, among them that skillful manipulator of the republic, Cicero. Caius [Julius] Cæsar, when he had conquered Pompey, though he used his victory with clemency, and granted to men of the opposite faction both life and honors, was suspected of aiming at royalty, and was assassinated in the curia by a party of noble senators, who had conspired to defend the liberty of the republic. His power was then coveted by Antony, a man of very different character, polluted and debased by every kind of vice, who was strenuously resisted by Cicero on the same plea of defending the liberty of the republic. At this juncture that other Cæsar, the adopted son of Caius, and afterward, as I said, known by the name of Augustus, had made his debut as a young man of remarkable genius. This youthful Cæsar was favored by Cicero, in order that his influence might counteract that of Antony; for he hoped that Cæsar would overthrow and blast the power of Antony, and establish a free state—so blind and unaware of the future was he: for that very young man, whose advancement and influence he was fostering, allowed Cicero to be killed as the seal of an alliance with Antony, and subjected to his own rule the very liberty of the republic in defense of which he had made so many orations.

31. THAT IT IS EFFRONTERY TO IMPUTE THE PRESENT TROUBLES TO CHRIST AND THE PROHIBITION OF POLYTHEISTIC WORSHIP SINCE EVEN WHEN THE GODS WERE WORSHIPED SUCH CALAMITIES BEFELL THE PEOPLE

Let those who have no gratitude to Christ for His great benefits blame their own gods for these heavy disasters. For certainly when these occurred the altars of the gods were kept blazing, and there rose the mingled fragrance of "Sabæan incense and fresh garlands"; the priests were clothed with honor, the shrines were maintained in splendor; sacrifices, games, sacred ecstasies, were common in the temples; while the blood of the citizens was being so freely shed, not only in remote places, but among the very altars of the gods. Cicero did not choose to seek sanctuary in a temple, because Mucius had sought it there in vain. But they who most unpardonably calumniate this Christian era are the very men who either themselves fled for asylum to the places specially dedicated to Christ, or were led there by the barbarians that they might be safe. In short, not to recapitulate the many instances I have cited, and not to add to their number others which it were tedious to enumerate, this one thing I am persuaded of, and this every impartial judgment will readily acknowledge, that if the human race had received Christianity before the Punic wars, and if the same desolating calamities which these wars brought upon Europe and Africa had followed the introduction of Christianity, there is no one of those who now accuse us who would not have attributed them to our religion. How intolerable would their accusations have been, at least so far as the Romans are concerned, if the Christian religion had been received and diffused prior to the invasion of the Gauls, or to the ruinous floods and fires which desolated Rome, or to those most calamitous of all events, the civil wars! And those other disasters, which were of so strange a nature that they were reckoned prodigies, had they happened since the Christian era, to whom but to the Christians would they have imputed these as crimes? I do not speak of those things which were rather surprising than hurtful—oxen speaking, unborn infants articulating some words in their mothers' wombs, serpents flying, hens and women being changed into the other sex; and other similar prodigies which, whether true or false, are recorded not in their imaginative, but in their historical works, and which do not injure, but only astonish, men. But when it rained earth, when it rained chalk, when it rained stones—not hailstones, but real stones—this certainly was calculated to do serious damage. We have read in their books that the fires of Etna, pouring down from the top of the mountain to the neighboring shore, caused the sea to boil, so that rocks were burned up, and the pitch of ships began to run—a phenomenon incredibly surprising, but at the same time no less hurtful. By the same violent heat, they relate that on another occasion Sicily was filled with cinders, so that the houses of the city Catina were destroyed and buried under them—a calamity which moved the Romans to pity them, and remit their tribute for that year. One may also read that Africa, which had by that time become a province of Rome, was visited by a prodigious multitude of locusts, which, after consuming the fruit and foliage of the trees, were driven into the sea in one vast and measureless cloud; so that when they were drowned and cast upon the shore, the air was polluted, and so serious a pestilence produced that in the kingdom of Masinissa alone they say there perished eight hundred thousand persons, besides a much greater number in the neighboring districts. At Utica they assure us that, of thirty thousand soldiers then garrisoning it, there survived only ten. Yet which of these disasters, suppose they happened now, would not be attributed to the Christian religion by those who thus thoughtlessly accuse us, and whom we are compelled to answer? And yet to their own gods they attribute none of these things, though they worship them for the sake of escaping lesser calamities of the same kind, and do not reflect that they who formerly worshiped them were not preserved from these serious disasters.

BOOK FOUR

ARGUMENT[1]

In this book it is proved that the extent and long duration of the Roman Empire is to be ascribed, not to Jove or the gods of the heathen, to whom individually scarce even single things and the very basest functions were believed to be entrusted, but to the one true God, the author of felicity, by whose power and judgment earthly kingdoms are founded and maintained.

---

1. In Augustine's letter to Evodius (169), which was written toward the end of the year 415, he mentions that this fourth book and the following one were begun and finished during that same year.

1. OF THE THINGS WHICH HAVE BEEN DISCUSSED IN THE FIRST BOOK

Having begun to speak of the city of God, I have thought it necessary first of all to reply to its enemies, who, eagerly pursuing earthly joys and gaping after transitory things, throw the blame of all the sorrow they suffer in them—rather through the compassion of God in admonishing than His severity in punishing—on the Christian religion, which is the one salutary and true religion. And since there is among them also an unlearned rabble, they are stirred up as by the authority of the learned to hate us more bitterly, thinking in their inexperience that things which have happened unwontedly in their days were not wont to happen in other times gone by; and whereas this opinion of theirs is confirmed even by those who know that it is false, and yet dissemble their knowledge in order that they may seem to have just cause for murmuring against us, it was necessary, from books in which their authors recorded and published the history of bygone times that it might be known, to demonstrate that it is far otherwise than they think; and at the same time to teach that the false gods, whom they openly worshiped, or still worship in secret, are most unclean spirits, and most malignant and deceitful demons, even to such a pitch that they take delight in crimes which, whether real or only fictitious, are yet their own, which it has been their will to have celebrated in honor of them at their own festivals; so that human infirmity cannot be called back from the perpetration of damnable deeds, so long as authority is furnished for imitating them that seems even divine. These things we have proved, not from our own conjectures, but partly from recent memory, because we ourselves have seen such things celebrated, and to such deities, partly from the writings of those who have left these things on record to posterity, not as if in reproach but as in honor of their own gods. Thus Varro, a most learned man among them, and of the weightiest authority, when he made separate books concerning things human and things divine, distributing some among the human, others among the divine, according to the special dignity of each, placed the scenic plays not at all among things human, but among things divine; though, certainly, if only there were good and honest men in the state, the scenic plays ought not to be allowed even among things human. And this he did not on his own authority, but because, being born and educated at Rome, he found them among the divine things. Now as we briefly stated in the end of the first book what we intended afterward to discuss, and as we have disposed of a part of this in the next two books, we see what our readers will expect us now to take up.

2. OF THOSE THINGS WHICH ARE CONTAINED IN BOOKS SECOND AND THIRD

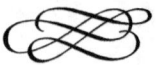

We had promised, then, that we would say something against those who attribute the calamities of the Roman republic to our religion, and that we would recount the evils, as many and great as we could remember or might deem sufficient, which that city, or the provinces belonging to its empire, had suffered before their sacrifices were prohibited, all of which would beyond doubt have been attributed to us, if our religion had either already shone on them, or had thus prohibited their sacrilegious rites. These things we have, as we think, fully disposed of in the second and third books, treating in the second of evils in morals, which alone or chiefly are to be accounted evils; and in the third, of those which only fools dread to undergo—namely, those of the body or of outward things—which for the most part the good also suffer. But those evils by which they themselves become evil, they take, I do not say patiently, but with pleasure. And how few evils have I related concerning that one city and its empire! Not even all down to the time of Cæsar Augustus. What if I had chosen to recount and enlarge on those evils, not which men have inflicted on each other, such as the devastations and destructions of war, but which happen in earthly things, from the elements of the world itself. Of such evils Apuleius speaks briefly in one passage of that book which he wrote, *De Mundo,* saying that all earthly things are subject to change, overthrow, and destruction.[1] For, to use his own words, by excessive earthquakes the ground has burst asunder, and cities with their inhabitants have been clean destroyed: by sudden rains whole regions have been washed away; those also which formerly had been continents have been insulated by strange and new-come waves, and others, by the subsiding of the sea, have been made passable by the foot of man: by winds and storms cities have been overthrown; fires have flashed forth from the clouds, by which regions in the East being burned up have perished; and on the western coasts the like destructions have been caused by the bursting forth of waters and floods. So, formerly, from the lofty craters of Etna, rivers of fire kindled by God have flowed like a torrent down the steeps. If I had wished to collect from history wherever I could, these and similar instances, where should I have finished what happened even in those times before the name of Christ had put down those of their idols, so vain and hurtful to true salvation? I promised that I should also point out which of their customs, and for what cause, the true God, in whose power all kingdoms are, had deigned to favor to the enlargement of their empire; and how those whom they think gods can have profited them nothing, but much rather hurt them by deceiving and beguiling them; so that it seems to me I must now speak of these things, and chiefly of the increase of the Roman Empire. For I have already said not a little, especially in the second book, about the many evils introduced into their manners by the hurtful deceits of the demons whom they worshiped as gods. But throughout all the three books already completed, where it appeared suitable, we have set forth how much succor God, through the name of Christ, to whom the barbarians beyond the custom of war paid so much honor, has bestowed on the good and bad, according as it is written, "Who maketh His sun to rise on the good and the evil, and giveth rain to the just and the unjust."[2]

---

1. *Cf. Bacon's Essay on the Vicissitudes of Things.*
2. Matt. 5:45.

3. WHETHER THE GREAT EXTENT OF THE EMPIRE, WHICH HAS BEEN ACQUIRED ONLY BY WARS, IS TO BE RECKONED AMONG THE GOOD THINGS EITHER OF THE WISE OR THE HAPPY

Now, therefore, let us see how it is that they dare to ascribe the very great extent and duration of the Roman Empire to those gods whom they contend that they worship honorably, even by the obsequies of vile games and the ministry of vile men: although I should like first to inquire for a little what reason, what prudence, there is in wishing to glory in the greatness and extent of the empire, when you cannot point out the happiness of men who are always rolling, with dark fear and cruel lust, in warlike slaughters and in blood, which, whether shed in civil or foreign war, is still human blood; so that their joy may be compared to glass in its fragile splendor, of which one is horribly afraid lest it should be suddenly broken in pieces. That this may be more easily discerned, let us not come to nought by being carried away with empty boasting, or blunt the edge of our attention by loud-sounding names of things, when we hear of peoples, kingdoms, provinces. But let us suppose a case of two men; for each individual man, like one letter in a language, is as it were the element of a city or kingdom, however far spreading in its occupation of the earth. Of these two men let us suppose that one is poor, or rather of middling circumstances; the other very rich. But the rich man is anxious with fears, pining with discontent, burning with covetousness, never secure, always uneasy, panting from the perpetual strife of his enemies, adding to his patrimony indeed by these miseries to an immense degree, and by these additions also heaping up most bitter cares. But that other man of moderate wealth is contented with a small and compact estate, most dear to his own family, enjoying the sweetest peace with his kindred neighbors and friends, in piety religious, benignant in mind, healthy in body, in life frugal, in manners chaste, in conscience secure. I know not whether anyone can be such a fool, that he dare hesitate which to prefer. As, therefore, in the case of these two men, so in two families, in two nations, in two kingdoms, this test of tranquility holds good; and if we apply it vigilantly and without prejudice, we shall quite easily see where the mere show of happiness dwells, and where real felicity. Wherefore if the true God is worshiped, and if He is served with genuine rites and true virtue, it is advantageous that good men should long reign both far and wide. Nor is this advantageous so much to themselves, as to those over whom they reign. For, so far as concerns themselves, their piety and probity, which are great gifts of God, suffice to give them true felicity, enabling them to live well the life that now is, and afterward to receive that which is eternal. In this world, therefore, the dominion of good men is profitable, not so much for themselves as for human affairs. But the dominion of bad men is hurtful chiefly to themselves who rule, for they destroy their own souls by greater license in wickedness; while those who are put under them in service are not hurt except by their own iniquity. For to the just all the evils imposed on them by unjust rulers are not the punishment of crime, but the test of virtue. Therefore the good man, although he is a slave, is free; but the bad man, even if he reigns, is a slave, and that not of one man, but, what is far more grievous, of as many masters as he has vices; of which vices when the divine Scripture treats, it says, "For of whom any man is overcome, to the same he is also the bond slave."[1]

---

1. 2 Pet. 2:19.

4. HOW LIKE KINGDOMS WITHOUT JUSTICE ARE TO ROBBERIES

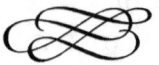

Justice being taken away, then, what are kingdoms but great robberies? For what are robberies themselves, but little kingdoms? The band itself is made up of men; it is ruled by the authority of a prince, it is knit together by the pact of the confederacy; the booty is divided by the law agreed on. If, by the admittance of abandoned men, this evil increases to such a degree that it holds places, fixes abodes, takes possession of cities, and peoples, it assumes the more plainly the name of a kingdom, because the reality is now manifestly conferred on it, not by the removal of covetousness, but by the addition of impunity. Indeed, that was an apt and true reply which was given to Alexander the Great by a pirate who had been seized. For when that king had asked the man what he meant by keeping hostile possession of the sea, he answered with bold pride, "What you mean by seizing the whole earth; but because I do it with a petty ship, I am called a robber, while you who do it with a great fleet are styled emperor."[1]

---

1. Nonius Marcellus borrows this anecdote from Cicero *De Rep. 3*.

5. OF THE RUNAWAY GLADIATORS WHOSE POWER BECAME LIKE THAT OF ROYAL DIGNITY

I shall not therefore stay to inquire what sort of men Romulus gathered together, seeing he deliberated much about them—how, being assumed out of that life they led into the fellowship of his city, they might cease to think of the punishment they deserved, the fear of which had driven them to greater villainies; so that henceforth they might be made more peaceable members of society. But this I say, that the Roman Empire, which by subduing many nations had already grown great and an object of universal dread, was itself greatly alarmed, and only with much difficulty avoided a disastrous overthrow, because a mere handful of gladiators in Campania, escaping from the games, had recruited a great army, appointed three generals, and most widely and cruelly devastated Italy. Let them say what god aided these men, so that from a small and contemptible band of robbers they attained to a kingdom, feared even by the Romans, who had such great forces and fortresses. Or will they deny that they were divinely aided because they did not last long?[1] As if, indeed, the life of any man whatever lasted long. In that case, too, the gods aid no one to reign, since all individuals quickly die; nor is sovereign power to be reckoned a benefit, because in a little time in every man, and thus in all of them one by one, it vanishes like a vapor. For what does it matter to those who worshiped the gods under Romulus, and are long since dead, that after their death the Roman Empire has grown so great, while they plead their causes before the powers beneath? Whether those causes are good or bad, it matters not to the question before us. And this is to be understood of all those who carry with them the heavy burden of their actions, having in the few days of their life swiftly and hurriedly passed over the stage of the imperial office, although the office itself has lasted through long spaces of time, being filled by a constant succession of dying men. If, however, even those benefits which last only for the shortest time are to be ascribed to the aid of the gods, these gladiators were not a little aided, who broke the bonds of their servile condition, fled, escaped, raised a great and most powerful army, obedient to the will and orders of their chiefs and much feared by the Roman majesty, and remaining unsubdued by several Roman generals, seized many places, and, having won very many victories, enjoyed whatever pleasures they wished, and did what their lust suggested, and, until at last they were conquered, which was done with the utmost difficulty, lived sublime and dominant. But let us come to greater matters.

---

1. It was extinguished by Crassus in its third year.

6. CONCERNING THE COVETOUSNESS OF NINUS, WHO WAS THE FIRST WHO MADE WAR ON HIS NEIGHBORS, THAT HE MIGHT RULE MORE WIDELY

Justinus, who wrote Greek or rather foreign history in Latin, and briefly, like Trogus Pompeius whom he followed, begins his work thus: "In the beginning of the affairs of peoples and nations the government was in the hands of kings, who were raised to the height of this majesty not by courting the people, but by the knowledge good men had of their moderation. The people were held bound by no laws; the decisions of the princes were instead of laws. It was the custom to guard rather than to extend the boundaries of the empire; and kingdoms were kept within the bounds of each ruler's native land. Ninus king of the Assyrians first of all, through new lust of empire, changed the old and, as it were, ancestral custom of nations. He first made war on his neighbors, and wholly subdued as far as to the frontiers of Libya the nations as yet untrained to resist." And a little after he says: "Ninus established by constant possession the greatness of the authority he had gained. Having mastered his nearest neighbors, he went on to others, strengthened by the accession of forces, and by making each fresh victory the instrument of that which followed, subdued the nations of the whole East." Now, with whatever fidelity to fact either he or Trogus may in general have written —for that they sometimes told lies is shown by other more trustworthy writers—yet it is agreed among other authors, that the kingdom of the Assyrians was extended far and wide by King Ninus. And it lasted so long, that the Roman Empire has not yet attained the same age; for, as those write who have treated of chronological history, this kingdom endured for 1,240 years from the first year in which Ninus began to reign, until it was transferred to the Medes. But to make war on your neighbors, and thence to proceed to others, and through mere lust of dominion to crush and subdue people who do you no harm, what else is this to be called than great robbery?

7. WHETHER EARTHLY KINGDOMS IN THEIR RISE AND FALL HAVE BEEN EITHER AIDED OR DESERTED BY THE HELP OF THE GODS

If this kingdom was so great and lasting without the aid of the gods, why is the ample territory and long duration of the Roman Empire to be ascribed to the Roman gods? For whatever is the cause in it, the same is in the other also. But if they contend that the prosperity of the other also is to be attributed to the aid of the gods, I ask of which? For the other nations whom Ninus overcame did not then worship other gods. Or if the Assyrians had gods of their own, who, so to speak, were more skillful workmen in the construction and preservation of the empire, whether are they dead, since they themselves have also lost the empire; or, having been defrauded of their pay, or promised a greater, have they chosen rather to go over to the Medes, and from them again to the Persians, because Cyrus invited them, and promised them something still more advantageous? This nation, indeed, since the time of the kingdom of Alexander the Macedonian, which was as brief in duration as it was great in extent, has preserved its own empire, and at this day occupies no small territories in the East. If this is so, then either the gods are unfaithful, who desert their own and go over to their enemies, which Camillus, who was but a man, did not do, when, being victor and subduer of a most hostile state, although he had felt that Rome, for whom he had done so much, was ungrateful, yet afterward, forgetting the injury and remembering his native land, he freed her again from the Gauls; or they are not so strong as gods ought to be, since they can be overcome by human skill or strength. Or if, when they carry on war among themselves, the gods are not overcome by men, but some gods who are peculiar to certain cities are perchance overcome by other gods, it follows that they have quarrels among themselves which they uphold, each for his own part. Therefore a city ought not to worship its own gods, but rather others who aid their own worshipers. Finally, whatever may have been the case as to this change of sides, or flight, or migration, or failure in battle on the part of the gods, the name of Christ had not yet been proclaimed in those parts of the earth when these kingdoms were lost and transferred through great destructions in war. For if, after more than twelve hundred years, when the kingdom was taken away from the Assyrians, the Christian religion had there already preached another eternal kingdom, and put a stop to the sacrilegious worship of false gods, what else would the foolish men of that nation have said, but that the kingdom which had been so long preserved, could be lost for no other cause than the desertion of their own religions and the reception of Christianity? In which foolish speech that might have been uttered, let those we speak of observe their own likeness, and blush, if there is any sense of shame in them, because they have uttered similar complaints; although the Roman Empire is afflicted rather than changed—a thing which has befallen it in other times also, before the name of Christ was heard, and it has been restored after such affliction—a thing which even in these times is not to be despaired of. For who knows the will of God concerning this matter?

8. WHICH OF THE GODS CAN THE ROMANS SUPPOSE PRESIDED OVER THE INCREASE AND PRESERVATION OF THEIR EMPIRE, WHEN THEY HAVE BELIEVED THAT EVEN THE CARE OF SINGLE THINGS COULD SCARCELY BE COMMITTED TO SINGLE GODS?

Next let us ask, if they please, out of so great a crowd of gods which the Romans worship, whom in especial, or what gods they believe to have extended and preserved that empire. Now, surely of this work, which is so excellent and so very full of the highest dignity, they dare not ascribe any part to the goddess Cloacina;[1] or to Volupia, who has her appellation from voluptuousness; or to Libentina, who has her name from lust; or to Vaticanus, who presides over the screaming of infants; or to Cunina, who rules over their cradles. But how is it possible to recount in one part of this book all the names of gods or goddesses, which they could scarcely comprise in great volumes, distributing among these divinities their peculiar offices about single things? They have not even thought that the charge of their lands should be committed to any one god: but they have entrusted their farms to Rusina; the ridges of the mountains to Jugatinus; over the downs they have set the goddess Collatina; over the valleys, Vallonia. Nor could they even find one Segetia so competent, that they could commend to her care all their corn crops at once; but so long as their seed corn was still under the ground, they would have the goddess Seia set over it; then, whenever it was above ground and formed straw, they set over it the goddess Segetia; and when the grain was collected and stored, they set over it the goddess Tutilina, that it might be kept safe. Who would not have thought that goddess Segetia sufficient to take care of the standing corn until it had passed from the first green blades to the dry ears? Yet she was not enough for men, who loved a multitude of gods, that the miserable soul, despising the chaste embrace of the one true God, should be prostituted to a crowd of demons. Therefore they set Proserpina over the germinating seeds; over the joints and knots of the stems, the god Nodotus; over the sheaths enfolding the ears, the goddess Voluntina; when the sheaths opened that the spike might shoot forth, it was ascribed to the goddess Patelana; when the stems stood all equal with new ears, because the ancients described this equalizing by the term *hostire*, it was ascribed to the goddess Hostilina; when the grain was in flower, it was dedicated to the goddess Flora; when full of milk, to the god Lacturnus; when maturing, to the goddess Matuta; when the crop was runcated—that is, removed from the soil—to the goddess Runcina.

Nor do I yet recount them all, for I am sick of all this, though it gives them no shame. Only, I have said these very few things, in order that it may be understood they dare by no means say that the Roman Empire has been established, increased, and preserved by their deities, who had all their own functions assigned to them in such a way, that no general oversight was entrusted to any one of them. When, therefore, could Segetia take care of the empire, who was not allowed to take care of the corn and the trees? When could Cunina take thought about war, whose oversight was not allowed to go beyond the cradles of the babies? When could Nodotus give help in battle, who had nothing to do even with the sheath of the ear, but only with the knots of the joints? Everyone sets a porter at the door of his house, and because he is a man, he is quite sufficient; but these people have set three gods, Forculus to the doors, Cardea to the hinge, Limentinus to the threshold.[2] Thus Forculus could not at the same time take care also of the hinge and the threshold.

---

1. Cloacina, supposed by Lactantius (*De Falsa Relig.* 1.20), Cyprian (*De Idol. Vanit.*), and Augustine (see below, 4.23) to be the goddess of the *cloaca*, or sewage of Rome. Others, however, suppose it to be equivalent to Cluacina, a title given to Venus, because the Romans after the end of the Sabine war purified themselves (*cluere*) in the vicinity of her statue.
2. "Forculum foribus, Cardeam cardini, Limentinum limini."

9. WHETHER THE GREAT EXTENT AND LONG DURATION OF THE ROMAN EMPIRE SHOULD BE ASCRIBED TO JOVE, WHOM HIS WORSHIPERS BELIEVE TO BE THE CHIEF GOD

Therefore omitting, or passing by for a little, that crowd of petty gods, we ought to inquire into the part performed by the great gods, whereby Rome has been made so great as to reign so long over so many nations. Doubtless, therefore, this is the work of Jove. For they will have it that he is the king of all the gods and goddesses, as is shown by his scepter and by the Capitol on the lofty hill. Concerning that god they publish a saying which, although that of a poet, is most apt, "All things are full of Jove."[1] Varro believes that this god is worshiped, although called by another name, even by those who worship one God alone without any image. But if this is so, why has he been so badly used at Rome (and indeed by other nations too), that an image of him should be made?—a thing which was so displeasing to Varro himself, that although he was overborne by the perverse custom of so great a city, he had not the least hesitation in both saying and writing, that those who have appointed images for the people have both taken away fear and added error.

---

1. Virgil *Eclogue* 3.60.

10. WHAT OPINIONS THOSE HAVE FOLLOWED WHO HAVE SET DIVERSE GODS OVER DIVERSE PARTS OF THE WORLD

Why, also, is Juno united to him as his wife, who is called at once "sister and yokefellow"?[1] Because, say they, we have Jove in the ether, Juno in the air; and these two elements are united, the one being superior, the other inferior. It is not he, then, of whom it is said, "All things are full of Jove," if Juno also fills some part. Does each fill either, and are both of this couple in both of these elements, and in each of them at the same time? Why, then, is the ether given to Jove, the air to Juno? Besides, these two should have been enough. Why is it that the sea is assigned to Neptune, the earth to Pluto? And that these also might not be left without mates, Salacia is joined to Neptune, Proserpine to Pluto. For they say that, as Juno possesses the lower part of the heavens—that is, the air—so Salacia possesses the lower part of the sea, and Proserpine the lower part of the earth. They seek how they may patch up these fables, but they find no way. For if these things were so, their ancient sages would have maintained that there are three chief elements of the world, not four, in order that each of the elements might have a pair of gods. Now, they have positively affirmed that the ether is one thing, the air another. But water, whether higher or lower, is surely water. Suppose it ever so unlike, can it ever be so much so as no longer to be water? And the lower earth, by whatever divinity it may be distinguished, what else can it be than earth? Lo, then, since the whole physical world is complete in these four or three elements, where shall Minerva be? What should she possess, what should she fill? For she is placed in the Capitol along with these two, although she is not the offspring of their marriage. Or if they say that she possesses the higher part of the ether—and on that account the poets have feigned that she sprang from the head of Jove—why then is she not rather reckoned queen of the gods, because she is superior to Jove? Is it because it would be improper to set the daughter before the father? Why, then, is not that rule of justice observed concerning Jove himself toward Saturn? Is it because he was conquered? Have they fought then? By no means, say they; that is an old wife's fable. Lo, we are not to believe fables, and must hold more worthy opinions concerning the gods! Why, then, do they not assign to the father of Jove a seat, if not of higher, at least of equal honor? Because Saturn, say they, is length of time.[2] Therefore they who worship Saturn worship Time; and it is insinuated that Jupiter, the king of the gods, was born of Time. For is anything unworthy said when

Jupiter and Juno are said to have been sprung from Time, if he is the heaven and she is the earth, since both heaven and earth have been made, and are therefore not eternal? For their learned and wise men have this also in their books. Nor is that saying taken by Virgil out of poetic figments, but out of the books of philosophers,

> *Then Ether, the Father Almighty, in copious showers descended*
> *Into his spouse's glad bosom, making it fertile*[3]

—that is, into the bosom of Tellus, or the earth. Although here, also, they will have it that there are some differences, and think that in the earth herself Terra is one thing, Tellus another, and Tellumo another. And they have all these as gods, called by their own names, distinguished by their own offices, and venerated with their own altars and rites. This same earth also they call the mother of the gods, so that even the fictions of the poets are more tolerable, if, according, not to their poetical but sacred books, Juno is not only the sister and wife, but also the mother of Jove. The same earth they worship as Ceres, and also as Vesta; while yet they more frequently affirm that Vesta is nothing else than fire, pertaining to the hearths, without which the city cannot exist; and therefore virgins are wont to serve her, because as nothing is born of a virgin, so nothing is born of fire; but all this nonsense ought to be completely abolished and extinguished by Him who is born of a virgin. For who can bear that, while they ascribe to the fire so much honor, and, as it were, chastity, they do not blush sometimes even to call Vesta Venus, so that honored virginity may vanish in her handmaidens? For if Vesta is Venus, how can virgins rightly serve her by abstaining from venery? Are there two Venuses, the one a virgin, the other not a maid? Or rather, are there three, one the goddess of virgins, who is also called Vesta, another the goddess of wives, and another of harlots? To her also the Phenicians offered a gift by prostituting their daughters before they united them to husbands.[4] Which of these is the wife of Vulcan? Certainly not the virgin, since she has a husband. Far be it from us to say it is the harlot, lest we should seem to wrong the son of Juno and fellow worker of Minerva. Therefore it is to be understood that she belongs to the married people; but we would not wish them to imitate her in what she did with Mars. "Again," say they, "you return to fables." What sort of justice is that, to be angry with us because we say such things of their gods, and not to be angry with themselves, who in their theatres most willingly behold the crimes of their gods? And —a thing incredible, if it were not thoroughly well proved—these very theatric representations of the crimes of their gods have been instituted in honor of these same gods.

---

1. Virgil *Æneid* 1.47.
2. Cicero *De Nat. Deor.* 2.25.
3. Virgil *Georg.* 2.325–326.
4. Eusebius *De Præp. Evang.* 1.10.

11. CONCERNING THE MANY GODS WHOM THE PAGAN DOCTORS DEFEND AS BEING ONE AND THE SAME JOVE

Let them therefore assert as many things as ever they please in physical reasonings and disputations. One while, let Jupiter be the soul of this corporeal world, who fills and moves that whole mass, constructed and compacted out of four, or as many elements as they please; another while, let him yield to his sister and brothers their parts of it: now let him be the ether, that from above he may embrace Juno, the air spread out beneath; again, let him be the whole heaven along with the air, and impregnate with fertilizing showers and seeds the earth, as his wife, and, at the same time, his mother (for this is not vile in divine beings); and yet again (that it may not be necessary to run through them all), let him, the one god, of whom many think it has been said by a most noble poet,

> *For God pervadeth all things,*
> *All lands, and the tracts of the sea, and the*
> *depth of the heavens*[1]

—let it be him who in the ether is Jupiter; in the air, Juno; in the sea, Neptune; in the lower parts of the sea, Salacia; in the earth, Pluto; in the lower part of the earth, Proserpine; on the domestic hearths, Vesta; in the furnace of the workmen, Vulcan; among the stars, Sol and Luna, and the Stars; in divination, Apollo; in merchandise, Mercury; in Janus, the initiator; in Terminus, the terminator; Saturn, in time; Mars and Bellona, in war; Liber, in vineyards; Ceres, in cornfields; Diana, in forests; Minerva, in learning. Finally, let it be him who is in that crowd, as it were, of plebeian gods: let him preside under the name of Liber over the seed of men, and under that of Libera over that of women: let him be Diespiter, who brings forth the birth to the light of day: let him be the goddess Mena, whom they set over the menstruation of women: let him be Lucina, who is invoked by women in childbirth: let him bring help to those who are being born, by taking them up from the bosom of the earth, and let him be called Ops: let him open the mouth in the crying babe, and be called the god Vaticanus: let him lift it from the earth, and be called the goddess Levana; let him watch over cradles, and be called the goddess Cunina: let it be no other than he who is in those goddesses, who sing the fates of the newborn, and are called Carmentes: let him preside over fortuitous events, and be called Fortuna: in the goddess Rumina, let him milk out the breast to the little one, because the ancients termed the breast *ruma:* in the goddess Potina, let him administer drink: in the goddess Educa, let him supply food: from the terror of infants, let him be styled Paventia: from the hope which comes, Venilia: from voluptuousness, Volupia: from action, Agenor: from the stimulants by which man is spurred on to much action, let him be named the goddess Stimula: let him be the goddess Strenia, for making strenuous; Numeria, who teaches to number; Camœna, who teaches to sing: let him be both the god Consus for granting counsel, and the goddess Sentia for inspiring sentences: let him be the goddess Juventas, who, after the robe of boyhood is laid aside, takes charge of the beginning of the youthful age: let him be Fortuna Barbata, who endues adults with a beard, whom they have not chosen to honor; so that this divinity, whatever it may be, should at least be a male god, named either Barbatus, from *barba,* like Nodotus, from *nodus;* or, certainly, not Fortuna, but because he has beards, Fortunius: let him, in the god Jugatinus, yoke couples in marriage; and when the girdle of the virgin wife is loosed, let him be invoked as the goddess Virginiensis: let him be Mutunus or Tuternus, who, among the Greeks, is called Priapus. If they are not ashamed of it, let all these which I have named, and whatever others I have not named (for I have not thought fit to name all), let all these gods and goddesses be that one Jupiter, whether, as some will have it, all these are parts of him, or are his powers, as those think who are pleased to consider him the soul of the world, which is the opinion of most of their doctors, and these the greatest. If these things are so (how evil they may be I do not yet meanwhile inquire), what would they lose, if they, by a more prudent abridgment, should worship one god? For what part of him could be contemned if he himself should be worshiped? But if they are afraid lest parts of him should be angry at being passed by or neglected, then it is not the case, as they will have it, that this whole is as the life of one living being, which contains all the gods together, as if they were its virtues, or members, or parts; but each part has its own life separate from the rest, if it is so that one can be angered, appeased, or stirred up more than another. But if it is said that all together—that is, the whole Jove himself—would be offended if his parts were not also worshiped singly and minutely, it is foolishly spoken. Surely none of them could be passed by if he who singly possesses them all should be worshiped. For, to omit other things which are innumerable, when they say that all the stars are parts of Jove, and are all alive, and have rational souls, and therefore without controversy are gods, can they not see how many they do not worship, to how many they do not build temples or set up altars, and to how very few, in fact, of the stars they have thought of setting them up and offering sacrifice? If, therefore, those are displeased who are not severally worshiped, do they not fear to live with only a few appeased, while all heaven is displeased? But if they worship all the stars because they are part of Jove whom they worship, by the same compendious method they could supplicate them all in him alone. For in this way no one would be displeased, since in him alone all would be supplicated. No one would be contemned, instead of there being just cause of displeasure given to the much greater number who are passed by in the worship offered to some; especially when Priapus, stretched out in vile nakedness, is preferred to those who shine from their supernal abode.

---

1. Virgil *Georg.* 4.221–222.

12. CONCERNING THE OPINION OF THOSE WHO HAVE THOUGHT THAT GOD IS THE SOUL OF THE WORLD, AND THE WORLD IS THE BODY OF GOD

Ought not men of intelligence, and indeed men of every kind, to be stirred up to examine the nature of this opinion? For there is no need of excellent capacity for this task, that putting away the desire of contention, they may observe that if God is the soul of the world, and the world is as a body to Him, who is the soul, He must be one living being consisting of soul and body, and that this same God is a kind of womb of nature containing all things in Himself, so that the lives and souls of all living things are taken, according to the manner of each one's birth, out of His soul which vivifies that whole mass, and therefore nothing at all remains which is not a part of God. And if this is so, who cannot see what impious and irreligious consequences follow, such as that whatever one may trample, he must trample a part of God, and in slaying any living creature, a part of God must be slaughtered? But I am unwilling to utter all that may occur to those who think of it, yet cannot be spoken without irreverence.

13. CONCERNING THOSE WHO ASSERT THAT ONLY RATIONAL ANIMALS ARE PARTS OF THE ONE GOD

But if they contend that only rational animals, such as men, are parts of God, I do not really see how, if the whole world is God, they can separate beasts from being parts of Him. But what need is there of striving about that? Concerning the rational animal himself—that is, man—what more unhappy belief can be entertained than that a part of God is whipped when a boy is whipped? And who, unless he is quite mad, could bear the thought that parts of God can become lascivious, iniquitous, impious, and altogether damnable? In brief, why is God angry at those who do not worship Him, since these offenders are parts of Himself? It remains, therefore, that they must say that all the gods have their own lives; that each one lives for himself, and none of them is a part of any one; but that all are to be worshiped—at least as many as can be known and worshiped; for they are so many it is impossible that all can be so. And of all these, I believe that

Jupiter, because he presides as king, is thought by them to have both established and extended the Roman Empire. For if he has not done it, what other god do they believe could have attempted so great a work, when they must all be occupied with their own offices and works, nor can one intrude on that of another? Could the kingdom of men then be propagated and increased by the king of the gods?

14. THE ENLARGEMENT OF KINGDOMS IS UNSUITABLY ASCRIBED TO JOVE; FOR IF, AS THEY WILL HAVE IT, VICTORIA IS A GODDESS, SHE ALONE WOULD SUFFICE FOR THIS BUSINESS

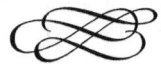

Here, first of all, I ask, why even the kingdom itself is not some god? For why should not it also be so, if Victory is a goddess? Or what need is there of Jove himself in this affair, if Victory favors and is propitious, and always goes to those whom she wishes to be victorious? With this goddess favorable and propitious, even if Jove was idle and did nothing, what nations could remain unsubdued, what kingdom would not yield? But perhaps it is displeasing to good men to fight with most wicked unrighteousness, and provoke with voluntary war neighbors who are peaceable and do no wrong, in order to enlarge a kingdom? If they feel thus, I entirely approve and praise them.

15. WHETHER IT IS SUITABLE FOR GOOD MEN TO WISH TO RULE MORE WIDELY

Let them ask, then, whether it is quite fitting for good men to rejoice in extended empire. For the iniquity of those with whom just wars are carried on favors the growth of a kingdom, which would certainly have been small if the peace and justice of neighbors had not by any wrong provoked the carrying on of war against them; and human affairs being thus more happy, all kingdoms would have been small, rejoicing in neighborly concord; and thus there would have been very many kingdoms of nations in the world, as there are very many houses of citizens in a city. Therefore, to carry on war and extend a kingdom over wholly subdued nations seems to bad men to be felicity, to good men necessity. But because it would be worse that the injurious should rule over those who are more righteous, therefore even that is not unsuitably called felicity. But beyond doubt it is greater felicity to have a good neighbor at peace, than to conquer a bad one by making war. Your wishes are bad, when you desire that one whom you hate or fear should be in such a condition that you can conquer him. If, therefore, by carrying on wars that were just, not impious or unrighteous, the Romans could have acquired so great an empire, ought they not to worship as a goddess even the injustice of foreigners? For we see that this has cooperated much in extending the empire, by making foreigners so unjust that they became people with whom just wars might be carried on, and the empire increased. And why may not injustice, at least that of foreign nations, also be a goddess, if Fear and Dread and Ague have deserved to be Roman gods? By these two, therefore—that is, by foreign injustice, and the goddess Victoria, for injustice stirs up causes of wars, and Victoria brings these same wars to a happy termination—the empire has increased, even although Jove has been idle. For what part could Jove have here, when those things which might be thought to be his benefits are held to be gods, called gods, worshiped as gods, and are themselves invoked for their own parts? He also might have some part here, if he himself might be called Empire, just as she is called Victory. Or if empire is the gift of Jove, why may not victory also be held to be his gift? And it certainly would have been held to be so, had he been recognized and worshiped, not as a stone in the Capitol, but as the true King of kings and Lord of lords.

16. WHAT WAS THE REASON WHY THE ROMANS, IN DETAILING SEPARATE GODS FOR ALL THINGS AND ALL MOVEMENTS OF THE MIND, CHOSE TO HAVE THE TEMPLE OF QUIET OUTSIDE THE GATES

But I wonder very much, that while they assigned to separate gods single things, and (well-nigh) all movements of the mind; that while they invoked the goddess Agenoria, who should excite to action; the goddess Stimula, who should stimulate to unusual action; the goddess Murcia, who should not move men beyond measure, but make them, as Pomponius says, *murcid*—that is, too slothful and inactive; the goddess Strenua, who should make them strenuous; and that while they offered to all these gods and goddesses solemn and public worship, they should yet have been unwilling to give public acknowledgment to her whom they name Quies because she makes men quiet, but built her temple outside the Colline gate. Whether was this a symptom of an unquiet mind, or rather was it thus intimated that he who should persevere in worshiping that crowd, not, to be sure, of gods, but of demons, could not dwell with quiet; to which the true Physician calls, saying, "Learn of Me, for I am meek and lowly in heart, and ye shall find rest unto your souls"?

17. WHETHER, IF THE HIGHEST POWER BELONGS TO JOVE, VICTORIA ALSO OUGHT TO BE WORSHIPED

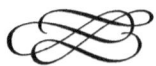

Or do they say, perhaps, that Jupiter sends the goddess Victoria, and that she, as it were acting in obedience to the king of the gods, comes to those to whom he may have dispatched her, and takes up her quarters on their side? This is truly said, not of Jove, whom they, according to their own imagination, feign to be king of the gods, but of Him who is the true eternal King, because he sends, not Victory, who is no person, but His angel, and causes whom He pleases to conquer; whose counsel may be hidden, but cannot be unjust. For if Victory is a goddess, why is not Triumph also a god, and joined to Victory either as husband, or brother, or son? Indeed, they have imagined such things concerning the gods, that if the poets had feigned the like, and they should have been discussed by us, they would have replied that they were laughable figments of the poets not to be attributed to true deities. And yet they themselves did not laugh when they were, not reading in the poets, but worshiping in the temples such doating follies. Therefore they should entreat Jove alone for all things, and supplicate him only. For if Victory is a goddess, and is under him as her king, wherever he might have sent her, she could not dare to resist and do her own will rather than his.

18. WITH WHAT REASON THEY WHO THINK FELICITY AND FORTUNE GODDESSES HAVE DISTINGUISHED THEM

What shall we say, besides, of the idea that Felicity also is a goddess? She has received a temple; she has merited an altar; suitable rites of worship are paid to her. She alone, then, should be worshiped. For where she is present, what good thing can be absent? But what does a man wish, that he thinks Fortune also a goddess and worships her? Is felicity one thing, fortune another? Fortune, indeed, may be bad as well as good; but felicity, if it could be bad, would not be felicity. Certainly we ought to think all the gods of either sex (if they also have sex) are only good. This says Plato; this say other philosophers; this say all estimable rulers of the republic and the nations. How is it, then, that the goddess Fortune is sometimes good, sometimes bad? Is it perhaps the case that when she is bad she is not a goddess, but is suddenly changed into a malignant demon? How many Fortunes are there then? Just as many as there are men who are fortunate, that is, of good fortune. But since there must also be very many others who at the very same time are men of bad fortune, could she, being one and the same Fortune, be at the same time both bad and good—the one to these, the other to those? She who is the goddess, is she always good? Then she herself is felicity. Why, then, are two names given her? Yet this is tolerable; for it is customary that one thing should be called by two names. But why different temples, different altars, different rituals? There is a reason, say they, because Felicity is she whom the good have by previous merit; but fortune, which is termed good without any trial of merit, befalls both good and bad men fortuitously, whence also she is named Fortune. How, therefore, is she good, who without any discernment comes—both to the good and to the bad? Why is she worshiped, who is thus blind, running at random on anyone whatever, so that for the most part she passes by her worshipers, and cleaves to those who despise her? Or if her worshipers profit somewhat, so that they are seen by her and loved, then she follows merit, and does not come fortuitously. What, then, becomes of that definition of fortune? What becomes of the opinion that she has received her very name from fortuitous events? For it profits one nothing to worship her if she is truly fortune. But if she distinguishes her worshipers, so that she may benefit them, she is not fortune. Or does Jupiter send her too, whither he pleases? Then let him alone be worshiped; because Fortune is not able to resist him when he commands her, and sends her where he pleases. Or, at least, let the bad worship her, who do not choose to have merit by which the goddess Felicity might be invited.

19. CONCERNING FORTUNA MULIEBRIS

To this supposed deity, whom they call Fortuna,[1] they ascribe so much, indeed, that they have a tradition that the image of her, which was dedicated by the Roman matrons, and called Fortuna Muliebris, has spoken, and has said, once and again, that the matrons pleased her by their homage; which, indeed, if it is true, ought not to excite our wonder. For it is not so difficult for malignant demons to deceive, and they ought the rather to advert to their wits and wiles, because it is that goddess who comes by haphazard who has spoken, and not she who comes to reward merit. For Fortuna was loquacious, and Felicitas mute; and for what other reason but that men might not care to live rightly, having made Fortuna their friend, who could make them fortunate without any good desert? And truly, if Fortuna speaks, she should at least speak, not with a womanly, but with a manly voice; lest they themselves who have dedicated the image should think so great a miracle has been worked by feminine loquacity.

---

1. The feminine Fortune.

20. CONCERNING VIRTUE AND FAITH, WHICH THE PAGANS HAVE HONORED WITH TEMPLES AND SACRED RITES, PASSING BY OTHER GOOD QUALITIES, WHICH OUGHT LIKEWISE TO HAVE BEEN WORSHIPED, IF DEITY WAS RIGHTLY ATTRIBUTED TO THESE

They have made Virtue also a goddess, which, indeed, if it could be a goddess, had been preferable to many. And now, because it is not a goddess, but a gift of God, let *it* be obtained by prayer from Him, by whom alone it can be given, and the whole crowd of false gods vanishes. But why is Faith believed to be a goddess, and why does she herself receive temple and altar? For whoever prudently acknowledges her makes his own self an abode for her. But how do they know what faith is, of which it is the prime and greatest function that the true God may be believed in? But why had not virtue sufficed? Does it not include faith also? Forasmuch as they have thought proper to distribute virtue into four divisions—prudence, justice, fortitude, and temperance—and as each of these divisions has its own virtues, faith is among the parts of justice, and has the chief place with as many of us as know what that saying means, "The just shall live by faith."[1] But if Faith is a goddess, I wonder why these keen lovers of a multitude of gods have wronged so many other goddesses, by passing them by, when they could have dedicated temples and altars to them likewise. Why has temperance not deserved to be a goddess, when some Roman princes have obtained no small glory on account of her? Why, in fine, is fortitude not a goddess, who aided Mucius when he thrust his right hand into the flames; who aided Curtius, when for the sake of his country he threw himself headlong into the yawning earth; who aided Decius the sire, and Decius the son, when they devoted themselves for the army?—though we might question whether these men had *true* fortitude, if this concerned our present discussion. Why have prudence and wisdom merited no place among the gods? Is it because they are all worshiped under the general name of Virtue itself? Then they could thus worship the true God also, of whom all the other gods are thought to be parts. But in that one name of virtue is comprehended both faith and chastity, which yet have obtained separate altars in temples of their own.

---

1. Hab. 2:4.

21. THAT ALTHOUGH NOT UNDERSTANDING THEM TO BE THE GIFTS OF GOD, THEY OUGHT AT LEAST TO HAVE BEEN CONTENT WITH VIRTUE AND FELICITY

These, not verity but vanity has made goddesses. For these are gifts of the true God, not themselves goddesses. However, where virtue and felicity are, what else is sought for? What can suffice the man whom virtue and felicity do not suffice? For surely virtue comprehends all things we need do, felicity all things we need wish for. If Jupiter, then, was worshiped in order that he might give these two things—because, if extent and duration of empire is something good, it pertains to this same felicity—why is it not understood that they are not goddesses, but the gifts of God? But if they are judged to be goddesses, then at least that other great crowd of gods should not be sought after. For, having considered all the offices which their fancy has distributed among the various gods and goddesses, let them find out, if they can, anything which could be bestowed by any god whatever on a man possessing virtue, possessing felicity. What instruction could be sought either from Mercury or Minerva, when Virtue already possessed all in herself? Virtue, indeed, is defined by the ancients as itself the art of living well and rightly. Hence, because virtue is called in Greek ἀρετή, it has been thought the Latins have derived from it the term *art*. But if Virtue cannot come except to the clever, what need was there of the god Father Catius, who should make men cautious, that is, acute, when Felicity could confer this? Because, to be born clever belongs to felicity. Whence, although goddess Felicity could not be worshiped by one not yet born, in order that, being made his friend, she might bestow this on him, yet she might confer this favor on parents who were her worshipers, that clever children should be born to them. What need had women in childbirth to invoke Lucina, when, if Felicity should be present, they would have, not only a good delivery, but good children too? What need was there to commend the children to the goddess Ops when they were being born; to the god Vaticanus in their birth cry; to the goddess Cunina when lying cradled; to the goddess Rumina when sucking; to the god Statilinus when standing; to the goddess Adeona when coming; to Abeona when going away; to the goddess Mens that they might have a good mind; to the god Volumnus, and the goddess Volumna, that they might wish for good things; to the nuptial gods, that they might make good matches; to the rural gods, and chiefly to the goddess Fructesca herself, that they might receive the most abundant fruits; to Mars and Bellona, that they might carry on war well; to the goddess

Victoria, that they might be victorious; to the god Honor, that they might be honored; to the goddess Pecunia, that they might have plenty money; to the god Æsculanus, and his son Argentinus, that they might have brass and silver coin? For they set down Æsculanus as the father of Argentinus for this reason, that brass coin began to be used before silver. But I wonder Argentinus has not begotten Aurinus, since gold coin also has followed. Could they have him for a god, they would prefer Aurinus both to his father Argentinus and his grandfather Æsculanus, just as they set Jove before Saturn. Therefore, what necessity was there on account of these gifts, either of soul, or body, or outward estate, to worship and invoke so great a crowd of gods, all of whom I have not mentioned, nor have they themselves been able to provide for all human benefits, minutely and singly methodized, minute and single gods, when the one goddess Felicity was able, with the greatest ease, compendiously to bestow the whole of them? Nor should any other be sought after, either for the bestowing of good things, or for the averting of evil. For why should they invoke the goddess Fessonia for the weary; for driving away enemies, the goddess Pellonia; for the sick, as a physician, either Apollo or Æsculapius, or both together if there should be great danger? Neither should the god Spiniensis be entreated that he might root out the thorns from the fields; nor the goddess Rubigo that the mildew might not come—Felicitas alone being present and guarding, either no evils would have arisen, or they would have been quite easily driven away. Finally, since we treat of these two goddesses, Virtue and Felicity, if felicity is the reward of virtue, she is not a goddess, but a gift of God. But if she is a goddess, why may she not be said to confer virtue itself, inasmuch as it is a great felicity to attain virtue?

22. CONCERNING THE KNOWLEDGE OF THE WORSHIP DUE TO THE GODS, WHICH VARRO GLORIES IN HAVING HIMSELF CONFERRED ON THE ROMANS

What is it, then, that Varro boasts he has bestowed as a very great benefit on his fellow citizens, because he not only recounts the gods who ought to be worshiped by the Romans, but also tells what pertains to each of them? "Just as it is of no advantage," he says, "to know the name and appearance of any man who is a physician, and not know that he is a physician, so," he says, "it is of no advantage to know well that Æsculapius is a god, if you are not aware that he can bestow the gift of health, and consequently do not know why you ought to supplicate him." He also affirms this by another comparison, saying, "No one is able, not only to live well, but even to live at all, if he does not know who is a smith, who a baker, who a weaver, from whom he can seek any utensil, whom he may take for a helper, whom for a leader, whom for a teacher"; asserting, "that in this way it can be doubtful to no one, that thus the knowledge of the gods is useful, if one can know what force, and faculty, or power any god may have in any thing. For from this we may be able," he says, "to know what god we ought to call to, and invoke for any cause; lest we should do as too many are wont to do, and desire water from Liber, and wine from Lymphs." Very useful, forsooth! Who would not give this man thanks if he could show true things, and if he could teach that the one true God, from whom all good things are, is to be worshiped by men?

23. CONCERNING FELICITY, WHOM THE ROMANS, WHO VENERATE MANY GODS, FOR A LONG TIME DID NOT WORSHIP WITH DIVINE HONOR, THOUGH SHE ALONE WOULD HAVE SUFFICED INSTEAD OF ALL

But how does it happen, if their books and rituals are true, and Felicity is a goddess, that she herself is not appointed as the only one to be worshiped, since she could confer all things, and all at once make men happy? For who wishes anything for any other reason than that he may become happy? Why was it left to Lucullus to dedicate a temple to so great a goddess at so late a date, and after so many Roman rulers? Why did Romulus himself, ambitious as he was of founding a fortunate city, not erect a temple to this goddess before all others? Why did he supplicate the other gods for anything, since he would have lacked nothing had she been with him? For even he himself would neither have been first a king, then afterward, as they think, a god, if this goddess had not been propitious to him. Why, therefore, did he appoint as gods for the Romans, Janus, Jove, Mars, Picus, Faunus, Tibernus, Hercules, and others, if there were more of them? Why did Titus Tatius add Saturn, Ops, Sun, Moon, Vulcan, Light, and whatever others he added, among whom was even the goddess Cloacina, while Felicity was neglected? Why did Numa appoint so many gods and so many goddesses without this one? Was it perhaps because he could not see her among so great a crowd? Certainly King Hostilius would not have introduced the new gods Fear and Dread to be propitiated, if he could have known or might have worshiped this goddess. For, in presence of Felicity, Fear and Dread would have disappeared—I do not say propitiated, but put to flight. Next, I ask, how is it that the Roman Empire had already immensely increased before anyone worshiped Felicity? Was the empire, therefore, more great than happy? For how could true felicity be there, where there was not true piety? For piety is the genuine worship of the true God, and not the worship of as many demons as there are false gods. Yet even afterward, when Felicity had already been taken into the number of the gods, the great infelicity of the civil wars ensued. Was Felicity perhaps justly indignant, both because she was invited so late, and was invited not to honor, but rather to reproach, because along with her were worshiped Priapus, and Cloacina, and Fear and Dread, and Ague, and others which were not gods to be worshiped, but the crimes of the worshipers? Last of all, if it seemed good to worship so great a goddess along with a most unworthy crowd, why at least was she not worshiped in a more honorable way than the rest? For is it not intolerable that Felicity is placed neither among the gods *Consentes*, whom they allege to be admitted into the council of Jupiter, nor among the gods whom they term *Select*? Some temple might be made for her which might be preeminent, both in loftiness of site and dignity of style. Why, indeed, not something better than is made for Jupiter himself? For who gave the kingdom even to Jupiter but Felicity? I am supposing that when he reigned he was happy. Felicity, however, is certainly more valuable than a kingdom. For no one doubts that a man might easily be found who may fear to be made a king; but no one is found who is unwilling to be happy. Therefore, if it is thought they can be consulted by augury, or in any other way, the gods themselves should be consulted about this thing, whether they may wish to give place to Felicity. If, perchance, the place should already be occupied by the temples and altars of others, where a greater and more lofty temple might be built to Felicity, even Jupiter himself might give way, so that Felicity might rather obtain the very pinnacle of the Capitoline hill. For there is not anyone who would resist Felicity, except, which is impossible, one who might wish to be unhappy. Certainly, if he should be consulted, Jupiter would in no case do what those three gods, Mars, Terminus, and Juventas, did, who positively refused to give place to their superior and king. For, as their books record, when king Tarquin wished to construct the Capitol, and perceived that the place which seemed to him to be the most worthy and suitable was preoccupied by other gods, not daring to do anything contrary to their pleasure, and believing that they would willingly give place to a god who was so great, and was their own master, because there were many of them there when the Capitol was founded, he inquired by augury whether they chose to give place to Jupiter, and they were all willing to remove thence except those whom I have named, Mars, Terminus, and Juventas; and therefore the Capitol was built in such a way that these three also might be within it, yet with such obscure signs that even the most learned men could scarcely know this. Surely, then, Jupiter himself would by no means despise Felicity, as he was himself despised by Terminus, Mars, and Juventas. But even they themselves who had not given place to Jupiter, would certainly give place to Felicity, who had made Jupiter king over them. Or if they should not give place, they would act thus not out of contempt of her, but because they chose rather to be obscure in the house of Felicity, than to be eminent without her in their own places.

Thus the goddess Felicity being established in the largest and loftiest place, the citizens should learn whence the furtherance of every good desire should be sought. And so, by the persuasion of nature herself, the superfluous multitude of other gods being abandoned, Felicity alone would be worshiped, prayer would be made to her alone, her temple alone would be frequented by the citizens who wished to be happy, which no one of them would not wish; and thus felicity, who was sought for from all the gods, would be sought for only from her own self. For who wishes to receive from any god anything else than felicity, or what he supposes to tend to felicity? Wherefore, if Felicity has it in her power to be with what man she pleases (and she has it if she is a goddess), what folly is it, after all, to seek from any other god her whom you can obtain by request from her own self! Therefore they ought to honor this goddess above other gods, even by dignity of place. For, as we read in their own authors, the ancient Romans paid greater honors to I know not what Summanus, to whom they attributed nocturnal thunderbolts, than to Jupiter, to whom diurnal thunderbolts were held to pertain. But, after a famous and conspicuous temple had been built to Jupiter, owing to the dignity of the building, the multitude resorted to him in so great numbers, that scarce one can be found who remembers even to have read the name of Summanus, which now he cannot once hear named. But if Felicity is not a goddess, because, as is true, it is a gift of God, that god must be sought who has power to give it, and that hurtful multitude of false gods must be abandoned which the vain multitude of foolish men follows after, making gods to itself of the gifts of God, and offending Himself whose gifts they are by the stubbornness of a proud will. For he cannot be free from infelicity who worships Felicity as a goddess, and forsakes God, the giver of felicity; just as he cannot be free from hunger who licks a painted loaf of bread, and does not buy it of the man who has a real one.

24. THE REASONS BY WHICH THE PAGANS ATTEMPT TO DEFEND THEIR WORSHIPING AMONG THE GODS THE DIVINE GIFTS THEMSELVES

We may, however, consider their reasons. Is it to be believed, say they, that our forefathers were besotted even to such a degree as not to know that these things are divine gifts, and not gods? But as they knew that such things are granted to no one, except by some god freely bestowing them, they called the gods whose names they did not find out by the names of those things which they deemed to be given by them; sometimes slightly altering the name for that purpose, as, for example, from war they have named Bellona, not *bellum;* from cradles, Cunina, not *cunæ;* from standing corn, Segetia, not *seges;* from apples, Pomona, not *pomum;* from oxen, Bubona, not *bos.* Sometimes, again, with no alteration of the word, just as the things themselves are named, so that the goddess who gives money is called Pecunia, and money is not thought to be itself a goddess: so of

Virtus, who gives virtue; Honor, who gives honor; Concordia, who gives concord; Victoria, who gives victory. So, they say, when Felicitas is called a goddess, what is meant is not the thing itself which is given, but that deity by whom felicity is given.

25. CONCERNING THE ONE GOD ONLY TO BE WORSHIPED, WHO, ALTHOUGH HIS NAME IS UNKNOWN, IS YET DEEMED TO BE THE GIVER OF FELICITY

Having had that reason rendered to us, we shall perhaps much more easily persuade, as we wish, those whose heart has not become too much hardened. For if now human infirmity has perceived that felicity cannot be given except by some god; if this was perceived by those who worshiped so many gods, at whose head they set Jupiter himself; if, in their ignorance of the name of Him by whom felicity was given, they agreed to call Him by the name of that very thing which they believed He gave—then it follows that they thought that felicity could not be given even by Jupiter himself, whom they already worshiped, but certainly by him whom they thought fit to worship under the name of Felicity itself. I thoroughly affirm the statement that they believed felicity to be given by a certain God whom they knew not: let Him therefore be sought after, let Him be worshiped, and it is enough. Let the train of innumerable demons be repudiated, and let this God suffice every man whom his gift suffices. For him, I say, God the giver of felicity will not be enough to worship, for whom felicity itself is not enough to receive. But let him for whom it suffices (and man has nothing more he ought to wish for) serve the one God, the giver of felicity. This God is not he whom they call Jupiter. For if they acknowledged him to be the giver of felicity, they would not seek, under the name of Felicity itself, for another god or goddess by whom felicity might be given; nor could they tolerate that Jupiter himself should be worshiped with such infamous attributes. For he is said to be the debaucher of the wives of others; he is the shameless lover and ravisher of a beautiful boy.

26. OF THE SCENIC PLAYS, THE CELEBRATION OF WHICH THE GODS HAVE EXACTED FROM THEIR WORSHIPERS

"But," says Cicero, "Homer invented these things, and transferred things human to the gods: I would rather transfer things divine to us."[1] The poet, by ascribing such crimes to the gods, has justly displeased the grave man. Why, then, are the scenic plays, where these crimes are habitually spoken of, acted, exhibited, in honor of the gods, reckoned among things divine by the most learned men? Cicero should exclaim, not against the inventions of the poets, but against the customs of the ancients. Would not they have exclaimed in reply, What have we done? The gods themselves have loudly demanded that these plays should be exhibited in their honor, have fiercely exacted them, have menaced destruction unless this was performed, have avenged its neglect with great severity, and have manifested pleasure at the reparation of such neglect. Among their virtuous and wonderful deeds the following is related. It was announced in a dream to Titus Latinius, a Roman rustic, that he should go to the senate and tell them to recommence the games of Rome, because on the first day of their celebration a condemned criminal had been led to punishment in sight of the people, an incident so sad as to disturb the gods who were seeking amusement from the games. And when the peasant who had received this intimation was afraid on the following day to deliver it to the senate, it was renewed next night in a severer form: he lost his son, because of his neglect. On the third night he was warned that a yet graver punishment was impending, if he should still refuse obedience. When even thus he did not dare to obey, he fell into a virulent and horrible disease. But then, on the advice of his friends, he gave information to the magistrates, and was carried in a litter into the senate, and having, on declaring his dream, immediately recovered strength, went away on his own feet whole.[2] The senate, amazed at so great a miracle, decreed that the games should be renewed at fourfold cost. What sensible man does not see that men, being put upon by malignant demons, from whose domination nothing save the grace of God through Jesus Christ our Lord sets free, have been compelled by force to exhibit to such gods as these, plays which, if well advised, they should condemn as shameful? Certain it is that in these plays the poetic crimes of the gods are celebrated, yet they are plays which were reestablished by decree of the senate, under compulsion of the gods. In these plays the most shameless actors celebrated Jupiter as the corrupter of chastity, and thus gave him pleasure. If that was a fiction, he would have been moved to anger; but if he was delighted with the representation of his crimes, even although fabulous, then, when he happened to be worshiped, who but the devil could be served? Is it so that he could found, extend, and preserve the Roman Empire, who was more vile than any Roman man whatever, to whom such things were displeasing? Could he give felicity who was so infelicitously worshiped, and who, unless he should be thus worshiped, was yet more infelicitously provoked to anger?

---

1. Cicero Tusc. Disp. 1.26.
2. Livy 2.36; Cicero *De Divinat.* 26.

27. CONCERNING THE THREE KINDS OF GODS ABOUT WHICH THE PONTIFF SCÆVOLA HAS DISCOURSED

It is recorded that the very learned pontiff Scævola[1] had distinguished about three kinds of gods—one introduced by the poets, another by the philosophers, another by the statesmen. The first kind he declares to be trifling, because many unworthy things have been invented by the poets concerning the gods; the second does not suit states, because it contains some things that are superfluous, and some, too, which it would be prejudicial for the people to know. It is no great matter about the superfluous things, for it is a common saying of skillful lawyers, "Superfluous things do no harm."[2] But what are those things which do harm when brought before the multitude? "These," he says, "that Hercules, Æsculapius, Castor and Pollux, are not gods; for it is declared by learned men that these were but men, and yielded to the common lot of mortals." What else? "That states have not the true images of the gods; because the true God has neither sex, nor age, nor definite corporeal members." The pontiff is not willing that the people should know these things; for he does not think they are false. He thinks it expedient, therefore, that states should be deceived in matters of religion; which Varro himself does not even hesitate to say in his books about things divine. Excellent religion! to which the weak, who requires to be delivered, may flee for succor; and when he seeks for the truth by which he may be delivered, it is believed to be expedient for him that he be deceived. And, truly, in these same books, Scævola is not silent as to his reason for rejecting the poetic sort of gods—to wit, "because they so disfigure the gods that they could not bear comparison even with good men, when they make one to commit theft, another adultery; or, again, to say or do something else basely and foolishly; as that three goddesses contested (with each other) the prize of beauty, and the two vanquished by Venus destroyed Troy; that Jupiter turned himself into a bull or swan that he might copulate with someone; that a goddess married a man, and Saturn devoured his children; that, in fine, there is nothing that could be imagined, either of the miraculous or vicious, which may not be found there, and yet is far removed from the nature of the gods." O chief pontiff Scævola, take away the plays if you are able; instruct the people that they may not offer such honors to the immortal gods, in which, if they like, they may admire the crimes of the gods, and, so far as it is possible, may, if they please, imitate them. But if the people shall have answered you, you, O pontiff, have brought these things in among us, then ask the gods themselves at whose instigation you have ordered these things, that they may not order such things to be offered to them. For if they are bad, and therefore in no way to be believed concerning the majority of the gods, the greater is the wrong done the gods about whom they are feigned with impunity. But they do not hear you, they are demons, they teach wicked things, they rejoice in vile things; not only do they not count it a wrong if these things are feigned about them, but it is a wrong they are quite unable to bear if they are not acted at their stated festivals. But now, if you would call on Jupiter against them, chiefly for that reason that more of his crimes are wont to be acted in the scenic plays, is it not the case that, although you call him god Jupiter, by whom this whole world is ruled and administered, it is he to whom the greatest wrong is done by you, because you have thought he ought to be worshiped along with them, and have styled him their king?

---

1. Called by Cicero (*De Oratore* 1.39) the most eloquent of lawyers, and the best skilled lawyer among eloquent men.
2. "Superflua non nocent."

28. WHETHER THE WORSHIP OF THE GODS HAS BEEN OF SERVICE TO THE ROMANS IN OBTAINING AND EXTENDING THE EMPIRE

Therefore such gods, who are propitiated by such honors, or rather are impeached by them (for it is a greater crime to delight in having such things said of them falsely, than even if they could be said truly), could never by any means have been able to increase and preserve the Roman Empire. For if they could have done it, they would rather have bestowed so grand a gift on the Greeks, who, in this kind of divine things—that is, in scenic plays—have worshiped them more honorably and worthily, although they have not exempted themselves from those slanders of the poets, by whom they saw the gods torn in pieces, giving them licence to ill-use any man they pleased, and have not deemed the scenic players themselves to be base, but have held them worthy even of distinguished honor. But just as the Romans were able to have gold money, although they did not worship a god Aurinus, so also they could have silver and brass coin, and yet worship neither Argentinus nor his father Æsculanus; and so of all the rest, which it would be irksome for me to detail. It follows, therefore, both that they could not by any means attain such dominion if the true God was unwilling; and that if these gods, false and many, were unknown or contemned, and He alone was known and worshiped with sincere faith and virtue, they would both have a better kingdom here, whatever might be its extent, and whether they might have one here or not, would afterward receive an eternal kingdom.

29. OF THE FALSITY OF THE AUGURY BY WHICH THE STRENGTH AND STABILITY OF THE ROMAN EMPIRE WAS CONSIDERED TO BE INDICATED

For what kind of augury is that which they have declared to be most beautiful, and to which I referred a little ago, that Mars, and Terminus, and Juventas would not give place even to Jove, the king of the gods? For thus, they say, it was signified that the nation dedicated to Mars—that is, the Roman—should yield to none the place it once occupied; likewise, that on account of the god Terminus, no one would be able to disturb the Roman frontiers; and also, that the Roman youth, because of the goddess Juventas, should yield to no one. Let them see, therefore, how they can hold him to be the king of their gods, and the giver of their own kingdom, if these auguries set him down for an adversary, to whom it would have been honorable not to yield. However, if these things are true, they need not be at all afraid. For they are not going to confess that the gods who would not yield to

Jove have yielded to Christ. For, without altering the boundaries of the empire, Jesus Christ has proved Himself able to drive them, not only from their temples, but from the hearts of their worshipers. But, before Christ came in the flesh, and, indeed, before these things which we have quoted from their books could have been written, but yet after that auspice was made under King Tarquin, the Roman army has been diverse times scattered or put to flight, and has shown the falseness of the auspice, which they derived from the fact that the goddess Juventas had not given place to Jove; and the nation dedicated to Mars was trodden down in the city itself by the invading and triumphant Gauls; and the boundaries of the empire, through the falling away of many cities to Hannibal, had been hemmed into a narrow space. Thus the beauty of the auspices is made void, and there has remained only the contumacy against Jove, not of gods, but of demons. For it is one thing not to have yielded, and another to have returned whither you have yielded. Besides, even afterward, in the oriental regions, the boundaries of the Roman Empire were changed by the will of Hadrian; for he yielded up to the Persian Empire those three noble provinces, Armenia, Mesopotamia, and Assyria. Thus that god Terminus, who according to these books was the guardian of the Roman frontiers, and by that most beautiful auspice had not given place to Jove, would seem to have been more afraid of Hadrian, a king of men, than of the king of the gods. The aforesaid provinces having also been taken back again, almost within our own recollection the frontier fell back, when Julian, given up to the oracles of their gods, with immoderate daring ordered the victualing ships to be set on fire. The army being thus left destitute of provisions, and he himself also being presently killed by the enemy, and the legions being hard pressed, while dismayed by the loss of their commander, they were reduced to such extremities that no one could have escaped, unless by articles of peace the boundaries of the empire had then been established where they still remain; not, indeed, with so great a loss as was suffered by the concession of Hadrian, but still at a considerable sacrifice. It was a vain augury, then, that the god Terminus did not yield to Jove, since he yielded to the will of Hadrian, and yielded also to the rashness of Julian, and the necessity of Jovinian. The more intelligent and grave Romans have seen these things, but have had little power against the custom of the state, which was bound to observe the rites of the demons; because even they themselves, although they perceived that these things were vain, yet thought that the religious worship which is due to God should be paid to the nature of things which is established under the rule and government of the one true God, "serving," as says the apostle, "the creature more than the Creator, who is blessed forevermore."[1] The help of this true God was necessary to send holy and truly pious men, who would die for the true religion that they might remove the false from among the living.

---

1. Rom. 1:25.

30. WHAT KIND OF THINGS EVEN THEIR WORSHIPERS HAVE OWNED THEY HAVE THOUGHT ABOUT THE GODS OF THE NATIONS

Cicero the augur laughs at auguries, and reproves men for regulating the purposes of life by the cries of crows and jackdaws.[1] But it will be said that an Academic philosopher, who argues that all things are uncertain, is unworthy to have any authority in these matters. In the second book of his *De Natura Deorum*,[2] he introduces Lucilius Balbus, who, after showing that superstitions have their origin in physical and philosophical truths, expresses his indignation at the setting up of images and fabulous notions, speaking thus: "Do you not therefore see that from true and useful physical discoveries the reason may be drawn away to fabulous and imaginary gods? This gives birth to false opinions and turbulent errors, and superstitions well-nigh old-wifeish. For both the forms of the gods, and their ages, and clothing, and ornaments, are made familiar to us; their genealogies, too, their marriages, kinships, and all things about them, are debased to the likeness of human weakness. They are even introduced as having perturbed minds; for we have accounts of the lusts, cares, and angers of the gods. Nor, indeed, as the fables go, have the gods been without their wars and battles. And that not only when, as in Homer, some gods on either side have defended two opposing armies, but they have even carried on wars on their own account, as with the Titans or with the Giants. Such things it is quite absurd either to say or to believe: they are utterly frivolous and groundless." Behold, now, what is confessed by those who defend the gods of the nations. Afterward he goes on to say that some things belong to superstition, but others to religion, which he thinks good to teach according to the Stoics. "For not only the philosophers," he says, "but also our forefathers, have made a distinction between superstition and religion. For those," he says, "who spent whole days in prayer, and offered sacrifice, that their children might outlive them, are called superstitious."[3] Who does not see that he is trying, while he fears the public prejudice, to praise the religion of the ancients, and that he wishes to disjoin it from superstition, but cannot find out how to do so? For if those who prayed and sacrificed all day were called superstitious by the ancients, were those also called so who instituted (what he blames) the images of the gods of diverse age and distinct clothing, and invented the genealogies of gods, their marriages, and kinships? When, therefore, these things are found fault with as superstitious, he implicates in that fault the ancients who instituted and worshiped such images. No, he implicates himself, who, with whatever eloquence he may strive to extricate himself and be free, was yet under the necessity of venerating these images; nor dared he so much as whisper in a discourse to the people what in this disputation he plainly sounds forth. Let us Christians, therefore, give thanks to the Lord our God—not to heaven and earth, as that author argues, but to Him who has made heaven and earth; because these superstitions, which that Balbus, like a babbler,[4] scarcely reprehends, He, by the most deep lowliness of Christ, by the preaching of the apostles, by the faith of the martyrs dying for the truth and living with the truth, has overthrown, not only in the hearts of the religious, but even in the temples of the superstitious, by their own free service.

---

1. Cicero De Divinat. 2.37.
2. Cicero *De Nat. Deor.* 2.28.
3. Superstition, from *superstes.* Against this etymology of Cicero, see Lactantius *Inst. Div.* 4.28.
4. Balbus, from *balbutiens,* stammering, babbling.

31. Concerning the Opinions of Varro, Who, While Reprobating the Popular Belief, Thought That Their Worship Should Be Confined to One God, Though He Was Unable to Discover the True God

What says Varro himself, whom we grieve to have found, although not by his own judgment, placing the scenic plays among things divine? When in many passages he is exhorting, like a religious man, to the worship of the gods, does he not in doing so admit that he does not in his own judgment believe those things which he relates that the Roman state has instituted; so that he does not hesitate to affirm that if he were founding a new state, he could enumerate the gods and their names better by the rule of nature? But being born into a nation already ancient, he says that he finds himself bound to accept the traditional names and surnames of the gods, and the histories connected with them, and that his purpose in investigating and publishing these details is to incline the people to worship the gods, and not to despise them. By which words this most acute man sufficiently indicates that he does not publish all things, because they would not only have been contemptible to himself, but would have seemed despicable even to the rabble, unless they had been passed over in silence. I should be thought to conjecture these things, unless he himself, in another passage, had openly said, in speaking of religious rites, that many things are true which it is not only not useful for the common people to know, but that it is expedient that the people should think otherwise, even though falsely, and therefore the Greeks have shut up the religious ceremonies and mysteries in silence, and within walls. In this he no doubt expresses the policy of the so-called wise men by whom states and peoples are ruled. Yet by this crafty device the malign demons are wonderfully delighted, who possess alike the deceivers and the deceived, and from whose tyranny nothing sets free save the grace of God through Jesus Christ our Lord.

The same most acute and learned author also says, that those alone seem to him to have perceived what God is, who have believed Him to be the soul of the world, governing it by design and reason.[1] And by this, it appears, that although he did not attain to the truth—for the true God is not a soul, but the maker and author of the soul—yet if he could have been free to go against the prejudices of custom, he could have confessed and counseled others that the one God ought to be worshiped, who governs the world by design and reason; so that on this subject only this point would remain to be debated with him, that he had called Him a soul, and not rather the creator of the soul. He says, also, that the ancient Romans, for more than 170 years, worshiped the gods without an image.[2] "And if this custom," he says, "could have remained till now, the gods would have been more purely worshiped." In favor of this opinion, he cites as a witness among others the Jewish nation; nor does he hesitate to conclude that passage by saying of those who first consecrated images for the people, that they have both taken away religious fear from their fellow citizens, and increased error, wisely thinking that the gods easily fall into contempt when exhibited under the stolidity of images. But as he does not say they have transmitted error, but that they have increased it, he therefore wishes it to be understood that there was error already when there were no images. Wherefore, when he says they alone have perceived what God is who have believed Him to be the governing soul of the world, and thinks that the rites of religion would have been more purely observed without images, who fails to see how near he has come to the truth? For if he had been able to do anything against so inveterate an error, he would certainly have given it as his opinion both that the one God should be worshiped, and that He should be worshiped without an image; and having so nearly discovered the truth, perhaps he might easily have been put in mind of the mutability of the soul, and might thus have perceived that the true God is that immutable nature which made the soul itself. Since these things are so, whatever ridicule such men have poured in their writings against the plurality of the gods, they have done so rather as compelled by the secret will of God to confess them, than as trying to persuade others. If, therefore, any testimonies are adduced by us from these writings, they are adduced for the confutation of those who are unwilling to consider from how great and malignant a power of the demons the singular sacrifice of the shedding of the most holy blood, and the gift of the imparted Spirit, can set us free.

---

1. See Cicero *De Nat. Deor.* 1.2.
2. Plutarch's *Numa* 8.

32. IN WHAT INTEREST THE PRINCES OF THE NATIONS WISHED FALSE RELIGIONS TO CONTINUE AMONG THE PEOPLE SUBJECT TO THEM

Varro says also, concerning the generations of the gods, that the people have inclined to the poets rather than to the natural philosophers; and that therefore their forefathers—that is, the ancient Romans—believed both in the sex and the generations of the gods, and settled their marriages; which certainly seems to have been done for no other cause except that it was the business of such men as were prudent and wise to deceive the people in matters of religion, and in that very thing not only to worship, but also to imitate the demons, whose greatest lust is to deceive. For just as the demons cannot possess any but those whom they have deceived with guile, so also men in princely office, not indeed being just, but like demons, have persuaded the people in the name of religion to receive as true those things which they themselves knew to be false; in this way, as it were, binding them up more firmly in civil society, so that they might in like manner possess them as subjects. But who that was weak and unlearned could escape the deceits of both the princes of the state and the demons?

33. THAT THE TIMES OF ALL KINGS AND KINGDOMS ARE ORDAINED BY THE JUDGMENT AND POWER OF THE TRUE GOD

Therefore that God, the author and giver of felicity, because He alone is the true God, Himself gives earthly kingdoms both to good and bad. Neither does He do this rashly, and, as it were, fortuitously—because He is God, not fortune—but according to the order of things and times, which is hidden from us, but thoroughly known to Himself; which same order of times, however, He does not serve as subject to it, but Himself rules as lord and appoints as governor. Felicity He gives only to the good. Whether a man be a subject or a king makes no difference; he may equally either possess or not possess it. And it shall be full in that life where kings and subjects exist no longer. And therefore earthly kingdoms are given by Him both to the good and the bad; lest His worshipers, still under the conduct of a very weak mind, should covet these gifts from Him as some great things. And this is the mystery of the Old Testament, in which the New was hidden, that there even earthly gifts are promised: those who were spiritual understanding even then, although not yet openly declaring, both the eternity which was symbolized by these earthly things, and in what gifts of God true felicity could be found.

34. CONCERNING THE KINGDOM OF THE JEWS, WHICH WAS FOUNDED BY THE ONE AND TRUE GOD, AND PRESERVED BY HIM AS LONG AS THEY REMAINED IN THE TRUE RELIGION

Therefore, that it might be known that these earthly good things, after which those pant who cannot imagine better things, remain in the power of the one God Himself, not of the many false gods whom the Romans have formerly believed worthy of worship, He multiplied His people in Egypt from being very few, and delivered them out of it by wonderful signs. Nor did their women invoke Lucina when their offspring was being incredibly multiplied; and that nation having increased incredibly, He Himself delivered, He Himself saved them from the hands of the Egyptians, who persecuted them, and wished to kill all their infants. Without the goddess Rumina they sucked; without Cunina they were cradled; without Educa and Potina they took food and drink; without all those puerile gods they were educated; without the nuptial gods they were married; without the worship of Priapus they had conjugal intercourse; without invocation of Neptune the divided sea opened up a way for them to pass over, and overwhelmed with its returning waves their enemies who pursued them. Neither did they consecrate any goddess Mannia when they received manna from heaven; nor, when the smitten rock poured forth water to them when they thirsted, did they worship Nymphs and Lymphs. Without the mad rites of Mars and Bellona they carried on war; and while, indeed, they did not conquer without victory, yet they did not hold it to be a goddess, but the gift of their God. Without Segetia they had harvests; without Bubona, oxen; honey without Mellona; apples without Pomona: and, in a word, everything for which the Romans thought they must supplicate so great a crowd of false gods, they received much more happily from the one true God. And if they had not sinned against Him with impious curiosity, which seduced them like magic arts, and drew them to strange gods and idols, and at last led them to kill Christ, their kingdom would have remained to them, and would have been, if not more spacious, yet more happy, than that of Rome. And now that they are dispersed through almost all lands and nations, it is through the providence of that one true God; that whereas the images, altars, groves, and temples of the false gods are everywhere overthrown, and their sacrifices prohibited, it may be shown from their books how this has been foretold by their prophets so long before; lest, perhaps, when they should be read in ours, they might seem to be invented by us. But now, reserving what is to follow for the following book, we must here set a bound to the prolixity of this one.

BOOK FIVE

ARGUMENT[1]

Augustine first discusses the doctrine of fate, for the sake of confuting those who are disposed to refer to fate the power and increase of the Roman Empire, which could not be attributed to false gods, as has been shown in the preceding book. After that, he proves that there is no contradiction between God's prescience and our free will. He then speaks of the manners of the ancient Romans, and shows in what sense it was due to the virtue of the Romans themselves, and in how far to the counsel of God, that He increased their dominion, though they did not worship Him. Finally, he explains what is to be accounted the true happiness of the Christian emperors.

Since, then, it is established that the complete attainment of all we desire is that which constitutes felicity, which is no goddess, but a gift of God, and that therefore men can worship no god save Him who is able to make them happy—and were Felicity herself a goddess, she would with reason be the only object of worship—since, I say, this is established, let us now go on to consider why God, who is able to give with all other things those good gifts which can be possessed by men who are not good, and consequently not happy, has seen fit to grant such extended and long-continued dominion to the Roman Empire; for that this was not effected by that multitude of false gods which they worshiped, we have both already adduced, and shall, as occasion offers, yet adduce considerable proof.

---

1. Written in the year 415.

1. THAT THE CAUSE OF THE ROMAN EMPIRE, AND OF ALL KINGDOMS, IS NEITHER FORTUITOUS NOR CONSISTS IN THE POSITION OF THE STARS1

The cause, then, of the greatness of the Roman Empire is neither fortuitous nor fatal, according to the judgment or opinion of those who call those things *fortuitous* which either have no causes, or such causes as do not proceed from some intelligible order, and those things *fatal* which happen independently of the will of God and man, by the necessity of a certain *order*. In a word, human kingdoms are established by divine Providence. And if anyone attributes their existence to fate, because he calls the will or the power of God itself by the name of fate, let him keep his opinion, but correct his language. For why does he not say at first what he will say afterward, when someone shall put the question to him: what he means by *fate*? For when men hear that word, according to the ordinary use of the language, they simply understand by it the virtue of that particular position of the stars which may exist at the time when anyone is born or conceived, which some separate altogether from the will of God, while others affirm that this also is dependent on that will. But those who are of opinion that, apart from the will of God, the stars determine what we shall do, or what good things we shall possess, or what evils we shall suffer, must be refused a hearing by all, not only by those who hold the true religion, but by those who wish to be the worshipers of any gods whatsoever, even false gods. For what does this opinion really amount to but this, that no god whatever is to be worshiped or prayed to? Against these, however, our present disputation is not intended to be directed, but against those who, in defense of those whom they think to be gods, oppose the Christian religion. They, however, who make the position of the stars depend on the divine will, and in a manner decree what character each man shall have, and what good or evil shall happen to him, if they think that these same stars have that power conferred upon them by the supreme power of God, in order that they may determine these things according to their will, do a great injury to the celestial sphere, in whose most brilliant senate, and most splendid senate house, as it were, they suppose that wicked deeds are decreed to be done—such deeds as that, if any terrestrial state should decree them, it would be condemned to overthrow by the decree of the whole human race. What judgment, then, is left to God concerning the deeds of men, who is Lord both of the stars and of men, when to these deeds a celestial necessity is attributed? Or, if they do not say that the stars, though they have indeed received a certain power from God, who is supreme, determine those things according to their own discretion, but simply that His commands are fulfilled by them instrumentally in the application and enforcing of such necessities, are we thus to think concerning God even what it seemed unworthy that we should think concerning the will of the stars? But, if the stars are said rather to signify these things than to effect them, so that that *position of the stars* is, as it were, a kind of speech predicting, not causing future things—for this has been the opinion of men of no ordinary learning—certainly the mathematicians are not wont so to speak saying, for example, Mars in such or such a position *signifies* a homicide, but *makes* a homicide. But, nevertheless, though we grant that they do not speak as they ought, and that we ought to accept as the proper form of speech that employed by the philosophers in predicting those things which they think they discover in the position of the stars, how comes it that they have never been able to assign any cause why, in the life of twins, in their actions, in the events which befall them, in their professions, arts, honors, and other things pertaining to human life, also in their very death, there is often so great a difference, that, as far as these things are concerned, many entire strangers are more like them than they are like each other, though separated at birth by the smallest interval of time, but at conception generated by the same act of copulation, and at the same moment?

2. ON THE DIFFERENCE IN THE HEALTH OF TWINS

Cicero says that the famous physician Hippocrates has left in writing that he had suspected that a certain pair of brothers were twins, from the fact that they both took ill at once, and their disease advanced to its crisis and subsided in the same time in each of them.[1] Posidonius the Stoic, who was much given to astrology, used to explain the fact by supposing that they had been born and conceived under the same constellation. In this question the conjecture of the physician is by far more worthy to be accepted, and approaches much nearer to credibility, since, according as the parents were affected in body at the time of copulation, so might the first elements of the fœtuses have been affected, so that all that was necessary for their growth and development up till birth having been supplied from the body of the same mother, they might be born with like constitutions.

Thereafter, nourished in the same house, on the same kinds of food, where they would have also the same kinds of air, the same locality, the same quality of water—which, according to the testimony of medical science, have a very great influence, good or bad, on the condition of bodily health—and where they would also be accustomed to the same kinds of exercise, they would have bodily constitutions so similar that they would be similarly affected with sickness at the same time and by the same causes. But, to wish to adduce that particular position of the stars which existed at the time when they were born or conceived as the cause of their being simultaneously affected with sickness, manifests the greatest arrogance, when so many beings of most diverse kinds, in the most diverse conditions, and subject to the most diverse events, may have been conceived and born at the same time, and in the same district, lying under the same sky. But we know that twins do not only act differently, and travel to very different places, but that they also suffer from different kinds of sickness; for which Hippocrates would give what is in my opinion the simplest reason, namely, that, through diversity of food and exercise, which arises not from the constitution of the body, but from the inclination of the mind, they may have come to be different from each other in respect of health. Moreover, Posidonius, or any other asserter of the fatal influence of the stars, will have enough to do to find anything to say to this, if he be unwilling to impose upon the minds of the uninstructed in things of which they are ignorant. But, as to what they attempt to make out from that very small interval of time elapsing between the births of twins, on account of that point in the heavens where the mark of the natal hour is placed, and which they call the "horoscope," it is either disproportionately small to the diversity which is found in the dispositions, actions, habits, and fortunes of twins, or it is disproportionately great when compared with the estate of twins, whether low or high, which is the same for both of them, the cause for whose greatest difference they place, in every case, in the hour on which one is born; and, for this reason, if the one is born so immediately after the other that there is no change in the horoscope, I demand an entire similarity in all that respects them both, which can never be found in the case of any twins. But if the slowness of the birth of the second give time for a change in the horoscope, I demand different parents, which twins can never have.

---

1. This fact is not recorded in any of the extant works of Hippocrates or Cicero. Vives supposes it may have found place in Cicero's book *De Fato*.

3. CONCERNING THE ARGUMENTS WHICH NIGIDIUS THE MATHEMATICIAN DREW FROM THE POTTER'S WHEEL, IN THE QUESTION ABOUT THE BIRTH OF TWINS

It is to no purpose, therefore, that that famous fiction about the potter's wheel is brought forward, which tells of the answer which Nigidius is said to have given when he was perplexed with this question, and on account of which he was called *Figulus*.[1] For, having whirled round the potter's wheel with all his strength, he marked it with ink, striking it twice with the utmost rapidity, so that the strokes seemed to fall on the very same part of it. Then, when the rotation had ceased, the marks which he had made were found upon the rim of the wheel at no small distance apart. Thus, said he, considering the great rapidity with which the celestial sphere revolves, even though twins were born with as short an interval between their births as there was between the strokes which I gave this wheel, that brief interval of time is equivalent to a very great distance in the celestial sphere. Hence, said he, come whatever dissimilitudes may be remarked in the habits and fortunes of twins. This argument is more fragile than the vessels which are fashioned by the rotation of that wheel. For if there is so much significance in the heavens which cannot be comprehended by observation of the constellations, that, in the case of twins, an inheritance may fall to the one and not to the other, why, in the case of others who are not twins, do they dare, having examined their constellations, to declare such things as pertain to that secret which no one can comprehend, and to attribute them to the precise moment of the birth of each individual? Now, if such predictions in connection with the natal hours of others who are not twins are to be vindicated on the ground that they are founded on the observation of more extended spaces in the heavens, while those very small moments of time which separated the births of twins, and correspond to minute portions of celestial space, are to be connected with trifling things about which the mathematicians are not wont to be consulted—for who would consult them as to when he is to sit, when to walk abroad, when and on what he is to dine? How can we be justified in so speaking, when we can point out such manifold diversity both in the habits, doings, and destinies of twins?

---

1. That is, the potter.

4. CONCERNING THE TWINS ESAU AND JACOB, WHO WERE VERY UNLIKE EACH OTHER BOTH IN THEIR CHARACTER AND ACTIONS

In the time of the ancient fathers, to speak concerning illustrious persons, there were born two twin brothers, the one so immediately after the other, that the first took hold of the heel of the second. So great a difference existed in their lives and manners, so great a dissimilarity in their actions, so great a difference in their parents' love for them respectively, that the very contrast between them produced even a mutual hostile antipathy. Do we mean, when we say that they were so unlike each other, that when the one was walking the other was sitting, when the one was sleeping the other was waking—which differences are such as are attributed to those minute portions of space which cannot be appreciated by those who note down the position of the stars which exists at the moment of one's birth, in order that the mathematicians may be consulted concerning it? One of these twins was for a long time a hired servant; the other never served.

One of them was beloved by his mother; the other was not so. One of them lost that honor which was so much valued among their people; the other obtained it. And what shall we say of their wives, their children, and their possessions? How different they were in respect to all these! If, therefore, such things as these are connected with those minute intervals of time which elapse between the births of twins, and are not to be attributed to the constellations, wherefore are they predicted in the case of others from the examination of their constellations? And if, on the other hand, these things are said to be predicted, because they are connected, not with minute and inappreciable moments, but with intervals of time which can be observed and noted down, what purpose is that potter's wheel to serve in this matter, except it be to whirl round men who have hearts of clay, in order that they may be prevented from detecting the emptiness of the talk of the mathematicians?

5. IN WHAT MANNER THE MATHEMATICIANS ARE CONVICTED OF PROFESSING A VAIN SCIENCE

Do not those very persons whom the medical sagacity of Hippocrates led him to suspect to be twins, because their disease was observed by him to develop to its crisis and to subside again in the same time in each of them—do not these, I say, serve as a sufficient refutation of those who wish to attribute to the influence of the stars that which was owing to a similarity of bodily constitution? For wherefore were they both sick of the same disease, and at the same time, and not the one after the other in the order of their birth? (For certainly they could not both be born at the same time.) Or, if the fact of their having been born at different times by no means necessarily implies that they must be sick at different times, why do they contend that the difference in the time of their births was the cause of their difference in other things? Why could they travel in foreign parts at different times, marry at different times, beget children at different times, and do many other things at different times, by reason of their having been born at different times, and yet could not, for the same reason, also be sick at different times? For if a difference in the moment of birth changed the horoscope, and occasioned dissimilarity in all other things, why has that simultaneousness which belonged to their conception remained in their attacks of sickness? Or, if the destinies of health are involved in the time of conception, but those of other things be said to be attached to the time of birth, they ought not to predict anything concerning health from examination of the constellations of birth, when the hour of conception is not also given, that its constellations may be inspected. But if they say that they predict attacks of sickness without examining the horoscope of conception, because these are indicated by the moments of birth, how could they inform either of these twins when he would be sick, from the horoscope of his birth, when the other also, who had not the same horoscope of birth, must of necessity fall sick at the same time? Again, I ask, if the distance of time between the births of twins is so great as to occasion a difference of their constellations on account of the difference of their horoscopes, and therefore of all the cardinal points to which so much influence is attributed, that even from such change there comes a difference of destiny, how is it possible that this should be so, since they cannot have been conceived at different times? Or, if two conceived at the same moment of time could have different destinies with respect to their births, why may not also two born at the same moment of time have different destinies for life and for death? For if the one moment in which both were conceived did not hinder that the one should be born before the other, why, if two are born at the same moment, should anything hinder them from dying at the same moment? If a simultaneous conception allows of twins being differently affected in the *womb*, why should not simultaneousness of birth allow of any two individuals having different fortunes in the *world*? And thus would all the fictions of this art, or rather delusion, be swept away. What strange circumstance is this, that two children conceived at the same time, no, at the same moment, under the same position of the stars, have different fates which bring them to different hours of birth, while two children, born of two different mothers, at the same moment of time, under one and the same position of the stars, cannot have different fates which shall conduct them by necessity to diverse manners of life and of death? Are they at conception as yet without destinies, because they can only have them if they be born? What, therefore, do they mean when they say that, if the hour of the conception be found, many things can be predicted by these astrologers?—from which also arose that story which is reiterated by some, that a certain sage chose an hour in which to lie with his wife, in order to secure his begetting an illustrious son. From this opinion also came that answer of Posidonius, the great astrologer and also philosopher, concerning those twins who were attacked with sickness at the same time, namely, "That this had happened to them because they were conceived at the same time, and *born* at the same time." For certainly he added "conception," lest it should be said to him that they could not both be born at the same time, knowing that at any rate they must both have been conceived at the same time; wishing thus to show that he did not attribute the fact of their being similarly and simultaneously affected with sickness to the similarity of their bodily constitutions as its proximate cause, but that he held that even in respect of the similarity of their health, they were bound together by a sidereal connection. If, therefore, the time of conception has so much to do with the similarity of destinies, these same destinies ought not to be changed by the circumstances of birth; or, if the destinies of twins be said to be changed because they are born at different times, why should we not rather understand that they had been already changed in order that they might be born at different times? Does not, then, the will of men living in the world change the destinies of birth, when the order of birth can change the destinies they had at conception?

6. CONCERNING TWINS OF DIFFERENT SEXES

But even in the very conception of twins, which certainly occurs at the same moment in the case of both, it often happens that the one is conceived a male, and the other a female. I know two of different sexes who are twins. Both of them are alive, and in the flower of their age; and though they resemble each other in body, as far as difference of sex will permit, still they are very different in the whole scope and purpose of their lives (consideration being had of those differences which necessarily exist between the lives of males and females)—the one holding the office of a count, and being almost constantly away from home with the army in foreign service; the other never leaving her country's soil, or her native district. Still more—and this is more incredible, if the destinies of the stars are to be believed in, though it is not wonderful if we consider the wills of men, and the free gifts of God—he is married; she is a sacred virgin: he has begotten a numerous offspring; she has never even married. But is not the virtue of the horoscope very great? I think I have said enough to show the absurdity of that. But, say those astrologers, whatever be the virtue of the horoscope in other respects, it is certainly of significance with respect to birth. But why not also with respect to conception, which takes place undoubtedly with one act of copulation? And, indeed, so great is the force of nature, that after a woman has once conceived, she ceases to be liable to conception. Or were they, perhaps, changed at birth, either he into a male, or she into a female, because of the difference in their horoscopes? But, while it is not altogether absurd to say that certain sidereal influences have some power to cause differences in bodies alone—as, for instance, we see that the seasons of the year come round by the approaching and receding of the sun, and that certain kinds of things are increased in size or diminished by the waxings and wanings of the moon, such as sea urchins, oysters, and the wonderful tides of the ocean—it does not follow that the *wills of men* are to be made subject to the position of the stars. The astrologers, however, when they wish to bind our actions also to the constellations, only set us on investigating whether, even in these bodies, the changes may not be attributable to some other than a sidereal cause. For what is there which more intimately concerns a body than its sex? And yet, under the same position of the stars, twins of different sexes may be conceived. Wherefore, what greater absurdity can be affirmed or believed than that the position of the stars, which was the same for both of them at the time of conception, could not cause that the one child should not have been of a different sex from her brother, with whom she had a common constellation, while the position of the stars which existed at the hour of their birth could cause that she should be separated from him by the great distance between marriage and holy virginity?

7. CONCERNING THE CHOOSING OF A DAY FOR MARRIAGE, OR FOR PLANTING, OR SOWING

Now, will anyone bring forward this, that in choosing certain particular days for particular actions, men bring about certain new destinies for their actions? That man, for instance, according to this doctrine, was not born to have an illustrious son, but rather a contemptible one, and therefore, being a man of learning, he choose an hour in which to lie with his wife. He made, therefore, a destiny which he did not have before, and from that destiny of his own making something began to be fatal which was not contained in the destiny of his natal hour. Oh, singular stupidity! A day is chosen on which to marry; and for this reason, I believe, that unless a day be chosen, the marriage may fall on an unlucky day, and turn out an unhappy one. What then becomes of what the stars have already decreed at the hour of birth? Can a man be said to change by an act of choice that which has already been determined for him, while that which he himself has determined in the choosing of a day cannot be changed by another power? Thus, if men alone, and not all things under heaven, are subject to the influence of the stars, why do they choose some days as suitable for planting vines or trees, or for sowing grain, other days as suitable for taming beasts on, or for putting the males to the females, that the cows and mares may be impregnated, and for suchlike things? If it be said that certain chosen days have an influence on these things, because the constellations rule over all terrestrial bodies, animate and inanimate, according to differences in moments of time, let it be considered what innumerable multitudes of beings are born or arise, or take their origin at the very same instant of time, which come to ends so different, that they may persuade any little boy that these observations about days are ridiculous. For who is so mad as to dare affirm that all trees, all herbs, all beasts, serpents, birds, fishes, worms, have each separately their own moments of birth or commencement? Nevertheless, men are wont, in order to try the skill of the mathematicians, to bring before them the constellations of dumb animals, the constellations of whose birth they diligently observe at home with a view to this discovery; and they prefer those mathematicians to all others, who say from the inspection of the constellations that they indicate the birth of a beast and not of a man. They also dare tell what kind of beast it is, whether it is a wool-bearing beast, or a beast suited for carrying burdens, or one fit for the plow, or for watching a house; for the astrologers are also tried with respect to the fates of dogs, and their answers concerning these are followed by shouts of admiration on the part of those who consult them. They so deceive men as to make them think that during the birth of a man the births of all other beings are suspended, so that not even a fly comes to life at the same time that he is being born, under the same region of the heavens. And if this be admitted with respect to the fly, the reasoning cannot stop there, but must ascend from flies till it lead them up to camels and elephants. Nor are they willing to attend to this, that when a day has been chosen whereon to sow a field, so many grains fall into the ground simultaneously, germinate simultaneously, spring up, come to perfection, and ripen simultaneously; and yet, of all the ears which are coeval, and, so to speak, *congerminal,* some are destroyed by mildew, some are devoured by the birds, and some are pulled by men. How can they say that all these had their different constellations, which they see coming to so different ends? Will they confess that it is folly to choose days for such things, and to affirm that they do not come within the sphere of the celestial decree, while they subject men alone to the stars, on whom alone in the world God has bestowed free wills? All these things being considered, we have good reason to believe that, when the astrologers give very many wonderful answers, it is to be attributed to the occult inspiration of spirits not of the best kind, whose care it is to insinuate into the minds of men, and to confirm in them, those false and noxious opinions concerning the fatal influence of the stars, and not to their marking and inspecting of horoscopes, according to some kind of art which in reality has no existence.

8. CONCERNING THOSE WHO CALL BY THE NAME OF FATE, NOT THE POSITION OF THE STARS, BUT THE CONNECTION OF CAUSES WHICH DEPENDS ON THE WILL OF GOD

But, as to those who call by the name of fate, not the disposition of the stars as it may exist when any creature is conceived, or born, or commences its existence, but the whole connection and train of causes which makes everything become what it does become, there is no need that I should labor and strive with them in a merely verbal controversy, since they attribute the so-called order and connection of causes to the will and power of God most high, who is most rightly and most truly believed to know all things before they come to pass, and to leave nothing unordained; from whom are all powers, although the wills of all are not from Him. Now, that it is chiefly the will of God most high, whose power extends itself irresistibly through all things which they call fate, is proved by the following verses, of which, if I mistake not, Annæus Seneca is the author:

Father supreme, Thou ruler of the lofty heavens,
Lead me where'er it is Thy pleasure; I will give
A prompt obedience, making no delay,
Lo! here I am. Promptly I come to do Thy sovereign will;
If Thy command shall thwart my inclination, I will still
Follow Thee groaning, and the work assigned,
With all the suffering of a mind repugnant,
Will perform, being evil; which, had I been good,
I should have undertaken and performed, though hard,
With virtuous cheerfulness.
The Fates do lead the man that follows willing;
But the man that is unwilling, him they drag.[1]

Most evidently, in this last verse, he calls that "fate" which he had before called "the will of the Father supreme," whom, he says, he is ready to obey that he may be led, being willing, not dragged, being unwilling, since "the Fates do lead the man that follows willing; but the man that is unwilling, him they drag."

The following Homeric lines, which Cicero translates into Latin, also favor this opinion:

> *Such are the minds of men, as is the light*
> *Which Father Jove himself doth pour*
> *Illustrious o'er the fruitful earth.*[2]

Not that Cicero wishes that a poetical sentiment should have any weight in a question like this; for when he says that the Stoics, when asserting the power of fate, were in the habit of using these verses from Homer, he is not treating concerning the opinion of that poet, but concerning that of those philosophers, since by these verses, which they quote in connection with the controversy which they hold about fate, is most distinctly manifested what it is which they reckon fate, since they call by the name of Jupiter him whom they reckon the supreme god, from whom, they say, hangs the whole chain of fates.

---

1. Seneca *Ep.* 107.
2. Homer *Odyssey* 18.136–137.

9. CONCERNING THE FOREKNOWLEDGE OF GOD AND THE FREE WILL OF MAN, IN OPPOSITION TO THE DEFINITION OF CICERO

The manner in which Cicero addresses himself to the task of refuting the Stoics shows that he did not think he could effect anything against them in argument unless he had first demolished divination.[1] And this he attempts to accomplish by denying that there is any knowledge of future things, and maintains with all his might that there is no such knowledge either in God or man, and that there is no prediction of events. Thus he both denies the foreknowledge of God, and attempts by vain arguments, and by opposing to himself certain oracles very easy to be refuted, to overthrow all prophecy, even such as is clearer than the light (though even these oracles are not refuted by him).

But, in refuting these conjectures of the mathematicians, his argument is triumphant, because truly these are such as destroy and refute themselves. Nevertheless, they are far more tolerable who assert the fatal influence of the stars than they who deny the foreknowledge of future events. For, to confess that God exists, and at the same time to deny that He has foreknowledge of future things, is the most manifest folly. This Cicero himself saw, and therefore attempted to assert the doctrine embodied in the words of Scripture, "The fool hath said in his heart, There is no God."[2] That, however, he did not do in his own person, for he saw how odious and offensive such an opinion would be; and therefore, in his book on the nature of the gods,[3] he makes Cotta dispute concerning this against the Stoics, and preferred to give his own opinion in favor of Lucilius Balbus, to whom he assigned the defense of the Stoical position, rather than in favor of Cotta, who maintained that no divinity exists. However, in his book on divination, he in his own person most openly opposes the doctrine of the prescience of future things. But all this he seems to do in order that he may not grant the doctrine of fate, and by so doing destroy free will. For he thinks that, the knowledge of future things being once conceded, fate follows as so necessary a consequence that it cannot be denied.

But, let these perplexing debatings and disputations of the philosophers go on as they may, we, in order that we may confess the most high and true God Himself, do confess His will, supreme power, and prescience. Neither let us be afraid lest, after all, we do not do by will that which we do by will, because He, whose foreknowledge is infallible, foreknew that we would do it. It was this which Cicero was afraid of, and therefore opposed foreknowledge. The Stoics also maintained that all things do not come to pass by necessity, although they contended that all things happen according to destiny. What is it, then, that Cicero feared in the prescience of future things? Doubtless it was this—that if all future things have been foreknown, they will happen in the order in which they have been foreknown; and if they come to pass in this order, there is a certain order of things foreknown by God; and if a certain order of things, then a certain order of causes, for nothing can happen which is not preceded by some efficient cause. But if there is a certain order of causes according to which everything happens which does happen, then by fate, says he, all things happen which do happen. But if this be so, then is there nothing in our own power, and there is no such thing as freedom of will; and if we grant that, says he, the whole economy of human life is subverted. In vain are laws enacted. In vain are reproaches, praises, chidings, exhortations had recourse to; and there is no justice whatever in the appointment of rewards for the good, and punishments for the wicked. And that consequences so disgraceful, and absurd, and pernicious to humanity may not follow, Cicero chooses to reject the foreknowledge of future things, and shuts up the religious mind to this alternative, to make choice between two things, either that something is in our own power, or that there is foreknowledge—both of which cannot be true; but if the one is affirmed, the other is thereby denied. He therefore, like a truly great and wise man, and one who consulted very much and very skillfully for the good of humanity, of those two chose the freedom of the will, to confirm which he denied the foreknowledge of future things; and thus, wishing to make men free he makes them sacrilegious. But the religious mind chooses both, confesses both, and maintains both by the faith of piety. But how so? says Cicero; for the knowledge of future things being granted, there follows a chain of consequences which ends in this, that there can be nothing depending on our own free wills. And further, if there is anything depending on our wills, we must go backward by the same steps of reasoning till we arrive at the conclusion that there is no foreknowledge of future things. For we go backward through all the steps in the following order: If there is free will, all things do not happen according to fate; if all things do not happen according to fate, there is not a certain order of causes; and if there is not a certain order of causes, neither is there a certain order of things foreknown by God—for things cannot come to pass except they are preceded by efficient causes—but, if there is no fixed and certain order of causes foreknown by God, all things cannot be said to happen according as He foreknew that they would happen. And further, if it is not true that all things happen just as they have been foreknown by Him, there is not, says he, in God any foreknowledge of future events.

Now, against the sacrilegious and impious darings of reason, we assert both that God knows all things before they come to pass, and that we do by our free will whatsoever we know and feel to be done by us only because we will it. But that all things come to pass by fate, we do not say; no we affirm that nothing comes to pass by fate; for we demonstrate that the name of fate, as it is wont to be used by those who speak of fate, meaning thereby the position of the stars at the time of each one's conception or birth, is an unmeaning word, for astrology itself is a delusion. But an order of causes in which the highest efficiency is attributed to the will of God, we neither deny nor do we designate it by the name of fate, unless, perhaps, we may understand fate to mean that which is spoken, deriving it from *fari*, to speak; for we cannot deny that it is written in the sacred Scriptures, "God hath spoken once; these two things have I heard, that power belongeth unto God. Also unto Thee, O God, belongeth mercy: for Thou wilt render unto every man according to his works."[4] Now the expression "once has He spoken" is to be understood as meaning "immovably," that is, unchangeably has He spoken, inasmuch as He knows unchangeably all things which shall be, and all things which He will do. We might, then, use the word *fate* in the sense it bears when derived from *fari*, to speak, had it not already come to be understood in another sense, into which I am unwilling that the hearts of men should unconsciously slide. But it does not follow that, though there is for God a certain order of all causes, there must therefore be nothing depending on the free exercise of our own wills, for our wills themselves are included in that order of causes which is certain to God, and is embraced by His foreknowledge, for human wills are also causes of human actions; and He who foreknew all the causes of things would certainly among those causes not have been ignorant of our wills. For even that very concession which Cicero himself makes is enough to refute him in this argument. For what does it help him to say that nothing takes place without a cause, but that every cause is not fatal, there being a fortuitous cause, a natural cause, and a voluntary cause? It is sufficient that he confesses that whatever happens must be preceded by a cause. For we say that those causes which are called fortuitous are not a mere name for the absence of causes, but are only latent, and we attribute them either to the will of the true God, or to that of spirits of some kind or other. And as to natural causes, we by no means separate them from the will of Him who is the author and framer of all nature. But now as to voluntary causes. They are referable either to God, or to angels, or to men, or to animals of whatever description, if indeed those instinctive movements of animals devoid of reason, by which, in accordance with their own nature, they seek or shun various things, are to be called wills. And when I speak of the wills of angels, I mean either the wills of good angels, whom we call the angels of God, or of the wicked angels, whom we call the angels of the devil, or demons. Also by the wills of men I mean the wills either of the good or of the wicked. And from this we conclude that there are no efficient causes of all things which come to pass unless voluntary causes, that is, such as belong to that nature which is the spirit of life. For the air or wind is called spirit, but, inasmuch as it is a body, it is not the spirit of life. The spirit of life, therefore, which quickens all things, and is the creator of every body, and of every created spirit, is God Himself, the uncreated spirit. In His supreme will resides the power which acts on the wills of all created spirits, helping the good, judging the evil, controlling all, granting power to some, not granting it to others. For, as He is the creator of all natures, so also is He the bestower of all powers, not of all wills; for wicked wills are not from Him, being contrary to nature, which is from Him. As to bodies, they are more subject to wills: some to our wills, by which I mean the wills of all living mortal creatures, but more to the wills of men than of beasts. But all of them are most of all subject to the will of God, to whom all wills also are subject, since they have no power except what He has bestowed upon them. The cause of things, therefore, which makes but is not made, is God; but all other causes both make and are made. Such are all created spirits, and especially the rational. Material causes, therefore, which may rather be said to be made than to make, are not to be reckoned among efficient causes, because they can only do what the wills of spirits do by them. How, then, does an order of causes which is certain to the foreknowledge of God necessitate that there should be nothing which is dependent on our wills, when our wills themselves have a very important place in the order of causes? Cicero, then, contends with those who call this order of causes fatal, or rather designate this order itself by the name of fate; to which we have an abhorrence, especially on account of the word, which men have become accustomed to understand as meaning what is not true. But, whereas he denies that the order of all causes is most certain, and perfectly clear to the prescience of God, we detest his opinion more than the Stoics do. For he either denies that God exists—which, indeed, in an assumed personage, he has labored to do, in his book *De Natura Deorum*—or if he confesses that He exists, but denies that He is prescient of future things, what is that but just "the fool saying in his heart there is no God"? For one who is not prescient of all future things is not God. Wherefore our wills also have just so much power as God willed and foreknew that they should have; and therefore whatever power they have, they have it within most certain limits; and whatever they are to do, they are most assuredly to do, for He whose foreknowledge is infallible foreknew that they would have the power to do it, and would do it. Wherefore, if I should choose to apply the name of fate to anything at all, I should rather say that fate belongs to the weaker of two parties, will to the stronger, who has the other in his power, than that the freedom of our will is excluded by that order of causes, which, by an unusual application of the word peculiar to themselves, the Stoics call *Fate*.

---

1. *Cicero De Divinat.* 2.
2. Ps. 14:1.
3. Book 3.
4. Ps. 62:11–12.

10. WHETHER OUR WILLS ARE RULED BY NECESSITY

Wherefore, neither is that necessity to be feared, for dread of which the Stoics labored to make such distinctions among the causes of things as should enable them to rescue certain things from the dominion of necessity, and to subject others to it. Among those things which they wished not to be subject to necessity they placed our wills, knowing that they would not be free if subjected to necessity. For if that is to be called our necessity which is not in our power, but even though we be unwilling effects what it can effect—as, for instance, the necessity of death—it is manifest that our wills by which we live uprightly or wickedly are not under such a necessity; for we do many things which, if we were not willing, we should certainly not do. This is primarily true of the act of willing itself—for if we will, it is; if we will not, it is not—for we should not will if we were unwilling. But if we define necessity to be that according to which we say that it is necessary that anything be of such or such a nature, or be done in such and such a manner, I know not why we should have any dread of that necessity taking away the freedom of our will. For we do not put the life of God or the foreknowledge of God under necessity if we should say that it is necessary that God should live forever, and foreknow all things; as neither is His power diminished when we say that He cannot die or fall into error—for this is in such a way impossible to Him, that if it were possible for Him, He would be of less power. But assuredly He is rightly called omnipotent, though He can neither die nor fall into error. For He is called omnipotent on account of His doing what He wills, not on account of His suffering what He wills not; for if that should befall Him, He would by no means be omnipotent. Wherefore, He cannot do some things for the very reason that He is omnipotent. So also, when we say that it is necessary that, when we will, we will by free choice, in so saying we both affirm what is true beyond doubt, and do not still subject our wills thereby to a necessity which destroys liberty. Our wills, therefore, *exist* as *wills*, and do themselves whatever we do by willing, and which would not be done if we were unwilling. But when anyone suffers anything, being unwilling by the will of another, even in that case will retains its essential validity—we do not mean the will of the party who inflicts the suffering, for we resolve it into the power of God. For if a will should simply exist, but not be able to do what it wills, it would be overborne by a more powerful will. Nor would this be the case unless there had existed will, and that not the will of the other party, but the will of him who willed, but was not able to accomplish what he willed. Therefore, whatsoever a man suffers contrary to his own will, he ought not to attribute to the will of men, or of angels, or of any created spirit, but rather to His will who gives power to wills. It is not the case, therefore, that because God foreknew what would be in the power of our wills, there is for that reason nothing in the power of our wills. For he who foreknew this did not foreknow nothing. Moreover, if He who foreknew what would be in the power of our wills did not foreknow nothing, but something, assuredly, even though He did foreknow, there is something in the power of our wills. Therefore we are by no means compelled, either, retaining the prescience of God, to take away the freedom of the will, or, retaining the freedom of the will, to deny that He is prescient of future things, which is impious. But we embrace both. We faithfully and sincerely confess both. The former, that we may believe well; the latter, that we may live well. For he lives ill who does not believe well concerning God. Wherefore, be it far from us, in order to maintain our freedom, to deny the prescience of Him by whose help we are or shall be free. Consequently, it is not in vain that laws are enacted, and that reproaches, exhortations, praises, and vituperations are had recourse to; for these also He foreknew, and they are of great avail, even as great as He foreknew that they would be of. Prayers, also, are of avail to procure those things which He foreknew that He would grant to those who offered them; and with justice have rewards been appointed for good deeds, and punishments for sins. For a man does not therefore sin because God foreknew that he would sin. No, it cannot be doubted but that it is the man himself who sins when he does sin, because He, whose foreknowledge is infallible, foreknew not that fate, or fortune, or something else would sin, but that the man himself would sin, who, if he wills not, sins not. But if he shall not will to sin, even this did God foreknow.

11. CONCERNING THE UNIVERSAL PROVIDENCE OF GOD IN THE LAWS OF WHICH ALL THINGS ARE COMPREHENDED

Therefore God supreme and true, with His Word and Holy Spirit (which three are one), one God omnipotent, creator and maker of every soul and of every body; by whose gift all are happy who are happy through verity and not through vanity; who made man a rational animal consisting of soul and body, who, when he sinned, neither permitted him to go unpunished, nor left him without mercy; who has given to the good and to the evil, being in common with stones, vegetable life in common with trees, sensuous life in common with brutes, intellectual life in common with angels alone; from whom is every mode, every species, every order; from whom are measure, number, weight; from whom is everything which has an existence in nature, of whatever kind it be, and of whatever value; from whom are the seeds of forms and the forms of seeds, and the motion of seeds and of forms; who gave also to flesh its origin, beauty, health, reproductive fecundity, disposition of members, and the salutary concord of its parts; who also to the irrational soul has given memory, sense, appetite, but to the rational soul, in addition to these, has given intelligence and will; who has not left, not to speak of heaven and earth, angels and men, but not even the entrails of the smallest and most contemptible animal, or the feather of a bird, or the little flower of a plant, or the leaf of a tree, without a harmony, and, as it were, a mutual peace among all its parts; that God can never be believed to have left the kingdoms of men, their dominations and servitudes, outside of the laws of His providence.

12. BY WHAT VIRTUES THE ANCIENT ROMANS MERITED THAT THE TRUE GOD, ALTHOUGH THEY DID NOT WORSHIP HIM, SHOULD ENLARGE THEIR EMPIRE

Wherefore let us go on to consider what virtues of the Romans they were which the true God, in whose power are also the kingdoms of the earth, condescended to help in order to raise the empire, and also for what reason He did so. And, in order to discuss this question on clearer ground, we have written the former books, to show that the power of those gods, who, they thought, were to be worshiped with such trifling and silly rites, had nothing to do in this matter; and also what we have already accomplished of the present volume, to refute the doctrine of fate, lest anyone who might have been already persuaded that the Roman Empire was not extended and preserved by the worship of these gods, might still be attributing its extension and preservation to some kind of fate, rather than to the most powerful will of God most high. The ancient and primitive Romans, therefore, though their history shows us that, like all the other nations, with the sole exception of the Hebrews, they worshiped false gods, and sacrificed victims, not to God, but to demons, have nevertheless this commendation bestowed on them by their historian, that they were "greedy of praise, prodigal of wealth, desirous of great glory, and content with a moderate fortune."[1] Glory they most ardently loved: for it they wished to live, for it they did not hesitate to die. Every other desire was repressed by the strength of their passion for that one thing. At length their country itself, because it seemed inglorious to serve, but glorious to rule and to command, they first earnestly desired to be free, and then to be mistress. Hence it was that, not enduring the domination of kings, they put the government into the hands of two chiefs, holding office for a year, who were called consuls, not kings or lords.[2] But royal pomp seemed inconsistent with the administration of a ruler (*regentis*), or the benevolence of one who consults (that is, for the public good) (*consulentis*), but rather with the haughtiness of a lord (*dominantis*). King Tarquin, therefore, having been banished, and the consular government having been instituted, it followed, as the same author already alluded to says in his praises of the Romans, that "the state grew with amazing rapidity after it had obtained liberty, so great a desire of glory had taken possession of it." That eagerness for praise and desire of glory, then, was that which accomplished those many wonderful things, laudable, doubtless, and glorious according to human judgment. The same Sallust praises the great men of his own time, Marcus Cato, and Caius Cæsar, saying that for a long time the republic had no one great in virtue, but that within his memory there had been these two men of eminent virtue, and very different pursuits. Now, among the praises which he pronounces on Cæsar he put this, that he wished for a great empire, an army, and a new war, that he might have a sphere where his genius and virtue might shine forth. Thus it was ever the prayer of men of heroic character that Bellona would excite miserable nations to war, and lash them into agitation with her bloody scourge, so that there might be occasion for the display of their valor. This, forsooth, is what that desire of praise and thirst for glory did. Wherefore, by the love of liberty in the first place, afterward also by that of domination and through the desire of praise and glory, they achieved many great things; and their most eminent poet testifies to their having been prompted by all these motives:

> Porsenna there, with pride elate,
> Bids Rome to Tarquin ope her gate;
> With arms he hems the city in,
> Æneas's sons stand firm to win.[3]

At that time it was their greatest ambition either to die bravely or to live free; but when liberty was obtained, so great a desire of glory took possession of them, that liberty alone was not enough unless domination also should be sought, their great ambition being that which the same poet puts into the mouth of Jupiter:

> *Nay, Juno's self, whose wild alarms*
> *Set ocean, earth, and heaven in arms,*
> *Shall change for smiles her moody frown,*
> *And vie with me in zeal to crown*
> *Rome's sons, the nation of the gown.*
> *So stands my will. There comes a day,*
> *While Rome's great ages hold their way,*
> *When old Assaracus's sons*
> *Shall quit them on the myrmidons,*
> *O'er Phthia and Mycenæ reign,*
> *And humble Argos to their chain.*[4]

Which things, indeed, Virgil makes Jupiter predict as future, while, in reality, he was only himself passing in review in his own mind, things which were already done, and which were beheld by him as present realities. But I have mentioned them with the intention of showing that, next to liberty, the Romans so highly esteemed domination, that it received a place among those things on which they bestowed the greatest praise. Hence also it is that that poet, preferring to the arts of other nations those arts which peculiarly belong to the Romans, namely, the arts of ruling and commanding, and of subjugating and vanquishing nations, says,

> *Others, belike, with happier grace,*
> *From bronze or stone shall call the face,*
> *Plead doubtful causes, map the skies,*
> *And tell when planets set or rise;*
> *But Roman thou, do thou control*
> *The nations far and wide;*
> *Be this thy genius, to impose*

The rule of peace on vanquished foes,
Show pity to the humble soul,
And crush the sons of pride.[5]

These arts they exercised with the more skill the less they gave themselves up to pleasures, and to enervation of body and mind in coveting and amassing riches, and through these corrupting morals, by extorting them from the miserable citizens and lavishing them on base stage players. Hence these men of base character, who abounded when Sallust wrote and Virgil sang these things, did not seek after honors and glory by these arts, but by treachery and deceit. Wherefore the same says, "But at first it was rather ambition than avarice that stirred the minds of men, which vice, however, is nearer to virtue. For glory, honor, and power are desired alike by the good man and by the ignoble; but the former," he says, "strives onward to them by the true way, while the other, knowing nothing of the good arts, seeks them by fraud and deceit."[6] And what is meant by seeking the attainment of glory, honor, and power by good arts, is to seek them by virtue, and not by deceitful intrigue; for the good and the ignoble man alike desire these things, but the good man strives to overtake them by the true way. The way is virtue, along which he presses as to the goal of possession—namely, to glory, honor, and power. Now that this was a sentiment engrained in the Roman mind, is indicated even by the temples of their gods; for they built in very close proximity the temples of Virtue and Honor, worshiping as gods the gifts of God. Hence we can understand what they who were good thought to be the end of virtue, and to what they ultimately referred it, namely, to honor; for, as to the bad, they had no virtue though they desired honor, and strove to possess it by fraud and deceit. Praise of a higher kind is bestowed upon Cato, for he says of him, "The less he sought glory, the more it followed him."[7] We say praise of a higher kind; for the glory with the desire of which the Romans burned is the judgment of men thinking well of men. And therefore virtue is better, which is content with no human judgment save that of one's own conscience. Whence the apostle says, "For this is our glory, the testimony of our conscience."[8] And in another place he says, "But let every one prove his own work, and then he shall have glory in himself, and not in another."[9] That glory, honor, and power, therefore, which they desired for themselves, and to which the good sought to attain by good arts, should not be sought after by virtue, but virtue by them. For there is no true virtue except that which is directed toward that end in which is the highest and ultimate good of man. Wherefore even the honors which Cato sought he ought not to have sought, but the state ought to have conferred them on him unsolicited, on account of his virtues.

But, of the two great Romans of that time, Cato was he whose virtue was by far the nearest to the true idea of virtue. Wherefore, let us refer to the opinion of Cato himself, to discover what was the judgment he had formed concerning the condition of the state both then and in former times. "I do not think," he says, "that it was by arms that our ancestors made the republic great from being small. Had that been the case, the republic of our day would have been by far more flourishing than that of their times, for the number of our allies and citizens is far greater; and, besides, we possess a far greater abundance of armor and of horses than they did. But it was other things than these that made them great, and we have none of them: industry at home, just government without, a mind free in deliberation, addicted neither to crime nor to lust. Instead of these, we have luxury and avarice, poverty in the state, opulence among citizens; we laud riches, we follow laziness; there is no difference made between the good and the bad; all the rewards of virtue are got possession of by intrigue. And no wonder, when every individual consults only for his own good, when you are the slaves of pleasure at home, and, in public affairs, of money and favor, no wonder that an onslaught is made upon the unprotected republic."[10]

He who hears these words of Cato or of Sallust probably thinks that such praise bestowed on the ancient Romans was applicable to all of them, or, at least, to very many of them. It is not so; otherwise the things which Cato himself writes, and which I have quoted in the second book of this work, would not be true. In that passage he says, that even from the very beginning of the state wrongs were committed by the more powerful, which led to the separation of the people from the fathers, besides which there were other internal dissensions; and the only time at which there existed a just and moderate administration was after the banishment of the kings, and that no longer than while they had cause to be afraid of Tarquin, and were carrying on the grievous war which had been undertaken on his account against Etruria; but afterward the fathers oppressed the people as slaves, flogged them as the kings had done, drove them from their land, and, to the exclusion of all others, held the government in their own hands alone. And to these discords, while the fathers were wishing to rule, and the people were unwilling to serve, the second Punic war put an end; for again great fear began to press upon their disquieted minds, holding them back from those distractions by another and greater anxiety, and bringing them back to civil concord. But the great things which were then achieved were accomplished through the administration of a few men, who were good in their own way. And by the wisdom and forethought of these few good men, which first enabled the republic to endure these evils and mitigated them, it waxed greater and greater. And this the same historian affirms, when he says that, reading and hearing of the many illustrious achievements of the Roman people in peace and in war, by land and by sea, he wished to understand what it was by which these great things were specially sustained. For he knew that very often the Romans had with a small company contended with great legions of the enemy; and he knew also that with small resources they had carried on wars with opulent kings. And he says that, after having given the matter much consideration, it seemed evident to him that the preeminent virtue of a few citizens had achieved the whole, and that that explained how poverty overcame wealth, and small numbers great multitudes. But, he adds, after that the state had been corrupted by luxury and indolence, again the republic, by its own greatness, was able to bear the vices of its magistrates and generals. Wherefore even the praises of Cato are only applicable to a few; for only a few were possessed of that virtue which leads men to pursue after glory, honor, and power by the true way—that is, by virtue itself. This industry at home, of which Cato speaks, was the consequence of a desire to enrich the public treasury, even though the result should be poverty at home; and therefore, when he speaks of the evil arising out of the corruption of morals, he reverses the expression, and says, "Poverty in the state, riches at home."

---

1. *Sallust De Conj. Cat. 7.*
2. Augustine notes that the name consul is derived from *consulere,* and thus signifies a more benign rule than that of a *rex* (from *regere*), or *dominus* (from *dominari*).
3. Virgil *Æneid* 8.646.
4. Ibid., 1.279.
5. Ibid., 6.847.
6. *Sallust De Conj. Cat. 11.*
7. Ibid., 54.
8. 2 Cor. 1:12.
9. Gal. 6:4.
10. *Sallust De Conj. Cat. 52.*

13. CONCERNING THE LOVE OF PRAISE, WHICH, THOUGH IT IS A VICE, IS RECKONED A VIRTUE, BECAUSE BY IT GREATER VICE IS RESTRAINED

Wherefore, when the kingdoms of the East had been illustrious for a long time, it pleased God that there should also arise a Western empire, which, though later in time, should be more illustrious in extent and greatness. And, in order that it might overcome the grievous evils which existed among other nations, He purposely granted it to such men as, for the sake of honor, and praise, and glory, consulted well for their country, in whose glory they sought their own, and whose safety they did not hesitate to prefer to their own, suppressing the desire of wealth and many other vices for this one vice, namely, the love of praise. For he has the soundest perception who recognizes that even the love of praise is a vice; nor has this escaped the perception of the poet Horace, who says,

You're bloated by ambition? take advice:

*Yon book will ease you if you read it
   thrice.*[1]

And the same poet, in a lyric song, has thus spoken with the desire of repressing the passion for domination:

*Rule an ambitious spirit, and thou hast
A wider kingdom than if thou shouldst
   join
To distant Gades Lybia, and thus
Shouldst hold in service either
   Carthaginian.*[2]

Nevertheless, they who restrain baser lusts, not by the power of the Holy Spirit obtained by the faith of piety, or by the love of intelligible beauty, but by desire of human praise, or, at all events, restrain them better by the love of such praise, are not indeed yet holy, but only less base. Even Tully [Cicero] was not able to conceal this fact; for, in the same books which he wrote, *De Republica*, when speaking concerning the education of a chief of the state, who ought, he says, to be nourished on glory, goes on to say that their ancestors did many wonderful and illustrious things through desire of glory. So far, therefore, from resisting this vice, they even thought that it ought to be excited and kindled up, supposing that that would be beneficial to the republic. But not even in his books on philosophy does Tully dissimulate this poisonous opinion, for he there avows it more clearly than day. For when he is speaking of those studies which are to be pursued with a view to the true good, and not with the vainglorious desire of human praise, he introduces the following universal and general statement:

Honor nourishes the arts, and all are stimulated to the prosecution of studies by glory; and those pursuits are always neglected which are generally discredited.[3]

---

1. Horace *Ep.* 1.50.36–37.
2. Horace *Carm.* 2.2.
3. Cicero *Tusc. Disp.* 1.2.

14. CONCERNING THE ERADICATION OF THE LOVE OF HUMAN PRAISE, BECAUSE ALL THE GLORY OF THE RIGHTEOUS IS IN GOD

It is, therefore, doubtless far better to resist this desire than to yield to it, for the purer one is from this defilement, the more like is he to God; and, though this vice be not thoroughly eradicated from his heart—for it does not cease to tempt even the minds of those who are making good progress in virtue—at any rate, let the desire of glory be surpassed by the love of righteousness, so that, if there be seen anywhere "lying neglected things which are generally discredited," if they are good, if they are right, even the love of human praise may blush and yield to the love of truth. For so hostile is this vice to pious faith, if the love of glory be greater in the heart than the fear or love of God, that the Lord said, "How can ye believe, who look for glory from one another, and do not seek the glory which is from God alone?"[1] Also, concerning some who had believed on Him, but were afraid to confess Him openly, the evangelist says, "They loved the praise of men more than the praise of God";[2] which did not the holy apostles, who, when they proclaimed the name of Christ in those places where it was not only discredited, and therefore neglected—according as Cicero says, "Those things are always neglected which are generally discredited"—but was even held in the utmost detestation, holding to what they had heard from the good Master, who was also the Physician of minds, "If anyone shall deny Me before men, him will I also deny before My Father who is in heaven, and before the angels of God,"[3] amid maledictions and reproaches, and most grievous persecutions and cruel punishments, were not deterred from the preaching of human salvation by the noise of human indignation. And when, as they did and spoke divine things, and lived divine lives, conquering, as it were, hard hearts, and introducing into them the peace of righteousness, great glory followed them in the church of Christ, they did not rest in that as in the end of their virtue, but, referring that glory itself to the glory of God, by whose grace they were what they were, they sought to kindle, also by that same flame, the minds of those for whose good they consulted, to the love of Him, by whom they could be made to be what they themselves were. For their Master had taught them not to seek to be good for the sake of human glory, saying, "Take heed that ye do not your righteousness before men to be seen of them, or otherwise ye shall not have a reward from your Father who is in heaven."[4] But again, lest, understanding this wrongly, they should, through fear of pleasing men, be less useful through concealing their goodness, showing for what end they ought to make it known, He says, "Let your works shine before men, that they may see your good deeds, and glorify your Father who is in heaven."[5] Not, observe, "that ye may be seen by them, that is, in order that their eyes may be directed upon you"—for of yourselves you are nothing—but "that they may glorify your Father who is in heaven," by fixing their regards on whom they may become such as you are. These the martyrs followed, who surpassed the Scævolas, and the Curtiuses, and the Deciuses, both in true virtue, because in true piety, and also in the greatness of their number. But since those Romans were in an earthly city, and had before them, as the end of all the offices undertaken in its behalf, its safety, and a kingdom, not in heaven, but in earth—not in the sphere of eternal life, but in the sphere of demise and succession, where the dead are succeeded by the dying—what else but glory should they love, by which they wished even after death to live in the mouths of their admirers?

---

1. John 5:44.
2. John 12:43.
3. Matt. 10:33.
4. Matt. 6:1.
5. Matt. 5:16.

15. CONCERNING THE TEMPORAL REWARD WHICH GOD GRANTED TO THE VIRTUES OF THE ROMANS

Now, therefore, with regard to those to whom God did not purpose to give eternal life with His holy angels in His own celestial city, to the society of which that true piety which does not render the service of religion, which the Greeks call λατρεία, to any save the true God conducts, if He had also withheld from them the terrestrial glory of that most excellent empire, a reward would not have been rendered to their good arts—that is, their virtues—by which they sought to attain so great glory. For as to those who seem to do some good that they may receive glory from men, the Lord also says, "Verily I say unto you, they have received their reward."[1] So also these despised their own private affairs for the sake of the republic, and for its treasury resisted avarice, consulted for the good of their country with a spirit of freedom, addicted neither to what their laws pronounced to be crime nor to lust. By all these acts, as by the true way, they pressed forward to honors, power, and glory; they were honored among almost all nations; they imposed the laws of their empire upon many nations; and at this day, both in literature and history, they are glorious among almost all nations. There is no reason why they should complain against the justice of the supreme and true God —"they have received their reward."

---

1. Matt. 6:2.

16. CONCERNING THE REWARD OF THE HOLY CITIZENS OF THE CELESTIAL CITY, TO WHOM THE EXAMPLE OF THE VIRTUES OF THE ROMANS ARE USEFUL

But the reward of the saints is far different, who even here endured reproaches for that city of God which is hateful to the lovers of this world. That city is eternal. There none are born, for none die. There is true and full felicity—not a goddess, but a gift of God. Thence we receive the pledge of faith while on our pilgrimage we sigh for its beauty. There rises not the sun on the good and the evil, but the Sun of righteousness protects the good alone. There no great industry shall be expended to enrich the public treasury by suffering privations at home, for there is the common treasury of truth. And, therefore, it was not only for the sake of recompensing the citizens of Rome that her empire and glory had been so signally extended, but also that the citizens of that eternal city, during their pilgrimage here, might diligently and soberly contemplate these examples, and see what a love they owe to the supernal country on account of life eternal, if the terrestrial country was so much beloved by its citizens on account of human glory.

17. TO WHAT PROFIT THE ROMANS CARRIED ON WARS, AND HOW MUCH THEY CONTRIBUTED TO THE WELL-BEING OF THOSE WHOM THEY CONQUERED

For, as far as this life of mortals is concerned, which is spent and ended in a few days, what does it matter under whose government a dying man lives, if they who govern do not force him to impiety and iniquity? Did the Romans at all harm those nations, on whom, when subjugated, they imposed their laws, except in as far as that was accomplished with great slaughter in war? Now, had it been done with consent of the nations, it would have been done with greater success, but there would have been no glory of conquest, for neither did the Romans themselves live exempt from those laws which they imposed on others. Had this been done without Mars and Bellona, so that there should have been no place for victory, no one conquering where no one had fought, would not the condition of the Romans and of the other nations have been one and the same, especially if that had been done at once which afterward was done most humanely and most acceptably, namely, the admission of all to the rights of Roman citizens who belonged to the Roman Empire, and if that had been made the privilege of all which was formerly the privilege of a few, with this one condition, that the humbler class who had no lands of their own should live at the public expense—an alimentary impost, which would have been paid with a much better grace by them into the hands of good administrators of the republic, of which they were members, by their own hearty consent, than it would have been paid with had it to be extorted from them as conquered men? For I do not see what it makes for the safety, good morals, and certainly not for the dignity, of men, that some have conquered and others have been conquered, except that it yields them that most insane pomp of human glory, in which "they have received their reward," who burned with excessive desire of it, and carried on most eager wars. For do not their lands pay tribute? Have they any privilege of learning what the others are not privileged to learn? Are there not many senators in the other countries who do not even know Rome by sight? Take away outward show,[1] and what are all men after all but men? But even though the perversity of the age should permit that all the better men should be more highly honored than others, neither thus should human honor be held at a great price, for it is smoke which has no weight. But let us avail ourselves even in these things of the kindness of God. Let us consider how great things they despised, how great things they endured, what lusts they subdued for the sake of human glory, who merited that glory, as it were, in reward for such virtues; and let this be useful to us even in suppressing pride, so that, as that city in which it has been promised us to reign as far surpasses this one as heaven is distant from the earth, as eternal life surpasses temporal joy, solid glory empty praise, or the society of angels the society of mortals, or the glory of Him who made the sun and moon the light of the sun and moon, the citizens of so great a country may not seem to themselves to have done anything very great, if, in order to obtain it, they have done some good works or endured some evils, when those men for this terrestrial country already obtained, did such great things, suffered such great things. And especially are all these things to be considered, because the remission of sins which collects citizens to the celestial country has something in it to which a shadowy resemblance is found in that asylum of Romulus, whither escape from the punishment of all manner of crimes congregated that multitude with which the state was to be founded.

---

1. Jactantia.

18. HOW FAR CHRISTIANS OUGHT TO BE FROM BOASTING, IF THEY HAVE DONE ANYTHING FOR THE LOVE OF THE ETERNAL COUNTRY, WHEN THE ROMANS DID SUCH GREAT THINGS FOR HUMAN GLORY AND A TERRESTRIAL CITY

What great thing, therefore, is it for that eternal and celestial city to despise all the charms of this world, however pleasant, if for the sake of this terrestrial city Brutus could even put to death his son—a sacrifice which the heavenly city compels no one to make? But certainly it is more difficult to put to death one's sons, than to do what is required to be done for the heavenly country, even to distribute to the poor those things which were looked upon as things to be massed and laid up for one's children, or to let them go, if there arise any temptation which compels us to do so, for the sake of faith and righteousness. For it is not earthly riches which make us or our sons happy; for they must either be lost by us in our lifetime, or be possessed when we are dead, by whom we know not, or perhaps by whom we would not. But it is God who makes us happy, who is the true riches of minds. But of Brutus, even the poet who celebrates his praises testifies that it was the occasion of unhappiness to him that he slew his son, for he says,

> *And call his own rebellious seed*
> *For menaced liberty to bleed.*
> *Unhappy father! howsoe'er*
> *The deed be judged by after days.*[1]

But in the following verse he consoles him in his unhappiness, saying,

> *His country's love shall all o'erbear.*

There are those two things, namely, liberty and the desire of human praise, which compelled the Romans to admirable deeds. If, therefore, for the liberty of dying men, and for the desire of human praise which is sought after by mortals, sons could be put to death by a father, what great thing is it, if, for the true liberty which has made us free from the dominion of sin, and death, and the devil—not through the desire of human praise, but through the earnest desire of freeing men, not from King Tarquin, but from demons and the prince of the demons—we should, I do not say put to death our sons, but reckon among our sons Christ's poor ones? If, also, another Roman chief, surnamed Torquatus, slew his son, not because he fought against his country, but because, being challenged by an enemy, he through youthful impetuosity fought, though for his country, yet contrary to orders which he his father had given as general; and this he did, notwithstanding that his son was victorious, lest there should be more evil in the example of authority despised, than good in the glory of slaying an enemy; if, I say, Torquatus acted thus, wherefore should they boast themselves, who, for the laws of a celestial country, despise all earthly good things, which are loved far less than sons? If Furius Camillus, who was condemned by those who envied him, notwithstanding that he had thrown off from the necks of his countrymen the yoke of their most bitter enemies, the Veientes, again delivered his ungrateful country from the Gauls, because he had no other in which he could have better opportunities for living a life of glory; if Camillus did thus, why should he be extolled as having done some great thing, who, having, it may be, suffered in the church at the hands of carnal enemies most grievous and dishonoring injury, has not betaken himself to heretical enemies, or himself raised some heresy against her, but has rather defended her, as far as he was able, from the most pernicious perversity of heretics, since there is not another church, I say not in which one can live a life of glory, but in which eternal life can be obtained? If Mucius, in order that peace might be made with King Porsenna, who was pressing the Romans with a most grievous war, when he did not succeed in slaying Porsenna, but slew another by mistake for him, reached forth his right hand and laid it on a red-hot altar, saying that many such as he saw him to be had conspired for his destruction, so that Porsenna, terrified at his daring, and at the thought of a conspiracy of such as he, without any delay recalled all his warlike purposes, and made peace; if, I say, Mucius did this, who shall speak of his meritorious claims to the kingdom of heaven, if for it he may have given to the flames not one hand, but even his whole body, and that not by his own spontaneous act, but because he was persecuted by another? If Curtius, spurring on his steed, threw himself all armed into a precipitous gulf, obeying the oracles of their gods, which had commanded that the Romans should throw into that gulf the best thing which they possessed, and they could only understand thereby that, since they excelled in men and arms, the gods had commanded that an armed man should be cast headlong into that destruction; if he did this, shall we say that that man has done a great thing for the eternal city who may have died by a like death, not, however, precipitating himself spontaneously into a gulf, but having suffered this death at the hands of some enemy of his faith, more especially when he has received from his Lord, who is also King of his country, a more certain oracle, "Fear not them who kill the body, but cannot kill the soul"?[2] If the Decii dedicated themselves to death, consecrating themselves in a form of words, as it were, that falling, and pacifying by their blood the wrath of the gods, they might be the means of delivering the Roman army; if they did this, let not the holy martyrs carry themselves proudly, as though they had done some meritorious thing for a share in that country where are eternal life and felicity, if even to the shedding of their blood, loving not only the brethren for whom it was shed, but, according as had been commanded them, even their enemies by whom it was being shed, they have vied with one another in faith of love and love of faith. If Marcus Pulvillus, when engaged in dedicating a temple to Jupiter, Juno, and Minerva, received with such indifference the false intelligence which was brought to him of the death of his son, with the intention of so agitating him that he should go away, and thus the glory of dedicating the temple should fall to his colleague; if he received that intelligence with such indifference that he even ordered that his son should be cast out unburied, the love of glory having overcome in his heart the grief of bereavement, how shall anyone affirm that he had done a great thing for the preaching of the gospel, by which the citizens of the heavenly city are delivered from diverse errors and gathered together from diverse wanderings, to whom his Lord has said, when anxious about the burial of his father, "Follow Me, and let the dead bury their dead"?[3] Regulus, in order not to break his oath, even with his most cruel enemies, returned to them from Rome itself, because (as he is said to have replied to the Romans when they wished to retain him) he could not have the dignity of an honorable citizen at Rome after having been a slave to the Africans, and the Carthaginians put him to death with the utmost tortures, because he had spoken against them in the senate. If Regulus acted thus, what tortures are not to be despised for the sake of good faith toward that country to whose beatitude faith itself leads? Or what will a man have rendered to the Lord for all He has bestowed upon him, if, for the faithfulness he owes to Him, he shall have suffered such things as Regulus suffered at the hands of his most ruthless enemies for the good faith which he owed to them? And how shall a Christian dare vaunt himself of his voluntary poverty, which he has chosen in order that during the pilgrimage of this life he may walk the more disencumbered on the way which leads to the country where the true riches are, even God Himself; how, I say, shall he vaunt himself for this, when he hears or reads that Lucius Valerius, who died when he was holding the office of consul, was so poor that his funeral expenses were paid with money collected by the people? Or when he hears that Quintius Cincinnatus, who, possessing only four acres of land, and cultivating them with his own hands, was taken from the plow to be made dictator—an office more honorable even than that of consul—and that, after having won great glory by conquering the enemy, he preferred notwithstanding to continue in his poverty? Or how shall he boast of having done a great thing, who has not been prevailed upon by the offer of any reward of this world to renounce his connection with that heavenly and eternal country, when he hears that Fabricius could not be prevailed on to forsake the Roman city by the great gifts offered to him by Pyrrhus king of the Epirots, who promised him the fourth part of his kingdom, but preferred to abide there in his poverty as a private individual? For if, when their republic—that is, the interest of the people, the interest of the country, the common interest

—was most prosperous and wealthy, they themselves were so poor in their own houses, that one of them, who had already been twice a consul, was expelled from that senate of poor men by the censor, because he was discovered to possess ten pounds weight of silverplate—since, I say, those very men by whose triumphs the public treasury was enriched were so poor, ought not all Christians, who make common property of their riches with a far nobler purpose, even that (according to what is written in the Acts of the Apostles) they may distribute to each one according to his need, and that no one may say that anything is his own, but that all things may be their common possession[4]—ought they not to understand that they should not vaunt themselves, because they do that to obtain the society of angels, when those men did well-nigh the same thing to preserve the glory of the Romans?

How could these, and whatever like things are found in the Roman history, have become so widely known, and have been proclaimed by so great a fame, had not the Roman Empire, extending far and wide, been raised to its greatness by magnificent successes? Wherefore, through that empire, so extensive and of so long continuance, so illustrious and glorious also through the virtues of such great men, the reward which they sought was rendered to their earnest aspirations, and also examples are set before us, containing necessary admonition, in order that we may be stung with shame if we shall see that we have not held fast those virtues for the sake of the most glorious city of God, which are, in whatever way, resembled by those virtues which they held fast for the sake of the glory of a terrestrial city, and that, too, if we shall feel conscious that we have held them fast, we may not be lifted up with pride, because, as the apostle says, "The sufferings of the present time are not worthy to be compared to the glory which shall be revealed in us."[5] But so far as regards human and temporal glory, the lives of these ancient Romans were reckoned sufficiently worthy. Therefore, also, we see, in the light of that truth which, veiled in the Old Testament, is revealed in the New, namely, that it is not in view of terrestrial and temporal benefits, which divine Providence grants promiscuously to good and evil, that God is to be worshiped, but in view of eternal life, everlasting gifts, and of the society of the heavenly city itself; in the light of this truth we see that the Jews were most righteously given as a trophy to the glory of the Romans; for we see that these Romans, who rested on earthly glory, and sought to obtain it by virtues, such as they were, conquered those who, in their great depravity, slew and rejected the giver of true glory, and of the eternal city.

---

1. Virgil *Æneid* 6.820.
2. Matt. 10:28.
3. Matt. 8:22.
4. Acts 2:45.
5. Rom. 8:18.

19. CONCERNING THE DIFFERENCE BETWEEN TRUE GLORY AND THE DESIRE OF DOMINATION

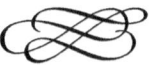

There is assuredly a difference between the desire of human glory and the desire of domination; for, though he who has an overweening delight in human glory will be also very prone to aspire earnestly after domination, nevertheless they who desire the true glory even of human praise strive not to displease those who judge well of them. For there are many good moral qualities, of which many are competent judges, although they are not possessed by many; and by those good moral qualities those men press on to glory, honor, and domination, of whom Sallust says, "But they press on by the true way."

But whosoever, without possessing that desire of glory which makes one fear to displease those who judge his conduct, desires domination and power, very often seeks to obtain what he loves by most open crimes. Therefore he who desires glory presses on to obtain it either by the true way, or certainly by deceit and artifice, wishing to appear good when he is not. Therefore to him who possesses virtues it is a great virtue to despise glory; for contempt of it is seen by God, but is not manifest to human judgment. For whatever anyone does before the eyes of men in order to show himself to be a despiser of glory, if they suspect that he is doing it in order to get greater praise—that is, greater glory—he has no means of demonstrating to the perceptions of those who suspect him that the case is really otherwise than they suspect it to be. But he who despises the judgment of praisers, despises also the rashness of suspectors. Their salvation, indeed, he does not despise, if he is truly good; for so great is the righteousness of that man who receives his virtues from the Spirit of God, that he loves his very enemies, and so loves them that he desires that his haters and detractors may be turned to righteousness, and become his associates, and that not in an earthly but in a heavenly country. But with respect to his praisers, though he sets little value on their praise, he does not set little value on their love; neither does he elude their praise, lest he should forfeit their love. And, therefore, he strives earnestly to have their praises directed to Him from whom everyone receives whatever in him is truly praiseworthy. But he who is a despiser of glory, but is greedy of domination, exceeds the beasts in the vices of cruelty and luxuriousness. Such, indeed, were certain of the Romans, who, wanting the love of esteem, wanted not the thirst for domination; and that there were many such, history testifies. But it was Nero Cæsar who was the first to reach the summit, and, as it were, the citadel, of this vice; for so great was his luxuriousness, that one would have thought there was nothing manly to be dreaded in him, and such his cruelty, that, had not the contrary been known, no one would have thought there was anything effeminate in his character. Nevertheless power and domination are not given even to such men save by the providence of the most high God, when He judges that the state of human affairs is worthy of such lords. The divine utterance is clear on this matter; for the Wisdom of God thus speaks: "By Me kings reign, and tyrants possess the land."[1] But, that it may not be thought that by "tyrants" is meant, not wicked and impious kings, but brave men, in accordance with the ancient use of the word, as when Virgil says,

> *For know that treaty may not stand*
> *Where king greets king and joins not*
> *hand,*[2]

in another place it is most unambiguously said of God, that He "maketh the man who is a hypocrite to reign on account of the perversity of the people."[3] Wherefore, though I have, according to my ability, shown for what reason God, who alone is true and just, helped forward the Romans, who were good according to a certain standard of an earthly state, to the acquirement of the glory of so great an empire, there may be, nevertheless, a more hidden cause, known better to God than to us, depending on the diversity of the merits of the human race. Among all who are truly pious, it is at all events agreed that no one without true piety—that is, true worship of the true God—can have true virtue; and that it is not true virtue which is the slave of human praise. Though, nevertheless, they who are not citizens of the eternal city, which is called the city of God in the sacred Scriptures, are more useful to the earthly city when they possess even that virtue than if they had not even that. But there could be nothing more fortunate for human affairs than that, by the mercy of God, they who are endowed with true piety of life, if they have the skill for ruling people, should also have the power. But such men, however great virtues they may possess in this life, attribute it solely to the grace of God that He has bestowed it on them—willing, believing, seeking. And, at the same time, they understand how far they are short of that perfection of righteousness which exists in the society of those holy angels for which they are striving to fit themselves. But however much that virtue may be praised and cried up, which without true piety is the slave of human glory, it is not at all to be compared even to the feeble beginnings of the virtue of the saints, whose hope is placed in the grace and mercy of the true God.

---

1. Prov. 8:15.
2. Virgil *Æneid* 7.266.
3. Job 34:30.

20. THAT IT IS AS SHAMEFUL FOR THE VIRTUES TO SERVE HUMAN GLORY AS BODILY PLEASURE

Philosophers—who place the end of human good in virtue itself, in order to put to shame certain other philosophers, who indeed approve of the virtues, but measure them all with reference to the end of bodily pleasure, and think that this pleasure is to be sought for its own sake, but the virtues on account of pleasure—are wont to paint a kind of word picture, in which Pleasure sits like a luxurious queen on a royal seat, and all the virtues are subjected to her as slaves, watching her nod, that they may do whatever she shall command. She commands Prudence to be ever on the watch to discover how Pleasure may rule, and be safe. Justice she orders to grant what benefits she can, in order to secure those friendships which are necessary for bodily pleasure; to do wrong to no one, lest, on account of the breaking of the laws, Pleasure be not able to live in security. Fortitude she orders to keep her mistress, that is, Pleasure, bravely in her mind, if any affliction befall her body which does not occasion death, in order that by remembrance of former delights she may mitigate the poignancy of present pain. Temperance she commands to take only a certain quantity even of the most favorite food, lest, through immoderate use, anything prove hurtful by disturbing the health of the body, and thus Pleasure, which the Epicureans make to consist chiefly in the health of the body, be grievously offended. Thus the virtues, with the whole dignity of their glory, will be the slaves of Pleasure, as of some imperious and disreputable woman.

There is nothing, say our philosophers, more disgraceful and monstrous than this picture, and which the eyes of good men can less endure. And they say the truth. But I do not think that the picture would be sufficiently becoming, even if it were made so that the virtues should be represented as the slaves of human glory; for, though that glory be not a luxurious woman, it is nevertheless puffed up, and has much vanity in it. Wherefore it is unworthy of the solidity and firmness of the virtues to represent them as serving this glory, so that Prudence shall provide nothing, Justice distribute nothing, Temperance moderate nothing, except to the end that men may be pleased and vainglory served. Nor will they be able to defend themselves from the charge of such baseness, while they, by way of being despisers of glory, disregard the judgment of other men, seem to themselves wise, and please themselves. For their virtue—if, indeed, it is virtue at all—is only in another way subjected to human praise; for he who seeks to please himself seeks still to please man. But he who, with true piety toward God, whom he loves, believes, and hopes in, fixes his attention more on those things in which he displeases himself, than on those things, if there are any such, which please himself, or rather, not himself, but the truth, does not attribute that by which he can now please the truth to anything but to the mercy of Him whom he has feared to displease, giving thanks for what in him is healed, and pouring out prayers for the healing of that which is yet unhealed.

21. THAT THE ROMAN DOMINION WAS GRANTED BY HIM FROM WHOM IS ALL POWER, AND BY WHOSE PROVIDENCE ALL THINGS ARE RULED

These things being so, we do not attribute the power of giving kingdoms and empires to any save to the true God, who gives happiness in the kingdom of heaven to the pious alone, but gives kingly power on earth both to the pious and the impious, as it may please Him, whose good pleasure is always just. For though we have said something about the principles which guide His administration, insofar as it has seemed good to Him to explain it, nevertheless it is too much for us, and far surpasses our strength, to discuss the hidden things of men's hearts, and by a clear examination to determine the merits of various kingdoms. He, therefore, who is the one true God, who never leaves the human race without just judgment and help, gave a kingdom to the Romans when He would, and as great as He would, as He did also to the Assyrians, and even the Persians, by whom, as their own books testify, only two gods are worshiped, the one good and the other evil—to say nothing concerning the Hebrew people, of whom I have already spoken as much as seemed necessary, who, as long as they were a kingdom, worshiped none save the true God. The same, therefore, who gave to the Persians harvests, though they did not worship the goddess Segetia, who gave the other blessings of the earth, though they did not worship the many gods which the Romans supposed to preside, each one over some particular thing, or even many of them over each several thing—He, I say, gave the Persians dominion, though they worshiped none of those gods to whom the Romans believed themselves indebted for the empire. And the same is true in respect of men as well as nations. He who gave power to Marius gave it also to Caius Cæsar; He who gave it to Augustus gave it also to Nero; He also who gave it to the most benignant emperors, the Vespasians, father and son, gave it also to the cruel Domitian; and, finally, to avoid the necessity of going over them all, He who gave it to the Christian Constantine gave it also to the apostate Julian, whose gifted mind was deceived by a sacrilegious and detestable curiosity, stimulated by the love of power. And it was because he was addicted through curiosity to vain oracles, that, confident of victory, he burned the ships which were laden with the provisions necessary for his army, and therefore, engaging with hot zeal in rashly audacious enterprises, he was soon slain, as the just consequence of his recklessness, and left his army unprovisioned in an enemy's country, and in such a predicament that it never could have escaped, save by altering the boundaries of the Roman Empire, in violation of that omen of the god Terminus of which I spoke in the preceding book; for the god Terminus yielded to necessity, though he had not yielded to Jupiter. Manifestly these things are ruled and governed by the one God according as He pleases; and if His motives are hid, are they therefore unjust?

22. THE DURATIONS AND ISSUES OF WAR DEPEND ON THE WILL OF GOD

Thus also the durations of wars are determined by Him as He may see meet, according to His righteous will, and pleasure, and mercy, to afflict or to console the human race, so that they are sometimes of longer, sometimes of shorter duration. The war of the Pirates and the third Punic war were terminated with incredible celerity. Also the war of the fugitive gladiators, though in it many Roman generals and the consuls were defeated, and Italy was terribly wasted and ravaged, was nevertheless ended in the third year, having itself been, during its continuance, the end of much. The Picentes, the Marsi, and the Peligni, not distant but Italian nations, after a long and most loyal servitude under the Roman yoke, attempted to raise their heads into liberty, though many nations had now been subjected to the Roman power, and Carthage had been overthrown. In this Italian war the Romans were very often defeated, and two consuls perished, besides other noble senators; nevertheless this calamity was not protracted over a long space of time, for the fifth year put an end to it. But the second Punic war, lasting for the space of eighteen years, and occasioning the greatest disasters and calamities to the republic, wore out and wellnigh consumed the strength of the Romans; for in two battles about seventy thousand Romans fell.[1] The first Punic war was terminated after having been waged for three-and-twenty years. The Mithridatic war was waged for forty years. And that no one may think that in the early and much belauded times of the Romans they were far braver and more able to bring wars to a speedy termination, the Samnite war was protracted for nearly fifty years; and in this war the Romans were so beaten that they were even put under the yoke. But because they did not love glory for the sake of justice, but seemed rather to have loved justice for the sake of glory, they broke the peace and the treaty which had been concluded. These things I mention, because many, ignorant of past things, and some also dissimulating what they know, if in Christian times they see any war protracted a little longer than they expected, straightway make a fierce and insolent attack on our religion, exclaiming that, but for it, the deities would have been supplicated still, according to ancient rites; and then, by that bravery of the Romans, which, with the help of Mars and Bellona, speedily brought to an end such great wars, this war also would be speedily terminated. Let them, therefore, who have read history recollect what long-continued wars, having various issues and entailing woeful slaughter, were waged by the ancient Romans, in accordance with the general truth that the earth, like the tempestuous deep, is subject to agitations from tempests—tempests of such evils, in various degrees—and let them sometimes confess what they do not like to own, and not, by madly speaking against God, destroy themselves and deceive the ignorant.

---

1. Of the Thrasymene Lake and Cannæ.

23. CONCERNING THE WAR IN WHICH RADAGAISUS, KING OF THE GOTHS, A WORSHIPER OF DEMONS, WAS CONQUERED IN ONE DAY, WITH ALL HIS MIGHTY FORCES

Nevertheless they do not mention with thanksgiving what God has very recently, and within our own memory, wonderfully and mercifully done, but as far as in them lies they attempt, if possible, to bury it in universal oblivion. But should we be silent about these things, we should be in like manner ungrateful. When Radagaisus, king of the Goths, having taken up his position very near to the city, with a vast and savage army, was already close upon the Romans, he was in one day so speedily and so thoroughly beaten, that, while not even one Roman was wounded, much less slain, far more than a hundred thousand of his army were prostrated, and he himself and his sons, having been captured, were forthwith put to death, suffering the punishment they deserved. For had so impious a man, with so great and so impious a host, entered the city, whom would he have spared? What tombs of the martyrs would he have respected? In his treatment of what person would he have manifested the fear of God? Whose blood would he have refrained from shedding? Whose chastity would he have wished to preserve inviolate? But how loud would they not have been in the praises of their gods! How insultingly they would have boasted, saying that Radagaisus had conquered, that he had been able to achieve such great things, because he propitiated and won over the gods by daily sacrifices—a thing which the Christian religion did not allow the Romans to do! For when he was approaching to those places where he was overwhelmed at the nod of the supreme Majesty, as his fame was everywhere increasing, it was being told us at Carthage that the pagans were believing, publishing, and boasting, that he, on account of the help and protection of the gods friendly to him, because of the sacrifices which he was said to be daily offering to them, would certainly not be conquered by those who were not performing such sacrifices to the Roman gods, and did not even permit that they should be offered by anyone. And now these wretched men do not give thanks to God for his great mercy, who, having determined to chastise the corruption of men, which was worthy of far heavier chastisement than the corruption of the barbarians, tempered His indignation with such mildness as, in the first instance, to cause that the king of the Goths should be conquered in a wonderful manner, lest glory should accrue to demons, whom he was known to be supplicating, and thus the minds of the weak should be overthrown; and then, afterward, to cause that, when Rome was to be taken, it should be taken by those barbarians who, contrary to any custom of all former wars, protected, through reverence for the Christian religion, those who fled for refuge to the sacred places, and who so opposed the demons themselves, and the rites of impious sacrifices, that they seemed to be carrying on a far more terrible war with them than with men. Thus did the true Lord and Governor of things both scourge the Romans mercifully, and, by the marvelous defeat of the worshipers of demons, show that those sacrifices were not necessary even for the safety of present things; so that, by those who do not obstinately hold out, but prudently consider the matter, true religion may not be deserted on account of the urgencies of the present time, but may be more clung to in most confident expectation of eternal life.

24. WHAT WAS THE HAPPINESS OF THE CHRISTIAN EMPERORS, AND HOW FAR IT WAS TRUE HAPPINESS

For neither do we say that certain Christian emperors were therefore happy because they ruled a long time, or, dying a peaceful death, left their sons to succeed them in the empire, or subdued the enemies of the republic, or were able both to guard against and to suppress the attempt of hostile citizens rising against them. These and other gifts or comforts of this sorrowful life even certain worshipers of demons have merited to receive, who do not belong to the kingdom of God to which these belong; and this is to be traced to the mercy of God, who would not have those who believe in Him desire such things as the highest good. But we say that they are happy if they rule justly; if they are not lifted up amid the praises of those who pay them sublime honors, and the obsequiousness of those who salute them with an excessive humility, but remember that they are men; if they make their power the handmaid of His majesty by using it for the greatest possible extension of His worship; if they fear, love, worship God; if more than their own they love that kingdom in which they are not afraid to have partners; if they are slow to punish, ready to pardon; if they apply that punishment as necessary to government and defense of the republic, and not in order to gratify their own enmity; if they grant pardon, not that iniquity may go unpunished, but with the hope that the transgressor may amend his ways; if they compensate with the lenity of mercy and the liberality of benevolence for whatever severity they may be compelled to decree; if their luxury is as much restrained as it might have been unrestrained; if they prefer to govern depraved desires rather than any nation whatever; and if they do all these things, not through ardent desire of empty glory, but through love of eternal felicity, not neglecting to offer to the true God, who is their God, for their sins, the sacrifices of humility, contrition, and prayer. Such Christian emperors, we say, are happy in the present time by hope, and are destined to be so in the enjoyment of the reality itself, when that which we wait for shall have arrived.

25. CONCERNING THE PROSPERITY WHICH GOD GRANTED TO THE CHRISTIAN EMPEROR CONSTANTINE

For the good God, lest men, who believe that He is to be worshiped with a view to eternal life, should think that no one could attain to all this high estate, and to this terrestrial dominion, unless he should be a worshiper of the demons—supposing that these spirits have great power with respect to such things—for this reason He gave to the Emperor Constantine, who was not a worshiper of demons, but of the true God Himself, such fullness of earthly gifts as no one would even dare wish for. To him also He granted the honor of founding a city,[1] a companion to the Roman Empire, the daughter, as it were, of Rome itself, but without any temple or image of the demons. He reigned for a long period as sole emperor, and unaided held and defended the whole Roman world. In conducting and carrying on wars he was most victorious; in overthrowing tyrants he was most successful. He died at a great age, of sickness and old age, and left his sons to succeed him in the empire.[2] But again, lest any emperor should become a Christian in order to merit the happiness of Constantine, when everyone should be a Christian for the sake of eternal life, God took away Jovian far sooner than Julian, and permitted that Gratian should be slain by the sword of a tyrant. But in his case there was far more mitigation of the calamity than in the case of the great Pompey, for he could not be avenged by Cato, whom he had left, as it were, heir to the civil war. But Gratian, though pious minds require not such consolations, was avenged by Theodosius, whom he had associated with himself in the empire, though he had a little brother of his own, being more desirous of a faithful alliance than of extensive power.

---

1. Constantinople.
2. Constantius, Constantine, and Constans.

26. ON THE FAITH AND PIETY OF THEODOSIUS AUGUSTUS

And on this account, Theodosius not only preserved during the lifetime of Gratian that fidelity which was due to him, but also, after his death, he, like a true Christian, took his little brother Valentinian under his protection, as joint emperor, after he had been expelled by Maximus, the murderer of his father. He guarded him with paternal affection, though he might without any difficulty have got rid of him, being entirely destitute of all resources, had he been animated with the desire of extensive empire, and not with the ambition of being a benefactor. It was therefore a far greater pleasure to him, when he had adopted the boy, and preserved to him his imperial dignity, to console him by his very humanity and kindness. Afterward, when that success was rendering Maximus terrible, Theodosius, in the midst of his perplexing anxieties, was not drawn away to follow the suggestions of a sacrilegious and unlawful curiosity, but sent to John, whose abode was in the desert of Egypt—for he had learned that this servant of God (whose fame was spreading abroad) was endowed with the gift of prophecy—and from him he received assurance of victory. Immediately the slayer of the tyrant Maximus, with the deepest feelings of compassion and respect, restored the boy Valentinianus to his share in the empire from which he had been driven. Valentinianus being soon after slain by secret assassination, or by some other plot or accident, Theodosius, having again received a response from the prophet, and placing entire confidence in it, marched against the tyrant Eugenius, who had been unlawfully elected to succeed that emperor, and defeated his very powerful army, more by prayer than by the sword. Some soldiers who were at the battle reported to me that all the missiles they were throwing were snatched from their hands by a vehement wind, which blew from the direction of Theodosius's army upon the enemy; nor did it only drive with greater velocity the darts which were hurled against them, but also turned back upon their own bodies the darts which they themselves were throwing. And therefore the poet Claudian, although an alien from the name of Christ, nevertheless says in his praises of him, "O prince, too much beloved by God, for thee Æolus pours armed tempests from their caves; for thee the air fights, and the winds with one accord obey thy bugles."[1] But the victor, as he had believed and predicted, overthrew the statues of Jupiter, which had been, as it were, consecrated by I know not what kind of rites against him, and set up in the Alps. And the thunderbolts of these statues, which were made of gold, he mirthfully and graciously presented to his couriers who (as the joy of the occasion permitted) were jocularly saying that they would be most happy to be struck by such thunderbolts. The sons of his own enemies, whose fathers had been slain not so much by his orders as by the vehemence of war, having fled for refuge to a church, though they were not yet Christians, he was anxious, taking advantage of the occasion, to bring over to Christianity, and treated them with Christian love. Nor did he deprive them of their property, but, besides allowing them to retain it, bestowed on them additional honors. He did not permit private animosities to affect the treatment of any man after the war. He was not like Cinna, and Marius, and Sylla, and other such men, who wished not to finish civil wars even when they were finished, but rather grieved that they had arisen at all, than wished that when they were finished they should harm anyone. Amid all these events, from the very commencement of his reign, he did not cease to help the troubled church against the impious by most just and merciful laws, which the heretical Valens, favoring the Arians, had vehemently afflicted. Indeed, he rejoiced more to be a member of this church than he did to be a king upon the earth. The idols of the Gentiles he everywhere ordered to be overthrown, understanding well that not even terrestrial gifts are placed in the power of demons, but in that of the true God. And what could be more admirable than his religious humility, when, compelled by the urgency of certain of his intimates, he avenged the grievous crime of the Thessalonians, which at the prayer of the bishops he had promised to pardon, and, being laid hold of by the discipline of the church, did penance in such a way that the sight of his imperial loftiness prostrated made the people who were interceding for him weep more than the consciousness of offense had made them fear it when enraged? These and other similar good works, which it would be long to tell, he carried with him from this world of time, where the greatest human nobility and loftiness are but vapor. Of these works the reward is eternal happiness, of which God is the giver, though only to those who are sincerely pious. But all other blessings and privileges of this life, as the world itself, light, air, earth, water, fruits, and the soul of man himself, his body, senses, mind, life, He lavishes on good and bad alike. And among these blessings is also to be reckoned the possession of an empire, whose extent He regulates according to the requirements of His providential government at various times. Whence, I see, we must now answer those who, being confuted and convicted by the most manifest proofs, by which it is shown that for obtaining these terrestrial things, which are all the foolish desire to have, that multitude of false gods is of no use, attempt to assert that the gods are to be worshiped with a view to the interest, not of the present life, but of that which is to come after death. For as to those who, for the sake of the friendship of this world, are willing to worship vanities, and do not grieve that they are left to their puerile understandings, I think they have been sufficiently answered in these five books; of which books, when I had published the first three, and they had begun to come into the hands of many, I heard that certain persons were preparing against them an answer of some kind or other in writing. Then it was told me that they had already written their answer, but were waiting a time when they could publish it without danger. Such persons I would advise not to desire what cannot be of any advantage to them; for it is very easy for a man to seem to himself to have answered arguments, when he has only been unwilling to be silent. For what is more loquacious than vanity? And though it be able, if it like, to shout more loudly than the truth, it is not, for all that, more powerful than the truth. But let men consider diligently all the things that we have said, and if, perchance, judging without party spirit, they shall clearly perceive that they are such things as may rather be shaken than torn up by their most impudent garrulity, and, as it were, satirical and mimic levity, let them restrain their absurdities, and let them choose rather to be corrected by the wise than to be lauded by the foolish. For if they are waiting an opportunity, not for liberty to speak the truth, but for license to revile, may not that befall them which Tully says concerning someone, "Oh, wretched man! who was at liberty to sin"?[2] Wherefore, whoever he be who deems himself happy because of license to revile, he would be far happier if that were not allowed him at all; for he might all the while, laying aside empty boast, be contradicting those to whose views he is opposed by way of free consultation with them, and be listening, as it becomes him, honorably, gravely, candidly, to all that can be adduced by those whom he consults by friendly disputation.

---

1. "Panegyr. de tertio Honorii consulatu."
2. Cicero *Tusc. Disp.* 5.19.

BOOK SIX

ARGUMENT

Hitherto the argument has been conducted against those who believe that the gods are to be worshiped for the sake of temporal advantages, now it is directed against those who believe that they are to be worshiped for the sake of eternal life. Augustine devotes the five following books to the confutation of this latter belief, and first of all shows how mean an opinion of the gods was held by Varro himself, the most esteemed writer on heathen theology. Of this theology Augustine adopts Varro's division into three kinds, mythical, natural, and civil; and at once demonstrates that neither the mythical nor the civil can contribute anything to the happiness of the future life.

In the five former books, I think I have sufficiently disputed against those who believe that the many false gods, which the Christian truth shows to be useless images, or unclean spirits and pernicious demons, or certainly creatures, not the Creator, are to be worshiped for the advantage of this mortal life, and of terrestrial affairs, with that rite and service which the Greeks call λατρεία, and which is due to the one true God. And who does not know that, in the face of excessive stupidity and obstinacy, neither these five nor any other number of books whatsoever could be enough, when it is esteemed the glory of vanity to yield to no amount of strength on the side of truth—certainly to his destruction over whom so heinous a vice tyrannizes? For, notwithstanding all the assiduity of the physician who attempts to effect a cure, the disease remains unconquered, not through any fault of his, but because of the incurableness of the sick man. But those who thoroughly weigh the things which they read, having understood and considered them, without any, or with no great and excessive degree of that obstinacy which belongs to a long-cherished error, will more readily judge that, in the five books already finished, we have done more than the necessity of the question demanded, than that we have given it less discussion than it required. And they cannot have doubted but that all the hatred which the ignorant attempt to bring upon the Christian religion on account of the disasters of this life, and the destruction and change which befall terrestrial things, while the learned do not merely dissimulate, but encourage that hatred, contrary to their own consciences, being possessed by a mad impiety;

they cannot have doubted, I say, but that this hatred is devoid of right reflection and reason, and full of most light temerity, and most pernicious animosity.

1. OF THOSE WHO MAINTAIN THAT THEY WORSHIP THE GODS NOT FOR THE SAKE OF TEMPORAL BUT ETERNAL ADVANTAGES

Now, as, in the next place (as the promised order demands), those are to be refuted and taught who contend that the gods of the nations, which the Christian truth destroys, are to be worshiped not on account of this life, but on account of that which is to be after death, I shall do well to commence my disputation with the truthful oracle of the holy psalm, "Blessed is the man whose hope is the LORD God, and who respecteth not vanities and lying follies."[1] Nevertheless, in all vanities and lying follies the philosophers are to be listened to with far more toleration, who have repudiated those opinions and errors of the people; for the people set up images to the deities, and either feigned concerning those whom they call immortal gods many false and unworthy things, or believed them, already feigned, and, when believed, mixed them up with their worship and sacred rites.

With those men who, though not by free avowal

of their convictions, do still testify that they disapprove of those things by their muttering disapprobation during disputations on the subject, it may not be very far amiss to discuss the following question: Whether for the sake of the life which is to be after death, we ought to worship, not the one God who made all creatures spiritual and corporeal, but those many gods who, as some of these philosophers hold, were made by that one God, and placed by Him in their respective sublime spheres, and are therefore considered more excellent and more noble than all the others?[2] But who will assert that it must be affirmed and contended that those gods, certain of whom I have mentioned in the fourth book,[3] to whom are distributed, each to each, the charges of minute things, do bestow eternal life? But will those most skilled and most acute men, who glory in having written for the great benefit of men, to teach on what account each god is to be worshiped, and what is to be sought from each, lest with most disgraceful absurdity, such as a mimic is wont for the sake of merriment to exhibit, water should be sought from Liber, wine from the Lymphs—will those men indeed affirm to any man supplicating the immortal gods, that when he shall have asked wine from the Lymphs, and they shall have answered him, "We have water, seek wine from Liber," he may rightly say, "If ye have not wine, at least give me eternal life"? What more monstrous than this absurdity? Will not these Lymphs—for they are wont to be very easily made laugh[4]—laughing loudly (if they do not attempt to deceive like demons), answer the suppliant, "O man, dost thou think that we have life (*vitam*) in our power, who thou hearest have not even the vine (*vitem*)?" It is therefore most impudent folly to seek and hope for eternal life from such gods as are asserted so to preside over the separate minute concernments of this most sorrowful and short life, and whatever is useful for supporting and propping it, as that if anything which is under the care and power of one be sought from another, it is so incongruous and absurd that it appears very like to mimic drollery—which, when it is done by mimics knowing what they are doing, is deservedly laughed at in the theatre, but when it is done by foolish persons, who do not know better, is more deservedly ridiculed in the world. Wherefore, as concerns those gods which the states have established, it has been cleverly invented and handed down to memory by learned men, what god or goddess is to be supplicated in relation to every particular thing—what, for instance, is to be sought from Liber, what from the Lymphs, what from Vulcan, and so of all the rest, some of whom I have mentioned in the fourth book, and some I have thought right to omit. Further, if it is an error to seek wine from Ceres, bread from Liber, water from Vulcan, fire from the Lymphs, how much greater absurdity ought it to be thought, if supplication be made to any one of these for eternal life?

Wherefore, if, when we were inquiring what gods or goddesses are to be believed to be able to confer earthly kingdoms upon men, all things having been discussed, it was shown to be very far from the truth to think that even terrestrial kingdoms are established by any of those many false deities, is it not most insane impiety to believe that eternal life, which is, without any doubt or comparison, to be preferred to all terrestrial kingdoms, can be given to anyone by any of these gods? For the reason why such gods seemed to us not to be able to give even an earthly kingdom was not because they are very great and exalted, while that is something small and abject, which they, in their so great sublimity, would not condescend to care for, but because, however deservedly any one may, in consideration of human frailty, despise the falling pinnacles of an earthly kingdom, these gods have presented such an appearance as to seem most unworthy to have the granting and preserving of even those entrusted to them; and consequently, if (as we have taught in the two last books of our work, where this matter is treated of) no god out of all that crowd, either belonging to, as it were, the plebeian or to the noble gods, is fit to give mortal kingdoms to mortals, how much less is he able to make immortals of mortals?

And more than this, if, according to the opinion of those with whom we are now arguing, the gods are to be worshiped, not on account of the present life, but of that which is to be after death, then, certainly, they are not to be worshiped on account of those particular things which are distributed and portioned out (not by any law of rational truth, but by mere vain conjecture) to the power of such gods, as they believe they ought to be worshiped, who contend that their worship is necessary for all the desirable things of this mortal life, against whom I have disputed sufficiently, as far as I was able, in the five preceding books. These things being so, if the age itself of those who worshiped the goddess Juventas should be characterized by remarkable vigor, while her despisers should either die within the years of youth, or should, during that period, grow cold as with the torpor of old age; if bearded Fortuna should cover the cheeks of her worshipers more handsomely and more gracefully than all others, while we should see those by whom she was despised either altogether beardless or ill-bearded; even then we should most rightly say, that thus far these several gods had power, limited in some way by their functions, and that, consequently, neither ought eternal life to be sought from Juventas, who could not give a beard, nor ought any good thing after this life to be expected from Fortuna Barbata, who has no power even in this life to give the age itself at which the beard grows. But now, when their worship is necessary not even on account of those very things which they think are subjected to their power—for many worshipers of the goddess Juventas have not been at all vigorous at that age, and many who do not worship her rejoice in youthful strength; and also many suppliants of Fortuna Barbata have either not been able to attain to any beard at all, not even an ugly one, although they who adore her in order to obtain a beard are ridiculed by her bearded despisers—is the human heart really so foolish as to believe that that worship of the gods, which it acknowledges to be vain and ridiculous with respect to those very temporal and swiftly passing gifts, over each of which one of these gods is said to preside, is fruitful in results with respect to eternal life? And that they are able to give eternal life has not been affirmed even by those who, that they might be worshiped by the silly populace, distributed in minute division among them these temporal occupations, that none of them might sit idle; for they had supposed the existence of an exceedingly great number.

---

1. Ps. 40:4.
2. Plato, in the *Timæus*.
3. See above, 4.11, 4.21.
4. See Virgil *Ecl.* 3.9.

2. WHAT WE ARE TO BELIEVE THAT VARRO THOUGHT CONCERNING THE GODS OF THE NATIONS, WHOSE VARIOUS KINDS AND SACRED RITES HE HAS SHOWN TO BE SUCH THAT HE WOULD HAVE ACTED MORE REVERENTLY TOWARD THEM HAD HE BEEN ALTOGETHER SILENT CONCERNING THEM

Who has investigated those things more carefully than Marcus Varro? Who has discovered them more learnedly? Who has considered them more attentively? Who has distinguished them more acutely? Who has written about them more diligently and more fully? Who, though he is less pleasing in his eloquence, is nevertheless so full of instruction and wisdom, that in all the erudition which we call secular, but they liberal, he will teach the student of things as much as Cicero delights the student of words. And even Tully himself renders him such testimony, as to say in his

Academic books that he had held that disputation which is there carried on with Marcus Varro, "a man," he adds, "unquestionably the acutest of all men, and, without any doubt, the most learned."[1] He does not say the most eloquent or the most fluent, for in reality he was very deficient in this faculty, but he says, "of all men the most acute." And in those books—that is, the Academic—where he contends that all things are to be doubted, he adds of him, "without any doubt the most learned." In truth, he was so certain concerning this thing, that he laid aside that doubt which he is wont to have recourse to in all things, as if, when about to dispute in favor of the doubt of the Academics, he had, with respect to this one thing, forgotten that he was an Academic. But in the first book, when he extols the literary works of the same Varro, he says, "Us straying and wandering in our own city like strangers, thy books, as it were, brought home, that at length we might come to know of who we were and where we were. Thou hast opened up to us the age of the country, the distribution of seasons, the laws of sacred things, and of the priests; thou hast opened up to us domestic and public discipline; thou hast pointed out to us the proper places for religious ceremonies, and hast informed us concerning sacred places. Thou hast shown us the names, kinds, offices, causes of all divine and human things."[2]

This man, then, of so distinguished and excellent acquirements, and, as Terentian briefly says of him in a most elegant verse,

Varro, a man universally informed,[3]

who read so much that we wonder when he had time to write, wrote so much that we can scarcely believe anyone could have read it all—this man, I say, so great in talent, so great in learning, had he had been an opposer and destroyer of the so-called divine things of which he wrote, and had he said that they pertained to superstition rather than to religion, might perhaps, even in that case, not have written so many things which are ridiculous, contemptible, detestable. But when he so worshiped these same gods, and so vindicated their worship, as to say, in that same literary work of his, that he was afraid lest they should perish, not by an assault by enemies, but by the negligence of the citizens, and that from this ignominy they are being delivered by him, and are being laid up and preserved in the memory of the good by means of such books, with a zeal far more beneficial than that through which Metellus is declared to have rescued the sacred things of Vesta from the flames, and Æneas to have rescued the Penates from the burning of Troy; and when he nevertheless, gives forth such things to be read by succeeding ages as are deservedly judged by wise and unwise to be unfit to be read, and to be most hostile to the truth of religion; what ought we to think but that a most acute and learned man—not, however made free by the Holy Spirit—was overpowered by the custom and laws of his state, and, not being able to be silent about those things by which he was influenced, spoke of them under pretense of commending religion?

1. Of the four books *De Acad.*, dedicated to Varro, only a part of the first is extant.
2. *Cicero De Quæst. Acad. 1.3.*
3. In his book *De Metris,* chapter on *phalæcian* verses.

3. VARRO'S DISTRIBUTION OF HIS BOOK WHICH HE COMPOSED CONCERNING THE ANTIQUITIES OF HUMAN AND DIVINE THINGS

He wrote forty-one books of antiquities. These he divided into human and divine things. Twenty-five he devoted to human things, sixteen to divine things; following this plan in that division—namely, to give six books to each of the four divisions of human things. For he directs his attention to these considerations: who perform, where they perform, when they perform, what they perform. Therefore in the first six books he wrote concerning men; in the second six, concerning places; in the third six, concerning times; in the fourth and last six, concerning things. Four times six, however, make only twenty-four. But he placed at the head of them one separate work, which spoke of all these things conjointly.

In divine things, the same order he preserved throughout, as far as concerns those things which are performed to the gods. For sacred things are performed by men in places and times. These four things I have mentioned he embraced in twelve books, allotting three to each. For he wrote the first three concerning men, the following three concerning places, the third three concerning times, and the fourth three concerning sacred rites—showing who should perform, where they should perform, when they should perform, what they should perform, with most subtle distinction. But because it was necessary to say—and that especially was expected—to whom they should perform sacred rites, he wrote concerning the gods themselves the last three books; and these five times three made fifteen. But they are in all, as we have said, sixteen. For he put also at the beginning of these one distinct book, speaking by way of introduction of all which follows; which being finished, he proceeded to subdivide the first three in that fivefold distribution which pertain to men, making the first concerning high priests, the second concerning augurs, the third concerning the fifteen men presiding over the sacred ceremonies.[1] The second three he made concerning places, speaking in one of them concerning their chapels, in the second concerning their temples, and in the third concerning religious places. The next three which follow these, and pertain to times—that is, to festival days—he distributed so as to make one concerning holidays, the other concerning the circus games, and the third concerning scenic plays. Of the fourth three, pertaining to sacred things, he devoted one to consecrations, another to private, the last to public, sacred rites. In the three which remain, the gods themselves follow this pompous train, as it were, for whom all this culture has been expended. In the first book are the certain gods, in the second the uncertain, in the third, and last of all, the chief and select gods.

---

1. Tarquin the Proud, having bought the books of the sibyl, appointed two men to preserve and interpret them (Dionysius of Halicarnassus *Antiq.* 4.62). These were afterward increased to ten, while the plebeians were contending for larger privileges; and subsequently five more were added.

4. THAT FROM THE DISPUTATION OF VARRO, IT FOLLOWS THAT THE WORSHIPERS OF THE GODS REGARD HUMAN THINGS AS MORE ANCIENT THAN DIVINE THINGS

In this whole series of most beautiful and most subtle distributions and distinctions, it will most easily appear evident from the things we have said already, and from what is to be said hereafter, to any man who is not, in the obstinacy of his heart, an enemy to himself, that it is vain to seek and to hope for, and even most impudent to wish for eternal life. For these institutions are either the work of men or of demons—not of those whom they call good demons, but, to speak more plainly, of unclean, and, without controversy, malign spirits, who with wonderful slyness and secretness suggest to the thoughts of the impious, and sometimes openly present to their understandings, noxious opinions, by which the human mind grows more and more foolish, and becomes unable to adapt itself to and abide in the immutable and eternal truth, and seek to confirm these opinions by every kind of fallacious attestation in their power. This very same

Varro testifies that he wrote first concerning human things, but afterward concerning divine things, because the states existed first, and afterward these things were instituted by them. But the true religion was not instituted by any earthly state, but plainly it established the celestial city. It, however, is inspired and taught by the true God, the giver of eternal life to His true worshipers.

The following is the reason Varro gives when he confesses that he had written first concerning human things, and afterward of divine things, because these divine things were instituted by men: "As the painter is before the painted tablet, the mason before the edifice, so states are before those things which are instituted by states." But he says that he would have written first concerning the gods, afterward concerning men, if he had been writing concerning the whole nature of the gods—as if he were really writing concerning some portion of, and not all, the nature of the gods; or as if, indeed, some portion of, though not all, the nature of the gods ought not to be put before that of men. How, then, comes it that in those three last books, when he is diligently explaining the certain, uncertain, and select gods, he seems to pass over no portion of the nature of the gods? Why, then, does he say, "If we had been writing on the whole nature of the gods, we would first have finished the divine things before we touched the human"? For he either writes concerning the whole nature of the gods, or concerning some portion of it, or concerning no part of it at all. If concerning it all, it is certainly to be put before human things; if concerning some part of it, why should it not, from the very nature of the case, precede human things? Is not even some part of the gods to be preferred to the whole of humanity? But if it is too much to prefer a part of the divine to all human things, that part is certainly worthy to be preferred to the Romans at least. For he writes the books concerning human things, not with reference to the whole world, but only to Rome; which books he says he had properly placed, in the order of writing, before the books on divine things, like a painter before the painted tablet, or a mason before the building, most openly confessing that, as a picture or a structure, even these divine things were instituted by men. There remains only the third supposition, that he is to be understood to have written concerning no divine nature, but that he did not wish to say this openly, but left it to the intelligent to infer; for when one says "not all," usage understands that to mean "some," but it *may* be understood as meaning "none," because that which is *none* is neither all nor some. In fact, as he himself says, if he had been writing concerning all the nature of the gods, its due place would have been before human things in the order of writing. But, as the truth declares, even though Varro is silent, the divine nature should have taken precedence of Roman things, though it were not *all,* but only *some.* But it is properly put after, therefore it is *none.* His arrangement, therefore, was due, not to a desire to give human things priority to divine things, but to his unwillingness to prefer false things to true. For in what he wrote on human things, he followed the history of affairs; but in what he wrote concerning those things which they call divine, what else did he follow but mere conjectures about vain things? This, doubtless, is what, in a subtle manner, he wished to signify; not only writing concerning divine things after the human, but even giving a reason why he did so; for if he had suppressed this, some, perchance, would have defended his doing so in one way, and some in another. But in that very reason he has rendered, he has left nothing for men to conjecture at will, and has sufficiently proved that he preferred men to the institutions of men, not the nature of men to the nature of the gods. Thus he confessed that, in writing the books concerning divine things, he did not write concerning the truth which belongs to nature, but the falseness which belongs to error; which he has elsewhere expressed more openly (as I have mentioned in the fourth book[1]), saying that, had he been founding a new city himself, he would have written according to the order of nature; but as he had only found an old one, he could not but follow its custom.

---

1. See above, 4.31.

5. CONCERNING THE THREE KINDS OF THEOLOGY ACCORDING TO VARRO, NAMELY, ONE FABULOUS, THE OTHER NATURAL, THE THIRD CIVIL

Now what are we to say of this proposition of his, namely, that there are three kinds of theology, that is, of the account which is given of the gods; and of these, the one is called mythical, the other physical, and the third civil? Did the Latin usage permit, we should call the kind which he has placed first in order *fabular*,[1] but let us call it *fabulous*,[2] for mythical is derived from the Greek μῦθος, a fable; but that the second should be called *natural*, the usage of speech now admits; the third he himself has designated in Latin, calling it *civil*.[3] Then he says, "They call that kind *mythical* which the poets chiefly use; *physical*, that which the philosophers use; *civil*, that which the people use. As to the first I have mentioned," says he, "in it are many fictions, which are contrary to the dignity and nature of the immortals. For we find in it that one god has been born from the head, another from the thigh, another from drops of blood; also, in this we find that gods have stolen, committed adultery, served men; in a word, in this all manner of things are attributed to the gods, such as may befall, not merely any man, but even the most contemptible man." He certainly, where he could, where he dared, where he thought he could do it with impunity, has manifested, without any of the haziness of ambiguity, how great injury was done to the nature of the gods by lying fables; for he was speaking, not concerning natural theology, not concerning civil, but concerning fabulous theology, which he thought he could freely find fault with.

Let us see, now, what he says concerning the second kind. "The second kind which I have explained," he says, "is that concerning which philosophers have left many books, in which they treat such questions as these: what gods there are, where they are, of what kind and character they are, since what time they have existed, or if they have existed from eternity; whether they are of fire, as Heraclitus believes; or of number, as Pythagoras; or of atoms, as Epicurus says; and other such things, which men's ears can more easily hear inside the walls of a school than outside in the Forum." He finds fault with nothing in this kind of theology which they call *physical,* and which belongs to philosophers, except that he has related their controversies among themselves, through which there has arisen a multitude of dissentient sects. Nevertheless he has removed this kind from the Forum, that is, from the populace, but he has shut it up in schools. But that first kind, most false and most base, he has not removed from the citizens. Oh, the religious ears of the people, and among them even those of the Romans, that are not able to bear what the philosophers dispute concerning the gods! But when the poets sing and stage players act such things as are derogatory to the dignity and the nature of the immortals, such as may befall not a man merely, but the most contemptible man, they not only bear, but willingly listen to. Nor is this all, but they even consider that these things please the gods, and that they are propitiated by them.

But someone may say, Let us distinguish these two kinds of theology, the mythical and the physical—that is, the fabulous and the natural—from this civil kind about which we are now speaking. Anticipating this, he himself has distinguished them. Let us see now how he explains the civil theology itself. I see, indeed, why it should be distinguished as fabulous, even because it is false, because it is base, because it is unworthy. But to wish to distinguish the natural from the civil, what else is that but to confess that the civil itself is false? For if that be natural, what fault has it that it should be excluded? And if this which is called civil be not natural, what merit has it that it should be admitted? This, in truth, is the cause why he wrote first concerning human things, and afterward concerning divine things; since in divine things he did not follow nature, but the institution of men. Let us look at this civil theology of his. "The third kind," says he, "is that which citizens in cities, and especially the priests, ought to know and to administer. From it is to be known what god each one may suitably worship, what sacred rites and sacrifices each one may suitably perform." Let us still attend to what follows. "The first theology," he says, "is especially adapted to the theatre, the second to the world, the third to the city." Who does not see to which he gives the palm? Certainly to the second, which he said above is that of the philosophers. For he testifies that this pertains to the world, than which they think there is nothing better. But those two theologies, the first and the third—to wit, those of the theatre and of the city—has he distinguished them or united them? For although we see that the city is in the world, we do not see that it follows that any things belonging to the city pertain to the world. For it is possible that such things may be worshiped and believed in the city, according to false opinions, as have no existence either in the world or out of it. But where is the theatre but in the city? Who instituted the theatre but the state? For what purpose did it constitute it but for scenic plays? And to what class of things do scenic plays belong but to those divine things concerning which these books of Varro's are written with so much ability?

---

1. Fabulare.
2. Fabulosum.
3. Civile.

6. CONCERNING THE MYTHIC, THAT IS, THE FABULOUS, THEOLOGY, AND THE CIVIL, AGAINST VARRO

O Marcus Varro! you are the most acute, and without doubt the most learned, but still a man, not God—now lifted up by the Spirit of God to see and to announce divine things, you see, indeed, that divine things are to be separated from human trifles and lies, but you fear to offend those most corrupt opinions of the populace, and their customs in public superstitions, which you yourself, when you consider them on all sides, perceive, and all your literature loudly pronounces to be abhorrent from the nature of the gods, even of such gods as the frailty of the human mind supposes to exist in the elements of this world. What can the most excellent human talent do here? What can human learning, though manifold, avail you in this perplexity? You desire to worship the natural gods; you are compelled to worship the civil. You have found some of the gods to be fabulous, on whom you vomit forth very freely what you think, and, whether you will or not, you wet therewith even the civil gods. You say, forsooth, that the fabulous are adapted to the theatre, the natural to the world, and the civil to the city; though the world is a divine work, but cities and theatres are the works of men, and though the gods who are laughed at in the theatre are not other than those who are adored in the temples; and you do not exhibit games in honor of other gods than those to whom you immolate victims. How much more freely and more subtly would you have decided these had you said that some gods are natural, others established by men; and concerning those who have been so established, the literature of the poets gives one account, and that of the priests another—both of which are, nevertheless, so friendly the one to the other, through fellowship in falsehood, that they are both pleasing to the demons, to whom the doctrine of the truth is hostile.

That theology, therefore, which they call natural, being put aside for a moment, as it is afterward to be discussed, we ask if anyone is really content to seek a hope for eternal life from poetical, theatrical, scenic gods? Perish the thought! The true God avert so wild and sacrilegious a madness! What, is eternal life to be asked from those gods whom these things pleased, and whom these things propitiate, in which their own crimes are represented? No one, as I think, has arrived at such a pitch of headlong and furious impiety. So then, neither by the fabulous nor by the civil theology does anyone obtain eternal life. For the one sows base things concerning the gods by feigning them, the other reaps by cherishing them; the one scatters lies, the other gathers them together; the one pursues divine things with false crimes, the other incorporates among divine things the plays which are made up of these crimes; the one sounds abroad in human songs impious fictions concerning the gods, the other consecrates these for the festivities of the gods themselves; the one sings the misdeeds and crimes of the gods, the other loves them; the one gives forth or feigns, the other either attests the true or delights in the false. Both are base; both are damnable. But the one which is theatrical teaches public abomination, and that one which is of the city adorns itself with that abomination. Shall eternal life be hoped for from these, by which this short and temporal life is polluted? Does the society of wicked men pollute our life if they insinuate themselves into our affections, and win our assent? And does not the society of demons pollute the life, who are worshiped with their own crimes? —if with true crimes, how wicked the demons! if with false, how wicked the worship!

When we say these things, it may perchance seem to someone who is very ignorant of these matters that only those things concerning the gods which are sung in the songs of the poets and acted on the stage are unworthy of the divine majesty, and ridiculous, and too detestable to be celebrated, while those sacred things which not stage players but priests perform are pure and free from all unseemliness. Had this been so, never would anyone have thought that these theatrical abominations should be celebrated in their honor, never would the gods themselves have ordered them to be performed to them. But men are in nowise ashamed to perform these things in the theatres, because similar things are carried on in the temples. In short, when the aforementioned author attempted to distinguish the civil theology from the fabulous and natural, as a sort of third and distinct kind, he wished it to be understood to be rather tempered by both than separated from either. For he says that those things which the poets write are less than the people ought to follow, while what the philosophers say is more than it is expedient for the people to pry into. "Which," says he, "differ in such a way, that nevertheless not a few things from both of them have been taken to the account of the civil theology; wherefore we will indicate what the civil theology has in common with that of the poet, though it ought to be more closely connected with the theology of philosophers." Civil theology is therefore not quite disconnected from that of the poets. Nevertheless, in another place, concerning the generations of the gods, he says that the people are more inclined toward the poets than toward the physical theologians. For in this place he said what ought to be done; in that other place, what was really done. He said that the latter had written for the sake of utility, but the poets for the sake of amusement. And hence the things from the poets' writings, which the people ought not to follow, are the crimes of the gods; which, nevertheless, amuse both the people and the gods. For, for amusement's sake, he says, the poets write, and not for that of utility; nevertheless they write such things as the gods will desire, and the people perform.

7. CONCERNING THE LIKENESS AND AGREEMENT OF THE FABULOUS AND CIVIL THEOLOGIES

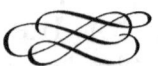

That theology, therefore, which is fabulous, theatrical, scenic, and full of all baseness and unseemliness, is taken up into the civil theology; and part of that theology, which in its totality is deservedly judged to be worthy of reprobation and rejection, is pronounced worthy to be cultivated and observed; not at all an incongruous part, as I have undertaken to show, and one which, being alien to the whole body, was unsuitably attached to and suspended from it, but a part entirely congruous with, and most harmoniously fitted to the rest, as a member of the same body. For what else do those images, forms, ages, sexes, characteristics of the gods show? If the poets have Jupiter with a beard and Mercury beardless, have not the priests the same? Is the Priapus of the priests less obscene than the Priapus of the players? Does he receive the adoration of worshipers in a different form from that in which he moves about the stage for the amusement of spectators? Is not Saturn old and Apollo young in the shrines where their images stand as well as when represented by actors' masks? Why are Forculus, who presides over doors, and Limentinus, who presides over thresholds and lintels, male gods, and Cardea between them feminine, who presides over hinges? Are not those things found in books on divine things, which grave poets have deemed unworthy of their verses? Does the Diana of the theatre carry arms, while the Diana of the city is simply a virgin? Is the stage Apollo a lyrist, but the Delphic Apollo ignorant of this art? But these things are decent compared with the more shameful things. What was thought of Jupiter himself by those who placed his wet nurse in the Capitol? Did they not bear witness to Euhemerus, who, not with the garrulity of a fable teller, but with the gravity of a historian who had diligently investigated the matter, wrote that all such gods had been men and mortals? And they who appointed the Epulones as parasites at the table of Jupiter, what else did they wish for but mimic sacred rites? For if any mimic had said that parasites of Jupiter were made use of at his table, he would assuredly have appeared to be seeking to call forth laughter. Varro said it—not when he was mocking, but when he was commending the gods did he say it. His books on divine, not on human, things testify that he wrote this—not where he set forth the scenic games, but where he explained the Capitoline laws. In a word, he is conquered, and confesses that, as they made the gods with a human form, so they believed that they are delighted with human pleasures.

For also malign spirits were not so wanting to their own business as not to confirm noxious opinions in the minds of men by converting them into sport. Whence also is that story about the sacristan of Hercules, which says that, having nothing to do, he took to playing at dice as a pastime, throwing them alternately with the one hand for Hercules, with the other for himself, with this understanding, that if he should win, he should from the funds of the temple prepare himself a supper, and hire a mistress; but if Hercules should win the game, he himself should, at his own expense, provide the same for the pleasure of Hercules. Then, when he had been beaten by himself, as though by Hercules, he gave to the god Hercules the supper he owed him, and also the most noble harlot Larentina. But she, having fallen asleep in the temple, dreamed that Hercules had had intercourse with her, and had said to her that she would find her payment with the youth whom she should first meet on leaving the temple, and that she was to believe this to be paid to her by Hercules. And so the first youth that met her on going out was the wealthy Tarutius, who kept her a long time, and when he died left her his heir. She, having obtained a most ample fortune, that she should not seem ungrateful for the divine hire, in her turn made the Roman people her heir, which she thought to be most acceptable to the deities; and, having disappeared, the will was found. By which meritorious conduct they say that she gained divine honors.

Now had these things been feigned by the poets and acted by the mimics, they would without any doubt have been said to pertain to the fabulous theology, and would have been judged worthy to be separated from the dignity of the civil theology. But when these shameful things—not of the poets, but of the people; not of the mimics, but of the sacred things; not of the theatres, but of the temples, that is, not of the fabulous, but of the civil theology—are reported by so great an author, not in vain do the actors represent with theatrical art the baseness of the gods, which is so great; but surely in vain do the priests attempt, by rites called sacred, to represent their nobleness of character, which has no existence. There are sacred rites of Juno; and these are celebrated in her beloved island, Samos, where she was given in marriage to Jupiter. There are sacred rites of Ceres, in which Proserpine is sought for, having been carried off by Pluto. There are sacred rites of Venus, in which, her beloved Adonis being slain by a boar's tooth, the lovely youth is lamented. There are sacred rites of the mother of the gods, in which the beautiful youth Atys, loved by her, and castrated by her through a woman's jealousy, is deplored by men who have suffered the like calamity, whom they call Galli. Since, then, these things are more unseemly than all scenic abomination, why is it that they strive to separate, as it were, the fabulous fictions of the poet concerning the gods, as, forsooth, pertaining to the theatre, from the civil theology which they wish to belong to the city, as though they were separating from noble and worthy things, things unworthy and base? Wherefore there is more reason to thank the stage actors, who have spared the eyes of men and have not laid bare by theatrical exhibition all the things which are hid by the walls of the temples. What good is to be thought of their sacred rites which are concealed in darkness, when those which are brought forth into the light are so detestable? And certainly they themselves have seen what they transact in secret through the agency of mutilated and effeminate men. Yet they have not been able to conceal those same men miserably and vile enervated and corrupted. Let them persuade whom they can that they transact anything holy through such men, who, they cannot deny, are numbered, and live among their sacred things. We know not what they transact, but we know through whom they transact; for we know what things are transacted on the stage, where never, even in a chorus of harlots, has one who is mutilated or an effeminate appeared. And, nevertheless, even these things are acted by vile and infamous characters; for, indeed, they ought not to be acted by men of good character. What, then, are those sacred rites, for the performance of which holiness has chosen such men as not even the obscenity of the stage has admitted?

8. CONCERNING THE INTERPRETATIONS, CONSISTING OF NATURAL EXPLANATIONS, WHICH THE PAGAN TEACHERS ATTEMPT TO SHOW FOR THEIR GODS

But all these things, they say, have certain physical, that is, natural interpretations, showing their natural meaning; as though in this disputation we were seeking physics and not theology, which is the account, not of nature, but of God. For although He who is the true God is God, not by opinion, but by nature, nevertheless all nature is not God; for there is certainly a nature of man, of a beast, of a tree, of a stone—none of which is God. For if, when the question is concerning the mother of the gods—that from which the whole system of interpretation starts certainly is—that the mother of the gods is the earth, why do we make further inquiry? Why do we carry our investigation through all the rest of it? What can more manifestly favor them who say that all those gods were men? For they are earthborn in the sense that the earth is their mother. But in the true theology the earth is the work, not the mother, of God. But in whatever way their sacred rites may be interpreted, and whatever reference they may have to the nature of things, it is not according to nature, but contrary to nature, that men should be effeminates. This disease, this crime, this abomination, has a recognized place among those sacred things, though even depraved men will scarcely be compelled by torments to confess they are guilty of it. Again, if these sacred rites, which are proved to be fouler than scenic abominations, are excused and justified on the ground that they have their own interpretations, by which they are shown to symbolize the nature of things, why are not the poetical things in like manner excused and justified? For many have interpreted even these in like fashion, to such a degree that even that which they say is the most monstrous and most horrible—namely, that Saturn devoured his own children—has been interpreted by some of them to mean that length of time, which is signified by the name of Saturn, consumes whatever it begets; or that, as the same Varro thinks, Saturn belongs to seeds which fall back again into the earth from whence they spring. And so one interprets it in one way, and one in another. And the same is to be said of all the rest of this theology.

And, nevertheless, it is called the fabulous theology, and is censured, cast off, rejected, together with all such interpretations belonging to it. And not only by the natural theology, which is that of the philosophers, but also by this civil theology, concerning which we are speaking, which is asserted to pertain to cities and peoples, it is judged worthy of repudiation, because it has invented unworthy things concerning the gods. Of which, I know, this is the secret: that those most acute and learned men, by whom those things were written, understood that both theologies ought to be rejected—to wit, both that fabulous and this civil one—but the former they dared to reject, the latter they dared not; the former they set forth to be censured, the latter they showed to be very like it; not that it might be chosen to be held in preference to the other, but that it might be understood to be worthy of being rejected together with it. And thus, without danger to those who feared to censure the civil theology, both of them being brought into contempt, that theology which they call natural might find a place in better disposed minds; for the civil and the fabulous are both fabulous and both civil. He who shall wisely inspect the vanities and obscenities of both will find that they are both fabulous; and he who shall direct his attention to the scenic plays pertaining to the fabulous theology in the festivals of the civil gods, and in the divine rites of the cities, will find they are both civil. How, then, can the power of giving eternal life be attributed to any of those gods whose own images and sacred rites convict them of being most like to the fabulous gods, which are most openly reprobated, in forms, ages, sex, characteristics, marriages, generations, rites; in all which things they are understood either to have been men, and to have had their sacred rites and solemnities instituted in their honor according to the life or death of each of them, the demons suggesting and confirming this error, or certainly most foul spirits, who, taking advantage of some occasion or other, have stolen into the minds of men to deceive them?

9. CONCERNING THE SPECIAL OFFICES OF THE GODS

And as to those very offices of the gods, so meanly and so minutely portioned out, so that they say that they ought to be supplicated, each one according to his special function—about which we have spoken much already, though not all that is to be said concerning it—are they not more consistent with mimic buffoonery than divine majesty? If anyone should use two nurses for his infant, one of whom should give nothing but food, the other nothing but drink, as these make use of two goddesses for this purpose, Educa and Potina, he should certainly seem to be foolish, and to do in his house a thing worthy of a mimic. They would have Liber to have been named from "liberation," because through him males at the time of copulation are liberated by the emission of the seed. They also say that Libera (the same in their opinion as Venus) exercises the same function in the case of women, because they say that they also emit seed; and they also say that on this account the same part of the male and of the female is placed in the temple, that of the male to Liber, and that of the female to Libera. To these things they add the women assigned to Liber, and the wine for exciting lust. Thus the Bacchanalia are celebrated with the utmost insanity, with respect to which Varro himself confesses that such things would not be done by the Bacchanals except their minds were highly excited. These things, however, afterward displeased a saner senate, and it ordered them to be discontinued. Here, at length, they perhaps perceived how much power unclean spirits, when held to be gods, exercise over the minds of men. These things, certainly, were not to be done in the theatres; for there they play, not rave, although to have gods who are delighted with such plays is very like raving.

But what kind of distinction is this which he makes between the religious and the superstitious man, saying that the gods are feared[1] by the superstitious man, but are reverenced[2] as parents by the religious man, not feared as enemies; and that they are all so good that they will more readily spare those who are impious than hurt one who is innocent? And yet he tells us that three gods are assigned as guardians to a woman after she has been delivered, lest the god Silvanus come in and molest her; and that in order to signify the presence of these protectors, three men go round the house during the night, and first strike the threshold with a hatchet, next with a pestle, and the third time sweep it with a brush, in order that these symbols of agriculture having been exhibited, the god Silvanus might be hindered from entering, because neither are trees cut down or pruned without a hatchet, neither is grain ground without a pestle, nor corn heaped up without a besom. Now from these three things three gods have been named: Intercidona, from the cut[3] made by the hatchet; Pilumnus, from the pestle; Diverra, from the besom; by which guardian gods the woman who has been delivered is preserved against the power of the god Silvanus. Thus the guardianship of kindly disposed gods would not avail against the malice of a mischievous god, unless they were three to one, and fought against him, as it were, with the opposing emblems of cultivation, who, being an inhabitant of the woods, is rough, horrible, and uncultivated. Is this the innocence of the gods? Is this their concord? Are these the health-giving deities of the cities, more ridiculous than the things which are laughed at in the theatres?

When a male and a female are united, the god Jugatinus presides. Well, let this be borne with. But the married woman must be brought home: the god Domiducus also is invoked. That she may be in the house, the god Domitius is introduced. That she may remain with her husband, the goddess Manturnæ is used. What more is required? Let human modesty be spared. Let the lust of flesh and blood go on with the rest, the secret of shame being respected. Why is the bedchamber filled with a crowd of deities, when even the groomsmen[4] have departed? And, moreover, it is so filled, not that in consideration of their presence more regard may be paid to chastity, but that by their help the woman, naturally of the weaker sex, and trembling with the novelty of her situation, may the more readily yield her virginity. For there are the goddess Virginiensis, and the god-father Subigus, and the goddess-mother Prema, and the goddess Pertunda, and Venus, and Priapus.[5] What is this? If it was absolutely necessary that a man, laboring at this work, should be helped by the gods, might not some one god or goddess have been sufficient? Was Venus not sufficient alone, who is even said to be named from this, that without her power a woman does not cease to be a virgin? If there is any shame in men, which is not in the deities, is it not the case that, when the married couple believe that so many gods of either sex are present, and busy at this work, they are so much affected with shame, that the man is less moved, and the woman more reluctant? And certainly, if the goddess Virginiensis is present to loose the virgin's zone, if the god Subigus is present that the virgin may be got under the man, if the goddess Prema is present that, having been got under him, she may be kept down, and may not move herself, what has the goddess Pertunda to do there? Let her blush; let her go forth. Let the husband himself do something. It is disgraceful that anyone but himself should do that from which she gets her name. But perhaps she is tolerated because she is said to be a goddess, and not a god. For if she were believed to be a male, and were called Pertundus, the husband would demand more help against him for the chastity of his wife than the newly delivered woman against Silvanus. But why am I saying this, when Priapus, too, is there, a male to excess, upon whose immense and most unsightly member the newly married bride is commanded to sit, according to the most honorable and most religious custom of matrons?

Let them go on, and let them attempt with all the subtlety they can to distinguish the civil theology from the fabulous, the cities from the theatres, the temples from the stages, the sacred things of the priests from the songs of the poets, as honorable things from base things, truthful things from fallacious, grave from light, serious from ludicrous, desirable things from things to be rejected, we understand what they do. They are aware that that theatrical and fabulous theology hangs by the civil, and is reflected back upon it from the songs of the poets as from a mirror; and thus, that theology having been exposed to view which they do not dare to condemn, they more freely assail and censure that picture of it, in order that those who perceive what they mean may detest this very face itself of which that is the picture—which, however, the gods themselves, as though seeing themselves in the same mirror, love so much, that it is better seen in both of them who and what they are. Whence, also, they have compelled their worshipers, with terrible commands, to dedicate to them the uncleanness of the fabulous theology, to put them among their solemnities, and reckon them among divine things; and thus they have both shown themselves more manifestly to be most impure spirits, and have made that rejected and reprobated theatrical theology a member and a part of this, as it were, chosen and approved theology of the city, so that, though the whole is disgraceful and false, and contains in it fictitious gods, one part of it is in the literature of the priests, the other in the songs of the poets. Whether it may have other parts is another question. At present, I think, I have sufficiently shown, on account of the division of Varro, that the theology of the city and that of the theatre belong to one civil theology. Wherefore, because they are both equally disgraceful, absurd, shameful, false, far be it from religious men to hope for eternal life from either the one or the other.

In fine, even Varro himself, in his account and enumeration of the gods, starts from the moment of a man's conception. He commences the series of those gods who take charge of man with Janus, carries it on to the death of the man decrepit with age, and terminates it with the goddess Nænia, who is sung at the funerals of the aged. After that, he begins to give an account of the other gods, whose province is not man himself, but man's belongings, as food, clothing, and all that is necessary for this life; and, in the case of all these, he explains what is the special office of each, and for what each ought to be supplicated. But with all this scrupulous and comprehensive diligence, he has neither proved the existence, nor so much as mentioned the name, of any god from whom eternal life is to be sought—the one object for which we are Christians. Who, then, is so stupid as not to perceive that this man, by setting forth and opening up so diligently the civil theology, and by exhibiting its likeness to that fabulous, shameful, and disgraceful theology, and also by teaching that that fabulous sort is also a part of this other, was laboring to obtain a place in the minds of men for none but that natural theology, which he says pertains to philosophers, with such subtlety that he censures the fabulous, and, not daring openly to censure the civil, shows its censurable character by simply exhibiting it; and thus, both being reprobated by the judgment of men of right understanding, the natural alone remains to be chosen? But concerning this in its own place, by the help of the true God, we have to discuss more diligently.

---

1. Timeri.
2. Vereri.
3. Intercido, I cut or cleave.
4. Paranymphi.
5. Cf. Tertullian *Ad Nat.* 2.11; Arnobius *Contra Gent.* 4; Lactantius *Inst. Div.* 1.20.

10. CONCERNING THE LIBERTY OF SENECA, WHO MORE VEHEMENTLY CENSURED THE CIVIL THEOLOGY THAN VARRO DID THE FABULOUS

That liberty, in truth, which this man wanted, so that he did not dare to censure that theology of the city, which is very similar to the theatrical, so openly as he did the theatrical itself, was, though not fully, yet in part possessed by Annæus Seneca, whom we have some evidence to show to have flourished in the times of our apostles. It was in part possessed by him, I say, for he possessed it in writing, but not in living. For in that book which he wrote against superstition,[1] he more copiously and vehemently censured that civil and urban theology than Varro the theatrical and fabulous. For, when speaking concerning images, he says, "They dedicate images of the sacred and inviolable immortals in most worthless and motionless matter. They give them the appearance of man, beasts, and fishes, and some make them of mixed sex, and heterogeneous bodies. They call them deities, when they are such that if they should get breath and should suddenly meet them, they would be held to be monsters." Then, a while afterward, when extolling the natural theology, he had expounded the sentiments of certain philosophers, he opposes to himself a question, and says, "Here someone says, Shall I believe that the heavens and the earth are gods, and that some are above the moon and some below it? Shall I bring forward either Plato or the peripatetic Strato, one of whom made God to be without a body, the other without a mind?" In answer to which he says, "And, really, what truer do the dreams of Titus Tatius, or Romulus, or Tullus Hostilius appear to thee? Tatius declared the divinity of the goddess Cloacina; Romulus that of Picus and Tiberinus; Tullus Hostilius that of Pavor and Pallor, the most disagreeable affections of men, the one of which is the agitation of the mind under fright, the other that of the body, not a disease, indeed, but a change of color." Will you rather believe that these are deities, and receive them into heaven? But with what freedom he has written concerning the rites themselves, cruel and shameful! "One," he says, "castrates himself, another cuts his arms. Where will they find room for the fear of these gods when angry, who use such means of gaining their favor when propitious? But gods who wish to be worshiped in this fashion should be worshiped in none. So great is the frenzy of the mind when perturbed and driven from its seat, that the gods are propitiated by men in a manner in which not even men of the greatest ferocity and fable-renowned cruelty vent their rage. Tyrants have lacerated the limbs of some; they never ordered anyone to lacerate his own. For the gratification of royal lust, some have been castrated; but no one ever, by the command of his lord, laid violent hands on himself to emasculate himself. They kill themselves in the temples. They supplicate with their wounds and with their blood. If anyone has time to see the things they do and the things they suffer, he will find so many things unseemly for men of respectability, so unworthy of freemen, so unlike the doings of sane men, that no one would doubt that they are mad, had they been mad with the minority; but now the multitude of the insane is the defense of their sanity."

He next relates those things which are wont to be done in the Capitol, and with the utmost intrepidity insists that they are such things as one could only believe to be done by men making sport, or by madmen. For having spoken with derision of this, that in the Egyptian sacred rites Osiris, being lost, is lamented for, but straightway, when found, is the occasion of great joy by his reappearance, because both the losing and the finding of him are feigned; and yet that grief and that joy which are elicited thereby from those who have lost nothing and found nothing are real; having I say, so spoken of this, he says, "Still there is a fixed time for this frenzy. It is tolerable to go mad once in the year. Go into the Capitol. One is suggesting divine commands[2] to a god; another is telling the hours to Jupiter; one is a lictor; another is an anointer, who with the mere movement of his arms imitates one anointing. There are women who arrange the hair of

Juno and Minerva, standing far away not only from her image, but even from her temple. These move their fingers in the manner of hairdressers. There are some women who hold a mirror. There are some who are calling the gods to assist them in court. There are some who are holding up documents to them, and are explaining to them their cases. A learned and distinguished comedian, now old and decrepit, was daily playing the mimic in the Capitol, as though the gods would gladly be spectators of that which men had ceased to care about. Every kind of artificers working for the immortal gods is dwelling there in idleness." And a little after he says, "Nevertheless these, though they give themselves up to the gods for purposes superflous enough, do not do so for any abominable or infamous purpose. There sit certain women in the Capitol who think they are beloved by Jupiter; nor are they frightened even by the look of the, if you will believe the poets, most wrathful Juno."

This liberty Varro did not enjoy. It was only the poetical theology he seemed to censure. The civil, which this man cuts to pieces, he was not bold enough to impugn. But if we attend to the truth, the temples where these things are performed are far worse than the theatres where they are represented. Whence, with respect to these sacred rites of the civil theology, Seneca preferred, as the best course to be followed by a wise man, to feign respect for them in act, but to have no real regard for them at heart. "All which things," he says, "a wise man will observe as being commanded by the laws, but not as being pleasing to the gods." And a little after he says, "And what of this, that we unite the gods in marriage, and that not even naturally, for we join brothers and sisters? We marry Bellona to Mars, Venus to Vulcan, Salacia to Neptune. Some of them we leave unmarried, as though there were no match for them, which is surely needless, especially when there are certain unmarried goddesses, as Populonia, or Fulgora, or the goddess Rumina, for whom I am not astonished that suitors have been awanting. All this ignoble crowd of gods, which the superstition of ages has amassed, we ought," he says, "to adore in such a way as to remember all the while that its worship belongs rather to custom than to reality." Wherefore, neither those laws nor customs instituted in the civil theology that which was pleasing to the gods, or which pertained to reality. But this man, whom philosophy had made, as it were, free, nevertheless, because he was an illustrious senator of the Roman people, worshiped what he censured, did what he condemned, adored what he reproached, because, forsooth, philosophy had taught him something great—namely, not to be superstitious in the world, but, on account of the laws of cities and the customs of men, to be an actor, not on the stage, but in the temples—conduct the more to be condemned, that those things which he was deceitfully acting he so acted that the people thought he was acting sincerely. But a stage actor would rather delight people by acting plays than take them in by false pretenses.

---

1. Mentioned also by Tertullian (*Apol.* 12), but not extant.
2. Numina. Another reading is *nomina;* and with either reading another translation is admissible: "One is announcing to a god the names (or gods) who salute him."

11. WHAT SENECA THOUGHT CONCERNING THE JEWS

Seneca, among the other superstitions of civil theology, also found fault with the sacred things of the Jews, and especially the sabbaths, affirming that they act uselessly in keeping those seventh days, whereby they lose through idleness about the seventh part of their life, and also many things which demand immediate attention are damaged. The Christians, however, who were already most hostile to the Jews, he did not dare to mention, either for praise or blame, lest, if he praised them, he should do so against the ancient custom of his country, or, perhaps, if he should blame them, he should do so against his own will.

When he was speaking concerning those Jews, he said, "When, meanwhile, the customs of that most accursed nation have gained such strength that they have been now received in all lands, the conquered have given laws to the conquerors." By these words he expresses his astonishment; and, not knowing what the providence of God was leading him to say, subjoins in plain words an opinion by which he showed what he thought about the meaning of those sacred institutions: "For," he says, "those, however, know the cause of their rites, while the greater part of the people know not why they perform theirs." But concerning the solemnities of the Jews, either why or how far they were instituted by divine authority, and afterward, in due time, by the same authority taken away from the people of God, to whom the mystery of eternal life was revealed, we have both spoken elsewhere, especially when we were treating against the Manichæans, and also intend to speak in this work in a more suitable place.

12. THAT WHEN ONCE THE VANITY OF THE GODS OF THE NATIONS HAS BEEN EXPOSED, IT CANNOT BE DOUBTED THAT THEY ARE UNABLE TO BESTOW ETERNAL LIFE ON ANYONE, WHEN THEY CANNOT AFFORD HELP EVEN WITH RESPECT TO THE THINGS OF THIS TEMPORAL LIFE

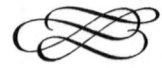

Now, since there are three theologies, which the Greeks call respectively mythical, physical, and political, and which may be called in Latin fabulous, natural, and civil; and since neither from the fabulous, which even the worshipers of many and false gods have themselves most freely censured, nor from the civil, of which that is convicted of being a part, or even worse than it, can eternal life be hoped for from any of these theologies—if anyone thinks that what has been said in this book is not enough for him, let him also add to it the many and various dissertations concerning God as the giver of felicity, contained in the former books, especially the fourth one.

For to what but to felicity should men consecrate

themselves, were felicity a goddess? However, as it is not a goddess, but a gift of God, to what God but the giver of happiness ought we to consecrate ourselves, who piously love eternal life, in which there is true and full felicity? But I think, from what has been said, no one ought to doubt that none of those gods is the giver of happiness, who are worshiped with such shame, and who, if they are not so worshiped, are more shamefully enraged, and thus confess that they are most foul spirits. Moreover, how can he give eternal life who cannot give happiness? For we mean by eternal life that life where there is endless happiness. For if the soul live in eternal punishments, by which also those unclean spirits shall be tormented, that is rather eternal death than eternal life. For there is no greater or worse death than when death never dies. But because the soul from its very nature, being created immortal, cannot be without some kind of life, its utmost death is alienation from the life of God in an eternity of punishment. So, then, He only who gives true happiness gives eternal life, that is, an endlessly happy life. And since those gods whom this civil theology worships have been proved to be unable to give this happiness, they ought not to be worshiped on account of those temporal and terrestrial things, as we showed in the five former books, much less on account of eternal life, which is to be after death, as we have sought to show in this one book especially, while the other books also lend it their cooperation. But since the strength of inveterate habit has its roots very deep, if anyone thinks that I have not disputed sufficiently to show that this civil theology ought to be rejected and shunned, let him attend to another book which, with God's help, is to be joined to this one.

BOOK SEVEN

ARGUMENT

In this book it is shown that eternal life is not obtained by the worship of Janus, Jupiter, Saturn, and the other "select gods" of the civil theology.

It will be the duty of those who are endowed with quicker and better understandings, in whose case the former books are sufficient, and more than sufficient, to effect their intended object, to bear with me with patience and equanimity while I attempt with more than ordinary diligence to tear up and eradicate depraved and ancient opinions hostile to the truth of piety, which the long-continued error of the human race has fixed very deeply in unenlightened minds; cooperating also in this, according to my little measure, with the grace of Him who, being the true God, is able to accomplish it, and on whose help I depend in my work; and, for the sake of others, such should not deem superfluous what they feel to be no longer necessary for themselves. A very great matter is at stake when the true and truly holy divinity is commended to men as that which they ought to seek after and to worship; not, however, on account of the transitory vapor of mortal life, but on account of life eternal, which alone is blessed, although the help necessary for this frail life we are now living is also afforded us by it.

1. WHETHER, SINCE IT IS EVIDENT THAT DEITY IS NOT TO BE FOUND IN THE CIVIL THEOLOGY, WE ARE TO BELIEVE THAT IT IS TO BE FOUND IN THE SELECT GODS

If there is anyone whom the sixth book, which I have last finished, has not persuaded that this divinity, or, so to speak, deity—for this word also our authors do not hesitate to use, in order to translate more accurately that which the Greeks call θεότης—if there is anyone, I say, whom the sixth book has not persuaded that this divinity or deity is not to be found in that theology which they call civil, and which Marcus Varro has explained in sixteen books—that is, that the happiness of eternal life is not attainable through the worship of gods such as states have established to be worshiped, and that in such a form—perhaps, when he has read this book, he will not have anything further to desire in order to the clearing up of this question. For it is possible that someone may think that at least the select and chief gods, whom Varro comprised in his last book, and of whom we have not spoken sufficiently, are to be worshiped on account of the blessed life, which is none other than eternal. In respect to which matter I do not say what Tertullian said, perhaps more wittily than truly, "If gods are selected like onions, certainly the rest are rejected as bad."[1] I do not say this, for I see that even from among the select, some are selected for some greater and more excellent office: as in warfare, when recruits have been elected, there are some again elected from among those for the performance of some greater military service; and in the church, when persons are elected to be overseers, certainly the rest are not rejected, since all good Christians are deservedly called elect; in the erection of a building cornerstones are elected, though the other stones, which are destined for other parts of the structure, are not rejected; grapes are elected for eating, while the others, which we leave for drinking, are not rejected. There is no need of adducing many illustrations, since the thing is evident. Wherefore the selection of certain gods from among many affords no proper reason why either he who wrote on this subject, or the worshipers of the gods, or the gods themselves, should be spurned. We ought rather to seek to know what gods these are, and for what purpose they may appear to have been selected.

---

1. Tertullian *Apol.* 13, "Nec electio sine reprobatione"; and *Ad Nat.* 2.9, "Si dei ut bulbi seliguntur, qui non seliguntur, reprobi pronuntiantur."

2. WHO ARE THE SELECT GODS, AND WHETHER THEY ARE HELD TO BE EXEMPT FROM THE OFFICES OF THE COMMONER GODS

The following gods, certainly, Varro signalizes as select, devoting one book to this subject: Janus, Jupiter, Saturn, Genius, Mercury, Apollo, Mars, Vulcan, Neptune, Sol, Orcus, Father Liber, Tellus, Ceres, Juno, Luna, Diana, Minerva, Venus, Vesta; of which twenty gods, twelve are males, and eight females. Whether are these deities called select, because of their higher spheres of administration in the world, or because they have become better known to the people, and more worship has been expended on them? If it be on account of the greater works which are performed by them in the world, we ought not to have found them among that, as it were, plebeian crowd of deities, which has assigned to it the charge of minute and trifling things. For, first of all, at the conception of a fœtus, from which point all the works commence which have been distributed in minute detail to many deities, Janus himself opens the way for the reception of the seed; there also is Saturn, on account of the seed itself; there is Liber,[1] who liberates the male by the effusion of the seed; there is Libera, whom they also would have to be Venus, who confers this same benefit on the woman, namely, that she also be liberated by the emission of the seed; all these are of the number of those who are called select. But there is also the goddess Mena, who presides over the menses; though the daughter of Jupiter, ignoble nevertheless. And this province of the menses the same author, in his book on the select gods, assigns to Juno herself, who is even queen among the select gods; and here, as Juno Lucina, along with the same Mena, her stepdaughter, she presides over the same blood. There also are two gods, exceedingly obscure, Vitumnus and Sentinus—the one of whom imparts life to the fœtus, and the other sensation; and, of a truth, they bestow, most ignoble though they be, far more than all those noble and select gods bestow. For, surely, without life and sensation, what is the whole fœtus which a woman carries in her womb, but a most vile and worthless thing, no better than slime and dust?

---

1. Cicero (*De Nat. Deor.* 2) distinguishes this Liber from Liber Bacchus, son of Jupiter and Semele.

3. HOW THERE IS NO REASON WHICH CAN BE SHOWN FOR THE SELECTION OF CERTAIN GODS, WHEN THE ADMINISTRATION OF MORE EXALTED OFFICES IS ASSIGNED TO MANY INFERIOR GODS

What is the cause, therefore, which has driven so many select gods to these very small works, in which they are excelled by Vitumnus and Sentinus, though little known and sunk in obscurity, inasmuch as they confer the munificent gifts of life and sensation? For the select Janus bestows an entrance, and, as it were, a door[1] for the seed; the select Saturn bestows the seed itself; the select Liber bestows on men the emission of the same seed; Libera, who is Ceres or Venus, confers the same on women; the select Juno confers (not alone, but together with Mena, the daughter of Jupiter) the menses, for the growth of that which has been conceived; and the obscure and ignoble Vitumnus confers life, while the obscure and ignoble Sentinus confers sensation—which two last things are as much more excellent than the others, as they themselves are excelled by reason and intellect. For as those things which reason and understand are preferable to those which, without intellect and reason, as in the case of cattle, live and feel; so also those things which have been endowed with life and sensation are deservedly preferred to those things which neither live nor feel. Therefore Vitumnus the life giver,[2] and Sentinus the sense giver,[3] ought to have been reckoned among the select gods, rather than Janus the admitter of seed, and Saturn the giver or sower of seed, and Liber and Libera the movers and liberators of seed; which seed is not worth a thought, unless it attain to life and sensation. Yet these select gifts are not given by select gods, but by certain unknown, and, considering their dignity, neglected gods. But if it be replied that Janus has dominion over all beginnings, and therefore the opening of the way for conception is not without reason assigned to him; and that Saturn has dominion over all seeds, and therefore the sowing of the seed whereby a human being is generated cannot be excluded from his operation; that Liber and Libera have power over the emission of all seeds, and therefore preside over those seeds which pertain to the procreation of men; that Juno presides over all purgations and births, and therefore she has also charge of the purgations of women and the births of human beings; if they give this reply, let them find an answer to the question concerning Vitumnus and Sentinus, whether they are willing that these likewise should have dominion over all things which live and feel. If they grant this, let them observe in how sublime a position they are about to place them. For to spring from seeds is in the earth and of the earth, but to live and feel are supposed to be properties even of the sidereal gods. But if they say that only such things as come to life in flesh, and are supported by senses, are assigned to Sentinus, why does not that God who made all things live and feel, bestow on flesh also life and sensation, in the universality of His operation conferring also on fœtuses this gift? And what, then, is the use of Vitumnus and Sentinus? But if these, as it were, extreme and lowest things have been committed by Him who presides universally over life and sense to these gods as to servants, are these select gods then so destitute of servants, that they could not find any to whom even they might commit those things, but with all their dignity, for which they are, it seems, deemed worthy to be selected, were compelled to perform their work along with ignoble ones? Juno is select queen of the gods, and the sister and wife of Jupiter; nevertheless she is Iterduca, the conductor, to boys, and performs this work along with a most ignoble pair—the goddesses Abeona and Adeona. There they have also placed the goddess Mena, who gives to boys a good mind, and she is not placed among the select gods; as if anything greater could be bestowed on a man than a good mind. But Juno is placed among the select because she is Iterduca and Domiduca (she who conducts one on a journey, and who conducts him home again); as if it is of any advantage for one to make a journey, and to be conducted home again, if his mind is not good. And yet the goddess who bestows that gift has not been placed by the selectors among the select gods, though she ought indeed to have been preferred even to Minerva, to whom, in this minute distribution of work, they have allotted the memory of boys. For who will doubt that it is a far better thing to have a good mind, than ever so great a memory? For no one is bad who has a good mind;[4] but some who are very bad are possessed of an admirable memory, and are so much the worse, the less they are able to forget the bad things which they think. And yet Minerva is among the select gods, while the goddess Mena is hidden by a worthless crowd. What shall I say concerning Virtus? What concerning Felicitas?—concerning whom I have already spoken much in the fourth book;[5] to whom, though they held them to be goddesses, they have not thought fit to assign a place among the select gods, among whom they have given a place to Mars and Orcus, the one the causer of death, the other the receiver of the dead.

Since, therefore, we see that even the select gods themselves work together with the others, like a senate with the people, in all those minute works which have been minutely portioned out among many gods; and since we find that far greater and better things are administered by certain gods who have not been reckoned worthy to be selected than by those who are called select, it remains that we suppose that they were called select and chief, not on account of their holding more exalted offices in the world, but because it happened to them to become better known to the people. And even Varro himself says, that in that way obscurity had fallen to the lot of some father gods and mother goddesses,[6] as it fails to the lot of man. If, therefore, Felicity ought not perhaps to have been put among the select gods, because they did not attain to that noble position by merit, but by chance, Fortune at least should have been placed among them, or rather before them; for they say that that goddess distributes to everyone the gifts she receives, not according to any rational arrangement, but according as chance may determine. She ought to have held the uppermost place among the select gods, for among them chiefly it is that she shows what power she has. For we see that they have been selected not on account of some eminent virtue or rational happiness, but by that random power of Fortune which the worshipers of these gods think that she exerts. For that most eloquent man Sallust also may perhaps have the gods themselves in view when he says: "But, in truth, fortune rules in everything; it renders all things famous or obscure, according to caprice rather than according to truth."[7] For they cannot discover a reason why Venus should have been made famous, while Virtus has been made obscure, when the divinity of both of them has been solemnly recognized by them, and their merits are not to be compared. Again, if she has deserved a noble position on account of the fact that she is much sought after—for there are more who seek after Venus than after Virtus—why has Minerva been celebrated while Pecunia has been left in obscurity, although throughout the whole human race avarice allures a far greater number than skill? And even among those who are skilled in the arts, you will rarely find a man who does not practice his own art for the purpose of pecuniary gain; and that for the sake of which anything is made, is always valued more than that which is made for the sake of something else. If, then, this selection of gods has been made by the judgment of the foolish multitude, why has not the goddess Pecunia been preferred to Minerva, since there are many artificers for the sake of money? But if this distinction has been made by the few wise, why has Virtus been preferred to Venus, when reason by far prefers the former? At all events, as I have already said, Fortune herself—who, according to those who attribute most influence to her, renders all things famous or obscure according to caprice rather than according to the truth—since she has been able to exercise so much power even over the gods, as, according to her capricious judgment, to render those of them famous whom she would, and those obscure whom she would; Fortune herself ought to occupy the place of preeminence among the select gods, since over them also she has such preeminent power. Or must we suppose that the reason why she is not among the select is simply this, that even Fortune herself has had an adverse fortune? She was adverse, then, to herself, since, while ennobling others, she herself has remained obscure.

---

1. Januam.
2. Vivificator.
3. Sensificator.
4. As we say, right-minded.

5. See above, 4.21; 4.23.
6. The father Saturn and the mother Ops, e.g., being more obscure than their son Jupiter and daughter Juno.
7. *Sallust De Conj. Cat. 8.*

4. THE INFERIOR GODS, WHOSE NAMES ARE NOT ASSOCIATED WITH INFAMY, HAVE BEEN BETTER DEALT WITH THAN THE SELECT GODS, WHOSE INFAMIES ARE CELEBRATED

However, anyone who eagerly seeks for celebrity and renown, might congratulate those select gods, and call them fortunate, were it not that he saw that they have been selected more to their injury than to their honor. For that low crowd of gods have been protected by their very meanness and obscurity from being overwhelmed with infamy. We laugh, indeed, when we see them distributed by the mere fiction of human opinions, according to the special works assigned to them, like those who farm small portions of the public revenue, or like workmen in the street of the silversmiths,[1] where one vessel, in order that it may go out perfect, passes through the hands of many, when it might have been finished by one perfect workman. But the only reason why the combined skill of many workmen was thought necessary, was, that it is better that each part of an art should be learned by a special workman, which can be done speedily and easily, than that they should all be compelled to be perfect in one art throughout all its parts, which they could only attain slowly and with difficulty. Nevertheless there is scarcely to be found one of the nonselect gods who has brought infamy on himself by any crime, while there is scarce any one of the select gods who has not received upon himself the brand of notable infamy. These latter have descended to the humble works of the others, while the others have not come up to their sublime crimes. Concerning Janus, there does not readily occur to my recollection anything infamous; and perhaps he was such a one as lived more innocently than the rest, and further removed from misdeeds and crimes. He kindly received and entertained Saturn when he was fleeing; he divided his kingdom with his guest, so that each of them had a city for himself,[2] the one Janiculum, and the other Saturnia. But those seekers after every kind of unseemliness in the worship of the gods have disgraced him, whose life they found to be less disgracful than that of the other gods, with an image of monstrous deformity, making it sometimes with two faces, and sometimes, as it were, double, with four faces.[3] Did they wish that, as the most of the select gods had lost shame[4] through the perpetration of shameful crimes, his greater innocence should be marked by a greater number of faces?[5]

---

1. Vicus argentarius.
2. Virgil *Æneid*, 8.357–358.

3. Quadrifrons.
4. Frons.
5. *"Quanto iste innocentior esset, tanto frontosior appareret"*; being used for the shamelessness of innocence, as we use "face" for the shamelessness of impudence.

5. CONCERNING THE MORE SECRET DOCTRINE OF THE PAGANS, AND CONCERNING THE PHYSICAL INTERPRETATIONS

But let us hear their own physical interpretations by which they attempt to color, as with the appearance of profounder doctrine, the baseness of most miserable error. Varro, in the first place, commends these interpretations so strongly as to say, that the ancients invented the images, badges, and adornments of the gods, in order that when those who went to the mysteries should see them with their bodily eyes, they might with the eyes of their mind see the soul of the world, and its parts, that is, the true gods; and also that the meaning which was intended by those who made their images with the human form, seemed to be this—namely, that the mind of mortals, which is in a human body, is very like to the immortal mind,[1] just as vessels might be placed to represent the gods, as, for instance, a wine vessel might be placed in the temple of Liber, to signify wine, that which is contained being signified by that which contains. Thus by an image which had the human form the rational soul was signified, because the human form is the vessel, as it were, in which that nature is wont to be contained which they attribute to God, or to the gods. These are the mysteries of doctrine to which that most learned man penetrated in order that he might bring them forth to the light. But, O you most acute man, have you lost among those mysteries that prudence which led you to form the sober opinion, that those who first established those images for the people took away fear from the citizens and added error, and that the ancient Romans honored the gods more chastely without images? For it was through consideration of them that you were emboldened to speak these things against the later Romans. For if those most ancient Romans also had worshiped images, perhaps you would have suppressed by the silence of fear all those sentiments (true sentiments, nevertheless) concerning the folly of setting up images, and would have extolled more loftily, and more loquaciously, those mysterious doctrines consisting of these vain and pernicious fictions. Your soul, so learned and so clever (and for this I grieve much for you), could never through these mysteries have reached its God; that is, the God by whom, not with whom, it was made, of whom it is not a part, but a work—that God who is not the soul of all things, but who made every soul, and in whose light alone every soul is blessed, if it be not ungrateful for His grace.

But the things which follow in this book will show what is the nature of these mysteries, and what value is to be set upon them. Meanwhile, this most learned man confesses as his opinion that the soul of the world and its parts are the true gods, from which we perceive that his theology (to wit, that same natural theology to which he pays great regard) has been able, in its completeness, to extend itself even to the nature of the rational soul. For in this book (concerning the select gods) he says a very few things by anticipation concerning the natural theology; and we shall see whether he has been able in that book, by means of physical interpretations, to refer to this natural theology that civil theology, concerning which he wrote last when treating of the select gods. Now, if he has been able to do this, the whole is natural; and in that case, what need was there for distinguishing so carefully the civil from the natural? But if it has been distinguished by a veritable distinction, then, since not even this natural theology with which he is so much pleased is true (for though it has reached as far as the soul, it has not reached to the true God who made the soul), how much more contemptible and false is that civil theology which is chiefly occupied about what is corporeal, as will be shown by its very interpretations, which they have with such diligence sought out and enucleated, some of which I must necessarily mention!

---

1. Cicero *Tusc. Disp.* 5.13.

6. CONCERNING THE OPINION OF VARRO, THAT GOD IS THE SOUL OF THE WORLD, WHICH NEVERTHELESS, IN ITS VARIOUS PARTS, HAS MANY SOULS WHOSE NATURE IS DIVINE

The same Varro, then, still speaking by anticipation, says that he thinks that God is the soul of the world (which the Greeks call κόσμος), and that this world itself is God; but as a wise man, though he consists of body and mind, is nevertheless called wise on account of his mind, so the world is called God on account of mind, although it consists of mind and body. Here he seems, in some fashion at least, to acknowledge one God; but that he may introduce more, he adds that the world is divided into two parts, heaven and earth, which are again divided each into two parts, heaven into ether and air, earth into water and land, of all which the ether is the highest, the air second, the water third, and the earth the lowest. All these four parts, he says, are full of souls; those which are in the ether and air being immortal, and those which are in the water and on the earth mortal. From the highest part of the heavens to the orbit of the moon there are souls, namely, the stars and planets; and these are not only understood to be gods, but are seen to be such. And between the orbit of the moon and the commencement of the region of clouds and winds there are aerial souls; but these are seen with the mind, not with the eyes, and are called heroes, and lares, and genii. This is the natural theology which is briefly set forth in these anticipatory statements, and which satisfied not Varro only, but many philosophers besides. This I must discuss more carefully, when, with the help of God, I shall have completed what I have yet to say concerning the civil theology, as far as it concerns the select gods.

7. WHETHER IT IS REASONABLE TO SEPARATE JANUS AND TERMINUS AS TWO DISTINCT DEITIES

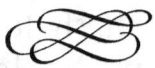

Who, then, is Janus, with whom Varro commences? He is the world. Certainly a very brief and unambiguous reply. Why, then, do they say that the beginnings of things pertain to him, but the ends to another whom they call Terminus? For they say that two months have been dedicated to these two gods, with reference to beginnings and ends—January to Janus, and February to Terminus—over and above those ten months which commence with March and end with December. And they say that that is the reason why the Terminalia are celebrated in the month of February, the same month in which the sacred purification is made which they call Februum, and from which the month derives its name.[1] Do the beginnings of things, therefore, pertain to the world, which is Janus, and not also the ends, since another god has been placed over them? Do they not own that all things which they say begin in this world also come to an end in this world? What folly it is, to give him only half power in work, when in his image they give him two faces! Would it not be a far more elegant way of interpreting the two-faced image, to say that Janus and Terminus are the same, and that the one face has reference to beginnings, the other to ends? For one who works ought to have respect to both. For he who in every forthputting of activity does not look back on the beginning, does not look forward to the end. Wherefore it is necessary that prospective intention be connected with retrospective memory. For how shall one find how to finish anything, if he has forgotten what it was which he had begun? But if they thought that the blessed life is begun in this world, and perfected beyond the world, and for that reason attributed to Janus, that is, to the world, only the power of beginnings, they should certainly have preferred Terminus to him, and should not have shut him out from the number of the select gods. Yet even now, when the beginnings and ends of temporal things are represented by these two gods, more honor ought to have been given to Terminus. For the greater joy is that which is felt when anything is finished; but things begun are always cause of much anxiety until they are brought to an end, which end he who begins anything very greatly longs for, fixes his mind on, expects, desires; nor does anyone ever rejoice over anything he has begun, unless it be brought to an end.

1. An interesting account of the changes made in the Roman year by Numa is given in Plutarch's life of that king. Ovid also (*Fasti* 2) explains the derivation of February, telling us that it was the last month of the old year, and took its name from the lustrations performed then: "*Februa Romani dixere piamina patres.*"

8. FOR WHAT REASON THE WORSHIPERS OF JANUS HAVE MADE HIS IMAGE WITH TWO FACES, WHEN THEY WOULD SOMETIMES HAVE IT BE SEEN WITH FOUR

But now let the interpretation of the two-faced image be produced. For they say that it has two faces, one before and one behind, because our gaping mouths seem to resemble the world: whence the Greeks call the palate οὐρανός, and some Latin poets,[1] he says, have called the heavens *palatum* [the palate]; and from the gaping mouth, they say, there is a way out in the direction of the teeth, and a way in in the direction of the gullet. See what the world has been brought to on account of a Greek or a poetical word for our palate! Let this god be worshiped only on account of saliva, which has two open doorways under the heavens of the palate—one through which part of it may be spit out, the other through which part of it may be swallowed down. Besides, what is more absurd than not to find in the world itself two doorways opposite to each other, through which it may either receive anything into itself, or cast it out from itself; and to seek of our throat and gullet, to which the world has no resemblance, to make up an image of the world in Janus, because the world is said to resemble the *palate*, to which Janus bears no likeness? But when they make him four-faced, and call him double Janus, they interpret this as having reference to the four quarters of the world, as though the world looked out on anything, like Janus through his four faces. Again, if Janus is the world, and the world consists of four quarters, then the image of the two-faced Janus is false. Or if it is true, because the whole world is sometimes understood by the expression east and west, will anyone call the world double when north and south also are mentioned, as they call Janus double when he has four faces? They have no way at all of interpreting, in relation to the world, four doorways by which to go in and to come out as they did in the case of the two-faced Janus, where they found, at any rate in the human mouth, something which answered to what they said about him; unless perhaps Neptune come to their aid, and hand them a fish, which, besides the mouth and gullet, has also the openings of the gills, one on each side. Nevertheless, with all the doors, no soul escapes this vanity but that one which hears the truth saying, "I am the door."[2]

---

1. Ennius, in Cicero *De Nat. Deor.* 2.18.
2. John 10:9.

9. CONCERNING THE POWER OF JUPITER, AND A COMPARISON OF JUPITER WITH JANUS

But they also show whom they would have Jove (who is also called Jupiter) understood to be. He is the god, say they, who has the power of the causes by which anything comes to be in the world. And how great a thing this is, that most noble verse of Virgil testifies:

> *Happy is he who has learned the causes of things.*[1]

But why is Janus preferred to him? Let that most acute and most learned man answer us this question. "Because," says he, "Janus has dominion over first things, Jupiter over highest[2] things. Therefore Jupiter is deservedly held to be the king of all things; for highest things are better than first things: for although first things precede in time, highest things excel by dignity."

Now this would have been rightly said had the

first parts of things which are done been distinguished from the highest parts; as, for instance, it is the beginning of a thing done to set out, the highest part to arrive. The commencing to learn is the first part of a thing begun, the acquirement of knowledge is the highest part. And so of all things: the beginnings are first, the ends highest. This matter, however, has been already discussed in connection with Janus and Terminus. But the causes which are attributed to Jupiter are things effecting, not things effected; and it is impossible for them to be prevented in time by things which are made or done, or by the beginnings of such things; for the thing which makes is always prior to the thing which is made. Therefore, though the beginnings of things which are made or done pertain to Janus, they are nevertheless not prior to the efficient causes which they attribute to Jupiter. For as nothing takes place without being preceded by an efficient cause, so without an efficient cause nothing begins to take place. Verily, if the people call this god Jupiter, in whose power are all the causes of all natures which have been made, and of all natural things, and worship him with such insults and infamous criminations, they are guilty of more shocking sacrilege than if they should totally deny the existence of any god. It would therefore be better for them to call some other god by the name of Jupiter—someone worthy of base and criminal honors; substituting instead of Jupiter some vain fiction (as Saturn is said to have had a stone given to him to devour instead of his son), which they might make the subject of their blasphemies, rather than speak of *that* god as both thundering and committing adultery—ruling the whole world, and laying himself out for the commission of so many licentious acts—having in his power nature and the highest causes of all natural things, but not having his own causes good.

Next, I ask what place they find any longer for this Jupiter among the gods, if Janus is the world; for Varro defined the true gods to be the soul of the world, and the parts of it. And therefore whatever falls not within this definition is certainly not a true god, according to them. Will they then say that Jupiter is the soul of the world, and Janus the body—that is, this visible world? If they say this, it will not be possible for them to affirm that Janus is a god. For even, according to them, the body of the world is not a god, but the soul of the world and its parts. Wherefore Varro, seeing this, says that he thinks God is the soul of the world, and that this world itself is God; but that as a wise man though he consists of soul and body, is nevertheless called wise from the soul, so the world is called God from the soul, though it consists of soul and body. Therefore the body of the world alone is not God, but either the soul of it alone, or the soul and the body together, yet so as that it is God not by virtue of the body, but by virtue of the soul. If, therefore, Janus is the world, and Janus is a god, will they say, in order that Jupiter may be a god, that he is some part of Janus? For they are wont rather to attribute universal existence to Jupiter; whence the saying, "All things are full of Jupiter."[3] Therefore they must think Jupiter also, in order that he may be a god, and especially king of the gods, to be the world, that he may rule over the other gods—according to them, his parts. To this effect, also, the same Varro expounds certain verses of Valerius Soranus[4] in that book which he wrote apart from the others concerning the worship of the gods. These are the verses:

> *Almighty Jove, progenitor of kings, and*
> *   things, and gods,*
> *And eke the mother of the gods, god one*
> *   and all.*

But in the same book he expounds these verses by saying that as the male emits seed, and the female receives it, so Jupiter, whom they believed to be the world, both emits all seeds from himself and receives them into himself. For which reason, he says, Soranus wrote, "Jove, progenitor and mother"; and with no less reason said that one and all were the same. For the world is one, and in that one are all things.

---

1. Virgil *Georg.* 2.470.
2. Summa, which also includes the meaning "last."
3. Virgil (*Ecl.* 3.60), who borrows the expression from the *Phœnomena* of Aratus.
4. Soranus lived about 100 B.C. See Smith's *Dictionary*.

10. WHETHER THE DISTINCTION BETWEEN JANUS AND JUPITER IS A PROPER ONE

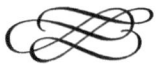

Since, therefore, Janus is the world, and Jupiter is the world, wherefore are Janus and Jupiter two gods, while the world is but one? Why do they have separate temples, separate altars, different rites, dissimilar images? If it be because the nature of beginnings is one, and the nature of causes another, and the one has received the name of Janus, the other of Jupiter; is it then the case, that if one man has two distinct offices of authority, or two arts, two judges or two artificers are spoken of, because the nature of the offices or the arts is different? So also with respect to one god: if he have the power of beginnings and of causes, must he therefore be thought to be two gods, because beginnings and causes are two things? But if they think that this is right, let them also affirm that Jupiter is as many gods as they have given him surnames, on account of many powers; for the things from which these surnames are applied to him are many and diverse. I shall mention a few of them.

11. CONCERNING THE SURNAMES OF JUPITER, WHICH ARE REFERRED NOT TO MANY GODS, BUT TO ONE AND THE SAME GOD

They have called him Victor, Invictus, Opitulus, Impulsor, Stator, Centumpeda, Supinalis, Tigillus, Almus, Ruminus, and other names which it were long to enumerate. But these surnames they have given to one god on account of diverse causes and powers, but yet have not compelled him to be, on account of so many things, as many gods. They gave him these surnames because he conquered all things; because he was conquered by none; because he brought help to the needy; because he had the power of impelling, stopping, stablishing, throwing on the back; because as a beam[1] he held together and sustained the world; because he nourished all things; because, like the pap,[2] he nourished animals. Here, we perceive, are some great things and some small things; and yet it is one who is said to perform them all. I think that the causes and the beginnings of things, on account of which they have thought that the one world is two gods, Jupiter and Janus, are nearer to each other than the holding together of the world, and the giving of the pap to animals; and yet, on account of these two works so far apart from each other, both in nature and dignity, there has not been any necessity for the existence of two gods; but one Jupiter has been called, on account of the one Tigillus, on account of the other Ruminus. I am unwilling to say that the giving of the pap to sucking animals might have become Juno rather than Jupiter, especially when there was the goddess Rumina to help and to serve her in this work; for I think it may be replied that Juno herself is nothing else than Jupiter, according to those verses of Valerius Soranus, where it has been said:

> "Almighty Jove, progenitor of kings, and
>   things, and gods,
> And eke the mother of the gods," etc.

Why, then, was he called Ruminus, when they who may perchance inquire more diligently may find that he is also that goddess Rumina?

If, then, it was rightly thought unworthy of the majesty of the gods, that in one ear of corn one god should have the care of the joint, another that of the husk, how much more unworthy of that majesty is it, that one thing, and that of the lowest kind, even the giving of the pap to animals that they may be nourished, should be under the care of two gods, one of whom is Jupiter himself, the very king of all things, who does this not along with his own wife, but with some ignoble Rumina (unless perhaps he himself is Rumina, being Ruminus for males and Rumina for females)! I should certainly have said that they had been unwilling to apply to Jupiter a feminine name, had he not been styled in these verses "progenitor and mother," and had I not read among other surnames of his that of Pecunia [money], which we found as a goddess among those petty deities, as I have already mentioned in the fourth book. But since both males and females have money [*pecuniam*], why has he not been called both Pecunius and Pecunia? That is their concern.

---

1. Tigillus.
2. Ruma.

12. THAT JUPITER IS ALSO CALLED PECUNIA

How elegantly they have accounted for this name! "He is also called Pecunia," say they, "because all things belong to him." Oh, how grand an explanation of the name of a deity! Yes; he to whom all things belong is most meanly and most contumeliously called Pecunia. In comparison of all things which are contained by heaven and earth, what are all things together which are possessed by men under the name of money?[1] And this name, forsooth, has avarice given to Jupiter, that whoever was a lover of money might seem to himself to love not an ordinary god, but the very king of all things himself. But it would be a far different thing if he had been called Riches. For riches are one thing, money another. For we call rich the wise, the just, the good, who have either no money or very little. For they are more truly rich in possessing virtue, since by it, even as respects things necessary for the body, they are content with what they have. But we call the greedy poor, who are always craving and always wanting. For they may possess ever so great an amount of money; but whatever be the abundance of that, they are not able but to want. And we properly call God Himself rich; not, however, in money, but in omnipotence. Therefore they who have abundance of money are called rich, but inwardly needy if they are greedy. So also, those who have no money are called poor, but inwardly rich if they are wise.

What, then, ought the wise man to think of this theology, in which the king of the gods receives the name of that thing "which no wise man has desired"?[2] For had there been anything wholesomely taught by this philosophy concerning eternal life, how much more appropriately would that god who is the ruler of the world have been called by them, not money, but wisdom, the love of which purges from the filth of avarice, that is, of the love of money!

---

1. Pecunia, that is, property; the original meaning of *pecunia* being property in cattle, then property or wealth of any kind. Cf. Augustine *De Discipl. Christ.* 6.
2. Sallust *De Conj. Cat.* 11.

13. THAT WHEN IT IS EXPOUNDED WHAT SATURN IS, WHAT GENIUS IS, IT COMES TO THIS, THAT BOTH OF THEM ARE SHOWN TO BE JUPITER

But why speak more of this Jupiter, with whom perchance all the rest are to be identified; so that, he being all, the opinion as to the existence of many gods may remain as a mere opinion, empty of all truth? And they are all to be referred to him, if his various parts and powers are thought of as so many gods, or if the principle of mind which they think to be diffused through all things has received the names of many gods from the various parts which the mass of this visible world combines in itself, and from the manifold administration of nature. For what is Saturn also? "One of the principal gods," he says, "who has dominion over all sowings." Does not the exposition of the verses of Valerius Soranus teach that Jupiter is the world, and that he emits all seeds from himself, and receives them into himself?

It is he, then, with whom is the dominion of all sowings. What is Genius? "He is the god who is set over, and has the power of begetting, all things." Who else than the world do they believe to have this power, to which it has been said:

Almighty Jove, progenitor and mother?

And when in another place he says that Genius is the rational soul of everyone, and therefore exists separately in each individual, but that the corresponding soul of the world is God, he just comes back to this same thing—namely, that the soul of the world itself is to be held to be, as it were, the universal genius. This, therefore, is what he calls Jupiter. For if every genius is a god, and the soul of every man a genius, it follows that the soul of every man is a god. But if very absurdity compels even these theologians themselves to shrink from this, it remains that they call that genius god by special and preeminent distinction, whom they call the soul of the world, and therefore Jupiter.

14. CONCERNING THE OFFICES OF MERCURY AND MARS

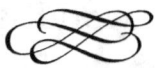

But they have not found how to refer Mercury and Mars to any parts of the world, and to the works of God which are in the elements; and therefore they have set them at least over human works, making them assistants in speaking and in carrying on wars. Now Mercury, if he has also the power of the speech of the gods, rules also over the king of the gods himself, if Jupiter, as he receives from him the faculty of speech, also speaks according as it is his pleasure to permit him—which surely is absurd; but if it is only the power over human speech which is held to be attributed to him, then we say it is incredible that Jupiter should have condescended to give the pap not only to children, but also to beasts—from which he has been surnamed Ruminus—and yet should have been unwilling that the care of our speech, by which we excel the beasts, should pertain to him. And thus speech itself both belongs to Jupiter, and is Mercury. But if speech itself is said to be Mercury, as those things which are said concerning him by way of interpretation show it to be—for he is said to have been called Mercury, that is, he who runs between,[1] because speech runs between men; they say also that the Greeks call him Ἑρμῆς, because speech, or interpretation, which certainly belongs to speech, is called by them ἑρμηνεία; also he is said to preside over payments, because speech passes between sellers and buyers; the wings, too, which he has on his head and on his feet, they say mean that speech passes winged through the air; he is also said to have been called the messenger,[2] because by means of speech all our thoughts are expressed[3]—if, therefore, speech itself is Mercury, then, even by their own confession, he is not a god. But when they make to themselves gods of such as are not even demons, by praying to unclean spirits, they are possessed by such as are not gods, but demons. In like manner, because they have not been able to find for Mars any element or part of the world in which he might perform some works of nature of whatever kind, they have said that he is the god of war, which is a work of men, and that not one which is considered desirable by them. If, therefore, Felicitas should give perpetual peace, Mars would have nothing to do. But if war itself is Mars, as speech is Mercury, I wish it were as true that there were no war to be falsely called a god, as it is true that it is not a god.

---

1. "Quasi medius currens."
2. Nuncius.
3. Enunciantur.

15. CONCERNING CERTAIN STARS WHICH THE PAGANS HAVE CALLED BY THE NAMES OF THEIR GODS

But possibly these stars which have been called by their names are these gods. For they call a certain star Mercury, and likewise a certain other star Mars. But among those stars which are called by the names of gods, is that one which they call Jupiter, and yet with them Jupiter is the world. There also is that one they call Saturn, and yet they give to him no small property besides —namely, all seeds. There also is that brightest of them all which is called by them Venus, and yet they will have this same Venus to be also the moon —not to mention how Venus and Juno are said by them to contend about that most brilliant star, as though about another golden apple. For some say that Lucifer belongs to Venus, and some to Juno. But, as usual, Venus conquers. For by far the greatest number assign that star to Venus, so much so that there is scarcely found one of them who thinks otherwise. But since they call Jupiter the king of all, who will not laugh to see his star so far surpassed in brilliancy by the star of Venus? For it ought to have been as much more brilliant than the rest, as he himself is more powerful. They answer that it only appears so because it is higher up, and very much farther away from the earth. If, therefore, its greater dignity has deserved a higher place, why is Saturn higher in the heavens than Jupiter? Was the vanity of the fable which made Jupiter king not able to reach the stars? And has Saturn been permitted to obtain at least in the heavens, what he could not obtain in his own kingdom nor in the Capitol?

But why has Janus received no star? If it is because he is the world, and they are all in him, the world is also Jupiter's, and yet he has one. Did Janus compromise his case as best he could, and instead of the one star which he does not have among the heavenly bodies, accept so many faces on earth? Again, if they think that on account of the stars alone Mercury and Mars are parts of the world, in order that they may be able to have them for gods, since speech and war are not parts of the world, but acts of men, how is it that they have made no altars, established no rites, built no temples for Aries, and Taurus, and Cancer, and Scorpio, and the rest which they number as the celestial signs, and which consist not of single stars, but each of them of many stars, which also they say are situated above those already mentioned in the highest part of the heavens, where a more constant motion causes the stars to follow an undeviating course? And why have they not reckoned them as gods, I do not say among those select gods, but not even among those, as it were, plebeian gods?

16. CONCERNING APOLLO AND DIANA, AND THE OTHER SELECT GODS WHOM THEY WOULD HAVE TO BE PARTS OF THE WORLD

Although they would have Apollo to be a diviner and physician, they have nevertheless given him a place as some part of the world. They have said that he is also the sun; and likewise they have said that Diana, his sister, is the moon, and the guardian of roads. Whence also they will have her be a virgin, because a road brings forth nothing. They also make both of them have arrows, because those two planets send their rays from the heavens to the earth. They make Vulcan to be the fire of the world; Neptune the waters of the world; Father Dis, that is, Orcus, the earthy and lowest part of the world. Liber and Ceres they set over seeds—the former over the seeds of males, the latter over the seeds of females; or the one over the fluid part of seed, but the other over the dry part. And all this together is referred to the world, that is, to Jupiter, who is called "progenitor and mother," because he emitted all seeds from himself, and received them into himself. For they also make this same Ceres to be the Great Mother, who they say is none other than the earth, and call her also Juno. And therefore they assign to her the second causes of things, notwithstanding that it has been said to Jupiter, "progenitor and mother of the gods"; because, according to them, the whole world itself is Jupiter's. Minerva, also, because they set her over human arts, and did not find even a star in which to place her, has been said by them to be either the highest ether, or even the moon. Also Vesta herself they have thought to be the highest of the goddesses, because she is the earth; although they have thought that the milder fire of the world, which is used for the ordinary purposes of human life, not the more violent fire, such as belongs to Vulcan, is to be assigned to her. And thus they will have all those select gods to be the world and its parts—some of them the whole world, others of them its parts; the whole of it Jupiter—its parts, Genius, Mater Magna, Sol and Luna, or rather Apollo and Diana, and so on. And sometimes they make one god many things; sometimes one thing many gods. Many things are one god in the case of Jupiter; for both the whole world is Jupiter, and the sky alone is Jupiter, and the star alone is said and held to be Jupiter. Juno also is mistress of second causes—Juno is the air, Juno is the earth; and had she won it over Venus, Juno would have been the star. Likewise Minerva is the highest ether, and Minerva is likewise the moon, which they suppose to be in the lowest limit of the ether. And also they make one thing many gods in this way. The world is both

Janus and Jupiter; also the earth is Juno, and Mater Magna, and Ceres.

17. THAT EVEN VARRO HIMSELF PRONOUNCED HIS OWN OPINIONS REGARDING THE GODS AMBIGUOUS

And the same is true with respect to all the rest, as is true with respect to those things which I have mentioned for the sake of example. They do not explain them, but rather involve them. They rush hither and thither, to this side or to that, according as they are driven by the impulse of erratic opinion; so that even Varro himself has chosen rather to doubt concerning all things, than to affirm anything. For, having written the first of the three last books concerning the certain gods, and having commenced in the second of these to speak of the uncertain gods, he says: "I ought not to be censured for having stated in this book the doubtful opinions concerning the gods. For he who, when he has read them, shall think that they both ought to be, and can be, conclusively judged of, will do so himself. For my own part, I can be more easily led to doubt the things which I have written in the first book, than to attempt to reduce all the things I shall write in this one to any orderly system." Thus he makes uncertain not only that book concerning the uncertain gods, but also that other concerning the certain gods. Moreover, in that third book concerning the select gods, after having exhibited by anticipation as much of the natural theology as he deemed necessary, and when about to commence to speak of the vanities and lying insanities of the civil theology, where he was not only without the guidance of the truth of things, but was also pressed by the authority of tradition, he says: "I will write in this book concerning the public gods of the Roman people, to whom they have dedicated temples, and whom they have conspicuously distinguished by many adornments; but, as Xenophon of Colophon writes, I will state what I think, not what I am prepared to maintain: it is for man to think those things, for God to know them."

It is not, then, an account of things comprehended and most certainly believed which he promised, when about to write those things which were instituted by men. He only timidly promises an account of things which are but the subject of doubtful opinion. Nor, indeed, was it possible for him to affirm with the same certainty that Janus was the world, and such like things; or to discover with the same certainty such things as how Jupiter was the son of Saturn, while Saturn was made subject to him as king; he could, I say, neither affirm nor discover such things with the same certainty with which he knew such things as that the world existed, that the heavens and earth existed, the heavens bright with stars, and the earth fertile through seeds; or with the same perfect conviction with which he believed that this universal mass of nature is governed and administered by a certain invisible and mighty force.

18. A MORE CREDIBLE CAUSE OF THE RISE OF PAGAN ERROR

A far more credible account of these gods is given, when it is said that they were men, and that to each one of them sacred rites and solemnities were instituted, according to his particular genius, manners, actions, circumstances; which rites and solemnities, by gradually creeping through the souls of men, which are like demons, and eager for things which yield them sport, were spread far and wide; the poets adorning them with lies, and false spirits seducing men to receive them. For it is far more likely that some youth, either impious himself, or afraid of being slain by an impious father, being desirous to reign, dethroned his father, than that (according to Varro's interpretation) Saturn was overthrown by his son Jupiter: for cause, which belongs to Jupiter, is before seed, which belongs to Saturn. For had this been so, Saturn would never have been before Jupiter, nor would he have been the father of Jupiter. For cause always precedes seed, and is never generated from seed. But when they seek to honor by natural interpretation most vain fables or deeds of men, even the acutest men are so perplexed that we are compelled to grieve for their folly also.

19. CONCERNING THE INTERPRETATIONS WHICH COMPOSE THE REASON OF THE WORSHIP OF SATURN

They said, says Varro, that Saturn was wont to devour all that sprang from him, because seeds returned to the earth from whence they sprang. And when it is said that a lump of earth was put before Saturn to be devoured instead of Jupiter, it is signified, he says, that before the art of plowing was discovered, seeds were buried in the earth by the hands of men. The earth itself, then, and not seeds, should have been called Saturn, because it in a manner devours what it has brought forth, when the seeds which have sprung from it return again into it. And what has Saturn's receiving of a lump of earth instead of Jupiter to do with this, that the seeds were covered in the soil by the hands of men? Was the seed kept from being devoured, like other things, by being covered with the soil? For what they say would imply that he who put on the soil took away the seed, as Jupiter is said to have been taken away when the lump of soil was offered to Saturn instead of him, and not rather that the soil, by covering the seed, only caused it to be devoured the more eagerly. Then, in that way, Jupiter is the seed, and not the cause of the seed, as was said a little before.

But what shall men do who cannot find anything wise to say, because they are interpreting foolish things? Saturn has a pruning knife. That, says Varro, is on account of agriculture. Certainly in Saturn's reign there as yet existed no agriculture, and therefore the former times of Saturn are spoken of, because, as the same Varro interprets the fables, the primeval men lived on those seeds which the earth produced spontaneously. Perhaps he received a pruning knife when he had lost his scepter—that he who had been a king, and lived at ease during the first part of his time, should become a laborious workman while his son occupied the throne. Then he says that boys were wont to be immolated to him by certain peoples, the Carthaginians, for instance; and also that adults were immolated by some nations, for example the Gauls—because, of all seeds, the human race is the best. What need we say more concerning this most cruel vanity? Let us rather attend to and hold by this, that these interpretations are not carried up to the true God—a living, incorporeal, unchangeable nature, from whom a blessed life enduring forever may be obtained—but that they end in things which are corporeal, temporal, mutable, and mortal. And whereas it is said in the fables that Saturn castrated his father Cœlus, this signifies, says Varro, that the divine seed belongs to Saturn, and not to Cœlus; for this reason, as far as a reason can be discovered, namely, that in heaven[1] nothing is born from seed. But, lo! Saturn, if he is the son of Cœlus, is the son of Jupiter. For they affirm times without number, and that emphatically, that the heavens[2] are Jupiter. Thus those things which come not of the truth, do very often, without being impelled by anyone, themselves overthrow one another. He says that Saturn was called Κρόνος, which in the Greek tongue signifies a space of time,[3] because, without that, seed cannot be productive. These and many other things are said concerning Saturn, and they are all referred to seed. But Saturn surely, with all that great power, might have sufficed for seed. Why are other gods demanded for it, especially Liber and Libera, that is, Ceres—concerning whom again, as far as seed is concerned, he says as many things as if he had said nothing concerning Saturn?

---

1. Cælo.
2. Cælum.
3. Χρόνος.

20. CONCERNING THE RITES OF ELEUSINIAN CERES

Now among the rites of Ceres, those Eleusinian rites are much famed which were in the highest repute among the Athenians, of which Varro offers no interpretation except with respect to corn, which Ceres discovered, and with respect to Proserpine, whom Ceres lost, Orcus having carried her away. And this Proserpine herself, he says, signifies the fecundity of seeds. But as this fecundity departed at a certain season, while the earth wore an aspect of sorrow through the consequent sterility, there arose an opinion that the daughter of Ceres, that is, fecundity itself, who was called Proserpine, from *proserpere* (to creep forth, to spring), had been carried away by Orcus, and detained among the inhabitants of the nether world; which circumstance was celebrated with public mourning. But since the same fecundity again returned, there arose joy because Proserpine had been given back by Orcus, and thus these rites were instituted. Then Varro adds, that many things are taught in the mysteries of Ceres which only refer to the discovery of fruits.

21. CONCERNING THE SHAMEFULNESS OF THE RITES WHICH ARE CELEBRATED IN HONOR OF LIBER

Now as to the rites of Liber, whom they have set over liquid seeds, and therefore not only over the liquors of fruits, among which wine holds, so to speak, the primacy, but also over the seeds of animals: as to these rites, I am unwilling to undertake to show to what excess of turpitude they had reached, because that would entail a lengthened discourse, though I am not unwilling to do so as a demonstration of the proud stupidity of those who practice them. Among other rites which I am compelled from the greatness of their number to omit, Varro says that in Italy, at the places where roads crossed each other, the rites of Liber were celebrated with such unrestrained turpitude, that the private parts of a man were worshiped in his honor. Nor was this abomination transacted in secret that some regard at least might be paid to modesty, but was openly and wantonly displayed. For during the festival of Liber this obscene member, placed on a car, was carried with great honor, first over the crossroads in the country, and then into the city. But in the town of Lavinium a whole month was devoted to Liber alone, during the days of which all the people gave themselves up to the most dissolute conversation, until that member had been carried through the forum and brought to rest in its own place; on which unseemly member it was necessary that the most honorable matron should place a wreath in the presence of all the people. Thus, forsooth, was the god Liber to be appeased in order to the growth of seeds. Thus was enchantment to be driven away from fields, even by a matron's being compelled to do in public what not even a harlot ought to be permitted to do in a theatre, if there were matrons among the spectators. For these reasons, then, Saturn alone was not believed to be sufficient for seeds—namely, that the impure mind might find occasions for multiplying the gods; and that, being righteously abandoned to uncleanliness by the one true God, and being prostituted to the worship of many false gods, through an avidity for ever greater and greater uncleanness, it should call these sacrilegious rites sacred things, and should abandon itself to be violated and polluted by crowds of foul demons.

22. CONCERNING NEPTUNE, AND SALACIA, AND VENILIA

Now Neptune had Salacia to wife, who they say is the nether waters of the sea. Wherefore was Venilia also joined to him? Was it not simply through the lust of the soul desiring a greater number of demons to whom to prostitute itself, and not because this goddess was necessary to the perfection of their sacred rites? But let the interpretation of this illustrious theology be brought forward to restrain us from this censuring by rendering a satisfactory reason. Venilia, says this theology, is the wave which comes to the shore, Salacia the wave which returns into the sea. Why, then, are there two goddesses, when it is one wave which comes and returns? Certainly it is mad lust itself, which in its eagerness for many deities resembles the waves which break on the shore. For though the water which goes is not different from that which returns, still the soul which goes and returns not is defiled by two demons, whom it has taken occasion by this false pretext to invite. I ask you, O Varro, and you who have read such works of learned men, and think you have learned something great—I ask you to interpret this, I do not say in a manner consistent with the eternal and unchangeable nature which alone is God, but only in a manner consistent with the doctrine concerning the soul of the world and its parts, which you think to be the true gods. It is a somewhat more tolerable thing that you have made that part of the soul of the world which pervades the sea your god Neptune. Is the wave, then, which comes to the shore and returns to the main, two parts of the world, or two parts of the soul of the world? Who of you is so silly as to think so? Why, then, have they made to you two goddesses? The only reason seems to be, that your wise ancestors have provided, not that many gods should rule you, but that many of such demons as are delighted with those vanities and falsehoods should possess you. But why has that Salacia, according to this interpretation, lost the lower part of the sea, seeing that she was represented as subject to her husband? For in saying that she is the receding wave, you have put her on the surface. Was she enraged at her husband for taking Venilia as a concubine, and thus drove him from the upper part of the sea?

23. CONCERNING THE EARTH, WHICH VARRO AFFIRMS TO BE A GODDESS, BECAUSE THAT SOUL OF THE WORLD WHICH HE THINKS TO BE GOD PERVADES ALSO THIS LOWEST PART OF HIS BODY, AND IMPARTS TO IT A DIVINE FORCE

Surely the earth, which we see full of its own living creatures, is one; but for all that, it is but a mighty mass among the elements, and the lowest part of the world. Why, then, would they have it to be a goddess? Is it because it is fruitful? Why, then, are not men rather held to be gods, who render it fruitful by cultivating it; but though they plow it, do not adore it? But, say they, the part of the soul of the world which pervades it makes it a goddess. As if it were not a far more evident thing, no, a thing which is not called in question, that there is a soul in man. And yet men are not held to be gods, but (a thing to be sadly lamented), with wonderful and pitiful delusion, are subjected to those who are not gods, and than whom they themselves are better, as the objects of deserved worship and adoration. And certainly the same Varro, in the book concerning the select gods, affirms that there are three grades of soul in universal nature. One which pervades all the living parts of the body, and has not sensation, but only the power of life—that principle which penetrates into the bones, nails, and hair. By this principle in the world trees are nourished, and grow without being possessed of sensation, and live in a manner peculiar to themselves. The second grade of soul is that in which there is sensation. This principle penetrates into the eyes, ears, nostrils, mouth, and the organs of sensation. The third grade of soul is the highest and is called mind, where intelligence has its throne. This grade of soul no mortal creatures except man are possessed of. Now this part of the soul of the world, Varro says, is called God, and in us is called Genius. And the stones and earth in the world, which we see, and which are not pervaded by the power of sensation, are, as it were, the bones and nails of God. Again, the sun, moon, and stars, which we perceive, and by which he perceives, are his organs of perception. Moreover, the ether is his mind; and by the virtue which is in it, which penetrates into the stars, it also makes them gods; and because it penetrates through them into the earth, it makes it the goddess Tellus, whence again it enters and permeates the sea and ocean, making them the god Neptune.

Let him return from this, which he thinks to be natural theology, back to that from which he went out, in order to rest from the fatigue occasioned by the many turnings and windings of his path. Let him return, I say, let him return to the civil theology. I wish to detain him there a while. I have somewhat to say which has to do with that theology. I am not yet saying, that if the earth and stones are similar to our bones and nails, they are in like manner devoid of intelligence, as they are devoid of sensation. Nor am I saying that, if our bones and nails are said to have intelligence, because they are in a man who has intelligence, he who says that the things analogous to these in the world are gods, is as stupid as he is who says that our bones and nails are men. We shall perhaps have occasion to dispute these things with the philosophers. At present, however, I wish to deal with Varro as a political theologian. For it is possible that, though he may seem to have wished to lift up his head, as it were, into the liberty of natural theology, the consciousness that the book with which he was occupied was one concerning a subject belonging to civil theology, may have caused him to relapse into the point of view of that theology, and to say this in order that the ancestors of his nation, and other states, might not be believed to have bestowed on Neptune an irrational worship. What I am to say is this: since the earth is one, why has not that part of the soul of the world which permeates the earth made it that one goddess which he calls Tellus? But had it done so, what then had become of Orcus, the brother of Jupiter and Neptune, whom they call Father Dis?[1] And where, in that case, had been his wife Proserpine, who, according to another opinion given in the same book, is called, not the fecundity of the earth, but its lower part?[2]

But if they say that part of the soul of the world, when it permeates the upper part of the earth, makes the god Father Dis, but when it pervades the nether part of the same the goddess Proserpine; what, in that case, will that Tellus be? For all that which she was has been divided into these two parts, and these two gods; so that it is impossible to find what to make or where to place her as a third goddess, except it be said that those divinities Orcus and Proserpine are the one goddess Tellus, and that they are not three gods, but one or two, while notwithstanding they are called three, held to be three, worshiped as three, having their own several altars, their own shrines, rites, images, priests, while their own false demons also through these things defile the prostituted soul. Let this further question be answered: What part of the earth does a part of the soul of the world permeate in order to make the god Tellumo? No, says he; but the earth being one and the same, has a double life—the masculine, which produces seed, and the feminine, which receives and nourishes the seed. Hence it has been called Tellus from the feminine principle, and Tellumo from the masculine. Why, then, do the priests, as he indicates, perform divine service to four gods, two others being added—namely, to Tellus, Tellumo, Altor, and Rusor? We have already spoken concerning Tellus and Tellumo. But why do they worship Altor?[3] Because, says he, all that springs of the earth is nourished by the earth. Wherefore do they worship Rusor?[4] Because all things return back again to the place whence they proceeded.

---

1. See above, 7.16.
2. *Varro De Ling. Lat. 5.68.*
3. Nourisher.
4. Returner.

24. CONCERNING THE SURNAMES OF TELLUS AND THEIR SIGNIFICATIONS, WHICH, ALTHOUGH THEY INDICATE MANY PROPERTIES, OUGHT NOT TO HAVE ESTABLISHED THE OPINION THAT THERE IS A CORRESPONDING NUMBER OF GODS

The one earth, then, on account of this fourfold virtue, ought to have had four surnames, but not to have been considered as four gods—as Jupiter and Juno, though they have so many surnames, are for all that only single deities—for by all these surnames it is signified that a manifold virtue belongs to one god or to one goddess; but the multitude of surnames does not imply a multitude of gods. But as sometimes even the vilest women themselves grow tired of those crowds which they have sought after under the impulse of wicked passion, so also the soul, become vile, and prostituted to impure spirits, sometimes begins to loathe to multiply to itself gods to whom to surrender itself to be polluted by them, as much as it once delighted in so doing. For Varro himself, as if ashamed of that crowd of gods, would make Tellus to be one goddess. "They say," says he, "that whereas the one great mother has a tympanum, it is signified that she is the orb of the earth; whereas she has towers on her head, towns are signified; and whereas seats are fixed round about her, it is signified that while all things move, she moves not. And their having made the Galli to serve this goddess, signifies that they who are in need of seed ought to follow the earth for in it all seeds are found. By their throwing themselves down before her, it is taught," he says, "that they who cultivate the earth should not sit idle, for there is always something for them to do. The sound of the cymbals signifies the noise made by the throwing of iron utensils, and by men's hands, and all other noises connected with agricultural operations; and these cymbals are of brass, because the ancients used brazen utensils in their agriculture before iron was discovered. They place beside the goddess an unbound and tame lion, to show that there is no kind of land so wild and so excessively barren as that it would be profitless to attempt to bring it in and cultivate it." Then he adds that, because they gave many names and surnames to mother Tellus, it came to be thought that these signified many gods. "They think," says he, "that Tellus is Ops, because the earth is improved by labor; Mother, because it brings forth much; Great, because it brings forth seed; Proserpine, because fruits creep forth from it; Vesta, because it is invested with herbs. And thus," says he, "they not at all absurdly identify other goddesses with the earth." If, then, it is one goddess (though, if the truth were consulted, it is not even that), why do they nevertheless separate it into many? Let there be many names of one goddess, and let there not be as many goddesses as there are names.

But the authority of the erring ancients weighs heavily on Varro, and compels him, after having expressed this opinion, to show signs of uneasiness; for he immediately adds, "With which things the opinion of the ancients, who thought that there were really many goddesses, does not conflict." How does it not conflict, when it is entirely a different thing to say that one goddess has many names, and to say that there are many goddesses? But it is possible, he says, that the same thing may both be one, and yet have in it a plurality of things. I grant that there are many things in one man; are there therefore in him many men? In like manner, in one goddess there are many things; are there therefore also many goddesses? But let them divide, unite, multiply, reduplicate, and implicate as they like.

These are the famous mysteries of Tellus and the Great Mother, all of which are shown to have reference to mortal seeds and to agriculture. Do these things, then—namely, the tympanum, the towers, the Galli, the tossing to and fro of limbs, the noise of cymbals, the images of lions—do these things, having this reference and this end, promise eternal life? Do the mutilated Galli, then, serve this Great Mother in order to signify that they who are in need of seed should follow the earth, as though it were not rather the case that this very service caused them to want seed? For whether do they, by following this goddess, acquire seed, being in want of it, or, by following her, lose seed when they have it? Is this to interpret or to deprecate? Nor is it considered to what a degree malign demons have gained the upper hand, inasmuch as they have been able to exact such cruel rites without having dared to promise any great things in return for them. Had the earth not been a goddess, men would have, by laboring, laid their hands on *it* in order to obtain seed through it, and would not have laid violent hands on themselves in order to lose seed on account of it. Had it not been a goddess, it would have become so fertile by the hands of others, that it would not have compelled a man to be rendered barren by his own hands; nor that in the festival of Liber an honorable matron put a wreath on the private parts of a man in the sight of the multitude, where perhaps her husband was standing by blushing and perspiring, if there is any shame left in men; and that in the celebration of marriages the newly married bride was ordered to sit upon Priapus. These things are bad enough, but they are small and contemptible in comparison with that most cruel abomination, or most abominable cruelty, by which either set is so deluded that neither perishes of its wound. There the enchantment of fields is feared; here the amputation of members is not feared. There the modesty of the bride is outraged, but in such a manner as that neither her fruitfulness nor even her virginity is taken away; here a man is so mutilated that he is neither changed into a woman nor remains a man.

25. THE INTERPRETATION OF THE MUTILATION OF ATYS WHICH THE DOCTRINE OF THE GREEK SAGES SET FORTH

Varro has not spoken of that Atys, nor sought out any interpretation for him, in memory of whose being loved by Ceres the Gallus is mutilated. But the learned and wise Greeks have by no means been silent about an interpretation so holy and so illustrious. The celebrated philosopher Porphyry has said that Atys signifies the flowers of spring, which is the most beautiful season, and therefore was mutilated because the flower falls before the fruit appears.[1] They have not, then, compared the man himself, or rather that semblance of a man they called Atys, to the flower, but his male organs—these, indeed, fell while he was living. Did I say fell? No, truly they did not fall, nor were they plucked off, but torn away. Nor when that flower was lost did any fruit follow, but rather sterility. What, then, do they say is signified by the castrated Atys himself, and whatever remained to him after his castration? To what do they refer that? What interpretation does that give rise to? Do they, after vain endeavors to discover an interpretation, seek to persuade men that that is rather to be believed which report has made public, and which has also been written concerning his having been a mutilated man? Our Varro has very properly opposed this, and has been unwilling to state it; for it certainly was not unknown to that most learned man.

---

1. *In the book De Ratione Naturali Deorum.*

26. CONCERNING THE ABOMINATION OF THE SACRED RITES OF THE GREAT MOTHER

Concerning the effeminates consecrated to the same Great Mother, in defiance of all the modesty which belongs to men and women, Varro has not wished to say anything, nor do I remember to have read anywhere aught concerning them. These effeminates, no later than yesterday, were going through the streets and places of Carthage with anointed hair, whitened faces, relaxed bodies, and feminine gait, exacting from the people the means of maintaining their ignominious lives. Nothing has been said concerning them. Interpretation failed, reason blushed, speech was silent. The Great Mother has surpassed all her sons, not in greatness of deity, but of crime. To this monster not even the monstrosity of Janus is to be compared. His deformity was only in his image; hers was the deformity of cruelty in her sacred rites. He has a redundancy of members in stone images; she inflicts the loss of members on men. This abomination is not surpassed by the licentious deeds of Jupiter, so many and so great. He, with all his seductions of women, only disgraced heaven with one Ganymede; she, with so many avowed and public effeminates, has both defiled the earth and outraged heaven. Perhaps we may either compare Saturn to this Magna Mater, or even set him before her in this kind of abominable cruelty, for he mutilated his father. But at the festivals of Saturn, men could rather be slain by the hands of others than mutilated by their own. He devoured his sons, as the poets say, and the natural theologists interpret this as they list. History says he slew them. But the Romans never received, like the Carthaginians, the custom of sacrificing their sons to him. This Great Mother of the gods, however, has brought mutilated men into Roman temples, and has preserved that cruel custom, being believed to promote the strength of the Romans by emasculating their men. Compared with this evil, what are the thefts of Mercury, the wantonness of Venus, and the base and flagitious deeds of the rest of them, which we might bring forward from books, were it not that they are daily sung and danced in the theatres? But what are these things to so great an evil—an evil whose magnitude was only proportioned to the greatness of the Great Mother—especially as these are said to have been invented by the poets—as if the poets had also invented this that they are acceptable to the gods? Let it be imputed, then, to the audacity and impudence of the poets that these things have been sung and written of. But that they have been incorporated into the body of divine rites and honors, the deities themselves demanding and extorting that incorporation, what is that but the crime of the gods? No, more, the confession of demons and the deception of wretched men? But as to this that the Great Mother is considered to be worshiped in the appropriate form when she is worshiped by the consecration of mutilated men, this is not an invention of the poets; no, they have rather shrunk from it with horror than sung of it. Ought anyone, then, to be consecrated to these select gods, that he may live blessedly after death, consecrated to whom he could not live decently before death, being subjected to such foul superstitions, and bound over to unclean demons? But all these things, says Varro, are to be referred to the world.[1] Let him consider if it be not rather to the unclean.[2] But why not refer that to the world which is demonstrated to be in the world? We, however, seek for a mind which, trusting to true religion, does not adore the world as its god, but for the sake of God praises the world as a work of God, and, purified from mundane defilements, comes pure[3] to God Himself who founded the world.[4]

---

1. Mundum.
2. Immundum.
3. Mundus.
4. Mundum.

27. CONCERNING THE FIGMENTS OF THE PHYSICAL THEOLOGISTS, WHO NEITHER WORSHIP THE TRUE DIVINITY, NOR PERFORM THE WORSHIP WHEREWITH THE TRUE DIVINITY SHOULD BE SERVED

We see that these select gods have, indeed, become more famous than the rest; not, however, that their merits may be brought to light, but that their opprobrious deeds may not be hid. Whence it is more credible that they were men, as not only poetic but also historical literature has handed down. For this which Virgil says,

> *Then from Olympus's heights came down*
> *Good Saturn, exiled from his throne*
> *By Jove, his mightier heir;*[1]

and what follows with reference to this affair, is fully related by the historian Euhemerus, and has been translated into Latin by Ennius. And as they who have written before us in the Greek or in the Latin tongue against such errors as these have said much concerning this matter, I have thought it unnecessary to dwell upon it. When I consider those physical reasons, then, by which learned and acute men attempt to turn human things into divine things, all I see is that they have been able to refer these things only to temporal works and to that which has a corporeal nature, and even though invisible still mutable; and this is by no means the true God. But if this worship had been performed as the symbolism of ideas at least congruous with religion, though it would indeed have been cause of grief that the true God was not announced and proclaimed by its symbolism, nevertheless it could have been in some degree borne with, when it did not occasion and command the performance of such foul and abominable things. But since it is impiety to worship the body or the soul for the true God, by whose indwelling alone the soul is happy, how much more impious is it to worship those things through which neither soul nor body can obtain either salvation or human honor? Wherefore if with temple, priest, and sacrifice, which are due to the true God, any element of the world be worshiped, or any created spirit, even though not impure and evil, that worship is still evil, not because the things are evil by which the worship is performed, but because those things ought only to be used in the worship of Him to whom alone such worship and service are due. But if anyone insist that he worships the one true God—that is, the Creator of every soul and of every body—with stupid and monstrous idols, with human victims, with putting a wreath on the male organ, with the wages of unchastity, with the cutting of limbs, with emasculation, with the consecration of effeminates, with impure and obscene plays, such a one does not sin because he worships One who ought not to be worshiped, but because he worships Him who ought to be worshiped in a way in which He ought not to be worshiped. But he who worships with such things —that is, foul and obscene things—and that not the true God, namely, the maker of soul and body, but a creature, even though not a wicked creature, whether it be soul or body, or soul and body together, twice sins against God, because he both worships for God what is not God, and also worships with such things as neither God nor what is not God ought to be worshiped with. It is, indeed, manifest how these pagans worship—that is, how shamefully and criminally they worship; but what or whom they worship would have been left in obscurity, had not their history testified that those same confessedly base and foul rites were rendered in obedience to the demands of the gods, who exacted them with terrible severity. Wherefore it is evident beyond doubt that this whole civil theology is occupied in inventing means for attracting wicked and most impure spirits, inviting them to visit senseless images, and through these to take possession of stupid hearts.

---

1. Virgil *Æneid* 8.319–320.

28. THAT THE DOCTRINE OF VARRO CONCERNING THEOLOGY IS IN NO PART CONSISTENT WITH ITSELF

To what purpose, then, is it that this most learned and most acute man Varro attempts, as it were, with subtle disputation, to reduce and refer all these gods to heaven and earth? He cannot do it. They go out of his hands like water; they shrink back; they slip down and fall. For when about to speak of the females, that is, the goddesses, he says, "Since, as I observed in the first book concerning places, heaven and earth are the two origins of the gods, on which account they are called celestials and terrestrials, and as I began in the former books with heaven, speaking of Janus, whom some have said to be heaven, and others the earth, so I now commence with Tellus in speaking concerning the goddesses." I can understand what embarrassment so great a mind was experiencing. For he is influenced by the perception of a certain plausible resemblance, when he says that the heaven is that which does, and the earth that which suffers, and therefore attributes the masculine principle to the one, and the feminine to the other, not considering that it is rather He who made both heaven and earth who is the maker of both activity and passivity. On this principle he interprets the celebrated mysteries of the Samothracians, and promises, with an air of great devoutness, that he will by writing expound these mysteries, which have not been so much as known to his countrymen, and will send them his exposition. Then he says that he had from many proofs gathered that, in those mysteries, among the images one signifies heaven, another the earth, another the patterns of things, which Plato calls ideas. He makes Jupiter to signify heaven, Juno the earth, Minerva the ideas. Heaven, by which anything is made; the earth, from which it is made; and the pattern, according to which it is made. But, with respect to the last, I am forgetting to say that Plato attributed so great an importance to these ideas as to say, not that anything was made by heaven according to them, but that according to them heaven itself was made.[1] To return, however—it is to be observed that Varro has, in the book on the select gods, lost that theory of these gods, in whom he has, as it were, embraced all things. For he assigns the male gods to heaven, the females to earth; among which latter he has placed Minerva, whom he had before placed above heaven itself. Then the male god Neptune is in the sea, which pertains rather to earth than to heaven. Last of all, Father Dis, who is called in Greek Πλούτων, another male god, brother of both (Jupiter and Neptune), is also held to be a god of the earth, holding the upper region of the earth himself, and allotting the nether region to his wife Proserpine. How, then, do they attempt to refer the gods to heaven, and the goddesses to earth? What solidity, what consistency, what sobriety has this disputation? But that Tellus is the origin of the goddesses—the great mother, to wit, beside whom there is continually the noise of the mad and abominable revelry of effeminates and mutilated men, and men who cut themselves, and indulge in frantic gesticulations—how is it, then, that Janus is called the head of the gods, and Tellus the head of the goddesses? In the one case error does not make one head, and in the other frenzy does not make a sane one. Why do they vainly attempt to refer these to the world? Even if they could do so, no pious person worships the world for the true God. Nevertheless, plain truth makes it evident that they are not able even to do this. Let them rather identify them with dead men and most wicked demons, and no further question will remain.

---

1. In the *Timæus*.

29. THAT ALL THINGS WHICH THE PHYSICAL THEOLOGISTS HAVE REFERRED TO THE WORLD AND ITS PARTS, THEY OUGHT TO HAVE REFERRED TO THE ONE TRUE GOD

For all those things which, according to the account given of those gods, are referred to the world by so-called physical interpretation, may, without any religious scruple, be rather assigned to the true God, who made heaven and earth, and created every soul and every body; and the following is the manner in which we see that this may be done. We worship God—not heaven and earth, of which two parts this world consists, nor the soul or souls diffused through all living things—but God who made heaven and earth, and all things which are in them; who made every soul, whatever be the nature of its life, whether it have life without sensation and reason, or life with sensation, or life with both sensation and reason.

30. HOW PIETY DISTINGUISHES THE CREATOR FROM THE CREATURES, SO THAT, INSTEAD OF ONE GOD, THERE ARE NOT WORSHIPED AS MANY GODS AS THERE ARE WORKS OF THE ONE AUTHOR

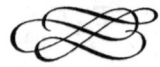

And now, to begin to go over those works of the one true God, on account of which these have made to themselves many and false gods, while they attempt to give an honorable interpretation to their many most abominable and most infamous mysteries—we worship that God who has appointed to the natures created by Him both the beginnings and the end of their existing and moving; who holds, knows, and disposes the causes of things; who has created the virtue of seeds; who has given to what creatures He would a rational soul, which is called mind; who has bestowed the faculty and use of speech; who has imparted the gift of foretelling future things to whatever spirits it seemed to Him good; who also Himself predicts future things, through whom He pleases, and through whom He will, removes diseases; who, when the human race is to be corrected and chastised by wars, regulates also the beginnings, progress, and ends of these wars; who has created and governs the most vehement and most violent fire of this world, in due relation and proportion to the other elements of immense nature; who is the governor of all the waters; who has made the sun brightest of all material lights, and has given him suitable power and motion; who has not withdrawn, even from the inhabitants of the nether world, His dominion and power; who has appointed to mortal natures their suitable seed and nourishment, dry or liquid; who establishes and makes fruitful the earth; who bountifully bestows its fruits on animals and on men; who knows and ordains, not only principal causes, but also subsequent causes; who has determined for the moon her motion; who affords ways in heaven and on earth for passage from one place to another; who has granted also to human minds, which He has created, the knowledge of the various arts for the help of life and nature; who has appointed the union of male and female for the propagation of offspring; who has favored the societies of men with the gift of terrestrial fire for the simplest and most familiar purposes, to burn on the hearth and to give light. These are, then, the things which that most acute and most learned man Varro has labored to distribute among the select gods, by I know not what physical interpretation, which he has got from other sources, and also conjectured for himself. But these things the one true God makes and does, but as *the same* God—that is, as He who is wholly everywhere, included in no space, bound by no chains, mutable in no part of His being, filling heaven and earth with omnipresent power, not with a needy nature. Therefore He governs all things in such a manner as to allow them to perform and exercise their own proper movements. For although they can be nothing without Him, they are not what He is. He does also many things through angels; but only from Himself does He beatify angels. So also, though He send angels to men for certain purposes, He does not for all that beatify men by the good inherent in the angels, but by Himself, as He does the angels themselves.

31. WHAT BENEFITS GOD GIVES TO THE FOLLOWERS OF THE TRUTH TO ENJOY OVER AND ABOVE HIS GENERAL BOUNTY

For, besides such benefits as, according to this administration of nature of which we have made some mention, He lavishes on good and bad alike, we have from Him a great manifestation of great love, which belongs only to the good. For although we can never sufficiently give thanks to Him, that we are, that we live, that we behold heaven and earth, that we have mind and reason by which to seek after Him who made all these things, nevertheless, what hearts, what number of tongues, shall affirm that they are sufficient to render thanks to Him for this, that He has not wholly departed from us, laden and overwhelmed with sins, averse to the contemplation of His light, and blinded by the love of darkness, that is, of iniquity, but has sent to us His own Word, who is His only Son, that by His birth and suffering for us in the flesh, which He assumed, we might know how much God valued man, and that by that unique sacrifice we might be purified from all our sins, and that, love being shed abroad in our hearts by His Spirit, we might, having surmounted all difficulties, come into eternal rest, and the ineffable sweetness of the contemplation of Himself?

32. THAT AT NO TIME IN THE PAST WAS THE MYSTERY OF CHRIST'S REDEMPTION WANTING, BUT WAS AT ALL TIMES DECLARED, THOUGH IN VARIOUS FORMS

This mystery of eternal life, even from the beginning of the human race, was, by certain signs and sacraments suitable to the times, announced through angels to those to whom it was meet. Then the Hebrew people was congregated into one republic, as it were, to perform this mystery; and in that republic was foretold, sometimes through men who understood what they spoke, and sometimes through men who understood not, all that had transpired since the advent of Christ until now, and all that will transpire. This same nation, too, was afterward dispersed through the nations, in order to testify to the Scriptures in which eternal salvation in Christ had been declared. For not only the prophecies which are contained in words, nor only the precepts for the right conduct of life, which teach morals and piety, and are contained in the sacred Writings—not only these, but also the rites, priesthood, tabernacle or temple, altars, sacrifices, ceremonies, and whatever else belongs to that service which is due to God, and which in Greek is properly called λατρεία—all these signified and fore-announced those things which we who believe in Jesus Christ unto eternal life believe to have been fulfilled, or behold in process of fulfillment, or confidently believe shall yet be fulfilled.

33. THAT ONLY THROUGH THE CHRISTIAN RELIGION COULD THE DECEIT OF MALIGN SPIRITS, WHO REJOICE IN THE ERRORS OF MEN, HAVE BEEN MANIFESTED

This, the only true religion, has alone been able to manifest that the gods of the nations are most impure demons, who desire to be thought gods, availing themselves of the names of certain defunct souls, or the appearance of mundane creatures, and with proud impurity rejoicing in things most base and infamous, as though in divine honors, and envying human souls their conversion to the true God. From whose most cruel and most impious dominion a man is liberated when he believes on Him who has afforded an example of humility, following which men may rise as great as was that pride by which they fell. Hence are not only those gods, concerning whom we have already spoken much, and many others belonging to different nations and lands, but also those of whom we are now treating, who have been selected as it were into the senate of the gods—selected, however, on account of the notoriousness of their crimes, not on account of the dignity of their virtues—whose sacred things Varro attempts to refer to certain natural reasons, seeking to make base things honorable, but cannot find how to square and agree with these reasons, because these are not the causes of those rites, which he thinks, or rather wishes to be thought to be so. For had not only these, but also all others of this kind, been real causes, even though they had nothing to do with the true God and eternal life, which is to be sought in religion, they would, by affording some sort of reason drawn from the nature of things, have mitigated in some degree that offense which was occasioned by some turpitude or absurdity in the sacred rites, which was not understood. This he attempted to do in respect to certain fables of the theatres, or mysteries of the shrines; but he did not acquit the theatres of likeness to the shrines, but rather condemned the shrines for likeness to the theatres. However, he in some way made the attempt to soothe the feelings shocked by horrible things, by rendering what he would have to be natural interpretations.

34. CONCERNING THE BOOKS OF NUMA POMPILIUS, WHICH THE SENATE ORDERED TO BE BURNED, IN ORDER THAT THE CAUSES OF SACRED RIGHTS THEREIN ASSIGNED SHOULD NOT BECOME KNOWN

But, on the other hand, we find, as the same most learned man has related, that the causes of the sacred rites which were given from the books of Numa Pompilius could by no means be tolerated, and were considered unworthy, not only to become known to the religious by being read, but even to lie written in the darkness in which they had been concealed. For now let me say what I promised in the third book of this work to say in its proper place. For, as we read in the same Varro's book on the worship of the gods, "A certain one Terentius had a field at the Janiculum, and once, when his plowman was passing the plow near to the tomb of Numa Pompilius, he turned up from the ground the books of Numa, in which were written the causes of the sacred institutions; which books he carried to the prætor, who, having read the beginnings of them, referred to the senate what seemed to be a matter of so much importance. And when the chief senators had read certain of the causes why this or that rite was instituted, the senate assented to the dead Numa, and the conscript fathers, as though concerned for the interests of religion, ordered the prætor to burn the books."[1] Let each one believe what he thinks; no, let every champion of such impiety say whatever mad contention may suggest. For my part, let it suffice to suggest that the causes of those sacred things which were written down by King Numa Pompilius, the institutor of the Roman rites, ought never to have become known to people or senate, or even to the priests themselves; and also that Numa himself attained to these secrets of demons by an illicit curiosity, in order that he might write them down, so as to be able, by reading, to be reminded of them. However, though he was king, and had no cause to be afraid of anyone, he neither dared to teach them to anyone, nor to destroy them by obliteration, or any other form of destruction. Therefore, because he was unwilling that anyone should know them, lest men should be taught infamous things, and because he was afraid to violate them, lest he should enrage the demons against himself, he buried them in what he thought a safe place, believing that a plow could not approach his sepulchre. But the senate, fearing to condemn the religious solemnities of their ancestors, and therefore compelled to assent to Numa, were nevertheless so convinced that those books were pernicious, that they did not order them to be buried again, knowing that human curiosity would thereby be excited to seek with far greater eagerness after the matter already divulged, but ordered the scandalous relics to be destroyed with fire; because, as they thought it was now a necessity to perform those sacred rites, they judged that the error arising from ignorance of their causes was more tolerable than the disturbance which the knowledge of them would occasion the state.

---

1. Plutarch's *Numa;* Livy 40.29.

35. CONCERNING THE HYDROMANCY THROUGH WHICH NUMA WAS BEFOOLED BY CERTAIN IMAGES OF DEMONS SEEN IN THE WATER

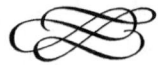

For Numa himself also, to whom no prophet of God, no holy angel was sent, was driven to have recourse to hydromancy, that he might see the images of the gods in the water (or, rather, appearances whereby the demons made sport of him), and might learn from them what he ought to ordain and observe in the sacred rites. This kind of divination, says Varro, was introduced from the Persians, and was used by Numa himself, and at an after time by the philosopher Pythagoras. In this divination, he says, they also inquire at the inhabitants of the nether world, and make use of blood; and this the Greeks call νεκρομαντεία. But whether it be called necromancy or hydromancy it is the same thing, for in either case the dead are supposed to foretell future things. But by what artifices these things are done, let themselves consider; for I am unwilling to say that these artifices were wont to be prohibited by the laws, and to be very severely punished even in the Gentile states, before the advent of our Saviour. I am unwilling, I say, to affirm this, for perhaps even such things were then allowed. However, it was by these arts that Pompilius learned those sacred rites which he gave forth as facts, while he concealed their causes; for even he himself was afraid of that which he had learned. The senate also caused the books in which those causes were recorded to be burned. What is it, then, to me, that Varro attempts to adduce all sorts of fanciful physical interpretations, which if these books had contained, they would certainly not have been burned? For otherwise the conscript fathers would also have burned those books which Varro published and dedicated to the high priest Cæsar.[1] Now Numa is said to have married the nymph Egeria, because (as Varro explains it in the forementioned book) he carried forth[2] water wherewith to perform his hydromancy. Thus facts are wont to be converted into fables through false colorings. It was by that hydromancy, then, that that overcurious Roman king learned both the sacred rites which were to be written in the books of the priests and also the causes of those rites—which latter, however, he was unwilling that anyone besides himself should know. Wherefore he made these causes, as it were, to die along with himself, taking care to have them written by themselves, and removed from the knowledge of men by being buried in the earth. Wherefore the things which are written in those books were either abominations of demons, so foul and noxious as to render that whole civil theology execrable even in the eyes of such men as those senators, who had accepted so many shameful things in the sacred rites themselves, or they were nothing else than the accounts of dead men, whom, through the lapse of ages, almost all the Gentile nations had come to believe to be immortal gods; while those same demons were delighted even with such rites, having presented themselves to receive worship under pretense of being those very dead men whom they had caused to be thought immortal gods by certain fallacious miracles, performed in order to establish that belief. But, by the hidden providence of the true God, these demons were permitted to confess these things to their friend Numa, having been gained by those arts through which necromancy could be performed, and yet were not constrained to admonish him rather at his death to burn than to bury the books in which they were written. But, in order that these books might be unknown, the demons could not resist the plow by which they were thrown up, or the pen of Varro, through which the things which were done in reference to this matter have come down even to our knowledge. For they are not able to effect anything which they are not allowed; but they are permitted to influence those whom God, in His deep and just judgment, according to their deserts, gives over either to be simply afflicted by them, or to be also subdued and deceived. But how pernicious these writings were judged to be, or how alien from the worship of the true Divinity, may be understood from the fact that the senate preferred to burn what Pompilius had hid, rather than to fear what he feared, so that he could not dare to do that. Wherefore let him who does not desire to live a pious life even now, seek eternal life by means of such rites. But let him who does not wish to have fellowship with malign demons have no fear for the noxious superstition wherewith they are worshiped, but let him recognize the true religion by which they are unmasked and vanquished.

---

1. Cf. Lactantius *Inst. Div.* 1.6.
2. Egesserit.

BOOK EIGHT

ARGUMENT

Augustine comes now to the third kind of theology, that is, the natural, and takes up the question, whether the worship of the gods of the natural theology is of any avail toward securing blessedness in the life to come. This question he prefers to discuss with the Platonists, because the Platonic system is "facile princeps" among philosophies, and makes the nearest approximation to Christian truth. In pursuing this argument, he first refutes Apuleius, and all who maintain that the demons should be worshiped as messengers and mediators between gods and men; demonstrating that by no possibility can men be reconciled to good gods by demons, who are the slaves of vice, and who delight in and patronize what good and wise men abhor and condemn—the blasphemous fictions of poets, theatrical exhibitions, and magical arts.

1. THAT THE QUESTION OF NATURAL THEOLOGY IS TO BE DISCUSSED WITH THOSE PHILOSOPHERS WHO SOUGHT A MORE EXCELLENT WISDOM

We shall require to apply our mind with far greater intensity to the present question than was requisite in the solution and unfolding of the questions handled in the preceding books; for it is not with ordinary men, but with philosophers that we must confer concerning the theology which they call natural. For it is not like the fabulous, that is, the theatrical; nor the civil, that is, the urban theology: the one of which displays the crimes of the gods, while the other manifests their criminal desires, which demonstrate them to be rather malign demons than gods. It is, we say, with philosophers we have to confer with respect to this theology—men whose very name, if rendered into Latin, signifies those who profess the love of wisdom. Now, if wisdom is God, who made all things, as is attested by the divine authority and truth,[1] then the philosopher is a lover of God. But since the thing itself, which is called by this name, exists not in all who glory in the name—for it does not follow, of course, that all who are called philosophers are lovers of true wisdom—we must needs select from the number of those with whose opinions we have been able to acquaint ourselves by reading, some with whom we may not unworthily engage in the treatment of this question. For I have not in this work undertaken to refute all the vain opinions of the philosophers, but only such as pertain to theology, which Greek word we understand to mean an account or explanation of the divine nature. Nor, again, have I undertaken to refute all the vain theological opinions of all the philosophers, but only of such of them as, agreeing in the belief that there is a divine nature, and that this divine nature is concerned about human affairs, do nevertheless deny that the worship of the one unchangeable God is sufficient for the obtaining of a blessed life after death, as well as at the present time; and hold that, in order to obtain that life, many gods, created, indeed, and appointed to their several spheres by that one God, are to be worshiped. These approach nearer to the truth than even Varro; for, while he saw no difficulty in extending natural theology in its entirety even to the world and the soul of the world, these acknowledge God as existing above all that is of the nature of soul, and as the Creator not only of this visible world, which is often called heaven and earth, but also of every soul whatsoever, and as Him who gives blessedness to the rational soul—of which kind is the human soul—by participation in His own unchangeable and incorporeal light. There is no one, who has even a slender knowledge of these things, who does not know of the Platonic philosophers, who derive their name from their master Plato. Concerning this Plato, then, I will briefly state such things as I deem necessary to the present question, mentioning beforehand those who preceded him in time in the same department of literature.

---

1. Wisd. of Sol. 7:24–27.

2. CONCERNING THE TWO SCHOOLS OF PHILOSOPHERS, THAT IS, THE ITALIC AND IONIC, AND THEIR FOUNDERS

As far as concerns the literature of the Greeks, whose language holds a more illustrious place than any of the languages of the other nations, history mentions two schools of philosophers, the one called the Italic school, originating in that part of Italy which was formerly called Magna Græcia; the other called the Ionic school, having its origin in those regions which are still called by the name of Greece. The Italic school had for its founder Pythagoras of Samos, to whom also the term "philosophy" is said to owe its origin. For whereas formerly those who seemed to excel others by the laudable manner in which they regulated their lives were called sages, Pythagoras, on being asked what he professed, replied that he was a philosopher, that is, a student or lover of wisdom; for it seemed to him to be the height of arrogance to profess oneself a sage.[1] The founder of the Ionic school, again, was

Thales of Miletus, one of those seven who were styled the "seven sages," of whom six were distinguished by the kind of life they lived, and by certain maxims which they gave forth for the proper conduct of life. Thales was distinguished as an investigator into the nature of things; and, in order that he might have successors in his school, he committed his dissertations to writing. That, however, which especially rendered him eminent was his ability, by means of astronomical calculations, even to predict eclipses of the sun and moon. He thought, however, that water was the first principle of things, and that of it all the elements of the world, the world itself, and all things which are generated in it, ultimately consist. Over all this work, however, which, when we consider the world, appears so admirable, he set nothing of the nature of divine mind. To him succeeded Anaximander, his pupil, who held a different opinion concerning the nature of things; for he did not hold that all things spring from one principle, as Thales did, who held that principle to be water, but thought that each thing springs from its own proper principle. These principles of things he believed to be infinite in number, and thought that they generated innumerable worlds, and all the things which arise in them. He thought, also, that these worlds are subject to a perpetual process of alternate dissolution and regeneration, each one continuing for a longer or shorter period of time, according to the nature of the case; nor did he, any more than Thales, attribute anything to a divine mind in the production of all this activity of things. Anaximander left as his successor his disciple

Anaximenes, who attributed all the causes of things to an infinite air. He neither denied nor ignored the existence of gods, but, so far from believing that the air was made by them, he held, on the contrary, that they sprang from the air. Anaxagoras, however, who was his pupil, perceived that a divine mind was the productive cause of all things which we see, and said that all the various kinds of things, according to their several modes and species, were produced out of an infinite matter consisting of homogeneous particles, but by the efficiency of a divine mind. Diogenes, also, another pupil of Anaximenes, said that a certain air was the original substance of things out of which all things were produced, but that it was possessed of a divine reason, without which nothing could be produced from it. Anaxagoras was succeeded by his disciple Archelaus, who also thought that all things consisted of homogeneous particles, of which each particular thing was made, but that those particles were pervaded by a divine mind, which perpetually energized all the eternal bodies, namely, those particles, so that they are alternately united and separated. Socrates, the master of Plato, is said to have been the disciple of Archelaus; and on Plato's account it is that I have given this brief historical sketch of the whole history of these schools.

---

1. Sapiens, that is, a wise man, one who had attained to wisdom.

3. OF THE SOCRATIC PHILOSOPHY

Socrates is said to have been the first who directed the entire effort of philosophy to the correction and regulation of manners, all who went before him having expended their greatest efforts in the investigation of physical, that is, natural phenomena. However, it seems to me that it cannot be certainly discovered whether Socrates did this because he was wearied of obscure and uncertain things, and so wished to direct his mind to the discovery of something manifest and certain, which was necessary in order to the obtaining of a blessed life—that one great object toward which the labor, vigilance, and industry of all philosophers seem to have been directed—or whether (as some yet more favorable to him suppose) he did it because he was unwilling that minds defiled with earthly desires should essay to raise themselves upward to divine things. For he saw that the causes of things were sought for by them—which causes he believed to be ultimately reducible to nothing else than the will of the one true and supreme God—and on this account he thought they could only be comprehended by a purified mind; and therefore that all diligence ought to be given to the purification of the life by good morals, in order that the mind, delivered from the depressing weight of lusts, might raise itself upward by its native vigor to eternal things, and might, with purified understanding, contemplate that nature which is incorporeal and unchangeable light, where live the causes of all created natures. It is evident, however, that he hunted out and pursued, with a wonderful pleasantness of style and argument, and with a most pointed and insinuating urbanity, the foolishness of ignorant men, who thought that they knew this or that—sometimes confessing his own ignorance, and sometimes dissimulating his knowledge, even in those very moral questions to which he seems to have directed the whole force of his mind. And hence there arose hostility against him, which ended in his being calumniously impeached, and condemned to death. Afterward, however, that very city of the Athenians, which had publicly condemned him, did publicly bewail him—the popular indignation having turned with such vehemence on his accusers, that one of them perished by the violence of the multitude, while the other only escaped a like punishment by voluntary and perpetual exile.

Illustrious, therefore, both in his life and in his death, Socrates left very many disciples of his philosophy, who vied with one another in desire for proficiency in handling those moral questions which concern the chief good (*summum bonum*), the possession of which can make a man blessed; and because, in the disputations of Socrates, where he raises all manner of questions, makes assertions, and then demolishes them, it did not evidently appear what he held to be the chief good, everyone took from these disputations what pleased him best, and everyone placed the final good[1] in whatever it appeared to himself to consist. Now, that which is called the final good is that at which, when one has arrived, he is blessed. But so diverse were the opinions held by those followers of Socrates concerning this final good, that (a thing scarcely to be credited with respect to the followers of one master) some placed the chief good in pleasure, as Aristippus, others in virtue, as Antisthenes. Indeed, it were tedious to recount the various opinions of various disciples.

---

1. Finem boni.

4. CONCERNING PLATO, THE CHIEF AMONG THE DISCIPLES OF SOCRATES, AND HIS THREEFOLD DIVISION OF PHILOSOPHY

But, among the disciples of Socrates, Plato was the one who shone with a glory which far excelled that of the others, and who not unjustly eclipsed them all. By birth, an Athenian of honorable parentage, he far surpassed his fellow disciples in natural endowments, of which he was possessed in a wonderful degree. Yet, deeming himself and the Socratic discipline far from sufficient for bringing philosophy to perfection, he traveled as extensively as he was able, going to every place famed for the cultivation of any science of which he could make himself master. Thus he learned from the Egyptians whatever they held and taught as important; and from Egypt, passing into those parts of Italy which were filled with the fame of the Pythagoreans, he mastered, with the greatest facility, and under the most eminent teachers, all the Italic philosophy which was then in vogue. And, as he had a peculiar love for his master Socrates, he made him the speaker in all his dialogues, putting into his mouth whatever he had learned, either from others, or from the efforts of his own powerful intellect, tempering even his moral disputations with the grace and politeness of the Socratic style. And, as the study of wisdom consists in action and contemplation, so that one part of it may be called active, and the other contemplative—the active part having reference to the conduct of life, that is, to the regulation of morals, and the contemplative part to the investigation into the causes of nature and into pure truth—Socrates is said to have excelled in the active part of that study, while Pythagoras gave more attention to its contemplative part, on which he brought to bear all the force of his great intellect. To Plato is given the praise of having perfected philosophy by combining both parts into one. He then divides it into three parts—the first moral, which is chiefly occupied with action; the second natural, of which the object is contemplation; and the third rational, which discriminates between the true and the false. And though this last is necessary both to action and contemplation, it is contemplation, nevertheless, which lays peculiar claim to the office of investigating the nature of truth. Thus this tripartite division is not contrary to that which made the study of wisdom to consist in action and contemplation. Now, as to what Plato thought with respect to each of these parts—that is, what he believed to be the end of all actions, the cause of all natures, and the light of all intelligences—it would be a question too long to discuss, and about which we ought not to make any rash affirmation. For, as Plato liked and constantly affected the well-known method of his master Socrates, namely, that of dissimulating his knowledge or his opinions, it is not easy to discover clearly what he himself thought on various matters, any more than it is to discover what were the real opinions of Socrates. We must, nevertheless, insert into our work certain of those opinions which he expresses in his writings, whether he himself uttered them, or narrates them as expressed by others, and seems himself to approve of—opinions sometimes favorable to the true religion, which our faith takes up and defends, and sometimes contrary to it, as, for example, in the questions concerning the existence of one God or of many, as it relates to the truly blessed life which is to be after death. For those who are praised as having most closely followed Plato, who is justly preferred to all the other philosophers of the Gentiles, and who are said to have manifested the greatest acuteness in understanding him, do perhaps entertain such an idea of God as to admit that in Him are to be found the cause of existence, the ultimate reason for the understanding, and the end in reference to which the whole life is to be regulated. Of which three things, the first is understood to pertain to the natural, the second to the rational, and the third to the moral part of philosophy. For if man has been so created as to attain, through that which is most excellent in him, to that which excels all things—that is, to the one true and absolutely good God, without whom no nature exists, no doctrine instructs, no exercise profits—let Him be sought in whom all things are secure to us, let Him be discovered in whom all truth becomes certain to us, let Him be loved in whom all becomes right to us.

5. THAT IT IS ESPECIALLY WITH THE PLATONISTS THAT WE MUST CARRY ON OUR DISPUTATIONS ON MATTERS OF THEOLOGY, THEIR OPINIONS BEING PREFERABLE TO THOSE OF ALL OTHER PHILOSOPHERS

If, then, Plato defined the wise man as one who imitates, knows, loves this God, and who is rendered blessed through fellowship with Him in His own blessedness, why discuss with the other philosophers? It is evident that none come nearer to us than the Platonists. To them, therefore, let that fabulous theology give place which delights the minds of men with the crimes of the gods; and that civil theology also, in which impure demons, under the name of gods, have seduced the peoples of the earth given up to earthly pleasures, desiring to be honored by the errors of men, and by filling the minds of their worshipers with impure desires, exciting them to make the representation of their crimes one of the rites of their worship, while they themselves found in the spectators of these exhibitions a most pleasing spectacle—a theology in which, whatever was honorable in the temple, was defiled by its mixture with the obscenity of the theatre, and whatever was base in the theatre was vindicated by the abominations of the temples. To these philosophers also the interpretations of Varro must give place, in which he explains the sacred rites as having reference to heaven and earth, and to the seeds and operations of perishable things; for, in the first place, those rites have not the signification which he would have men believe is attached to them, and therefore truth does not follow him in his attempt so to interpret them; and even if they had this signification, still those things ought not to be worshiped by the rational soul as its god which are placed below it in the scale of nature, nor ought the soul to prefer to itself as gods things to which the true God has given it the preference. The same must be said of those writings pertaining to the sacred rites, which Numa Pompilius took care to conceal by causing them to be buried along with himself, and which, when they were afterward turned up by the plow, were burned by order of the senate. And, to treat Numa with all honor, let us mention as belonging to the same rank as these writings that which Alexander of Macedon wrote to his mother as communicated to him by Leo, an Egyptian high priest. In this letter not only Picus and Faunus, and Æneas and Romulus, or even Hercules and Æsculapius and Liber, born of Semele, and the twin sons of Tyndareus, or any other mortals who have been deified, but even the principal gods themselves,[1] to whom Cicero, in his Tusculan questions,[2] alludes without mentioning their names, Jupiter, Juno, Saturn, Vulcan, Vesta, and many others whom Varro attempts to identify with the parts or the elements of the world, are shown to have been men. There is, as we have said, a similarity between this case and that of Numa; for the priest being afraid because he had revealed a mystery, earnestly begged of Alexander to command his mother to burn the letter which conveyed these communications to her. Let these two theologies, then, the fabulous and the civil, give place to the Platonic philosophers, who have recognized the true God as the author of all things, the source of the light of truth, and the bountiful bestower of all blessedness. And not these only, but to these great acknowledgers of so great a God, those philosophers must yield who, having their mind enslaved to their body, supposed the principles of all things to be material; as Thales, who held that the first principle of all things was water; Anaximenes, that it was air; the Stoics, that it was fire; Epicurus, who affirmed that it consisted of atoms, that is to say, of minute corpuscules; and many others whom it is needless to enumerate, but who believed that bodies, simple or compound, animate or inanimate, but nevertheless bodies, were the cause and principle of all things. For some of them—as, for instance, the Epicureans—believed that living things could originate from things without life; others held that all things living or without life spring from a living principle, but that, nevertheless, all things, being material, spring from a material principle. For the Stoics thought that fire, that is, one of the four material elements of which this visible world is composed, was both living and intelligent, the maker of the world and of all things contained in it—that it was in fact God. These and others like them have only been able to suppose that which their hearts enslaved to sense have vainly suggested to them. And yet they have within themselves something which they could not see: they represented to themselves inwardly things which they had seen without, even when they were not seeing them, but only thinking of them. But this representation in thought is no longer a body, but only the similitude of a body; and that faculty of the mind by which this similitude of a body is seen is neither a body nor the similitude of a body; and the faculty which judges whether the representation is beautiful or ugly is without doubt superior to the object judged of. This principle is the understanding of man, the rational soul; and it is certainly not a body, since that similitude of a body which it beholds and judges of is itself not a body. The soul is neither earth, nor water, nor air, nor fire, of which four bodies, called the four elements, we see that this world is composed. And if the soul is not a body, how should God, its Creator, be a body? Let all those philosophers, then, give place, as we have said, to the Platonists, and those also who have been ashamed to say that God is a body, but yet have thought that our souls are of the same nature as God. They have not been staggered by the great changeableness of the soul—an attribute which it would be impious to ascribe to the divine nature—but they say it is the body which changes the soul, for in itself it is unchangeable. As well might they say, "Flesh is wounded by some body, for in itself it is invulnerable." In a word, that which is unchangeable can be changed by nothing, so that that which can be changed by the body cannot properly be said to be immutable.

---

1. Dii majorum gentium.
2. Cicero Tusc. Disp. 1.13.

6. CONCERNING THE MEANING OF THE PLATONISTS IN THAT PART OF PHILOSOPHY CALLED PHYSICAL

These philosophers, then, whom we see not undeservedly exalted above the rest in fame and glory, have seen that no material body is God, and therefore they have transcended all bodies in seeking for God. They have seen that whatever is changeable is not the most high God, and therefore they have transcended every soul and all changeable spirits in seeking the Supreme. They have seen also that, in every changeable thing, the form which makes it that which it is, whatever be its mode or nature, can only *be* through Him who truly *is*, because He is unchangeable. And therefore, whether we consider the whole body of the world, its figure, qualities, and orderly movement, and also all the bodies which are in it; or whether we consider all life, either that which nourishes and maintains, as the life of trees, or that which, besides this, has also sensation, as the life of beasts; or that which adds to all these intelligence, as the life of man; or that which does not need the support of nutriment, but only maintains, feels, understands, as the life of angels—all can only *be* through Him who absolutely *is*. For to Him it is not one thing to *be*, and another to live, as though He could *be*, not living; nor is it to Him one thing to live, and another thing to understand, as though He could live, not understanding; nor is it to Him one thing to understand, another thing to be blessed, as though He could understand and not be blessed. But to Him to live, to understand, to be blessed, are to *be*. They have understood, from this unchangeableness and this simplicity, that all things must have been made by Him, and that He could Himself have been made by none. For they have considered that whatever *is* is either body or life, and that life is something better than body, and that the nature of body is sensible, and that of life intelligible. Therefore they have preferred the intelligible nature to the sensible. We mean by sensible things such things as can be perceived by the sight and touch of the body; by intelligible things, such as can be understood by the sight of the mind. For there is no corporeal beauty, whether in the condition of a body, as figure, or in its movement, as in music, of which it is not the mind that judges. But this could never have been, had there not existed in the mind itself a superior form of these things, without bulk, without noise of voice, without space and time. But even in respect of these things, had the mind not been mutable, it would not have been possible for one to judge better than another with regard to sensible forms.

He who is clever judges better than he who is slow, he who is skilled than he who is unskillful, he who is practiced than he who is unpracticed; and the same person judges better after he has gained experience than he did before. But that which is capable of more and less is mutable; whence able men, who have thought deeply on these things, have gathered that the first form is not to be found in those things whose form is changeable. Since, therefore, they saw that body and mind might be more or less beautiful in form, and that, if they wanted form, they could have no existence, they saw that there is some existence in which is the first form, unchangeable, and therefore not admitting of degrees of comparison, and in that they most rightly believed was the first principle of things which was not made, and by which all things were made. Therefore that which is known of God He manifested to them when His invisible things were seen by them, being understood by those things which have been made; also His eternal power and Godhead by whom all visible and temporal things have been created.[1] We have said enough upon that part of theology which they call physical, that is, natural.

---

1. Rom. 1:19–20.

7. HOW MUCH THE PLATONISTS ARE TO BE HELD AS EXCELLING OTHER PHILOSOPHERS IN LOGIC, THAT IS, RATIONAL PHILOSOPHY

Then, again, as far as regards the doctrine which treats of that which they call logic, that is, rational philosophy, far be it from us to compare them with those who attributed to the bodily senses the faculty of discriminating truth, and thought, that all we learn is to be measured by their untrustworthy and fallacious rules. Such were the Epicureans, and all of the same school. Such also were the Stoics, who ascribed to the bodily senses that expertness in disputation which they so ardently love, called by them dialectic, asserting that from the senses the mind conceives the notions (ἔννοιαι) of those things which they explicate by definition. And hence is developed the whole plan and connection of their learning and teaching. I often wonder, with respect to this, how they can say that none are beautiful but the wise; for by what bodily sense have they perceived that beauty, by what eyes of the flesh have they seen wisdom's comeliness of form? Those, however, whom we justly rank before all others, have distinguished those things which are conceived by the mind from those which are perceived by the senses, neither taking away from the senses anything to which they are competent, nor attributing to them anything beyond their competency. And the light of our understandings, by which all things are learned by us, they have affirmed to be that selfsame God by whom all things were made.

8. THAT THE PLATONISTS HOLD THE FIRST RANK IN MORAL PHILOSOPHY ALSO

The remaining part of philosophy is morals, or what is called by the Greeks ἠθική, in which is discussed the question concerning the chief good—that which will leave us nothing further to seek in order to be blessed, if only we make all our actions refer to it, and seek it not for the sake of something else, but for its own sake. Therefore it is called the end, because we wish other things on account of it, but itself only for its own sake. This beatific good, therefore, according to some, comes to a man from the body, according to others, from the mind, and, according to others, from both together. For they saw that man himself consists of soul and body; and therefore they believed that from either of these two, or from both together, their well-being must proceed, consisting in a certain final good, which could render them blessed, and to which they might refer all their actions, not requiring anything ulterior to which to refer that good itself. This is why those who have added a third kind of good things, which they call extrinsic—as honor, glory, wealth, and the like—have not regarded them as part of the final good, that is, to be sought after for their own sake, but as things which are to be sought for the sake of something else, affirming that this kind of good is good to the good, and evil to the evil. Wherefore, whether they have sought the good of man from the mind or from the body, or from both together, it is still only from man they have supposed that it must be sought. But they who have sought it from the body have sought it from the inferior part of man; they who have sought it from the mind, from the superior part; and they who have sought it from both, from the whole man. Whether, therefore, they have sought it from any part, or from the whole man, still they have only sought it from man; nor have these differences, being three, given rise only to three dissentient sects of philosophers, but to many. For diverse philosophers have held diverse opinions, both concerning the good of the body, and the good of the mind, and the good of both together. Let, therefore, all these give place to those philosophers who have not affirmed that a man is blessed by the enjoyment of the body, or by the enjoyment of the mind, but by the enjoyment of God—enjoying Him, however, not as the mind does the body or itself, or as one friend enjoys another, but as the eye enjoys light, if, indeed, we may draw any comparison between these things. But what the nature of this comparison is, will, if God help me, be shown in another place, to the best of my ability. At present, it is sufficient to mention that Plato determined the final good to be to live according to virtue, and affirmed that he only can attain to virtue who knows and imitates God—which knowledge and imitation are the only cause of blessedness. Therefore he did not doubt that to philosophize is to love God, whose nature is incorporeal. Whence it certainly follows that the student of wisdom, that is, the philosopher, will then become blessed when he shall have begun to enjoy God. For though he is not necessarily blessed who enjoys that which he loves (for many are miserable by loving that which ought not to be loved, and still more miserable when they enjoy it), nevertheless no one is blessed who does not enjoy that which he loves. For even they who love things which ought not to be loved do not count themselves blessed by loving merely, but by enjoying them. Who, then, but the most miserable will deny that he is blessed, who enjoys that which he loves, and loves the true and highest good? But the true and highest good, according to Plato, is God, and therefore he would call him a philosopher who loves God; for philosophy is directed to the obtaining of the blessed life, and he who loves God is blessed in the enjoyment of God.

9. CONCERNING THAT PHILOSOPHY WHICH HAS COME NEAREST TO THE CHRISTIAN FAITH

Whatever philosophers, therefore, thought concerning the supreme God, that He is both the maker of all created things, the light by which things are known, and the good in reference to which things are to be done; that we have in Him the first principle of nature, the truth of doctrine, and the happiness of life—whether these philosophers may be more suitably called Platonists, or whether they may give some other name to their sect; whether, we say, that only the chief men of the Ionic school, such as Plato himself, and they who have well understood him, have thought thus; or whether we also include the Italic school, on account of Pythagoras and the Pythagoreans, and all who may have held like opinions; and, lastly, whether also we include all who have been held wise men and philosophers among all nations who are discovered to have seen and taught this, be they

Atlantics, Libyans, Egyptians, Indians, Persians, Chaldæans, Scythians, Gauls, Spaniards, or of other nations—we prefer these to all other philosophers, and confess that they approach nearest to us.

10. THAT THE EXCELLENCY OF THE CHRISTIAN RELIGION IS ABOVE ALL THE SCIENCE OF PHILOSOPHERS

For although a Christian man instructed only in ecclesiastical literature may perhaps be ignorant of the very name of Platonists, and may not even know that there have existed two schools of philosophers speaking the Greek tongue, to wit, the Ionic and Italic, he is nevertheless not so deaf with respect to human affairs, as not to know that philosophers profess the study, and even the possession, of wisdom. He is on his guard, however, with respect to those who philosophize according to the elements of this world, not according to God, by whom the world itself was made; for he is warned by the precept of the apostle, and faithfully hears what has been said, "Beware that no one deceive you through philosophy and vain deceit, according to the elements of the world."[1] Then, that he may not suppose that all philosophers are such as do this, he hears the same apostle say concerning certain of them, "Because that which is known of God is manifest among them, for God has manifested it to them. For His invisible things from the creation of the world are clearly seen, being understood by the things which are made, also His eternal power and Godhead."[2] And, when speaking to the Athenians, after having spoken a mighty thing concerning God, which few are able to understand, "In Him we live, and move, and have our being,"[3] he goes on to say, "as certain also of your own have said." He knows well, too, to be on his guard against even these philosophers in their errors. For where it has been said by him, "that God has manifested to them by those things which are made His invisible things, that they might be seen by the understanding," there it has also been said that they did not rightly worship God Himself, because they paid divine honors, which are due to Him alone, to other things also to which they ought not to have paid them—"because, knowing God, they glorified Him not as God: neither were thankful, but became vain in their imaginations, and their foolish heart was darkened. Professing themselves to be wise, they became fools, and changed the glory of the incorruptible God into the likeness of the image of corruptible man, and of birds, and four-footed beasts, and creeping things"[4]—where the apostle would have us understand him as meaning the Romans, and Greeks, and Egyptians, who gloried in the name of wisdom; but concerning this we will dispute with them afterward. With respect, however, to that wherein they agree with us, we prefer them to all others, namely, concerning the one God, the author of this universe, who is not only above every body, being incorporeal, but also above all souls, being incorruptible—our principle, our light, our good. And though the Christian man, being ignorant of their writings, does not use in disputation words which he has not learned—not calling that part of philosophy natural (which is the Latin term), or physical (which is the Greek one), which treats of the investigation of nature; or that part rational, or logical, which deals with the question how truth may be discovered; or that part moral, or ethical, which concerns morals, and shows how good is to be sought, and evil to be shunned—he is not, therefore, ignorant that it is from the one true and supremely good God that we have that nature in which we are made in the image of God, and that doctrine by which we know Him and ourselves, and that grace through which, by cleaving to Him, we are blessed. This, therefore, is the cause why we prefer these to all the others, because, while other philosophers have worn out their minds and powers in seeking the causes of things, and endeavoring to discover the right mode of learning and of living, these, by knowing God, have found where resides the cause by which the universe has been constituted, and the light by which truth is to be discovered, and the fountain at which felicity is to be drunk. All philosophers, then, who have had these thoughts concerning God, whether Platonists or others, agree with us. But we have thought it better to plead our cause with the Platonists, because their writings are better known. For the Greeks, whose tongue holds the highest place among the languages of the Gentiles, are loud in their praises of these writings; and the Latins, taken with their excellence, or their renown, have studied them more heartily than other writings, and, by translating them into our tongue, have given them greater celebrity and notoriety.

---

1. Col. 2:8.
2. Rom. 1:19–20.
3. Acts 17:28.
4. Rom. 1:21–23.

11. HOW PLATO HAS BEEN ABLE TO APPROACH SO NEARLY TO CHRISTIAN KNOWLEDGE

Certain partakers with us in the grace of Christ wonder when they hear and read that Plato had conceptions concerning God, in which they recognize considerable agreement with the truth of our religion. Some have concluded from this, that when he went to Egypt he had heard the prophet Jeremiah, or, while traveling in the same country, had read the prophetic Scriptures, which opinion I myself have expressed in certain of my writings.[1] But a careful calculation of dates, contained in chronological history, shows that Plato was born about a hundred years after the time in which Jeremiah prophesied, and, as he lived eighty-one years, there are found to have been about seventy years from his death to that time when Ptolemy, king of Egypt, requested the prophetic Scriptures of the Hebrew people to be sent to him from Judæa, and committed them to seventy Hebrews, who also knew the Greek tongue, to be translated and kept. Therefore, on that voyage of his, Plato could neither have seen Jeremiah, who was dead so long before, nor have read those same Scriptures which had not yet been translated into the Greek language, of which he was a master, unless, indeed, we say that, as he was most earnest in the pursuit of knowledge, he also studied those writings through an interpreter, as he did those of the Egyptians—not, indeed, writing a translation of them (the facilities for doing which were only gained even by Ptolemy in return for munificent acts of kindness,[2] though fear of his kingly authority might have seemed a sufficient motive), but learning as much as he possibly could concerning their contents by means of conversation. What warrants this supposition are the opening verses of Genesis: "In the beginning God made the heaven and earth. And the earth was invisible, and without order; and darkness was over the abyss: and the Spirit of God moved over the waters."[3] For in the *Timæus*, when writing on the formation of the world, he says that God first united earth and fire; from which it is evident that he assigns to fire a place in heaven. This opinion bears a certain resemblance to the statement, "In the beginning God made heaven and earth." Plato next speaks of those two intermediary elements, water and air, by which the other two extremes, namely, earth and fire, were mutually united; from which circumstance he is thought to have so understood the words, "The Spirit of God moved over the waters." For, not paying sufficient attention to the designations given by those Scriptures to the Spirit of God, he may have thought that the four elements are spoken of in that place, because the air also is called spirit.[4] Then, as to Plato's saying that the philosopher is a lover of God, nothing shines forth more conspicuously in those sacred Writings. But the most striking thing in this connection, and that which most of all inclines me almost to assent to the opinion that Plato was not ignorant of those writings, is the answer which was given to the question elicited from the holy Moses when the words of God were conveyed to him by the angel; for, when he asked what was the name of that God who was commanding him to go and deliver the Hebrew people out of Egypt, this answer was given: "I am who am; and thou shalt say to the children of Israel, He who *is* sent me unto you";[5] as though compared with Him that truly *is*, because He is unchangeable, those things which have been created mutable *are* not—a truth which Plato zealously held, and most diligently commended. And I know not whether this sentiment is anywhere to be found in the books of those who were before Plato, unless in that book where it is said, "I am who am; and thou shalt say to the children of Israel, *Who is* sent me unto you."

---

1. Augustine, De Doctrina Christiana 2.43. Cf. *Retract.* 2.4.2.
2. Liberating Jewish slaves, and sending gifts to the temple. See Josephus *Ant.* 12.2.
3. Gen. 1:1–2.
4. Spiritus.
5. Exod. 3:14.

12. THAT EVEN THE PLATONISTS, THOUGH THEY SAY THESE THINGS CONCERNING THE ONE TRUE GOD, NEVERTHELESS THOUGHT THAT SACRED RITES WERE TO BE PERFORMED IN HONOR OF MANY GODS

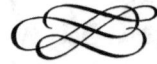

But we need not determine from what source he learned these things—whether it was from the books of the ancients who preceded him, or, as is more likely, from the words of the apostle: "Because that which is known of God, has been manifested among them, for God hath manifested it to them. For His invisible things from the creation of the world are clearly seen, being understood by those things which have been made, also His eternal power and Godhead."[1] From whatever source he may have derived this knowledge, then, I think I have made it sufficiently plain that I have not chosen the Platonic philosophers undeservedly as the parties with whom to discuss; because the question we have just taken up concerns the natural theology—the question, namely, whether sacred rites are to be performed to one God, or to many, for the sake of the happiness which is to be after death. I have specially chosen them because their juster thoughts concerning the one God who made heaven and earth, have made them illustrious among philosophers. This has given them such superiority to all others in the judgment of posterity, that, though Aristotle, the disciple of Plato, a man of eminent abilities, inferior in eloquence to Plato, yet far superior to many in that respect, had founded the Peripatetic sect—so called because they were in the habit of walking about during their disputations—and though he had, through the greatness of his fame, gathered very many disciples into his school, even during the life of his master; and though Plato at his death was succeeded in his school, which was called the Academy, by Speusippus, his sister's son, and Xenocrates, his beloved disciple, who, together with their successors, were called from this name of the school, Academics; nevertheless the most illustrious recent philosophers, who have chosen to follow Plato, have been unwilling to be called Peripatetics, or Academics, but have preferred the name of Platonists. Among these were the renowned Plotinus, Iamblichus, and Porphyry, who were Greeks, and the African Apuleius, who was learned both in the Greek and Latin tongues. All these, however, and the rest who were of the same school, and also Plato himself, thought that sacred rites ought to be performed in honor of many gods.

---

1. Rom. 1:20.

13. CONCERNING THE OPINION OF PLATO, ACCORDING TO WHICH HE DEFINED THE GODS AS BEINGS ENTIRELY GOOD AND THE FRIENDS OF VIRTUE

Therefore, although in many other important respects they differ from us, nevertheless with respect to this particular point of difference, which I have just stated, as it is one of great moment, and the question on hand concerns it, I will first ask them to what gods they think that sacred rites are to be performed—to the good or to the bad, or to both the good and the bad? But we have the opinion of Plato affirming that all the gods are good, and that there is not one of the gods bad. It follows, therefore, that these are to be performed to the good, for then they are performed to gods; for if they are not good, neither are they gods. Now, if this be the case (for what else ought we to believe concerning the gods?), certainly it explodes the opinion that the bad gods are to be propitiated by sacred rites in order that they may not harm us, but the good gods are to be invoked in order that they may assist us. For there are no bad gods, and it is to the good that, as they say, the due honor of such rites is to be paid. Of what character, then, are those gods who love scenic displays, even demanding that a place be given them among divine things, and that they be exhibited in their honor? The power of these gods proves that they exist, but their liking such things proves that they are bad. For it is well known what Plato's opinion was concerning scenic plays. He thinks that the poets themselves, because they have composed songs so unworthy of the majesty and goodness of the gods, ought to be banished from the state. Of what character, therefore, are those gods who contend with Plato himself about those scenic plays? He does not suffer the gods to be defamed by false crimes; the gods command those same crimes to be celebrated in their own honor.

In fine, when they ordered these plays to be inaugurated, they not only demanded base things, but also did cruel things, taking from Titus Latinius his son, and sending a disease upon him because he had refused to obey them, which they removed when he had fulfilled their commands. Plato, however, bad though they were, did not think they were to be feared; but, holding to his opinion with the utmost firmness and constancy, does not hesitate to remove from a well-ordered state all the sacrilegious follies of the poets, with which these gods are delighted because they themselves are impure. But Labeo places this same Plato (as I have mentioned already in the second book[1]) among the demigods. Now Labeo thinks that the bad deities are to be propitiated with bloody victims, and by fasts accompanied with the same, but the good deities with plays, and all other things which are associated with joyfulness. How comes it, then, that the demigod Plato so persistently dares to take away those pleasures, because he deems them base, not from the demigods but from the gods, and these the good gods? And, moreover, those very gods themselves do certainly refute the opinion of Labeo, for they showed themselves in the case of Latinius to be not only wanton and sportive, but also cruel and terrible. Let the Platonists, therefore, explain these things to us, since, following the opinion of their master, they think that all the gods are good and honorable, and friendly to the virtues of the wise, holding it unlawful to think otherwise concerning any of the gods. We will explain it, say they. Let us then attentively listen to them.

---

1. See above, 2.14.

14. OF THE OPINION OF THOSE WHO HAVE SAID THAT RATIONAL SOULS ARE OF THREE KINDS, TO WIT, THOSE OF THE CELESTIAL GODS, THOSE OF THE AERIAL DEMONS, AND THOSE OF TERRESTRIAL MEN

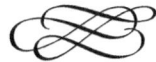

There is, say they, a threefold division of all animals endowed with a rational soul, namely, into gods, men, and demons. The gods occupy the loftiest region, men the lowest, the demons the middle region. For the abode of the gods is heaven, that of men the earth, that of the demons the air. As the dignity of their regions is diverse, so also is that of their natures; therefore the gods are better than men and demons. Men have been placed below the gods and demons, both in respect of the order of the regions they inhabit, and the difference of their merits. The demons, therefore, who hold the middle place, as they are inferior to the gods, than whom they inhabit a lower region, so they are superior to men, than whom they inhabit a loftier one. For they have immortality of body in common with the gods, but passions of the mind in common with men. On which account, say they, it is not wonderful that they are delighted with the obscenities of the theatre, and the fictions of the poets, since they are also subject to human passions, from which the gods are far removed, and to which they are altogether strangers. Whence we conclude that it was not the gods, who are all good and highly exalted, that Plato deprived of the pleasure of theatric plays, by reprobating and prohibiting the fictions of the poets, but the demons.

Of these things many have written: among others Apuleius, the Platonist of Madaura, who composed a whole work on the subject, titled, *Concerning the God of Socrates*. He there discusses and explains of what kind that deity was who attended on Socrates, a sort of familiar, by whom it is said he was admonished to desist from any action which would not turn out to his advantage. He asserts most distinctly, and proves at great length, that it was not a god but a demon; and he discusses with great diligence the opinion of Plato concerning the lofty estate of the gods, the lowly estate of men, and the middle estate of demons. These things being so, how did Plato dare to take away, if not from the gods, whom he removed from all human contagion, certainly from the demons, all the pleasures of the theatre, by expelling the poets from the state? Evidently in this way he wished to admonish the human soul, although still confined in these moribund members, to despise the shameful commands of the demons, and to detest their impurity, and to choose rather the splendor of virtue. But if Plato showed himself virtuous in answering and prohibiting these things, then certainly it was shameful of the demons to command them. Therefore either Apuleius is wrong, and Socrates' familiar did not belong to this class of deities, or Plato held contradictory opinions, now honoring the demons, now removing from the well-regulated state the things in which they delighted, or Socrates is not to be congratulated on the friendship of the demon, of which Apuleius was so ashamed that he titled his book *On the God of Socrates*, while according to the tenor of his discussion, wherein he so diligently and at such length distinguishes gods from demons, he ought not to have titled it, *Concerning the God*, but *Concerning the Demon of Socrates*. But he preferred to put this into the discussion itself rather than into the title of his book. For, through the sound doctrine which has illuminated human society, all, or almost all, men have such a horror at the name of demons, that everyone who before reading the dissertation of Apuleius, which sets forth the dignity of demons, should have read the title of the book, *On the Demon of Socrates*, would certainly have thought that the author was not a sane man. But what did even Apuleius find to praise in the demons, except subtlety and strength of body and a higher place of habitation? For when he spoke generally concerning their manners, he said nothing that was good, but very much that was bad. Finally, no one, when he has read that book, wonders that they desired to have even the obscenity of the stage among divine things, or that, wishing to be thought gods, they should be delighted with the crimes of the gods, or that all those sacred solemnities, whose obscenity occasions laughter, and whose shameful cruelty causes horror, should be in agreement with their passions.

15. THAT THE DEMONS ARE NOT BETTER THAN MEN BECAUSE OF THEIR AERIAL BODIES, OR ON ACCOUNT OF THEIR SUPERIOR PLACE OF ABODE

Wherefore let not the mind truly religious, and submitted to the true God, suppose that demons are better than men, because they have better bodies. Otherwise it must put many beasts before itself which are superior to us both in acuteness of the senses, in ease and quickness of movement, in strength and in long-continued vigor of body. What man can equal the eagle or the vulture in strength of vision? Who can equal the dog in acuteness of smell? Who can equal the hare, the stag, and all the birds in swiftness? Who can equal in strength the lion or the elephant? Who can equal in length of life the serpents, which are affirmed to put off old age along with their skin, and to return to youth again? But as we are better than all these by the possession of reason and understanding, so we ought also to be better than the demons by living good and virtuous lives. For divine Providence gave to them bodies of a better quality than ours, that that in which we excel them might in this way be commended to us as deserving to be far more cared for than the body, and that we should learn to despise the bodily excellence of the demons compared with goodness of life, in respect of which we are better than they, knowing that we too shall have immortality of body—not an immortality tortured by eternal punishment, but that which is consequent on purity of soul.

But now, as regards loftiness of place, it is altogether ridiculous to be so influenced by the fact that the demons inhabit the air, and we the earth, as to think that on that account they are to be put before us; for in this way we put all the birds before ourselves. But the birds, when they are weary with flying, or require to repair their bodies with food, come back to the earth to rest or to feed, which the demons, they say, do not. Are they, therefore, inclined to say that the birds are superior to us, and the demons superior to the birds? But if it be madness to think so, there is no reason why we should think that, on account of their inhabiting a loftier element, the demons have a claim to our religious submission. But as it is really the case that the birds of the air are not only not put before us who dwell on the earth; but are even subjected to us on account of the dignity of the rational soul which is in us, so also it is the case that the demons, though they are aerial, are not better than we who are terrestrial because the air is higher than the earth, but, on the contrary, men are to be put before demons because their despair is not to be compared to the hope of pious men. Even that law of Plato's, according to which he mutually orders and arranges the four elements, inserting between the two extreme elements —namely, fire, which is in the highest degree mobile, and the immovable earth—the two middle ones, air and water, that by how much the air is higher up than the water, and the fire than the air, by so much also are the waters higher than the earth —this law, I say, sufficiently admonishes us not to estimate the merits of animated creatures according to the grades of the elements. And Apuleius himself says that man is a terrestrial animal in common with the rest, who is nevertheless to be put far before aquatic animals, though Plato puts the waters themselves before the land. By this he would have us understand that the same order is not to be observed when the question concerns the merits of animals, though it seems to be the true one in the gradation of bodies; for it appears to be possible that a soul of a higher order may inhabit a body of a lower, and a soul of a lower order a body of a higher.

16. WHAT APULEIUS THE PLATONIST THOUGHT CONCERNING THE MANNERS AND ACTIONS OF DEMONS

The same Apuleius, when speaking concerning the manners of demons, said that they are agitated with the same perturbations of mind as men; that they are provoked by injuries, propitiated by services and by gifts, rejoice in honors, are delighted with a variety of sacred rites, and are annoyed if any of them be neglected. Among other things, he also says that on them depend the divinations of augurs, soothsayers, and prophets, and the revelations of dreams, and that from them also are the miracles of the magicians. But, when giving a brief definition of them, he says, "Demons are of an animal nature, passive in soul, rational in mind, aerial in body, eternal in time." "Of which five things, the three first are common to them and us, the fourth peculiar to themselves, and the fifth common to them with the gods."[1] But I see that they have in common with the gods two of the first things, which they have in common with us. For he says that the gods also are animals; and when he is assigning to every order of beings its own element, he places us among the other terrestrial animals which live and feel upon the earth. Wherefore, if the demons are animals as to genus, this is common to them, not only with men, but also with the gods and with beasts; if they are rational as to their mind, this is common to them with the gods and with men; if they are eternal in time, this is common to them with the gods only; if they are passive as to their soul, this is common to them with men only; if they are aerial in body, in this they are alone. Therefore it is no great thing for them to be of an animal nature, for so also are the beasts; in being rational as to mind, they are not above ourselves, for so are we also; and as to their being eternal as to time, what is the advantage of that if they are not blessed? For better is temporal happiness than eternal misery. Again, as to their being passive in soul, how are they in this respect above us, since we also are so, but would not have been so had we not been miserable? Also, as to their being aerial in body, how much value is to be set on that, since a soul of any kind whatsoever is to be set above every body? And therefore religious worship, which ought to be rendered from the soul, is by no means due to that thing which is inferior to the soul. Moreover, if he had, among those things which he says belong to demons, enumerated virtue, wisdom, happiness, and affirmed that they have those things in common with the gods, and, like them, eternally, he would assuredly have attributed to them something greatly to be desired, and much to be prized. And even in that case it would not have been our duty to worship them like God on account of these things, but rather to worship Him from whom we know they had received them. But how much less are they really worthy of divine honor—those aerial animals who are only rational that they may be capable of misery, passive that they may be actually miserable, and eternal that it may be impossible for them to end their misery!

---

1. *Apuleius De Deo Socratis.*

17. WHETHER IT IS PROPER THAT MEN SHOULD WORSHIP THOSE SPIRITS FROM WHOSE VICES IT IS NECESSARY THAT THEY BE FREED

Wherefore, to omit other things, and confine our attention to that which he says is common to the demons with us, let us ask this question: if all the four elements are full of their own animals, the fire and the air of immortal, and the water and the earth of mortal ones, why are the souls of demons agitated by the whirlwinds and tempests of passions?—for the Greek word πάθος means perturbation, whence he chose to call the demons "passive in soul," because the word passion, which is derived from πάθος, signified a commotion of the mind contrary to reason. Why, then, are these things in the minds of demons which are not in beasts? For if anything of this kind appears in beasts, it is not perturbation, because it is not contrary to reason, of which they are devoid. Now it is foolishness or misery which is the cause of these perturbations in the case of men, for we are not yet blessed in the possession of that perfection of wisdom which is promised to us at last, when we shall be set free from our present mortality. But the gods, they say, are free from these perturbations, because they are not only eternal, but also blessed; for they also have the same kind of rational souls, but most pure from all spot and plague. Wherefore, if the gods are free from perturbation because they are blessed, not miserable animals, and the beasts are free from them because they are animals which are capable neither of blessedness nor misery, it remains that the demons, like men, are subject to perturbations because they are not blessed but miserable animals. What folly, therefore, or rather what madness, to submit ourselves through any sentiment of religion to demons, when it belongs to the true religion to deliver us from that depravity which makes us like to them! For Apuleius himself, although he is very sparing toward them, and thinks they are worthy of divine honors, is nevertheless compelled to confess that they are subject to anger; and the true religion commands us not to be moved with anger, but rather to resist it. The demons are won over by gifts; and the true religion commands us to favor no one on account of gifts received. The demons are flattered by honors; but the true religion commands us by no means to be moved by such things. The demons are haters of some men and lovers of others, not in consequence of a prudent and calm judgment, but because of what he calls their "passive soul"; whereas the true religion commands us to love even our enemies. Lastly, the true religion commands us to put away all disquietude of heart and agitation of mind, and also all commotions and tempests of the soul, which Apuleius asserts to be continually swelling and surging in the souls of demons. Why, therefore, except through foolishness and miserable error, should you humble yourself to worship a being to whom you desire to be unlike in your life? And why should you pay religious homage to him whom you are unwilling to imitate, when it is the highest duty of religion to imitate Him whom you worship?

18. WHAT KIND OF RELIGION THAT IS WHICH TEACHES THAT MEN OUGHT TO EMPLOY THE ADVOCACY OF DEMONS IN ORDER TO BE RECOMMENDED TO THE FAVOR OF THE GOOD GODS

In vain, therefore, have Apuleius, and they who think with him, conferred on the demons the honor of placing them in the air, between the ethereal heavens and the earth, that they may carry to the gods the prayers of men, to men the answers of the gods: for Plato held, they say, that no god has intercourse with man. They who believe these things have thought it unbecoming that men should have intercourse with the gods, and the gods with men, but a befitting thing that the demons should have intercourse with both gods and men, presenting to the gods the petitions of men, and conveying to men what the gods have granted; so that a chaste man, and one who is a stranger to the crimes of the magic arts, must use as patrons, through whom the gods may be induced to hear him, demons who love these crimes, although the very fact of his not loving them ought to have recommended him to them as one who deserved to be listened to with greater readiness and willingness on their part. They love the abominations of the stage, which chastity does not love. They love, in the sorceries of the magicians, "*a thousand arts of inflicting harm*,"[1] which innocence does not love. Yet both chastity and innocence, if they wish to obtain anything from the gods, will not be able to do so by their own merits, except their enemies act as mediators on their behalf. Apuleius need not attempt to justify the fictions of the poets, and the mockeries of the stage. If human modesty can act so faithlessly toward itself as not only to love shameful things, but even to think that they are pleasing to the divinity, we can cite on the other side their own highest authority and teacher, Plato.

---

1. Virgil *Æneid* 7.338.

19. OF THE IMPIETY OF THE MAGIC ART, WHICH IS DEPENDENT ON THE ASSISTANCE OF MALIGN SPIRITS

Moreover, against those magic arts, concerning which some men, exceedingly wretched and exceedingly impious, delight to boast, may not public opinion itself be brought forward as a witness? For why are those arts so severely punished by the laws, if they are the works of deities who ought to be worshiped? Shall it be said that the Christians have ordained those laws by which magic arts are punished? With what other meaning, except that these sorceries are without doubt pernicious to the human race, did the most illustrious poet say,

> By heaven, I swear, and your dear life,
> Unwillingly these arms I wield,
> And take, to meet the coming strife,
> Enchantment's sword and shield.[1]

And that also which he says in another place concerning magic arts,

> *I've seen him to another place transport the standing corn,*[2]

has reference to the fact that the fruits of one field are said to be transferred to another by these arts which this pestiferous and accursed doctrine teaches. Does not Cicero inform us that, among the laws of the Twelve Tables, that is, the most ancient laws of the Romans, there was a law written which appointed a punishment to be inflicted on him who should do this?[3] Lastly, was it before Christian judges that Apuleius himself was accused of magic arts?[4] Had he known these arts to be divine and pious, and congruous with the works of divine power, he ought not only to have confessed, but also to have professed them, rather blaming the laws by which these things were prohibited and pronounced worthy of condemnation, while they ought to have been held worthy of admiration and respect. For by so doing, either he would have persuaded the judges to adopt his own opinion, or, if they had shown their partiality for unjust laws, and condemned him to death notwithstanding his praising and commending such things, the demons would have bestowed on his soul such rewards as he deserved, who, in order to proclaim and set forth their divine works, had not feared the loss of his human life. As our martyrs, when that religion was charged on them as a crime, by which they knew they were made safe and most glorious throughout eternity, did not choose, by denying it, to escape temporal punishments, but rather by confessing, professing, and proclaiming it, by enduring all things for it with fidelity and fortitude, and by dying for it with pious calmness, put to shame the law by which that religion was prohibited, and caused its revocation. But there is extant a most copious and eloquent oration of this Platonic philosopher, in which he defends himself against the charge of practicing these arts, affirming that he is wholly a stranger to them, and only wishing to show his innocence by denying such things as cannot be innocently committed. But all the miracles of the magicians, who he thinks are justly deserving of condemnation, are performed according to the teaching and by the power of demons. Why, then, does he think that they ought to be honored? For he asserts that they are necessary, in order to present our prayers to the gods, and yet their works are such as we must shun if we wish our prayers to reach the true God. Again, I ask, what kind of prayers of men does he suppose are presented to the good gods by the demons? If magical prayers, they will have none such; if lawful prayers, they will not receive them through such beings. But if a sinner who is penitent pour out prayers, especially if he has committed any crime of sorcery, does he receive pardon through the intercession of those demons by whose instigation and help he has fallen into the sin he mourns? Or do the demons themselves, in order that they may merit pardon for the penitent, first become penitents because they have deceived them? This no one ever said concerning the demons; for had this been the case, they would never have dared to seek for themselves divine honors. For how should they do so who desired by penitence to obtain the grace of pardon; seeing that such detestable pride could not exist along with a humility worthy of pardon?

---

1. Virgil *Æneid* 4.492–493.
2. Virgil *Ecl.* 8.99.
3. Pliny (*Hist. Nat.* 28.2) *and others quote the law as running: "Qui fruges incantasit, qui malum carmen incantasit . . . neu alienam segetem pelexeris."*
4. Before Claudius, the prefect of Africa, a heathen.

20. WHETHER WE ARE TO BELIEVE THAT THE GOOD GODS ARE MORE WILLING TO HAVE INTERCOURSE WITH DEMONS THAN WITH MEN

But does any urgent and most pressing cause compel the demons to mediate between the gods and men, that they may offer the prayers of men, and bring back the answers from the gods? And if so, what, pray, is that cause, what is that so great necessity? Because, say they, no god has intercourse with man. Most admirable holiness of God, which has no intercourse with a supplicating man, and yet has intercourse with an arrogant demon! Which has no intercourse with a penitent man, and yet has intercourse with a deceiving demon! Which has no intercourse with a man fleeing for refuge to the divine nature, and yet has intercourse with a demon feigning divinity! Which has no intercourse with a man seeking pardon, and yet has intercourse with a demon persuading to wickedness! Which has no intercourse with a man expelling the poets by means of philosophical writings from a well-regulated state, and yet has intercourse with a demon requesting from the princes and priests of a state the theatrical performance of the mockeries of the poets! Which has no intercourse with the man who prohibits the ascribing of crime to the gods, and yet has intercourse with a demon who takes delight in the fictitious representation of their crimes! Which has no intercourse with a man punishing the crimes of the magicians by just laws, and yet has intercourse with a demon teaching and practicing magical arts! Which has no intercourse with a man shunning the imitation of a demon, and yet has intercourse with a demon lying in wait for the deception of a man!

21. WHETHER THE GODS USE THE DEMONS AS MESSENGERS AND INTERPRETERS, AND WHETHER THEY ARE DECEIVED BY THEM WILLINGLY, OR WITHOUT THEIR OWN KNOWLEDGE

But herein, no doubt, lies the great necessity for this absurdity, so unworthy of the gods, that the ethereal gods, who are concerned about human affairs, would not know what terrestrial men were doing unless the aerial demons should bring them intelligence, because the ether is suspended far away from the earth and far above it, but the air is contiguous both to the ether and to the earth. O admirable wisdom! what else do these men think concerning the gods who, they say, are all in the highest degree good, but that they are concerned about human affairs, lest they should seem unworthy of worship, while, on the other hand, from the distance between the elements, they are ignorant of terrestrial things? It is on this account that they have supposed the demons to be necessary as agents, through whom the gods may inform themselves with respect to human affairs, and through whom, when necessary, they may succor men; and it is on account of this office that the demons themselves have been held as deserving of worship. If this be the case, then a demon is better known by these good gods through nearness of body, than a man is by goodness of mind. O mournful necessity, or shall I not rather say detestable and vain error, that I may not impute vanity to the divine nature! For if the gods can, with their minds free from the hindrance of bodies, see our mind, they do not need the demons as messengers from our mind to them; but if the ethereal gods, by means of their bodies, perceive the corporeal indices of minds, as the countenance, speech, motion, and thence understand what the demons tell them, then it is also possible that they may be deceived by the falsehoods of demons. Moreover, if the divinity of the gods cannot be deceived by the demons, neither can it be ignorant of our actions. But I would they would tell me whether the demons have informed the gods that the fictions of the poets concerning the crimes of the gods displease Plato, concealing the pleasure which they themselves take in them; or whether they have concealed both, and have preferred that the gods should be ignorant with respect to this whole matter, or have told both, as well the pious prudence of Plato with respect to the gods as their own lust, which is injurious to the gods; or whether they have concealed Plato's opinion, according to which he was unwilling that the gods should be defamed with falsely alleged crimes through the impious license of the poets, while they have not been ashamed nor afraid to make known their own wickedness, which makes them love theatrical plays, in which the infamous deeds of the gods are celebrated. Let them choose which they will of these four alternatives, and let them consider how much evil any one of them would require them to think of the gods. For if they choose the first, they must then confess that it was not possible for the good gods to dwell with the good Plato, though he sought to prohibit things injurious to them, while they dwelt with evil demons, who exulted in their injuries; and this because they suppose that the good gods can only know a good man, placed at so great a distance from them, through the mediation of evil demons, whom they could know on account of their nearness to themselves.[1] If they shall choose the second, and shall say that both these things are concealed by the demons, so that the gods are wholly ignorant both of Plato's most religious law and the sacrilegious pleasure of the demons, what, in that case, can the gods know to any profit with respect to human affairs through these mediating demons, when they do not know those things which are decreed, through the piety of good men, for the honor of the good gods against the lust of evil demons? But if they shall choose the third, and reply that these intermediary demons have communicated, not only the opinion of Plato, which prohibited wrongs to be done to the gods, but also their own delight in these wrongs, I would ask if such a communication is not rather an insult? Now the gods, hearing both and knowing both, not only permit the approach of those malign demons, who desire and do things contrary to the dignity of the gods and the religion of Plato, but also, through these wicked demons, who are near to them, send good things to the good Plato, who is far away from them; for they inhabit such a place in the concatenated series of the elements, that they can come into contact with those by whom they are accused, but not with him by whom they are defended—knowing the truth on both sides, but not being able to change the weight of the air and the earth. There remains the fourth supposition; but it is worse than the rest. For who will suffer it to be said that the demons have made known the calumnious fictions of the poets concerning the immortal gods, and also the disgraceful mockeries of the theatres, and their own most ardent lust after, and most sweet pleasure in these things, while they have concealed from them that Plato, with the gravity of a philosopher, gave it as his opinion that all these things ought to be removed from a well-regulated republic; so that the good gods are now compelled, through such messengers, to know the evil doings of the most wicked beings, that is to say, of the messengers themselves, and are not allowed to know the good deeds of the philosophers, though the former are for the injury, but these latter for the honor of the gods themselves?

---

1. Another reading: "whom they could not know, though near to themselves."

22. THAT WE MUST, NOTWITHSTANDING THE OPINION OF APULEIUS, REJECT THE WORSHIP OF DEMONS

None of these four alternatives, then, is to be chosen; for we dare not suppose such unbecoming things concerning the gods as the adoption of any one of them would lead us to think. It remains, therefore, that no credence whatever is to be given to the opinion of Apuleius and the other philosophers of the same school, namely, that the demons act as messengers and interpreters between the gods and men to carry our petitions from us to the gods, and to bring back to us the help of the gods. On the contrary, we must believe them to be spirits most eager to inflict harm, utterly alien from righteousness, swollen with pride, pale with envy, subtle in deceit; who dwell indeed in this air as in a prison, in keeping with their own character, because, cast down from the height of the higher heaven, they have been condemned to dwell in this element as the just reward of irretrievable transgression. But, though the air is situated above the earth and the waters, they are not on that account superior in merit to men, who, though they do not surpass them as far as their earthly bodies are concerned, do nevertheless far excel them through piety of mind—they having made choice of the true God as their helper. Over many, however, who are manifestly unworthy of participation in the true religion, they tyrannize as over captives whom they have subdued—the greatest part of whom they have persuaded of their divinity by wonderful and lying signs, consisting either of deeds or of predictions. Some, nevertheless, who have more attentively and diligently considered their vices, they have not been able to persuade that they are gods, and so have feigned themselves to be messengers between the gods and men. Some, indeed, have thought that not even this latter honor ought to be acknowledged as belonging to them, not believing that they were gods, because they saw that they were wicked, whereas the gods, according to their view, are all good. Nevertheless they dared not say that they were wholly unworthy of all divine honor, for fear of offending the multitude, by whom, through inveterate superstition, the demons were served by the performance of many rites, and the erection of many temples.

23. WHAT HERMES TRISMEGISTUS THOUGHT CONCERNING IDOLATRY, AND FROM WHAT SOURCE HE KNEW THAT THE SUPERSTITIONS OF EGYPT WERE TO BE ABOLISHED

The Egyptian Hermes, whom they call Trismegistus, had a different opinion concerning those demons. Apuleius, indeed, denies that they are gods; but when he says that they hold a middle place between the gods and men, so that they seem to be necessary for men as mediators between them and the gods, he does not distinguish between the worship due to them and the religious homage due to the supernal gods. This Egyptian, however, says that there are some gods made by the supreme God, and some made by men. Anyone who hears this, as I have stated it, no doubt supposes that it has reference to images, because they are the works of the hands of men; but he asserts that visible and tangible images are, as it were, only the bodies of the gods, and that there dwell in them certain spirits, which have been invited to come into them, and which have power to inflict harm, or to fulfill the desires of those by whom di-

THE CITY OF GOD | 711

vine honors and services are rendered to them. To unite, therefore, by a certain art, those invisible spirits to visible and material things, so as to make, as it were, animated bodies, dedicated and given up to those spirits who inhabit them—this, he says, is to make gods, adding that men have received this great and wonderful power. I will give the words of this Egyptian as they have been translated into our tongue: "And, since we have undertaken to discourse concerning the relationship and fellowship between men and the gods, know, O Æsculapius, the power and strength of man. As the Lord and Father, or that which is highest, even God, is the maker of the celestial gods, so man is the maker of the gods who are in the temples, content to dwell near to men."[1] And a little after he says, "Thus humanity, always mindful of its nature and origin, perseveres in the imitation of divinity; and as the Lord and Father made eternal gods, that they should be like Himself, so humanity fashioned its own gods according to the likeness of its own countenance." When this Æsculapius, to whom especially he was speaking, had answered him, and had said, "Dost thou mean the statues, O Trismegistus?"—"Yes, the statues," replied he, "however unbelieving thou art, O Æsculapius—the statues, animated and full of sensation and spirit, and who do such great and wonderful things—the statues prescient of future things, and foretelling them by lot, by prophet, by dreams, and many other things, who bring diseases on men and cure them again, giving them joy or sorrow according to their merits. Dost thou not know, O Æsculapius, that Egypt is an image of heaven, or, more truly, a translation and descent of all things which are ordered and transacted there, that it is, in truth, if we may say so, to be the temple of the whole world? And yet, as it becomes the prudent man to know all things beforehand, ye ought not to be ignorant of this, that there is a time coming when it shall appear that the Egyptians have all in vain, with pious mind, and with most scrupulous diligence, waited on the divinity, and when all their holy worship shall come to nought, and be found to be in vain."

Hermes then follows out at great length the statements of this passage, in which he seems to predict the present time, in which the Christian religion is overthrowing all lying figments with a vehemence and liberty proportioned to its superior truth and holiness, in order that the grace of the true Saviour may deliver men from those gods which man has made, and subject them to that God by whom man was made. But when Hermes predicts these things, he speaks as one who is a friend to these same mockeries of demons, and does not clearly express the name of Christ. On the contrary, he deplores, as if it had already taken place, the future abolition of those things by the observance of which there was maintained in Egypt a resemblance of heaven—he bears witness to Christianity by a kind of mournful prophecy. Now it was with reference to such that the apostle said, that "knowing God, they glorified Him not as God, neither were thankful, but became vain in their imaginations, and their foolish heart was darkened; professing themselves to be wise, they became fools, and changed the glory of the incorruptible God into the likeness of the image of corruptible man,"[2] and so on, for the whole passage is too long to quote. For Hermes makes many such statements agreeable to the truth concerning the one true God who fashioned this world. And I know not how he has become so bewildered by that "darkening of the heart" as to stumble into the expression of a desire that men should always continue in subjection to those gods which he confesses to be made by men, and to bewail their future removal; as if there could be anything more wretched than mankind tyrannized over by the work of his own hands, since man, by worshiping the works of his own hands, may more easily cease to be man, than the works of his hands can, through his worship of them, become gods. For it can sooner happen that man, who has received an honorable position, may, through lack of understanding, become comparable to the beasts, than that the works of man may become preferable to the work of God, made in His own image, that is, to man himself. Wherefore deservedly is man left to fall away from Him who made Him, when he prefers to himself that which he himself has made.

For these vain, deceitful, pernicious, sacrilegious things did the Egyptian Hermes sorrow, because he knew that the time was coming when they should be removed. But his sorrow was as impudently expressed as his knowledge was impudently obtained; for it was not the Holy Spirit who revealed these things to him, as He had done to the holy prophets, who, foreseeing these things, said with exultation, "If a man shall make gods, lo, they are no gods";[3] and in another place, "And it shall come to pass in that day, saith the LORD, that I will cut off the names of the idols out of the land, and they shall no more be remembered."[4] But the holy Isaiah prophesies expressly concerning Egypt in reference to this matter, saying, "And the idols of Egypt shall be moved at His presence, and their heart shall be overcome in them,"[5] and other things to the same effect. And with the prophet are to be classed those who rejoiced that that which they knew was to come had actually come—as Simeon, or Anna, who immediately recognized Jesus when He was born, or Elisabeth, who in the Spirit recognized Him when He was conceived, or Peter, who said by the revelation of the Father, "Thou art Christ, the Son of the living God."[6] But to this Egyptian those spirits indicated the time of their own destruction, who also, when the Lord was present in the flesh, said with trembling, "Art Thou come hither to destroy us before the time?"[7] meaning by destruction before the time, either that very destruction which they expected to come, but which they did not think would come so suddenly as it appeared to have done, or only that destruction which consisted in their being brought into contempt by being made known. And, indeed, this was a destruction before the time, that is, before the time of judgment, when they are to be punished with eternal damnation, together with all men who are implicated in their wickedness, as the true religion declares, which neither errs nor leads into error; for it is not like him who, blown hither and thither by every wind of doctrine, and mixing true things with things which are false, bewails as about to perish a religion which he afterward confesses to be error.

---

1. These quotations are from a dialogue between Hermes and Æsculapius, which is said to have been translated into Latin by Apuleius.
2. Rom. 1:21.
3. Jer. 16:20.
4. Zech. 13:2.
5. Isa. 19:1.
6. Matt. 16:16.
7. Matt. 8:29.

24. HOW HERMES OPENLY CONFESSED THE ERROR OF HIS FOREFATHERS, THE COMING DESTRUCTION OF WHICH HE NEVERTHELESS BEWAILED

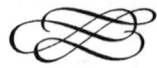

After a long interval, Hermes again comes back to the subject of the gods which men have made, saying as follows: "But enough on this subject. Let us return to man and to reason, that divine gift on account of which man has been called a rational animal. For the things which have been said concerning man, wonderful though they are, are less wonderful than those which have been said concerning reason. For man to discover the divine nature, and to make it, surpasses the wonder of all other wonderful things. Because, therefore, our forefathers erred very far with respect to the knowledge of the gods, through incredulity and through want of attention to their worship and service, they invented this art of making gods; and this art once invented, they associated with it a suitable virtue borrowed from universal nature, and being incapable of making souls, they evoked those of demons or of angels, and united them with these holy images and divine mysteries, in order that through these souls the images might have power to do good or harm to men." I know not whether the demons themselves could have been made, even by adjuration, to confess as he has confessed in these words: "Because our forefathers erred very far with respect to the knowledge of the gods, through incredulity and through want of attention to their worship and service, they invented the art of making gods." Does he say that it was a moderate degree of error which resulted in their discovery of the art of making gods, or was he content to say "they erred"? No; he must needs add "very far," and say, *They erred very far.* It was this great error and incredulity, then, of their forefathers who did not attend to the worship and service of the gods, which was the origin of the art of making gods. And yet this wise man grieves over the ruin of this art at some future time, as if it were a divine religion. Is he not verily compelled by divine influence, on the one hand, to reveal the past error of his forefathers, and by a diabolical influence, on the other hand, to bewail the future punishment of demons? For if their forefathers, by erring very far with respect to the knowledge of the gods, through incredulity and aversion of mind from their worship and service, invented the art of making gods, what wonder is it that all that is done by this detestable art, which is opposed to the divine religion, should be taken away by that religion, when truth corrects error, faith refutes incredulity, and conversion rectifies aversion?

For if he had only said, without mentioning the

cause, that his forefathers had discovered the art of making gods, it would have been our duty, if we paid any regard to what is right and pious, to consider and to see that they could never have attained to this art if they had not erred from the truth, if they had believed those things which are worthy of God, if they had attended to divine worship and service. However, if we alone should say that the causes of this art were to be found in the great error and incredulity of men, and aversion of the mind erring from and unfaithful to divine religion, the impudence of those who resist the truth were in some way to be borne with; but when he who admires in man, above all other things, this power which it has been granted him to practice and sorrows because a time is coming when all those figments of gods invented by men shall even be commanded by the laws to be taken away—when even this man confesses nevertheless, and explains the causes which led to the discovery of this art, saying that their ancestors, through great error and incredulity, and through not attending to the worship and service of the gods, invented this art of making gods—what ought we to say, or rather to do, but to give to the Lord our God all the thanks we are able, because He has taken away those things by causes the contrary of those which led to their institution? For that which the prevalence of error instituted, the way of truth took away; that which incredulity instituted, faith took away; that which aversion from divine worship and service instituted, conversion to the one true and holy God took away. Nor was this the case only in Egypt, for which country alone the spirit of the demons lamented in Hermes, but in all the earth, which sings to the Lord a new song,[1] as the truly holy and truly prophetic Scriptures have predicted, in which it is written, "Sing unto the LORD a new song; sing unto the LORD, all the earth." For the title of this psalm is, "When the house was built after the captivity." For a house is being built to the Lord in all the earth, even the city of God, which is the holy church, after that captivity in which demons held captive those men who, through faith in God, became living stones in the house. For although man made gods, it did not follow that he who made them was not held captive by them, when, by worshiping them, he was drawn into fellowship with them—into the fellowship not of stolid idols, but of cunning demons; for what are idols but what they are represented to be in the same Scriptures, "They have eyes, but they do not see,"[2] and, though artistically fashioned, are still without life and sensation? But unclean spirits, associated through that wicked art with these same idols, have miserably taken captive the souls of their worshipers, by bringing them down into fellowship with themselves. Whence the apostle says, "We know that an idol is nothing, but those things which the Gentiles sacrifice they sacrifice to demons, and not to God; and I would not ye should have fellowship with demons."[3] After this captivity, therefore, in which men were held by malign demons, the house of God is being built in all the earth; whence the title of that psalm in which it is said, "Sing unto the LORD a new song; sing unto the LORD, all the earth. Sing unto the LORD, bless His name; declare well His salvation from day to day. Declare His glory among the nations, among all people His wonderful things. For great is the LORD, and much to be praised: He is terrible above all gods. For all the gods of the nations are demons: but the LORD made the heavens."[4]

Wherefore he who sorrowed because a time was coming when the worship of idols should be abolished, and the domination of the demons over those who worshiped them, wished, under the influence of a demon, that that captivity should always continue, at the cessation of which that psalm celebrates the building of the house of the Lord in all the earth. Hermes foretold these things with grief, the prophet with joyfulness; and because the Spirit is victorious who sang these things through the ancient prophets, even Hermes himself was compelled in a wonderful manner to confess, that those very things which he wished not to be removed, and at the prospect of whose removal he was sorrowful, had been instituted, not by prudent, faithful, and religious, but by erring and unbelieving men, averse to the worship and service of the gods. And although he calls them gods, nevertheless, when he says that they were made by such men as we certainly ought not to be, he shows, whether he will or not, that they are not to be worshiped by those who do not resemble these image makers, that is, by prudent, faithful, and religious men, at the same time also making it manifest that the very men who made them involved themselves in the worship of those as gods who were not gods. For true is the saying of the prophet, "If a man *make* gods, lo, they are no gods."[5] Such gods, therefore, acknowledged by such worshipers and made by such men, did Hermes call "gods made by men," that is to say, demons, through some art of I know not what description, bound by the chains of their own lusts to images. But, nevertheless, he did not agree with that opinion of the Platonic Apuleius, of which we have already shown the incongruity and absurdity, namely, that they were interpreters and intercessors between the gods whom God made, and men whom the same God made, bringing to God the prayers of men, and from God the gifts given in answer to these prayers. For it is exceedingly stupid to believe that gods whom men have made have more influence with gods whom God has made than men themselves have, whom the very same God has made. And consider, too, that it is a demon which, bound by a man to an image by means of an impious art, has been made a god, but a god to such a man only, not to every man. What kind of god, therefore, is that which no man would make but one erring, incredulous, and averse to the true God? Moreover, if the demons which are worshiped in the temples, being introduced by some kind of strange art into images, that is, into visible representations of themselves, by those men who by this art made gods when they were straying away from, and were averse to the worship and service of the gods—if, I say, those demons are neither mediators nor interpreters between men and the gods, both on account of their own most wicked and base manners, and because men, though erring, incredulous, and averse from the worship and service of the gods, are nevertheless beyond doubt better than the demons whom they themselves have evoked, then it remains to be affirmed that what power they possess they possess as demons, doing harm by bestowing pretended benefits—harm all the greater for the deception—or else openly and undisguisedly doing evil to men. They cannot, however, do anything of this kind unless where they are permitted by the deep and secret providence of God, and then only so far as they are permitted. When, however, they are permitted, it is not because they, being midway between men and the gods, have through the friendship of the gods great power over men; for these demons cannot possibly be friends to the good gods who dwell in the holy and heavenly habitation, by whom we mean holy angels and rational creatures, whether thrones, or dominations, or principalities, or powers, from whom they are as far separated in disposition and character as vice is distant from virtue, wickedness from goodness.

---

1. Ps. 96:1.
2. Ps. 115:5, etc.
3. 1 Cor. 10:19–20.
4. Ps. 96:1–5.
5. Jer. 16:20.

25. CONCERNING THOSE THINGS WHICH MAY BE COMMON TO THE HOLY ANGELS AND TO MEN

Wherefore we must by no means seek, through the supposed mediation of demons, to avail ourselves of the benevolence or beneficence of the gods, or rather of the good angels, but through resembling them in the possession of a good will, through which we are with them, and live with them, and worship with them the same God, although we cannot see them with the eyes of our flesh. But it is not in locality we are distant from them, but in merit of life, caused by our miserable unlikeness to them in will, and by the weakness of our character; for the mere fact of our dwelling on earth under the conditions of life in the flesh does not prevent our fellowship with them. It is only prevented when we, in the impurity of our hearts, mind earthly things. But in this present time, while we are being healed that we may eventually be as they are, we are brought near to them by faith, if by their assistance we believe that He who is their blessedness is also ours.

26. THAT ALL THE RELIGION OF THE PAGANS HAS REFERENCE TO DEAD MEN

It is certainly a remarkable thing how this Egyptian, when expressing his grief that a time was coming when those things would be taken away from Egypt, which he confesses to have been invented by men erring, incredulous, and averse to the service of divine religion, says, among other things, "Then shall that land, the most holy place of shrines and temples, be full of sepulchres and dead men," as if, in sooth, if these things were not taken away, men would not die! As if dead bodies could be buried elsewhere than in the ground! As if, as time advanced, the number of sepulchres must not necessarily increase in proportion to the increase of the number of the dead! But they who are of a perverse mind, and opposed to us, suppose that what he grieves for is that the memorials of our martyrs were to succeed to their temples and shrines, in order, forsooth, that they may have grounds for thinking that gods were worshiped by the pagans in temples, but that dead men are worshiped by us in sepulchres. For with such blindness do impious men, as it were, stumble over mountains, and will not see the things which strike their own eyes, that they do not attend to the fact that in all the literature of the pagans there are not found any or scarcely any gods, who have not been men, to whom, when dead, divine honors have been paid. I will not enlarge on the fact that Varro says that all dead men are thought by them to be gods—Manes—and proves it by those sacred rites which are performed in honor of almost all the dead, among which he mentions funeral games, considering this the very highest proof of divinity, because games are only wont to be celebrated in honor of divinities. Hermes himself, of whom we are now treating, in that same book in which, as if foretelling future things, he says with sorrow, "Then shall that land, the most holy place of shrines and temples, be full of sepulchres and dead men," testifies that the gods of Egypt were dead men. For, having said that their forefathers, erring very far with respect to the knowledge of the gods, incredulous and inattentive to the divine worship and service, invented the art of making gods, with which art, when invented, they associated the appropriate virtue which is inherent in universal nature, and by mixing up that virtue with this art, they called forth the souls of demons or of angels (for they could not make souls), and caused them to take possession of, or associate themselves with holy images and divine mysteries, in order that through these souls the images might have power to do good or harm to men; having said this, he goes on, as it were, to prove it by illustrations, saying, "Thy grandsire, O Æsculapius, the first discoverer of medicine, to whom a temple was consecrated in a mountain of Libya, near to the shore of the crocodiles, in which temple lies his earthly man, that is, his body—for the better part of him, or rather the whole of him, if the whole man is in the intelligent life, went back to heaven—affords even now by his divinity all those helps to infirm men which formerly he was wont to afford to them by the art of medicine." He says, therefore that a dead man was worshiped as a god in that place where he had his sepulchre. He deceives men by a falsehood, for the man "went back to heaven." Then he adds, "Does not Hermes, who was my grandsire, and whose name I bear, abiding in the country which is called by his name, help and preserve all mortals who come to him from every quarter?" For this elder Hermes, that is, Mercury, who, he says, was his grandsire, is said to be buried in Hermopolis, that is, in the city called by his name; so here are two gods whom he affirms to have been men, Æsculapius and Mercury. Now concerning Æsculapius, both the Greeks and the Latins think the same thing; but as to Mercury, there are many who do not think that he was formerly a mortal, though Hermes testifies that he was his grandsire. But are these two different individuals who were called by the same name? I will not dispute much whether they are different individuals or not. It is sufficient to know that this Mercury of whom Hermes speaks is, as well as Æsculapius, a god who once was a man, according to the testimony of this same Trismegistus, esteemed so great by his countrymen, and also the grandson of Mercury himself.

Hermes goes on to say, "But do we know how many good things Isis, the wife of Osiris, bestows when she is propitious, and what great opposition she can offer when enraged?" Then, in order to show that there were gods made by men through this art, he goes on to say, "For it is easy for earthly and mundane gods to be angry, being made and composed by men out of either nature"; thus giving us to understand that he believed that demons were formerly the souls of dead men, which, as he says, by means of a certain art invented by men very far in error, incredulous, and irreligious, were caused to take possession of images, because they who made such gods were not able to make souls. When, therefore, he says "either nature," he means soul and body—the demon being the soul, and the image the body. What, then, becomes of that mournful complaint, that the land of Egypt, the most holy place of shrines and temples, was to be full of sepulchres and dead men? Verily, the fallacious spirit, by whose inspiration Hermes spoke these things, was compelled to confess through him that even already that land was full of sepulchres and of dead men, whom they were worshiping as gods. But it was the grief of the demons which was expressing itself through his mouth, who were sorrowing on account of the punishments which were about to fall upon them at the tombs of the martyrs. For in many such places they are tortured and compelled to confess, and are cast out of the bodies of men, of which they had taken possession.

27. CONCERNING THE NATURE OF THE HONOR WHICH THE CHRISTIANS PAY TO THEIR MARTYRS

But, nevertheless, we do not build temples, and ordain priests, rites, and sacrifices for these same martyrs; for they are not our gods, but their God is our God. Certainly we honor their reliquaries, as the memorials of holy men of God who strove for the truth even to the death of their bodies, that the true religion might be made known, and false and fictitious religions exposed. For if there were some before them who thought that these religions were really false and fictitious, they were afraid to give expression to their convictions. But who ever heard a priest of the faithful, standing at an altar built for the honor and worship of God over the holy body of some martyr, say in the prayers, I offer to thee a sacrifice, O Peter, or O Paul, or O Cyprian? For it is to God that sacrifices are offered at their tombs—the God who made them both men and martyrs, and associated them with holy angels in celestial honor; and the reason why we pay such honors to their memory is, that by so doing we may both give thanks to the true God for their victories, and, by recalling them afresh to remembrance, may stir ourselves up to imitate them by seeking to obtain like crowns and palms, calling to our help that same God on whom they called. Therefore, whatever honors the religious may pay in the places of the martyrs, they are but honors rendered to their memory,[1] not sacred rites or sacrifices offered to dead men as to gods. And even such as bring thither food—which, indeed, is not done by the better Christians, and in most places of the world is not done at all—do so in order that it may be sanctified to them through the merits of the martyrs, in the name of the Lord of the martyrs, first presenting the food and offering prayer, and thereafter taking it away to be eaten, or to be in part bestowed upon the needy.[2] But he who knows the one sacrifice of Christians, which is the sacrifice offered in those places, also knows that these are not sacrifices offered to the martyrs. It is, then, neither with divine honors nor with human crimes, by which they worship their gods, that we honor our martyrs; neither do we offer sacrifices to them, or convert the crimes of the gods into their sacred rites. For let those who will and can read the letter of Alexander to his mother Olympias, in which he tells the things which were revealed to him by the priest Leo, and let those who have read it recall to memory what it contains, that they may see what great abominations have been handed down to memory, not by poets, but by the mystic writings of the Egyptians, concerning the goddess Isis, the wife of Osiris, and the parents of both, all of whom, according to these writings, were royal personages. Isis, when sacrificing to her parents, is said to have discovered a crop of barley, of which she brought some ears to the king her husband, and his councillor Mercurius, and hence they identify her with Ceres. Those who read the letter may there see what was the character of those people to whom when dead sacred rites were instituted as to gods, and what those deeds of theirs were which furnished the occasion for these rites. Let them not once dare to compare in any respect those people, though they hold them to be gods, to our holy martyrs, though we do not hold them to be gods. For we do not ordain priests and offer sacrifices to our martyrs, as they do to their dead men, for that would be incongruous, undue, and unlawful, such being due only to God; and thus we do not delight them with their own crimes, or with such shameful plays as those in which the crimes of the gods are celebrated, which are either real crimes committed by them at a time when they were men, or else, if they never were men, fictitious crimes invented for the pleasure of noxious demons. The god of Socrates, if he had a god, cannot have belonged to this class of demons. But perhaps they who wished to excel in this art of making gods, imposed a god of this sort on a man who was a stranger to, and innocent of, any connection with that art. What need we say more? No one who is even moderately wise imagines that demons are to be worshiped on account of the blessed life which is to be after death. But perhaps they will say that all the gods are good, but that of the demons some are bad and some good, and that it is the good who are to be worshiped, in order that through them we may attain to the eternally blessed life. To the examination of this opinion we will devote the following book.

---

1. Ornamenta memoriarum.
2. Cf. Augustine *Confessions* 6.2.

BOOK NINE

ARGUMENT

Having in the preceding book shown that the worship of demons must be abjured, since they in a thousand ways proclaim themselves to be wicked spirits, Augustine in this book meets those who allege a distinction among demons, some being evil, while others are good; and, having exploded this distinction, he proves that to no demon, but to Christ alone, belongs the office of providing men with eternal blessedness.

1. THE POINT AT WHICH THE DISCUSSION HAS ARRIVED, AND WHAT REMAINS TO BE HANDLED

Some have advanced the opinion that there are both good and bad gods; but some, thinking more respectfully of the gods, have attributed to them so much honor and praise as to preclude the supposition of any god being wicked. But those who have maintained that there are wicked gods as well as good ones have included the demons under the name "gods," and sometimes, though more rarely, have called the gods demons; so that they admit that Jupiter, whom they make the king and head of all the rest, is called a demon by Homer.[1] Those, on the other hand, who maintain that the gods are all good, and far more excellent than the men who are justly called good, are moved by the actions of the demons, which they can neither deny nor impute to the gods whose goodness they affirm, to distinguish between gods and demons; so that, whenever they find anything offensive in the deeds or sentiments by which unseen spirits manifest their power, they believe this to proceed not from the gods, but from the demons. At the same time they believe that, as no god can hold direct intercourse with men, these demons hold the position of mediators, ascending with prayers, and returning with gifts. This is the opinion of the Platonists, the ablest and most esteemed of their philosophers, with whom we therefore chose to debate this question—whether the worship of a number of gods is of any service toward obtaining blessedness in the future life. And this is the reason why, in the preceding book, we have inquired how the demons, who take pleasure in such things as good and wise men loathe and execrate, in the sacrilegious and immoral fictions which the poets have written not of men, but of the gods themselves, and in the wicked and criminal violence of magical arts, can be regarded as more nearly related and more friendly to the gods than men are, and can mediate between good men and the good gods; and it has been demonstrated that this is absolutely impossible.

---

1. See Plutarch, on the Cessation of Oracles.

2. WHETHER AMONG THE DEMONS, INFERIOR TO THE GODS, THERE ARE ANY GOOD SPIRITS UNDER WHOSE GUARDIANSHIP THE HUMAN SOUL MIGHT REACH TRUE BLESSEDNESS

This book, then, ought, according to the promise made in the end of the preceding one, to contain a discussion, not of the difference which exists among the gods, who, according to the Platonists, are all good, nor of the difference between gods and demons, the former of whom they separate by a wide interval from men, while the latter are placed intermediately between the gods and men, but of the difference, since they make one, among the demons themselves. This we shall discuss so far as it bears on our theme. It has been the common and usual belief that some of the demons are bad, others good; and this opinon, whether it be that of the Platonists or any other sect, must by no means be passed over in silence, lest someone suppose he ought to cultivate the good demons in order that by their mediation he may be accepted by the gods, all of whom he believes to be good, and that he may live with them after death;

whereas he would thus be ensnared in the toils of wicked spirits, and would wander far from the true God, with whom alone, and in whom alone, the human soul, that is to say, the soul that is rational and intellectual, is blessed.

3. WHAT APULEIUS ATTRIBUTES TO THE DEMONS, TO WHOM, THOUGH HE DOES NOT DENY THEM REASON, HE DOES NOT ASCRIBE VIRTUE

What, then, is the difference between good and evil demons? For the Platonist Apuleius, in a treatise on this whole subject,[1] while he says a great deal about their aerial bodies, has not a word to say of the spiritual virtues with which, if they were good, they must have been endowed. Not a word has he said, then, of that which could give them happiness; but proof of their misery he has given, acknowledging that their mind, by which they rank as reasonable beings, is not only not imbued and fortified with virtue so as to resist all unreasonable passions, but that it is somehow agitated with tempestuous emotions, and is thus on a level with the mind of foolish men. His own words are: "It is this class of demons the poets refer to, when, without serious error, they feign that the gods hate and love individuals among men, prospering and ennobling some, and opposing and distressing others. Therefore pity, indignation, grief, joy, every human emotion is experienced by the demons, with the same mental disturbance, and the same tide of feeling and thought. These turmoils and tempests banish them far from the tranquility of the celestial gods." Can there be any doubt that in these words it is not some inferior part of their spiritual nature, but the very mind by which the demons hold their rank as rational beings, which he says is tossed with passion like a stormy sea? They cannot, then, be compared even to wise men, who with undisturbed mind resist these perturbations to which they are exposed in this life, and from which human infirmity is never exempt, and who do not yield themselves to approve of or perpetrate anything which might deflect them from the path of wisdom and law of rectitude. They resemble in character, though not in bodily appearance, wicked and foolish men. I might indeed say they are worse, inasmuch as they have grown old in iniquity, and incorrigible by punishment. Their mind, as Apuleius says, is a sea tossed with tempest, having no rallying point of truth or virtue in their soul from which they can resist their turbulent and depraved emotions.

---

1. Apuleius De Deo Socratis.

4. THE OPINION OF THE PERIPATETICS AND STOICS ABOUT MENTAL EMOTIONS

Among the philosophers there are two opinions about these mental emotions, which the Greeks call πάθη, while some of our own writers, as Cicero, call them perturbations,[1] some affections, and some, to render the Greek word more accurately, passions. Some say that even the wise man is subject to these perturbations, though moderated and controlled by reason, which imposes laws upon them, and so restrains them within necessary bounds. This is the opinion of the Platonists and Aristotelians; for Aristotle was Plato's disciple, and the founder of the Peripatetic school. But others, as the Stoics, are of opinion that the wise man is not subject to these perturbations. But Cicero, in his book *De Finibus*, shows that the Stoics are here at variance with the Platonists and Peripatetics rather in words than in reality; for the Stoics decline to apply the term "goods" to external and bodily advantages,[2] because they reckon that the only good is virtue, the art of living well, and this exists only in the mind. The other philosophers, again, use the simple and customary phraseology, and do not scruple to call these things goods, though in comparison of virtue, which guides our life, they are little and of small esteem. And thus it is obvious that, whether these outward things are called goods or advantages, they are held in the same estimation by both parties, and that in this matter the Stoics are pleasing themselves merely with a novel phraseology. It seems, then, to me that in this question, whether the wise man is subject to mental passions, or wholly free from them, the controversy is one of words rather than of things; for I think that, if the reality and not the mere sound of the words is considered, the Stoics hold precisely the same opinion as the Platonists and Peripatetics. For, omitting for brevity's sake other proofs which I might adduce in support of this opinion, I will state but one which I consider conclusive. Aulus Gellius, a man of extensive erudition, and gifted with an eloquent and graceful style, relates, in his work titled *Noctes Atticæ*[3] that he once made a voyage with an eminent Stoic philosopher; and he goes on to relate fully and with gusto what I shall barely state, that when the ship was tossed and in danger from a violent storm, the philosopher grew pale with terror. This was noticed by those on board, who, though themselves threatened with death, were curious to see whether a philosopher would be agitated like other men. When the tempest had passed over, and as soon as their security gave them freedom to resume their talk, one of the passengers, a rich and luxurious Asiatic, begins to banter the philosopher, and rally him because he had even become pale with fear, while he himself had been unmoved by the impending destruction. But the philosopher availed himself of the reply of Aristippus the Socratic, who, on finding himself similarly bantered by a man of the same character, answered, "You had no cause for anxiety for the soul of a profligate debauchee, but I had reason to be alarmed for the soul of Aristippus." The rich man being thus disposed of, Aulus Gellius asked the philosopher, in the interests of science and not to annoy him, what was the reason of his fear? And he, willing to instruct a man so zealous in the pursuit of knowledge, at once took from his wallet a book of Epictetus the Stoic,[4] in which doctrines were advanced which precisely harmonized with those of Zeno and Chrysippus, the founders of the Stoical school. Aulus Gellius says that he read in this book that the Stoics maintain that there are certain impressions made on the soul by external objects which they call *phantasiæ,* and that it is not in the power of the soul to determine whether or when it shall be invaded by these. When these impressions are made by alarming and formidable objects, it must needs be that they move the soul even of the wise man, so that for a little he trembles with fear, or is depressed by sadness, these impressions anticipating the work of reason and self-control; but this does not imply that the mind accepts these evil impressions, or approves or consents to them. For this consent is, they think, in a man's power; there being this difference between the mind of the wise man and that of the fool, that the fool's mind yields to these passions and consents to them, while that of the wise man, though it cannot help being invaded by them, yet retains with unshaken firmness a true and steady persuasion of those things which it ought rationally to desire or avoid. This account of what Aulus Gellius relates that he read in the book of Epictetus about the sentiments and doctrines of the Stoics I have given as well as I could, not, perhaps, with his choice language, but with greater brevity, and, I think, with greater clearness. And if this be true, then there is no difference, or next to none, between the opinion of the Stoics and that of the other philosophers regarding mental passions and perturbations, for both parties agree in maintaining that the mind and reason of the wise man are not subject to these. And perhaps what the Stoics mean by asserting this, is that the wisdom which characterizes the wise man is clouded by no error and sullied by no taint, but, with this reservation that his wisdom remains undisturbed, he is exposed to the impressions which the goods and ills of this life (or, as they prefer to call them, the advantages or disadvantages) make upon them. For we need not say that if that philosopher had thought nothing of those things which he thought he was forthwith to lose, life and bodily safety, he would not have been so terrified by his danger as to betray his fear by the pallor of his cheek. Nevertheless, he might suffer this mental disturbance, and yet maintain the fixed persuasion that life and bodily safety, which the violence of the tempest threatened to destroy, are not those good things which make their possessors good, as the possession of righteousness does. But insofar as they persist that we must call them not goods but advantages, they quarrel about words and neglect things. For what difference does it make whether goods or advantages be the better name, while the Stoic no less than the Peripatetic is alarmed at the prospect of losing them, and while, though they name them differently, they hold them in like esteem? Both parties assure us that, if urged to the commission of some immorality or crime by the threatened loss of these goods or advantages, they would prefer to lose such things as preserve bodily comfort and security rather than commit such things as violate righteousness. And thus the mind in which this resolution is well grounded suffers no perturbations to prevail with it in opposition to reason, even though they assail the weaker parts of the soul; and not only so, but it rules over them, and, while it refuses its consent and resists them, administers a reign of virtue. Such a character is ascribed to Æneas by Virgil when he says,

> *He stands immovable by tears,*
> *Nor tenderest words with pity hears.*[5]

---

1. Cicero *De Fin.* 3.20; *Tusc. Disp.* 3.4.
2. *The distinction between bona and commoda is thus given by Seneca (Ep. 87, ad fin.): "Commodum est quod plus usus est quam molestiæ; bonum sincerum debet esse et ab omni parte innoxium."*
3. Aulus Gellius *Noctes Atticæ* 19.1.
4. See Diogenes Laertius 2.71.
5. Virgil *Æneid* 4.449.

5. THAT THE PASSIONS WHICH ASSAIL THE SOULS OF CHRISTIANS DO NOT SEDUCE THEM TO VICE, BUT EXERCISE THEIR VIRTUE

We need not at present give a careful and copious exposition of the doctrine of Scripture, the sum of Christian knowledge, regarding these passions. It subjects the mind itself to God, that He may rule and aid it, and the passions, again, to the mind, to moderate and bridle them, and turn them to righteous uses. In our ethics, we do not so much inquire whether a pious soul is angry, as why he is angry; not whether he is sad, but what is the cause of his sadness; not whether he fears, but what he fears. For I am not aware that any right-thinking person would find fault with anger at a wrongdoer which seeks his amendment, or with sadness which intends relief to the suffering, or with fear lest one in danger be destroyed. The Stoics, indeed, are accustomed to condemn compassion.[1] But how much more honorable had it been in that Stoic we have been telling of, had he been disturbed by compassion prompting him to relieve a fellow creature, than to be disturbed by the fear of shipwreck! Far better and more humane, and more consonant with pious sentiments, are the words of Cicero in praise of Cæsar, when he says, "Among your virtues none is more admirable and agreeable than your compassion."[2] And what is compassion but a fellow feeling for another's misery, which prompts us to help him if we can? And this emotion is obedient to reason, when compassion is shown without violating right, as when the poor are relieved, or the penitent forgiven. Cicero, who knew how to use language, did not hesitate to call this a virtue, which the Stoics are not ashamed to reckon among the vices, although, as the book of the eminent Stoic, Epictetus, quoting the opinions of Zeno and Chrysippus, the founders of the school, has taught us, they admit that passions of this kind invade the soul of the wise man, whom they would have to be free from all vice. Whence it follows that these very passions are not judged by them to be vices, since they assail the wise man without forcing him to act against reason and virtue; and that, therefore, the opinion of the Peripatetics or Platonists and of the Stoics is one and the same. But, as Cicero says,[3] mere logomachy is the bane of these pitiful Greeks, who thirst for contention rather than for truth. However, it may justly be asked, whether our subjection to these affections, even while we follow virtue, is a part of the infirmity of this life. For the holy angels feel no anger while they punish those whom the eternal law of God consigns to punishment, no fellow feeling with misery while they relieve the miserable, no fear while they aid those who are in danger; and yet ordinary language ascribes to them also these mental emotions, because, though they have none of our weakness, their acts resemble the actions to which these emotions move us; and thus even God Himself is said in Scripture to be angry, and yet without any perturbation. For this word is used of the effect of His vengeance, not of the disturbing mental affection.

---

1. Seneca *De Clem.* 2.4–5.
2. Cicero *Pro. Lig.* 12.
3. Cicero *De Oratore* 1.11.47.

6. OF THE PASSIONS WHICH, ACCORDING TO APULEIUS, AGITATE THE DEMONS WHO ARE SUPPOSED BY HIM TO MEDIATE BETWEEN GODS AND MEN

Deferring for the present the question about the holy angels, let us examine the opinion of the Platonists, that the demons who mediate between gods and men are agitated by passions. For if their mind, though exposed to their incursion, still remained free and superior to them, Apuleius could not have said that their hearts are tossed with passions as the sea by stormy winds.[1] Their mind, then—that superior part of their soul whereby they are rational beings, and which, if it actually exists in them, should rule and bridle the turbulent passions of the inferior parts of the soul—this mind of theirs, I say, is, according to the Platonist referred to, tossed with a hurricane of passions. The mind of the demons, therefore, is subject to the emotions of fear, anger, lust, and all similar affections. What part of them, then, is free, and endued with wisdom, so that they are pleasing to the gods, and the fit guides of men into purity of life, since their very highest part, being the slave of passion and subject to vice, only makes them more intent on deceiving and seducing, in proportion to the mental force and energy of desire they possess?

---

1. *Apuleius De Deo Socratis.*

7. THAT THE PLATONISTS MAINTAIN THAT THE POETS WRONG THE GODS BY REPRESENTING THEM AS DISTRACTED BY PARTY FEELING, TO WHICH THE DEMONS, AND NOT THE GODS, ARE SUBJECT

But if anyone says that it is not of all the demons, but only of the wicked, that the poets, not without truth, say that they violently love or hate certain men—for it was of them Apuleius said that they were driven about by strong currents of emotion—how can we accept this interpretation, when Apuleius, in the very same connection, represents all the demons, and not only the wicked, as intermediate between gods and men by their aerial bodies? The fiction of the poets, according to him, consists in their making gods of demons, and giving them the names of gods, and assigning them as allies or enemies to individual men, using this poetical license, though they profess that the gods are very different in character from the demons, and far exalted above them by their celestial abode and wealth of beatitude. This, I say, is the poets' fiction, to say that these are gods who are not gods, and that, under the names of gods, they fight among themselves about the men whom they love or hate with keen partisan feeling. Apuleius says that this is not far from the truth, since, though they are wrongfully called by the names of the gods, they are described in their own proper character as demons. To this category, he says, belongs the Minerva of Homer, "who interposed in the ranks of the Greeks to restrain Achilles." For that this was Minerva he supposes to be poetical fiction; for he thinks that Minerva is a goddess, and he places her among the gods whom he believes to be all good and blessed in the sublime ethereal region, remote from intercourse with men. But that there was a demon favorable to the Greeks and adverse to the Trojans, as another, whom the same poet mentions under the name of Venus or Mars (gods exalted above earthly affairs in their heavenly habitations), was the Trojans' ally and the foe of the Greeks, and that these demons fought for those they loved against those they hated—in all this he owned that the poets stated something very like the truth. For they made these statements about beings to whom he ascribes the same violent and tempestuous passions as disturb men, and who are therefore capable of loves and hatreds not justly formed, but formed in a party spirit, as the spectators in races or hunts take fancies and prejudices. It seems to have been the great fear of this Platonist that the poetical fictions should be believed of the gods, and not of the demons who bore their names.

8. HOW APULEIUS DEFINES THE GODS WHO DWELL IN HEAVEN, THE DEMONS WHO OCCUPY THE AIR, AND MEN WHO INHABIT EARTH

The definition which Apuleius gives of demons, and in which he of course includes all demons, is that they are in nature animals, in soul subject to passion, in mind reasonable, in body aerial, in duration eternal. Now in these five qualities he has named absolutely nothing which is proper to good men and not also to bad. For when Apuleius had spoken of the celestials first, and had then extended his description so as to include an account of those who dwell far below on the earth, that, after describing the two extremes of rational being, he might proceed to speak of the intermediate demons, he says, "Men, therefore, who are endowed with the faculty of reason and speech, whose soul is immortal and their members mortal, who have weak and anxious spirits, dull and corruptible bodies, dissimilar characters, similar ignorance, who are obstinate in their audacity, and persistent in their hope, whose labor is vain, and whose fortune is ever on the wane, their race immortal, themselves perishing, each generation replenished with creatures whose life is swift and their wisdom slow, their death sudden and their life a wail—these are the men who dwell on the earth."[1] In recounting so many qualities which belong to the large proportion of men, did he forget that which is the property of the few when he speaks of their wisdom being slow? If this had been omitted, this his description of the human race, so carefully elaborated, would have been defective. And when he commended the excellence of the gods, he affirmed that they excelled in that very blessedness to which he thinks men must attain by wisdom. And therefore, if he had wished us to believe that some of the demons are good, he should have inserted in his description something by which we might see that they have, in common with the gods, some share of blessedness, or, in common with men, some wisdom. But, as it is, he has mentioned no good quality by which the good may be distinguished from the bad. For although he refrained from giving a full account of their wickedness, through fear of offending, not themselves but their worshipers, for whom he was writing, yet he sufficiently indicated to discerning readers what opinion he had of them; for only in the one article of the eternity of their bodies does he assimilate them to the gods, all of whom, he asserts, are good and blessed, and absolutely free from what he himself calls the stormy passions of the demons; and as to the soul, he quite plainly affirms that they resemble men and not the gods, and that this resemblance lies not in the possession of wisdom, which even men can attain to, but in the perturbation of passions which sway the foolish and wicked, but is so ruled by the good and wise that they prefer not to admit rather than to conquer it. For if he had wished it to be understood that the demons resembled the gods in the eternity not of their bodies but of their souls, he would certainly have admitted men to share in this privilege, because, as a Platonist, he of course must hold that the human soul is eternal. Accordingly, when describing this race of living beings, he said that their souls were immortal, their members mortal. And, consequently, if men have not eternity in common with the gods because they have mortal bodies, demons have eternity in common with the gods because their bodies are immortal.

---

1. Ibid.

9. WHETHER THE INTERCESSION OF THE DEMONS CAN SECURE FOR MEN THE FRIENDSHIP OF THE CELESTIAL GODS

How, then, can men hope for a favorable introduction to the friendship of the gods by such mediators as these, who are, like men, defective in that which is the better part of every living creature, namely, the soul, and who resemble the gods only in the body, which is the inferior part? For a living creature or animal consists of soul and body, and of these two parts the soul is undoubtedly the better; even though vicious and weak, it is obviously better than even the soundest and strongest body, for the greater excellence of its nature is not reduced to the level of the body even by the pollution of vice, as gold, even when tarnished, is more precious than the purest silver or lead. And yet these mediators, by whose interposition things human and divine are to be harmonized, have an eternal body in common with the gods, and a vicious soul in common with men—as if the religion by which these demons are to unite gods and men were a bodily, and not a spiritual, matter. What wickedness, then, or punishment has suspended these false and deceitful mediators, as it were head downward, so that their inferior part, their body, is linked to the gods above, and their superior part, the soul, bound to men beneath; united to the celestial gods by the part that serves, and miserable, together with the inhabitants of earth, by the part that rules? For the body is the servant, as Sallust says: "We use the soul to rule, the body to obey";[1] adding, "the one we have in common with the gods, the other with the brutes." For he was here speaking of men; and they have, like the brutes, a mortal body. These demons, whom our philosophic friends have provided for us as mediators with the gods, may indeed say of the soul and body, the one we have in common with the gods, the other with men; but, as I said, they are as it were suspended and bound head downward, having the slave, the body, in common with the gods, the master, the soul, in common with miserable men—their inferior part exalted, their superior part depressed. And therefore, if anyone supposes that, because they are not subject, like terrestrial animals, to the separation of soul and body by death, they therefore resemble the gods in their eternity, their body must not be considered a chariot of an eternal triumph, but rather the chain of an eternal punishment.

---

1. *Sallust De Conj. Cat. 1.*

10. THAT, ACCORDING TO PLOTINUS, MEN, WHOSE BODY IS MORTAL, ARE LESS WRETCHED THAN DEMONS, WHOSE BODY IS ETERNAL

Plotinus, whose memory is quite recent,[1] enjoys the reputation of having understood Plato better than any other of his disciples. In speaking of human souls, he says, "The Father in compassion made their bonds mortal";[2] that is to say, he considered it due to the Father's mercy that men, having a mortal body, should not be forever confined in the misery of this life. But of this mercy the demons have been judged unworthy, and they have received, in conjunction with a soul subject to passions, a body not mortal like man's, but eternal. For they should have been happier than men if they had, like men, had a mortal body, and, like the gods, a blessed soul. And they should have been equal to men, if in conjunction with a miserable soul they had at least received, like men, a mortal body, so that death might have freed them from trouble, if, at least, they should have attained some degree of piety. But, as it is, they are not only no happier than men, having, like them, a miserable soul, they are also more wretched, being eternally bound to the body; for he does not leave us to infer that by some progress in wisdom and piety they can become gods, but expressly says that they are demons forever.

---

1. Plotinus died in A.D. 270. For his relation to Plato, see Augustine's *Contra Acad.* 3.41.
2. Plotinus *Enn.* 4.3.12.

11. OF THE OPINION OF THE PLATONISTS, THAT THE SOULS OF MEN BECOME DEMONS WHEN DISEMBODIED

He[1] says, indeed, that the souls of men are demons, and that men become Lares if they are good, Lemures or Larvæ if they are bad, and Manes if it is uncertain whether they deserve well or ill. Who does not see at a glance that this is a mere whirlpool sucking men to moral destruction? For, however wicked men have been, if they suppose they shall become Larvæ or divine Manes, they will become the worse the more love they have for inflicting injury; for, as the Larvæ are hurtful demons made out of wicked men, these men must suppose that after death they will be invoked with sacrifices and divine honors that they may inflict injuries. But this question we must not pursue. He also states that the blessed are called in Greek εὐδαίμονες, because they are good souls, that is to say, good demons, confirming his opinion that the souls of men are demons.

1. Apuleius, not Plotinus.

12. OF THE THREE OPPOSITE QUALITIES BY WHICH THE PLATONISTS DISTINGUISH BETWEEN THE NATURE OF MEN AND THAT OF DEMONS

But at present we are speaking of those beings whom he described as being properly intermediate between gods and men, in nature animals, in mind rational, in soul subject to passion, in body aerial, in duration eternal. When he had distinguished the gods, whom he placed in the highest heaven, from men, whom he placed on earth, not only by position but also by the unequal dignity of their natures, he concluded in these words: "You have here two kinds of animals: the gods, widely distinguished from men by sublimity of abode, perpetuity of life, perfection of nature; for their habitations are separated by so wide an interval that there can be no intimate communication between them, and while the vitality of the one is eternal and indefeasible, that of the others is fading and precarious, and while the spirits of the gods are exalted in bliss, those of men are sunk in miseries."[1]

Here I find three opposite qualities ascribed to the extremes of being, the highest and lowest. For, after mentioning the three qualities for which we are to admire the gods, he repeated, though in other words, the same three as a foil to the defects of man. The three qualities are "sublimity of abode, perpetuity of life, perfection of nature." These he again mentioned so as to bring out their contrasts in man's condition. As he had mentioned "sublimity of abode," he says, "their habitations are separated by so wide an interval"; as he had mentioned "perpetuity of life," he says, that "while divine life is eternal and indefeasible, human life is fading and precarious"; and as he had mentioned "perfection of nature," he says, that "while the spirits of the gods are exalted in bliss, those of men are sunk in miseries." These three things, then, he predicates of the gods, exaltation, eternity, blessedness; and of man he predicates the opposite, lowliness of habitation, mortality, misery.

---

1. *Apuleius De Deo Socratis.*

13. HOW THE DEMONS CAN MEDIATE BETWEEN GODS AND MEN IF THEY HAVE NOTHING IN COMMON WITH BOTH, BEING NEITHER BLESSED LIKE THE GODS, NOR MISERABLE LIKE MEN

If, now, we endeavor to find between these opposites the mean occupied by the demons, there can be no question as to their local position; for, between the highest and lowest place, there is a place which is rightly considered and called the middle place. The other two qualities remain, and to them we must give greater care, that we may see whether they are altogether foreign to the demons, or how they are so bestowed upon them without infringing upon their mediate position. We may dismiss the idea that they are foreign to them. For we cannot say that the demons, being rational animals, are neither blessed nor wretched, as we say of the beasts and plants, which are void of feeling and reason, or as we say of the middle place, that it is neither the highest nor the lowest. The demons, being rational, must be either miserable or blessed. And, in like manner, we cannot say that they are neither mortal nor immortal; for all living things either live eternally or end life in death. Our author, besides, stated that the demons are eternal. What remains for us to suppose, then, but that these mediate beings are assimilated to the gods in one of the two remaining qualities, and to men in the other? For if they received both from above, or both from beneath, they should no longer be mediate, but either rise to the gods above, or sink to men beneath. Therefore, as it has been demonstrated that they must possess these two qualities, they will hold their middle place if they receive one from each party. Consequently, as they cannot receive their eternity from beneath, because it is not there to receive, they must get it from above; and accordingly they have no choice but to complete their mediate position by accepting misery from men.

According to the Platonists, then, the gods, who occupy the highest place, enjoy eternal blessedness, or blessed eternity; men, who occupy the lowest, a mortal misery, or a miserable mortality; and the demons, who occupy the mean, a miserable eternity, or an eternal misery. As to those five things which Apuleius included in his definition of demons, he did not show, as he promised, that the demons are mediate. For three of them, that their nature is animal, their mind rational, their soul subject to passions, he said that they have in common with men; one thing, their eternity, in common with the gods; and one proper to themselves, their aerial body. How, then, are they intermediate, when they have three things in common with the lowest, and only one in common with the highest? Who does not see that the intermediate position is abandoned in proportion as they tend to, and are depressed toward, the lowest extreme? But perhaps we are to accept them as intermediate because of their one property of an aerial body, as the two extremes have each their proper body, the gods an ethereal, men a terrestrial body, and because two of the qualities they possess in common with man they possess also in common with the gods, namely, their animal nature and rational mind. For Apuleius himself, in speaking of gods and men, said, "You have two animal natures." And Platonists are wont to ascribe a rational mind to the gods. Two qualities remain, their liability to passion, and their eternity—the first of which they have in common with men, the second with the gods; so that they are neither wafted to the highest nor depressed to the lowest extreme, but perfectly poised in their intermediate position. But then, this is the very circumstance which constitutes the eternal misery, or miserable eternity, of the demons. For he who says that their soul is subject to passions would also have said that they are miserable, had he not blushed for their worshipers. Moreover, as the world is governed, not by fortuitous haphazard, but, as the Platonists themselves avow, by the providence of the supreme God, the misery of the demons would not be eternal unless their wickedness were great.

If, then, the blessed are rightly styled *eudemons*, the demons intermediate between gods and men are not eudemons. What, then, is the local position of those good demons, who, above men but beneath the gods, afford assistance to the former, minister to the latter? For if they are good and eternal, they are doubtless blessed. But eternal blessedness destroys their intermediate character, giving them a close resemblance to the gods, and widely separating them from men. And therefore the Platonists will in vain strive to show how the good demons, if they are both immortal and blessed, can justly be said to hold a middle place between the gods, who are immortal and blessed, and men, who are mortal and miserable. For if they have both immortality and blessedness in common with the gods, and neither of these in common with men, who are both miserable and mortal, are they not rather remote from men and united with the gods, than intermediate between them? They would be intermediate if they held one of their qualities in common with the one party, and the other with the other, as man is a kind of mean between angels and beasts—the beast being an irrational and mortal animal, the angel a rational and immortal one, while man, inferior to the angel and superior to the beast, and having in common with the one mortality, and with the other reason, is a rational and mortal animal. So, when we seek for an intermediate between the blessed immortals and miserable mortals, we should find a being which is either mortal and blessed, or immortal and miserable.

14. WHETHER MEN, THOUGH MORTAL, CAN ENJOY TRUE BLESSEDNESS

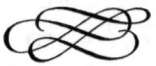

It is a great question among men, whether man can be mortal and blessed. Some, taking the humbler view of his condition, have denied that he is capable of blessedness so long as he continues in this mortal life; others, again, have spurned this idea, and have been bold enough to maintain that, even though mortal, men may be blessed by attaining wisdom. But if this be the case, why are not these wise men constituted mediators between miserable mortals and the blessed immortals, since they have blessedness in common with the latter, and mortality in common with the former? Certainly, if they are blessed, they envy no one (for what more miserable than envy?), but seek with all their might to help miserable mortals on to blessedness, so that after death they may become immortal, and be associated with the blessed and immortal angels.

15. OF THE MAN CHRIST JESUS, THE MEDIATOR BETWEEN GOD AND MEN

But if, as is much more probable and credible, it must needs be that all men, so long as they are mortal, are also miserable, we must seek an intermediate who is not only man, but also God, that, by the interposition of His blessed mortality, He may bring men out of their mortal misery to a blessed immortality. In this intermediate two things are requisite, that He become mortal, and that He do not continue mortal. He did become mortal, not rendering the divinity of the Word infirm, but assuming the infirmity of flesh. Neither did He continue mortal in the flesh, but raised it from the dead; for it is the very fruit of His mediation that those, for the sake of whose redemption He became the Mediator, should not abide eternally in bodily death. Wherefore it became the Mediator between us and God to have both a transient mortality and a permanent blessedness, that by that which is transient He might be assimilated to mortals, and might translate them from mortality to that which is permanent. Good angels, therefore, cannot mediate between miserable mortals and blessed immortals, for they themselves also are both blessed and immortal; but evil angels can mediate, because they are immortal like the one party, miserable like the other. To these is opposed the good Mediator, who, in opposition to their immortality and misery, has chosen to be mortal for a time, and has been able to continue blessed in eternity. It is thus He has destroyed, by the humility of His death and the benignity of His blessedness, those proud immortals and hurtful wretches, and has prevented them from seducing to misery by their boast of immortality those men whose hearts He has cleansed by faith, and whom He has thus freed from their impure dominion.

Man, then, mortal and miserable, and far removed from the immortal and the blessed, what medium shall he choose by which he may be united to immortality and blessedness? The immortality of the demons, which might have some charm for man, is miserable; the mortality of Christ, which might offend man, exists no longer. In the one there is the fear of an eternal misery; in the other, death, which could not be eternal, can no longer be feared, and blessedness, which is eternal, must be loved. For the immortal and miserable mediator interposes himself to prevent us from passing to a blessed immortality, because that which hinders such a passage, namely, misery, continues in him; but the mortal and blessed Mediator interposed Himself, in order that, having passed through mortality, He might of mortals make immortals (showing His power to do this in His own resurrection), and from being miserable to raise them to the blessed company from the number of whom He had Himself never departed. There is, then, a wicked mediator, who separates friends, and a good Mediator, who reconciles enemies. And those who separate are numerous, because the multitude of the blessed are blessed only by their participation in the one God; of which participation the evil angels being deprived, they are wretched, and interpose to hinder rather than to help to this blessedness, and by their very number prevent us from reaching that one beatific good, to obtain which we need not many but one Mediator, the uncreated Word of God, by whom all things were made, and in partaking of whom we are blessed. I do not say that He is Mediator because He is the Word, for as the Word He is supremely blessed and supremely immortal, and therefore far from miserable mortals; but He is Mediator as He is man, for by His humanity He shows us that, in order to obtain that blessed and beatific good, we need not seek other mediators to lead us through the successive steps of this attainment, but that the blessed and beatific God, having Himself become a partaker of our humanity, has afforded us ready access to the participation of His divinity. For in delivering us from our mortality and misery, He does not lead us to the immortal and blessed angels, so that we should become immortal and blessed by participating in their nature, but He leads us straight to that Trinity, by participating in which the angels themselves are blessed. Therefore, when He chose to be in the form of a servant, and lower than the angels, that He might be our Mediator, He remained higher than the angels, in the form of God—Himself at once the way of life on earth and life itself in heaven.

16. WHETHER IT IS REASONABLE IN THE PLATONISTS TO DETERMINE THAT THE CELESTIAL GODS DECLINE CONTACT WITH EARTHLY THINGS AND INTERCOURSE WITH MEN, WHO THEREFORE REQUIRE THE INTERCESSION OF THE DEMONS

That opinion, which the same Platonist avers that Plato uttered, is not true, "that no god holds intercourse with men."[1] And this, he says, is the chief evidence of their exaltation, that they are never contaminated by contact with men. He admits, therefore, that the demons are contaminated; and it follows that they cannot cleanse those by whom they are themselves contaminated, and thus all alike become impure, the demons by associating with men, and men by worshiping the demons. Or, if they say that the demons are not contaminated by associating and dealing with men, then they are better than the gods, for the gods, were they to do so, would be contaminated. For this, we are told, is the glory of the gods, that they are so highly exalted that no human intercourse can sully them. He affirms, indeed, that the supreme God, the Creator of all things, whom we call the true God, is spoken of by Plato as the only God whom the poverty of human speech fails even passably to describe; and that even the wise, when their mental energy is as far as possible delivered from the trammels of connection with the body, have only such gleams of insight into His nature as may be compared to a flash of lightning illuminating the darkness. If, then, this supreme God, who is truly exalted above all things, does nevertheless visit the minds of the wise, when emancipated from the body, with an intelligible and ineffable presence, though this be only occasional, and as it were a swift flash of light athwart the darkness, why are the other gods so sublimely removed from all contact with men, as if they would be polluted by it—as if it were not a sufficient refutation of this to lift up our eyes to those heavenly bodies which give the earth its needful light? If the stars, though they, by his account, are visible gods, are not contaminated when we look at them, neither are the demons contaminated when men see them quite closely. But perhaps it is the human voice, and not the eye, which pollutes the gods; and therefore the demons are appointed to mediate and carry men's utterances to the gods, who keep themselves remote through fear of pollution? What am I to say of the other senses? For by smell neither the demons, who are present, nor the gods, though they were present and inhaling the exhalations of living men, would be polluted if they are not contaminated with the effluvia of the carcasses offered in sacrifice. As for taste, they are pressed by no necessity of repairing bodily decay, so as to be reduced to ask food from men. And touch is in their own power. For while it may seem that contact is so called, because the sense of touch is specially concerned in it, yet the gods, if so minded, might mingle with men, so as to see and be seen, hear and be heard; and where is the need of touching? For men would not dare to desire this, if they were favored with the sight or conversation of gods or good demons; and if through excessive curiosity they should desire it, how could they accomplish their wish without the consent of the god or demon, when they cannot touch so much as a sparrow unless it be caged?

There is, then, nothing to hinder the gods from mingling in a bodily form with men, from seeing and being seen, from speaking and hearing. And if the demons do thus mix with men, as I said, and are not polluted, while the gods, were they to do so, should be polluted, then the demons are less liable to pollution than the gods. And if even the demons are contaminated, how can they help men to attain blessedness after death, if, so far from being able to cleanse them, and present them clean to the unpolluted gods, these mediators are themselves polluted? And if they cannot confer this benefit on men, what good can their friendly mediation do? Or shall its result be, not that men find entrance to the gods, but that men and demons abide together in a state of pollution, and consequently of exclusion from blessedness? Unless, perhaps, someone may say that, like sponges or things of that sort, the demons themselves, in the process of cleansing their friends, become themselves the filthier in proportion as the others become clean. But if this is the solution, then the gods, who shun contact or intercourse with men for fear of pollution, mix with demons who are far more polluted. Or perhaps the gods, who cannot cleanse men without polluting themselves, can without pollution cleanse the demons who have been contaminated by human contact? Who can believe such follies, unless the demons have practiced their deceit upon him? If seeing and being seen is contamination, and if the gods, whom Apuleius himself calls visible, "the brilliant lights of the world,"[2] and the other stars, are seen by men, are we to believe that the demons, who cannot be seen unless they please, are safer from contamination? Or if it is only the seeing and not the being seen which contaminates, then they must deny that these gods of theirs, these brilliant lights of the world, see men when their rays beam upon the earth. Their rays are not contaminated by lighting on all manner of pollution, and are we to suppose that the gods would be contaminated if they mixed with men, and even if contact were needed in order to assist them? For there is contact between the earth and the sun's or moon's rays, and yet this does not pollute the light.

---

1. Ibid.
2. Virgil *Georg.* 1.5.

17. THAT TO OBTAIN THE BLESSED LIFE, WHICH CONSISTS IN PARTAKING OF THE SUPREME GOOD, MAN NEEDS SUCH MEDIATION AS IS FURNISHED NOT BY A DEMON, BUT BY CHRIST ALONE

I am considerably surprised that such learned men, men who pronounce all material and sensible things to be altogether inferior to those that are spiritual and intelligible, should mention bodily contact in connection with the blessed life. Is that sentiment of Plotinus forgotten—"We must fly to our beloved fatherland. There is the Father, there our all. What fleet or flight shall convey us thither? Our way is, to become like God"?[1] If, then, one is nearer to God the more like he is to Him, there is no other distance from God than unlikeness to Him. And the soul of man is unlike that incorporeal and unchangeable and eternal essence, in proportion as it craves things temporal and mutable. And as the things beneath, which are mortal and impure, cannot hold intercourse with the immortal purity which is above, a mediator is indeed needed to remove this difficulty; but not a mediator who resembles the highest order of being by possessing an immortal body, and the lowest by having a diseased soul, which makes him rather grudge that we be healed than help our cure. We need a Mediator who, being united to us here below by the mortality of His body, should at the same time be able to afford us truly divine help in cleansing and liberating us by means of the immortal righteousness of His spirit, whereby He remained heavenly even while here upon earth. Far be it from the incontaminable God to fear pollution from the man[2] He assumed, or from the men among whom He lived in the form of a man. For, though His incarnation showed us nothing else, these two wholesome facts were enough, that true divinity cannot be polluted by flesh, and that demons are not to be considered better than ourselves because they have not flesh.[3] This, then, as Scripture says, is the "Mediator between God and man, the man Christ Jesus,"[4] of whose divinity, whereby He is equal to the Father, and humanity, whereby He has become like us, this is not the place to speak as fully as I could.

---

1. Augustine apparently quotes from memory from two passages of the *Ennead* (1.6.8; 2.3).
2. Or, humanity.
3. Cf. *De Trin.* 13.22.
4. 1 Tim. 2:5.

18. THAT THE DECEITFUL DEMONS, WHILE PROMISING TO CONDUCT MEN TO GOD BY THEIR INTERCESSION, MEAN TO TURN THEM FROM THE PATH OF TRUTH

As to the demons, these false and deceitful mediators, who, though their uncleanness of spirit frequently reveals their misery and malignity, yet, by virtue of the levity of their aerial bodies and the nature of the places they inhabit, do contrive to turn us aside and hinder our spiritual progress; they do not help us toward God, but rather prevent us from reaching Him. Since even in the bodily way, which is erroneous and misleading, and in which righteousness does not walk—for we must rise to God not by bodily ascent, but by incorporeal or spiritual conformity to Him—in this bodily way, I say, which the friends of the demons arrange according to the weight of the various elements, the aerial demons being set between the ethereal gods and earthy men, they imagine the gods to have this privilege, that by this local interval they are preserved from the pollution of human contact. Thus they believe that the demons are contaminated by men rather than men cleansed by the demons, and that the gods themselves should be polluted unless their local superiority preserved them. Who is so wretched a creature as to expect purification by a way in which men are contaminating, demons contaminated, and gods contaminable? Who would not rather choose that way whereby we escape the contamination of the demons, and are cleansed from pollution by the incontaminable God, so as to be associated with the uncontaminated angels?

19. THAT EVEN AMONG THEIR OWN WORSHIPERS THE NAME "DEMON" HAS NEVER A GOOD SIGNIFICATION

But as some of these demonolators, as I may call them, and among them Labeo, allege that those whom they call demons are by others called angels, I must, if I would not seem to dispute merely about words, say something about the good angels. The Platonists do not deny their existence, but prefer to call them good demons. But we, following Scripture, according to which we are Christians, have learned that some of the angels are good, some bad, but never have we read in Scripture of good demons; but wherever this or any cognate term occurs, it is applied only to wicked spirits. And this usage has become so universal, that, even among those who are called pagans, and who maintain that demons as well as gods should be worshiped, there is scarcely a man, no matter how well read and learned, who would dare to say by way of praise to his slave, "You have a demon"; or who could doubt that the man to whom he said this would consider it a curse? Why, then, are we to subject ourselves to the necessity of explaining away what we have said when we have given offense by using the word "demon," with which everyone, or almost everyone, connects a bad meaning, while we can so easily evade this necessity by using the word "angel"?

20. OF THE KIND OF KNOWLEDGE WHICH PUFFS UP THE DEMONS

However, the very origin of the name suggests something worthy of consideration, if we compare it with the divine books. They are called demons from a Greek word meaning knowledge.[1] Now the apostle, speaking with the Holy Spirit, says, "Knowledge puffeth up, but charity buildeth up."[2] And this can only be understood as meaning that without charity knowledge does no good, but inflates a man or magnifies him with an empty windiness. The demons, then, have knowledge without charity, and are thereby so inflated or proud, that they crave those divine honors and religious services which they know to be due to the true God, and still, as far as they can, exact these from all over whom they have influence. Against this pride of the demons, under which the human race was held subject as its merited punishment, there was exerted the mighty influence of the humility of God, who appeared in the form of a servant; but men, resembling the demons in pride, but not in knowledge, and being puffed up with uncleanness, failed to recognize Him.

---

1. δαίμων = δαήμων, knowing; so Plato *Cratylus* 398.B.
2. 1 Cor. 8:1.

21. TO WHAT EXTENT THE LORD WAS PLEASED TO MAKE HIMSELF KNOWN TO THE DEMONS

The devils themselves knew this manifestation of God so well, that they said to the Lord though clothed with the infirmity of flesh, "What have we to do with Thee, Jesus of Nazareth? Art Thou come to destroy us before the time?"[1] From these words, it is clear that they had great knowledge, and no charity. They feared His power to punish, and did not love His righteousness. He made known to them so much as He pleased, and He was pleased to make known so much as was needful. But He made Himself known not as to the holy angels, who know Him as the Word of God, and rejoice in His eternity, which they partake, but as was requisite to strike with terror the beings from whose tyranny He was going to free those who were predestined to His kingdom and the glory of it, eternally true and truly eternal. He made Himself known, therefore, to the demons, not by that which is life eternal, and the unchangeable light which illumines the pious, whose souls are cleansed by the faith that is in Him, but by some temporal effects of His power, and evidences of His mysterious presence, which were more easily discerned by the angelic senses even of wicked spirits than by human infirmity. But when He judged it advisable gradually to suppress these signs, and to retire into deeper obscurity, the prince of the demons doubted whether He were the Christ, and endeavored to ascertain this by tempting Him, insofar as He permitted Himself to be tempted, that He might adapt the manhood He wore to be an example for our imitation. But after that temptation, when, as Scripture says, He was ministered to[2] by the angels who are good and holy, and therefore objects of terror to the impure spirits, He revealed more and more distinctly to the demons how great He was, so that, even though the infirmity of His flesh might seem contemptible, none dared to resist His authority.

---

1. Mark 1:24.
2. Matt. 4:3–11.

22. THE DIFFERENCE BETWEEN THE KNOWLEDGE OF THE HOLY ANGELS AND THAT OF THE DEMONS

The good angels, therefore, hold cheap all that knowledge of material and transitory things which the demons are so proud of possessing—not that they are ignorant of these things, but because the love of God, whereby they are sanctified, is very dear to them, and because, in comparison of that not merely immaterial but also unchangeable and ineffable beauty, with the holy love of which they are inflamed, they despise all things which are beneath it, and all that is not it, that they may with every good thing that is in them enjoy that good which is the source of their goodness. And therefore they have a more certain knowledge even of those temporal and mutable things, because they contemplate their principles and causes in the word of God, by which the world was made—those causes by which one thing is approved, another rejected, and all arranged. But the demons do not behold in the wisdom of God these eternal, and, as it were, cardinal causes of things temporal, but only foresee a larger part of the future than men do, by reason of their greater acquaintance with the signs which are hidden from us. Sometimes, too, it is their own intentions they predict. And, finally, the demons are frequently, the angels never, deceived. For it is one thing, by the aid of things temporal and changeable, to conjecture the changes that may occur in time, and to modify such things by one's own will and faculty—and this is to a certain extent permitted to the demons—it is another thing to foresee the changes of times in the eternal and immutable laws of God, which live in His wisdom, and to know the will of God, the most infallible and powerful of all causes, by participating in His spirit; and this is granted to the holy angels by a just discretion. And thus they are not only eternal, but blessed. And the good wherein they are blessed is God, by whom they were created. For without end they enjoy the contemplation and participation of Him.

23. THAT THE NAME OF GODS IS FALSELY GIVEN TO THE GODS OF THE GENTILES, THOUGH SCRIPTURE APPLIES IT BOTH TO THE HOLY ANGELS AND JUST MEN

If the Platonists prefer to call these angels gods rather than demons, and to reckon them with those whom Plato, their founder and master, maintains were created by the supreme God,[1] they are welcome to do so, for I will not spend strength in fighting about words. For if they say that these beings are immortal, and yet created by the supreme God, blessed but by cleaving to their Creator and not by their own power, they say what we say, whatever name they call these beings by. And that this is the opinion either of all or the best of the Platonists can be ascertained by their writings. And regarding the name itself, if they see fit to call such blessed and immortal creatures gods, this need not give rise to any serious discussion between us, since in our own Scriptures we read, "The God of gods, the LORD hath spoken";[2] and again, "Confess to the God of gods";[3] and again, "He is a great King above all gods."[4] And where it is said, "He is to be feared above all gods," the reason is forthwith added, for it follows, "for all the gods of the nations are idols, but the LORD made the heavens."[5] He said, "above all gods," but added, "of the nations"; that is to say, above all those whom the nations count gods, in other words, demons. By them He is to be feared with that terror in which they cried to the Lord, "Hast Thou come to destroy us?" But where it is said, "the God of gods," it cannot be understood as the god of the demons; and far be it from us to say that "great King above all gods" means "great King above all demons." But the same Scripture also calls men who belong to God's people "gods": "I have said, Ye are gods, and all of you children of the Most High."[6] Accordingly, when God is styled God of gods, this may be understood of these gods; and so, too, when He is styled a great King above all gods.

Nevertheless, someone may say, if men are called gods because they belong to God's people, whom He addresses by means of men and angels, are not the immortals, who already enjoy that felicity which men seek to attain by worshiping God, much more worthy of the title? And what shall we reply to this, if not that it is not without reason that in Holy Scripture men are more expressly styled gods than those immortal and blessed spirits to whom we hope to be equal in the resurrection, because there was a fear that the weakness of unbelief, being overcome with the excellence of these beings, might presume to constitute some of them a god? In the case of men this was a result that need not be guarded against. Besides, it was right that the men belonging to God's people should be more expressly called gods, to assure and certify them that He who is called God of gods is their God; because, although those immortal and blessed spirits who dwell in the heavens are called gods, yet they are not called gods of gods, that is to say, gods of the men who constitute God's people, and to whom it is said, "I have said, Ye are gods, and all of you the children of the Most High." Hence the saying of the apostle, "Though there be that are called gods, whether in heaven or in earth, as there be gods many and lords many, but to us there is but one God, the Father, of whom are all things, and we in Him; and one Lord Jesus Christ, by whom are all things, and we by Him."[7]

We need not, therefore, laboriously contend about the name, since the reality is so obvious as to admit of no shadow of doubt. That which we say, that the angels who are sent to announce the will of God to men belong to the order of blessed immortals, does not satisfy the Platonists, because they believe that this ministry is discharged, not by those whom they call gods, in other words, not by blessed immortals, but by demons, whom they dare not affirm to be blessed, but only immortal, or if they do rank them among the blessed immortals, yet only as good demons, and not as gods who dwell in the heaven of heavens remote from all human contact. But, though it may seem mere wrangling about a name, yet the name of demon is so detestable that we cannot bear in any sense to apply it to the holy angels. Now, therefore, let us close this book in the assurance that, whatever we call these immortal and blessed spirits, who yet are only creatures, they do not act as mediators to introduce to everlasting felicity miserable mortals, from whom they are severed by a twofold distinction. And those others who are mediators, insofar as they have immortality in common with their superiors, and misery in common with their inferiors (for they are justly miserable in punishment of their wickedness), cannot bestow upon us, but rather grudge that we should possess, the blessedness from which they themselves are excluded. And so the friends of the demons have nothing considerable to allege why we should rather worship them as our helpers than avoid them as traitors to our interests. As for those spirits who are good, and who are therefore not only immortal but also blessed, and to whom they suppose we should give the title of gods, and offer worship and sacrifices for the sake of inheriting a future life, we shall, by God's help, endeavor in the following book to show that these spirits, call them by what name, and ascribe to them what nature you will, desire that religious worship be paid to God alone, by whom they were created, and by whose communications of Himself to them they are blessed.

---

1. Timæus.
2. Ps. 1:1.
3. Ps. 136:2.
4. Ps. 95:3.
5. Ps. 96:5–6.
6. Ps. 82:6.
7. 1 Cor. 8:5–6.

BOOK TEN

ARGUMENT

In this book Augustine teaches that the good angels wish God alone, whom they themselves serve, to receive that divine honor which is rendered by sacrifice, and which is called latreia. He then goes on to dispute against Porphyry about the principle and way of the soul's cleansing and deliverance.

1. THAT THE PLATONISTS THEMSELVES HAVE DETERMINED THAT GOD ALONE CAN CONFER HAPPINESS EITHER ON ANGELS OR MEN, BUT THAT IT YET REMAINS A QUESTION WHETHER THOSE SPIRITS WHOM THEY DIRECT US TO WORSHIP, THAT WE MAY OBTAIN HAPPINESS, WISH SACRIFICE TO BE OFFERED TO THEMSELVES, OR TO THE ONE GOD ONLY

It is the decided opinion of all who use their brains, that all men desire to be happy. But who are happy, or how they become so, these are questions about which the weakness of human understanding stirs endless and angry controversies, in which philosophers have wasted their strength and expended their leisure. To adduce and discuss their various opinions would be tedious, and is unnecessary. The reader may remember what we said in the eighth book, while making a selection of the philosophers with whom we might discuss the question regarding the future life of happiness, whether we can reach it by paying divine honors to the one true God, the Creator of all gods, or by worshiping many gods, and he will not expect us to repeat here the same argument, especially as, even if he has forgotten it, he may refresh his memory by reperusal. For we made selection of the Platonists, justly esteemed the noblest of the philosophers, because they had the wit to perceive that the human soul, immortal and rational, or intellectual, as it is, cannot be happy except by partaking of the light of that God by whom both itself and the world were made; and also that the happy life which all men desire cannot be reached by any who does not cleave with a pure and holy love to that one supreme good, the unchangeable God. But as even these philosophers, whether accommodating to the folly and ignorance of the people, or, as the apostle says, "becoming vain in their imaginations,"[1] supposed or allowed others to suppose that many gods should be worshiped, so that some of them considered that divine honor by worship and sacrifice should be rendered even to the demons (an error I have already exploded), we must now, by God's help, ascertain what is thought about our religious worship and piety by those immortal and blessed spirits, who dwell in the heavenly places among dominations, principalities, powers, whom the Platonists call gods, and some either good demons, or, like us, angels—that is to say, to put it more plainly, whether the angels desire us to offer sacrifice and worship, and to consecrate our possessions and ourselves, to them or only to God, theirs and ours.

For this is the worship which is due to the Divinity, or, to speak more accurately, to the Deity; and, to express this worship in a single word as there does not occur to me any Latin term sufficiently exact, I shall avail myself, whenever necessary, of a Greek word. Λατρεία, whenever it occurs in Scripture, is rendered by the word "service." But that service which is due to men, and in reference to which the apostle writes that servants must be subject to their own masters,[2] is usually designated by another word in Greek,[3] whereas the service which is paid to God alone by worship, is always, or almost always, called λατρεία in the usage of those who wrote from the divine oracles. This cannot so well be called simply "cultus," for in that case it would not seem to be due exclusively to God; for the same word is applied to the respect we pay either to the memory or the living presence of men. From it, too, we derive the words "agriculture," "colonist," and others.[4] And the heathen call their gods "cœlicolæ," not because they worship heaven, but because they dwell in it, and as it were colonize it—not in the sense in which we call those colonists who are attached to their native soil to cultivate it under the rule of the owners, but in the sense in which the great master of the Latin language says, "There was an ancient city inhabited by Tyrian colonists."[5] He called them colonists, not because they cultivated the soil, but because they inhabited the city. So, too, cities that have hived off from larger cities are called colonies. Consequently, while it is quite true that, using the word in a special sense, "cult" can be rendered to none but God, yet, as the word is applied to other things besides, the cult due to God cannot in Latin be expressed by this word alone.

The word "religion" might seem to express more definitely the worship due to God alone, and therefore Latin translators have used this word to represent θρησκεία; yet, as not only the uneducated, but also the best instructed, use the word "religion" to express human ties, and relationships, and affinities, it would inevitably introduce ambiguity to use this word in discussing the worship of God, unable as we are to say that religion is nothing else than the worship of God, without contradicting the common usage which applies this word to the observance of social relationships. "Piety," again, or, as the Greeks say, εὐσέβεια, is commonly understood as the proper designation of the worship of God. Yet this word also is used of dutifulness to parents. The common people, too, use it of works of charity, which, I suppose, arises from the circumstance that God enjoins the performance of such works, and declares that He is pleased with them instead of, or in preference to, sacrifices. From this usage it has also come to pass that God Himself is called pious,[6] in which sense the Greeks never use εὐσεβεῖν, though εὐσέβεια is applied to works of charity by their common people also. In some passages of Scripture, therefore, they have sought to preserve the distinction by using not εὐσέβεια, the more general word, but θεοσέβεια, which literally denotes the worship of God. We, on the other hand, cannot express either of these ideas by one word. This worship, then, which in Greek is called λατρεία, and in Latin *servitus* [service], but the service due to God only; this worship, which in Greek is called θρησκεία, and in Latin *religio*, but the religion by which we are bound to God only; this worship, which they call θεοσέβεια, but which we cannot express in one word, but call it the worship of God—this, we say, belongs only to that God who is the true God, and who makes His worshipers gods.[7] And therefore, whoever these immortal and blessed inhabitants of heaven be, if they do not love us, and wish us to be blessed, then we ought not to worship them; and if they do love us and desire our happiness, they cannot wish us to be made happy by any other means than they themselves have enjoyed—for how could they wish our blessedness to flow from one source, theirs from another?

---

1. Rom. 1:21.
2. Eph. 6:5.
3. Namely, δουλεία: Cf. *Quæst. in Exod.* 94; *Quæst. in Gen.* 21; *Contra Faust.* 15.9, etc.
4. Agricolæ, coloni, incolæ.
5. Virgil *Æneid* 1.12.
6. 2 Chron. 30:9; Eccles. 11:13; Jth. 7:20.
7. Ps. 82:6.

2. THE OPINION OF PLOTINUS THE PLATONIST REGARDING ENLIGHTENMENT FROM ABOVE

But with these more estimable philosophers we have no dispute in this matter. For they perceived, and in various forms abundantly expressed in their writings, that these spirits have the same source of happiness as ourselves—a certain intelligible light, which is their God, and is different from themselves, and illumines them that they may be penetrated with light, and enjoy perfect happiness in the participation of God. Plotinus, commenting on Plato, repeatedly and strongly asserts that not even the soul which they believe to be the soul of the world, derives its blessedness from any other source than we do, namely, from that Light which is distinct from it and created it, and by whose intelligible illumination it enjoys light in things intelligible. He also compares those spiritual things to the vast and conspicuous heavenly bodies, as if God were the sun, and the soul the moon; for they suppose that the moon derives its light from the sun. That great Platonist, therefore, says that the rational soul, or rather the intellectual soul—in which class he comprehends the souls of the blessed immortals who inhabit heaven—has no nature superior to it save God, the Creator of the world and the soul itself, and that these heavenly spirits derive their blessed life, and the light of truth, from the same source as ourselves, agreeing with the gospel where we read, "There was a man sent from God whose name was John; the same came for a witness to bear witness of that Light, that through Him all might believe. He was not that Light, but that he might bear witness of the Light. That was the true Light which lighteth every man that cometh into the world";[1] a distinction which sufficiently proves that the rational or intellectual soul such as John had cannot be its own light, but needs to receive illumination from another, the true Light. This John himself avows when he delivers his witness: "We have all received of His fullness."[2]

---

1. John 1:6–9.
2. John 1:16.

3. THAT THE PLATONISTS, THOUGH KNOWING SOMETHING OF THE CREATOR OF THE UNIVERSE, HAVE MISUNDERSTOOD THE TRUE WORSHIP OF GOD, BY GIVING DIVINE HONOR TO ANGELS, GOOD OR BAD

This being so, if the Platonists, or those who think with them, knowing God, glorified Him as God and gave thanks, if they did not become vain in their own thoughts, if they did not originate or yield to the popular errors, they would certainly acknowledge that neither could the blessed immortals retain, nor we miserable mortals reach, a happy condition without worshiping the one God of gods, who is both theirs and ours. To Him we owe the service which is called in Greek λατρεία, whether we render it outwardly or inwardly; for we are all His temple, each of us severally and all of us together, because He condescends to inhabit each individually and the whole harmonious body, being no greater in all than in each, since He is neither expanded nor divided. Our heart when it rises to Him is His altar; the priest who intercedes for us is His only begotten; we sacrifice to Him bleeding victims when we contend for His truth even unto blood; to Him we offer the sweetest incense when we come before Him burning with holy and pious love; to Him we devote and surrender ourselves and His gifts in us; to Him, by solemn feasts and on appointed days, we consecrate the memory of His benefits, lest through the lapse of time ungrateful oblivion should steal upon us; to Him we offer on the altar of our heart the sacrifice of humility and praise, kindled by the fire of burning love. It is that we may see Him, so far as He can be seen; it is that we may cleave to Him, that we are cleansed from all stain of sins and evil passions, and are consecrated in His name. For He is the fountain of our happiness, He the end of all our desires. Being attached to Him, or rather let me say, reattached—for we had detached ourselves and lost hold of Him—being, I say, reattached to Him,[1] we tend toward Him by love, that we may rest in Him, and find our blessedness by attaining that end. For our good, about which philosophers have so keenly contended, is nothing else than to be united to God. It is, if I may say so, by spiritually embracing Him that the intellectual soul is filled and impregnated with true virtues. We are enjoined to love this good with all our heart, with all our soul, with all our strength. To this good we ought to be led by those who love us, and to lead those we love. Thus are fulfilled those two commandments on which hang all the Law and the Prophets: "Thou shalt love the Lord thy God with all thy heart, and with all thy mind, and with all thy soul"; and "Thou shalt love thy neighbor as thyself."[2] For, that man might be intelligent in his self-love, there was appointed for him an end to which he might refer all his actions, that he might be blessed. For he who loves himself wishes nothing else than this. And the end set before him is "to draw near to God."[3] And so, when one who has this intelligent self-love is commanded to love his neighbor as himself, what else is enjoined than that he shall do all in his power to commend to him the love of God? This is the worship of God, this is true religion, this right piety, this the service due to God only. If any immortal power, then, no matter with what virtue endowed, loves us as himself, he must desire that we find our happiness by submitting ourselves to Him, in submission to whom he himself finds happiness. If he does not worship God, he is wretched, because deprived of God; if he worships God, he cannot wish to be worshiped in God's stead. On the contrary, these higher powers acquiesce heartily in the divine sentence in which it is written, "He that sacrificeth unto any god, save unto the LORD only, he shall be utterly destroyed."[4]

---

1. Augustine here remarks, in a clause that cannot be given in English, that the word *religio* is derived from *religere*.—So Cicero *De Nat. Deor.* 2.28.
2. Matt. 22:37–40.
3. Ps. 73:28.
4. Exod. 22:20.

4. THAT SACRIFICE IS DUE TO THE TRUE GOD ONLY

But, putting aside for the present the other religious services with which God is worshiped, certainly no man would dare to say that sacrifice is due to any but God. Many parts, indeed, of divine worship are unduly used in showing honor to men, whether through an excessive humility or pernicious flattery; yet, while this is done, those persons who are thus worshiped and venerated, or even adored, are reckoned no more than human; and whoever thought of sacrificing save to one whom he knew, supposed, or feigned to be a god? And how ancient a part of God's worship sacrifice is, those two brothers Cain and Abel sufficiently show, of whom God rejected the elder's sacrifice, and looked favorably on the younger's.

5. OF THE SACRIFICES WHICH GOD DOES NOT REQUIRE, BUT WISHED TO BE OBSERVED FOR THE EXHIBITION OF THOSE THINGS WHICH HE DOES REQUIRE

And who is so foolish as to suppose that the things offered to God are needed by Him for some uses of His own? Divine Scripture in many places explodes this idea. Not to be wearisome, suffice it to quote this brief saying from a psalm: "I have said to the LORD, Thou art my God: for Thou needest not my goodness."[1] We must believe, then, that God has no need, not only of cattle, or any other earthly and material thing, but even of man's righteousness, and that whatever right worship is paid to God profits not Him, but man. For no man would say he did a benefit to a fountain by drinking, or to the light by seeing. And the fact that the ancient church offered animal sacrifices, which the people of God nowadays read of without imitating, proves nothing else than this, that those sacrifices signified the things which we do for the purpose of drawing near to God, and inducing our neighbor to do the same. A sacrifice, therefore, is the visible sacrament or sacred sign of an invisible sacrifice. Hence that penitent in the psalm, or it may be the psalmist himself, entreating God to be merciful to his sins, says, "If Thou desiredst sacrifice, I would give it: Thou delightest not in whole burnt offerings. The sacrifice of God is a broken heart: a heart contrite and humble God will not despise."[2] Observe how, in the very words in which he is expressing God's refusal of sacrifice, he shows that God requires sacrifice. He does not desire the sacrifice of a slaughtered beast, but He desires the sacrifice of a contrite heart. Thus, that sacrifice which he says God does not wish, is the symbol of the sacrifice which God does wish. God does not wish sacrifices in the sense in which foolish people think He wishes them, namely, to gratify His own pleasure. For if He had not wished that the sacrifices He requires, as, for example, a heart contrite and humbled by penitent sorrow, should be symbolized by those sacrifices which He was thought to desire because pleasant to Himself, the old law would never have enjoined their presentation; and they were destined to be merged when the fit opportunity arrived, in order that men might not suppose that the sacrifices themselves, rather than the things symbolized by them, were pleasing to God or acceptable in us. Hence, in another passage from another psalm, he says, "If I were hungry, I would not tell thee; for the world is Mine and the fullness thereof. Will I eat the flesh of bulls, or drink the blood of goats?"[3]—as if He should say, "Supposing such things were necessary to Me, I would never ask thee for what I have in My own hand." Then He goes on to mention what these signify: "Offer unto God the sacrifice of praise, and pay thy vows unto the Most High. And call upon Me in the day of trouble: I will deliver thee, and thou shalt glorify Me."[4] So in another prophet: "Wherewith shall I come before the LORD, and bow myself before the high God? Shall I come before Him with burnt offerings, with calves of a year old? Will the LORD be pleased with thousands of rams, or with ten thousands of rivers of oil? Shall I give my firstborn for my transgression, the fruit of my body for the sin of my soul? Hath He showed thee, O man, what is good; and what doth the LORD require of thee, but to do justly, and to love mercy, and to walk humbly with thy God?"[5] In the words of this prophet, these two things are distinguished and set forth with sufficient explicitness, that God does not require these sacrifices for their own sakes, and that He does require the sacrifices which they symbolize. In the epistle titled "to the Hebrews" it is said, "To do good and to communicate, forget not: for with such sacrifices God is well pleased."[6] And so, when it is written, "I desire mercy rather than sacrifice,"[7] nothing else is meant than that one sacrifice is preferred to another; for that which in common speech is called sacrifice is only the symbol of the true sacrifice. Now mercy is the true sacrifice, and therefore it is said, as I have just quoted, "with such sacrifices God is well pleased." All the divine ordinances, therefore, which we read concerning the sacrifices in the service of the tabernacle or the temple, we are to refer to the love of God and our neighbor. For "on these two commandments," as it is written, "hang all the Law and the Prophets."⁸

---

1. Ps. 16:2.
2. Ps. 51:16–17.
3. Ps. 50:12–13.
4. Ps. 50:14–15.
5. Mic. 6:6–8.
6. Heb. 13:16.
7. Hos. 6:6.
8. Matt. 22:40.

6. OF THE TRUE AND PERFECT SACRIFICE

Thus a true sacrifice is every work which is done that we may be united to God in holy fellowship, and which has a reference to that supreme good and end in which alone we can be truly blessed.[1] And therefore even the mercy we show to men, if it is not shown for God's sake, is not a sacrifice. For, though made or offered by man, sacrifice is a divine thing, as those who called it *sacrifice*[2] meant to indicate. Thus man himself, consecrated in the name of God, and vowed to God, is a sacrifice insofar as he dies to the world that he may live to God. For this is a part of that mercy which each man shows to himself; as it is written, "Have mercy on thy soul by pleasing God."[3] Our body, too, as a sacrifice when we chasten it by temperance, if we do so as we ought, for God's sake, that we may not yield our members instruments of unrighteousness unto sin, but instruments of righteousness unto God.⁴ Exhorting to this sacrifice, the apostle says, "I beseech you, therefore, brethren, by the mercy of God, that ye present your bodies a living sacrifice, holy, acceptable to God, which is your reasonable service."⁵ If, then, the body, which, being inferior, the soul uses as a servant or instrument, is a sacrifice when it is used rightly, and with reference to God, how much more does the soul itself become a sacrifice when it offers itself to God, in order that, being inflamed by the fire of His love, it may receive of His beauty and become pleasing to Him, losing the shape of earthly desire, and being remolded in the image of permanent loveliness? And this, indeed, the apostle subjoins, saying, "And be not conformed to this world; but be ye transformed in the renewing of your mind, that ye may prove what is that good, and acceptable, and perfect will of God."⁶ Since, therefore, true sacrifices are works of mercy to ourselves or others, done with a reference to God, and since works of mercy have no other object than the relief of distress or the conferring of happiness, and since there is no happiness apart from that good of which it is said, "It is good for me to be very near to God,"⁷ it follows that the whole redeemed city, that is to say, the congregation or community of the saints, is offered to God as our sacrifice through the great High Priest, who offered Himself to God in His passion for us, that we might be members of this glorious head, according to the form of a servant. For it was this form He offered, in this He was offered, because it is according to it He is Mediator, in this He is our Priest, in this the Sacrifice. Accordingly, when the apostle had exhorted us to present our bodies a living sacrifice, holy, acceptable to God, our reasonable service, and not to be conformed to the world, but to be transformed in the renewing of our mind, that we might prove what is that good, and acceptable, and perfect will of God, that is to say, the true sacrifice of ourselves, he says, "For I say, through the grace of God which is given unto me, to every man that is among you, not to think of himself more highly than he ought to think, but to think soberly, according as God hath dealt to every man the measure of faith. For, as we have many members in one body, and all members have not the same office, so we, being many, are one body in Christ, and every one members one of another, having gifts differing according to the grace that is given to us."[8] This is the sacrifice of Christians: we, being many, are one body in Christ. And this also is the sacrifice which the church continually celebrates in the sacrament of the altar, known to the faithful, in which she teaches that she herself is offered in the offering she makes to God.

---

1. On the service rendered to the church by this definition, see Waterland's *Works* 5.124.
2. Literally, a sacred action.
3. Ecclus. 30:24.
4. Rom. 6:13.
5. Rom. 12:1.
6. Rom. 12:2.
7. Ps. 73:28.
8. Rom. 12:3–6.

7. OF THE LOVE OF THE HOLY ANGELS, WHICH PROMPTS THEM TO DESIRE THAT WE WORSHIP THE ONE TRUE GOD, AND NOT THEMSELVES

It is very right that these blessed and immortal spirits, who inhabit celestial dwellings, and rejoice in the communications of their Creator's fullness, firm in His eternity, assured in His truth, holy by His grace, since they compassionately and tenderly regard us miserable mortals, and wish us to become immortal and happy, do not desire us to sacrifice to themselves, but to Him whose sacrifice they know themselves to be in common with us. For we and they together are the one city of God, to which it is said in the psalm, "Glorious things are spoken of thee, O city of God";[1] the human part sojourning here below, the angelic aiding from above. For from that heavenly city, in which God's will is the intelligible and unchangeable law, from that heavenly council chamber—for they sit in counsel regarding us—that Holy Scripture, descended to us by the ministry of angels, in which it is written, "He that sacrificeth unto any god, save unto the LORD only, he shall be utterly destroyed,"[2]—this Scripture, this law, these precepts, have been confirmed by such miracles, that it is sufficiently evident to whom these immortal and blessed spirits, who desire us to be like themselves, wish us to sacrifice.

---

1. Ps. 87:3.
2. Exod. 22:20.

8. OF THE MIRACLES WHICH GOD HAS CONDESCENDED TO ADHIBIT, THROUGH THE MINISTRY OF ANGELS, TO HIS PROMISES FOR THE CONFIRMATION OF THE FAITH OF THE GODLY

I should seem tedious were I to recount all the ancient miracles, which were worked in attestation of God's promises which He made to Abraham thousands of years ago, that in his seed all the nations of the earth should be blessed.[1] For who can but marvel that Abraham's barren wife should have given birth to a son at an age when not even a prolific woman could bear children; or, again, that when Abraham sacrificed, a flame from heaven should have run between the divided parts;[2] or that the angels in human form, whom he had hospitably entertained, and who had renewed God's promise of offspring, should also have predicted the destruction of Sodom by fire from heaven;[3] and that his nephew Lot should have been rescued from Sodom by the angels as the fire was just descending, while his wife, who looked back as she went, and was immediately turned into salt, stood as a sacred beacon warning us that no one who is being saved should long for what he is leaving? How striking also were the wonders done by Moses to rescue God's people from the yoke of slavery in Egypt, when the magi of the Pharaoh, that is, the king of Egypt, who tyrannized over this people, were suffered to do some wonderful things that they might be vanquished all the more signally! They did these things by the magical arts and incantations to which the evil spirits or demons are addicted; while Moses, having as much greater power as he had right on his side, and having the aid of angels, easily conquered them in the name of the Lord who made heaven and earth. And, in fact, the magicians failed at the third plague; whereas Moses, dealing out the miracles delegated to him, brought ten plagues upon the land, so that the hard hearts of Pharaoh and the Egyptians yielded, and the people were let go. But, quickly repenting, and essaying to overtake the departing Hebrews, who had crossed the sea on dry ground, they were covered and overwhelmed in the returning waters. What shall I say of those frequent and stupendous exhibitions of divine power, while the people were conducted through the wilderness? Of the waters which could not be drunk, but lost their bitterness, and quenched the thirsty, when at God's command a piece of wood was cast into them? Of the manna that descended from heaven to appease their hunger, and which begat worms and putrefied when anyone collected more than the appointed quantity, and yet, though double was gathered on the day before the Sabbath (it not being lawful to gather it on that day), remained fresh? Of the birds which filled the camp, and turned appetite into satiety when they longed for flesh, which it seemed impossible to supply to so vast a population? Of the enemies who met them, and opposed their passage with arms, and were defeated without the loss of a single Hebrew, when Moses prayed with his hands extended in the form of a cross? Of the seditious persons who arose among God's people, and separated themselves from the divinely ordered community, and were swallowed up alive by the earth, a visible token of an invisible punishment? Of the rock struck with the rod, and pouring out waters more than enough for all the host? Of the deadly serpents' bites, sent in just punishment of sin, but healed by looking at the lifted brazen serpent, so that not only were the tormented people healed, but a symbol of the crucifixion of death set before them in this destruction of death by death? It was this serpent which was preserved in memory of this event, and was afterward worshiped by the mistaken people as an idol, and was destroyed by the pious and God-fearing King Hezekiah, much to his credit.

---

1. Gen. 18:18.
2. Gen. 15:17. In his *Retractations* (2.43), Augustine says that he should not have spoken of this as miraculous, because it was an appearance seen in sleep.
3. Gen. 18.

9. OF THE ILLICIT ARTS CONNECTED WITH DEMONOLATRY, AND OF WHICH THE PLATONIST PORPHYRY ADOPTS SOME, AND DISCARDS OTHERS

These miracles, and many others of the same nature, which it were tedious to mention, were worked for the purpose of commending the worship of the one true God, and prohibiting the worship of a multitude of false gods. Moreover, they were worked by simple faith and godly confidence, not by the incantations and charms composed under the influence of a criminal tampering with the unseen world, of an art which they call either magic, or by the more abominable title necromancy, or the more honorable designation theurgy; for they wish to discriminate between those whom the people call magicians, who practice necromancy, and are addicted to illicit arts and condemned, and those others who seem to them to be worthy of praise for their practice of theurgy—the truth, however, being that both classes are the slaves of the deceitful rites of the demons whom they invoke under the names of angels.

For even Porphyry promises some kind of purgation of the soul by the help of theurgy, though he does so with some hesitation and shame, and denies that this art can secure to anyone a return to God; so that you can detect his opinion vacillating between the profession of philosophy and an art which he feels to be presumptuous and sacrilegious. For at one time he warns us to avoid it as deceitful, and prohibited by law, and dangerous to those who practice it; then again, as if in deference to its advocates, he declares it useful for cleansing one part of the soul, not, indeed, the intellectual part, by which the truth of things intelligible, which have no sensible images, is recognized, but the spiritual part, which takes cognizance of the images of things material. This part, he says, is prepared and fitted for intercourse with spirits and angels, and for the vision of the gods, by the help of certain theurgic consecrations, or, as they call them, mysteries. He acknowledges, however, that these theurgic mysteries impart to the intellectual soul no such purity as fits it to see its God, and recognize the things that truly exist. And from this acknowledgment we may infer what kind of gods these are, and what kind of vision of them is imparted by theurgic consecrations, if by it one cannot see the things which truly exist. He says, further, that the rational, or, as he prefers calling it, the intellectual soul, can pass into the heavens without the spiritual part being cleansed by theurgic art, and that this art cannot so purify the spiritual part as to give it entrance to immortality and eternity. And therefore, although he distinguishes angels from demons, asserting that the habitation of the latter is in the air, while the former dwell in the ether and empyrean, and although he advises us to cultivate the friendship of some demon, who may be able after our death to assist us, and elevate us at least a little above the earth—for he owns that it is by another way we must reach the heavenly society of the angels—he at the same time distinctly warns us to avoid the society of demons, saying that the soul, expiating its sin after death, execrates the worship of demons by whom it was entangled. And of theurgy itself, though he recommends it as reconciling angels and demons, he cannot deny that it treats with powers which either themselves envy the soul its purity, or serve the arts of those who do envy it. He complains of this through the mouth of some Chaldæan or other: "A good man in Chaldæa complains," he says, "that his most strenuous efforts to cleanse his soul were frustrated, because another man, who had influence in these matters, and who envied him purity, had prayed to the powers, and bound them by his conjuring not to listen to his request. Therefore," adds Porphyry, "what the one man bound, the other could not loose." And from this he concludes that theurgy is a craft which accomplishes not only good but evil among gods and men; and that the gods also have passions, and are perturbed and agitated by the emotions which Apuleius attributed to demons and men, but from which he preserved the gods by that sublimity of residence, which, in common with Plato, he accorded to them.

10. CONCERNING THEURGY, WHICH PROMISES A DELUSIVE PURIFICATION OF THE SOUL BY THE INVOCATION OF DEMONS

But here we have another and a much more learned Platonist than Apuleius, Porphyry, to wit, asserting that, by I know not what theurgy, even the gods themselves are subjected to passions and perturbations; for by adjurations they were so bound and terrified that they could not confer purity of soul—were so terrified by him who imposed on them a wicked command, that they could not by the same theurgy be freed from that terror, and fulfill the righteous behest of him who prayed to them, or do the good he sought. Who does not see that all these things are fictions of deceiving demons, unless he be a wretched slave of theirs, and an alien from the grace of the true Liberator? For if the Chaldæan had been dealing with good gods, certainly a well-disposed man, who sought to purify his own soul, would have had more influence with them than an evil-disposed man seeking to hinder him. Or, if the gods were just, and considered the man unworthy of the purification he sought, at all events they should not have been terrified by an envious person, nor hindered, as Porphyry avows, by the fear of a stronger deity, but should have simply denied the boon on their own free judgment. And it is surprising that that well-disposed Chaldæan, who desired to purify his soul by theurgical rites, found no superior deity who could either terrify the frightened gods still more, and force them to confer the boon, or compose their fears, and so enable them to do good without compulsion—even supposing that the good theurgist had no rites by which he himself might purge away the taint of fear from the gods whom he invoked for the purification of his own soul. And why is it that there is a god who has power to terrify the inferior gods, and none who has power to free them from fear? Is there found a god who listens to the envious man, and frightens the gods from doing good? And is there not found a god who listens to the well-disposed man, and removes the fear of the gods that they may do him good? O excellent theurgy! O admirable purification of the soul!—a theurgy in which the violence of an impure envy has more influence than the entreaty of purity and holiness. Rather let us abominate and avoid the deceit of such wicked spirits, and listen to sound doctrine. As to those who perform these filthy cleansings by sacrilegious rites, and see in their initiated state (as he further tells us, though we may question this vision) certain wonderfully lovely appearances of angels or gods, this is what the apostle refers to when he speaks of "Satan transforming himself into an angel of light."[1] For these are the delusive appearances of that spirit who longs to entangle wretched souls in the deceptive worship of many and false gods, and to turn them aside from the true worship of the true God, by whom alone they are cleansed and healed, and who, as was said of Proteus, "turns himself into all shapes,"[2] equally hurtful, whether he assaults us as an enemy, or assumes the disguise of a friend.

---

1. 2 Cor. 11:14.
2. Virgil *Georg.* 4.411.

11. OF PORPHYRY'S EPISTLE TO ANEBO, IN WHICH HE ASKS FOR INFORMATION ABOUT THE DIFFERENCES AMONG DEMONS

It was a better tone which Porphyry adopted in his letter to Anebo the Egyptian, in which, assuming the character of an inquirer consulting him, he unmasks and explodes these sacrilegious arts. In that letter, indeed, he repudiates all demons, whom he maintains to be so foolish as to be attracted by the sacrificial vapors, and therefore residing not in the ether, but in the air beneath the moon, and indeed in the moon itself. Yet he has not the boldness to attribute to all the demons all the deceptions and malicious and foolish practices which justly move his indignation. For, though he acknowledges that as a race demons are foolish, he so far accommodates himself to popular ideas as to call some of them benignant demons. He expresses surprise that sacrifices not only incline the gods, but also compel and force them to do what men wish; and he is at a loss to understand how the sun and moon, and other visible celestial bodies—for bodies he does not doubt that they are—are considered gods, if the gods are distinguished from the demons by their incorporeality; also, if they are gods, how some are called beneficent and others hurtful, and how they, being corporeal, are numbered with the gods, who are incorporeal. He inquires further, and still as one in doubt, whether diviners and wonder-workers are men of unusually powerful souls, or whether the power to do these things is communicated by spirits from without. He inclines to the latter opinion, on the ground that it is by the use of stones and herbs that they lay spells on people, and open closed doors, and do similar wonders. And on this account, he says, some suppose that there is a race of beings whose property it is to listen to men —a race deceitful, full of contrivances, capable of assuming all forms, simulating gods, demons, and dead men—and that it is this race which bring about all these things which have the appearance of good or evil, but that what is really good they never help us in, and are indeed unacquainted with, for they make wickedness easy, but throw obstacles in the path of those who eagerly follow virtue; and that they are filled with pride and rashness, delight in sacrificial odors, are taken with flattery. These and the other characteristics of this race of deceitful and malicious spirits, who come into the souls of men and delude their senses, both in sleep and waking, he describes not as things of which he is himself convinced, but only with so much suspicion and doubt as to cause him to speak of them as commonly received opinions. We should sympathize with this great philosopher in the difficulty he experienced in acquainting himself with and confidently assailing the whole fraternity of devils, which any Christian old woman would unhesitatingly describe and most unreservedly detest. Perhaps, however, he shrank from offending Anebo, to whom he was writing, himself the most eminent patron of these mysteries, or the others who marveled at these magical feats as divine works, and closely allied to the worship of the gods.

However, he pursues this subject, and, still in the character of an inquirer, mentions some things which no sober judgment could attribute to any but malicious and deceitful powers. He asks why, after the better class of spirits have been invoked, the worse should be commanded to perform the wicked desires of men; why they do not hear a man who has just left a woman's embrace, while they themselves make no scruple of tempting men to incest and adultery; why their priests are commanded to abstain from animal food for fear of being polluted by the corporeal exhalations, while they themselves are attracted by the fumes of sacrifices and other exhalations; why the initiated are forbidden to touch a dead body, while their mysteries are celebrated almost entirely by means of dead bodies; why it is that a man addicted to any vice should utter threats, not to a demon or to the soul of a dead man, but to the sun and moon, or some of the heavenly bodies, which he intimidates by imaginary terrors, that he may wring from them a real boon—for he threatens that he will demolish the sky, and such like impossibilities—that those gods, being alarmed, like silly children, with imaginary and absurd threats, may do what they are ordered. Porphyry further relates that a man, Chæremon, profoundly versed in these sacred or rather sacrilegious mysteries, had written that the famous Egyptian mysteries of Isis and her husband Osiris had very great influence with the gods to compel them to do what they were ordered, when he who used the spells threatened to divulge or do away with these mysteries, and cried with a threatening voice that he would scatter the members of Osiris if they neglected his orders. Not without reason is Porphyry surprised that a man should utter such wild and empty threats against the gods—not against gods of no account, but against the heavenly gods, and those that shine with sidereal light—and that these threats should be effectual to constrain them with resistless power, and alarm them so that they fulfill his wishes. Not without reason does he, in the character of an inquirer into the reasons of these surprising things, give it to be understood that they are done by that race of spirits which he previously described as if quoting other people's opinions—spirits who deceive not, as he said, by nature, but by their own corruption, and who simulate gods and dead men, but not, as he said, demons, for demons they really are. As to his idea that by means of herbs, and stones, and animals, and certain incantations and noises, and drawings, sometimes fanciful, and sometimes copied from the motions of the heavenly bodies, men create upon earth powers capable of bringing about various results, all that is only the mystification which these demons practice on those who are subject to them, for the sake of furnishing themselves with merriment at the expense of their dupes. Either, then, Porphyry was sincere in his doubts and inquiries, and mentioned these things to demonstrate and put beyond question that they were the work, not of powers which aid us in obtaining life, but of deceitful demons; or, to take a more favorable view of the philosopher, he adopted this method with the Egyptian who was wedded to these errors, and was proud of them, that he might not offend him by assuming the attitude of a teacher, nor discompose his mind by the altercation of a professed assailant, but, by assuming the character of an inquirer, and the humble attitude of one who was anxious to learn, might turn his attention to these matters, and show how worthy they are to be despised and relinquished. Toward the conclusion of his letter, he requests Anebo to inform him what the Egyptian wisdom indicates as the way to blessedness. But as to those who hold intercourse with the gods, and pester them only for the sake of finding a runaway slave, or acquiring property, or making a bargain of a marriage, or such things, he declares that their pretensions to wisdom are vain. He adds that these same gods, even granting that on other points their utterances were true, were yet so ill-advised and unsatisfactory in their disclosures about blessedness, that they cannot be either gods or good demons, but are either that spirit who is called the deceiver, or mere fictions of the imagination.

12. OF THE MIRACLES WORKED BY THE TRUE GOD THROUGH THE MINISTRY OF THE HOLY ANGELS

Since by means of these arts wonders are done which quite surpass human power, what choice have we but to believe that these predictions and operations, which seem to be miraculous and divine, and which at the same time form no part of the worship of the one God, in adherence to whom, as the Platonists themselves abundantly testify, all blessedness consists, are the pastime of wicked spirits, who thus seek to seduce and hinder the truly godly? On the other hand, we cannot but believe that all miracles, whether worked by angels or by other means, so long as they are so done as to commend the worship and religion of the one God in whom alone is blessedness, are worked by those who love us in a true and godly sort, or through their means, God Himself working in them. For we cannot listen to those who maintain that the invisible God works no visible miracles; for even they believe that He made the world, which surely they will not deny to be visible. Whatever marvel happens in this world, it is certainly less marvelous than this whole world itself—I mean the sky and earth, and all that is in them—and these God certainly made. But, as the Creator Himself is hidden and incomprehensible to man, so also is the manner of creation. Although, therefore, the standing miracle of this visible world is little thought of, because always before us, yet, when we arouse ourselves to contemplate it, it is a greater miracle than the rarest and most unheard-of marvels. For man himself is a greater miracle than any miracle done through his instrumentality. Therefore God, who made the visible heaven and earth, does not disdain to work visible miracles in heaven or earth, that He may thereby awaken the soul which is immersed in things visible to worship Himself, the Invisible. But the place and time of these miracles are dependent on His unchangeable will, in which things future are ordered as if already they were accomplished. For He moves things temporal without Himself moving in time, He does not in one way know things that are to be, and, in another, things that have been; neither does He listen to those who pray otherwise than as He sees those that will pray. For, even when His angels hear us, it is He Himself who hears us in them, as in His true temple not made with hands, as in those men who are His saints; and His answers, though accomplished in time, have been arranged by His eternal appointment.

13. OF THE INVISIBLE GOD, WHO HAS OFTEN MADE HIMSELF VISIBLE, NOT AS HE REALLY IS, BUT AS THE BEHOLDERS COULD BEAR THE SIGHT

Neither need we be surprised that God, invisible as He is, should often have appeared visibly to the patriarchs. For as the sound which communicates the thought conceived in the silence of the mind is not the thought itself, so the form by which God, invisible in His own nature, became visible, was not God Himself. Nevertheless it is He Himself who was seen under that form, as that thought itself is heard in the sound of the voice; and the patriarchs recognized that, though the bodily form was not God, they saw the invisible God. For, though Moses conversed with God, yet he said, "If I have found grace in Thy sight, show me Thyself, that I may see and know Thee."[1] And as it was fit that the law, which was given, not to one man or a few enlightened men, but to the whole of a populous nation, should be accompanied by awe-inspiring signs, great marvels were worked, by the ministry of angels, before the people on the mount where the law was being given to them through one man, while the multitude beheld the awful appearances. For the people of Israel believed Moses, not as the Lacedæmonians believed their Lycurgus, because he had received from Jupiter or Apollo the laws he gave them. For when the law which enjoined the worship of one God was given to the people, marvelous signs and earthquakes, such as the divine wisdom judged sufficient, were brought about in the sight of all, that they might know that it was the Creator who could thus use creation to promulgate His law.

---

1. Exod. 33:13.

14. THAT THE ONE GOD IS TO BE WORSHIPED NOT ONLY FOR THE SAKE OF ETERNAL BLESSINGS, BUT ALSO IN CONNECTION WITH TEMPORAL PROSPERITY, BECAUSE ALL THINGS ARE REGULATED BY HIS PROVIDENCE

The education of the human race, represented by the people of God, has advanced, like that of an individual, through certain epochs, or, as it were, ages, so that it might gradually rise from earthly to heavenly things, and from the visible to the invisible. This object was kept so clearly in view, that, even in the period when temporal rewards were promised, the one God was presented as the object of worship, that men might not acknowledge any other than the true Creator and Lord of the spirit, even in connection with the earthly blessings of this transitory life. For he who denies that all things, which either angels or men can give us, are in the hand of the one Almighty, is a madman. The Platonist Plotinus discourses concerning providence, and, from the beauty of flowers and foliage, proves that from the supreme God, whose beauty is unseen and ineffable, providence reaches down even to these earthly things here below; and he argues that all these frail and perishing things could not have so exquisite and elaborate a beauty, were they not fashioned by Him whose unseen and unchangeable beauty continually pervades all things.[1] This is proved also by the Lord Jesus, where He says, "Consider the lilies, how they grow; they toil not, neither do they spin. And yet I say unto you that Solomon in all his glory was not arrayed like one of these. But if God so clothe the grass of the field, which today is and tomorrow is cast into the oven, how much more shall He clothe you, O ye of little faith!"[2] It was best, therefore, that the soul of man, which was still weakly desiring earthly things, should be accustomed to seek from God alone even these petty temporal boons, and the earthly necessaries of this transitory life, which are contemptible in comparison with eternal blessings, in order that the desire even of these things might not draw it aside from the worship of Him, to whom we come by despising and forsaking such things.

---

1. Plotinus *Enn.* 3.2.13.
2. Matt. 6:28–30.

15. OF THE MINISTRY OF THE HOLY ANGELS, BY WHICH THEY FULFILL THE PROVIDENCE OF GOD

And so it has pleased divine Providence, as I have said, and as we read in the Acts of the Apostles,[1] that the law enjoining the worship of one God should be given by the disposition of angels. But among them the person of God Himself visibly appeared, not, indeed, in His proper substance, which ever remains invisible to mortal eyes, but by the infallible signs furnished by creation in obedience to its Creator. He made use, too, of the words of human speech, uttering them syllable by syllable successively, though in His own nature He speaks not in a bodily but in a spiritual way; not to sense, but to the mind; not in words that occupy time, but, if I may so say, eternally, neither beginning to speak nor coming to an end. And what He says is accurately heard, not by the bodily but by the mental ear of His ministers and messengers, who are immortally blessed in the enjoyment of His unchangeable truth; and the directions which they in some ineffable way receive, they execute without delay or difficulty in the sensible and visible world. And this law was given in conformity with the age of the world, and contained at the first earthly promises, as I have said, which, however, symbolized eternal ones; and these eternal blessings few understood, though many took a part in the celebration of their visible signs. Nevertheless, with one consent both the words and the visible rites of that law enjoin the worship of one God—not one of a crowd of gods, but Him who made heaven and earth, and every soul and every spirit which is other than Himself. He created; all else was created; and, both for being and well-being, all things need Him who created them.

---

1. Acts 7:53.

16. WHETHER THOSE ANGELS WHO DEMAND THAT WE PAY THEM DIVINE HONOR, OR THOSE WHO TEACH US TO RENDER HOLY SERVICE, NOT TO THEMSELVES, BUT TO GOD, ARE TO BE TRUSTED ABOUT THE WAY TO LIFE ETERNAL

What angels, then, are we to believe in this matter of blessed and eternal life—those who wish to be worshiped with religious rites and observances, and require that men sacrifice to them; or those who say that all this worship is due to one God, the Creator, and teach us to render it with true piety to Him, by the vision of whom they are themselves already blessed, and in whom they promise that we shall be so? For that vision of God is the beauty of a vision so great, and is so infinitely desirable, that Plotinus does not hesitate to say that he who enjoys all other blessings in abundance, and has not this, is supremely miserable.[1] Since, therefore, miracles are worked by some angels to induce us to worship this God, by others, to induce us to worship themselves; and since the former forbid us to worship these, while the latter dare not forbid us to worship God, which are we to listen to? Let the Platonists reply, or any philosophers, or the theurgists, or rather, *periurgists*[2]—for this name is good enough for those who practice such arts. In short, let all men answer—if, at least, there survives in them any spark of that natural perception which, as rational beings, they possess when created—let them, I say, tell us whether we should sacrifice to the gods or angels who order us to sacrifice to them, or to that One to whom we are ordered to sacrifice by those who forbid us to worship either themselves or these others. If neither the one party nor the other had worked miracles, but had merely uttered commands, the one to sacrifice to themselves, the other forbidding that, and ordering us to sacrifice to God, a godly mind would have been at no loss to discern which command proceeded from proud arrogance, and which from true religion. I will say more. If miracles had been worked only by those who demand sacrifice for themselves, while those who forbade this, and enjoined sacrificing to the one God only, thought fit entirely to forego the use of visible miracles, the authority of the latter was to be preferred by all who would use, not their eyes only, but their reason. But since God, for the sake of commending to us the oracles of His truth, has, by means of these immortal messengers, who proclaim His majesty and not their own pride, worked miracles of surpassing grandeur, certainty, and distinctness, in order that the weak among the godly might not be drawn away to false religion by those who require us to sacrifice to them and endeavor to convince us by stupendous appeals to our senses, who is so utterly unreasonable as not to choose and follow the truth, when he finds that it is heralded by even more striking evidences than falsehood?

As for those miracles which history ascribes to the gods of the heathen—I do not refer to those prodigies which at intervals happen from some unknown physical causes, and which are arranged and appointed by divine Providence, such as monstrous births, and unusual meteorological phenomena, whether startling only, or also injurious, and which are said to be brought about and removed by communication with demons, and by their most deceitful craft—but I refer to these prodigies which manifestly enough are worked by their power and force, as, that the household gods which Æneas carried from Troy in his flight moved from place to place; that Tarquin cut a whetstone with a razor; that the Epidaurian serpent attached himself as a companion to Æsculapius on his voyage to Rome; that the ship in which the image of the Phrygian mother stood, and which could not be moved by a host of men and oxen, was moved by one weak woman, who attached her girdle to the vessel and drew it, as proof of her chastity; that a vestal, whose virginity was questioned, removed the suspicion by carrying from the Tiber a sieve full of water without any of it dropping: these, then, and the like, are by no means to be compared for greatness and virtue to those which, we read, were worked among God's people. How much less can we compare those marvels, which even the laws of heathen nations prohibit and punish—I mean the magical and theurgic marvels, of which the great part are merely illusions practiced upon the senses, as the drawing down of the moon, "that," as Lucan says, "it may shed a stronger influence on the plants"?[3] And if some of these do seem to equal those which are worked by the godly, the end for which they are worked distinguishes the two, and shows that ours are incomparably the more excellent. For those miracles commend the worship of a plurality of gods, who deserve worship the less the more they demand it; but these of ours commend the worship of the one God, who, both by the testimony of His own Scriptures, and by the eventual abolition of sacrifices, proves that He needs no such offerings. If, therefore, any angels demand sacrifice for themselves, we must prefer those who demand it, not for themselves, but for God, the Creator of all, whom they serve. For thus they prove how sincerely they love us, since they wish by sacrifice to subject us, not to themselves, but to Him by the contemplation of whom they themselves are blessed, and to bring us to Him from whom they themselves have never strayed. If, on the other hand, any angels wish us to sacrifice, not to one, but to many, not, indeed, to themselves, but to the gods whose angels they are, we must in this case also prefer those who are the angels of the one God of gods, and who so bid us to worship Him as to preclude our worshiping any other. But, further, if it be the case, as their pride and deceitfulness rather indicate, that they are neither good angels nor the angels of good gods, but wicked demons, who wish sacrifice to be paid, not to the one only and supreme God, but to themselves, what better protection against them can we choose than that of the one God whom the good angels serve, the angels who bid us sacrifice, not to themselves, but to Him whose sacrifice we ourselves ought to be?

---

1. Plotinus *Enn.* 1.6.7.
2. Meaning, officious meddlers.
3. Lucan *Pharsal.* 6.503.

17. CONCERNING THE ARK OF THE COVENANT, AND THE MIRACULOUS SIGNS WHEREBY GOD AUTHENTICATED THE LAW AND THE PROMISE

On this account it was that the law of God, given by the disposition of angels, and which commanded that the one God of gods alone receive sacred worship, to the exclusion of all others, was deposited in the ark, called the ark of the testimony. By this name it is sufficiently indicated, not that God, who was worshiped by all those rites, was shut up and enclosed in that place, though His responses emanated from it along with signs appreciable by the senses, but that His will was declared from that throne. The law itself, too, was engraved on tables of stone, and, as I have said, deposited in the ark, which the priests carried with due reverence during the sojourn in the wilderness, along with the tabernacle, which was in like manner called the tabernacle of the testimony; and there was then an accompanying sign, which appeared as a cloud by day and as a fire by night; when the cloud moved, the camp was shifted, and where it stood the camp was pitched. Besides these signs, and the voices which proceeded from the place where the ark was, there were other miraculous testimonies to the law. For when the ark was carried across Jordan, on the entrance to the land of promise, the upper part of the river stopped in its course, and the lower part flowed on, so as to present both to the ark and the people dry ground to pass over. Then, when it was carried seven times round the first hostile and polytheistic city they came to, its walls suddenly fell down, though assaulted by no hand, struck by no battering ram. Afterward, too, when they were now resident in the land of promise, and the ark had, in punishment of their sin, been taken by their enemies, its captors triumphantly placed it in the temple of their favorite god, and left it shut up there, but, on opening the temple next day, they found the image they used to pray to fallen to the ground and shamefully shattered. Then, being themselves alarmed by portents, and still more shamefully punished, they restored the ark of the testimony to the people from whom they had taken it. And what was the manner of its restoration? They placed it on a wagon, and yoked to it cows from which they had taken the calves, and let them choose their own course, expecting that in this way the divine will would be indicated; and the cows without any man driving or directing them, steadily pursued the way to the Hebrews, without regarding the lowing of their calves, and thus restored the ark to its worshipers. To God these and such like wonders are small, but they are mighty to terrify and give wholesome instruction to men. For if philosophers, and especially the Platonists, are with justice esteemed wiser than other men, as I have just been mentioning, because they taught that even these earthly and insignificant things are ruled by divine Providence, inferring this from the numberless beauties which are observable not only in the bodies of animals, but even in plants and grasses, how much more plainly do these things attest the presence of divinity which happen at the time predicted, and in which that religion is commended which forbids the offering of sacrifice to any celestial, terrestrial, or infernal being, and commands it to be offered to God only, who alone blesses us by His love for us, and by our love to Him, and who, by arranging the appointed times of those sacrifices, and by predicting that they were to pass into a better sacrifice by a better Priest, testified that He has no appetite for these sacrifices, but through them indicated others of more substantial blessing—and all this not that He Himself may be glorified by these honors, but that we may be stirred up to worship and cleave to Him, being inflamed by His love, which is our advantage rather than His?

18. AGAINST THOSE WHO DENY THAT THE BOOKS OF THE CHURCH ARE TO BE BELIEVED ABOUT THE MIRACLES WHEREBY THE PEOPLE OF GOD WERE EDUCATED

Will someone say that these miracles are false, that they never happened, and that the records of them are lies? Whoever says so, and asserts that in such matters no records whatever can be credited, may also say that there are no gods who care for human affairs. For they have induced men to worship them only by means of miraculous works, which the heathen histories testify, and by which the gods have made a display of their own power rather than done any real service. This is the reason why we have not undertaken in this work, of which we are now writing the tenth book, to refute those who either deny that there is any divine power, or contend that it does not interfere with human affairs, but those who prefer their own god to our God, the Founder of the holy and most glorious city, not knowing that He is also the invisible and unchangeable Founder of this visible and changing world, and the truest bestower of the blessed life which resides not in things created, but in Himself. For thus speaks His most trustworthy prophet: "It is good for me to be united to God."[1] Among philosophers it is a question, what is that end and good to the attainment of which all our duties are to have a relation? The psalmist did not say, "It is good for me to have great wealth, or to wear imperial insignia, purple, scepter, and diadem"; or, as some even of the philosophers have not blushed to say, "It is good for me to enjoy sensual pleasure"; or, as the better men among them seemed to say, "My good is my spiritual strength"; but, "It is good for me to be united to God." This he had learned from Him whom the holy angels, with the accompanying witness of miracles, presented as the sole object of worship. And hence he himself became the sacrifice of God, whose spiritual love inflamed him, and into whose ineffable and incorporeal embrace he yearned to cast himself. Moreover, if the worshipers of many gods (whatever kind of gods they fancy their own to be) believe that the miracles recorded in their civil histories, or in the books of magic, or of the more respectable theurgy, were worked by these gods, what reason have they for refusing to believe the miracles recorded in those writings, to which we owe a credence as much greater as He is greater to whom alone these writings teach us to sacrifice?

---

1. Ps. 73:28.

19. ON THE REASONABLENESS OF OFFERING, AS THE TRUE RELIGION TEACHES, A VISIBLE SACRIFICE TO THE ONE TRUE AND INVISIBLE GOD

As to those who think that these visible sacrifices are suitably offered to other gods, but that invisible sacrifices, the graces of purity of mind and holiness of will, should be offered, as greater and better, to the invisible God, Himself greater and better than all others, they must be oblivious that these visible sacrifices are signs of the invisible, as the words we utter are the signs of things. And therefore, as in prayer or praise we direct intelligible words to Him to whom in our heart we offer the very feelings we are expressing, so we are to understand that in sacrifice we offer visible sacrifice only to Him to whom in our heart we ought to present ourselves an invisible sacrifice. It is then that the angels, and all those superior powers who are mighty by their goodness and piety, regard us with pleasure, and rejoice with us and assist us to the utmost of their power. But if we offer such worship to them, they decline it; and when on any mission to men they become visible to the senses, they positively forbid it. Examples of this occur in Holy Writ. Some fancied they should, by adoration or sacrifice, pay the same honor to angels as is due to God, and were prevented from doing so by the angels themselves, and ordered to render it to Him to whom alone they know it to be due. And the holy angels have in this been imitated by holy men of God. For Paul and Barnabas, when they had worked a miracle of healing in Lycaonia, were thought to be gods, and the Lycaonians desired to sacrifice to them, and they humbly and piously declined this honor, and announced to them the God in whom they should believe. And those deceitful and proud spirits, who exact worship, do so simply because they know it to be due to the true God. For that which they take pleasure in is not, as Porphyry says and some fancy, the smell of the victims, but divine honors. They have, in fact, plenty odors on all hands, and if they wished more, they could provide them for themselves. But the spirits who arrogate to themselves divinity are delighted not with the smoke of carcasses but with the suppliant spirit which they deceive and hold in subjection, and hinder from drawing near to God, preventing him from offering himself in sacrifice to God by inducing him to sacrifice to others.

20. OF THE SUPREME AND TRUE SACRIFICE WHICH WAS EFFECTED BY THE MEDIATOR BETWEEN GOD AND MEN

And hence that true Mediator, insofar as, by assuming the form of a servant, He became the Mediator between God and men, the man Christ Jesus, though in the form of God He received sacrifice together with the Father, with whom He is one God, yet in the form of a servant He chose rather to be than to receive a sacrifice, that not even by this instance anyone might have occasion to suppose that sacrifice should be rendered to any creature. Thus He is both the Priest who offers and the Sacrifice offered. And He designed that there should be a daily sign of this in the sacrifice of the church, which, being His body, learns to offer herself through Him. Of this true Sacrifice the ancient sacrifices of the saints were the various and numerous signs; and it was thus variously figured, just as one thing is signified by a variety of words, that there may be less weariness when we speak of it much. To this supreme and true sacrifice all false sacrifices have given place.

21. OF THE POWER DELEGATED TO DEMONS FOR THE TRIAL AND GLORIFICATION OF THE SAINTS, WHO CONQUER NOT BY PROPITIATING THE SPIRITS OF THE AIR, BUT BY ABIDING IN GOD

The power delegated to the demons at certain appointed and well-adjusted seasons, that they may give expression to their hostility to the city of God by stirring up against it the men who are under their influence, and may not only receive sacrifice from those who willingly offer it, but may also extort it from the unwilling by violent persecution—this power is found to be not merely harmless, but even useful to the church, completing as it does the number of martyrs, whom the city of God esteems as all the more illustrious and honored citizens, because they have strived even to blood against the sin of impiety. If the ordinary language of the church allowed it, we might more elegantly call these men our heroes. For this name is said to be derived from Juno, who in Greek is called Hêrê, and hence, according to the Greek myths, one of her sons was called Heros. And these fables mystically signified that Juno was mistress of the air, which they suppose to be inhabited by the demons and the heroes, understanding by heroes the souls of the well-deserving dead. But for a quite opposite reason would we call our martyrs heroes—supposing, as I said, that the usage of ecclesiastical language would admit of it—not because they lived along with the demons in the air, but because they conquered these demons or powers of the air, and among them Juno herself, be she what she may, not unsuitably represented, as she commonly is by the poets, as hostile to virtue, and jealous of men of mark aspiring to the heavens. Virgil, however, unhappily gives way, and yields to her; for, though he represents her as saying, "I am conquered by Æneas,"[1] Helenus gives Æneas himself this religious advice:

> *Pay vows to Juno: overbear*
> *Her queenly soul with gift and prayer.*[2]

In conformity with this opinion, Porphyry—expressing, however, not so much his own views as other people's—says that a good god or Genius cannot come to a man unless the evil genius has been first of all propitiated, implying that the evil deities had greater power than the good; for, until they have been appeased and give place, the good can give no assistance; and if the evil deities oppose, the good can give no help; whereas the evil can do injury without the good being able to prevent them. This is not the way of the true and truly holy religion; not thus do our martyrs conquer Juno, that is to say, the powers of the air, who envy the virtues of the pious. Our heroes, if we could so call them, overcome Hêrê, not by suppliant gifts, but by divine virtues. As Scipio, who conquered Africa by his valor, is more suitably styled Africanus than if he had appeased his enemies by gifts, and so won their mercy.

---

1. Virgil *Æneid* 7.310.
2. Ibid., 3.438–439.

22. WHENCE THE SAINTS DERIVE POWER AGAINST DEMONS AND TRUE PURIFICATION OF HEART

It is by true piety that men of God cast out the hostile power of the air which opposes godliness; it is by exorcising it, not by propitiating it; and they overcome all the temptations of the adversary by praying, not to him, but to their own God against him. For the devil cannot conquer or subdue any but those who are in league with sin; and therefore he is conquered in the name of Him who assumed humanity, and that without sin, that Himself being both Priest and Sacrifice, He might bring about the remission of sins, that is to say, might bring it about through the Mediator between God and men, the man Christ Jesus, by whom we are reconciled to God, the cleansing from sin being accomplished. For men are separated from God only by sins, from which we are in this life cleansed not by our own virtue, but by the divine compassion; through His indulgence, not through our own power. For, whatever virtue we call our own is itself bestowed upon us by His goodness. And we might attribute too much to ourselves while in the flesh, unless we lived in the receipt of pardon until we laid it down. This is the reason why there has been vouchsafed to us, through the Mediator, this grace, that we who are polluted by sinful flesh should be cleansed by the likeness of sinful flesh. By this grace of God, wherein He has shown His great compassion toward us, we are both governed by faith in this life, and, after this life, are led onward to the fullest perfection by the vision of immutable truth.

23. OF THE PRINCIPLES WHICH, ACCORDING TO THE PLATONISTS, REGULATE THE PURIFICATION OF THE SOUL

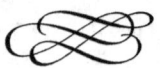

Even Porphyry asserts that it was revealed by divine oracles that we are not purified by any sacrifices[1] to sun or moon, meaning it to be inferred that we are not purified by sacrificing to any gods. For what mysteries can purify, if those of the sun and moon, which are esteemed the chief of the celestial gods, do not purify? He says, too, in the same place, that "principles" can purify, lest it should be supposed, from his saying that sacrificing to the sun and moon cannot purify, that sacrificing to some other of the host of gods might do so. And what he as a Platonist means by "principles," we know.[2] For he speaks of God the Father and God the Son, whom he calls (writing in Greek) the intellect or mind of the Father;[3] but of the Holy Spirit he says either nothing, or nothing plainly, for I do not understand what other he speaks of as holding the middle place between these two. For if, like Plotinus in his discussion regarding the three principal substances,[4] he wished us to understand by this third the soul of nature, he would certainly not have given it the middle place between these two, that is, between the Father and the Son. For Plotinus places the soul of nature after the intellect of the Father, while Porphyry, making it the mean, does not place it after, but between the others. No doubt he spoke according to his light, or as he thought expedient; but we assert that the Holy Spirit is the Spirit not of the Father only, nor of the Son only, but of both. For philosophers speak as they have a mind to, and in the most difficult matters do not scruple to offend religious ears; but we are bound to speak according to a certain rule, lest freedom of speech beget impiety of opinion about the matters themselves of which we speak.

---

1. Teletis.
2. The Platonists of the Alexandrian and Athenian schools, from Plotinus to Proclus, are at one in recognizing in God three principles or *hypostases:* (1) the One or the Good, which is the Father; (2) the Intelligence or Word, which is the Son; (3) the Soul, which is the universal principle of life. But as to the nature and order of these *hypostases,* the Alexandrians are no longer at one with the school of Athens. On the very subtle differences between the Trinity of Plotinus and that of Porphyry, consult M. Jules Simon 2.110 and M. Vacherot 2.37. —Saisset.
3. See below, 10.28.
4. Plotinus *Enn.* 5.1.

24. OF THE ONE ONLY TRUE PRINCIPLE WHICH ALONE PURIFIES AND RENEWS HUMAN NATURE

Accordingly, when we speak of God, we do not affirm two or three principles, no more than we are at liberty to affirm two or three gods; although, speaking of each, of the Father, or of the Son, or of the Holy Ghost, we confess that each is God: and yet we do not say, as the Sabellian heretics say, that the Father is the same as the Son, and the Holy Spirit the same as the Father and the Son; but we say that the Father is the Father of the Son, and the Son the Son of the Father, and that the Holy Spirit of the Father and the Son is neither the Father nor the Son. It was therefore truly said that man is cleansed only by a Principle, although the Platonists erred in speaking in the plural of *principles*. But Porphyry, being under the dominion of these envious powers, whose influence he was at once ashamed of and afraid to throw off, refused to recognize that Christ is the Principle by whose incarnation we are purified. Indeed he despised Him, because of the flesh itself which He assumed, that He might offer a sacrifice for our purification—a great mystery, unintelligible to Porphyry's pride, which that true and benignant Redeemer brought low by His humility, manifesting Himself to mortals by the mortality which He assumed, and which the malignant and deceitful mediators are proud of wanting, promising, as the boon of immortals, a deceptive assistance to wretched men. Thus the good and true Mediator showed that it is sin which is evil, and not the substance or nature of flesh; for this, together with the human soul, could without sin be both assumed and retained, and laid down in death, and changed to something better by resurrection. He showed also that death itself, although the punishment of sin, was submitted to by Him for our sakes without sin, and must not be evaded by sin on our part, but rather, if opportunity serves, be borne for righteousness' sake. For He was able to expiate sins by dying, because He both died, and not for sin of His own. But He has not been recognized by Porphyry as the Principle, otherwise he would have recognized Him as the Purifier. The Principle is neither the flesh nor the human soul in Christ but the Word by which all things were made. The flesh, therefore, does not by its own virtue purify, but by virtue of the Word by which it was assumed, when "the Word became flesh and dwelt among us."[1] For speaking mystically of eating His flesh, when those who did not understand Him were offended and went away, saying, "This is an hard saying, who can hear it?" He answered to the rest who remained, "It is the Spirit that quickeneth; the flesh profiteth nothing."[2] The Principle, therefore, having assumed a human soul and flesh, cleanses the soul and flesh of believers. Therefore, when the Jews asked Him who He was, He answered that He was the *Principle*.[3] And this we carnal and feeble men, liable to sin, and involved in the darkness of ignorance, could not possibly understand, unless we were cleansed and healed by Him, both by means of what we were, and of what we were not. For we were men, but we were not righteous; whereas in His incarnation there was a human nature, but it was righteous, and not sinful. This is the mediation whereby a hand is stretched to the lapsed and fallen; this is the seed "ordained by angels," by whose ministry the law also was given enjoining the worship of one God, and promising that this Mediator should come.

---

1. John 1:14.
2. John 6:60–64.
3. John 8:25; or "the beginning," following a different reading from ours.

25. THAT ALL THE SAINTS, BOTH UNDER THE LAW AND BEFORE IT, WERE JUSTIFIED BY FAITH IN THE MYSTERY OF CHRIST'S INCARNATION

It was by faith in this mystery, and godliness of life, that purification was attainable even by the saints of old, whether before the law was given to the Hebrews (for God and the angels were even then present as instructors), or in the periods under the law, although the promises of spiritual things, being presented in figure, seemed to be carnal, and hence the name of Old Testament. For it was then the prophets lived, by whom, as by angels, the same promise was announced; and among them was he whose grand and divine sentiment regarding the end and supreme good of man I have just now quoted, "It is good for me to cleave to God."[1] In this psalm the distinction between the Old and New Testaments is distinctly announced. For the psalmist says, that when he saw that the carnal and earthly promises were abundantly enjoyed by the ungodly, his feet were almost gone, his steps had well-nigh slipped; and that it seemed to him as if he had served God in vain, when he saw that those who despised God increased in that prosperity which he looked for at God's hand. He says, too, that, in investigating this matter with the desire of understanding why it was so, he had labored in vain, until he went into the sanctuary of God, and understood the end of those whom he had erroneously considered happy. Then he understood that they were cast down by that very thing, as he says, which they had made their boast, and that they had been consumed and perished for their iniquities; and that that whole fabric of temporal prosperity had become as a dream when one awakes, and suddenly finds himself destitute of all the joys he had imaged in sleep. And, as in this earth or earthy city they seemed to themselves to be great, he says, "O LORD, in Thy city Thou wilt reduce their image to nothing." He also shows how beneficial it had been for him to seek even earthly blessings only from the one true God, in whose power are all things, for he says, "As a beast was I before Thee, and I am always with Thee." "As a beast," he says, meaning that he was stupid. For I ought to have sought from Thee such things as the ungodly could not enjoy as well as I, and not those things which I saw them enjoying in abundance, and hence concluded I was serving Thee in vain, because they who declined to serve Thee had what I had not. Nevertheless, "I am always with Thee," because even in my desire for such things I did not pray to other gods. And consequently he goes on, "Thou hast holden me by my right hand, and by Thy counsel Thou hast guided me, and with glory hast taken me up"; as if all earthly advantages were left-hand blessings, though, when he saw them enjoyed by the wicked, his feet had almost gone. "For what," he says, "have I in heaven, and what have I desired from Thee upon earth?" He blames himself, and is justly displeased with himself; because, though he had in heaven so vast a possession (as he afterward understood), he yet sought from his God on earth a transitory and fleeting happiness—a happiness of mire, we may say. "My heart and my flesh," he says, "fail, O God of my heart." Happy failure, from things below to things above! And hence in another psalm He says, "My soul longeth, yea, even faileth, for the courts of the LORD."[2] Yet, though he had said of both his heart and his flesh that they were failing, he did not say, "O God of my heart and my flesh," but, "O God of my heart"; for by the heart the flesh is made clean. Therefore, says the Lord, "Cleanse that which is within, and the outside shall be clean also."[3] He then says that God Himself—not anything received from Him, but Himself—is his portion. "The God of my heart, and my portion forever." Among the various objects of human choice, God alone satisfied him. "For, lo," he says, "they that are far from Thee shall perish: Thou destroyest all them that go a-whoring from Thee"— that is, who prostitute themselves to many gods. And then follows the verse for which all the rest of the psalm seems to prepare: "It is good for me to cleave to God"—not to go far off; not to go a-whoring with a multitude of gods. And then shall this union with God be perfected, when all that is to be redeemed in us has been redeemed. But for the present we must, as he goes on to say, "place our hope in God." "For that which is seen," says the apostle, "is not hope. For what a man sees, why does he yet hope for? But if we hope for that we see not, then do we with patience wait for it."[4] Being, then, for the present established in this hope, let us do what the psalmist further indicates, and become in our measure angels or messengers of God, declaring His will, and praising His glory and His grace. For when he had said, "To place my hope in God," he goes on, "that I may declare all Thy praises in the gates of the daughter of Zion." This is the most glorious city of God; this is the city which knows and worships one God: she is celebrated by the holy angels, who invite us to their society, and desire us to become fellow citizens with them in this city; for they do not wish us to worship them as our gods, but to join them in worshiping their God and ours; nor to sacrifice to them, but, together with them, to become a sacrifice to God. Accordingly, whoever will lay aside malignant obstinacy, and consider these things, shall be assured that all these blessed and immortal spirits, who do not envy us (for if they envied they were not blessed), but rather love us, and desire us to be as blessed as themselves, look on us with greater pleasure, and give us greater assistance, when we join them in worshiping one God, Father, Son, and Holy Ghost, than if we were to offer to themselves sacrifice and worship.

1. Ps. 73:28.
2. Ps. 84:2.
3. Matt. 23:26.
4. Rom. 8:24–25.

26. OF PORPHYRY'S WEAKNESS IN WAVERING BETWEEN THE CONFESSION OF THE TRUE GOD AND THE WORSHIP OF DEMONS

I know not how it is so, but it seems to me that Porphyry blushed for his friends the theurgists; for he knew all that I have adduced, but did not frankly condemn polytheistic worship. He said, in fact, that there are some angels who visit earth, and reveal divine truth to theurgists, and others who publish on earth the things that belong to the Father, His height and depth. Can we believe, then, that the angels whose office it is to declare the will of the Father, wish us to be subject to any but Him whose will they declare? And hence, even this Platonist himself judiciously observes that we should rather imitate than invoke them. We ought not, then, to fear that we may offend these immortal and happy subjects of the one God by not sacrificing to them; for this they know to be due only to the one true God, in allegiance to whom they themselves find their blessedness, and therefore they will not have it given to them, either in figure or in the reality, which the mysteries of sacrifice symbolized. Such arrogance belongs to proud and wretched demons, whose disposition is diametrically opposite to the piety of those who are subject to God, and whose blessedness consists in attachment to Him. And, that we also may attain to this bliss, they aid us, as is fit, with sincere kindliness, and usurp over us no dominion, but declare to us Him under whose rule we are then fellow subjects. Why, then, O philosopher, do you still fear to speak freely against the powers which are inimical both to true virtue and to the gifts of the true God? Already you have discriminated between the angels who proclaim God's will, and those who visit theurgists, drawn down by I know not what art. Why do you still ascribe to these latter the honor of declaring divine truth? If they do not declare the will of the Father, what divine revelations can they make? Are not these the evil spirits who were bound over by the incantations of an envious man,[1] that they should not grant purity of soul to another, and could not, as you say, be set free from these bonds by a good man anxious for purity, and recover power over their own actions? Do you still doubt whether these are wicked demons; or do you, perhaps, feign ignorance, that you may not give offense to the theurgists, who have allured you by their secret rites, and have taught you, as a mighty boon, these insane and pernicious devilries? Do you dare to elevate above the air, and even to heaven, these envious powers, or pests, let me rather call them, less worthy of the name of sovereign than of slave, as you yourself own; and are you not ashamed to place them even among your sidereal gods, and so put a slight upon the stars themselves?

---

1. See above, 10.9.

27. OF THE IMPIETY OF PORPHYRY, WHICH IS WORSE THAN EVEN THE MISTAKE OF APULEIUS

How much more tolerable and accordant with human feeling is the error of your Platonist co-sectary Apuleius! for he attributed the diseases and storms of human passions only to the demons who occupy a grade beneath the moon, and makes even this avowal as by constraint regarding gods whom he honors; but the superior and celestial gods, who inhabit the ethereal regions, whether visible, as the sun, moon, and other luminaries, whose brilliancy makes them conspicuous, or invisible, but believed in by him, he does his utmost to remove beyond the slightest stain of these perturbations. It is not, then, from Plato, but from your Chaldæan teachers you have learned to elevate human vices to the ethereal and empyreal regions of the world and to the celestial firmament, in order that your theurgists might be able to obtain from your gods divine revelations; and yet you make yourself superior to these divine revelations by your intellectual life, which dispenses with these theurgic purifications as not needed by a philosopher. But, by way of rewarding your teachers, you recommend these arts to other men, who, not being philosophers, may be persuaded to use what you acknowledge to be useless to yourself, who are capable of higher things; so that those who cannot avail themselves of the virtue of philosophy, which is too arduous for the multitude, may, at your instigation, betake themselves to theurgists by whom they may be purified, not, indeed, in the intellectual, but in the spiritual part of the soul. Now, as the persons who are unfit for philosophy form incomparably the majority of mankind, more may be compelled to consult these secret and illicit teachers of yours than frequent the Platonic schools. For these most impure demons, pretending to be ethereal gods, whose herald and messenger you have become, have promised that those who are purified by theurgy in the spiritual part of their soul shall not indeed return to the Father, but shall dwell among the ethereal gods above the aerial regions. But such fancies are not listened to by the multitudes of men whom Christ came to set free from the tyranny of demons. For in Him they have the most gracious cleansing, in which mind, spirit, and body alike participate. For, in order that He might heal the whole man from the plague of sin, He took without sin the whole human nature. Would that you had known Him, and would that you had committed yourself for healing to Him rather than to your own frail and infirm human virtue, or to pernicious and curious arts! He would not have deceived you; for Him your own oracles, on your own showing, acknowledged holy and immortal. It is of Him, too, that the most famous poet speaks, poetically indeed, since he applies it to the person of another, yet truly, if you refer it to Christ, saying, "Under thine auspices, if any traces of our crimes remain, they shall be obliterated, and earth freed from its perpetual fear."[1] By which he indicates that, by reason of the infirmity which attaches to this life, the greatest progress in virtue and righteousness leaves room for the existence, if not of crimes, yet of the traces of crimes, which are obliterated only by that Saviour of whom this verse speaks. For that he did not say this at the prompting of his own fancy, Virgil tells us in almost the last verse of that fourth *Eclogue*, when he says, "The last age predicted by the Cumæan sibyl has now arrived"; whence it plainly appears that this had been dictated by the Cumæan sibyl. But those theurgists, or rather demons, who assume the appearance and form of gods, pollute rather than purify the human spirit by false appearances and the delusive mockery of unsubstantial forms. How can those whose own spirit is unclean cleanse the spirit of man? Were they not unclean, they would not be bound by the incantations of an envious man, and would neither be afraid nor grudge to bestow that hollow boon which they promise. But it is sufficient for our purpose that you acknowledge that the intellectual soul, that is, our mind, cannot be justified by theurgy; and that even the spiritual or inferior part of our soul cannot by this act be made eternal and immortal, though you maintain that it can be purified by it. Christ, however, promises life eternal; and therefore to Him the world flocks, greatly to your indignation, greatly also to your astonishment and confusion. What avails your forced avowal that theurgy leads men astray, and deceives vast numbers by its ignorant and foolish teaching, and that it is the most manifest mistake to have recourse by prayer and sacrifice to angels and principalities, when at the same time, to save yourself from the charge of spending labor in vain on such arts, you direct men to the theurgists, that by their means men, who do not live by the rule of the intellectual soul, may have their spiritual soul purified?

---

1. Virgil *Ecl.* 4.13–14.

28. HOW IT IS THAT PORPHYRY HAS BEEN SO BLIND AS NOT TO RECOGNIZE THE TRUE WISDOM—CHRIST

You drive men, therefore, into the most palpable error. And yet you are not ashamed of doing so much harm, though you call yourself a lover of virtue and wisdom. Had you been true and faithful in this profession, you would have recognized Christ, the virtue of God and the wisdom of God, and would not, in the pride of vain science, have revolted from His wholesome humility. Nevertheless you acknowledge that the spiritual part of the soul can be purified by the virtue of chastity without the aid of those theurgic arts and mysteries which you wasted your time in learning. You even say, sometimes, that these mysteries do not raise the soul after death, so that, after the termination of this life, they seem to be of no service even to the part you call spiritual; and yet you recur on every opportunity to these arts, for no other purpose, so far as I see, than to appear an accomplished theurgist, and gratify those who are curious in illicit arts, or else to inspire others with the same curiosity. But we give you all praise for saying that this art is to be feared, both on account of the legal enactments against it, and by reason of the danger involved in the very practice of it. And would that in this, at least, you were listened to by its wretched votaries, that they might be withdrawn from entire absorption in it, or might even be preserved from tampering with it at all! You say, indeed, that ignorance, and the numberless vices resulting from it, cannot be removed by any mysteries, but only by the πατρικὸς νοῦς, that is, the Father's mind or intellect conscious of the Father's will. But that Christ is this mind you do not believe; for Him you despise on account of the body He took of a woman and the shame of the cross; for your lofty wisdom spurns such low and contemptible things, and soars to more exalted regions. But He fulfills what the holy prophets truly predicted regarding Him: "I will destroy the wisdom of the wise, and bring to naught the prudence of the prudent."[1] For He does not destroy and bring to naught His own gift in them, but what they arrogate to themselves, and do not hold of Him. And hence the apostle, having quoted this testimony from the prophet, adds, "Where is the wise? Where is the scribe? Where is the disputer of this world? Hath not God made foolish the wisdom of this world? For after that, in the wisdom of God, the world by wisdom knew not God, it pleased God by the foolishness of preaching to save them that believe. For the Jews require a sign, and the Greeks seek after wisdom; but we preach Christ crucified, unto the Jews a stumbling block, and unto the Greeks foolishness; but unto them which are called, both Jews and Greeks, Christ the power of God, and the wisdom of God. Because the foolishness of God is wiser than men; and the weakness of God is stronger than men."[2] This is despised as a weak and foolish thing by those who are wise and strong in themselves; yet this is the grace which heals the weak, who do not proudly boast a blessedness of their own, but rather humbly acknowledge their real misery.

---

1. Isa. 29:14.
2. 1 Cor. 1:19–25.

29. OF THE INCARNATION OF OUR LORD JESUS CHRIST, WHICH THE PLATONISTS IN THEIR IMPIETY BLUSH TO ACKNOWLEDGE

You proclaim the Father and His Son, whom you call the Father's intellect or mind, and between these a third, by whom we suppose you mean the Holy Spirit, and in your own fashion you call these three Gods. In this, though your expressions are inaccurate, you do in some sort, and as through a veil, see what we should strive toward; but the incarnation of the unchangeable Son of God, whereby we are saved, and are enabled to reach the things we believe, or in part understand, this is what you refuse to recognize. You see in a fashion, although at a distance, although with filmy eye, the country in which we should abide; but the way to it you know not. Yet you believe in grace, for you say it is granted to few to reach God by virtue of intelligence. For you do not say, "Few have thought fit or have wished," but, "It has been granted to few"—distinctly acknowledging God's grace, not man's sufficiency. You also use this word more expressly, when, in accordance with the opinion of Plato, you make no doubt that in this life a man cannot by any means attain to perfect wisdom, but that whatever is lacking is in the future life made up to those who live intellectually, by God's providence and grace. Oh, had you but recognized the grace of God in Jesus Christ our Lord, and that very incarnation of His, wherein He assumed a human soul and body, you might have seemed the brightest example of grace![1] But what am I doing? I know it is useless to speak to a dead man—useless, at least, so far as regards you, but perhaps not in vain for those who esteem you highly, and love you on account of their love of wisdom or curiosity about those arts which you ought not to have learned; and these persons I address in your name. The grace of God could not have been more graciously commended to us than thus, that the only Son of God, remaining unchangeable in Himself, should assume humanity, and should give us the hope of His love, by means of the mediation of a human nature, through which we, from the condition of men, might come to Him who was so far off—the immortal from the mortal; the unchangeable from the changeable; the just from the unjust; the blessed from the wretched. And, as He had given us a natural instinct to desire blessedness and immortality, He Himself continuing to be blessed; but assuming mortality, by enduring what we fear, taught us to despise it, that what we long for He might bestow upon us.

But in order to your acquiescence in this truth, it is lowliness that is requisite, and to this it is extremely difficult to bend you. For what is there incredible, especially to men like you, accustomed to speculation, which might have predisposed you to believe in this—what is there incredible, I say, in the assertion that God assumed a human soul and body? You yourselves ascribe such excellence to the intellectual soul, which is, after all, the human soul, that you maintain that it can become consubstantial with that intelligence of the Father whom you believe in as the Son of God. What incredible thing is it, then, if some one soul be assumed by Him in an ineffable and unique manner for the salvation of many? Moreover, our nature itself testifies that a man is incomplete unless a body be united with the soul. This certainly would be more incredible, were it not of all things the most common; for we should more easily believe in a union between spirit and spirit, or, to use your own terminology, between the incorporeal and the incorporeal, even though the one were human, the other divine, the one changeable and the other unchangeable, than in a union between the corporeal and the incorporeal. But perhaps it is the unprecedented birth of a body from a virgin that staggers you? But, so far from this being a difficulty, it ought rather to assist you to receive our religion, that a miraculous person was born miraculously. Or, do you find a difficulty in the fact that, after His body had been given up to death, and had been changed into a higher kind of body by resurrection, and was now no longer mortal but incorruptible, He carried it up into heavenly places? Perhaps you refuse to believe this, because you remember that Porphyry, in these very books from which I have cited so much, and which treat of the return of the soul, so frequently teaches that a body of every kind is to be escaped from, in order that the soul may dwell in blessedness with God. But here, in place of following Porphyry, you ought rather to have corrected him, especially since you agree with him in believing such incredible things about the soul of this visible world and huge material frame. For, as scholars of Plato, you hold that the world is an animal, and a very happy animal, which you wish to be also everlasting. How, then, is it never to be loosed from a body, and yet never lose its happiness, if, in order to the happiness of the soul, the body must be left behind? The sun, too, and the other stars, you not only acknowledge to be bodies, in which you have the cordial assent of all seeing men, but also, in obedience to what you reckon a profounder insight, you declare that they are very blessed animals, and eternal, together with their bodies. Why is it, then, that when the Christian faith is pressed upon you, you forget, or pretend to ignore, what you habitually discuss or teach? Why is it that you refuse to be Christians, on the ground that you hold opinions which, in fact, you yourselves demolish? Is it not because Christ came in lowliness, and you are proud? The precise nature of the resurrection bodies of the saints may sometimes occasion discussion among those who are best read in the Christian Scriptures; yet there is not among us the smallest doubt that they shall be everlasting, and of a nature exemplified in the instance of Christ's risen body. But whatever be their nature, since we maintain that they shall be absolutely incorruptible and immortal, and shall offer no hindrance to the soul's contemplation, by which it is fixed in God, and as you say that among the celestials the bodies of the eternally blessed are eternal, why do you maintain that, in order to blessedness, every body must be escaped from? Why do you thus seek such a plausible reason for escaping from the Christian faith, if not because, as I again say, Christ is humble and you proud? Are you ashamed to be corrected? This is the vice of the proud. It is, forsooth, a degradation for learned men to pass from the school of Plato to the discipleship of Christ, who by His Spirit taught a fisherman to think and to say, "In the beginning was the Word, and the Word was with God, and the Word was God. The same was in the beginning with God. All things were made by Him; and without Him was not anything made that was made. In Him was life; and the life was the light of men. And the light shineth in darkness; and the darkness comprehended it not."[2] The old saint Simplicianus, afterward bishop of Milan, used to tell me that a certain Platonist was in the habit of saying that this opening passage of the holy gospel, titled "according to John," should be written in letters of gold, and hung up in all churches in the most conspicuous place. But the proud scorn to take God for their Master, because "the Word was made flesh and dwelt among us."[3] So that, with these miserable creatures, it is not enough that they are sick, but they boast of their sickness, and are ashamed of the medicine which could heal them. And, doing so, they secure not elevation, but a more disastrous fall.

---

1. According to another reading, "You might have seen it to be," etc.
2. John 1:1–5.
3. John 1:14.

30. PORPHYRY'S EMENDATIONS AND MODIFICATIONS OF PLATONISM

If it is considered unseemly to emend anything which Plato has touched, why did Porphyry himself make emendations, and these not a few —for it is very certain that Plato wrote that the souls of men return after death to the bodies of beasts?[1] Plotinus also, Porphyry's teacher, held this opinion;[2] yet Porphyry justly rejected it. He was of opinion that human souls return indeed into human bodies, but not into the bodies they had left, but other new bodies. He shrank from the other opinion, lest a woman who had returned into a mule might possibly carry her own son on her back. He did not shrink, however, from a theory which admitted the possibility of a mother coming back into a girl and marrying her own son. How much more honorable a creed is that which was taught by the holy and truthful angels, uttered by the prophets who were moved by God's Spirit, preached by Him who was foretold as the coming Saviour by His forerunning heralds, and by the apostles whom He sent forth, and who filled the whole world with the gospel—how much more honorable, I say, is the belief that souls return once for all to their own bodies, than that they return again and again to diverse bodies? Nevertheless Porphyry, as I have said, did considerably improve upon this opinion, insofar, at least, as he maintained that human souls could transmigrate only into human bodies, and made no scruple about demolishing the bestial prisons into which Plato had wished to cast them. He says, too, that God put the soul into the world that it might recognize the evils of matter, and return to the Father, and be forever emancipated from the polluting contact of matter. And although here is some inappropriate thinking (for the soul is rather given to the body that it may do good; for it would not learn evil unless it did it), yet he corrects the opinion of other Platonists, and that on a point of no small importance, inasmuch as he avows that the soul, which is purged from all evil and received to the Father's presence, shall never again suffer the ills of this life. By this opinion he quite subverted the favorite Platonic dogma, that as dead men are made out of living ones, so living men are made out of dead ones; and he exploded the idea which Virgil seems to have adopted from Plato, that the purified souls which have been sent into the Elysian fields (the poetic name for the joys of the blessed) are summoned to the river Lethe, that is, to the oblivion of the past,

> *That earthward they may pass once more,*
> *Remembering not the things before,*

> *And with a blind propension yearn
> To fleshly bodies to return.*[3]

This found no favor with Porphyry, and very justly; for it is indeed foolish to believe that souls should desire to return from that life, which cannot be very blessed unless by the assurance of its permanence, and to come back into this life, and to the pollution of corruptible bodies, as if the result of perfect purification were only to make defilement desirable. For if perfect purification effects the oblivion of all evils, and the oblivion of evils creates a desire for a body in which the soul may again be entangled with evils, then the supreme felicity will be the cause of infelicity, and the perfection of wisdom the cause of foolishness, and the purest cleansing the cause of defilement. And, however long the blessedness of the soul last, it cannot be founded on truth, if, in order to be blessed, it must be deceived. For it cannot be blessed unless it be free from fear. But, to be free from fear, it must be under the false impression that it shall be always blessed—the *false* impression, for it is destined to be also at some time miserable. How, then, shall the soul rejoice in truth, whose joy is founded on falsehood? Porphyry saw this, and therefore said that the purified soul returns to the Father, that it may never more be entangled in the polluting contact with evil. The opinion, therefore, of some Platonists, that there is a necessary revolution carrying souls away and bringing them round again to the same things, is false. But, were it true, what were the advantage of knowing it? Would the Platonists presume to allege their superiority to us, because we were in this life ignorant of what they themselves were doomed to be ignorant of when perfected in purity and wisdom in another and better life, and which they must be ignorant of if they are to be blessed? If it were most absurd and foolish to say so, then certainly we must prefer Porphyry's opinion to the idea of a circulation of souls through constantly alternating happiness and misery. And if this is just, here is a Platonist emending Plato, here is a man who saw what Plato did not see, and who did not shrink from correcting so illustrious a master, but preferred truth to Plato.

---

1. Cf. Eusebius *De Præp. Evang.* 13.16.
2. Plotinus *Enn.* 3.4.2.
3. Virgil *Æneid* 6.750–751.

31. AGAINST THE ARGUMENTS ON WHICH THE PLATONISTS GROUND THEIR ASSERTION THAT THE HUMAN SOUL IS CO-ETERNAL WITH GOD

Why, then, do we not rather believe the divinity in those matters, which human talent cannot fathom? Why do we not credit the assertion of divinity, that the soul is not co-eternal with God, but is created, and once was not? For the Platonists seemed to themselves to allege an adequate reason for their rejection of this doctrine, when they affirmed that nothing could be everlasting which had not always existed. Plato, however, in writing concerning the world and the gods in it, whom the Supreme made, most expressly states that they had a beginning and yet would have no end, but, by the sovereign will of the Creator, would endure eternally. But, by way of interpreting this, the Platonists have discovered that he meant a beginning, not of time, but of cause. "For as if a foot," they say, "had been always from eternity in dust, there would always have been a print underneath it; and yet no one would doubt that this print was made by the pressure of the foot, nor that, though the one was made by the other, neither was prior to the other; so," they say, "the world and the gods created in it have always been, their Creator always existing, and yet they were made." If, then, the soul has always existed, are we to say that its wretchedness has always existed? For if there is something in it which was not from eternity, but began in time, why is it impossible that the soul itself, though not previously existing, should begin to be in time? Its blessedness, too, which, as he owns, is to be more stable, and indeed endless, after the soul's experience of evils—this undoubtedly has a beginning in time, and yet is to be always, though previously it had no existence. This whole argumentation, therefore, to establish that nothing can be endless except that which has had no beginning, falls to the ground. For here we find the blessedness of the soul, which has a beginning, and yet has no end. And, therefore, let the incapacity of man give place to the authority of God; and let us take our belief regarding the true religion from the ever-blessed spirits, who do not seek for themselves that honor which they know to be due to their God and ours, and who do not command us to sacrifice save only to Him, whose sacrifice, as I have often said already, and must often say again, we and they ought together to be, offered through that Priest who offered Himself to death a sacrifice for us, in that human nature which He assumed, and according to which He desired to be our Priest.

32. OF THE UNIVERSAL WAY OF THE SOUL'S DELIVERANCE, WHICH PORPHYRY DID NOT FIND BECAUSE HE DID NOT RIGHTLY SEEK IT, AND WHICH THE GRACE OF CHRIST HAS ALONE THROWN OPEN

This is the religion which possesses the universal way for delivering the soul; for except by this way, none can be delivered. This is a kind of royal way, which alone leads to a kingdom which does not totter like all temporal dignities, but stands firm on eternal foundations. And when Porphyry says, toward the end of the first book *De Regressu Animæ*, that no system of doctrine which furnishes the universal way for delivering the soul has as yet been received, either from the truest philosophy, or from the ideas and practices of the Indians, or from the reasoning[1] of the Chaldæans, or from any source whatever, and that no historical reading had made him acquainted with that way, he manifestly acknowledges that there is such a way, but that as yet he was not acquainted with it. Nothing of all that he had so laboriously learned concerning the deliverance of the soul, nothing of all that he seemed to others, if not to himself, to know and believe, satisfied him. For he perceived that there was still wanting a commanding authority which it might be right to follow in a matter of such importance. And when he says that he had not learned from any truest philosophy a system which possessed the universal way of the soul's deliverance, he shows plainly enough, as it seems to me, either that the philosophy of which he was a disciple was not the truest, or that it did not comprehend such a way. And how can that be the truest philosophy which does not possess this way? For what else is the universal way of the soul's deliverance than that by which all souls universally are delivered, and without which, therefore, no soul is delivered? And when he says, in addition, "or from the ideas and practices of the Indians, or from the reasoning of the Chaldæans, or from any source whatever," he declares in the most unequivocal language that this universal way of the soul's deliverance was not embraced in what he had learned either from the Indians or the Chaldæans; and yet he could not forbear stating that it was from the Chaldæans he had derived these divine oracles of which he makes such frequent mention. What, therefore, does he mean by this universal way of the soul's deliverance, which had not yet been made known by any truest philosophy, or by the doctrinal systems of those nations which were considered to have great insight in things divine, because they indulged more freely in a curious and fanciful science and worship of angels? What is this universal way of which he acknowledges his ignorance, if not a way which does not belong to one nation as its special property, but is common to all, and divinely bestowed? Porphyry, a man of no mediocre abilities, does not question that such a way exists; for he believes that divine Providence could not have left men destitute of this universal way of delivering the soul. For he does not say that this way does not exist, but that this great boon and assistance has not yet been discovered, and has not come to his knowledge. And no wonder; for Porphyry lived in an age when this universal way of the soul's deliverance—in other words, the Christian religion—was exposed to the persecutions of idolaters and demon worshipers, and earthly rulers,[2] that the number of martyrs or witnesses for the truth might be completed and consecrated, and that by them proof might be given that we must endure all bodily sufferings in the cause of the holy faith, and for the commendation of the truth. Porphyry, being a witness of these persecutions, concluded that this way was destined to a speedy extinction, and that it, therefore, was not the universal way of the soul's deliverance, and did not see that the very thing that thus moved him, and deterred him from becoming a Christian, contributed to the confirmation and more effectual commendation of our religion.

This, then, is the universal way of the soul's deliverance, the way that is granted by the divine compassion to the nations universally. And no nation to which the knowledge of it has already come, or may hereafter come, ought to demand, "why so soon?" or, "why so late?"—for the design of Him who sends it is impenetrable by human capacity. This was felt by Porphyry when he confined himself to saying that this gift of God was not yet received, and had not yet come to his knowledge. For though this was so, he did not on that account pronounce that the way itself had no existence. This, I say, is the universal way for the deliverance of believers, concerning which the faithful Abraham received the divine assurance, "In thy seed shall all nations be blessed."[3] He, indeed, was by birth a Chaldæan; but, that he might receive these great promises, and that there might be propagated from him a seed "disposed by angels in the hand of a Mediator,"[4] in whom this universal way, thrown open to all nations for the deliverance of the soul, might be found, he was ordered to leave his country, and kindred, and father's house. Then was he himself, first of all, delivered from the Chaldæan superstitions, and by his obedience worshiped the one true God, whose promises he faithfully trusted. This is the universal way, of which it is said in holy prophecy, "God be merciful unto us, and bless us, and cause His face to shine upon us; that Thy way may be known upon earth, Thy saving health among all nations."[5] And hence, when our Saviour, so long after, had taken flesh of the seed of Abraham, He says of Himself, "I am the way, the truth, and the life."[6] This is the universal way, of which so long before it had been predicted, "And it shall come to pass in the last days, that the mountain of the LORD's house shall be established in the top of the mountains, and shall be exalted above the hills; and all nations shall flow unto it. And many people shall go and say, Come ye, and let us go up to the mountain of the LORD, to the house of the God of Jacob;

and He will teach us of His ways, and we will walk in His paths: for out of Zion shall go forth the law, and the word of the LORD from Jerusalem."[7] This way, therefore, is not the property of one, but of all nations. The law and the word of the Lord did not remain in Zion and Jerusalem, but issued thence to be universally diffused. And therefore the Mediator Himself, after His resurrection, says to His alarmed disciples, "These are the words which I spake unto you while I was yet with you, that all things must be fulfilled which were written in the law of Moses, and in the prophets, and in the Psalms, concerning me. Then opened He their understandings that they might understand the Scriptures, and said unto them, Thus it is written, and thus it behooved Christ to suffer, and to rise from the dead the third day: and that repentance and remission of sins should be preached in His name among all nations, beginning at Jerusalem."[8] This is the universal way of the soul's deliverance, which the holy angels and the holy prophets formerly disclosed where they could among the few men who found the grace of God, and especially in the Hebrew nation, whose commonwealth was, as it were, consecrated to prefigure and fore-announce the city of God which was to be gathered from all nations, by their tabernacle, and temple, and priesthood, and sacrifices. In some explicit statements, and in many obscure foreshadowings, this way was declared; but latterly came the Mediator Himself in the flesh, and His blessed apostles, revealing how the grace of the New Testament more openly explained what had been obscurely hinted to preceding generations, in conformity with the relation of the ages of the human race, and as it pleased God in His wisdom to appoint, who also bore them witness with signs and miracles, some of which I have cited above. For not only were there visions of angels, and words heard from those heavenly ministrants, but also men of God, armed with the word of simple piety, cast out unclean spirits from the bodies and senses of men, and healed deformities and sicknesses; the wild beasts of earth and sea, the birds of air, inanimate things, the elements, the stars, obeyed their divine commands; the powers of hell gave way before them, the dead were restored to life. I say nothing of the miracles peculiar and proper to the Saviour's own person, especially the nativity and the resurrection; in the one of which He worked only the mystery of a virgin maternity, while in the other He furnished an instance of the resurrection which all shall at last experience. This way purifies the whole man, and prepares the mortal in all his parts for immortality. For, to prevent us from seeking for one purgation for the part which Porphyry calls intellectual, and another for the part he calls spiritual, and another for the body itself, our most mighty and truthful Purifier and Saviour assumed the whole human nature. Except by this way, which has been present among men both during the period of the promises and of the proclamation of their fulfillment, no man has been delivered, no man is delivered, no man shall be delivered.

As to Porphyry's statement that the universal way of the soul's deliverance had not yet come to his knowledge by any acquaintance he had with history, I would ask, what more remarkable history can be found than that which has taken possession of the whole world by its authoritative voice? Or what more trustworthy than that which narrates past events, and predicts the future with equal clearness, and in the unfulfilled predictions of which we are constrained to believe by those that are already fulfilled? For neither Porphyry nor any Platonists can despise divination and prediction, even of things that pertain to this life and earthly matters, though they justly despise ordinary soothsaying and the divination that is connected with magical arts. They deny that these are the predictions of great men, or are to be considered important, and they are right; for they are founded, either on the foresight of subsidiary causes, as to a professional eye much of the course of a disease is foreseen by certain premonitory symptoms, or the unclean demons predict what they have resolved to do, that they may thus work upon the thoughts and desires of the wicked with an appearance of authority, and incline human frailty to imitate their impure actions. It is not such things that the saints who walk in the universal way care to predict as important, although, for the purpose of commending the faith, they knew and often predicted even such things as could not be detected by human observation, nor be readily verified by experience. But there were other truly important and divine events which they predicted, insofar as it was given them to know the will of God. For the incarnation of Christ, and all those important marvels that were accomplished in Him, and done in His name; the repentance of men and the conversion of their wills to God; the remission of sins, the grace of righteousness, the faith of the pious, and the multitudes in all parts of the world who believe in the true divinity; the overthrow of idolatry and demon worship, and the testing of the faithful by trials; the purification of those who persevered, and their deliverance from all evil; the day of judgment, the resurrection of the dead, the eternal damnation of the community of the ungodly, and the eternal kingdom of the most glorious city of God, ever blessed in the enjoyment of the vision of God—these things were predicted and promised in the Scriptures of this way; and of these we see so many fulfilled, that we justly and piously trust that the rest will also come to pass. As for those who do not believe, and consequently do not understand, that this is the way which leads straight to the vision of God and to eternal fellowship with Him, according to the true predictions and statements of the Holy Scriptures, they may storm at our position, but they cannot storm it.

And therefore, in these ten books, though not meeting, I dare say, the expectation of some, yet I have, as the true God and Lord has vouchsafed to aid me, satisfied the desire of certain persons, by refuting the objections of the ungodly, who prefer their own gods to the Founder of the holy city, about which we undertook to speak. Of these ten books, the first five were directed against those who think we should worship the gods for the sake of the blessings of this life, and the second five against those who think we should worship them for the sake of the life which is to be after death. And now, in fulfillment of the promise I made in the first book, I shall go on to say, as God shall aid me, what I think needs to be said regarding the origin, history, and deserved ends of the two cities, which, as already remarked, are in this world commingled and implicated with one another.

---

1. Inductio.
2. Namely, under Diocletian and Maximian.
3. Gen. 22:18.
4. Gal. 3:19.
5. Ps. 67:1–2.
6. John 14:6.
7. Isa. 2:2–3.
8. Luke 24:44–47.

BOOK ELEVEN

ARGUMENT

Here begins the second part[1] of this work, which treats of the origin, history, and destinies of the two cities, the earthly and the heavenly. In the first place, Augustine shows in this book how the two cities were formed originally, by the separation of the good and bad angels; and takes occasion to treat of the creation of the world, as it is described in Holy Scripture in the beginning of the book of Genesis.

---

1. Written in the year 416 or 417.

1. OF THIS PART OF THE WORK, WHEREIN WE BEGIN TO EXPLAIN THE ORIGIN AND END OF THE TWO CITIES

The city of God we speak of is the same to which testimony is borne by that Scripture, which excels all the writings of all nations by its divine authority, and has brought under its influence all kinds of minds, and this not by a casual intellectual movement, but obviously by an express providential arrangement. For there it is written, "Glorious things are spoken of thee, O city of God."[1] And in another psalm we read, "Great is the LORD, and greatly to be praised in the city of our God, in the mountain of His holiness, increasing the joy of the whole earth."[2] And, a little after, in the same psalm, "As we have heard, so have we seen in the city of the LORD of hosts, in the city of our God. God has established it forever." And in another, "There is a river the streams whereof shall make glad the city of our God, the holy place of the tabernacles of the Most High. God is in the midst of her, she shall not be moved."³ From these and similar testimonies, all of which it were tedious to cite, we have learned that there is a city of God, and its Founder has inspired us with a love which makes us covet its citizenship. To this Founder of the holy city the citizens of the earthly city prefer their own gods, not knowing that He is the God of gods, not of false, that is, of impious and proud gods, who, being deprived of His unchangeable and freely communicated light, and so reduced to a kind of poverty-stricken power, eagerly grasp at their own private privileges, and seek divine honors from their deluded subjects; but of the pious and holy gods, who are better pleased to submit themselves to one, than to subject many to themselves, and who would rather worship God than be worshiped as God. But to the enemies of this city we have replied in the ten preceding books, according to our ability and the help afforded by our Lord and King. Now, recognizing what is expected of me, and not unmindful of my promise, and relying, too, on the same succor, I will endeavor to treat of the origin, and progress, and deserved destinies of the two cities (the earthly and the heavenly, to wit), which, as we said, are in this present world commingled and, as it were, entangled together. And, first, I will explain how the foundations of these two cities were originally laid, in the difference that arose among the angels.

---

1. Ps. 87:3.

2. Ps. 48:1.
3. Ps. 46:4.

2. OF THE KNOWLEDGE OF GOD, TO WHICH NO MAN CAN ATTAIN SAVE THROUGH THE MEDIATOR BETWEEN GOD AND MEN, THE MAN CHRIST JESUS

It is a great and very rare thing for a man, after he has contemplated the whole creation, corporeal and incorporeal, and has discerned its mutability, to pass beyond it, and, by the continued soaring of his mind, to attain to the unchangeable substance of God, and, in that height of contemplation, to learn from God Himself that none but He has made all that is not of the divine essence. For God speaks with a man not by means of some audible creature dinning in his ears, so that atmospheric vibrations connect Him that makes with him that hears the sound, nor even by means of a spiritual being with the semblance of a body, such as we see in dreams or similar states; for even in this case He speaks as if to the ears of the body, because it is by means of the semblance of a body He speaks, and with the appearance of a real interval of space —for visions are exact representations of bodily objects. Not by these, then, does God speak, but by the truth itself, if anyone is prepared to hear with the mind rather than with the body. For He speaks to that part of man which is better than all else that is in him, and than which God Himself alone is better. For since man is most properly understood (or, if that cannot be, then, at least, *believed*) to be made in God's image, no doubt it is that part of him by which he rises above those lower parts he has in common with the beasts, which brings him nearer to the Supreme. But since the mind itself, though naturally capable of reason and intelligence, is disabled by besotting and inveterate vices not merely from delighting and abiding in, but even from tolerating His unchangeable light, until it has been gradually healed, and renewed, and made capable of such felicity, it had, in the first place, to be impregnated with faith, and so purified. And that in this faith it might advance the more confidently toward the truth, the truth itself, God, God's Son, assuming humanity without destroying His divinity,[1] established and founded this faith, that there might be a way for man to man's God through a God-man. For this is the Mediator between God and men, the man Christ Jesus. For it is as man that He is the Mediator and the Way. Since, if the way lies between him who goes, and the place whither he goes, there is hope of his reaching it; but if there be no way, or if he know not where it is, what boots [avails] it to know whither he should go? Now the only way that is infallibly secured against all mistakes is when the very same person is at once God and man, God our end, man our way.[2]

1. Homine assumto, non Deo consumto.
2. Quo itur Deus, qua itur homo.

3. OF THE AUTHORITY OF THE CANONICAL SCRIPTURES COMPOSED BY THE DIVINE SPIRIT

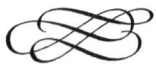

This Mediator, having spoken what He judged sufficient first by the prophets, then by His own lips, and afterward by the apostles, has besides produced the Scripture which is called canonical, which has paramount authority, and to which we yield assent in all matters of which we ought not to be ignorant, and yet cannot know of ourselves. For if we attain the knowledge of present objects by the testimony of our own senses,[1] whether internal or external, then, regarding objects remote from our own senses, we need others to bring their testimony, since we cannot know them by our own, and we credit the persons to whom the objects have been or are sensibly present. Accordingly, as in the case of visible objects which we have not seen, we trust those who have (and likewise with all sensible objects), so in the case of things which are perceived[2] by the mind and spirit, that is, which are remote from our own interior sense, it behooves us to trust those who have seen them set in that incorporeal light, or abidingly contemplate them.

---

1. A clause is here inserted to give the etymology of *præsentia* from *præ sensibus*.
2. Another derivation, *sententia* from *sensus*, the inward perception of the mind.

4. THAT THE WORLD IS NEITHER WITHOUT BEGINNING, NOR YET CREATED BY A NEW DECREE OF GOD, BY WHICH HE AFTERWARD WILLED WHAT HE HAD NOT BEFORE WILLED

Of all visible things, the world is the greatest; of all invisible, the greatest is God. But, that the world is, we see; that God is, we believe. That God made the world, we can believe from no one more safely than from God Himself. But where have we heard Him? Nowhere more distinctly than in the Holy Scriptures, where His prophet said, "In the beginning God created the heavens and the earth."[1] Was the prophet present when God made the heavens and the earth? No; but the wisdom of God, by whom all things were made, was there,[2] and wisdom insinuates itself into holy souls, and makes them the friends of God and His prophets, and noiselessly informs them of His works. They are taught also by the angels of God, who always behold the face of the Father,[3] and announce His will to whom it befits. Of these prophets was he who said and wrote, "In the beginning God created the heavens and the earth." And so fit a witness was he of God, that the same Spirit of God, who revealed these things to him, enabled him also so long before to predict that our faith also would be forthcoming.

But why did God choose then to create the heavens and earth which up to that time He had not made?[4] If they who put this question wish to make out that the world is eternal and without beginning, and that consequently it has not been made by God, they are strangely deceived, and rave in the incurable madness of impiety. For, though the voices of the prophets were silent, the world itself, by its well-ordered changes and movements, and by the fair appearance of all visible things, bears a testimony of its own, both that it has been created, and also that it could not have been created save by God, whose greatness and beauty are unutterable and invisible. As for those[5] who own, indeed, that it was made by God, and yet ascribe to it not a temporal but only a creational beginning, so that in some scarcely intelligible way the world should always have existed a created world, they make an assertion which seems to them to defend God from the charge of arbitrary hastiness, or of suddenly conceiving the idea of creating the world as a quite new idea, or of casually changing His will, though He be unchangeable. But I do not see how this supposition of theirs can stand in other respects, and chiefly in respect of the soul; for if they contend that it is coeternal with God, they will be quite at a loss to explain whence there has accrued to it new misery, which through a previous eternity had not existed. For if they said that its happiness and misery ceaselessly alternate, they must say, further, that this alternation will continue forever; whence will result this absurdity, that, though the soul is called blessed, it is not so in this, that it foresees its own misery and disgrace. And yet, if it does not foresee it, and supposes that it will be neither disgraced nor wretched, but always blessed, then it is blessed because it is deceived; and a more foolish statement one cannot make. But if their idea is that the soul's misery has alternated with its bliss during the ages of the past eternity, but that now, when once the soul has been set free, it will return henceforth no more to misery, they are nevertheless of opinion that it has never been truly blessed before, but begins at last to enjoy a new and uncertain happiness; that is to say, they must acknowledge that some new thing, and that an important and signal thing, happens to the soul which never in a whole past eternity happened it before. And if they deny that God's eternal purpose included this new experience of the soul, they deny that He is the Author of its blessedness, which is unspeakable impiety. If, on the other hand, they say that the future blessedness of the soul is the result of a new decree of God, how will they show that God is not chargeable with that mutability which displeases them? Further, if they acknowledge that it was created in time, but will never perish in time—that it has, like number,[6] a beginning but no end—and that, therefore, having once made trial of misery, and been delivered from it, it will never again return thereto, they will certainly admit that this takes place without any violation of the immutable counsel of God. Let them, then, in like manner believe regarding the world that it too could be made in time, and yet that God, in making it, did not alter His eternal design.

---

1. Gen. 1:1.
2. Prov. 8:27.
3. Matt. 18:10.
4. A common question among the Epicureans; urged by Velleius in Cicero *De Nat. Deor.* 1.9; adopted by the Manichæans and spoken to by Augustine in the *Confessions* 11.10, 12, also in *De Gen. contra Man.* 1.3.
5. The Neoplatonists.
6. Number begins at one, but runs on infinitely.

5. THAT WE OUGHT NOT TO SEEK TO COMPREHEND THE INFINITE AGES OF TIME BEFORE THE WORLD, NOR THE INFINITE REALMS OF SPACE

Next, we must see what reply can be made to those who agree that God is the Creator of the world, but have difficulties about the time of its creation, and what reply, also, they can make to difficulties we might raise about the place of its creation. For, as they demand why the world was created then and no sooner, we may ask why it was created just here where it is, and not elsewhere. For if they imagine infinite spaces of time before the world, during which God could not have been idle, in like manner they may conceive outside the world infinite realms of space, in which, if anyone says that the Omnipotent cannot hold His hand from working, will it not follow that they must adopt Epicurus's dream of innumerable worlds?—with this difference only, that he asserts that they are formed and destroyed by the fortuitous movements of atoms, while they will hold that they are made by God's hand, if they maintain that, throughout the boundless immensity of space, stretching interminably in every direction round the world, God cannot rest, and that the worlds which they suppose Him to make cannot be destroyed. For here the question is with those who, with ourselves, believe that God is spiritual, and the Creator of all existences but Himself. As for others, it is a condescension to dispute with them on a religious question, for they have acquired a reputation only among men who pay divine honors to a number of gods, and have become conspicuous among the other philosophers for no other reason than that, though they are still far from the truth, they are near it in comparison with the rest. While these, then, neither confine in any place, nor limit, nor distribute the divine substance, but, as is worthy of God, own it to be wholly though spiritually present everywhere, will they perchance say that this substance is absent from such immense spaces outside the world, and is occupied in one only (and that a very little one compared with the infinity beyond), the one, namely, in which is the world? I think they will not proceed to this absurdity. Since they maintain that there is but one world, of vast material bulk, indeed, yet finite, and in its own determinate position, and that this was made by the working of God, let them give the same account of God's resting in the infinite times before the world as they give of His resting in the infinite spaces outside of it. And as it does not follow that God set the world in the very spot it occupies and no other by accident rather than by divine reason, although no human reason can comprehend why it was so set, and though there was no merit in the spot chosen to give it the precedence of infinite others, so neither does it follow that we should suppose that God was guided by chance when He created the world in that and no earlier time, although previous times had been running by during an infinite past, and though there was no difference by which one time could be chosen in preference to another. But if they say that the thoughts of men are idle when they conceive infinite places, since there is no place beside the world, we reply that, by the same showing, it is vain to conceive of the past times of God's rest, since there is no time before the world.

6. THAT THE WORLD AND TIME HAD BOTH ONE BEGINNING, AND THE ONE DID NOT ANTICIPATE THE OTHER

For if eternity and time are rightly distinguished by this, that time does not exist without some movement and transition, while in eternity there is no change, who does not see that there could have been no time had not some creature been made, which by some motion could give birth to change—the various parts of which motion and change, as they cannot be simultaneous, succeed one another—and thus, in these shorter or longer intervals of duration, time would begin? Since then, God, in whose eternity is no change at all, is the Creator and Ordainer of time, I do not see how He can be said to have created the world after spaces of time had elapsed, unless it be said that prior to the world there was some creature by whose movement time could pass. And if the sacred and infallible Scriptures say that in the beginning God created the heavens and the earth, in order that it may be understood that He had made nothing previously—for if He had made anything before the rest, this thing would rather be said to have been made "in the beginning"—then assuredly the world was made, not in time, but simultaneously with time. For that which is made in time is made both after and before some time—after that which is past, before that which is future. But none could then be past, for there was no creature by whose movements its duration could be measured. But simultaneously with time the world was made, if in the world's creation change and motion were created, as seems evident from the order of the first six or seven days. For in these days the morning and evening are counted, until, on the sixth day, all things which God then made were finished, and on the seventh the rest of God was mysteriously and sublimely signalized. What kind of days these were it is extremely difficult, or perhaps impossible for us to conceive, and how much more to say!

7. OF THE NATURE OF THE FIRST DAYS, WHICH ARE SAID TO HAVE HAD MORNING AND EVENING, BEFORE THERE WAS A SUN

We see, indeed, that our ordinary days have no evening but by the setting, and no morning but by the rising, of the sun; but the first three days of all were passed without sun, since it is reported to have been made on the fourth day. And first of all, indeed, light was made by the word of God, and God, we read, separated it from the darkness, and called the light Day, and the darkness Night; but what kind of light that was, and by what periodic movement it made evening and morning, is beyond the reach of our senses; neither can we understand how it was, and yet must unhesitatingly believe it. For either it was some material light, whether proceeding from the upper parts of the world, far removed from our sight, or from the spot where the sun was afterward kindled; or under the name of light the holy city was signified, composed of holy angels and blessed spirits, the city of which the apostle says, "Jerusalem which is above is our eternal mother in heaven";[1] and in another place, "For ye are all the children of the light, and the children of the day; we are not of the night, nor of darkness."[2] Yet in some respects we may appropriately speak of a morning and evening of this day also. For the knowledge of the creature is, in comparison of the knowledge of the Creator, but a twilight; and so it dawns and breaks into morning when the creature is drawn to the praise and love of the Creator; and night never falls when the Creator is not forsaken through love of the creature. In fine, Scripture, when it would recount those days in order, never mentions the word "night." It never says, "Night was," but, "The evening and the morning were the first day." So of the second and the rest. And, indeed, the knowledge of created things contemplated by themselves is, so to speak, more colorless than when they are seen in the wisdom of God, as in the art by which they were made. Therefore evening is a more suitable figure than night; and yet, as I said, morning returns when the creature returns to the praise and love of the Creator. When it does so in the knowledge of itself, that is the first day; when in the knowledge of the firmament, which is the name given to the sky between the waters above and those beneath, that is the second day; when in the knowledge of the earth, and the sea, and all things that grow out of the earth, that is the third day; when in the knowledge of the greater and less luminaries, and all the stars, that is the fourth day; when in the knowledge of all animals that swim in the waters and that fly in the air, that is the fifth day; when in the knowledge of all animals that live on the earth, and of man himself, that is the sixth day.[3]

---

1. Gal. 4:26.
2. 1 Thess. 5:5.
3. *Cf. De Gen. ad Litt. 1 and 4.*

8. WHAT WE ARE TO UNDERSTAND OF GOD'S RESTING ON THE SEVENTH DAY, AFTER THE SIX DAYS' WORK

When it is said that God rested on the seventh day from all His works, and hallowed it, we are not to conceive of this in a childish fashion, as if work were a toil to God, who "spake and it was done"—spoke by the spiritual and eternal, not audible and transitory word. But God's rest signifies the rest of those who rest in God, as the joy of a house means the joy of those in the house who rejoice, though not the house, but something else, causes the joy. How much more intelligible is such phraseology, then, if the house itself, by its own beauty, makes the inhabitants joyful! For in this case we not only call it joyful by that figure of speech in which the thing containing is used for the thing contained (as when we say, "The theatres applaud," "The meadows low," meaning that the men in the one applaud, and the oxen in the other low), but also by that figure in which the cause is spoken of as if it were the effect, as when a letter is said to be joyful, because it makes its readers so. Most appropriately, therefore, the sacred narrative states that God rested, meaning thereby that those rest who are in Him, and whom He makes to rest. And this the prophetic narrative promises also to the men to whom it speaks, and for whom it was written, that they themselves, after those good works which God does in and by them, if they have managed by faith to get near to God in this life, shall enjoy in Him eternal rest. This was prefigured to the ancient people of God by the rest enjoined in their Sabbath law, of which, in its own place, I shall speak more at large.

9. WHAT THE SCRIPTURES TEACH US TO BELIEVE CONCERNING THE CREATION OF THE ANGELS

At present, since I have undertaken to treat of the origin of the holy city, and first of the holy angels, who constitute a large part of this city, and indeed the more blessed part, since they have never been expatriated, I will give myself to the task of explaining, by God's help, and as far as seems suitable, the Scriptures which relate to this point. Where Scripture speaks of the world's creation, it is not plainly said whether or when the angels were created; but if mention of them is made, it is implicitly under the name of "heaven," when it is said, "In the beginning God created the heavens and the earth," or perhaps rather under the name of "light," of which presently. But that they were wholly omitted, I am unable to believe, because it is written that God on the seventh day rested from all His works which He made; and this very book itself begins, "In the beginning God created the heavens and the earth," so that before heaven and earth God seems to have made nothing. Since, therefore, He began with the heavens and the earth—and the earth itself, as Scripture adds, was at first invisible and formless, light not being as yet made, and darkness covering the face of the deep (that is to say, covering an undefined chaos of earth and sea, for where light is not, darkness must needs be)—and then when all things, which are recorded to have been completed in six days, were created and arranged, how should the angels be omitted, as if they were not among the works of God, from which on the seventh day He rested? Yet, though the fact that the angels are the work of God is not omitted here, it is indeed not explicitly mentioned; but elsewhere Holy Scripture asserts it in the clearest manner. For in the Hymn of the Three Children in the Furnace it was said, "O all ye works of the Lord, bless ye the Lord";[1] and among these works mentioned afterward in detail, the angels are named. And in the psalm it is said, "Praise ye the LORD from the heavens, praise Him in the heights. Praise ye Him, all His angels; praise ye Him, all His hosts. Praise ye Him, sun and moon; praise Him, all ye stars of light. Praise Him, ye heaven of heavens; and ye waters that be above the heavens. Let them praise the name of the LORD; for He commanded, and they were created."[2] Here the angels are most expressly and by divine authority said to have been made by God, for of them among the other heavenly things it is said, "He commanded, and they were created." Who, then, will be bold enough to suggest that the angels were made after the six days' creation? If anyone is so foolish, his folly is disposed of by a Scripture of like authority, where God says, "When the stars were made, the angels praised me with a loud voice."[3] The angels therefore existed before the stars; and the stars were made the fourth day. Shall we then say that they were made the third day? Far from it; for we know what was made that day. The earth was separated from the water, and each element took its own distinct form, and the earth produced all that grows on it. On the second day, then? Not even on this; for on it the firmament was made between the waters above and beneath, and was called "Heaven," in which firmament the stars were made on the fourth day. There is no question, then, that if the angels are included in the works of God during these six days, they are that light which was called "Day," and whose unity Scripture signalizes by calling that day not the "first day," but "one day."[4] For the second day, the third, and the rest are not other days; but the same "one" day is repeated to complete the number six or seven, so that there should be knowledge both of God's works and of His rest. For when God said, "Let there be light, and there was light," if we are justified in understanding in this light the creation of the angels, then certainly they were created partakers of the eternal light which is the unchangeable wisdom of God, by which all things were made, and whom we call the only begotten Son of God; so that they, being illumined by the Light that created them, might themselves become light and be called "Day," in participation of that unchangeable Light and Day which is the Word of

God, by whom both themselves and all else were made. "The true Light, which lighteth every man that cometh into the world"[5]—this Light lights also every pure angel, that he may be light not in himself, but in God; from whom if an angel turn away, he becomes impure, as are all those who are called unclean spirits, and are no longer light in the Lord, but darkness in themselves, being deprived of the participation of Light eternal. For evil has no positive nature; but the loss of good has received the name "evil."[6]

---

1. Verse 35.
2. Ps. 148:1–5.
3. Job 38:7.
4. Vives here notes that the Greek theologians and Jerome held, with Plato, that spiritual creatures were made first, and used by God in the creation of things material. The Latin theologians and Basil held that God made all things at once.
5. John 1:9.
6. Mali enim nulla natura est: sed amissio boni, mali nomen accepit.

10. OF THE SIMPLE AND UNCHANGEABLE TRINITY, FATHER, SON, AND HOLY GHOST, ONE GOD, IN WHOM SUBSTANCE AND QUALITY ARE IDENTICAL

There is, accordingly, a good which is alone simple, and therefore alone unchangeable, and this is God. By this Good have all others been created, but not simple, and therefore not unchangeable. "Created," I say—that is, made, not begotten. For that which is begotten of the simple Good is simple as itself, and the same as itself. These two we call the Father and the Son; and both together with the Holy Spirit are one God; and to this Spirit the epithet Holy is in Scripture, as it were, appropriated. And He is another than the Father and the Son, for He is neither the Father nor the Son. I say "another," not "another thing," because He is equally with them the simple Good, unchangeable and coeternal. And this Trinity is one God; and nonetheless simple because a Trinity. For we do not say that the nature of the good is simple, because the Father alone possesses it, or the Son alone, or the Holy Ghost alone; nor do we say, with the Sabellian heretics, that it is only nominally a Trinity, and has no real distinction of persons; but we say it is simple, because it is what it has, with the exception of the relation of the persons to one another. For, in regard to this relation, it is true that the Father has a Son, and yet is not Himself the Son; and the Son has a Father, and is not Himself the Father. But, as regards Himself, irrespective of relation to the other, each is what He has; thus, He is in Himself living, for He has life, and is Himself the Life which He has.

It is for this reason, then, that the nature of the Trinity is called simple, because it has not anything which it can lose, and because it is not one thing and its contents another, as a cup and the liquor, or a body and its color, or the air and the light or heat of it, or a mind and its wisdom. For none of these is what it has: the cup is not liquor, nor the body color, nor the air light and heat, nor the mind wisdom. And hence they can be deprived of what they have, and can be turned or changed into other qualities and states, so that the cup may be emptied of the liquid of which it is full, the body be discolored, the air darken, the mind grow silly. The incorruptible body which is promised to the saints in the resurrection cannot, indeed, lose its quality of incorruption, but the bodily substance and the quality of incorruption are not the same thing. For the quality of incorruption resides entire in each several part, not greater in one and less in another; for no part is more incorruptible than another. The body, indeed, is itself greater in whole than in part; and one part of it is larger, another smaller, yet is not the larger more incorruptible than the smaller? The body, then, which is not in each of its parts a whole body, is one thing; incorruptibility, which is throughout complete, is another thing—for every part of the incorruptible body, however unequal to the rest otherwise, is equally incorrupt. For the hand, that is, is not more incorrupt than the finger because it is larger than the finger; so, though finger and hand are unequal, their incorruptibility is equal. Thus, although incorruptibility is inseparable from an incorruptible body, yet the substance of the body is one thing, the quality of incorruption another. And therefore the body is not what it has. The soul itself, too, though it be always wise (as it will be eternally when it is redeemed), will be so by participating in the unchangeable wisdom, which it is not; for though the air be never robbed of the light that is shed abroad in it, it is not on that account the same thing as the light. I do not mean that the soul is air, as has been supposed by some who could not conceive a spiritual nature;[1] but, with much dissimilarity, the two things have a kind of likeness, which makes it suitable to say that the immaterial soul is illumined with the immaterial light of the simple wisdom of God, as the material air is irradiated with material light, and that, as the air, when deprived of this light, grows dark (for material darkness is nothing else than air wanting light[2]), so the soul, deprived of the light of wisdom, grows dark.

According to this, then, those things which are essentially and truly divine are called simple, because in them quality and substance are identical, and because they are divine, or wise, or blessed in themselves, and without extraneous supplement. In Holy Scripture, it is true, the Spirit of wisdom is called "manifold"[3] because it contains many things in it; but what it contains it also is, and it being one is all these things. For neither are there many wisdoms, but one, in which are untold and infinite treasures of things intellectual, wherein are all invisible and unchangeable reasons of things visible and changeable which were created by it.[4] For God made nothing unwittingly; not even a human workman can be said to do so. But if He knew all that He made, He made only those things which He had known. Whence flows a very striking but true conclusion, that this world could not be known to us unless it existed, but could not have existed unless it had been known to God.

---

1. Plutarch (*De Plac. Phil.* 1.3 and 4.3) tells us that this opinion was held by Anaximenes of Miletus, the followers of Anaxagoras, and many of the Stoics. Diogenes the Cynic, as well as Diogenes of Apollonia, seems to have adopted the same opinion. See Zeller's *Stoics*, pp. 121 and 199.
2. "*Ubi lux non est, tenebræ sunt, non quia aliquid sunt tenebræ, sed ipsa lucis absentia tenebræ dicuntur.*"—Augustine *De Gen. contra Man.* 7.
3. Wisd. of Sol. 7:22.
4. The strongly Platonic tinge of this language is perhaps best preserved in a bare literal translation.

11. WHETHER THE ANGELS THAT FELL PARTOOK OF THE BLESSEDNESS WHICH THE HOLY ANGELS HAVE ALWAYS ENJOYED FROM THE TIME OF THEIR CREATION

And since these things are so, those spirits whom we call angels were never at any time or in any way darkness, but, as soon as they were made, were made light; yet they were not so created in order that they might exist and live in any way whatever, but were enlightened that they might live wisely and blessedly. Some of them, having turned away from this light, have not won this wise and blessed life, which is certainly eternal, and accompanied with the sure confidence of its eternity; but they have still the life of reason, though darkened with folly, and this they cannot lose even if they would. But who can determine to what extent they were partakers of that wisdom before they fell? And how shall we say that they participated in it equally with those who through it are truly and fully blessed, resting in a true certainty of eternal felicity? For if they had equally participated in this true knowledge, then the evil angels would have remained eternally blessed equally with the good, because they were equally expectant of it. For, though a life be never so long, it cannot be truly called eternal if it is destined to have an end; for it is called life inasmuch as it is lived, but eternal because it has no end. Wherefore, although everything eternal is not therefore blessed (for hellfire is eternal), yet if no life can be truly and perfectly blessed except it be eternal, the life of these angels was not blessed, for it was doomed to end, and therefore not eternal, whether they knew it or not. In the one case fear, in the other ignorance, prevented them from being blessed. And even if their ignorance was not so great as to breed in them a wholly false expectation, but left them wavering in uncertainty whether their good would be eternal or would some time terminate, this very doubt concerning so grand a destiny was incompatible with the plenitude of blessedness which we believe the holy angels enjoyed. For we do not so narrow and restrict the application of the term "blessedness" as to apply it to God only,[1] though doubtless He is so truly blessed that greater blessedness cannot be; and, in comparison of His blessedness, what is that of the angels, though, according to their capacity, they be perfectly blessed?

---

1. Vives remarks that the ancients defined blessedness as an absolutely perfect state in all good, peculiar to God. Perhaps Augustine had a reminiscence of the remarkable discussion in the *Tusc. Disp.* 5, and the definition, "*Neque ulla alia huic verbo, quum beatum dicimus, subjecta notio est, nisi, secretis malis omnibus, cumulata bonorum complexio.*"

12. A COMPARISON OF THE BLESSEDNESS OF THE RIGHTEOUS, WHO HAVE NOT YET RECEIVED THE DIVINE REWARD, WITH THAT OF OUR FIRST PARENTS IN PARADISE

And the angels are not the only members of the rational and intellectual creation whom we call blessed. For who will take upon him to deny that those first men in Paradise were blessed previously to sin, although they were uncertain how long their blessedness was to last, and whether it would be eternal (and eternal it would have been had they not sinned)—who, I say, will do so, seeing that even now we not unbecomingly call those blessed whom we see leading a righteous and holy life, in hope of immortality, who have no harrowing remorse of conscience, but obtain readily divine remission of the sins of their present infirmity? These, though they are certain that they shall be rewarded if they persevere, are not certain that they will persevere. For what man can know that he will persevere to the end in the exercise and increase of grace, unless he has been certified by some revelation from Him who, in His just and secret judgment, while He deceives none, informs few regarding this matter? Accordingly, so far as present comfort goes, the first man in Paradise was more blessed than any just man in this insecure state; but as regards the hope of future good, every man who not merely supposes, but certainly knows that he shall eternally enjoy the most high God in the company of angels, and beyond the reach of ill—this man, no matter what bodily torments afflict him, is more blessed than was he who, even in that great felicity of Paradise, was uncertain of his fate.[1]

---

1. With this chapter cf. the books *De Dono Persever.* and *De Corrept. et Gratia.*

13. WHETHER ALL THE ANGELS WERE SO CREATED IN ONE COMMON STATE OF FELICITY, THAT THOSE WHO FELL WERE NOT AWARE THAT THEY WOULD FALL, AND THAT THOSE WHO STOOD RECEIVED ASSURANCE OF THEIR OWN PERSEVERANCE AFTER THE RUIN OF THE FALLEN

From all this, it will readily occur to anyone that the blessedness which an intelligent being desires as its legitimate object results from a combination of these two things, namely, that it uninterruptedly enjoy the unchangeable good, which is God; and that it be delivered from all dubiety, and know certainly that it shall eternally abide in the same enjoyment. That it is so with the angels of light we piously believe; but that the fallen angels, who by their own default lost that light, did not enjoy this blessedness even before they sinned, reason bids us conclude. Yet if their life was of any duration before they fell, we must allow them a blessedness of some kind, though not that which is accompanied with foresight. Or, if it seems hard to believe that, when the angels were created, some were created in ignorance either of their perseverance or their fall, while others were most certainly assured of the eternity of their felicity—if it is hard to believe that they were not all from the beginning on an equal footing, until these who are now evil did of their own will fall away from the light of goodness, certainly it is much harder to believe that the holy angels are now uncertain of their eternal blessedness, and do not know regarding themselves as much as we have been able to gather regarding them from the Holy Scriptures. For what catholic Christian does not know that no new devil will ever arise among the good angels, as he knows that this present devil will never again return into the fellowship of the good? For the truth in the gospel promises to the saints and the faithful that they will be equal to the angels of God; and it is also promised them that they will "go away into life eternal."[1] But if we are certain that we shall never lapse from eternal felicity, while they are not certain, then we shall not be their equals, but their superiors. But as the truth never deceives, and as we shall be their equals, they must be certain of their blessedness. And because the evil angels could not be certain of that, since their blessedness was destined to come to an end, it follows either that the angels were unequal, or that, if equal, the good angels were assured of the eternity of their blessedness after the perdition of the others; unless, possibly, someone may say that the words of the Lord about the devil, "He was a murderer from the beginning, and abode not in the truth,"[2] are to be understood as if he was not only a murderer from the beginning of the human race, when man, whom he could kill by his deceit, was made, but also that he did not abide in the truth from the time of his own creation, and was accordingly never blessed with the holy angels, but refused to submit to his Creator, and proudly exulted as if in a private lordship of his own, and was thus deceived and deceiving. For the dominion of the Almighty cannot be eluded; and he who will not piously submit himself to things as they are, proudly feigns, and mocks himself with a state of things that does not exist; so that what the blessed apostle John says thus becomes intelligible: "The devil sinneth from the beginning"[3]—that is, from the time he was created he refused righteousness, which none but a will piously subject to God can enjoy. Whoever adopts this opinion at least disagrees with those heretics the Manichees, and with any other pestilential sect that may suppose that the devil has derived from some adverse evil principle a nature proper to himself. These persons are so befooled by error, that, although they acknowledge with ourselves the authority of the Gospels, they do not notice that the Lord did not say, "The devil was naturally a stranger to the truth," but, "The devil abode not in the truth," by which He meant us to understand that he had fallen from the truth, in which, if he had abode, he would have become a partaker of it, and have remained in blessedness along with the holy angels.[4]

---

1. Matt. 25:46.
2. John 8:44.
3. 1 John 3:8.
4. Cf. *De Gen. ad Litt.* 11.27 et seqq.

14. AN EXPLANATION OF WHAT IS SAID OF THE DEVIL, THAT HE DID NOT ABIDE IN THE TRUTH, BECAUSE THE TRUTH WAS NOT IN HIM

Moreover, as if we had been inquiring why the devil did not abide in the truth, our Lord subjoins the reason, saying, "because the truth is not in him." Now, it would be in him had he abode in it. But the phraseology is unusual. For, as the words stand, "He abode not in the truth, because the truth is not in him," it seems as if the truth's not being in him were the cause of his not abiding in it; whereas his not abiding in the truth is rather the cause of its not being in him. The same form of speech is found in the psalm: "I have called upon Thee, for Thou hast heard me, O God,"[1] where we should expect it to be said, "Thou hast heard me, O God, for I have called upon Thee." But when he had said, "I have called," then, as if someone were seeking proof of this, he demonstrates the effectual earnestness of his prayer by the effect of God's hearing it; as if he had said, "The proof that I have prayed is that Thou hast heard me."

---

1. Ps. 17:6.

15. HOW WE ARE TO UNDERSTAND THE WORDS, "THE DEVIL SINNETH FROM THE BEGINNING"

As for what John says about the devil, "The devil sinneth from the beginning,"[1] they[2] who suppose it is meant hereby that the devil was made with a sinful nature, misunderstand it; for if sin be natural, it is not sin at all. And how do they answer the prophetic proofs—either what Isaiah says when he represents the devil under the person of the king of Babylon, "How art thou fallen, O Lucifer, son of the morning!"[3] or what Ezekiel says, "Thou hast been in Eden, the garden of God; every precious stone was thy covering,"[4] where it is meant that he was sometime without sin; for a little after it is still more explicitly said, "Thou wast perfect in thy ways"? And if these passages cannot well be otherwise interpreted, we must understand by this one also, "He abode not in the truth," that he was once in the truth, but did not remain in it. And from this passage, "The devil sinneth from the beginning," it is not to be supposed that he sinned from the beginning of his created existence, but from the beginning of his sin, when by his pride he had once commenced to sin. There is a passage, too, in the book of Job, of which the devil is the subject: "This is the beginning of the creation of God, which He made to be a sport to His angels,"[5] which agrees with the psalm, where it is said, "There is that dragon which Thou hast made to be a sport therein."[6] But these passages are not to lead us to suppose that the devil was originally created to be the sport of the angels, but that he was doomed to this punishment after his sin. His beginning, then, is the handiwork of God; for there is no nature, even among the least, and lowest, and last of the beasts, which was not the work of Him from whom has proceeded all measure, all form, all order, without which nothing can be planned or conceived. How much more, then, is this angelic nature, which surpasses in dignity all else that He has made, the handiwork of the Most High!

---

1. 1 John 3:8.
2. The Manichæans.
3. Isa. 14:12.
4. Ezek. 28:13.
5. Job 40:14 (Septuagint).
6. Ps. 104:26.

16. OF THE RANKS AND DIFFERENCES OF THE CREATURES, ESTIMATED BY THEIR UTILITY, OR ACCORDING TO THE NATURAL GRADATIONS OF BEING

For, among those beings which exist, and which are not of God the Creator's essence, those which have life are ranked above those which have none; those that have the power of generation, or even of desiring, above those which want this faculty. And, among things that have life, the sentient are higher than those which have no sensation, as animals are ranked above trees. And, among the sentient, the intelligent are above those that have not intelligence—men, for example, above cattle. And, among the intelligent, the immortal such as the angels, above the mortal, such as men. These are the gradations according to the order of nature; but according to the utility each man finds in a thing, there are various standards of value, so that it comes to pass that we prefer some things that have no sensation to some sentient beings. And so strong is this preference, that, had we the power, we would abolish the latter from nature altogether, whether in ignorance of the place they hold in nature, or, though we know it, sacrificing them to our own convenience. Who, for example, would not rather have bread in his house than mice, gold than fleas? But there is little to wonder at in this, seeing that even when valued by men themselves (whose nature is certainly of the highest dignity), more is often given for a horse than for a slave, for a jewel than for a maid. Thus the reason of one contemplating nature prompts very different judgments from those dictated by the necessity of the needy, or the desire of the voluptuous; for the former considers what value a thing in itself has in the scale of creation, while necessity considers how it meets its need; reason looks for what the mental light will judge to be true, while pleasure looks for what pleasantly titilates the bodily sense. But of such consequence in rational natures is the weight, so to speak, of will and of love, that though in the order of nature angels rank above men, yet, by the scale of justice, good men are of greater value than bad angels.

17. THAT THE FLAW OF WICKEDNESS IS NOT NATURE, BUT CONTRARY TO NATURE, AND HAS ITS ORIGIN, NOT IN THE CREATOR, BUT IN THE WILL

It is with reference to the nature, then, and not to the wickedness of the devil, that we are to understand these words, "This is the beginning of God's handiwork";[1] for, without doubt, wickedness can be a flaw or vice[2] only where the nature previously was not vitiated. Vice, too, is so contrary to nature, that it cannot but damage it. And therefore departure from God would be no vice, unless in a nature whose property it was to abide with God. So that even the wicked will is a strong proof of the goodness of the nature. But God, as He is the supremely good Creator of good natures, so is He of evil wills the most just Ruler; so that, while they make an ill use of good natures, He makes a good use even of evil wills. Accordingly, He caused the devil (good by God's creation, wicked by his own will) to be cast down from his high position, and to become the mockery of His angels—that is, He caused his temptations to benefit those whom he wishes to injure by them. And because God, when He created him, was certainly not ignorant of his future malignity, and foresaw the good which He Himself would bring out of his evil, therefore says the psalm, "This leviathan whom Thou hast made to be a sport therein,"[3] that we may see that, even while God in His goodness created him good, He yet had already foreseen and arranged how He would make use of him when he became wicked.

---

1. Job. 40:14 (Septuagint).
2. It must be kept in view that "vice" has, in this passage, the meaning of sinful blemish.
3. Ps. 104:26.

18. OF THE BEAUTY OF THE UNIVERSE, WHICH BECOMES, BY GOD'S ORDINANCE, MORE BRILLIANT BY THE OPPOSITION OF CONTRARIES

For God would never have created any, I do not say angel, but even man, whose future wickedness He foreknew, unless He had equally known to what uses in behalf of the good He could turn him, thus embellishing the course of the ages, as it were an exquisite poem set off with antitheses. For what are called antitheses are among the most elegant of the ornaments of speech. They might be called in Latin "oppositions," or, to speak more accurately, "contrapositions"; but this word is not in common use among us,[1] though the Latin, and indeed the languages of all nations, avail themselves of the same ornaments of style. In the Second Epistle to the Corinthians the apostle Paul also makes a graceful use of antithesis, in that place where he says, "By the armor of righteousness on the right hand and on the left, by honor and dishonor, by evil report and good report: as deceivers, and yet true; as unknown, and yet well known; as dying, and, behold, we live; as chastened, and not killed; as sorrowful, yet always rejoicing; as poor, yet making many rich; as having nothing, and yet possessing all things."[2] As, then, these oppositions of contraries lend beauty to the language, so the beauty of the course of this world is achieved by the opposition of contraries, arranged, as it were, by an eloquence not of words, but of things. This is quite plainly stated in the book of Ecclesiasticus, in this way: "Good is set against evil, and life against death: so is the sinner against the godly. So look upon all the works of the Most High, and these are two and two, one against another."[3]

---

1. Quintilian uses it commonly in the sense of antithesis.
2. 2 Cor. 6:7–10.
3. Ecclus. 33:15.

19. WHAT, SEEMINGLY, WE ARE TO UNDERSTAND BY THE WORDS, "GOD DIVIDED THE LIGHT FROM THE DARKNESS"

Accordingly, though the obscurity of the divine word has certainly this advantage, that it causes many opinions about the truth to be started and discussed, each reader seeing some fresh meaning in it, yet, whatever is said to be meant by an obscure passage should be either confirmed by the testimony of obvious facts, or should be asserted in other and less ambiguous texts. This obscurity is beneficial, whether the sense of the author is at last reached after the discussion of many other interpretations, or whether, though that sense remain concealed, other truths are brought out by the discussion of the obscurity. To me it does not seem incongruous with the working of God, if we understand that the angels were created when that first light was made, and that a separation was made between the holy and the unclean angels, when, as is said, "God divided the light from the darkness; and God called the light Day, and the darkness He called Night." For He alone could make this discrimination, who was able also before they fell, to foreknow that they would fall, and that, being deprived of the light of truth, they would abide in the darkness of pride. For, so far as regards the day and night, with which we are familiar, He commanded those luminaries of heaven that are obvious to our senses to divide between the light and the darkness. "Let there be," He says, "lights in the firmament of the heaven, to divide the day from the night"; and shortly after He says, "And God made two great lights; the greater light to rule the day, and the lesser light to rule the night: the stars also. And God set them in the firmament of the heaven, to give light upon the earth, and to rule over the day and over the night, and to divide the light from the darkness."[1] But between that light, which is the holy company of the angels spiritually radiant with the illumination of the truth, and that opposing darkness, which is the noisome foulness of the spiritual condition of those angels who are turned away from the light of righteousness, only He Himself could divide, from whom their wickedness (not of nature, but of will), while yet it was future, could not be hidden or uncertain.

---

1. Gen. 1:14–18.

20. OF THE WORDS WHICH FOLLOW THE SEPARATION OF LIGHT AND DARKNESS, "AND GOD SAW THE LIGHT THAT IT WAS GOOD"

Then, we must not pass from this passage of Scripture without noticing that when God said, "Let there be light, and there was light," it was immediately added, "And God saw the light that it was good." No such expression followed the statement that He separated the light from the darkness, and called the light Day and the darkness Night, lest the seal of His approval might seem to be set on such darkness, as well as on the light. For when the darkness was not subject of disapprobation, as when it was divided by the heavenly bodies from this light which our eyes discern, the statement that God saw that it was good is inserted, not before, but after the division is recorded. "And God set them," so runs the passage, "in the firmament of the heaven, to give light upon the earth, and to rule over the day and over the night, and to divide the light from the darkness: and God saw that it was good." For He approved of both, because both were sinless. But where God said, "Let there be light, and there was light; and God saw the light that it was good"; and the narrative goes on, "and God divided the light from the darkness; and God called the light Day, and the darkness He called Night," there was not in this place subjoined the statement, "And God saw that it was good," lest both should be designated good, while one of them was evil, not by nature, but by its own fault. And therefore, in this case, the light alone received the approbation of the Creator, while the angelic darkness, though it had been ordained, was yet not approved.

21. OF GOD'S ETERNAL AND UNCHANGEABLE KNOWLEDGE AND WILL, WHEREBY ALL HE HAS MADE PLEASED HIM IN THE ETERNAL DESIGN AS WELL AS IN THE ACTUAL RESULT

For what else is to be understood by that invariable refrain, "And God saw that it was good," than the approval of the work in its design, which is the wisdom of God? For certainly God did not in the actual achievement of the work first learn that it was good, but, on the contrary, nothing would have been made had it not been first known by Him. While, therefore, He sees that that is good which, had He not seen it before it was made, would never have been made, it is plain that He is not discovering, but teaching that it is good. Plato, indeed, was bold enough to say that, when the universe was completed, God was, as it were, elated with joy.[1] And Plato was not so foolish as to mean by this that God was rendered more blessed by the novelty of His creation; but he wished thus to indicate that the work now completed met with its Maker's approval, as it had while yet in design. It is not as if the knowledge of God were of various kinds, knowing in different ways things which as yet are not, things which are, and things which have been. For not in our fashion does He look forward to what is future, nor at what is present, nor back upon what is past; but in a manner quite different and far and profoundly remote from our way of thinking. For He does not pass from this to that by transition of thought, but beholds all things with absolute unchangeableness; so that of those things which emerge in time, the future, indeed, are not yet, and the present are now, and the past no longer are; but all of these are by Him comprehended in His stable and eternal presence. Neither does He see in one fashion by the eye, in another by the mind, for He is not composed of mind and body; nor does His present knowledge differ from that which it ever was or shall be, for those variations of time, past, present, and future, though they alter our knowledge, do not affect His, "with whom is no variableness, neither shadow of turning."[2] Neither is there any growth from thought to thought in the conceptions of Him in whose spiritual vision all things which He knows are at once embraced. For as without any movement that time can measure, He Himself moves all temporal things, so He knows all times with a knowledge that time cannot measure. And therefore He saw that what He had made was good, when He saw that it was good to make it. And when He saw it made, He had not on that account a twofold nor any way increased knowledge of it; as if He had less knowledge before He made what He saw. For certainly He would not be the perfect worker He is, unless His knowledge were so perfect as to receive no addition from His finished works. Wherefore, if the only object had been to inform us who made the light, it had been enough to say, "God made the light"; and if further information regarding the means by which it was made had been intended, it would have sufficed to say, "And God said, Let there be light, and there was light," that we might know not only that God had made the world, but also that He had made it by the word. But because it was right that three leading truths regarding the creature be intimated to us, namely, who made it, by what means, and why, it is written, "God said, Let there be light, and there was light. And God saw the light that it was good." If, then, we ask who made it, it was "God." If, by what means, He said "Let it be," and it was. If we ask, why He made it, "it was good." Neither is there any author more excellent than God, nor any skill more efficacious than the word of God, nor any cause better than that good might be created by the good God. This also Plato has assigned as the most sufficient reason for the creation of the world, that good works might be made by a good God;[3] whether he read this passage, or, perhaps, was informed of these things by those who had read them, or, by his quick-sighted genius, penetrated to things spiritual and invisible through the things that are created, or was instructed regarding them by those who had discerned them.

1. The reference is to the *Timæus*, p. 37.C., where he says, "When the parent Creator perceived this created image of the eternal gods in life and motion, He was delighted, and in His joy considered how He might make it still more like its model."
2. Jas. 1:17.
3. The passage referred to is in the *Timæus*, p. 29.D.: "Let us say what was the cause of the Creator's forming this universe. He was good; and in the good no envy is ever generated about anything whatever. Therefore, being free from envy, He desired that all things should, as much as possible, resemble Himself."

22. OF THOSE WHO DO NOT APPROVE OF CERTAIN THINGS WHICH ARE A PART OF THIS GOOD CREATION OF A GOOD CREATOR, AND WHO THINK THAT THERE IS SOME NATURAL EVIL

This cause, however, of a good creation, namely, the goodness of God—this cause, I say, so just and fit, which, when piously and carefully weighed, terminates all the controversies of those who inquire into the origin of the world, has not been recognized by some heretics,[1] because there are, forsooth, many things, such as fire, frost, wild beasts, and so forth, which do not suit but injure this thin-blooded and frail mortality of our flesh, which is at present under just punishment. They do not consider how admirable these things are in their own places, how excellent in their own natures, how beautifully adjusted to the rest of creation, and how much grace they contribute to the universe by their own contributions as to a commonwealth; and how serviceable they are even to ourselves, if we use them with a knowledge of their fit adaptations—so that even poisons, which are destructive when used injudiciously, become wholesome and medicinal when used in conformity with their qualities and design; just as, on the other hand, those things which give us pleasure, such as food, drink, and the light of the sun, are found to be hurtful when immoderately or unseasonably used. And thus divine Providence admonishes us not foolishly to vituperate things, but to investigate their utility with care; and, where our mental capacity or infirmity is at fault, to believe that there is a utility, though hidden, as we have experienced that there were other things which we all but failed to discover. For this concealment of the use of things is itself either an exercise of our humility or a leveling of our pride; for no nature at all is evil, and this is a name for nothing but the want of good. But from things earthly to things heavenly, from the visible to the invisible, there are some things better than others; and for this purpose are they unequal, in order that they might all exist. Now God is in such sort a great worker in great things, that He is not less in little things—for these little things are to be measured not by their own greatness (which does not exist), but by the wisdom of their Designer; as, in the visible appearance of a man, if one eyebrow be shaved off, how nearly nothing is taken from the body, but how much from the beauty!—for that is not constituted by bulk, but by the proportion and arrangement of the members. But we do not greatly wonder that persons, who suppose that some evil nature has been generated and propagated by a kind of opposing principle proper to it, refuse to admit that the cause of the creation was this, that the good God produced a good creation. For they believe that He was driven to this enterprise of creation by the urgent necessity of repulsing the evil that warred against Him, and that He mixed His good nature with the evil for the sake of restraining and conquering it; and that this nature of His, being thus shamefully polluted, and most cruelly oppressed and held captive, He labors to cleanse and deliver it, and with all His pains does not wholly succeed; but such part of it as could not be cleansed from that defilement is to serve as a prison and chain of the conquered and incarcerated enemy. The Manichæans would not drivel, or rather, rave in such a style as this, if they believed the nature of God to be, as it is, unchangeable and absolutely incorruptible, and subject to no injury; and if, moreover, they held in Christian sobriety, that the soul which has shown itself capable of being altered for the worse by its own will, and of being corrupted by sin, and so, of being deprived of the light of eternal truth—that this soul, I say, is not a part of God, nor of the same nature as God, but is created by Him, and is far different from its Creator.

---

1. The Manichæans, to wit.

23. OF THE ERROR IN WHICH THE DOCTRINE OF ORIGEN IS INVOLVED

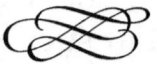

But it is much more surprising that some even of those who, with ourselves, believe that there is one only source of all things, and that no nature which is not divine can exist unless originated by that Creator, have yet refused to accept with a good and simple faith this so good and simple a reason of the world's creation, that a good God made it good; and that the things created, being different from God, were inferior to Him, and yet were good, being created by none other than He. But they say that souls, though not, indeed, parts of God, but created by Him, sinned by abandoning God; that, in proportion to their various sins, they merited different degrees of debasement from heaven to earth, and diverse bodies as prison houses; and that this is the world, and this the cause of its creation, not the production of good things, but the restraining of evil. Origen is justly blamed for holding this opinion. For in the books which he titles περὶ ἀρχῶν, that is, *Of Origins*, this is his sentiment, this his utterance. And I cannot sufficiently express my astonishment, that a man so erudite and well versed in ecclesiastical literature, should not have observed, in the first place, how opposed this is to the meaning of this authoritative Scripture, which, in recounting all the works of God, regularly adds, "And God saw that it was good"; and, when all were completed, inserts the words, "And God saw everything that He had made, and, behold, it was very good."[1] Was it not obviously meant to be understood that there was no other cause of the world's creation than that good creatures should be made by a good God? In this creation, had no one sinned, the world would have been filled and beautified with natures good without exception; and though there is sin, all things are not therefore full of sin, for the great majority of the heavenly inhabitants preserve their nature's integrity. And the sinful will, though it violated the order of its own nature, did not on that account escape the laws of God, who justly orders all things for good. For as the beauty of a picture is increased by well-managed shadows, so, to the eye that has skill to discern it, the universe is beautified even by sinners, though, considered by themselves, their deformity is a sad blemish.

In the second place, Origen, and all who think with him, ought to have seen that if it were the true opinion that the world was created in order that souls might, for their sins, be accommodated with bodies in which they should be shut up as in houses of correction, the more venial sinners receiving lighter and more ethereal bodies, while the grosser and graver sinners received bodies more crass and groveling, then it would follow that the devils, who are deepest in wickedness, ought, rather than even wicked men, to have earthly bodies, since these are the grossest and least ethereal of all. But in point of fact, that we might see that the deserts of souls are not to be estimated by the qualities of bodies, the wickedest devil possesses an ethereal body, while man, wicked, it is true, but with a wickedness small and venial in comparison with his, received even before his sin a body of clay. And what more foolish assertion can be advanced than that God, by this sun of ours, did not design to benefit the material creation, or lend luster to its loveliness, and therefore created one single sun for this single world, but that it so happened that one soul only had so sinned as to deserve to be enclosed in such a body as it is? On this principle, if it had chanced that not one, but two, yes, or ten, or a hundred had sinned similarly, and with a like degree of guilt, then this world would have one hundred suns. And that such is not the case, is due not to the considerate foresight of the Creator, contriving the safety and beauty of things material, but rather to the fact that so fine a quality of sinning was hit upon by only one soul, so that it alone has merited such a body. Manifestly persons holding such opinions should aim at confining, not souls of which they know not what they say, but themselves, lest they fall, and deservedly, far indeed from the truth. And as to these three answers which I formerly recommended when in the case of any creature the questions are put, "Who made it?" "By what means?" "Why?" that it should be replied, "God," "By the Word," "Because it was good"—as to these three answers, it is very questionable whether the Trinity itself is thus mystically indicated, that is, the Father, the Son, and the Holy Ghost, or whether there is some good reason for this acceptation in this passage of Scripture—this, I say, is questionable, and one can't be expected to explain everything in one volume.

---

1. Gen. 1:31.

24. OF THE DIVINE TRINITY, AND THE INDICATIONS OF ITS PRESENCE SCATTERED EVERYWHERE AMONG ITS WORKS

We believe, we maintain, we faithfully preach, that the Father begat the Word, that is, Wisdom, by which all things were made, the only begotten Son, one as the Father is one, eternal as the Father is eternal, and, equally with the Father, supremely good; and that the Holy Spirit is the Spirit alike of Father and of Son, and is Himself consubstantial and coeternal with both; and that this whole is a Trinity by reason of the individuality[1] of the persons, and one God by reason of the indivisible divine substance, as also one Almighty by reason of the indivisible omnipotence; yet so that, when we inquire regarding each singly, it is said that each is God and Almighty; and, when we speak of all together, it is said that there are not three Gods, nor three Almighties, but one God Almighty; so great is the indivisible unity of these Three, which requires that it be so stated. But, whether the Holy Spirit of the Father, and of the Son, who are both good, can be with propriety called the goodness of both, because He is common to both, I do not presume to determine hastily. Nevertheless, I would have less hesitation in saying that He is the holiness of both, not as if He were a divine attribute merely, but Himself also the divine substance, and the third person in the Trinity. I am the rather emboldened to make this statement, because, though the Father is a spirit, and the Son a spirit, and the Father holy, and the Son holy, yet the third person is distinctively called the Holy Spirit, as if He were the substantial holiness consubstantial with the other two. But if the divine goodness is nothing else than the divine holiness, then certainly it is a reasonable studiousness, and not presumptuous intrusion, to inquire whether the same Trinity be not hinted at in an enigmatical mode of speech, by which our inquiry is stimulated, when it is written who made each creature, and by what means, and why. For it is the Father of the Word who said, Let there be. And that which was made when He spoke was certainly made by means of the Word. And by the words, "God saw that it was good," it is sufficiently intimated that God made what was made not from any necessity, nor for the sake of supplying any want, but solely from His own goodness, that is, because it was good. And this is stated after the creation had taken place, that there might be no doubt that the thing made satisfied the goodness on account of which it was made. And if we are right in understanding that this goodness is the Holy Spirit, then the whole Trinity is revealed to us in the creation. In this, too, is the origin, the enlightenment, the blessedness of the holy city which is above among the holy angels. For if we inquire whence it is, God created it; or whence its wisdom, God illumined it; or whence its blessedness, God is its bliss. It has its form by subsisting in Him; its enlightenment by contemplating Him; its joy by abiding in Him. It is; it sees; it loves. In God's eternity is its life; in God's truth its light; in God's goodness its joy.

---

1. Proprietas.

25. OF THE DIVISION OF PHILOSOPHY INTO THREE PARTS

As far as one can judge, it is for the same reason that philosophers have aimed at a threefold division of science, or rather, were enabled to see that there was a threefold division (for they did not invent, but only discovered it), of which one part is called physical, another logical, the third ethical. The Latin equivalents of these names are now naturalized in the writings of many authors, so that these divisions are called natural, rational, and moral, on which I have touched slightly in the eighth book. Not that I would conclude that these philosophers, in this threefold division, had any thought of a trinity in God, although Plato is said to have been the first to discover and promulgate this distribution, and he saw that God alone could be the author of nature, the bestower of intelligence, and the kindler of love by which life becomes good and blessed. But certain it is that, though philosophers disagree both regarding the nature of things, and the mode of investigating truth, and of the good to which all our actions ought to tend, yet in these three great general questions all their intellectual energy is spent. And though there be a confusing diversity of opinion, every man striving to establish his own opinion in regard to each of these questions, yet no one of them all doubts that nature has some cause, science some method, life some end and aim. Then, again, there are three things which every artificer must possess if he is to effect anything—nature, education, practice. Nature is to be judged by capacity, education by knowledge, practice by its fruit. I am aware that, properly speaking, fruit is what one enjoys, use [practice] what one uses. And this seems to be the difference between them, that we are said to *enjoy* that which in itself, and irrespective of other ends, delights us; to use that which we seek for the sake of some end beyond. For which reason the things of time are to be used rather than enjoyed, that we may deserve to enjoy things eternal; and not as those perverse creatures who would fain enjoy money and use God—not spending money for God's sake, but worshiping God for money's sake. However, in common parlance, we both use fruits and enjoy uses. For we correctly speak of the "fruits of the field," which certainly we all use in the present life. And it was in accordance with this usage that I said that there were three things to be observed in a man, nature, education, practice. From these the philosophers have elaborated, as I said, the threefold division of that science by which a blessed life is attained: the natural having respect to nature, the rational to education, the moral to practice. If, then, we were ourselves the authors of our nature, we should have generated knowledge in ourselves, and should not require to reach it by education, that is, by learning it from others. Our love, too, proceeding from ourselves and returning to us, would suffice to make our life blessed, and would stand in need of no extraneous enjoyment. But now, since our nature has God as its requisite author, it is certain that we must have Him for our teacher that we may be wise; Him, too, to dispense to us spiritual sweetness that we may be blessed.

26. OF THE IMAGE OF THE SUPREME TRINITY, WHICH WE FIND IN SOME SORT IN HUMAN NATURE EVEN IN ITS PRESENT STATE

And we indeed recognize in ourselves the image of God, that is, of the supreme Trinity, an image which, though it be not equal to God, or rather, though it be very far removed from Him—being neither coeternal, nor, to say all in a word, consubstantial with Him—is yet nearer to Him in nature than any other of His works, and is destined to be yet restored, that it may bear a still closer resemblance. For we both are, and know that we are, and delight in our being, and our knowledge of it. Moreover, in these three things no true-seeming illusion disturbs us; for we do not come into contact with these by some bodily sense, as we perceive the things outside of us—colors, for example, by seeing, sounds by hearing, smells by smelling, tastes by tasting, hard and soft objects by touching—of all which sensible objects it is the images resembling them, but not themselves which we perceive in the mind and hold in the memory, and which excite us to desire the objects. But, without any delusive representation of images or phantasms, I am most certain that I am, and that I know and delight in this. In respect of these truths, I am not at all afraid of the arguments of the Academicians, who say, What if you are deceived? For if I am deceived, I am.[1] For he who is not, cannot be deceived; and if I am deceived, by this same token I am. And since I am if I am deceived, how am I deceived in believing that I am? for it is certain that I am if I am deceived. Since, therefore, I, the person deceived, should be, even if I were deceived, certainly I am not deceived in this knowledge that I am. And, consequently, neither am I deceived in knowing that I know. For, as I know that I am, so I know this also, that I know. And when I love these two things, I add to them a certain third thing, namely, my love, which is of equal moment. For neither am I deceived in this, that I love, since in those things which I love I am not deceived; though even if these were false, it would still be true that I *loved* false things. For how could I justly be blamed and prohibited from loving false things, if it were false that I loved them? But, since they are true and real, who doubts that when they are loved, the love of them is itself true and real? Further, as there is no one who does not wish to be happy, so there is no one who does not wish to be. For how can he be happy, if he is nothing?

---

1. This is one of the passages cited by Sir William Hamilton, along with the *"Cogito, ergo sum"* of Descartes, in confirmation of his proof, that insofar as we are *conscious* of certain modes of existence, insofar we possess an absolute certainty that we exist. See note A in Hamilton's *Reid*, p. 744.

27. OF EXISTENCE, AND KNOWLEDGE OF IT, AND THE LOVE OF BOTH

And truly the very fact of existing is by some natural spell so pleasant, that even the wretched are, for no other reason, unwilling to perish; and, when they feel that they are wretched, wish not that they themselves be annihilated, but that their misery be so. Take even those who, both in their own esteem, and in point of fact, are utterly wretched, and who are reckoned so, not only by wise men on account of their folly, but by those who count themselves blessed, and who think them wretched because they are poor and destitute —if anyone should give these men an immortality, in which their misery should be deathless, and should offer the alternative, that if they shrank from existing eternally in the same misery they might be annihilated, and exist nowhere at all, nor in any condition, on the instant they would joyfully, no exultantly, make election to exist always, even in such a condition, rather than not exist at all. The well-known feeling of such men witnesses to this. For when we see that they fear to die, and will rather live in such misfortune than end it by death, is it not obvious enough how nature shrinks from annihilation? And, accordingly, when they know that they must die, they seek, as a great boon, that this mercy be shown them, that they may a little longer live in the same misery, and delay to end it by death. And so they indubitably prove with what glad alacrity they would accept immortality, even though it secured to them endless destruction. What! do not even all irrational animals, to whom such calculations are unknown, from the huge dragons down to the least worms, all testify that they wish to exist, and therefore shun death by every movement in their power? No, the very plants and shrubs, which have no such life as enables them to shun destruction by movements we can see, do not they all seek in their own fashion to conserve their existence, by rooting themselves more and more deeply in the earth, that so they may draw nourishment, and throw out healthy branches toward the sky? In fine, even the lifeless bodies, which want not only sensation but seminal life, yet either seek the upper air or sink deep, or are balanced in an intermediate position, so that they may protect their existence in that situation where they can exist in most accordance with their nature.

And how much human nature loves the knowledge of its existence, and how it shrinks from being deceived, will be sufficiently understood from this fact, that every man prefers to grieve in a sane mind, rather than to be glad in madness. And this grand and wonderful instinct belongs to men alone of all animals; for, though some of them have keener eyesight than ourselves for this world's light, they cannot attain to that spiritual light with which our mind is somehow irradiated, so that we can form right judgments of all things. For our power to judge is proportioned to our acceptance of this light. Nevertheless, the irrational animals, though they have not knowledge, have certainly something resembling knowledge; whereas the other material things are said to be sensible, not because they have senses, but because they are the objects of our senses. Yet among plants, their nourishment and generation have some resemblance to sensible life. However, both these and all material things have their causes hidden in their nature; but their outward forms, which lend beauty to this visible structure of the world, are perceived by our senses, so that they seem to wish to compensate for their own want of knowledge by providing us with knowledge. But we perceive them by our bodily senses in such a way that we do not judge of them by these senses. For we have another and far superior sense, belonging to the inner man, by which we perceive what things are just, and what unjust—just by means of an intelligible idea, unjust by the want of it. This sense is aided in its functions neither by the eyesight, nor by the orifice of the ear, nor by the airholes of the nostrils, nor by the palate's taste, nor by any bodily touch. By it I am assured both that I am, and that I know this; and these two I love, and in the same manner I am assured that I love them.

28. WHETHER WE OUGHT TO LOVE THE LOVE ITSELF WITH WHICH WE LOVE OUR EXISTENCE AND OUR KNOWLEDGE OF IT, THAT SO WE MAY MORE NEARLY RESEMBLE THE IMAGE OF THE DIVINE TRINITY

We have said as much as the scope of this work demands regarding these two things, to wit, our existence, and our knowledge of it, and how much they are loved by us, and how there is found even in the lower creatures a kind of likeness of these things, and yet with a difference. We have yet to speak of the love wherewith they are loved, to determine whether this love itself is loved. And doubtless it is; and this is the proof. Because in men who are justly loved, it is rather love itself that is loved; for he is not justly called a good man who knows what is good, but who loves it. Is it not then obvious that we love in ourselves the very love wherewith we love whatever good we love? For there is also a love wherewith we love that which we ought not to love; and this love is hated by him who loves that wherewith he loves what ought to be loved. For it is quite possible for both to exist in one man. And this coexistence is good for a man, to the end that this love which conduces to our living well may grow, and the other, which leads us to evil may decrease, until our whole life be perfectly healed and transmuted into good. For if we were beasts, we should love the fleshly and sensual life, and this would be our sufficient good; and when it was well with us in respect of it, we should seek nothing beyond. In like manner, if we were trees, we could not, indeed, in the strict sense of the word, love anything; nevertheless we should seem, as it were, to long for that by which we might become more abundantly and luxuriantly fruitful. If we were stones, or waves, or wind, or flame, or anything of that kind, we should want, indeed, both sensation and life, yet should possess a kind of attraction toward our own proper position and natural order. For the specific gravity of bodies is, as it were, their love, whether they are carried downward by their weight, or upward by their levity. For the body is borne by its gravity, as the spirit by love, whithersoever it is borne.[1] But we are men, created in the image of our Creator, whose eternity is true, and whose truth is eternal, whose love is eternal and true, and who Himself is the eternal, true, and adorable Trinity, without confusion, without separation; and, therefore, while, as we run over all the works which He has established, we may detect, as it were, His footprints, now more and now less distinct even in those things that are beneath us, since they could not so much as exist, or be bodied forth in any shape, or follow and observe any law, had they not been made by Him who supremely is, and is supremely good and supremely wise; yet in ourselves beholding His image, let us, like that younger son of the gospel, come to ourselves, and arise and return to Him from whom by our sin we had departed. There our being will have no death, our knowledge no error, our love no mishap. But now, though we are assured of our possession of these three things, not on the testimony of others, but by our own consciousness of their presence, and because we see them with our own most truthful interior vision, yet, as we cannot of ourselves know how long they are to continue, and whether they shall never cease to be, and what issue their good or bad use will lead to, we seek for others who can acquaint us of these things, if we have not already found them. Of the trustworthiness of these witnesses, there will, not now, but subsequently, be an opportunity of speaking. But in this book let us go on as we have begun, with God's help, to speak of the city of God, not in its state of pilgrimage and mortality, but as it exists ever immortal in the heavens—that is, let us speak of the holy angels who maintain their allegiance to God, who never were, nor ever shall be, apostate, between whom and those who forsook light eternal and became darkness, God, as we have already said, made at the first a separation.

---

1. Cf. *Confessions* 13.9.

29. OF THE KNOWLEDGE BY WHICH THE HOLY ANGELS KNOW GOD IN HIS ESSENCE, AND BY WHICH THEY SEE THE CAUSES OF HIS WORKS IN THE ART OF THE WORKER, BEFORE THEY SEE THEM IN THE WORKS OF THE ARTIST

Those holy angels come to the knowledge of God not by audible words, but by the presence to their souls of immutable truth, that is, of the only begotten Word of God; and they know this Word Himself, and the Father, and their Holy Spirit, and that this Trinity is indivisible, and that the three persons of it are one substance, and that there are not three Gods but one God; and this they so know that it is better understood by them than we are by ourselves. Thus, too, they know the creature also, not in itself, but by this better way, in the wisdom of God, as if in the art by which it was created; and, consequently, they know themselves better in God than in themselves, though they have also this latter knowledge. For they were created, and are different from their Creator. In Him, therefore, they have, as it were, a noonday knowledge; in themselves, a twilight knowledge, according to our former explanations.[1] For there is a great difference between knowing a thing in the design in conformity to which it was made, and knowing it in itself—for example, the straightness of lines and correctness of figures is known in one way when mentally conceived, in another when described on paper; and justice is known in one way in the unchangeable truth, in another in the spirit of a just man. So is it with all other things—as, the firmament between the water above and below, which was called the heaven; the gathering of the waters beneath, and the laying bare of the dry land, and the production of plants and trees; the creation of sun, moon, and stars; and of the animals out of the waters, fowls, and fish, and monsters of the deep; and of everything that walks or creeps on the earth, and of man himself, who excels all that is on the earth—all these things are known in one way by the angels in the Word of God, in which they see the eternally abiding causes and reasons according to which they were made, and in another way in themselves: in the former, with a clearer knowledge; in the latter, with a knowledge dimmer, and rather of the bare works than of the design. Yet, when these works are referred to the praise and adoration of the Creator Himself, it is as if morning dawned in the minds of those who contemplate them.

---

1. See above, 11.7.

30. OF THE PERFECTION OF THE NUMBER SIX, WHICH IS THE FIRST OF THE NUMBERS WHICH IS COMPOSED OF ITS ALIQUOT PARTS

These works are recorded to have been completed in six days (the same day being six times repeated), because six is a perfect number—not because God required a protracted time, as if He could not at once create all things, which then should mark the course of time by the movements proper to them, but because the perfection of the works was signified by the number six. For the number six is the first which is made up of its own[1] parts, that is, of its sixth, third, and half, which are respectively one, two, and three, and which make a total of six. In this way of looking at a number, those are said to be its parts which exactly divide it, as a half, a third, a fourth, or a fraction with any denominator, for example , four is a part of nine, but not therefore an aliquot part; but one is, for it is the ninth part; and three is, for it is the third. Yet these two parts, the ninth and the third, or one and three, are far from making its whole sum of nine. So again, in the number ten, four is a part, yet does not divide it; but one is an aliquot part, for it is a tenth; so it has a fifth, which is two; and a half, which is five. But these three parts, a tenth, a fifth, and a half, or one, two, and five, added together, do not make ten, but eight. Of the number twelve, again, the parts added together exceed the whole; for it has a twelfth, that is, one; a sixth, or two; a fourth, which is three; a third, which is four; and a half, which is six. But one, two, three, four, and six make up, not twelve, but more, namely, sixteen. So much I have thought fit to state for the sake of illustrating the perfection of the number six, which is, as I said, the first which is exactly made up of its own parts added together; and in this number of days God finished His work.[2] And, therefore, we must not despise the science of numbers, which, in many passages of Holy Scripture, is found to be of eminent service to the careful interpreter.[3] Neither has it been without reason numbered among God's praises, "Thou hast ordered all things in number, and measure, and weight."[4]

---

1. Or aliquot parts.
2. Cf. Augustine *De Gen. ad Litt.* 4.2 and *De Trin.* 4.7.
3. For passages illustrating early opinions regarding numbers, see Smith's *Dictionary* Art.: Number.
4. Wisd. of Sol. 11:20.

31. OF THE SEVENTH DAY, IN WHICH COMPLETENESS AND REPOSE ARE CELEBRATED

But, on the seventh day (i.e., the same day repeated seven times, which number is also a perfect one, though for another reason), the rest of God is set forth, and then, too, we first hear of its being hallowed. So that God did not wish to hallow this day by His works, but by His rest, which has no evening, for it is not a creature; so that, being known in one way in the Word of God, and in another in itself, it should make a twofold knowledge, daylight and dusk (day and evening). Much more might be said about the perfection of the number seven, but this book is already too long, and I fear lest I should seem to catch at an opportunity of airing my little smattering of science more childishly than profitably. I must speak, therefore, in moderation and with dignity, lest, in too keenly following "number," I be accused of forgetting "weight" and "measure." Suffice it here to say, that three is the first whole number that is odd, four the first that is even, and of these two, seven is composed. On this account it is often put for all numbers together, as, "A just man falleth seven times, and riseth up again"[1]—that is, let him fall never so often, he will not perish (and this was meant to be understood not of sins, but of afflictions conducing to lowliness). Again, "Seven times a day will I praise Thee,"[2] which elsewhere is expressed thus, "I will bless the LORD *at all times.*"[3] And many such instances are found in the divine authorities, in which the number seven is, as I said, commonly used to express the whole, or the completeness of anything. And so the Holy Spirit, of whom the Lord says, "He will teach you all truth,"[4] is signified by this number.[5] In it is the rest of God, the rest His people find in Him. For rest is in the whole, that is, in perfect completeness, while in the part there is labor. And thus we labor as long as we know in part; "but when that which is perfect is come, then that which is in part shall be done away."[6] It is even with toil we search into the Scriptures themselves. But the holy angels, toward whose society and assembly we sigh while in this our toilsome pilgrimage, as they already abide in their eternal home, so do they enjoy perfect facility of knowledge and felicity of rest. It is without difficulty that they help us; for their spiritual movements, pure and free, cost them no effort.

---

1. Prov. 24:16.
2. Ps. 119:164.
3. Ps. 34:1.

4. John 16:13.
5. In Isa. 11:2, as he shows in his eighth sermon, where this subject is further pursued; otherwise, one might have supposed he referred to Rev. 3:1.
6. 1 Cor. 13:10.

32. OF THE OPINION THAT THE ANGELS WERE CREATED BEFORE THE WORLD

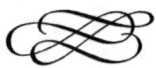

But if someone oppose our opinion, and say that the holy angels are not referred to when it is said, "Let there be light, and there was light"; if he suppose or teach that some material light, then first created, was meant, and that the angels were created, not only before the firmament dividing the waters and named "the heaven," but also before the time signified in the words, "In the beginning God created the heaven and the earth"; if he allege that this phrase, "In the beginning," does not mean that nothing was made before (for the angels were), but that God made all things by His Wisdom or Word, who is named in Scripture "the Beginning," as He Himself, in the gospel, replied to the Jews when they asked Him who He was, that He was the Beginning[1];—I will not contest the point, chiefly because it gives me the liveliest satisfaction to find the Trinity celebrated in the very beginning of the book of Genesis. For having said, "In the Beginning God created the heaven and the earth," meaning that the Father made them in the Son (as the psalm testifies where it says, "How manifold are Thy works, O LORD! in Wisdom hast Thou made them all"[2]), a little afterward mention is fitly made of the Holy Spirit also. For, when it had been told us what kind of earth God created at first, or what the mass or matter was which God, under the name of "heaven and earth," had provided for the construction of the world, as is told in the additional words, "And the earth was without form, and void; and darkness was upon the face of the deep," then, for the sake of completing the mention of the Trinity, it is immediately added, "And the Spirit of God moved upon the face of the waters." Let each one, then, take it as he pleases; for it is so profound a passage, that it may well suggest, for the exercise of the reader's tact, many opinions, and none of them widely departing from the rule of faith. At the same time, let none doubt that the holy angels in their heavenly abodes are, though not, indeed, coeternal with God, yet secure and certain of eternal and true felicity. To their company the Lord teaches that His little ones belong; and not only says, "They shall be equal to the angels of God,"[3] but shows, too, what blessed contemplation the angels themselves enjoy, saying, "Take heed that ye despise not one of these little ones: for I say unto you, that in heaven their angels do always behold the face of my Father which is in heaven."[4]

---

1. Augustine refers to John 8:25; see 10.24. He might rather have referred to Rev. 3:14.
2. Ps. 104:24.
3. Matt. 22:30.
4. Matt. 18:10.

33. OF THE TWO DIFFERENT AND DISSIMILAR COMMUNITIES OF ANGELS, WHICH ARE NOT INAPPROPRIATELY SIGNIFIED BY THE NAMES LIGHT AND DARKNESS

That certain angels sinned, and were thrust down to the lowest parts of this world, where they are, as it were, incarcerated till their final damnation in the day of judgment, the apostle Peter very plainly declares, when he says that "God spared not the angels that sinned, but cast them down to hell, and delivered them into chains of darkness to be reserved into judgment."[1] Who, then, can doubt that God, either in foreknowledge or in act, separated between these and the rest? And who will dispute that the rest are justly called "light"? For even we who are yet living by faith, hoping only and not yet enjoying equality with them, are already called "light" by the apostle: "For ye were sometimes darkness, but now are ye light in the Lord."[2] But as for these apostate angels, all who understand or believe them to be worse than unbelieving men are well aware that they are called "darkness." Wherefore, though light and darkness are to be taken in their literal signification in these passages of Genesis in which it is said, "God said, Let there be light, and there was light," and "God divided the light from the darkness," yet, for our part, we understand these two societies of angels—the one enjoying God, the other swelling with pride; the one to whom it is said, "Praise ye Him, all His angels,"[3] the other whose prince says, "All these things will I give Thee if Thou wilt fall down and worship me";[4] the one blazing with the holy love of God, the other reeking with the unclean lust of self-advancement. And since, as it is written, "God resisteth the proud, but giveth grace unto the humble,"[5] we may say, the one dwelling in the heaven of heavens, the other cast thence, and raging through the lower regions of the air; the one tranquil in the brightness of piety, the other tempest-tossed with beclouding desires; the one, at God's pleasure, tenderly succoring, justly avenging—the other, set on by its own pride, boiling with the lust of subduing and hurting; the one the minister of God's goodness to the utmost of their good pleasure, the other held in by God's power from doing the harm it would; the former laughing at the latter when it does good unwillingly by its persecutions, the latter envying the former when it gathers in its pilgrims. These two angelic communities, then, dissimilar and contrary to one another, the one both by nature good and by will upright, the other also good by nature but by will depraved, as they are exhibited in other and more explicit passages of Holy Writ, so I think they are spoken of in this book of Genesis under the names of light and darkness; and even if the author perhaps had a different meaning, yet our discussion of the obscure language has not been wasted time; for, though we have been unable to discover his meaning, yet we have adhered to the rule of faith, which is sufficiently ascertained by the faithful from other passages of equal authority. For, though it is the material works of God which are here spoken of, they have certainly a resemblance to the spiritual, so that Paul can say, "Ye are all the children of light, and the children of the day: we are not of the night, nor of darkness."[6] If, on the other hand, the author of Genesis saw in the words what we see, then our discussion reaches this more satisfactory conclusion, that the man of God, so eminently and divinely wise, or rather, that the Spirit of God who by him recorded God's works which were finished on the sixth day, may be supposed not to have omitted all mention of the angels whether he included them in the words "in the beginning," because He made them first, or, which seems most likely, because He made them in the only begotten Word. And, under these names heaven and earth, the whole creation is signified, either as divided into spiritual and material, which seems the more likely, or into the two great parts of the world in which all created things are contained, so that, first of all, the creation is presented in sum, and then its parts are enumerated according to the mystic number of the days.

1. 2 Pet. 2:4.
2. Eph. 5:8.
3. Ps. 148:2.
4. Matt. 4:9.
5. Jas. 4:6.
6. 1 Thess. 5:5.

34. OF THE IDEA THAT THE ANGELS WERE MEANT WHERE THE SEPARATION OF THE WATERS BY THE FIRMAMENT IS SPOKEN OF, AND OF THAT OTHER IDEA THAT THE WATERS WERE NOT CREATED

Some,[1] however, have supposed that the angelic hosts are somehow referred to under the name of waters, and that this is what is meant by, "Let there be a firmament in the midst of the waters":[2] that the waters above should be understood of the angels, and those below either of the visible waters, or of the multitude of bad angels, or of the nations of men. If this be so, then it does not here appear when the angels were created, but when they were separated. Though there have not been wanting men foolish and wicked enough[3] to deny that the waters were made by God, because it is nowhere written, "God said, Let there be waters." With equal folly they might say the same of the earth, for nowhere do we read, "God said, Let the earth be." But, say they, it is written, "In the beginning God created the heaven and the earth." Yes, and there the water is meant, for both are included in one word. For "the sea is His," as the psalm says, "and He made it; and His hands formed the dry land."[4] But those who would understand the angels by the waters above the skies have a difficulty about the specific gravity of the elements, and fear that the waters, owing to their fluidity and weight, could not be set in the upper parts of the world. So that, if they were to construct a man upon their own principles, they would not put in his head any moist humors, or "phlegm" as the Greeks call it, and which acts the part of water among the elements of our body. But, in God's handiwork, the head is the seat of the phlegm, and surely most fitly; and yet, according to their supposition, so absurdly that if we were not aware of the fact, and were informed by this same record that God had put a moist and cold and therefore heavy humor in the uppermost part of man's body, these world-weighers would refuse belief. And if they were confronted with the authority of Scripture, they would maintain that something else must be meant by the words. But, were we to investigate and discover all the details which are written in this divine Book regarding the creation of the world, we should have much to say, and should widely digress from the proposed aim of this work. Since, then, we have now said what seemed needful regarding these two diverse and contrary communities of angels, in which the origin of the two human communities (of which we intend to speak anon) is also found, let us at once bring this book also to a conclusion.

1. Augustine himself published this idea in his *Confessions* 13:32, but afterward retracted it, as "said without sufficient consideration" (*Retract.* 2.6.2). Epiphanius and Jerome ascribe it to Origen.
2. Gen. 1:6.
3. Namely, the Audians and Sampsæans, insignificant heretical sects mentioned by Theodoret and Epiphanius.
4. Ps. 95:5.

BOOK TWELVE

ARGUMENT

Augustine first institutes two inquiries regarding the angels; namely, whence is there in some a good, and in others an evil will? And what is the reason of the blessedness of the good, and the misery of the evil? Afterward he treats of the creation of man, and teaches that he is not from eternity, but was created, and by none other than God.

1. THAT THE NATURE OF THE ANGELS, BOTH GOOD AND BAD, IS ONE AND THE SAME

It has already, in the preceding book, been shown how the two cities originated among the angels. Before I speak of the creation of man, and show how the cities took their rise so far as regards the race of rational mortals, I see that I must first, so far as I can, adduce what may demonstrate that it is not incongruous and unsuitable to speak of a society composed of angels and men together; so that there are not four cities or societies—two, namely, of angels, and as many of men—but rather two in all, one composed of the good, the other of the wicked, angels or men indifferently.

That the contrary propensities in good and bad angels have arisen, not from a difference in their nature and origin, since God, the good Author and Creator of all essences, created them both, but from a difference in their wills and desires, it is impossible to doubt. While some steadfastly continued in that which was the common good of all, namely, in

God Himself, and in His eternity, truth, and love; others, being enamored rather of their own power, as if they could be their own good, lapsed to this private good of their own, from that higher and beatific good which was common to all, and, bartering the lofty dignity of eternity for the inflation of pride, the most assured verity for the slyness of vanity, uniting love for factious partisanship, they became proud, deceived, envious. The cause, therefore, of the blessedness of the good is adherence to God. And so the cause of the others' misery will be found in the contrary, that is, in their not adhering to God. Wherefore, if when the question is asked, why are the former blessed, it is rightly answered, because they adhere to God; and when it is asked, why are the latter miserable, it is rightly answered, because they do not adhere to God—then there is no other good for the rational or intellectual creature save God only. Thus, though it is not every creature that can be blessed (for beasts, trees, stones, and things of that kind have not this capacity), yet that creature which has the capacity cannot be blessed of itself, since it is created out of nothing, but only by Him by whom it has been created. For it is blessed by the possession of that whose loss makes it miserable. He, then, who is blessed not in another, but in himself, cannot be miserable, because he cannot lose himself.

Accordingly we say that there is no unchangeable good but the one, true, blessed God; that the things which He made are indeed good because from Him, yet mutable because made not out of Him, but out of nothing. Although, therefore, they are not the supreme good, for God is a greater good, yet those mutable things which can adhere to the immutable good, and so be blessed, are very good; for so completely is He their good, that without Him they cannot but be wretched. And the other created things in the universe are not better on this account, that they cannot be miserable. For no one would say that the other members of the body are superior to the eyes, because they cannot be blind. But as the sentient nature, even when it feels pain, is superior to the stony, which can feel none, so the rational nature, even when wretched, is more excellent than that which lacks reason or feeling, and can therefore experience no misery. And since this is so, then in this nature which has been created so excellent, that though it be mutable itself, it can yet secure its blessedness by adhering to the immutable good, the supreme God; and since it is not satisfied unless it be perfectly blessed, and cannot be thus blessed save in God—in this nature, I say, not to adhere to God, is manifestly a fault.[1] Now every fault injures the nature, and is consequently contrary to the nature. The creature, therefore, which cleaves to God, differs from those who do not, not by nature, but by fault; and yet by this very fault the nature itself is proved to be very noble and admirable. For that nature is certainly praised, the fault of which is justly blamed. For we justly blame the fault because it mars the praiseworthy nature. As, then, when we say that blindness is a defect of the eyes, we prove that sight belongs to the nature of the eyes; and when we say that deafness is a defect of the ears, hearing is thereby proved to belong to their nature;

so, when we say that it is a fault of the angelic creature that it does not cleave to God, we hereby most plainly declare that it pertained to its nature to cleave to God. And who can worthily conceive or express how great a glory that is, to cleave to God, so as to live to Him, to draw wisdom from Him, to delight in Him, and to enjoy this so great good, without death, error, or grief? And thus, since every vice is an injury of the nature, that very vice of the wicked angels, their departure from God, is sufficient proof that God created their nature so good, that it is an injury to it not to be with God.

---

1. Vitium: perhaps "fault" most nearly embraces all the uses of this word.

2. THAT THERE IS NO ENTITY CONTRARY TO THE DIVINE, BECAUSE NONENTITY SEEMS TO BE THAT WHICH IS WHOLLY OPPOSITE TO HIM WHO SUPREMELY AND ALWAYS IS

This may be enough to prevent anyone from supposing, when we speak of the apostate angels, that they could have another nature, derived, as it were, from some different origin, and not from God. From the great impiety of this error we shall disentangle ourselves the more readily and easily, the more distinctly we understand that which God spoke by the angel when He sent Moses to the children of Israel: "I am that I am."[1] For since God is the supreme existence, that is to say, supremely is, and is therefore unchangeable, the things that He made He empowered to be, but not to be supremely like Himself. To some He communicated a more ample, to others a more limited existence, and thus arranged the natures of beings in ranks. For as from *sapere* comes *sapientia*, so from *esse* comes *essentia*—a new word indeed, which the old Latin writers did not use, but which is naturalized in our day,[2] that our language may not want an equivalent for the Greek οὐσία. For this is expressed word for word by *essentia*. Consequently, to that nature which supremely is, and which created all else that exists, no nature is contrary save that which does not exist. For nonentity is the contrary of that which is. And thus there is no being contrary to God, the supreme Being, and Author of all beings whatsoever.

---

1. Exod. 3:14.
2. Quintilian calls it *dura*.

3. THAT THE ENEMIES OF GOD ARE SO, NOT BY NATURE, BUT BY WILL, WHICH, AS IT INJURES THEM, INJURES A GOOD NATURE; FOR IF VICE DOES NOT INJURE, IT IS NOT VICE

In Scripture they are called God's enemies who oppose His rule, not by nature, but by vice; having no power to hurt Him, but only themselves. For they are His enemies, not through their power to hurt, but by their will to oppose Him. For God is unchangeable, and wholly proof against injury. Therefore the vice which makes those who are called His enemies resist Him, is an evil not to God, but to themselves. And to them it is an evil, solely because it corrupts the good of their nature. It is not nature, therefore, but vice, which is contrary to God. For that which is evil is contrary to the good. And who will deny that God is the supreme good? Vice, therefore, is contrary to God, as evil to good. Further, the nature it vitiates is a good, and therefore to this good also it is contrary. But while it is contrary to God only as evil to good, it is contrary to the nature it vitiates, both as evil and as hurtful. For to

God no evils are hurtful; but only to natures mutable and corruptible, though, by the testimony of the vices themselves, originally good. For were they not good, vices could not hurt them. For how do they hurt them but by depriving them of integrity, beauty, welfare, virtue, and, in short, whatever natural good vice is wont to diminish or destroy? But if there be no good to take away, then no injury can be done, and consequently there can be no vice. For it is impossible that there should be a harmless vice. Whence we gather, that though vice cannot injure the unchangeable good, it can injure nothing but good; because it does not exist where it does not injure. This, then, may be thus formulated: vice cannot be in the highest good, and cannot be but in some good. Things solely good, therefore, can in some circumstances exist; things solely evil, never; for even those natures which are vitiated by an evil will, so far indeed as they are vitiated, are evil, but insofar as they are natures they are good. And when a vitiated nature is punished, besides the good it has in being a nature, it has this also, that it is not unpunished.[1] For this is just, and certainly everything just is a good. For no one is punished for natural but for voluntary vices. For even the vice which by the force of habit and long continuance has become a second nature, had its origin in the will. For at present we are speaking of the vices of the nature, which has a mental capacity for that enlightenment which discriminates between what is just and what is unjust.

---

1. With this may be compared the argument of Socrates in the *Gorgias,* in which it is shown that to escape punishment is worse than to suffer it, and that the greatest of evils is to do wrong and not be chastised.

4. OF THE NATURE OF IRRATIONAL AND LIFELESS CREATURES, WHICH IN THEIR OWN KIND AND ORDER DO NOT MAR THE BEAUTY OF THE UNIVERSE

But it is ridiculous to condemn the faults of beasts and trees, and other such mortal and mutable things as are void of intelligence, sensation, or life, even though these faults should destroy their corruptible nature; for these creatures received, at their Creator's will, an existence fitting them, by passing away and giving place to others, to secure that lowest form of beauty, the beauty of seasons, which in its own place is a requisite part of this world. For things earthly were neither to be made equal to things heavenly, nor were they, though inferior, to be quite omitted from the universe. Since, then, in those situations where such things are appropriate, some perish to make way for others that are born in their room, and the less succumb to the greater, and the things that are overcome are transformed into the quality of those that have the mastery, this is the appointed order of things transitory. Of this order the beauty does not strike us, because by our mortal frailty we are so involved in a part of it, that we cannot perceive the whole, in which these fragments that offend us are harmonized with the most accurate fitness and beauty. And therefore, where we are not so well able to perceive the wisdom of the Creator, we are very properly enjoined to believe it, lest in the vanity of human rashness we presume to find any fault with the work of so great an Artificer. At the same time, if we attentively consider even these faults of earthly things, which are neither voluntary nor penal, they seem to illustrate the excellence of the natures themselves, which are all originated and created by God; for it is that which pleases us in this nature which we are displeased to see removed by the fault—unless even the natures themselves displease men, as often happens when they become hurtful to them, and then men estimate them not by their nature, but by their utility; as in the case of those animals whose swarms scourged the pride of the Egyptians. But in this way of estimating, they may find fault with the sun itself; for certain criminals or debtors are sentenced by the judges to be set in the sun. Therefore it is not with respect to our convenience or discomfort, but with respect to their own nature, that the creatures are glorifying to their Artificer. Thus even the nature of the eternal fire, penal though it be to the condemned sinners, is most assuredly worthy of praise. For what is more beautiful than fire flaming, blazing, and shining? What more useful than fire for warming, restoring, cooking, though nothing is more destructive than fire burning and consuming? The same thing, then, when applied in one way, is destructive, but when applied suitably, is most beneficial. For who can find words to tell its uses throughout the whole world? We must not listen, then, to those who praise the light of fire but find fault with its heat, judging it not by its nature, but by their convenience or discomfort. For they wish to see, but not to be burned. But they forget that this very light which is so pleasant to them, disagrees with and hurts weak eyes; and in that heat which is disagreeable to them, some animals find the most suitable conditions of a healthy life.

5. THAT IN ALL NATURES, OF EVERY KIND AND RANK, GOD IS GLORIFIED

All natures, then, inasmuch as they are, and have therefore a rank and species of their own, and a kind of internal harmony, are certainly good. And when they are in the places assigned to them by the order of their nature, they preserve such being as they have received. And those things which have not received everlasting being are altered for better or for worse, so as to suit the wants and motions of those things to which the Creator's law has made them subservient; and thus they tend in the divine providence to that end which is embraced in the general scheme of the government of the universe. So that, though the corruption of transitory and perishable things brings them to utter destruction, it does not prevent their producing that which was designed to be their result. And this being so, God, who supremely is, and who therefore created every being which has not supreme existence (for that which was made of nothing could not be equal to Him, and indeed could not be at all had He not made it), is not to be found fault with on account of the creature's faults, but is to be praised in view of the natures He has made.

6. WHAT THE CAUSE OF THE BLESSEDNESS OF THE GOOD ANGELS IS, AND WHAT THE CAUSE OF THE MISERY OF THE WICKED

Thus the true cause of the blessedness of the good angels is found to be this, that they cleave to Him who supremely is. And if we ask the cause of the misery of the bad, it occurs to us, and not unreasonably, that they are miserable because they have forsaken Him who supremely is, and have turned to themselves who have no such essence. And this vice, what else is it called than pride? For "pride is the beginning of sin."[1] They were unwilling, then, to preserve their strength for God; and as adherence to God was the condition of their enjoying an ampler being, they diminished it by preferring themselves to Him. This was the first defect, and the first impoverishment, and the first flaw of their nature, which was created, not indeed supremely existent, but finding its blessedness in the enjoyment of the supreme Being; while by abandoning Him it should become, not indeed no nature at all, but a nature with a less ample existence, and therefore wretched.

If the further question be asked, "What was the efficient cause of their evil will?" there is none. For what is it which makes the will bad, when it is the will itself which makes the action bad? And consequently the bad will is the cause of the bad action, but nothing is the efficient cause of the bad will. For if anything is the cause, this thing either has or has not a will. If it has, the will is either good or bad. If good, who is so left to himself as to say that a good will makes a will bad? For in this case, a good will would be the cause of sin; a most absurd supposition. On the other hand, if this hypothetical thing has a bad will, I wish to know what made it so; and that we may not go on forever, I ask at once, what made the *first* evil will bad? For that is not the first which was itself corrupted by an evil will, but that is the first which was made evil by no other will. For if it were preceded by that which made it evil, that will was first which made the other evil. But if it is replied, "Nothing made it evil; it always was evil," I ask if it has been existing in some nature. For if not, then it did not exist at all; and if it did exist in some nature, then it vitiated and corrupted it, and injured it, and consequently deprived it of good. And therefore the evil will could not exist in an evil nature, but in a nature at once good and mutable, which this vice could injure. For if it did no injury, it was no vice; and consequently the will in which it was, could not be called evil. But if it did injury, it did it by taking away or diminishing good. And therefore there could not be from eternity, as was suggested, an evil will in that thing in which there had been previously a natural good, which the evil will was able to diminish by corrupting it. If, then, it was not from eternity, who, I ask, made it? The only thing that can be suggested in reply is, that something which itself had no will, made the will evil. I ask, then, whether this thing was superior, inferior, or equal to it? If superior, then it is better. How, then, has it no will, and not rather a good will? The same reasoning applies if it was equal; for so long as two things have equally a good will, the one cannot produce in the other an evil will. Then remains the supposition that that which corrupted the will of the angelic nature which first sinned, was itself an inferior thing without a will. But that thing, be it of the lowest and most earthly kind, is certainly itself good, since it is a nature and being, with a form and rank of its own in its own kind and order. How, then, can a good thing be the efficient cause of an evil will? How, I say, can good be the cause of evil? For when the will abandons what is above itself, and turns to what is lower, it becomes evil—not because that is evil to which it turns, but because the turning itself is wicked. Therefore it is not an inferior thing which has made the will evil, but it is itself which has become so by wickedly and inordinately desiring an inferior thing. For if two men, alike in physical and moral constitution, see the same corporal beauty, and one of them is excited by the sight to desire an illicit enjoyment while the other steadfastly maintains a modest restraint of his will, what do we suppose brings it about, that there is an evil will in the one and not in the other? What produces it in the man in whom it exists? Not the bodily beauty, for that was presented equally to the gaze of both, and yet did not produce in both an evil will. Did the flesh of the one cause the desire as he looked? But why did not the flesh of the other? Or was it the disposition? But why not the disposition of both? For we are supposing that both were of a like temperament of body and soul. Must we, then, say that the one was tempted by a secret suggestion of the evil spirit? As if it was not by his own will that he consented to this suggestion and to any inducement whatever! This consent, then, this evil will which he presented to the evil suasive influence —what was the cause of it, we ask? For, not to delay on such a difficulty as this, if both are tempted equally and one yields and consents to the temptation while the other remains unmoved by it, what other account can we give of the matter than this, that the one is willing, the other unwilling, to fall away from chastity? And what causes this but their own wills, in cases at least such as we are supposing, where the temperament is identical? The same beauty was equally obvious to the eyes of both; the same secret temptation pressed on both with equal violence. However minutely we examine the case, therefore, we can discern nothing which caused the will of the one to be evil. For if we say that the man himself made his will evil, what was the man himself before his will was evil but a good nature created by God, the unchangeable good? Here are two men who, before the temptation, were alike in body and soul, and of whom one yielded to the tempter who persuaded him, while the other could not be persuaded to desire that lovely body which was equally before the eyes of both. Shall we say of the successfully tempted man that he corrupted his own will, since he was certainly good before his will became bad? Then, why did he do so? Was it because his will was a nature, or because it was made of nothing? We shall find that the latter is the case. For if a nature is the cause of an evil will, what else can we say than that evil arises from good or that good is the cause of evil? And how can it come to pass that a nature, good though mutable, should produce any evil—that is to say, should make the will itself wicked?

---

1. Eccles. 10:13.

7. THAT WE OUGHT NOT TO EXPECT TO FIND ANY EFFICIENT CAUSE OF THE EVIL WILL

Let no one, therefore, look for an efficient cause of the evil will; for it is not efficient, but deficient, as the will itself is not an effecting of something, but a defect. For defection from that which supremely is, to that which has less of being—this is to begin to have an evil will. Now, to seek to discover the causes of these defections—causes, as I have said, not efficient, but deficient—is as if someone sought to see darkness, or hear silence. Yet both of these are known by us, and the former by means only of the eye, the latter only by the ear; but not by their positive actuality,[1] but by their want of it. Let no one then seek to know from me what I know that I do not know; unless he perhaps wishes to learn to be ignorant of that of which all we know is, that it cannot be known. For those things which are known not by their actuality, but by their want of it, are known, if our expression may be allowed and understood, by not knowing them, that by knowing them they may be not known. For when the eyesight surveys objects that strike the sense, it nowhere sees darkness but where it begins not to see. And so no other sense but the ear can perceive silence, and yet it is only perceived by not hearing. Thus, too, our mind perceives intelligible forms by understanding them; but when they are deficient, it knows them by not knowing them; for "who can understand defects?"[2]

---

1. Specie.
2. Ps. 19:12.

8. OF THE MISDIRECTED LOVE WHEREBY THE WILL FELL AWAY FROM THE IMMUTABLE TO THE MUTABLE GOOD

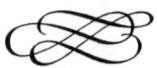

This I do know, that the nature of God can never, nowhere, nowise be defective, and that natures made of nothing can. These latter, however, the more being they have, and the more good they do (for then they do something positive), the more they have efficient causes; but insofar as they are defective in being, and consequently do evil (for then what is their work but vanity?), they have deficient causes. And I know likewise, that the will could not become evil, were it unwilling to become so; and therefore its failings are justly punished, being not necessary, but voluntary. For its defections are not to evil things, but are themselves evil; that is to say, are not toward things that are naturally and in themselves evil, but the defection of the will is evil, because it is contrary to the order of nature, and an abandonment of that which has supreme being for that which has less. For avarice is not a fault inherent in gold, but in the man who inordinately loves gold, to the detriment of justice, which ought to be held in incomparably higher regard than gold. Neither is luxury the fault of lovely and charming objects, but of the heart that inordinately loves sensual pleasures, to the neglect of temperance, which attaches us to objects more lovely in their spirituality, and more delectable by their incorruptibility. Nor yet is boasting the fault of human praise, but of the soul that is inordinately fond of the applause of men, and that makes light of the voice of conscience. Pride, too, is not the fault of him who delegates power, nor of power itself, but of the soul that is inordinately enamored of its own power, and despises the more just dominion of a higher authority. Consequently he who inordinately loves the good which any nature possesses, even though he obtain it, himself becomes evil in the good, and wretched because deprived of a greater good.

9. WHETHER THE ANGELS, BESIDES RECEIVING FROM GOD THEIR NATURE, RECEIVED FROM HIM ALSO THEIR GOOD WILL BY THE HOLY SPIRIT IMBUING THEM WITH LOVE

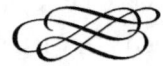

There is, then, no natural efficient cause or, if I may be allowed the expression, no essential cause, of the evil will, since itself is the origin of evil in mutable spirits, by which the good of their nature is diminished and corrupted; and the will is made evil by nothing else than defection from God—a defection of which the cause, too, is certainly deficient. But as to the good will, if we should say that there is no efficient cause of it, we must beware of giving currency to the opinion that the good will of the good angels is not created, but is coeternal with God. For if they themselves are created, how can we say that their good will was eternal? But if created, was it created along with themselves, or did they exist for a time without it? If along with themselves, then doubtless it was created by Him who created them, and, as soon as ever they were created, they attached themselves to Him who created them, with the love He created in them. And they are separated from the society of the rest, because they have continued in the same good will; while the others have fallen away to another will, which is an evil one, by the very fact of its being a falling away from the good; from which, we may add, they would not have fallen away had they been unwilling to do so. But if the good angels existed for a time without a good will, and produced it in themselves without God's interference, then it follows that they made themselves better than He made them. Away with such a thought! For without a good will, what were they but evil? Or if they were not evil, because they had not an evil will any more than a good one (for they had not fallen away from that which as yet they had not begun to enjoy), certainly they were not the same, not so good, as when they came to have a good will. Or if they could not make themselves better than they were made by Him who is surpassed by none in His work, then certainly, without His helpful operation, they could not come to possess that good will which made them better. And though their good will effected that they did not turn to themselves, who had a more stinted existence, but to Him who supremely is, and that, being united to Him, their own being was enlarged, and they lived a wise and blessed life by His communications to them, what does this prove but that the will, however good it might be, would have continued helplessly only to desire Him, had not He who had made their nature out of nothing, and yet capable of enjoying Him, first stimulated it to desire Him, and then filled it with Himself, and so made it better?

Besides, this too has to be inquired into, whether, if the good angels made their own will good, they did so with or without will? If without, then it was not their doing. If with, was the will good or bad? If bad, how could a bad will give birth to a good one? If good, then already they had a good will. And who made this will, which already they had, but He who created them with a good will, or with that chaste love by which they cleaved to Him, in one and the same act creating their nature, and endowing it with grace? And thus we are driven to believe that the holy angels never existed without a good will or the love of God. But the angels who, though created good, are yet evil now, became so by their own will. And this will was not made evil by their good nature, unless by its voluntary defection from good; for good is not the cause of evil, but a defection from good is. These angels, therefore, either received less of the grace of the divine love than those who persevered in the same; or if both were created equally good, then, while the one fell by their evil will, the others were more abundantly assisted, and attained to that pitch of blessedness at which they became certain they should never fall from it—as we have already shown in the preceding book.[1] We must therefore acknowledge, with the praise due to the Creator, that not only of holy men, but also of the holy angels, it can be said that "the love of God is shed abroad in their hearts by the Holy Ghost, which is given unto them."[2] And that not only of men, but primarily and principally of angels it is true, as it is written, "It is good to draw near to God."[3] And those who have this good in common, have, both with Him to whom they draw near, and with one another, a holy fellowship, and form one city of God —His living sacrifice, and His living temple. And I see that, as I have now spoken of the rise of this city among the angels, it is time to speak of the origin of that part of it which is hereafter to be united to the immortal angels, and which at present is being gathered from among mortal men, and is either sojourning on earth, or, in the persons of those who have passed through death, is resting in the secret receptacles and abodes of disembodied spirits. For from one man, whom God created as the first, the whole human race descended, according to the faith of Holy Scripture, which deservedly is of wonderful authority among all nations throughout the world; since, among its other true statements, it predicted, by its divine foresight, that all nations would give credit to it.

---

1. See above, 11.13.
2. Rom. 5:5.
3. Ps. 73:28.

10. OF THE FALSENESS OF THE HISTORY WHICH ALLOTS MANY THOUSAND YEARS TO THE WORLD'S PAST

Let us, then, omit the conjectures of men who know not what they say, when they speak of the nature and origin of the human race. For some hold the same opinion regarding men that they hold regarding the world itself, that they have always been. Thus Apuleius says when he is describing our race, "Individually they are mortal, but collectively, and as a race, they are immortal."[1] And when they are asked how, if the human race has always been, they vindicate the truth of their history, which narrates who were the inventors, and what they invented, and who first instituted the liberal studies and the other arts, and who first inhabited this or that region, and this or that island, they reply,[2] that most, if not all lands, were so desolated at intervals by fire and flood, that men were greatly reduced in numbers, and from these, again, the population was restored to its former numbers, and that thus there was at intervals a new beginning made, and though those things which had been interrupted and checked by the severe devastations were only renewed, yet they seemed to be originated then; but that man could not exist at all save as produced by man. But they say what they think, not what they know.

They are deceived, too, by those highly mendacious documents which profess to give the history of many thousand years, though, reckoning by the sacred Writings, we find that not six thousand years have yet passed.[3] And, not to spend many words in exposing the baselessness of these documents, in which so many thousands of years are accounted for, nor in proving that their authorities are totally inadequate, let me cite only that letter which Alexander the Great wrote to his mother Olympias,[4] giving her the narrative he had from an Egyptian priest, which he had extracted from their sacred archives, and which gave an account of kingdoms mentioned also by the Greek historians. In this letter of Alexander's a term of upward of five thousand years is assigned to the kingdom of Assyria; while in the Greek history only 1,300 years are reckoned from the reign of Bel himself, whom both Greek and Egyptian agree in counting the first king of Assyria. Then to the empire of the Persians and Macedonians this Egyptian assigned more than eight thousand years, counting to the time of Alexander, to whom he was speaking; while among the Greeks, 485 years are assigned to the Macedonians down to the death of Alexander, and to the Persians 233 years, reckoning to the termination of his conquests. Thus these give a much smaller number of years than the Egyptians; and indeed, though multiplied three times, the Greek chronology would still be shorter. For the Egyptians are said to have formerly reckoned only four months to their year;[5] so that one year, according to the fuller and truer computation now in use among them as well as among ourselves, would comprehend three of their old years. But not even thus, as I said, does the Greek history correspond with the Egyptian in its chronology. And therefore the former must receive the greater credit, because it does not exceed the true account of the duration of the world as it is given by our documents, which are truly sacred. Further, if this letter of Alexander, which has become so famous, differs widely in this matter of chronology from the probable credible account, how much less can we believe these documents which, though full of fabulous and fictitious antiquities, they would fain oppose to the authority of our well-known and divine books, which predicted that the whole world would believe them, and which the whole world accordingly has believed; which proved, too, that it had truly narrated past events by its prediction of future events, which have so exactly come to pass!

---

1. *Apuleius De Deo Socratis.*
2. Augustine no doubt refers to the interesting account given by Critias, near the beginning of the *Timæus*, of the conversation of Solon with the Egyptian priests.
3. Augustine here follows the chronology of Eusebius, who reckons 5,611 years from the creation to the taking of Rome by the Goths; adopting the Septuagint version of the patriarchal ages.

4. See above, 8.5.
5. It is not apparent to what Augustine refers. The Arcadians, according to Macrobius (*Saturn.* 1.7), divided their year into three months, and the Egyptians divided theirs into three seasons: each of these seasons having four months, it is possible that Augustine may have referred to this. See Wilkinson's excursus on the Egyptian year, in Rawlinson's *Herodotus* Book 2.

11. OF THOSE WHO SUPPOSE THAT THIS WORLD INDEED IS NOT ETERNAL, BUT THAT EITHER THERE ARE NUMBERLESS WORLDS, OR THAT ONE AND THE SAME WORLD IS PERPETUALLY RESOLVED INTO ITS ELEMENTS, AND RENEWED AT THE CONCLUSION OF FIXED CYCLES

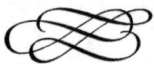

There are some, again, who, though they do not suppose that this world is eternal, are of opinion either that this is not the only world, but that there are numberless worlds or that indeed it is the only one, but that it dies, and is born again at fixed intervals, and this times without number;[1] but they must acknowledge that the human race existed before there were other men to beget them. For they cannot suppose that, if the whole world perish, some men would be left alive in the world, as they might survive in floods and conflagrations, which those other speculators suppose to be partial, and from which they can therefore reasonably argue that a few then survived whose posterity would renew the population; but as they believe that the world itself is renewed out of its own material, so they must believe that out of its elements the human race was produced, and then that the progeny of mortals sprang like that of other animals from their parents.

---

1. The former opinion was held by Democritus and his disciple Epicurus; the latter by Heraclitus, who supposed that "God amused Himself" by thus renewing worlds.

12. HOW THESE PERSONS ARE TO BE ANSWERED, WHO FIND FAULT WITH THE CREATION OF MAN ON THE SCORE OF ITS RECENT DATE

As to those who are always asking why man was not created during these countless ages of the infinitely extended past, and came into being so lately that, according to Scripture, less than six thousand years have elapsed since he began to be, I would reply to them regarding the creation of man, just as I replied regarding the origin of the world to those who will not believe that it is not eternal, but had a beginning, which even Plato himself most plainly declares, though some think his statement was not consistent with his real opinion.[1] If it offends them that the time that has elapsed since the creation of man is so short, and his years so few according to our authorities, let them take this into consideration, that nothing that has a limit is long, and that all the ages of time being finite, are very little, or indeed nothing at all, when compared to the interminable eternity. Consequently, if there had elapsed since the creation of man, I do not say five or six, but even sixty or six hundred thousand years, or sixty times as many, or six hundred or six hundred thousand times as many, or this sum multiplied until it could no longer be expressed in numbers, the same question could still be put, "Why was he not made before?" For the past and boundless eternity during which God abstained from creating man is so great, that, compare it with what vast and untold number of ages you please, so long as there is a definite conclusion of this term of time, it is not even as if you compared the minutest drop of water with the ocean that everywhere flows around the globe. For of these two, one indeed is very small, the other incomparably vast, yet both are finite; but that space of time which starts from some beginning, and is limited by some termination, be it of what extent it may, if you compare it with that which has no beginning, I know not whether to say we should count it the very minutest thing, or nothing at all. For, take this limited time, and deduct from the end of it, one by one, the briefest moments (as you might take day by day from a man's life, beginning at the day in which he now lives, back to that of his birth), and though the number of moments you must subtract in this backward movement be so great that no word can express it, yet this subtraction will some time carry you to the beginning. But if you take away from a time which has no beginning, I do not say brief moments one by one, nor yet hours, or days, or months, or years even in quantities, but terms of years so vast that they cannot be named by the most skillful arithmeticians—take away terms of years as vast as that which we have supposed to be gradually consumed by the deduction of moments—and take them away not once and again repeatedly, but always, and what do you effect, what do you make by your deduction, since you never reach the beginning, which has no existence? Wherefore, that which we now demand after five thousand odd years, our descendants might with like curiosity demand after six hundred thousand years, supposing these dying generations of men continue so long to decay and be renewed, and supposing posterity continues as weak and ignorant as ourselves. The same question might have been asked by those who have lived before us and while man was even newer upon earth. The first man himself in short might the day after or the very day of his creation have asked why he was created no sooner. And no matter at what earlier or later period he had been created, this controversy about the commencement of this world's history would have had precisely the same difficulties as it has now.

---

1. The Alexandrian Neoplatonists endeavored in this way to escape from the obvious meaning of the *Timæus*.

13. OF THE REVOLUTION OF THE AGES, WHICH SOME PHILOSOPHERS BELIEVE WILL BRING ALL THINGS ROUND AGAIN, AFTER A CERTAIN FIXED CYCLE, TO THE SAME ORDER AND FORM AS AT FIRST

This controversy some philosophers have seen no other approved means of solving than by introducing cycles of time, in which there should be a constant renewal and repetition of the order of nature;[1] and they have therefore asserted that these cycles will ceaselessly recur, one passing away and another coming, though they are not agreed as to whether one permanent world shall pass through all these cycles, or whether the world shall at fixed intervals die out, and be renewed so as to exhibit a recurrence of the same phenomena—the things which have been, and those which are to be, coinciding. And from this fantastic vicissitude they exempt not even the immortal soul that has attained wisdom, consigning it to a ceaseless transmigration between delusive blessedness and real misery. For how can that be truly called blessed which has no assurance of being so eternally, and is either in ignorance of the truth, and blind to the misery that is approaching, or, knowing it, is in misery and fear? Or if it passes to bliss, and leaves miseries forever, then there happens in time a new thing which time shall not end. Why not, then, the world also? Why may not man, too, be a similar thing? So that, by following the straight path of sound doctrine, we escape, I know not what circuitous paths, discovered by deceiving and deceived sages.

Some, too, in advocating these recurring cycles that restore all things to their original, cite in favor of their supposition what Solomon says in the book of Ecclesiastes: "What is that which hath been? It is that which shall be. And what is that which is done? It is that which shall be done: and there is no new thing under the sun. Who can speak and say, See, this is new? It hath been already of old time, which was before us."[2] This he said either of those things of which he had just been speaking—the succession of generations, the orbit of the sun, the course of rivers—or else of all kinds of creatures that are born and die. For men were before us, are with us, and shall be after us; and so all living things and all plants. Even monstrous and irregular productions, though differing from one another, and though some are reported as solitary instances, yet resemble one another generally, insofar as they are miraculous and monstrous, and, in this sense, have been, and shall be, and are no new and recent things under the sun. However, some would understand these words as meaning that in the predestination of God all things have already existed, and that thus there is no new thing under the sun. At all events, far be it from any true believer to suppose that by these words of Solomon those cycles are meant, in which, according to those philosophers, the same periods and events of time are repeated; as if, for example, the philosopher Plato, having taught in the school at Athens which is called the Academy, so, numberless ages before, at long but certain intervals, this same Plato, and the same school, and the same disciples existed, and so also are to be repeated during the countless cycles that are yet to be—far be it, I say, from us to believe this. For once Christ died for our sins; and, rising from the dead, He dies no more. "Death hath no more dominion over Him;[3] and we ourselves after the resurrection shall be "ever with the Lord,"[4] to whom we now say, as the sacred psalmist dictates, "Thou shalt keep us, O LORD, Thou shalt preserve us from this generation."[5] And that too which follows, is, I think, appropriate enough: "The wicked walk *in a circle*," not because their life is to recur by means of these circles, which these philosophers imagine, but because the path in which their false doctrine now runs is circuitous.

---

1. Antoninus says (2.14): "All things from eternity are of like forms, and come round in a circle." Cf. also 9.28, and the references to more ancient philosophical writers in Gataker's notes in these passages.
2. Eccles. 1:9–10. So Origen *De Prin.* 3.5 and 2.3.
3. Rom. 6:9.
4. 1 Thess. 4:16.
5. Ps. 12:7.

14. OF THE CREATION OF THE HUMAN RACE IN TIME, AND HOW THIS WAS EFFECTED WITHOUT ANY NEW DESIGN OR CHANGE OF PURPOSE ON GOD'S PART

What wonder is it if, entangled in these circles, they find neither entrance nor egress? For they know not how the human race, and this mortal condition of ours, took its origin, nor how it will be brought to an end, since they cannot penetrate the inscrutable wisdom of God. For, though Himself eternal, and without beginning, yet He caused time to have a beginning; and man, whom He had not previously made He made in time, not from a new and sudden resolution, but by His unchangeable and eternal design. Who can search out the unsearchable depth of this purpose, who can scrutinize the inscrutable wisdom, wherewith God, without change of will, created man, who had never before been, and gave him an existence in time, and increased the human race from one individual? For the psalmist himself, when he had first said, "Thou shalt keep us, O LORD, Thou shalt preserve us from this generation forever," and had then rebuked those whose foolish and impious doctrine preserves for the soul no eternal deliverance and blessedness, adds immediately, "The wicked walk in a circle." Then, as if it were said to him, "What then do you believe, feel, know? Are we to believe that it suddenly occurred to God to create man, whom He had never before made in a past eternity—God, to whom nothing new can occur, and in whom is no changeableness?" the psalmist goes on to reply, as if addressing God Himself, "According to the depth of Thy wisdom Thou hast multiplied the children of men." Let men, he seems to say, fancy what they please, let them conjecture and dispute as seems good to them, but you have multiplied the children of men according to the depth of your wisdom, which no man can comprehend. For this is a depth indeed, that God always has been, and that man, whom He had never made before, He willed to make in time, and this without changing His design and will.

15. WHETHER WE ARE TO BELIEVE THAT GOD, AS HE HAS ALWAYS BEEN SOVEREIGN LORD, HAS ALWAYS HAD CREATURES OVER WHOM HE EXERCISED HIS SOVEREIGNTY; AND IN WHAT SENSE WE CAN SAY THAT THE CREATURE HAS ALWAYS BEEN, AND YET CANNOT SAY IT IS COETERNAL

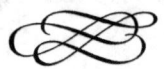

For my own part, indeed, as I dare not say that there ever was a time when the Lord God was not Lord,[1] so I ought not to doubt that man had no existence before time, and was first created in time. But when I consider what God could be the Lord of, if there was not always some creature, I shrink from making any assertion, remembering my own insignificance, and that it is written, "What man is he that can know the counsel of God? Or who can think what the will of the Lord is? For the thoughts of mortal men are timid, and our devices are but uncertain. For the corruptible body presseth down the soul, and the earthly tabernacle weigheth down the mind that museth upon many things."[2] Many things certainly do I muse upon in this earthly tabernacle, because the one thing which is true among the many, or beyond the many, I cannot find. If, then, among these many thoughts, I say that there have always been creatures for Him to be Lord of, who is always and ever has been Lord, but that these creatures have not always been the same, but succeeded one another (for we would not seem to say that any is coeternal with the Creator, an assertion condemned equally by faith and sound reason), I must take care lest I fall into the absurd and ignorant error of maintaining that by these successions and changes mortal creatures have always existed, whereas the immortal creatures had not begun to exist until the date of our own world, when the angels were created; if at least the angels are intended by that light which was first made, or, rather, by that heaven of which it is said, "In the beginning God created the heavens and the earth."[3] The angels at least did not exist before they were created; for if we say that they have always existed, we shall seem to make them coeternal with the Creator. Again, if I say that the angels were not created in time, but existed before all times, as those over whom God, who has ever been sovereign, exercised His sovereignty, then I shall be asked whether, if they were created before all time, they, being creatures, could possibly always exist. It may perhaps be replied, Why not *always*, since that which is in all time may very properly be said to be "always"? Now so true is it that these angels have existed in all time that even before time was they were created; if at least time began with the heavens, and the angels existed before the heavens. And if time was even before the heavenly bodies, not indeed marked by hours, days, months, and years—for these measures of time's periods which are commonly and properly called times, did manifestly begin with the motion of the heavenly bodies, and so God said, when He appointed them, "Let them be for signs, and for seasons, and for days, and for years"[4]—if, I say, time was before these heavenly bodies by some changing movement, whose parts succeeded one another and could not exist simultaneously, and if there was some such movement among the angels which necessitated the existence of time, and that they from their very creation should be subject to these temporal changes, then they have existed in all time, for time came into being along with them. And who will say that what was in all time, was not always?

But if I make such a reply, it will be said to me, "How, then, are they not coeternal with the Creator, if He and they always have been? How even can they be said to have been created, if we are to understand that they have always existed?" What shall we reply to this? Shall we say that both statements are true? That they always have been, since they have been in all time, they being created along with time, or time along with them, and yet that also they were created? For, similarly, we will not deny that time itself was created, though no one doubts that time has been in all time; for if it has not been in all time, then there was a time when there was no time. But the most foolish person could not make such an assertion. For we can reasonably say there was a time when Rome was not; there was a time when Jerusalem was not; there was a time when Abraham was not; there was a time when man was not, and so on: in fine, if the world was not made at the commencement of time, but after some time had elapsed, we can say there was a time when the world was not. But to say there was a time when time was not is as absurd as to say there was a man when there was no man; or, this world was when this world was not. For if we are not referring to the same object, the form of expression may be used, as, there was another man when this man was not. Thus we can reasonably say there was another time when this time was not; but not the merest simpleton could say there was a time when there was no time. As, then, we say that time was created, though we also say that it always has been, since in all time time has been, so it does not follow that if the angels have always been, they were therefore not created. For we say that they have always been, because they have been in all time; and we say they have been in all time, because time itself could nowise be without them. For where there is no creature whose changing movements admit of succession, there cannot be time at all. And consequently, even if they have always existed, they were created; neither, if they have always existed, are they therefore coeternal with the Creator. For He has always existed in unchangeable eternity; while they were created, and are said to have been always, because they have been in all time, time being impossible without the creature. But time passing away by its changefulness, cannot be coeternal with changeless eternity. And consequently, though the immortality of the angels does not pass in time, does not become past as if now it were not, nor has a future as if it were not yet, still their movements, which are the basis of time, do pass from future to past; and therefore they cannot be coeternal with the Creator, in whose movement we cannot say that there has been that which now is not, or shall be that which is not yet. Wherefore, if God always has been Lord, He has always had creatures under His dominion—creatures, however, not begotten of Him, but created by Him out of nothing; nor coeternal with Him, for He was before them though at no time without them, because He preceded them, not by the lapse of time, but by His abiding eternity. But if I make this reply to those who demand how He was always Creator, always Lord, if there were not always a subject creation; or how this was created, and not rather coeternal with its Creator, if it always was, I fear I may be accused of recklessly affirming what I know not, instead of teaching what I know. I return, therefore, to that which our Creator has seen fit that we should know; and those things which He has allowed the abler men to know in this life, or has reserved to be known in the next by the perfected saints, I acknowledge to be beyond my capacity. But I have thought it right to discuss these matters without making positive assertions, that they who read may be warned to abstain from hazardous questions, and may not deem themselves fit for everything. Let them rather endeavor to obey the wholesome injunction of the apostle, when he says, "For I say, through the grace given unto me, to every man that is among you, not to think of himself more highly than he ought to think; but to think soberly, according as God hath dealt to every man the measure of faith."[5] For if an infant receive nourishment suited to its strength, it becomes capable, as it grows, of taking more; but if its strength and capacity be overtaxed, it dwindles away in place of growing.

---

1. Cf. *De Trin.* 5.17.
2. Wisd. of Sol. 9:13–15.
3. Gen. 1:1.
4. Gen. 1:14.
5. Rom. 12:3.

16. HOW WE ARE TO UNDERSTAND GOD'S PROMISE OF LIFE ETERNAL, WHICH WAS UTTERED BEFORE THE "ETERNAL TIMES"

I own that I do not know what ages passed before the human race was created, yet I have no doubt that no created thing is coeternal with the Creator. But even the apostle speaks of time as eternal, and this with reference, not to the future, but, which is more surprising, to the past. For he says, "In hope of eternal life, which God that cannot lie promised before the eternal times, but hath in due times manifested His word."[1] You see he says that in the past there have been eternal times, which, however, were not coeternal with God. And since God before these eternal times not only existed, but also "promised" life eternal, which He manifested in its own times (that is to say, in due times), what else is this than His word? For this is life eternal. But then, how did He promise; for the promise was made to men, and yet they had no existence before eternal times? Does this not mean that, in His own eternity, and in His coeternal word, that which was to be in its own time was already predestined and fixed?

---

1. Titus 1:2–3. Augustine here follows the version of Jerome, and not the Vulgate. Cf. *Contra Priscill.* 6 and *De Gen. contra Man.* 4.4.

17. WHAT DEFENSE IS MADE BY SOUND FAITH REGARDING GOD'S UNCHANGEABLE COUNSEL AND WILL, AGAINST THE REASONINGS OF THOSE WHO HOLD THAT THE WORKS OF GOD ARE ETERNALLY REPEATED IN REVOLVING CYCLES THAT RESTORE ALL THINGS AS THEY WERE

Of this, too, I have no doubt, that before the first man was created, there never had been a man at all, neither this same man himself recurring by I know not what cycles, and having made I know not how many revolutions, nor any other of similar nature. From this belief I am not frightened by philosophical arguments, among which that is reckoned the most acute which is founded on the assertion that the infinite cannot be comprehended by any mode of knowledge. Consequently, they argue, God has in his own mind finite conceptions of all finite things which He makes. Now it cannot be supposed that His goodness was ever idle; for if it were, there should be ascribed to Him an awakening to activity in time, from a past eternity of inactivity, as if He repented of an idleness that had no beginning, and proceeded, therefore, to make a beginning of work. This being the case, they say it must be that the same things are always repeated, and that as they pass, so they are destined always to return, whether amid all these changes the world remains the same—the world which has always been, and yet was created—or that the world in these revolutions is perpetually dying out and being renewed; otherwise, if we point to a time when the works of God were begun, it would be believed that He considered His past eternal leisure to be inert and indolent, and therefore condemned and altered it as displeasing to Himself. Now if God is supposed to have been indeed always making temporal things, but different from one another, and one after the other, so that He thus came at last to make man, whom He had never made before, then it may seem that He made man not with knowledge (for they suppose no knowledge can comprehend the infinite succession of creatures), but at the dictate of the hour, as it struck him at the moment, with a sudden and accidental change of mind. On the other hand, say they, if those cycles be admitted, and if we suppose that the same temporal things are repeated, while the world either remains identical through all these rotations, or else dies away and is renewed, then there is ascribed to God neither the slothful ease of a past eternity, nor a rash and unforeseen creation. And if the same things be not thus repeated in cycles, then they cannot by any science or prescience be comprehended in their endless diversity. Even though reason could not refute, faith would smile at these argumentations, with which the godless endeavor to turn our simple piety from the right way, that we may walk with them "in a circle." But by the help of the Lord our God, even reason, and that readily enough, shatters these revolving circles which conjecture frames. For that which specially leads these men astray to refer their own circles to the straight path of truth, is, that they measure by their own human, changeable, and narrow intellect the divine mind, which is absolutely unchangeable, infinitely capacious, and without succession of thought, counting all things without number. So that saying of the apostle comes true of them, for, "comparing themselves with themselves, they do not understand."[1] For because they do, in virtue of a new purpose, whatever new thing has occurred to them to be done (their minds being changeable), they conclude it is so with God; and thus compare, not God—for they cannot conceive God, but think of one like themselves when they think of Him—not God, but themselves, and not with Him, but with themselves. For our part, we dare not believe that God is affected in one way when He works, in another when He rests. Indeed, to say that He is affected at all is an abuse of language, since it implies that there comes to be something in His nature which was not there before. For he who is affected is acted upon, and whatever is acted upon is changeable. His leisure, therefore, is no laziness, indolence, inactivity; as in His work is no labor, effort, industry. He can act while He reposes, and repose while He acts. He can begin a new work with (not a new, but) an eternal design; and what He has not made before, He does not now begin to make because He repents of His former repose. But when one speaks of His former repose and subsequent operation (and I know not how men can understand these things), this "former" and "subsequent" are applied only to the things created, which formerly did not exist, and subsequently came into existence. But in God the former purpose is not altered and obliterated by the subsequent and different purpose, but by one and the same eternal and unchangeable will He effected regarding the things He created, both that formerly, so long as they were not, they should not be, and that subsequently, when they began to be, they should come into existence. And thus, perhaps, He would show, in a very striking way, to those who have eyes for such things, how independent He is of what He makes, and how it is of His own gratuitous goodness He creates, since from eternity He dwelt without creatures in no less perfect a blessedness.

---

1. 2 Cor. 10:12. Here, and in *Enarrat. in Ps.* 34, and also in *Contra Faust.* 22.47, Augustine follows the Greek, and not the Vulgate.

18. AGAINST THOSE WHO ASSERT THAT THINGS THAT ARE INFINITE CANNOT BE COMPREHENDED BY THE KNOWLEDGE OF GOD

As for their other assertion, that God's knowledge cannot comprehend things infinite[1], it only remains for them to affirm, in order that they may sound the depths of their impiety, that God does not know all numbers. For it is very certain that they are infinite; since, no matter of what number you suppose an end to be made, this number can be, I will not say, increased by the addition of one more, but however great it be, and however vast be the multitude of which it is the rational and scientific expression, it can still be not only doubled, but even multiplied. Moreover, each number is so defined by its own properties, that no two numbers are equal. They are therefore both unequal and different from one another; and while they are simply finite, collectively they are infinite. Does God, therefore, not know numbers on account of this infinity; and does His knowledge extend only to a certain height in numbers, while of the rest He is ignorant? Who is so left to himself as to say so? Yet they can hardly pretend to put numbers out of the question, or maintain that they have nothing to do with the knowledge of God; for Plato,[2] their great authority, represents God as framing the world on numerical principles; and in our books also it is said to God, "Thou hast ordered all things in number, and measure, and weight."[3] The prophet also says, "who bringeth out their host by number."[4] And the Saviour says in the gospel, "The very hairs of your head are all numbered."[5] Far be it, then, from us to doubt that all number is known to Him "whose understanding," according to the psalmist, "is infinite."[6] The infinity of number, though there be no numbering of infinite numbers, is yet not incomprehensible by Him whose understanding is infinite. And thus, if everything which is comprehended is defined or made finite by the comprehension of him who knows it, then all infinity is in some ineffable way made finite to God, for it is comprehensible by His knowledge. Wherefore, if the infinity of numbers cannot be infinite to the knowledge of God, by which it is comprehended, what are we poor creatures that we should presume to fix limits to His knowledge, and say that unless the same temporal thing be repeated by the same periodic revolutions, God cannot either foreknow His creatures that He may make them, or know them when He has made them? God, whose knowledge is simply manifold, and uniform in its variety, comprehends all incomprehensibles with so incomprehensible a comprehension, that though He willed always to make His later works novel and unlike what went before them, He could not produce them without order and foresight, nor conceive them suddenly, but by His eternal foreknowledge.

---

1. That is, indefinite, or an indefinite succession of things.
2. Again in the *Timæus*.
3. Wisd. of Sol. 11:20.
4. Isa. 40:26.
5. Matt. 10:30.
6. Ps. 147:5.

19. OF WORLDS WITHOUT END, OR AGES OF AGES

I do not presume to determine whether God does so, and whether these times which are called "ages of ages"[1] are joined together in a continuous series, and succeed one another with a regulated diversity, and leave exempt from their vicissitudes only those who are freed from their misery, and abide without end in a blessed immortality; or whether these are called "ages of ages," that we may understand that the ages remain unchangeable in God's unwavering wisdom, and are the efficient causes, as it were, of those ages which are being spent in time. Possibly "ages" is used for "age," so that nothing else is meant by "ages of ages" than by "age of age," as nothing else is meant by "heavens of heavens" than by "heaven of heaven." For God called the firmament, above which are the waters, "heaven," and yet the psalm says, "Let the waters that are above the *heavens* praise the name of the

LORD."[2] Which of these two meanings we are to attach to "ages of ages," or whether there is not some other and better meaning still, is a very profound question; and the subject we are at present handling presents no obstacle to our meanwhile deferring the discussion of it, whether we may be able to determine anything about it, or may only be made more cautious by its further treatment, so as to be deterred from making any rash affirmations in a matter of such obscurity. For at present we are disputing the opinion that affirms the existence of those periodic revolutions by which the same things are always recurring at intervals of time. Now whichever of these suppositions regarding the "ages of ages" be the true one, it avails nothing for the substantiating of those cycles; for whether the ages of ages be not a repetition of the same world, but different worlds succeeding one another in a regulated connection, the ransomed souls abiding in well-assured bliss without any recurrence of misery, or whether the ages of ages be the eternal causes which rule what shall be and is in time, it equally follows, that those cycles which bring round the same things have no existence; and nothing more thoroughly explodes them than the fact of the eternal life of the saints.

---

1. De sæculis sæculorum.
2. Ps. 148:4.

20. OF THE IMPIETY OF THOSE WHO ASSERT THAT THE SOULS WHICH ENJOY TRUE AND PERFECT BLESSEDNESS MUST YET AGAIN AND AGAIN IN THESE PERIODIC REVOLUTIONS RETURN TO LABOR AND MISERY

What pious ears could bear to hear that after a life spent in so many and severe distresses (if, indeed, that should be called a life at all which is rather a death, so utter that the love of this present death makes us fear that death which delivers us from it), that after evils so disastrous, and miseries of all kinds have at length been expiated and finished by the help of true religion and wisdom, and when we have thus attained to the vision of God, and have entered into bliss by the contemplation of spiritual light and participation in His unchangeable immortality, which we burn to attain—that we must at some time lose all this, and that they who do lose it are cast down from that eternity, truth, and felicity to infernal mortality and shameful foolishness, and are involved in accursed woes, in which God is lost, truth held in detestation, and happiness sought in iniquitous impurities? And that this will happen endlessly again and again, recurring at fixed intervals, and in regularly returning periods? And that this everlasting and ceaseless revolution of definite cycles, which remove and restore true misery and deceitful bliss in turn, is contrived in order that God may be able to know His own works, since on the one hand He cannot rest from creating, and on the other, cannot know the infinite number of His creatures, if He always makes creatures? Who, I say, can listen to such things? Who can accept or suffer them to be spoken? Were they true, it were not only more prudent to keep silence regarding them, but even (to express myself as best I can) it were the part of wisdom not to know them. For if in the future world we shall not remember these things, and by this oblivion be blessed, why should we now increase our misery, already burdensome enough, by the knowledge of them? If, on the other hand, the knowledge of them will be forced upon us hereafter, now at least let us remain in ignorance, that in the present expectation we may enjoy a blessedness which the future reality is not to bestow; since in this life we are expecting to obtain life everlasting, but in the world to come are to discover it to be blessed, but not everlasting.

And if they maintain that no one can attain to the blessedness of the world to come, unless in this life he has been indoctrinated in those cycles in which bliss and misery relieve one another, how do they avow that the more a man loves God, the more readily he attains to blessedness—they who teach what paralyzes love itself? For who would not be more remiss and lukewarm in his love for a person whom he thinks he shall be forced to abandon, and whose truth and wisdom he shall come to hate; and this, too, after he has quite attained to the utmost and most blissful knowledge of Him that he is capable of? Can anyone be faithful in his love, even to a human friend, if he knows that he is destined to become his enemy?[1] God forbid that there be any truth in an opinion which threatens us with a real misery that is never to end, but is often and endlessly to be interrupted by intervals of fallacious happiness. For what happiness can be more fallacious and false than that in whose blaze of truth we yet remain ignorant that we shall be miserable, or in whose most secure citadel we yet fear that we shall be so? For if, on the one hand, we are to be ignorant of coming calamity, then our present misery is not so shortsighted for it is assured of coming bliss. If, on the other hand, the disaster that threatens is not concealed from us in the world to come, then the time of misery which is to be at last exchanged for a state of blessedness, is spent by the soul more happily than its time of happiness, which is to end in a return to misery. And thus our expectation of unhappiness is happy, but of happiness unhappy. And therefore, as we here suffer present ills, and hereafter fear ills that are imminent, it were truer to say that we shall always be miserable than that we can sometime be happy.

But these things are declared to be false by the loud testimony of religion and truth; for religion truthfully promises a true blessedness, of which we shall be eternally assured, and which cannot be interrupted by any disaster. Let us therefore keep to the straight path, which is Christ, and, with Him as our Guide and Saviour, let us turn away in heart and mind from the unreal and futile cycles of the godless. Porphyry, Platonist though he was, abjured the opinion of his school, that in these cycles souls are ceaselessly passing away and returning, either being struck with the extravagance of the idea, or sobered by his knowledge of Christianity. As I mentioned in the tenth book,[2] he preferred saying that the soul, as it had been sent into the world that it might know evil, and be purged and delivered from it, was never again exposed to such an experience after it had once returned to the Father. And if he abjured the tenets of his school, how much more ought we Christians to abominate and avoid an opinion so unfounded and hostile to our faith? But having disposed of these cycles and escaped out of them, no necessity compels us to suppose that the human race had no beginning in time, on the ground that there is nothing new in nature which, by I know not what cycles, has not at some previous period existed, and is not hereafter to exist again. For if the soul, once delivered, as it never was before, is never to return to misery, then there happens in its experience something which never happened before; and this, indeed, something of the greatest consequence, to wit, the secure entrance into eternal felicity. And if in an immortal nature there can occur a novelty, which never has been, nor ever shall be, reproduced by any cycle, why is it disputed that the same may occur in mortal natures? If they maintain that blessedness is no new experience to the soul, but only a return to that state in which it has been eternally, then at least its deliverance from misery is something new, since, by their own showing, the misery from which it is delivered is itself, too, a new experience. And if this new experience fell out by accident, and was not embraced in the order of things appointed by divine Providence, then where are those determinate and measured cycles in which no new thing happens, but all things are reproduced as they were before? If, however, this new experience was embraced in that providential order of nature (whether the soul was exposed to the evil of this world for the sake of discipline, or fell into it by sin), then it is possible for new things to happen which never happened before, and which yet are not extraneous to the order of nature. And if the soul is able by its own imprudence to create for itself a new misery, which was not unforeseen by the divine Providence, but was provided for in the order of nature along with the deliverance from it, how can we, even with all the rashness of human vanity, presume to deny that God can create new things—new to the world, but not to Him—which He never before created, but yet foresaw from all eternity? If they say that it is indeed true that ransomed souls return no more to misery, but that even so no new thing happens, since there always have been, now are, and ever shall be a succession of ransomed souls, they must at least grant that in this case there are new souls to whom the misery and the deliverance from it are new. For if they maintain that those souls out of which new men are daily being made (from whose bodies, if they have lived wisely, they are so delivered that they never return to misery) are not new, but have existed from eternity, they must logically admit that they are infinite. For however great a finite number of souls there were, that would not have sufficed to make perpetually new men from eternity—men whose souls were to be eternally freed from this mortal state, and never afterward to return to it. And our philosophers will find it hard to explain how there is an infinite number of souls in an order of nature which they require shall be finite, that it may be known by God.

And now that we have exploded these cycles which were supposed to bring back the soul at fixed periods to the same miseries, what can seem more in accordance with godly reason than to believe that it is possible for God both to create new things never before created, and in doing so, to preserve His will unaltered? But whether the number of eternally redeemed souls can be continually increased or not, let the philosophers themselves decide, who are so subtle in determining where infinity cannot be admitted. For our own part, our reasoning holds in either case. For if the number of souls can be indefinitely increased, what reason is there to deny that what had never before been created, could be created—since the number of ransomed souls never existed before, and has yet not only been once made, but will never cease to be anew coming into being? If, on the other hand, it be more suitable that the number of eternally ransomed souls be definite, and that this number will never be increased, yet this number, whatever it be, did assuredly never exist before, and it cannot increase, and reach the amount it signifies, without having some beginning; and this beginning never before existed. That this beginning, therefore, might be, the first man was created.

---

1. Cicero has the same *(De Amicitia 16):* "*Quonam modo quisquam amicus esse poterit, cui se putabit inimicum esse posse?*" He also quotes Scipio to the effect that no sentiment is more unfriendly to friendship than this, that we should love as if someday we were to hate.
2. See above, 10.30.

21. THAT THERE WAS CREATED AT FIRST BUT ONE INDIVIDUAL, AND THAT THE HUMAN RACE WAS CREATED IN HIM

Now that we have solved, as well as we could, this very difficult question about the eternal God creating new things, without any novelty of will, it is easy to see how much better it is that God was pleased to produce the human race from the one individual whom He created, than if He had originated it in several men. For as to the other animals, He created some solitary, and naturally seeking lonely places—as the eagles, kites, lions, wolves, and such like; others gregarious, which herd together, and prefer to live in company—as pigeons, starlings, stags, and little fallow deer, and the like: but neither class did He cause to be propagated from individuals, but called into being several at once. Man, on the other hand, whose nature was to be a mean between the angelic and bestial, He created in such sort, that if he remained in subjection to His Creator as his rightful

Lord, and piously kept His commandments, he should pass into the company of the angels, and obtain, without the intervention of death,[1] a blessed and endless immortality; but if he offended the Lord his God by a proud and disobedient use of his free will, he should become subject to death, and live as the beasts do—the slave of appetite, and doomed to eternal punishment after death. And therefore God created only one single man, not, certainly, that he might be a solitary bereft of all society, but that by this means the unity of society and the bond of concord might be more effectually commended to him, men being bound together not only by similarity of nature, but by family affection. And indeed He did not even create the woman that was to be given him as his wife, as he created the man, but created her out of the man, that the whole human race might derive from one man.

---

1. Coquæus remarks that this is leveled against the Pelagians.

22. THAT GOD FOREKNEW THAT THE FIRST MAN WOULD SIN, AND THAT HE AT THE SAME TIME FORESAW HOW LARGE A MULTITUDE OF GODLY PERSONS WOULD BY HIS GRACE BE TRANSLATED TO THE FELLOWSHIP OF THE ANGELS

And God was not ignorant that man would sin, and that, being himself made subject now to death, he would propagate men doomed to die, and that these mortals would run to such enormities in sin, that even the beasts devoid of rational will, and who were created in numbers from the waters and the earth, would live more securely and peaceably with their own kind than men, who had been propagated from one individual for the very purpose of commending concord. For not even lions or dragons have ever waged with their kind such wars as men have waged with one another.[1] But God foresaw also that by His grace a people would be called to adoption, and that they, being justified by the remission of their sins, would be united by the Holy Ghost to the holy angels in eternal peace, the last enemy, death, being destroyed; and He knew that this people would derive profit from the consideration that God had caused all men to be derived from one, for the sake of showing how highly He prizes unity in a multitude.

---

1. "Quando leoni
    Fortior eripuit vitam leo? quo nemore unquam
    Exspiravit aper majoris dentibus apri?
    Indica tigris agit rabida cum tigride pacem
    Perpetuam; sævis inter se convenit ursis.
    Ast homini," etc.
    Juvenal *Sat.* 15.160–165.
    —See also the very striking lines which precede these.

23. OF THE NATURE OF THE HUMAN SOUL CREATED IN THE IMAGE OF GOD

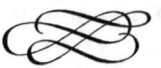

God, then, made man in His own image. For He created for him a soul endowed with reason and intelligence, so that he might excel all the creatures of earth, air, and sea, which were not so gifted. And when He had formed the man out of the dust of the earth, and had willed that his soul should be such as I have said—whether He had already made it, and now by breathing imparted it to man, or rather made it by breathing, so that that breath which God made by breathing (for what else is "to breathe" than to make breath?) is the soul[1]—He made also a wife for him, to aid him in the work of generating his kind, and her He formed of a bone taken out of the man's side, working in a divine manner. For we are not to conceive of this work in a carnal fashion, as if God worked as we commonly see artisans, who use their hands, and material furnished to them, that by their artistic skill they may fashion some material object. God's hand is God's power; and He, working invisibly, effects visible results. But this seems fabulous rather than true to men, who measure by customary and everyday works the power and wisdom of God, whereby He understands and produces without seeds even seeds themselves; and because they cannot understand the things which at the beginning were created, they are skeptical regarding them—as if the very things which they do know about human propagation, conceptions and births, would seem less incredible if told to those who had no experience of them; though these very things, too, are attributed by many rather to physical and natural causes than to the work of the divine mind.

---

1. See this further discussed in *De Gen. ad Litt.* 7.35 and in Delitzsch's *Biblical Psychology*.

24. WHETHER THE ANGELS CAN BE SAID TO BE THE CREATORS OF ANY, EVEN THE LEAST CREATURE

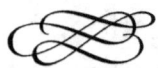

But in this book we have nothing to do with those who do not believe that the divine mind made or cares for this world. As for those who believe their own Plato, that all mortal animals—among whom man holds the preeminent place, and is near to the gods themselves—were created not by that most high God who made the world, but by other lesser gods created by the Supreme, and exercising a delegated power under His control—if only those persons be delivered from the superstition which prompts them to seek a plausible reason for paying divine honors and sacrificing to these gods as their creators, they will easily be disentangled also from this their error. For it is blasphemy to believe or to say (even before it can be understood) that any other than God is creator of any nature, be it never so small and mortal. And as for the angels, whom those Platonists prefer to call gods, although they do, so far as they are permitted and commissioned, aid in the production of the things around us, yet not on that account are we to call them creators, any more than we call gardeners the creators of fruits and trees.

25. THAT GOD ALONE IS THE CREATOR OF EVERY KIND OF CREATURE, WHATEVER ITS NATURE OR FORM

For whereas there is one form which is given from without to every bodily substance—such as the form which is constructed by potters and smiths, and that class of artists who paint and fashion forms like the body of animals—but another and internal form which is not itself constructed, but, as the efficient cause, produces not only the natural bodily forms, but even the life itself of the living creatures, and which proceeds from the secret and hidden choice of an intelligent and living nature—let that first-mentioned form be attributed to every artificer, but this latter to one only, God, the Creator and Originator who made the world itself and the angels, without the help of world or angels. For the same divine and, so to speak, creative energy, which cannot be made, but makes, and which gave to the earth and sky their roundness—this same divine, effective, and creative energy gave their roundness to the eye and to the apple; and the other natural objects which we anywhere see, received also their form, not from without, but from the secret and profound might of the Creator, who said, "Do not I fill heaven and earth?"[1] and whose wisdom it is that "reacheth from one end to another mightily; and sweetly doth she order all things."[2] Wherefore I know not what kind of aid the angels, themselves created first, afforded to the Creator in making other things. I cannot ascribe to them what perhaps they cannot do, neither ought I to deny them such faculty as they have. But, by their leave, I attribute the creating and originating work which gave being to all natures to God, to whom they themselves thankfully ascribe their existence. We do not call gardeners the creators of their fruits, for we read, "Neither is he that planteth anything, neither he that watereth, but God that giveth the increase."[3] No, not even the earth itself do we call a creator, though she seems to be the prolific mother of all things which she aids in germinating and bursting forth from the seed, and which she keeps rooted in her own breast; for we likewise read, "God giveth it a body, as it hath pleased Him, and to every seed his own body."[4] We ought not even to call a woman the creatress of her own offspring; for He rather is its creator who said to His servant, "Before I formed thee in the womb, I knew thee."[5] And although the various mental emotions of a pregnant woman do produce in the fruit of her womb similar qualities—as Jacob with his peeled wands caused piebald sheep to be produced—yet the mother as little creates her offspring as she created herself. Whatever bodily or seminal causes, then, may be used for the production of things, either by the cooperation of angels, men, or the lower animals, or by sexual generation; and whatever power the desires and mental emotions of the mother have to produce in the tender and plastic fœtus, corresponding lineaments and colors; yet the natures themselves, which are thus variously affected, are the production of none but the most high God. It is His occult power which pervades all things, and is present in all without being contaminated, which gives being to all that is, and modifies and limits its existence; so that without Him it would not be thus or thus, nor would have any being at all.[6] If, then, in regard to that outward form which the workman's hand imposes on his work, we do not say that Rome and Alexandria were built by masons and architects, but by the kings by whose will, plan, and resources they were built, so that the one has Romulus, the other Alexander, for its founder; with how much greater reason ought we to say that God alone is the Author of all natures, since He neither uses for His work any material which was not made by Him, nor any workmen who were not also made by Him, and since, if He were, so to speak, to withdraw from created things His creative power, they would straightway relapse into the nothingness in which they were before they were created? "Before," I mean, in respect of eternity, not of time. For what other creator could there be of time, than He who created those things whose movements make time?[7]

1. Jer. 23:24.
2. Wisd. of Sol. 8:1.
3. 1 Cor. 3:7.
4. 1 Cor. 15:38.
5. Jer. 1:5
6. Cf. *De Trin.* 3.13–16.
7. See above, 11.5.

26. OF THAT OPINION OF THE PLATONISTS, THAT THE ANGELS WERE THEMSELVES INDEED CREATED BY GOD, BUT THAT AFTERWARD THEY CREATED MAN'S BODY

It is obvious, that in attributing the creation of the other animals to those inferior gods who were made by the Supreme, he meant it to be understood that the immortal part was taken from God Himself, and that these minor creators added the mortal part; that is to say, he meant them to be considered the creators of our bodies, but not of our souls. But since Porphyry maintains that if the soul is to be purified, all entanglement with a body must be escaped from; and at the same time agrees with Plato and the Platonists in thinking that those who have not spent a temperate and honorable life return to mortal bodies as their punishment (to bodies of brutes in Plato's opinion, to human bodies in Porphyry's); it follows that those whom they would have us worship as our parents and authors, that they may plausibly call them gods, are, after all, but the forgers of our fetters and chains—not our creators, but our jailers and turnkeys, who lock us up in the most bitter and melancholy house of correction. Let the Platonists, then, either cease menacing us with our bodies as the punishment of our souls, or preaching that we are to worship as gods those whose work upon us they exhort us by all means in our power to avoid and escape from. But, indeed, both opinions are quite false. It is false that souls return again to this life to be punished; and it is false that there is any other creator of anything in heaven or earth, than He who made the heaven and the earth. For if we live in a body only to expiate our sins, how says Plato in another place, that the world could not have been the most beautiful and good, had it not been filled with all kinds of creatures, mortal and immortal?[1] But if our creation even as mortals be a divine benefit, how is it a punishment to be restored to a body, that is, to a divine benefit? And if God, as Plato continually maintains, embraced in His eternal intelligence the ideas both of the universe and of all the animals, how, then, should He not with His own hand make them all? Could He be unwilling to be the constructor of works, the idea and plan of which called for His ineffable and ineffably to be praised intelligence?

---

1. The Deity, desirous of making the universe in all respects resemble the most beautiful and entirely perfect of intelligible objects, formed it into one visible animal, containing within itself all the other animals with which it is naturally allied. —*Timæus* 11.

27. THAT THE WHOLE PLENITUDE OF THE HUMAN RACE WAS EMBRACED IN THE FIRST MAN, AND THAT GOD THERE SAW THE PORTION OF IT WHICH WAS TO BE HONORED AND REWARDED, AND THAT WHICH WAS TO BE CONDEMNED AND PUNISHED

With good cause, therefore, does the true religion recognize and proclaim that the same God who created the universal cosmos, created also all the animals, souls as well as bodies. Among the terrestrial animals man was made by Him in His own image, and, for the reason I have given, was made one individual, though he was not left solitary. For there is nothing so social by nature, so unsocial by its corruption, as this race. And human nature has nothing more appropriate, either for the prevention of discord, or for the healing of it, where it exists, than the remembrance of that first parent of us all, whom God was pleased to create alone, that all men might be derived from one, and that they might thus be admonished to preserve unity among their whole multitude. But from the fact that the woman was made for him from his side, it was plainly meant that we should learn how dear the bond between man and wife should be. These works of God do certainly seem extraordinary, because they are the first works. They who do not believe them ought not to believe any prodigies; for these would not be called prodigies did they not happen out of the ordinary course of nature. But is it possible that anything should happen in vain, however hidden be its cause, in so grand a government of divine Providence? One of the sacred psalmists says, "Come, behold the works of the LORD, what prodigies He hath wrought in the earth."[1] Why God made woman out of man's side, and what this first prodigy prefigured, I shall, with God's help, tell in another place. But at present, since this book must be concluded, let us merely say that in this first man, who was created in the beginning, there was laid the foundation, not indeed evidently, but in God's foreknowledge, of these two cities or societies, so far as regards the human race. For from that man all men were to be derived—some of them to be associated with the good angels in their reward, others with the wicked in punishment; all being ordered by the secret yet just judgment of God. For since it is written, "All the paths of the LORD are mercy and truth,"[2] neither can His grace be unjust, nor His justice cruel.

---

1. Ps. 46:8.
2. Ps. 25:10.

CONTENTS

TRANSLATOR'S PREFACE   1

BOOK ONE

Preface, explaining his design in undertaking this work   17

1. Of the adversaries of the name of Christ, whom the barbarians for Christ's sake spared when they stormed the city   19

2. That it is quite contrary to the usage of war, that the victors should spare the vanquished for the sake of their gods   22

3. That the Romans did not show their usual sagacity when they trusted that they would be benefited by the gods who had been unable to defend Troy   24

4. Of the asylum of Juno in Troy, which saved no one from the Greeks; and of the churches of the apostles, which protected from the barbarians all who fled to them   28

5. Cæsar's statement regarding the universal custom of an enemy when sacking a city   31

6. That not even the Romans, when they took cities, spared the conquered in their temples — 33

7. That the cruelties which occurred in the sack of Rome were in accordance with the custom of war, whereas the acts of clemency resulted from the influence of Christ's name — 36

8. Of the advantages and disadvantages which often indiscriminately accrue to good and wicked men — 38

9. Of the reasons for administering correction to bad and good together — 41

10. That the saints lose nothing in losing temporal goods — 46

11. Of the end of this life, whether it is material that it be long delayed — 52

12. Of the burial of the dead: that the denial of it to Christians does them no injury — 54

13. Reasons for burying the bodies of the saints — 57

14. Of the captivity of the saints, and that divine consolation never failed them therein — 60

15. Of Regulus, in whom we have an example of the voluntary endurance of captivity for the sake of religion; which yet did not profit him, though he was a worshiper of the gods — 62

16. Of the violation of the consecrated and other Christian virgins, to which they were subjected in captivity and to which their own will gave no consent; and whether this contaminated their souls — 66

17. Of suicide committed through fear of punishment or dishonor — 68

18. Of the violence which may be done to the body by another's lust, while the mind remains inviolate — 70

19. Of Lucretia, who put an end to her life because of the outrage done her — 73

20. That Christians have no authority for committing suicide in any circumstances whatever — 78

21. Of the cases in which we may put men to death without incurring the guilt of murder — 81

22. That suicide can never be prompted by magnanimity — 83

23. What we are to think of the example of Cato, who slew himself because unable to endure Cæsar's victory — 86

24. That in that virtue in which Regulus excels Cato, Christians are preeminently distinguished — 88

25. That we should not endeavor by sin to obviate sin — 91

26. That in certain peculiar cases the examples of the saints are not to be followed — 93

27. Whether voluntary death should be sought in order to avoid sin — 96

28. By what judgment of God the enemy was permitted to indulge his lust on the bodies of continent Christians — 99

29. What the servants of Christ should say in reply to the unbelievers who cast in their teeth that Christ did not rescue them from the fury of their enemies — 103

30. That those who complain of Christianity really desire to live without restraint in shameful luxury — 105

31. By what steps the passion for governing increased among the Romans — 107

32. Of the establishment of scenic entertainments — 109

33. That the overthrow of Rome has not corrected the vices of the Romans — 111

34. Of God's clemency in moderating the ruin of the city — 113

35. Of the sons of the church who are hidden among the wicked, and of false Christians within the church — 114

36. What subjects are to be handled in the following discourse — 116

BOOK TWO

1. Of the limits which must be put to the necessity of replying to an adversary — 121
2. Recapitulation of the contents of the first book — 123
3. That we need only to read history in order to see what calamities the Romans suffered before the religion of Christ began to compete with the worship of the gods — 126
4. That the worshipers of the gods never received from them any healthy moral precepts, and that in celebrating their worship all sorts of impurities were practiced — 128
5. Of the obscenities practiced in honor of the mother of the gods — 131
6. That the gods of the pagans never inculcated holiness of life — 134
7. That the suggestions of philosophers are precluded from having any moral effect, because they have not the authority which belongs to divine instruction, and because man's natural bias to evil induces him rather to follow the examples of the gods than to obey the precepts of men — 136
8. That the theatrical exhibitions publishing the shameful actions of the gods, propitiated rather than offended them — 139

9. That the poetical license which the Greeks, in obedience to their gods, allowed, was restrained by the ancient Romans — 141

10. That the devils, in suffering either false or true crimes to be laid to their charge, meant to do men a mischief — 144

11. That the Greeks admitted players to offices of state, on the ground that men who pleased the gods should not be contemptuously treated by their fellows — 146

12. That the Romans, by refusing to the poets the same license in respect of men which they allowed them in the case of the gods, showed a more delicate sensitiveness regarding themselves than regarding the gods — 149

13. That the Romans should have understood that gods who desired to be worshiped in licentious entertainments were unworthy of divine honor — 151

14. That Plato, who excluded poets from a well-ordered city, was better than these gods who desire to be honored by theatrical plays — 154

15. That it was vanity, not reason, which created some of the Roman gods — 158

16. That if the gods had really possessed any regard for righteousness, the Romans should have received good laws from them, instead of having to borrow them from other nations	160
17. Of the rape of the Sabine women, and other iniquities perpetrated in Rome's palmiest days	162
18. What the history of Sallust reveals regarding the life of the Romans, either when straitened by anxiety or relaxed in security	165
19. Of the corruption which had grown upon the Roman republic before Christ abolished the worship of the gods	169
20. Of the kind of happiness and life truly delighted in by those who inveigh against the Christian religion	172
21. Cicero's opinion of the Roman republic	175
22. That the Roman gods never took any steps to prevent the republic from being ruined by immorality	181
23. That the vicissitudes of this life are dependent not on the favor or hostility of demons, but on the will of the true God	184
24. Of the deeds of Sylla, in which the demons boasted that he had their help	188

25. How powerfully the evil spirits incite men to wicked actions, by giving them the quasidivine authority of their example … 192

26. That the demons gave in secret certain obscure instructions in morals, while in public their own solemnities inculcated all wickedness … 195

27. That the obscenities of those plays which the Romans consecrated in order to propitiate their gods, contributed largely to the overthrow of public order … 199

28. That the Christian religion is health giving … 201

29. An exhortation to the Romans to renounce paganism … 203

BOOK THREE

1. Of the ills which alone the wicked fear, and which the world continually suffered, even when the gods were worshiped … 209

2. Whether the gods, whom the Greeks and Romans worshiped in common, were justified in permitting the destruction of Ilium … 211

3. That the gods could not be offended by the adultery of Paris, this crime being so common among themselves … 214

4. Of Varro's opinion, that it is useful for men to feign themselves the offspring of the gods … 216

5. That it is not credible that the gods should have punished the adultery of Paris, seeing they showed no indignation at the adultery of the mother of Romulus   217

6. That the gods exacted no penalty for the fratricidal act of Romulus   219

7. Of the destruction of Ilium by Fimbria, a lieutenant of Marius   221

8. Whether Rome ought to have been entrusted to the Trojan gods   224

9. Whether it is credible that the peace during the reign of Numa was brought about by the gods   225

10. Whether it was desirable that the Roman empire should be increased by such a furious succession of wars, when it might have been quiet and safe by following in the peaceful ways of Numa   227

11. Of the statue of Apollo at Cumæ, whose tears are supposed to have portended disaster to the Greeks, whom the god was unable to succor   230

12. That the Romans added a vast number of gods to those introduced by Numa, and that their numbers helped them not at all   232

13. By what right or agreement the Romans obtained their first wives   234

14. Of the wickedness of the war waged by the Romans against the Albans, and of the victories won by the lust of power 238

15. What manner of life and death the Roman kings had 244

16. Of the first Roman consuls, the one of whom drove the other from the country, and shortly after perished at Rome by the hand of a wounded enemy, and so ended a career of unnatural murders 249

17. Of the disasters which vexed the Roman republic after the inauguration of the consulship, and of the nonintervention of the gods of Rome 252

18. The disasters suffered by the Romans in the Punic wars, which were not mitigated by the protection of the gods 259

19. Of the calamity of the second Punic war, which consumed the strength of both parties 263

20. Of the destruction of the Saguntines, who received no help from the Roman gods, though perishing on account of their fidelity to Rome 266

21. Of the ingratitude of Rome to Scipio, its deliverer, and of its manners during the period which Sallust describes as the best 270

22. Of the edict of Mithridates, commanding that all Roman citizens found in Asia should be slain — 273

23. Of the internal disasters which vexed the Roman republic, and followed a portentous madness which seized all the domestic animals — 275

24. Of the civil dissension occasioned by the sedition of the Gracchi — 277

25. Of the temple of Concord, which was erected by a decree of the senate on the scene of these seditions and massacres — 279

26. Of the various kinds of wars which followed the building of the temple of Concord — 281

27. Of the civil war between Marius and Sylla — 283

28. Of the victory of Sylla, the avenger of the cruelties of Marius — 285

29. A comparison of the disasters which Rome experienced during the Gothic and Gallic invasions, with those occasioned by the authors of the civil wars — 288

30. Of the connection of the wars which with great severity and frequency followed one another before the advent of Christ …… 290

31. That it is effrontery to impute the present troubles to Christ and the prohibition of polytheistic worship since even when the gods were worshiped such calamities befell the people …… 292

BOOK FOUR

1. Of the things which have been discussed in the first book …… 297

2. Of those things which are contained in books second and third …… 300

3. Whether the great extent of the empire, which has been acquired only by wars, is to be reckoned among the good things either of the wise or the happy …… 303

4. How like kingdoms without justice are to robberies …… 306

5. Of the runaway gladiators whose power became like that of royal dignity …… 308

6. Concerning the covetousness of Ninus, who was the first who made war on his neighbors, that he might rule more widely …… 311

7. Whether earthly kingdoms in their rise and fall have been either aided or deserted by the help of the gods …… 313

8. Which of the gods can the Romans suppose presided over the increase and preservation of their empire, when they have believed that even the care of single things could scarcely be committed to single gods?   316

9. Whether the great extent and long duration of the Roman empire should be ascribed to Jove, whom his worshipers believe to be the chief god   319

10. What opinions those have followed who have set diverse gods over diverse parts of the world   321

11. Concerning the many gods whom the pagan doctors defend as being one and the same Jove   325

12. Concerning the opinion of those who have thought that God is the soul of the world, and the world is the body of God   330

13. Concerning those who assert that only rational animals are parts of the one God   332

14. The enlargement of kingdoms is unsuitably ascribed to Jove; for if, as they will have it, Victoria is a goddess, she alone would suffice for this business   334

15. Whether it is suitable for good men to wish to rule more widely   335

16. What was the reason why the Romans, in detailing separate gods for all things and all movements of the mind, chose to have the temple of Quiet outside the gates — 337

17. Whether, if the highest power belongs to Jove, Victoria also ought to be worshiped — 339

18. With what reason they who think Felicity and Fortune goddesses have distinguished them — 341

19. Concerning Fortuna Muliebris — 344

20. Concerning Virtue and Faith, which the pagans have honored with temples and sacred rites, passing by other good qualities, which ought likewise to have been worshiped, if deity was rightly attributed to these — 346

21. That although not understanding them to be the gifts of God, they ought at least to have been content with Virtue and Felicity — 348

22. Concerning the knowledge of the worship due to the gods, which Varro glories in having himself conferred on the Romans — 352

23. Concerning Felicity, whom the Romans, who venerate many gods, for a long time did not worship with divine honor, though she alone would have sufficed instead of all — 354

24. The reasons by which the pagans attempt to defend their worshiping among the gods the divine gifts themselves — 359

25. Concerning the one God only to be worshiped, who, although his name is unknown, is yet deemed to be the giver of felicity — 361

26. Of the scenic plays, the celebration of which the gods have exacted from their worshipers — 363

27. Concerning the three kinds of gods about which the pontiff Scævola has discoursed — 366

28. Whether the worship of the gods has been of service to the Romans in obtaining and extending the empire — 369

29. Of the falsity of the augury by which the strength and stability of the Roman Empire was considered to be indicated — 371

30. What kind of things even their worshipers have owned they have thought about the gods of the nations — 374

31. Concerning the opinions of Varro, who, while reprobating the popular belief, thought that their worship should be confined to one God, though he was unable to discover the true God — 377

32. In what interest the princes of the nations wished false religions to continue among the people subject to them — 381

33. That the times of all kings and kingdoms are ordained by the judgment and power of the true God — 383

34. Concerning the kingdom of the Jews, which was founded by the one and true God, and preserved by Him as long as they remained in the true religion — 385

BOOK FIVE

1. That the cause of the Roman Empire, and of all kingdoms, is neither fortuitous nor consists in the position of the stars1 — 391

2. On the difference in the health of twins — 394

3. Concerning the arguments which Nigidius the mathematician drew from the potter's wheel, in the question about the birth of twins — 397

4. Concerning the twins Esau and Jacob, who were very unlike each other both in their character and actions — 399

5. In what manner the mathematicians are convicted of professing a vain science — 401

6. Concerning twins of different sexes — 405

7. Concerning the choosing of a day for marriage, or for planting, or sowing	408
8. Concerning those who call by the name of fate, not the position of the stars, but the connection of causes which depends on the will of God	412
9. Concerning the foreknowledge of God and the free will of man, in opposition to the definition of Cicero	415
10. Whether our wills are ruled by necessity	423
11. Concerning the universal providence of God in the laws of which all things are comprehended	427
12. By what virtues the ancient Romans merited that the true God, although they did not worship him, should enlarge their empire	429
13. Concerning the love of praise, which, though it is a vice, is reckoned a virtue, because by it greater vice is restrained	438
14. Concerning the eradication of the love of human praise, because all the glory of the righteous is in God	441
15. Concerning the temporal reward which God granted to the virtues of the Romans	444
16. Concerning the reward of the holy citizens of the celestial city, to whom the example of the virtues of the Romans are useful	446

17. To what profit the Romans carried on wars, and how much they contributed to the well-being of those whom they conquered   448

18. How far Christians ought to be from boasting, if they have done anything for the love of the eternal country, when the Romans did such great things for human glory and a terrestrial city   451

19. Concerning the difference between true glory and the desire of domination   459

20. That it is as shameful for the virtues to serve human glory as bodily pleasure   463

21. That the Roman dominion was granted by Him from whom is all power, and by whose providence all things are ruled   466

22. The durations and issues of war depend on the will of God   469

23. Concerning the war in which Radagaisus, king of the Goths, a worshiper of demons, was conquered in one day, with all his mighty forces   472

24. What was the happiness of the Christian emperors, and how far it was true happiness   475

25. Concerning the prosperity which God granted to the Christian emperor Constantine — 477

26. On the faith and piety of Theodosius Augustus — 479

BOOK SIX

1. Of those who maintain that they worship the gods not for the sake of temporal but eternal advantages — 489

2. What we are to believe that Varro thought concerning the gods of the nations, whose various kinds and sacred rites he has shown to be such that he would have acted more reverently toward them had he been altogether silent concerning them — 495

3. Varro's distribution of his book which he composed concerning the antiquities of human and divine things — 499

4. That from the disputation of Varro, it follows that the worshipers of the gods regard human things as more ancient than divine things — 502

5. Concerning the three kinds of theology according to Varro, namely, one fabulous, the other natural, the third civil — 506

6. Concerning the mythic, that is, the fabulous, theology, and the civil, against Varro — 510

7. Concerning the likeness and agreement of the fabulous and civil theologies — 514

8. Concerning the interpretations, consisting of natural explanations, which the pagan teachers attempt to show for their gods — 519

9. Concerning the special offices of the gods — 523

10. Concerning the liberty of Seneca, who more vehemently censured the civil theology than Varro did the fabulous — 530

11. What Seneca thought concerning the Jews — 536

12. That when once the vanity of the gods of the nations has been exposed, it cannot be doubted that they are unable to bestow eternal life on anyone, when they cannot afford help even with respect to the things of this temporal life — 538

BOOK SEVEN

1. Whether, since it is evident that Deity is not to be found in the civil theology, we are to believe that it is to be found in the select gods — 543

2. Who are the select gods, and whether they are held to be exempt from the offices of the commoner gods — 545

3. How there is no reason which can be shown for the selection of certain gods, when the administration of more exalted offices is assigned to many inferior gods 547

4. The inferior gods, whose names are not associated with infamy, have been better dealt with than the select gods, whose infamies are celebrated 554

5. Concerning the more secret doctrine of the pagans, and concerning the physical interpretations 557

6. Concerning the opinion of Varro, that God is the soul of the world, which nevertheless, in its various parts, has many souls whose nature is divine 560

7. Whether it is reasonable to separate Janus and Terminus as two distinct deities 562

8. For what reason the worshipers of Janus have made his image with two faces, when they would sometimes have it be seen with four 565

9. Concerning the power of Jupiter, and a comparison of Jupiter with Janus 567

10. Whether the distinction between Janus and Jupiter is a proper one 571

11. Concerning the surnames of Jupiter, which are referred not to many gods, but to one and the same god 573

12. That Jupiter is also called Pecunia 576

13. That when it is expounded what Saturn is, what Genius is, it comes to this, that both of them are shown to be Jupiter — 578

14. Concerning the offices of Mercury and Mars — 580

15. Concerning certain stars which the pagans have called by the names of their gods — 583

16. Concerning Apollo and Diana, and the other select gods whom they would have to be parts of the world — 586

17. That even Varro himself pronounced his own opinions regarding the gods ambiguous — 589

18. A more credible cause of the rise of pagan error — 592

19. Concerning the interpretations which compose the reason of the worship of Saturn — 594

20. Concerning the rites of Eleusinian Ceres — 597

21. Concerning the shamefulness of the rites which are celebrated in honor of Liber — 599

22. Concerning Neptune, and Salacia, and Venilia — 601

23. Concerning the earth, which Varro affirms to be a goddess, because that soul of the world which he thinks to be God pervades also this lowest part of his body, and imparts to it a divine force   603

24. Concerning the surnames of Tellus and their significations, which, although they indicate many properties, ought not to have established the opinion that there is a corresponding number of gods   608

25. The interpretation of the mutilation of Atys which the doctrine of the Greek sages set forth   612

26. Concerning the abomination of the sacred rites of the Great Mother   614

27. Concerning the figments of the physical theologists, who neither worship the true divinity, nor perform the worship wherewith the true divinity should be served   617

28. That the doctrine of Varro concerning theology is in no part consistent with itself   620

29. That all things which the physical theologists have referred to the world and its parts, they ought to have referred to the one true God   623

30. How piety distinguishes the Creator from the creatures, so that, instead of one God, there are not worshiped as many gods as there are works of the one author   624

31. What benefits God gives to the followers of the truth to enjoy over and above His general bounty   627

32. That at no time in the past was the mystery of Christ's redemption wanting, but was at all times declared, though in various forms   629

33. That only through the Christian religion could the deceit of malign spirits, who rejoice in the errors of men, have been manifested   631

34. Concerning the books of Numa Pompilius, which the senate ordered to be burned, in order that the causes of sacred rights therein assigned should not become known   633

35. Concerning the hydromancy through which Numa was befooled by certain images of demons seen in the water   636

BOOK EIGHT

1. That the question of natural theology is to be discussed with those philosophers who sought a more excellent wisdom	643
2. Concerning the two schools of philosophers, that is, the Italic and Ionic, and their founders	646
3. Of the Socratic philosophy	649
4. Concerning Plato, the chief among the disciples of Socrates, and his threefold division of philosophy	652
5. That it is especially with the Platonists that we must carry on our disputations on matters of theology, their opinions being preferable to those of all other philosophers	656
6. Concerning the meaning of the Platonists in that part of philosophy called physical	661
7. How much the Platonists are to be held as excelling other philosophers in logic, that is, rational philosophy	664
8. That the Platonists hold the first rank in moral philosophy also	666
9. Concerning that philosophy which has come nearest to the Christian faith	669
10. That the excellency of the Christian religion is above all the science of philosophers	671

11. How Plato has been able to approach so nearly to Christian knowledge   675

12. That even the Platonists, though they say these things concerning the one true God, nevertheless thought that sacred rites were to be performed in honor of many gods   678

13. Concerning the opinion of Plato, according to which he defined the gods as beings entirely good and the friends of virtue   680

14. Of the opinion of those who have said that rational souls are of three kinds, to wit, those of the celestial gods, those of the aerial demons, and those of terrestrial men   683

15. That the demons are not better than men because of their aerial bodies, or on account of their superior place of abode   687

16. What Apuleius the Platonist thought concerning the manners and actions of demons   690

17. Whether it is proper that men should worship those spirits from whose vices it is necessary that they be freed   693

18. What kind of religion that is which teaches that men ought to employ the advocacy of demons in order to be recommended to the favor of the good gods   696

19. Of the impiety of the magic art, which is dependent on the assistance of malign spirits   698

20. Whether we are to believe that the good gods are more willing to have intercourse with demons than with men   702

21. Whether the gods use the demons as messengers and interpreters, and whether they are deceived by them willingly, or without their own knowledge   704

22. That we must, notwithstanding the opinion of Apuleius, reject the worship of demons   708

23. What Hermes Trismegistus thought concerning idolatry, and from what source he knew that the superstitions of Egypt were to be abolished   710

24. How Hermes openly confessed the error of his forefathers, the coming destruction of which he nevertheless bewailed   716

25. Concerning those things which may be common to the holy angels and to men   723

26. That all the religion of the pagans has reference to dead men 725

27. Concerning the nature of the honor which the Christians pay to their martyrs 729

BOOK NINE

1. The point at which the discussion has arrived, and what remains to be handled 735

2. Whether among the demons, inferior to the gods, there are any good spirits under whose guardianship the human soul might reach true blessedness 737

3. What Apuleius attributes to the demons, to whom, though he does not deny them reason, he does not ascribe virtue 739

4. The opinion of the Peripatetics and Stoics about mental emotions 741

5. That the passions which assail the souls of Christians do not seduce them to vice, but exercise their virtue 746

6. Of the passions which, according to Apuleius, agitate the demons who are supposed by him to mediate between gods and men 749

7. That the Platonists maintain that the poets wrong the gods by representing them as distracted by party feeling, to which the demons, and not the gods, are subject 751

8. How Apuleius defines the gods who dwell in heaven, the demons who occupy the air, and men who inhabit earth — 753

9. Whether the intercession of the demons can secure for men the friendship of the celestial gods — 756

10. That, according to Plotinus, men, whose body is mortal, are less wretched than demons, whose body is eternal — 758

11. Of the opinion of the Platonists, that the souls of men become demons when disembodied — 760

12. Of the three opposite qualities by which the Platonists distinguish between the nature of men and that of demons — 762

13. How the demons can mediate between gods and men if they have nothing in common with both, being neither blessed like the gods, nor miserable like men — 764

14. Whether men, though mortal, can enjoy true blessedness — 768

15. Of the man Christ Jesus, the mediator between God and men — 769

16. Whether it is reasonable in the Platonists to determine that the celestial gods decline contact with earthly things and intercourse with men, who therefore require the intercession of the demons   773

17. That to obtain the blessed life, which consists in partaking of the supreme good, man needs such mediation as is furnished not by a demon, but by Christ alone   777

18. That the deceitful demons, while promising to conduct men to God by their intercession, mean to turn them from the path of truth   779

19. That even among their own worshipers the name "demon" has never a good signification   781

20. Of the kind of knowledge which puffs up the demons   783

21. To what extent the Lord was pleased to make Himself known to the demons   785

22. The difference between the knowledge of the holy angels and that of the demons   787

23. That the name of gods is falsely given to the gods of the Gentiles, though Scripture applies it both to the holy angels and just men   789

BOOK TEN

1. That the Platonists themselves have determined that God alone can confer happiness either on angels or men, but that it yet remains a question whether those spirits whom they direct us to worship, that we may obtain happiness, wish sacrifice to be offered to themselves, or to the one God only ... 795

2. The opinion of Plotinus the Platonist regarding enlightenment from above ... 800

3. That the Platonists, though knowing something of the creator of the universe, have misunderstood the true worship of God, by giving divine honor to angels, good or bad ... 802

4. That sacrifice is due to the true God only ... 805

5. Of the sacrifices which God does not require, but wished to be observed for the exhibition of those things which he does require ... 806

6. Of the true and perfect sacrifice ... 810

7. Of the love of the holy angels, which prompts them to desire that we worship the one true God, and not themselves ... 813

8. Of the miracles which God has condescended to adhibit, through the ministry of angels, to His promises for the confirmation of the faith of the godly ... 815

9. Of the illicit arts connected with demonolatry, and of which the Platonist Porphyry adopts some, and discards others — 818

10. Concerning theurgy, which promises a delusive purification of the soul by the invocation of demons — 821

11. Of Porphyry's epistle to Anebo, in which he asks for information about the differences among demons — 824

12. Of the miracles worked by the true God through the ministry of the holy angels — 829

13. Of the invisible God, who has often made Himself visible, not as He really is, but as the beholders could bear the sight — 831

14. That the one God is to be worshiped not only for the sake of eternal blessings, but also in connection with temporal prosperity, because all things are regulated by His providence — 833

15. Of the ministry of the holy angels, by which they fulfill the providence of God — 835

16. Whether those angels who demand that we pay them divine honor, or those who teach us to render holy service, not to themselves, but to God, are to be trusted about the way to life eternal — 837

17. Concerning the ark of the covenant, and the miraculous signs whereby God authenticated the law and the promise	842
18. Against those who deny that the books of the church are to be believed about the miracles whereby the people of God were educated	845
19. On the reasonableness of offering, as the true religion teaches, a visible sacrifice to the one true and invisible God	847
20. Of the supreme and true sacrifice which was effected by the Mediator between God and men	849
21. Of the power delegated to demons for the trial and glorification of the saints, who conquer not by propitiating the spirits of the air, but by abiding in God	851
22. Whence the saints derive power against demons and true purification of heart	854
23. Of the principles which, according to the Platonists, regulate the purification of the soul	856
24. Of the one only true principle which alone purifies and renews human nature	858
25. That all the saints, both under the law and before it, were justified by faith in the mystery of Christ's incarnation	861

26. Of Porphyry's weakness in wavering between the confession of the true God and the worship of demons 866

27. Of the impiety of Porphyry, which is worse than even the mistake of Apuleius 869

28. How it is that Porphyry has been so blind as not to recognize the true wisdom—Christ 873

29. Of the incarnation of our Lord Jesus Christ, which the Platonists in their impiety blush to acknowledge 876

30. Porphyry's emendations and modifications of Platonism 882

31. Against the arguments on which the Platonists ground their assertion that the human soul is co-eternal with God 886

32. Of the universal way of the soul's deliverance, which Porphyry did not find because he did not rightly seek it, and which the grace of Christ has alone thrown open 888

BOOK ELEVEN

1. Of this part of the work, wherein we begin to explain the origin and end of the two cities 899

2. Of the knowledge of God, to which no man can attain save through the Mediator between God and men, the man Christ Jesus 902

3. Of the authority of the canonical Scriptures composed by the Divine Spirit — 905

4. That the world is neither without beginning, nor yet created by a new decree of God, by which He afterward willed what He had not before willed — 907

5. That we ought not to seek to comprehend the infinite ages of time before the world, nor the infinite realms of space — 911

6. That the world and time had both one beginning, and the one did not anticipate the other — 914

7. Of the nature of the first days, which are said to have had morning and evening, before there was a sun — 916

8. What we are to understand of God's resting on the seventh day, after the six days' work — 919

9. What the Scriptures teach us to believe concerning the creation of the angels — 921

10. Of the simple and unchangeable Trinity, Father, Son, and Holy Ghost, one God, in whom substance and quality are identical — 925

11. Whether the angels that fell partook of the blessedness which the holy angels have always enjoyed from the time of their creation — 929

12. A comparison of the blessedness of the righteous, who have not yet received the divine reward, with that of our first parents in Paradise — 931

13. Whether all the angels were so created in one common state of felicity, that those who fell were not aware that they would fall, and that those who stood received assurance of their own perseverance after the ruin of the fallen — 933

14. An explanation of what is said of the devil, that he did not abide in the truth, because the truth was not in him — 937

15. How we are to understand the words, "the devil sinneth from the beginning" — 939

16. Of the ranks and differences of the creatures, estimated by their utility, or according to the natural gradations of being — 941

17. That the flaw of wickedness is not nature, but contrary to nature, and has its origin, not in the Creator, but in the will — 943

18. Of the beauty of the universe, which becomes, by God's ordinance, more brilliant by the opposition of contraries — 945

19. What, seemingly, we are to understand by the words, "God divided the light from the darkness" — 947

20. Of the words which follow the separation of light and darkness, "And God saw the light that it was good"   949

21. Of God's eternal and unchangeable knowledge and will, whereby all He has made pleased Him in the eternal design as well as in the actual result   951

22. Of those who do not approve of certain things which are a part of this good creation of a good Creator, and who think that there is some natural evil   955

23. Of the error in which the doctrine of Origen is involved   958

24. Of the divine Trinity, and the indications of its presence scattered everywhere among its works   962

25. Of the division of philosophy into three parts   965

26. Of the image of the supreme Trinity, which we find in some sort in human nature even in its present state   968

27. Of existence, and knowledge of it, and the love of both   971

28. Whether we ought to love the love itself with which we love our existence and our knowledge of it, that so we may more nearly resemble the image of the divine Trinity   974

29. Of the knowledge by which the holy angels know God in His essence, and by which they see the causes of His works in the art of the worker, before they see them in the works of the artist 977

30. Of the perfection of the number six, which is the first of the numbers which is composed of its aliquot parts 979

31. Of the seventh day, in which completeness and repose are celebrated 981

32. Of the opinion that the angels were created before the world 984

33. Of the two different and dissimilar communities of angels, which are not inappropriately signified by the names light and darkness 987

34. Of the idea that the angels were meant where the separation of the waters by the firmament is spoken of, and of that other idea that the waters were not created 991

BOOK TWELVE

1. That the nature of the angels, both good and bad, is one and the same 997

2. That there is no entity contrary to the divine, because nonentity seems to be that which is wholly opposite to Him who supremely and always is 1001

3. That the enemies of God are so, not by nature, but by will, which, as it injures them, injures a good nature; for if vice does not injure, it is not vice 1003

4. Of the nature of irrational and lifeless creatures, which in their own kind and order do not mar the beauty of the universe 1006

5. That in all natures, of every kind and rank, God is glorified 1009

6. What the cause of the blessedness of the good angels is, and what the cause of the misery of the wicked 1011

7. That we ought not to expect to find any efficient cause of the evil will 1016

8. Of the misdirected love whereby the will fell away from the immutable to the mutable good 1018

9. Whether the angels, besides receiving from God their nature, received from Him also their good will by the Holy Spirit imbuing them with love 1020

10. Of the falseness of the history which allots many thousand years to the world's past 1024

11. Of those who suppose that this world indeed is not eternal, but that either there are numberless worlds, or that one and the same world is perpetually resolved into its elements, and renewed at the conclusion of fixed cycles 1028

12. How these persons are to be answered, who find fault with the creation of man on the score of its recent date 1030

13. Of the revolution of the ages, which some philosophers believe will bring all things round again, after a certain fixed cycle, to the same order and form as at first 1033

14. Of the creation of the human race in time, and how this was effected without any new design or change of purpose on God's part 1036

15. Whether we are to believe that God, as he has always been sovereign Lord, has always had creatures over whom he exercised his sovereignty; and in what sense we can say that the creature has always been, and yet cannot say it is coeternal 1038

16. How we are to understand God's promise of life eternal, which was uttered before the "eternal times" 1044

17. What defense is made by sound faith regarding God's unchangeable counsel and will, against the reasonings of those who hold that the works of God are eternally repeated in revolving cycles that restore all things as they were   1046

18. Against those who assert that things that are infinite cannot be comprehended by the knowledge of God   1050

19. Of worlds without end, or ages of ages   1053

20. Of the impiety of those who assert that the souls which enjoy true and perfect blessedness must yet again and again in these periodic revolutions return to labor and misery   1055

21. That there was created at first but one individual, and that the human race was created in him   1062

22. That God foreknew that the first man would sin, and that He at the same time foresaw how large a multitude of godly persons would by His grace be translated to the fellowship of the angels   1064

23. Of the nature of the human soul created in the image of God   1066

24. Whether the angels can be said to be the creators of any, even the least creature   1068

25. That God alone is the Creator of every kind of creature, whatever its nature or form — 1070

26. Of that opinion of the Platonists, that the angels were themselves indeed created by God, but that afterward they created man's body — 1074

27. That the whole plenitude of the human race was embraced in the first man, and that God there saw the portion of it which was to be honored and rewarded, and that which was to be condemned and punished — 1076

ALSO AVAILABLE

Copyright © 2021 by Alicia Editions
Credits: Canva
All rights reserved.
No part of this book may be reproduced in any form or by any electronic or mechanical means, including information storage and retrieval systems, without written permission from the author, except for the use of brief quotations in a book review.

www.ingramcontent.com/pod-product-compliance
Lightning Source LLC
LaVergne TN
LVHW021046100526
838202LV00079B/4496